Economic and Financial Law & Policy – Shifting Insights & Values

Volume 1

Series editors
Koen Byttebier
Brussels, Belgium

Kim van der Borght
Brussels, Belgium

This book series focuses on presenting critical legal and interdisciplinary research regarding the tools and instruments of free-market-driven societies and their economies.

For the last few decades, the world markets have been in turmoil, to a large extent a result of value and policy choices which have been made since the late middle ages. As a result, on a global scale, economies and the legal systems giving form to them, have mainly if not exclusively become based on selfishness and greed, a reality which is moreover explicitly propagated by the theories of economic neo-liberalism.

It has nevertheless become clear in the recent past that said free market tools and mechanisms – such as private money creation by banks, next to the way huge corporations in general function and determine the outcome of economic processes – result in disastrous consequences, especially when remaining uncorrected by law and when not being submitted to clear public policy intervention measures.

Despite the evidence and growing understanding of the causes and consequences of neoliberal policy, few alternatives for the capitalist model as currently implemented, have so far been proposed.

In order to meet these concerns, this book series aims at offering an outlet for various forms of scientific research output, both monographs and edited collections.

The objective of every book of the series will hereby be to look critically at the legal methods and mechanisms shaping the free markets, and even to suggest alternatives for these.

Although the book series is initiated by legal scholars, it nevertheless aims to be truly multi- and interdisciplinary. The books series therefor welcomes and will incorporate all relevant disciplines, including law, economics, philosophy, ethics, religion, psychology, sociology, anthropology etc.

More information about this series at http://www.springer.com/series/15643

Koen Byttebier

Towards a New International Monetary Order

Springer

Koen Byttebier
Center for Economic Law and Governance
Free University of Brussels
Brussels, Belgium

Economic and Financial Law & Policy – Shifting Insights & Values
ISBN 978-3-319-52517-4 ISBN 978-3-319-52518-1 (eBook)
DOI 10.1007/978-3-319-52518-1

Library of Congress Control Number: 2017939564

Cover illustration, by Beatriz Acevedo: The bark of the White Mulberry (Morus alba) was historically one of the first sources for the creation of paper money. Ever since, money and it's role in monetary systems world wide have both facilitated and complicated human lives all over the world. The time is more than ripe to embark on a journey of re-exploring this role and its impact on socioeconomic relations and developments. This journey is symbolized by an illustration representing the White Mulberry, the 'tree where it all began'.

Printed on acid-free paper

This Springer imprint is published by Springer Nature
The registered company is Springer International Publishing AG
The registered company address is: Gewerbestrasse 11, 6330 Cham, Switzerland

"Because someone has made up the word 'wave', do I have to distinguish it from 'water'?"

– Kabir (1398–1448 or 1440–1518) –

Preface

Since the eruption of the 2008 financial crisis, I have focused my research to finding out why the monetary and financial system, so periodically, entails serious financial crises, going back as far as the Middle Ages during which the currently prevailing financial and monetary system took form.

One of the conclusions of my research has been that many of the monetary and financial problems still gripping the world economy up to the present date can to a large extent be blamed on the basic choice of values on which Western socioeconomic policies have been based since the late Middle Ages.

It is generally known that the decline of the Western Roman Empire in the fifth century all but stopped trade in the Western European territories and that its resuscitation in the Middle Ages has gone hand in hand with an historical choice for "egoism" and "greed" as driving forces for human behavior, in particular in the socioeconomic context.

Initially more a practical than a theoretical choice, the choice for greed and egoism as central socioeconomic values would gradually evolve into an elaborated economic doctrine, the so-called economic liberalism, which itself, during the past decades, has reappeared under its modern-day form of "economic neoliberalism."

Especially in the twentieth century, several attempts have been made to offer "alternatives" or "correctional methods" to the capitalist society shaped by economic liberalism, which since then, in the 1980s and 1990s, have been heavily opposed by the doctrine of economic neoliberalism. The latter would especially and more fiercely than ever in history put forward the idea that all theoretical and practical socioeconomic policies should be based on egoism and greed.

One of the conclusions of my research has been that said basically ethical choice may very well be one of the main causes of the numerous financial and economic problems that have poignantly manifested in the recent past.

This insight inevitably prompts the question what might be a possible alternative to the domination of economic neoliberalism and the unjust society it entails, especially within the scope of the monetary and financial system.

Furthermore, also on a more personal level, I have been able to witness the effects of the doctrine of economic neoliberalism myself. Having grown up in the 1970s and 1980s in a relatively poor laborer's family in "West Flanders," a rural part of Belgium, I personally experienced many of the detrimental consequences of the capitalist economy as reshaped by the philosophy of economic neoliberalism, not the least the striking contrast between the opportunities available to the middle and upper classes and those available to the poor classes of society.

Regretfully, I have to observe that society has in this regard rather retrogressed than progressed, an observation which, for instance, has been corroborated by relatively recent OECD findings (2014) on the access to higher education in Belgium.

It may hence be very clear that the theoretical models of economic neoliberalism which try to justify the several injustices characterizing the socioeconomic dynamics of the capitalist system by means of artificial doctrines, such as the theory of *voluntary association*, are irrelevant to those facing the severe oppression of capitalism.

It is therefore with an incomprehensibly cold cynicism that fervent "neoliberal" authors such as Ayn Rand dare to state that the numerous social injustices caused by capitalism, such as child slavery which still is present in many countries up to this very date, are not due to the forces of capitalism or the free market but to personal choices of parents who force their children to perform child labor (see further at marg. 123 of Chap. 3 of this book).

Also the doctrine of the *survival of the fittest* (in its neoliberal interpretation, not in the meaning Charles Darwin gave to the concept) does not make any sense in a society riddled with unequal opportunities as those prevailing in the present-day world being shaped by the ideas of economic neoliberalism.

It may furthermore be as appropriate to ban the idea of the *invisible hand* equally resolutely to the realm of mythology where it belongs (for instance, according to Joseph Stiglitz who rightfully has suggested that Adam Smith's doctrine is based on a mythical worldview).

Those who thoroughly study the ideas of economic neoliberalism and their practical consequences in daily life can but reach the conclusion that these ideas are diametrically opposed to the civilization model aspired to by law, religion, philosophy, and ethics ever since the Age of Enlightenment, especially the aim for more justice and equality in "interhuman" relations.

In my opinion, it is therefore mainly the unrestricted egoism promoted by neoliberal thinking itself that has resulted in the prevailing manifestly unjust world, which, above all and especially in a socioeconomic context, functions according to "the law of the jungle" and increasingly manifests itself as "a war of all against all."

An extremely worrying example of how economic neoliberalism, a.o., through techniques of liberalization and deregulation, is reshaping societies is the recent erosion of the systems formerly established in some Western countries to establish more justice and equality, such as social security and public services, as a result of which the modern welfare state model is being abandoned by more and more Western countries.

As worrisome are the findings by several researches that, in the prevailing neoliberal world order, the gaps between the poor and the rich are getting wider and deeper worldwide. The injustice this implies even adheres to the most classic Aristotelean meaning of a world where one group has monopolized "much too much" of what is good, leaving "way too little" of what is good for others (and one group of people has to experience too much of what is bad, while others hardly experience anything of what is bad). (See further under Sect. 3.6.2.2 of Chap. 3 of this book.)

More than ever, it is time for some serious reflection on the principles shaping our socioeconomic life to which the present book wants to add its own contribution.

An earlier Dutch version of this book was finished at the end of 2014 and was published under the title *Nu het gouden kalf verdronken is. Van hebzucht naar altruïsme als hoeksteen voor een Nieuwe Monetaire Wereldorde*[1], after which the book has been translated during the course of 2015 and the first half of 2016.

Based upon this Dutch version, the here introduced English version of the book has been prepared thanks to the efforts of Koen Vanbrabant (who prepared the translation of Chaps. 1 and 2 of the book) and Jan Willems (who prepared the translation of the next Chaps. 3–6 of the book); be it that, in light of further own insights and evolutions on a socioeconomic level, the text has at the same time further been adapted and deepened out.

The material has been updated until April 15, 2016.

Finally, I want to express my gratitude to the following people for their material and/or moral support: Armondo Linus Acosta, Francine Bernard, Julie Borgerhoff, Anne Claeys, Eduardo Fialho, Saurav Ghimire, Serge Gutwirth, Kristina Loguinova, Ann Maertens, Wilfried Rauws, Kim Van der Borght, Anne Marie Van der Eecken, and Tom Wera, next to my mother and sisters.

Ghent, Belgium
December 2014 and April 2016

Koen Byttebier

Reference

Byttebier K (2015) Nu het gouden kalf verdronken is. Van hebzucht naar altruïsme als hoeksteen voor een Nieuwe Monetaire Wereldorde. Maklu, Antwerp

---

[1] See Byttebier (2015).

Contents

List of Further Illustrations

List of Tables

Chapter 1
Introduction

For over two centuries capitalism has reigned supreme.[1] 1

Especially the writings of the Scottish moral philosopher Adam Smith (1723–1790), who was inspired by the philosophical schools of the Enlightenment, provided capitalism with the necessary ideological basis, which is probably one of the reasons why it has managed to develop into the dominant economic ideology on earth.

---

[1]An exact date on which capitalism originated can, of course, not be given (see Bernstein 2004, p. 19).

It has even been held that pinning down an exact date on which capitalism originated is more often than not a political exercise which always results in different outcomes. (See Heller 2011, p. 3.)

Some authors have argued that the first pre-capitalist practices already manifested in the Middle Ages, especially from the ninth century on, when interregional and international trade re-emerged in the Western world and the striving for more possessions became a life goal for many people. On and on, new ways of by-passing the interest-rules of the Catholic Church (which until then had posed an important barrier against such practices) hereby emerged. (See Vandewalle 1976, p. 7; see also Ripert 1951, p. 13, speaking of "***un capitalisme naissant***".)

In the world of ideas, one could argue that the founding fathers of Protestantism (Luther and Calvin), can also be considered as forerunners of the capitalist ideas as, due to their teachings, for instance the applying of interest to loans became an acceptable practice. Their ideas moreover caused a secession of the classic teachings of ancient philosophers, such as Plato and Aristotle, but also of those of important teachers of the Christian belief, such as Jesus Christ Himself, in addition to the church fathers of early Christianity and, later on, the so-called "scholastics", such as Thomas Aquinas, who have been among the last to oppose the application of unbridled money craving as the guiding principle of economics. (See furthermore Sect. 3.3.3.6.2 of Chap. 3 of this book.)

It is therefore hardly a coincidence that capitalism started its advance in the territories which were the first to adopt protestant doctrines, for instance the German territories (already in the sixteenth century) and later on Holland and the United Kingdom (especially in the seventeenth and eighteenth century). Capitalism became the most important economic system from the eighteenth century on and especially in the nineteenth and twentieth century. (Ripert 1951, p. 14; Fromm 1955, pp. 80 a.f.; Galbraith 1983, pp. 89 a.f.; Galbraith 1994, pp. 1 a.f.)

K. Byttebier, *Towards a New International Monetary Order*,
Economic and Financial Law & Policy – Shifting Insights & Values 1,
DOI 10.1007/978-3-319-52518-1_1

2 The current manifestation of capitalism is heavily supported by the underlying neo-liberal axiom that, in the economic domain, each individual must behave in the most egoistical way possible in order to enrich one's self as much as possible, thus feeding the economy with sufficient stimuli for productivity (and other types of activity)[2].

In this manner, capitalism primarily appeals to one of the lower values in human nature, namely the absolute assertion of the personal, individualistic (i.e. egoistic) interests, disregarding the impact of one's behavior on others or the environment.

One of the important (sub) doctrines of neo-liberalism is that the labor force of others may and even should be deployed to pursue the aforementioned goal: an unbridled expansion of personal fortune. As a consequence, a system which to a large extent functions according to the law of the jungle (in which the strong exploit the weak) has come to determine the socioeconomic relations.[3]

It has become sufficiently clear that this so-called "neo-liberal" doctrine, which, together with its predecessor, the "liberal" doctrine, has been implemented for more than two centuries, has managed to shape a world where a small financial "Power Elite" controls the economic power—and hence a substantial part of the planet's resources—in such a way that the rest of mankind has become subservient to them. This elite manages to do so by, *inter alia*, controlling a number of big and medium-sized enterprises, including private banks and other financial institutions, as well as through the democratically unjustifiable influence these enterprises exert on governments and parliaments (for instance to shape fiscal policy).

As a consequence, even though slavery in the sense of legally owning other human beings has throughout the ages been formally abolished in most countries, a great number of people still work within the (post-)modern capitalist societies as socioeconomic slaves, evidencing in a cynical way the classical (neo)liberal

---

[2]See *e.g.* Brook and Watkins (2012), pp. 75–77.

> The principle of productiveness says: Use your mind to create wealth. "Wealth" in this context refers to the creation of any material value – from a meal to a truck, to a medical operation, to a stock analysis, to a symphony. Productivity doesn't assume any particular level of ability. It says only: Do the best your mind is capable of. (Brook and Watkins 2012, p. 75.)

See also Rand (1992), p. 27; Stiglitz (2012), p. 78.

[3]Fromm (1955), pp. 84–85.

principle, generally known as Ricardo's "Iron Law of the Wages" which holds that labor should be remunerated as little as possible.[4]

Capital can in essence be considered as a savings surplus that is invested. It 3
forms the basis of the term "capitalism" and constitutes one of the major mechanisms of unbridled enrichment within the capitalist system.[5]

Massive business empires may be built by gathering capital, for instance by starting a company which aims to generate as much profit as possible by employing other people's labor at the lowest possible price and selling products and/or services on the market at the highest possible price. By applying this method to its fullest extent possible, capital suppliers may succeed in extracting gigantic fortunes from the business empires they thus create.

In particular, since the twentieth century, this effect has been enforced by all sorts of financial mechanisms, whereby providers of financial services and others, such as consultancy offices, law firms and capital planners, do not use their evident financial ingenuity to solve the problems created by capitalism (for instance the poverty we find in many countries and among large parts of the population), but rather to develop new fortune expansion techniques for large entrepreneurs.[6]

In this evolution, the classical dichotomy between "capital" and "labor" has according to some evolved into a new dichotomy simply dividing global societies into "the rich" and "the poor".

As no other as (John Kenneth) Galbraith has put it bluntly[7]:

---

[4]See the findings in Oxfam (2016), p. 4:

> One of the key trends underlying [the] huge concentration of wealth and incomes is the increasing return to capital versus labour. In almost all rich countries and in most developing countries, the share of national income going to workers has been falling. This means workers are capturing less and less of the gains from growth. In contrast, the owners of capital have seen their capital consistently grow (through interest payments, dividends, or retained profits) faster than the rate the economy has been growing. Tax avoidance by the owners of capital, and governments reducing taxes on capital gains have further added to these returns.

[5]Graff et al. (2014), p. 30.

[6]According to Stiglitz, they hereby also look for ways to keep their clients out of jail (see Stiglitz 2012, p. 42).

See also Oxfam (2014), p. 16:

> Large corporations can employ armies of specialist accountants to minimize their taxes and give them an unfair advantage over small businesses. Multinational corporations (MNCs), like Apple and Starbucks have been exposed for dodging billions in taxes, leading to unprecedented public pressure for reform.

See further Sachs (2011), p. 118.

Below in this book, some examples of how for instance the four major consultancy offices ("Price Waterhouse Coopers", "EY"—formally "Ernst and Young"—"Deloitte" and "KMPG"), in addition to numerous law firms, have supported methods of tax evasion will be further developed.

[7]Galbraith (1996), p. 7.

> On one side, there are now the rich, the comfortably endowed and those so aspiring, and on the other the economically less fortunate and the poor, along with the considerable number who, out of social concern or sympathy, seek to speak for them or for a more compassionate world.

4 In particular, during the last few decades, this capitalist system based on unbridled egoism has been neatly packaged into a religious system (*e.g.* by academic institutes such as the "F.A. Hayek Mont Pelerin Society" and later the "School of Chicago"), namely "economic neo-liberalism", which basically claims that the economy can only work efficiently by fully implementing the underlying premise of unbridled egoism.[8]

This has further increased the inherently disastrous effect of capitalism on our society in general.

It is probably hardly possible to put it any clearer than the Israeli historian Yuval Harari of the University of Jerusalem[9]:

> The new ethic promises paradise on condition that the rich remain greedy and spend their time making more money, and that the masses give free rein to their cravings and passions – and buy more and more. This is the first religion in history whose followers actually do what they are asked to do. How though, do we know that we'll really get paradise in return? We've seen it on television.

It could hereby even been held that the new religion of economic neo-liberalism even has its own credo ("Greed is good")[10] and its own prophets (modern bankers)[11].

5 The consequences of neo-liberal capitalism should by now be clear to everyone: the rich keep getting richer, at the cost of (*i*) the exploitation of the rest of the world population, (*ii*) grinding poverty for a major part of this population and (*iii*) an ever increasing threat to both the ecological balance and the safety of the planet.

6 In the absence of a unitary global fiscal policy, the fiscal and "parafiscal" system in most countries tends to increase these detrimental effects of capitalism.

In view of the mobility of capital, which during the past decades was enhanced by several (neo-)liberal treaties, the fiscal authorities of most (Western and Western inspired) countries do not manage to draw the main share of their income by taxing the proceeds of capital, hence primarily and heavily relying on taxing income from

---

[8]Steger (2013), p. 117.

Emmanuel Todd rightly pointed out that said neoliberal doctrine has lied at the basis of the European unification project. Todd argues that the success of this doctrine may be explained by the decline of traditional religious systems (especially Catholicism) in Europe which was replaced by a new ideology, namely the ideology worshipping the pursuit of money (see Todd 2015, pp. 53–54).

See also the observations of Mark Carney, Governor of the Bank of England, in Oxfam (2014), p. 55. See further Galbraith (1992), pp. 82 a.f.

[9]Harari (2014), p. 391.

[10]Tyler (2013), p. 36; Peterson (2011), p. 96; Krugman (2004), p. 110.

[11]Ferguson (1998), p. 17.

labor, which is intrinsically far less mobile and therefore much more vulnerable to taxation (and similar retribution systems implemented by government, such as mandatory social security contributions).

Also outside the scope of taxation policy, to a large extent under the impulse of the ruling financial "Power Elite", legislators and administrators of capitalist countries have globally chosen to team up with capital. **7**

The spirit of (economic) neo-liberalism which for instance, has shaped the European Union and its policies on two legal pillars which support the interests of big business, is a clear illustration of this.[12] The first of these pillars is the so-called "free movement of capital" which makes it possible to smoothly move production units to those areas where they can be organized in the cheapest way possible (i.e. where the laborers are available at the lowest price). The other pillar is the "free movement of persons" which, in turn, makes it possible to attract cheap laborers to one's own territory, in particular when it is difficult to move production itself.[13]

At present, the spirit of unbridled (neo)liberalism has globally affected all layers of society, measuring virtually any human activity merely in terms of either "cost price" or "profitability" (which happen to be the opposite sides of the same coin), and often a combination of both. **8**

It has even been argued that we live in "a financialized world", where the importance of anyone or anything is solely measured by the quantity of money he or it produces.[14]

One does not need to have a degree in economics to realize that implementing such an extreme profitability principle (instead of a solidarity principle), especially in sectors where this is not at all appropriate, for instance institutions for social services such as hospitals, homes for senior citizens, universities and other educational facilities, only has resulted in a situation where the cost of these services more and more has to be paid by their end users (i.e. patients, retired persons or their family, youngsters aspiring for an education,...), instead of through mechanisms of mutual solidarity.[15]

The underlying principle of solidarity, which historically formed the basis for this type of social services, is hereby more and more discarded in such a profitability approach. It need not surprise that, as a result, "neo-liberalized" capitalism has even further resulted in an ever-increasing economic inequality between the rich and the poor (see further, at marg. 145 a.f. of Chap. 3 of this book).

---

[12]Todd (2015), pp. 50 a.f. and pp. 85 a.f. (also: Todd 2015, pp. 45 a.f. and pp. 67 a.f.), having pointed out that: "***le langage de Maastricht était libéral, égalitaire, universaliste***", but that the result of its implementation has been the opposite and that "***Maastricht aboutit à celui de l'inégalité sous l'autorité transcendante d'une divinité cruelle, la monnaie***".

[13]An example of the latter are the cheap laborers from Eastern European countries being employed in Western European countries in difficult to relocate sectors such as retail, construction and agriculture.

[14]Huet (2010), p. 29. See also Harvey (2010), p. 29.

[15]Pinxten (2014); Pinxten and De Munter (2006), p. 15.

In a world shaped by this neo-liberal ideology, it hardly comes as a surprise that global society is headed—much like the Titanic on its collision course—for a social climate where quasi-paradoxically only the rich elite of society still has sufficient access to "social" services such as education, medical services and geriatric care.

9 Hence, there is some strong doubt about the validity of the thesis forwarded by neo-liberal schools holding that mankind has fundamentally benefited from a unitary implementation of unbridled egoism principle in all sectors of society.

It therefore does not come as a surprise that numerous prominent thinkers (among whom even some policy-makers, (former) bankers, etc.) have, in general, raised serious questions about the working premises of the capitalist economy and the correctness of the doctrine(s) of economic (neo-)liberalism, and in particular wonder how much longer mankind and the planet it inhabits can support this system with its many disastrous effects.

Some of these authors have expressed a fierce verdict on neo-liberal capitalism, referring to it as "the Capitalist Hell"[16] or "the neo-liberal madness,"[17] while another author has a somewhat milder verdict and merely compares it with "purgatory."[18]

10 Nonetheless, it is remarkable—although quite incomprehensible—how the neo-liberal way of thinking has won over the spirit of a major part of mankind since the 1980s (especially in Western and Western inspired countries).[19]

In present-day societies, for instance, this is quite apparent in the debate on reorganizing (European) government finances, where the major consensus is that austerity measures must primarily be implemented in social care (in its broad sense), and where there is hardly any resistance against the neo-Smithian arguments that "*everyone must tighten his belts*" and "*nobody may profit from other people's efforts.*" Meanwhile, ("corporatist") policymakers hardly raise any question about the fact that big business and its profits are highly protected from any noteworthy taxation, being safely housed in fiscal tax havens and refuge countries.[20]

In the meantime, the principle of "solidarity" remains still being preached by, for instance, (Catholic) church authorities. In those places where it can still be found, it is, however, mostly turned into a system of mandatory solidarity among the poor (in addition to the middle classes) that is imposed by state authorities through

---

[16]See Harari (2014), p. 368.

[17]Verhaeghe (2011).

[18]Bruckner (2002), p. 37.

[19]For an explanation, see Marcuse (1962), p. 85, a.o. holding that

> the manipulation of consciousness which has occurred throughout the orbit of contemporary industrial civilization has been described in the various interpretations of totalitarian and "popular cultures": co-ordination of the private and public existence of spontaneous and required reactions. The promotion of thoughtless leisure activities, the triumph of anti-intellectual ideologies, exemplify the trend.

[20]Sachs (2011), p. 118.

complicated fiscal and other regulations which to a large extent exempt the rich elite.[21]

As a result, the fact that government finances of an increasing number of countries are mainly supported by the poorer part of the population is incomprehensibly validated by policy-makers. It is moreover all the more astounding that the rich, when confronted with this paradox, claim they don't have to pay taxes since they are investing in employment and prosperity.

The neo-liberal doctrine has in this way even a ready explanation for the fact that, throughout the world and to an increasing degree, it is the poorer layers of the population who have to part with the biggest percentage of their income in order to finance their governments, while in contrast the rich(er) are mostly exempt from paying taxes, purportedly to allow them to re-invest their riches unhindered, but in reality: in order to become ever more rich (see further, at Sect. 3.4.6 of Chap. 3 of this book). **11**

When comparing the pros and the cons of exempting large fortunes and wages from taxation, governments worldwide seem to bear little or no consideration for the fact that accumulating wealth relies to a considerable degree on the use of collective services (*e.g.* roads, administrative services, education, health care,...), organized and paid by society at large (and, hence, out of money obtained through taxing especially the middle and lower classes of society).

During the past three decades the population at large in the Western world has endured in a rather stoic way how the implementation of neo-liberal doctrines has led to an increasing economic inequality, which now threatens mankind with a global destruction of public and social care mechanisms.[22] **12**

However, in various countries there have been occasional short outbursts of anger, mainly from the poorest layers of the population, which were hit most heavily by the 2008 financial crisis. These outbursts so far have manifested as riots, marches and manifestations in big cities such as London, Paris and various American cities, whereby the establishment and its capitalist economic system has severely been contested. One may also wonder to what extent acts of terrorism by people of the lower layers of society should also be considered as a form of protest against the prevailing, manifestly unjust social and economic world order.

In a world where the ghost image of poverty has reached a large part of the population in many countries, especially since the 2008 financial crisis[23], one can but question how long mankind will continue to cling to the credo of neo-liberal thinking, which constitutes the breeding ground for present-day capitalism in its many pernicious emanations.

---

[21]This raises the rhetorical question as to whether this really is what has been described in the teachings of Jesus Christ on which the said solidarity principle is historically based (see further, at marg. 31 a.f. of Chap. 3 of this book).

[22]Engelen et al. (2011), p. 49.

[23]By Emmanuel Tod referred to as "less painful" than the crisis of 1929, but however with far more enduring effects in the long run (see Todd 2015, pp. 33–34; also Todd 2015, p. 35).

In view of the ever-increasing poverty and the ever-increasing gap between rich and poor, one of the main priorities of authorities worldwide should, hence, become to avoid that the Marxian concepts of "impoverishment resulting in catastrophe" (partly endorsed by, for instance, John Kenneth Galbraith[24]) would turn into reality.

13 In spite of a lot of criticism, so far, very few truly alternative systems have been proposed to the capitalist system that is currently in force.

From an historical point of view, it was primarily Communism[25] that provided a certain counterbalance to capitalism for some time; yet it all but died during the last two decades of the twentieth century[26], presumably because of the major lack of freedom which has been typical in many former communist countries. Within capitalism, on the other hand, freedom as a value has been preserved, albeit primarily in a theoretical way, and not so much within socioeconomic life.

Currently there are still a few countries that continue to call themselves "communist", even though most of these appear to behave as ace students of the capitalist schools on the global markets.[27]

14 It should be clear that society should at the very least no longer intellectually accept the justification, more precisely the contrivance that defends the prevailing capitalist system.[28]

On the contrary, serious thought should be given to searching for (an) alternative system(s).

In view of the fact that the monetary system forms one of the bases of capitalism, further in the Chaps. 4 and 5 of this book, an attempt will be made to give a description of what an altruistically inspired monetary (and financial) system might look like. In contrast to the economic ethical vision of the neo-liberal schools, the aforementioned proposal will be based on the underlying observation that an unbridled egoism is not (or should not be) the only impulse determining human behavior, especially in social economic relationships. On the contrary, people may just as well behave altruistically, or at least strive to behave in an altruistic manner.

Hence, this reflection on a new monetary (and financial) system will be based upon reversing the goal that was set within the (neo)liberal doctrine (going back to Adam Smith): what if we were to sustain that even in his economic behavior man is also perfectly capable of being "altruistic". And if we were indeed to act in such an altruistic way, would this not result in a world much more just than the one which is the result of centuries of economic behavior based on the conviction that everyone needs to behave themselves as egoistically as possible in order to end up with a just economic order?

---

[24]Galbraith (1992), p. 53.

[25]Lloyd (2012), p. 359.

[26]See Berend (2006), p. 189, stating that

> the centrally planned economy, though transitorily rather successful, terminally failed at the end of the century.

[27]Yueh (2010), p. 26.

[28]Compare Galbraith (1996), pp. 60–61.

15 As said, the tentative reflections developed in the present book will mainly focus on a domain of legal science with which the author of this book is most familiar, namely that of monetary and financial law.

16 The implementation of a monetary system based on altruistic principles, as proposed in Chaps. 4 and 5 of this book, will hereby obviously have to cross the boundaries of the mere monetary and financial domain.

Hence, the proposals expressed in Chaps. 4 and 5 describe a *possible* framework for a new monetary and financial system based on altruism, which will also have to touch other economic domains (among which fiscality).

In other words, the system will have to be more than merely "monetary" in the traditional sense of the word. While hereafter "New Monetary World Order" as a working title for this new monetary system will be proposed, the working title might also be "New Economic and Monetary World Order" (or even "New Economic, Tax and Monetary World Order").

However, this is mainly a matter of semantics, and the reader is therefore beseeched to read the current book with an ample set of pragmatism concerning the regulatory role to be held by the world authorities to be instituted, as described further on in said in Chaps. 4 and 5.

17 As indicated by the proposed terminology, the new altruistically based monetary system will furthermore have to rely heavily on the basic principles of global collaboration and solidarity.

It has become completely illusory to believe that at this point in history any single country would be able to seriously oppose the battering ram of globalized capitalism which currently dominates the global socioeconomic relations.

18 A global altruistic monetary system (and hence also a global economy) will moreover necessarily have to choose labor over capital.

In the end, it is through labor that human beings develop themselves and may build themselves a worthy existence.[29]

---

[29] Compare Fromm (2013), p. 29 and pp. 33 a.f.

Erich Fromm has phrased this as follows:

> Labor is the self-expression of man, an expression of his individual, physical and mental powers. In this process of genuine activity, man develops himself, becomes himself; work is not only a means to an end – the product – but an end in itself, the meaningful expression of human energy. (See Fromm 2013, p. 34.)

Similar ideas have been brought forward by the Catholic Church:

> Work must not be understood only in the objective and material sense, but one must keep in mind its subjective dimension, insofar as it is always an expression of the person. Besides being a decisive paradigm for social life, work has all the dignity of being a context in which the person's natural and supernatural vocation must find fulfilment. (See Pontifical Council for Justice and Peace 2005, p. 101.)

In present-day neoliberal societies where the labor of the masses has been completely degraded as a means to make the rich of the planet ever the more rich and powerful, the question arises if, except maybe for artists, this truth still applies to anyone else.

An "altruistically" inspired economy and global monetary system (as opposed to the neo-Smithian "egoistic" one) will have to take this as one of the starting points and base its underlying monetary-economic goals on it.

In this approach, trying to gather fortune from capital (investments) is by definition evidence of a spirit of egoism, since capital by itself does not "work." On the contrary, it can only produce fortune by having others work (as cheaply as possible), while the capital backer (who works a lot less or at least is exempt of most of the "hard" labor) by definition takes an egoistic position towards the people he employs for his own profit, which is one of the basic premises of capitalism (as one can observe already by merely reading or rereading Adam Smith on this point).

It is self-evident that within the "New (Economic and) Monetary World Order", the system focus will have to shift drastically towards protecting labor (as opposed to protecting capital).[30]

19 In any case, such a fundamental re-orientation will suppose a landslide in economic and monetary thinking and behavior. At the very least, it will require an active choice in favor of "radical altruism" diametrically opposed to the ideal of "unbridled egoism" that lies at the base of the current economic and monetary thinking and behavior.

Such a landslide will also necessarily be required at the level of the national government machinery of the countries participating in the "New (Economic and) Monetary World Order," for instance at the level of fiscal and parafiscal policy.

The emphasis of fiscal and parafiscal systems will hereby have to shift from taxing mainly income from labor (plus common goods and services transactions) to taxing mainly income from capital (and large fortunes).

20 Before outlining such a blueprint for a more altruistic "New Monetary World Order", Chap. 2 of this book will first briefly outline the creation history of the monetary system and describe the major mechanisms of money creation and money use, in particular to the benefit of the reader who is less familiar with the workings of the monetary and financial mechanisms.

Chapter 3 of this book will then give an overview of a number of some (mainly Western) "schools of thought", which to various degrees focused in particular on the issue of fortune gathering and/or other financial issues, including the impact they had on the further development of the monetary system.[31]

These Chaps. 2 and 3 of this book hereby primarily aim to show that (*i*) money and the monetary system are essentially merely conventional systems adopted by mankind itself, while during the most recent centuries, (*ii*) the monetary system has been very strongly influenced by an ideology which has presented an (unbridled) egoism as determining value, namely "economic (neo)liberalism" which the whole of mankind seems to have endorsed.

21 However, the above choices have in no way resulted in new laws of nature "chiseled in imperishable stone", so that one may question these past choices

---

[30]Harribey et al. (2011), pp. 63–88, especially p. 79; Askenazy and Méhaut (2011), pp. 173–187.

[31]As to the relevance of this approach, see Galbraith (1987), p. 1.

(especially given their numerous disastrous effects) and, hopefully, might consider potential new choices, which would not lead to the end of the world as we know it.

Everyone hereby should thereby fully realize that money is nothing more than a figment of the human imagination and that any real transaction of goods and/or services could just as easily take place without any money involved, since money itself does not add any intrinsic value to the transactions of goods and services taking place in the real economy.

However, acting in complete consequence with this realization (in a "moneyless" society) would require a fundamental thought reversal, which cannot be undertaken by the few alone.

On the contrary, even a partial reversal (to which the further reflections developed in this book aim to be an incentive) can only take place if based on a growing collective consciousness.

Consequently, the reflections following hereafter have been undertaken with the **22**
aim of contributing to the awareness that the economy could be based on a different belief system, i.e. on a radical altruism rather than on an unbridled egoism.

References

Askenazy P, Méhaut P (2011) Redonner un avenir au travail. In: Les Économistes atterés (2011) Changer d'économie! Nos propositions pour 2012. Les liens qui libèrent, Paris, pp 173–187

Berend I (2006) An economic history of twentieth-century Europe. Cambridge University Press, Cambridge

Bernstein WJ (2004) The birth of plenty. How the prosperity of the modern world was created. McGraw-Hill, New York

Brook Y, Watkins D (2012) Free market revolution – how Ayn Rand's ideas can end big government. Palgrave Macmillan, New York

Bruckner P (2002) Misère de la prospérité – la religion marchande et ses ennemis. Bernard Grasset, Paris

Engelen E et al (2011) After the great complacence. Oxford University Press, Oxford

Ferguson N (1998) The house of Rothschild. Penguin Books, New York

Fromm E (1955) The sane society. A Fawcett Premier Book, Greenwich

Fromm E (2013) Marx's concept of man. Bloomsbury, London

Galbraith JK (1983) The anatomy of power. Houghton Mifflin Company, Boston

Galbraith JK (1987) Economics in perspective – a critical history. Houghton Mifflin Company, Boston

Galbraith JK (1992) The culture of contentment. Houghton Mifflin Company, Boston

Galbraith JK (1994) A journey through economic time – a firsthand view. Houghton Mifflin Company, Boston

Galbraith JK (1996) The good society – the humane agenda. Houghton Mifflin Company, Boston and New York

Graff M, Kenwood A, Lougheed A (2014) Growth of the international economy, 1820–2015. Routledge, London

Harari YN (2014) Sapiens – a brief history of humankind. Penguin Random House, London

Harribey JM, Quirion P, Rotillon Q (2011) Les enjeux d'une transformation écologique qui soit sociale. In: Les Économistes atterés (2011) Changer d'économie! Nos propositions pour 2012. Les liens qui libèrent, Paris, pp 63–88

Harvey D (2010) The enigma of capital and the crises of capitalism. Profile Books, London
Heller H (2011) The birth of capitalism: a twenty-first-century perspective. Pluto Press, London
Huet E (2010) Peter Thiel: don't blame technology for drop in middle class wages. http://www.forbes.com/sites/ellenhuet/2014/11/09/peter-thiel-dont-blame-technology-for-drop-in-middle-class-wages/
Krugman P (2004) The great unraveling: losing our way in the new century. W. W. Norton & Company, New York
Lloyd C (2012) What on earth happened? The complete story of the planet, life & people from the big bang to the present day. Bloomsbury, London
Marcuse H (1962) Eros and civilization – a philosophical inquiry into freud. Vintage Books (A division of Random House), New York
Oxfam (2014) Even it up – time to end extreme inequality. Oxfam GB, Oxford
Oxfam (2016) An economy for the 1%. How privilege and power in the economy drive extreme inequality and how this can be stopped. Oxfam briefing paper. https://www.oxfam.org/sites/www.oxfam.org/files/file_attachments/bp210-economy-one-percent-tax-havens-180116-en_0.pdf. Last consulted 18 Jan 2016
Peterson R (2011) Inside the investor's brain: the power of mind over money. Wiley, Hoboken
Pinxten R (2014) Schoon protest (want er is wel een alternatief). EPO Berchem
Pinxten R, De Munter K (2006) De culturele eeuw. Houtekiet, Antwerp
Pontifical Council for Justice and Peace (2005) Compendium of the Social Doctrine of the Church (to His Holiness Pope John Paul II Master of Social Doctrine and Evangelical Witness to Justice and Peace). Bloomsbury, London. http://www.vatican.va/roman_curia/pontifical_councils/justpeace/documents/rc_pc_justpeace_doc_20060526_compendio-dott-soc_en.html
Rand A (1992) The virtue of selfishness. New American Library (a division of Penguin Group), New York
Ripert G (1951) Aspects juridiques du capitalisme modern. Librairie Générale de droit et de jurisprudence, Paris
Sachs J (2011) The price of civilization: reawakening American virtue and prosperity. Random House, New York
Steger M (2013) Globalization a very short introduction. Oxford University Press, Oxford
Stiglitz J (2012) The price of inequality. Allen Lane (an imprint of Penguin Books), London
Todd E (2015) Qui est Charlie? Sociologie d'une crise religieuse. Éditions du Seuil, Paris (also: Todd E (2015) Wie is Charlie. Xenofobie en de nieuwe middenklasse. De Bezige Bij, Amsterdam and Antwerp)
Tyler G (2013) What went wrong: how the 1% hijacked the American middle class ... and what other countries got right. BenBella Books, Dallas
Vandewalle G (1976) De geschiedenis van het economisch denken. Kluwer, Deventer
Verhaeghe P (2011) De neo-liberale waanzin – Flexibel, efficiënt en... gestoord. Uitgeverij VUBPRESS, Brussels
Yueh L (2010) The economy of China. Edward Elgar, Cheltenham

Chapter 2
On the Conventional Nature of Money

2.1 Background

By now everyone is likely to be aware of the numerous worrisome events that have 1
taken place on the monetary and financial markets during the past decade.

Many refer to the combination of these worrisome events as "*the* financial crisis", although it would probably be better to speak about a sequence of successive financial crises which according to some even have resulted in an "economic recession". Recent research even seems to indicate that these events are evidence of a so-called "system failure" (that very well may be of a permanent nature).[1]

It has not been the intention to hereafter give an umpteenth journalistic view on 2
these events which evidence the failure of the current monetary and financial system.

One can find myriad publications doing just that. Many of them entail excellent further reading which can be strongly recommended.[2]

The present book merely aims to outline a number of personal considerations about money and the monetary system, including thoughts on the underlying causes of the aforementioned system failure (see in particular this chapter and Chap. 3).

As already mentioned in its Chap. 1, the present book will also make an attempt to conceive an alternative approach for the current organization of the monetary system (see in particular Chaps. 4 and 5).

---

[1] See especially Galbraith (1990).

[2] See *e.g.* Achterhuis (2011), p. 319; Engelen (2011); Boatright (2010), p. 592; Chérot and Frydman (2012), p. 302; de Bettignies and Lépineux (2009), p. 258; Harvey (2010), p. 296; Kerste et al. (2011); Giovanoli and Devos (2010), p. 610; Kerste et al. (2011), p. 225; Kirton et al. (2010), p. 345; Leader and David (2011), p. 519; Middelkoop (2009, 2014); Mishkin (2012), p. 832; Pagliari (2012), p. 274; Peil and Van Staveren (2009), p. 626; Piketty (2014), p. 696; Sedlacek (2011), p. 368; Shaxson (2012), p. 272.

K. Byttebier, *Towards a New International Monetary Order*,
Economic and Financial Law & Policy – Shifting Insights & Values 1,
DOI 10.1007/978-3-319-52518-1_2

3 The following quite revealing statement is attributed to Henry Ford (1863–1947)[3]:

> It is well enough that people of the nation do not understand our banking and monetary system, for if they did, I believe there would be a revolution before tomorrow morning.

After reading the present book, every reader will hopefully understand this statement, albeit that the intent of this book is not to call for a (violent) revolution, but for a democratically conceived and fundamental revision of the monetary (and financial) system, for which some lines of thinking will be proposed in Chaps. 4 and 5.

Perhaps bankers, described by some as the "prophets" of the neo-liberal religion, truly have prophetic gifts (see marg. 4 of Chap. 1 of this book), as evidenced by the following extract from a letter (with a content quite similar to the aforementioned quote by Ford). Said letter is attributed to the Rothschild brothers and deals with the significance of the banking and monetary system. It was purportedly addressed to some of the employees of the Rothschild brothers (New York, 1863)[4]:

> The few who understand the system will either be so interested in its profits or be so dependent upon its favors that there will be no opposition from that class, while on the other hand, the great body of people, mentally incapable of comprehending the tremendous advantage that capital derives from the system, will bear its burdens without complaint, and perhaps without even suspecting that the system is inimical to their interests.

4 The second chapter of this book therefore is necessarily one of "demystification".

Often the monetary and banking system is considered to be very complex. This is undoubtedly the case for the many, highly specialized financial products and services that have been created during the past decades and that, generally, constitute complicated agreements which, in particular when things go awry, become the object of equally complex rules and regulations, being issued by legislators and/or supervisory authorities at a huge cost for society.[5]

---

[3]http://www.brainyquote.com/quotes/quotes/h/henryford136294.html#MU7bvrjhhrdCGGBu.99/; see also http://www.themoneymasters.com/the-money-masters/famous-quotations-on-banking/.

[4]http://www.themoneymasters.com/the-money-masters/famous-quotations-on-banking/.

[5]In the documentary "*Capitalism – a love story*" film maker Michael Moore goes looking for the underlying causes of the financial crisis of 2008. When interviewing several financial and financial law specialists, he asks them to explain certain complex financial products. This leads to embarrassing moments when the specialist cannot provide the answers to the said questions.

For a general overview of some of the numerous documentaries and movies on the subject of the financial crisis of 2008, see http://documentaries.about.com/od/populardocsubjects/tp/EconomicDocumentaries.htm.

Yet the mechanism at the base of the monetary and banking system, at least when looked into from an elementary historical angle, is inherently not so complex.[6]

As this chapter and Chap. 3 of this book intend to demonstrate, the present-day monetary and financial system is simply a very handy, albeit perverse mechanism used by the capital backers of the banking and monetary system to acquire as much wealth as possible for themselves, without any significant concern for the immense sorrow this causes to the rest of mankind.

The second chapter of this book is furthermore the result of a(n elementary) **5**
research trip through the history of the monetary and banking system, above all aiming at demonstrating that, in essence, money is nothing else than that which "we"—mankind—consider to be money.

Yuval Noah Harari refers to this as to a continuous "*trust in the fabrications of the collective imagination*"[7].

The said historical analysis above all aims at demonstrating that money has an intrinsic changeable nature, and hence that "we"—mankind—might just as well "choose" to use something else as money instead of what we currently use.[8]

As already mentioned, this browsing through the (uncommonly fascinating) **6**
history of the banking and monetary system must necessarily remain concise, so during our tour we only look at a number of major milestones.

The primary intent hereof is to explain the essentially conventional, and therefore even somewhat "arbitrary," nature of the monetary mechanism, and not to provide a high degree of historical detail.

The reader should hereby above all avoid getting the impression that the monetary system has been created in a thought-out or premeditated way, as this was not (or hardly) the case.

---

[6] This insight is expressed as follows by John Kenneth Galbraith:

> The study of money, above all other fields in economics, is one in which complexity is used to disguise truth or to evade truth, not to reveal it. The process by which banks create money is so simple the mind is repelled. With something so important, a deeper mystery seems only decent. (see Galbraith 1975, pp. 18–19), also quoted on http://www.themoneymasters.com/the-money-masters/famous-quotations-on-banking/.

See furthermore Galbraith (1990), p. 19:

> The rule is that financial operations do not lend themselves to innovation. What is recurrently so described and celebrated is, without exception, a small variation on an established design, one that owes its distinctive character to the aforementioned brevity of the financial memory. The world of finance hails the invention of the wheel over and over again, often in a slightly more unstable version. All financial innovation involves, in one form or another, the creation of debt secured in greater or lesser adequacy by real assets.

[7] Harari (2014), pp. 200–201.

[8] See, for instance, the recent development of "bitcoins" as an alternative for government issued money used in certain internet transactions.

On the contrary, the process through which money has evolved to what it is today, has been a very gradual one, and in particular one of (a lot of) trial and error.[9]

2.2 The Essentially Conventional Nature of (the) Money (System)

2.2.1 Money as a Conventional Instrument Since Its Very Creation

7 In essence, money is a purely conventional system (in the widest sense of the term) which relies on a significant degree of mutual trust between the people who handle it, as is the case for any agreement.[10] As such, money and the monetary system are part of the so-called "social contract" underlying the societal order.[11]

In this approach, money is whatever mankind (or a certain organized society, for instance "a state"), considers to be money.[12]

This basic premise also implies that, as any conventional mechanism, money is inherently variable. Mankind's current vision of money is not necessarily forever frozen in time, since the social contract which deals with money can be modified, just like any other contract.

Put otherwise, within the monetary and financial system, there is no (unalterable) law that would be established forever.

8 Money and the set of legal rules that have further shaped today's money and monetary system, are moreover the result of historical developments.

9 Whoever takes the trouble to study the history of money and the monetary system in some depth will soon notice this "evolutionary" (and therefore, by definition, inherently variable) nature of money (and the monetary system).

It will hereby become as clear that these changes often did not take place in leaps and bounds, but rather gradually.

---

[9]One could even argue that, throughout all human endeavor, "trial and error" has been the usual "method" or rather "process" of creating societal systems, and for coming up with solutions to problems arising from living together (see Popper 1940, p. 403).

On the subject of the history of money and the banking system, see especially Bogaert et al. (2000) (also available in Dutch and French; see Bogaert, Kuran-van Hentenryk and Van der Wee 1991; Bogaert, Kuran-van Hentenryk and Van der Wee 1991); see also Galbraith (1975); Galbraith (1990).

[10]Harari (2014), p. 201.

[11]The term "contract" is here not so much used in its traditional legal meaning of a "private law agreement" between two or more persons, but in the sense of a set of norms adopted by a society by means of all kinds of international and state law mechanisms. As is the case for private law agreements, such mechanisms are themselves also subject to change and evolution.

[12]For further reading, see especially Galbraith (1975) and Galbraith (1990). Compare Brook and Watkins (2012), p. 77.

In some cases, these historical changes (resulting in the forms of money and the monetary system in use today) were motivated by the search for answers to problems arisen with former money (use). 10

Especially moments of financial crisis often caused tinkering with the monetary system in force at a given time. *On the one hand*, this resulted in the gradual establishment of a monetary system embedded in legal regulations. *On the other hand*, this contributed to the creation of a gradually increasingly globalized approach, as a result of which present-day money is in most countries in the world based on the same underlying philosophy (namely economic neo-liberalism).

It should therefore come as no surprise that money and the monetary system do not constitute a philosophically neutral commodity, but are to a large extent the fruit of a view, or better yet, of a combination of various views on society. This nevertheless does not contradict the starting premise that money and the monetary system are not the fruit of one premeditated and abstract (economic/philosophical) doctrine, but rather of a gradual and evolutionary process which throughout the ages has been fertilized by theoretical, philosophical, religious, ideological, political and other considerations, often during or subsequent to (financial) crises.

It is, as said, not the intention of the current book to give a comprehensive or detailed outline of the genesis of money and/or its history.[13] 11

We can instead make do with an outline of a number of major milestones, for the sole purpose (as mentioned above, at marg. 6 of this chapter) of showing that money has always had a conventional (intrinsically variable) and to a certain extent even "arbitrary" nature.

Consequently, the forms of money we know today (in addition to the underlying mechanisms of money creation), should in no way be considered to be "immutable".

Allegedly, it is not possible to trace an exact creation date for money or for the economy based on a monetary system. 12

On the contrary, it seems that different societies—in economic terms we might speak of "national economies"—adopted the "money" mechanism at specific moments in history.

The aforementioned "process" (which presumably occurred several times, in different parts of the world and at different times[14]) most probably interacted with the transition from a nomadic lifestyle to an agrarian society. 13

While an intensive commercial system (based upon money and a monetary system) was not needed to satisfy the economic needs of nomadic societies (consisting of relatively small, nomadic tribes mostly living off the proceeds of hunting and fruit gathering), the situation changed once societies evolved into agrarian ones, composed by larger, sedentary groups of people.[15]

---

[13] See the vast literature on this subject, *e.g.* Galbraith (1975); Galbraith (1990); Alvard (2013), p. 216; Bogaert et al. (2000), p. 422; Davies (2002), p. 720; Nussbaum (1950), p. 618; Fase and Vleminckx (1995), p. 192; Korteweg (1970); Kleinpeter (2000), pp. 59–64; Crockett (1981).

[14] Harari (2014), p. 197.

[15] Harari (2014), p. 194; Pinxten and De Munter (2006), pp. 47–48.

In these "agrarian" oriented societies, the individual became increasingly reliant on (barter) trade to satisfy his needs.[16]

The increasing use of barter trading in its own turn formed the breeding ground for the ascent of money (and the financial system). Direct barter trade hereby gradually evolved into a system of "indirect barter." A particular good, which usually had little or no intrinsic use, hereby began to function as the good against which all other goods and services could be exchanged.[17]

Thus money came into being.[18]

14 The intrinsically conventional nature of money was quite evident from the very beginning: money was "created" when a consensus grew within a given society that choosing a good against which all other goods and services could be exchanged, would be beneficial for sound economic trade planning.

2.2.2 *Origins of Coin-Based Monetary Systems*

15 The aforementioned so-called "social contracts" concerning the use of money were not only based on a consensus on the use of money as a generally accepted (= universal) means of exchange for the acquisition of other goods and services, but also about which material good might be appropriate to serve as money.

In the first stages of this money genesis process, various goods have been assigned as money. Different societies used different goods for this purpose.

However, throughout the centuries and all over the world, a strong preference would arise for the use of metal (often so-called "precious metals"[19]), mostly because these could be easily "coined". It therefore does not come as a surprise that the monetary system had already become a full-fledged coin system[20] in *e.g.* the Ancient Greek[21] and Roman[22] civilizations, being in essence agrarian societies which conducted trade and had most of the (hand) labor done by slaves[23].

---

[16]Harari (2014), p. 195. See also Pinxten and De Munter (2006), pp. 57 a.f.

[17]Ferguson (2009), p. 24.

[18]According to Plato, society itself originated when (coin) money came into use. In this approach, indirect trade economy is what gave shape to the economy and state organization (see Plato 1987, p. 61).

See also Galbraith (1975), pp. 7 a.f.

[19]See further Graeber (2012), p. 26; Ferguson (2009), p. 27; Korteweg (1970), p. 35.

[20]Bogaert et al. (2000), pp. 19 a.f.

See also Martin (2013), p. 15; Harari (2014), pp. 200 a.f.; Mandel (1962), pp. 254–258.

[21]Bogaert et al. (2000), pp. 23 a.f.

[22]Bogaert et al. (2000), pp. 44 a.f.

[23]Galbraith (1987), p. 9.

Slavery still expresses the love of capitalism, especially of the rich and the powerful, to exploit other people's labor as cheaply as possible (in order to get themselves as rich as possible), a love that regretfully still prevails in modern societies.

While large parts of the world evolved towards a coin based monetary system, coining—i.e. the creation of money out of metal—became to an increasing extent the prerogative of state (or other public) authorities.[24] **16**

As mankind organized itself increasingly into basic organizational legal structures, many of those structures started to gradually organize their own monetary system. Making abstraction of the name given to such organized "social structures," they usually had in common that a group of people considered themselves to be part of the same structure (*e.g.* a country, a sovereign city or region, etc.), generally controlled by a central leadership, often having sovereign claims on a given territory, where people who were not part of this structure did not have free access, but needed authorization from the central leadership.

It need not surprise that in society models relying on coin-based economies, the coining gradually became a prerogative of such central leadership. In such cases, only the ruler (sovereign, emperor, king, prince...) could coin money, which was evidenced by the fact that the coins in such an economy often bore the picture of its sovereign.[25]

This formula proved to be very successful. Coin-based money systems hereby gradually gained more and more confidence in view of the fact that the government became responsible for the money coining.[26]

In some cases, rulers responsible for issuing coin money, gradually wielded the coining even as a source of income. When such rulers needed (more) money themselves, they bought precious metal and minted coins with a fineness and weight that yielded them a profit. As a result, the value of the metal used in the coins became lower than the face value of the coins themselves[27], which could reduce trust in such "alloy" coin money.[28] **17**

This for instance happened in Ancient Rome, where at a certain point in time even local authorities refused to accept money issued by the state and, gradually, also the soldiers of the Roman legions lost confidence in the coin money, which, eventually, hardly contained any gold at all. This attributed to the understaffing of the Roman legions and would consequently contribute to the fall of the Western Roman Empire itself.[29]

During this historical evolution towards money creation based on coinage by the government, the conventional nature of the money system was essentially not **18**

---

[24]Graeber (2012), p. 27.

[25]Graeber (2012), pp. 27 a.f.

[26]Harari (2014), pp. 203–204; Vandewalle (1976), p. 8.

[27]Vandewalle (1976), p. 8.

[28]Galbraith (1975), pp. 8–9.

[29]Eagleton and Williams (2007), pp. 54 a.f.; Pfister (1941), p. 211; Breasted s.d., p. 125; Galbraith (1975), p. 9.

This clearly illustrates that "currency" (= money issued by the government) at all times is to be embedded in the social contract on which the state authority itself is based (see *e.g.* Vandewalle 1976, pp. 9 a.f.). When this trust is lost, the population will refuse to use the currency, which in turn, in extreme cases, can disrupt the organization of society itself.

altered, especially taking into account that a legal society structure itself may be considered as the outcome of a social contract.[30]

In this approach, a group of people keeps subjecting itself to a certain organizational legal structure to shape their society because they voluntarily choose to do so. In the course of time, they have "agreed" on the outlook of the organizational legal structure of society.[31]

In other words, the monetary system, originating within and by any organizational legal structure shaping society, is itself part of this social contract. More specifically, the money created by the government is accepted by the population on account of the trust that the people have in the authority of the government and its ability to maintain the purchasing power such money represents.[32]

Conversely, the power of the sovereign became also increasingly relying on the trust that his population put in his monetary system[33]. In this way, the historical tone for an ever increasing interdependence between money and power was set already at an early stage in the history of money.

2.2.3 *Money Within Modern States*

19 In contemporary societies, where the most common organizational legal structure that shapes societies is the so-called modern (central) (nation) "state", the creation of money is allegedly part of the sovereign state authority.[34]

Hence, the public bodies or administrations authorized under the constitution of such a modern state determine what constitutes money and what the legal organization of the monetary system looks like[35], using procedures that are to a greater or lesser degree "democratic".[36]

---

[30] Galbraith (1975), pp. 8 a.f.

[31] See Rousseau:

> Si donc on écarte du pacte social ce qui n'est pas de son essence, on trouvera qu'il se réduit aux termes suivants. Chacun de nous met and commun sa personne et toute sa puissance sous la suprême direction de la volonté générale; et nous recevons and corps chaque membre comme partie indivisible du tout. À l'instant, au lieu de la personne particulière de chaque contractant, cet acte d'association produit un corps moral et collectif compose d'autant de membres que l'assemblée a de voix, lequel reçoit de ce même acte son unité, son moi commun, sa vie et sa volonté. Cette personne publique qui se forme ainsi par l'union de toutes les autres prenait autrefois le nom de Cité, et prend maintenant celui de République ou de corps politique, lequel est appelé par ses membres État quand il est passif, Souverain quand il est actif, Puissance and le comparant à ses semblables. (Rousseau 2001, p. 53; see also Rolland 1940, p. 53; Brimo 1968, pp. 95 a.f.).

[32] See the historical examples summed up by Harari (2014), pp. 203–205.

[33] Harari (2014), pp. 203–204.

[34] See furthermore Martin (2013), pp. 66 a.f.; Shuster (1973), pp. 3 a.f.

[35] Harari (2014), pp. 200 a.f.

[36] For further reading, see Shuster (1973).

In many of these "modern" states (especially in the Western world), this legal organization of the money and of the monetary system is based on a more or less cohesive system of laws (or other "law-making" instruments with similar legal force). As a result, the monetary system is (or ever has been) voted in, or at least supported by, a democratically elected parliament, so that it is a reflection of the will of society.[37]

Even in such a formalized society model, where the conventional nature of 20
money and the monetary system is supported by the "social contract," their changing characteristic remains an essential characteristic.

Moreover, it appears that (nation) states in general have not been able to monopolize the creation of money entirely. On the contrary, throughout history, there have been several forms of so-called "privately" created money. This fact even still strongly determines the processes of money creation within contemporary societies where privately created money, both in numbers and in general societal impact, has become far more important than money issued by public authorities (see especially Sect. 2.5).[38]

2.3 Evolution of the Conventional Nature of the Monetary System in the Middle Ages

2.3.1 The Early Medieval Banking System

2.3.1.1 Predecessors of the Medieval Banking System

As has been pointed out in Sect. 2.2, already early in Western history, coins 21
composed of precious metals became gradually accepted as money in most parts of the world (usually under the auspices of a public authority).[39] Even so, the essentially conventional nature of money and the monetary system remained quite evident throughout Western history, in particular in light of the banking system that arose during the Middle Ages (especially as of the eleventh and twelfth centuries on).[40]

Without entering in too much detail,[41] some interesting key moments in this particular phase of the genesis of the currently prevailing monetary and financial system will hereafter be dealt with.

The emergence of the modern Western private banking system can be traced 22
back to the Middle Ages[42] (the period from 500 to 1500 AD).[43]

[37]Deweirdt et al. (1997), p. 27, pointing out the political symbol meaning of money.

[38]Harari (2014), p. 201.

[39]Galbraith (1975), p. 10.

[40]Eagleton and Williams (2007), pp. 77 a.f.

[41]See further Martin (2013), p. 32; Graeber (2012), p. 534.

[42]Martin (2013), pp. 88 a.f.

[43]Graff et al. (2014), p. 9.

Although also in Classic Antiquity there already had been some forerunners of the medieval banks and hence of today's modern banking system,[44] the latter has principally been shaped by a number of developments which have occurred in the Middle Ages.[45]

23 In medieval Western Europe, mainly from the twelfth century onwards,[46] there were institutions of all sorts that engaged in one way or another in monetary transactions.[47]

These institutions can be considered as the predecessors of the current banks.

For instance, there were the so-called "money changers." In an era when many cities and regions used their own local coins and inter-regional and international trade became increasingly important,[48] these money changers more and more played a crucial role in society.

Another example of institutions dealing with money professionally were the "jewelers" (also-called "gold and/or silversmiths"). Gold and silversmiths especially played an important role in the manufacture and storage of money, especially in areas and periods in which private individuals were allowed to have precious metals minted into coins.[49]

Also the so-called "pawn shops" have played a pioneer role in the genesis of modern banking.[50]

Moreover, within large mercantile houses arose affiliates responsible for preserving, transporting and exchanging money (a typical example was the mercantile house of the famous Italian Medici family[51]).

---

44 Bogaert et al. (2000), p. 19:

> The trade of banker (. . .) appeared for the first time in Greek history towards the end of the fifth century B.C., following the invention of money in Lydia in the last years of the seventh century B.C.

See also Galbraith (1975), p. 8; Ferguson (2009), p. 25.

45 Mankiw (2011), p. 627.

46 Bogaert et al. (2000), p. 71.

47 Bogaert et al. (2000), pp. 75 a.f.; see also Vandewalle (1976), p. 8.

48 Bogaert et al. (2000), p. 83.

49 Middelkoop (2014), p. 51.

50 Bogaert et al. (2000), p. 75.

51 Graeber (2012), pp. 291–292; Ferguson (1998); Bogaert et al. (2000), p. 111; Galbraith (1987), pp. 37 a.f.; Bogaert et al. (2000), pp. 95 a.f.; Middelkoop (2014), p. 52.

> Though others had tried before them, the Medici were the first bankers to make the transition from financial success to hereditary status and power. They achieved this by learning a crucial lesson: in finance small is seldom beautiful. By making their bank bigger and more diversified than any previous institution, they found a way of spreading their risks. And by engaging in currency trading as well as lending, they reduced their vulnerability to defaults. (Ferguson 2009, pp. 48–49.)

Initially also ecclesiastical institutions, *e.g.* convents and abbeys,[52] have played an important role in money circulation, in particular the "Order of the Poor Knights of Christ and the Temple of Solomon" (Lat.: "*Pauperes commilitones Christi Templique Solomonici*"), better known as "the Templars"[53]. Their main monasteries in Paris and London have even been referred to as "the principal banking houses" of their time and were both major lenders of money and major cashiers for various ecclesiastical and secular powers.[54] **24**

When some of the clients of the Templar banking houses faced increasing (re-) payment difficulties, they started to blame their problems on the banking houses themselves and viewed them as a threat to their power. This would motivate Philip IV the Fair, then King of France (1258–1314) to plead with Pope Clement V (1264–1314) for the dissolution of the Knights Templar, in its own turn leading to the papal bull "*Vox in Excelso*". Afterwards the role of the clergy in the financial sector largely disappeared, and they were gradually replaced by worldly "financial" institutions (in particular the ones mentioned in marg. 23 of this chapter).[55]

Out of the wide amalgam of institutions listed in marg. 23 of this chapter would gradually emerge the forerunners of today's banks in (using modern terminology) a process of continuous interaction between private and government initiative. **25**

2.3.1.2 The Medieval Mechanism of Coin Deposits

The institutions listed in the aforementioned marg. 23 of this chapter saw the light at a time when money creation—in essence, the coinage of precious metals (gold, silver, bronze, copper ...) into coins—was increasingly performed by or under the auspices of local sovereigns. Although a lot of variation prevailed, one common factor was that, in most cases, the strongest authoritative body in a specific region often arrogated coinage.[56] **26**

To put it in modern terminology: in such monetary systems, coinage became based on government authority. Otherwise put, money creation had gotten basically in public hands, as at that time in Western history, there was not yet other money besides coins.

With regard to this publically created coin money, the diverse institutions mentioned in marg. 23 of this chapter offered a variety of "financial services",

[52]Bogaert et al. (2000), p. 81.

[53]Delisle (1975), p. 248; Graeber (2012), p. 291; Bogaert et al. (2000), p. 103; Van Houtte (1942), p. 95.

[54]Eagleton and Williams (2007), p. 81; Van Houtte (1942), p. 95; Zilioli and Selmayr (2001), p. 40. See also; Le mystère sans fin des Templiers. In: Le Vif—l'espress (hors série), January 22nd 2016.

[55]Barber (1978), p. 311; Hamblin and Seely (2007), p. 125; Van Houtte (1942), pp. 95–96.

[56]Eagleton and Williams (2007), p. 77; Martin (2013), p. 74; Galbraith (1975), pp. 8 a.f.

such as the exchange, storage, transportation, coining and melting down of said coins.

As a result, in their respective professional capacity, these types of institutions often accumulated large quantities of coin money (mostly for the benefit of their clients).

In other words, these institutions increasingly functioned as “custodians” of the (cash) money on behalf of their clients (especially merchants, but also other well-off people), who for various practical reasons—many of them related to safety[57]—no longer wanted to keep their own (cash) money (= their coins), but entrusted its custody to said institutions.[58]

Thus came into existence an economic specialism, namely that of “custody” of (cash) money (= coins), in which we can recognize the predecessor of the current deposit function of the banking system, still one of the bases of the present-day financial and monetary system, hence of the prevailing private money creation system itself (see also further, under Sect. 2.5).

27 Since the task of such custodian institution(s) was initially limited to keeping and guarding the entrusted coins, under the commitment to return them to the depositor at the latter’s simple request, they did not yet play a true “bankers’ role”.

In modern terms, the function these institutions performed could be considered a mere “cashier’s function”.[59]

It goes without saying that a sound administration was a crucial element for the success of the respective service suppliers, besides offering guarantees for adequate surveillance (among others, by means of safes, of employing guards and through other security services).

28 However, some further evolutions of this custody function would prove to be of decisive importance for the development of the banking system. Once again, these evolutions were hardly based on preconceived, abstract concepts or systems,[60] but rather occurred simply while responding to practical opportunities and/or looking for ways to meet the growing needs of the clients of these respective professional “coin custodians”.

29 During these development phases of the modern banking system, an essential characteristic of the “primal form” of the contract of deposit for coins became gradually tinkered with.

The classic contract of deposit goes back to Roman law and essentially applies to a very specific type of agreement, whereby a depository receives a specific item from the depositor under the obligation to give back that very same item (and not

---

[57]Among which the risks and inconveniences of moving (huge amounts of) coins (see Eagleton and Williams 2007, p. 81).

[58]Bogaert, Kuran-van Hentenryk and Van der Wee (2000), p. 83.

[59]Bogaert, Kuran-van Hentenryk and Van der Wee (2000), p. 83.

[60]Martin (2013), p. 111.

another one), unmodified (and in principle even unused), whenever he is asked to do so by the depositor.[61]

Yet this basic characteristic of the deposit contract was soon found no longer to be essential for the deposit of money.

As explained above, money in the Middle Ages meant coins minted by or under the auspices of a (local) government authority. However, when a depositor deposited such a sum of money, i.e. a certain number of coins, he did not necessarily expect to get back those very same coins, but rather the same quantity of coins of the same kind—or possibly even other types of coins for a same total value.

Pretty soon, this principle of "fungibility" became prevalent for money deposits (in coins), even though this meant a departure from the classic deposit contract in a strict legal sense of the word.

The depository thus ended up in a position where he could "use" the coins entrusted to him by a particular co-contractor, on the condition that he managed to meet any repayment request from his co-contractor at any given time (consisting of the same quantity of other coins of the same kind, or possibly in coins of a different kind, provided their value was the same).

Moreover, the co-contractors of a professional coin depository tended to leave the coins in the custody of the depository for increasingly long periods because they did not need the coins themselves (otherwise put: as such co-contractors started to acquire more and more wealth, they also started to "save" money, or, in economic terms, they started to postpone its basic use of spending it), while a parallel payment system developed based on the debt instruments issued by the depositaries (see further, at marg. 38 of this chapter). The professional depositaries thus accumulated increasingly large stocks of coins which they could "use," on the condition that they were at all times able to honor any repayment requests from their clients.

2.3.1.3 The Medieval Mechanism of Lending Coin Money

As during the aforementioned processes (referred to above, at marg. 29 of this chapter), more and more "depositors" kept delaying their requests for repayment, thus extending the average deposit period of the coins handed over to their depository, the basis was created for a new economic activity for the depository, namely the "lending" of said coins to third parties. **30**

As already mentioned, this evolution required a departure from the classic contract of deposit. Little reservation against such practice seems to have been raised, which may be explained by the fact that, throughout the ages, commercial

[61]It goes without saying that this characteristic is essential to the deposit of specific objects.

For instance, when someone deposits a coat (to which he is attached), he expects to receive back that same coat, in the same condition. Obviously he will not settle for another coat, save in very exceptional circumstances, for instance if the depository would instead offer him a much nicer, more expensive coat. However, the latter situation would require a new contract between depositor and depository.

law has been shown to easily drop the strictness of classic, civil law requirements in cases where this is useful for commercial practice.[62] As a result the depository institutions which so far mainly had profiled themselves as depositaries of coin money, gradually developed into "loaners" of the latter to third parties in need of credit.

Initially, this lending activity was restricted by the so-called "papal prohibition on interest charging" and later in time, on "usury"[63], which was one of the reasons that such institutionalized "money-lending" against payment of interests, initially, fell mostly into Jewish hands, since Jews were not subject to the aforementioned papal prohibition on interest-charging[64]. (See also further, under Sect. 3.3.3 of Chap. 3 of this book.)

However, soon commercial practice sought for practices allowing depositories to escape the strict (papal) rules on the charging of interest (a topic which will be further explored in more detail in Chap. 3 of this book).

Thus, the predecessors of modern banks evolved into institutions which not only accepted coins in deposit (under the obligation of repaying an equivalent amount when so requested), but also started to loan out these coins to third parties in need of credit.[65]

31 In this evolution whereby depositories evolved into loaners of coin money, the "practical experience" of such a professional depository who also lent the coins entrusted to him to third parties, had to ensure a sound treasury management, since at all times he had to have sufficient coins in stock to be able to honor repayment requests from his (original) clients/"depositors."[66]

2.3.2 The Medieval Evolution Towards Privately Issued Paper Money

32 A second development would gradually resolve the economic restriction on the lending capacity of the specialized institutions referred to at marg. 31 of this chapter.

This development concerned the methods of proof used in the legal relationship between the professional depositaries and their clients-depositors.

33 Initially, when entering into a classic contract of deposit, very often an equally classic document of proof was drafted by the depository.

---

[62] Byttebier and Wera (2016), p. 2.

[63] See also Byttebier and Flamée (2012), p. 22.

[64] Byttebier and Flamée (2012), p. 25.

[65] Bogaert, Kuran-van Hentenryk and Van der Wee (2000), p. 83; Middelkoop (2014), p. 51. See also Galbraith (1987), pp. 140 a.f.

[66] As will be made clear in what follows, this has remained one of the main principles of modern-day banking.

For instance, the depositor of a certain sum of money—i.e. a certain number of coins—thus received a debt instrument in his name (which was usually not freely transferable, except under strict conditions imposed by civil law) mentioning a precise description of the restitution obligation of the depository. This kind of debt instrument, moreover, initially merely served as a method of proof of the right of the depositor to be repaid a specific number of coins or a number of coins for an equivalent nominal amount (and, consequently, of the corresponding obligation of the depository to repay the coin money).[67]

This commercial use would gradually evolve. As the earlier mentioned principle of "fungibility" of the coins to be returned became more important (see above, at marg. 29 of this chapter), the debt titles also changed form. Gradually, the debt titles were no longer made out in the name of the depositor, but got issued "to bearer". In addition, in order to facilitate the handling of the reimbursement requests at the counter of the depository, the debt titles which served as proof of the restitution obligation of the depository of the coins, got written out in advance for rounded figures. Whoever "deposited" a certain amount of coins, henceforth received in exchange several pre-issued debt titles written out for rounded amounts, adding up to the value of the deposited coins.[68]

Translated into more modern (financial) terminology, the situation of the fore- **34**
runners of modern banks at the point in history reached in the foregoing marg. 33 of this chapter, can be described as follows: private entities, initially functioning within the economy as professional depositaries of cash coins (at the time: the only form of money) started to issue—for reasons of proof—written documents granting the holder a right to repayment of coins for a nominal value (i.e. equivalent to the amount mentioned in the document). In order to facilitate the counter activity of the depository, there was an evolution towards the development of paper documents (debt instruments) mentioning rounded values and these eventually got issued to bearer.

The "pay-to-bearer" nature of the abovementioned paper documents had as an **35**
interesting side effect that the (initial) holders of such documents could fairly easily transfer them to third parties.

The general rule for pay-to-bearer documents is—in most law systems still—that its mere possession provides a sufficient legal value of proving the title contained in it.[69] As a result, the transfer of such pay-to-bearer paper can easily be accomplished by physically handing it over to a third party. The said proof of debt documents were moreover issued (eventually: to bearer) by relatively trustworthy parties, i.e. professional coin money depositaries which generally attached great importance to

[67]Bogaert, Kuran-van Hentenryk and Van der Wee (2000), p. 153; Eagleton and Williams (2007), p. 81.

[68]Eagleton and Williams (2007), p. 177; Bogaert, Kuran-van Hentenryk and Van der Wee (2000), p. 165.

[69]Martin (2013), p. 97; Weatherford (1997), pp. 123 a.f.

their market reputation, in particular as to their repayment capacity (in modern terms: they strove for a high level of "liquidity" and "solvency").

This eventually led to a practice whereby the proof-of-debt documents themselves gradually started to function as an appropriate instrument of payment themselves.

The debtor of a payment obligation towards a third party who was at the same time the holder of proof-of-debt documents issued by a professional depository of coin money (thus being himself a creditor of this depository) had two options: either (*i*) exchange the proof-of-debt documents for coin money at the depository's/issuer's, and pay his own creditor with that coin money; or (*ii*) if the third-party creditor agreed, hand over the debt instrument itself to his creditor in order to settle his debt (which legally speaking amounted to a system of tender payment by transfer of a claim); in such a case, the latter creditor himself became the rightful holder of the debenture documents and, in case he himself needed to pay his own creditor, he in turn got confronted with the same choice as the first-mentioned debtor himself had been (and further so, as Galbraith describes, "*ad infinitum*").[70]

36 As confidence in the issuers/depositaries of the mentioned debt instruments grew, the practice of repayment of debt through tender payment of such debenture documents issued by professional custodians of coin money also became more and more common (with less and less need to bring the underlying coins back into circulation).[71]

In this way, the debenture documents issued by professional custodians of coin money evolved into payment instruments themselves, more precisely into "privately emitted paper money".

A fundamental requirement for this system to work was that there had to be sufficient trust in the repayment capacity (liquidity and solvency) of the (private) issuers of the said debt instruments; without it, holders of such debenture documents would obviously be very likely to resort back to the underlying coin money.

37 It is hard to underline just how important this evolution has been as pivotal in the genesis of a real banking system (still lying at the basis of the modern banking and monetary system).

Martin[72] has phrased this as follows:

> It was here – in the creation of a private payments system – that the invention of modern banking originated. Such a humble birth may sound disappointing. Today, the banking sector's unglamorous routine of providing payments services takes a distant second place in the popular imagination to the exciting business of lending and trading. But their ability to finance and settle payments is the more fundamental activity. This is banks' specifically monetary role, and what makes them special.

---

[70]Galbraith (1975), p. 20.

[71]Martin (2013), pp. 100 a.f.

Comp. Galbraith (1975), pp. 18–19, in this regard having pointed out that

> the process by which banks create money is so simple that the mind is repelled. Where something so important is involved, a deeper mystery seems only decent.

[72]Martin (2013), p. 101.

2.3.3 *Medieval Private Paper Money Creation Based on Lending*

The practice described under Sect. 2.3.2 of using the aforementioned debenture documents soon was followed by another development. **38**

In their daily practice, issuers of bearer debenture documents started to experience that (*i*) the exchange of these documents for coins by their holders got more and more postponed in time, and (*ii*) on the contrary, the debenture documents evolved to a means of payment of debts themselves, while the holders no longer felt a need for an (immediate) exchange for coins.

This growing realization added a new dimension to the lending activity of coin depositories.[73]

Thus far (and as explained above), the lending activity of said coin depositories had been based on loaning out (the underlying) coins to parties in need of credit.

However, gradually a new lending technique would evolve whereby the issuer of the aforementioned debenture documents simply provided newly issued debenture documents (which did not rely on additionally deposited coins) to a counterparty in need of a credit.

As a consequence—and by definition—such issuer of bearer debenture documents would bring into circulation higher values (or amounts) of documents than he had coins in stock (cash). By definition, his cash resources consisting of coins became smaller than the value of the debenture documents put into circulation by him.[74]

The success of the technique of private (paper) money creation based on the lending activities of coin depositories, would furthermore be influenced by the evolution of the so-called "church prohibition on charging interest" (see further, under Sect. 3.3.3 of Chap. 3 of this book).[75] **39**

---

[73]Bleaney and Greenaway (1996), p. 382; Crockett (1981), p. 19.

[74]Galbraith (1987), p. 142; see also Galbraith (1977), pp. 164–166, having summarized this evolution as follows:

> With banks came the power, given to few private citizens, to create money.

[75]This church prohibition on charging interest had already been in vigor in the Western European (Catholic) territories since the early Middle Ages, but got more and more contested in the later Middle Ages, first in practice and then also in thought. As a result, it became for early bankers more and more lucrative to engage in massive lending (especially by issuing privately emitted paper money exceeding their cash reserve of coin money). They hereby started making agreements with the borrower, whereby the latter agreed not only to repay the capital made available, but also an additional interest, thus acting in defiance of the church restrictions on charging interest. This however gave a boost to the development of private paper money, as it prompted bankers to grant more and more credits in order to increase their profits (see Galbraith 1975, p. 13).

Moreover, the technique of interest generating credits also allowed for an increasingly "reckless" way of granting credits, as the interest mechanism made it possible to compensate losses from non-refunded credit with the gains of effectively repaid credit. This led to a proper free riding

40 It has probably not been a coincidence that the aforementioned technique of granting credit against interest by issuing amounts of paper money above the coin reserves of the issuers thereof, took a very strong hold in the early Protestant areas, i.e. in some areas of Germany (in the sixteenth century)[76] and in the Netherlands and the UK (in the seventeenth and eighteenth century).

This may, to some extent, be explained by the fact that renowned scholars such as Luther and later Calvin were among the first "Christian thinkers" endeavoring to make the practice of refundable credits and/or charging interest acceptable for Christians.

Hence, the mentioned territories were able to evolve into "capitalist powers *avant la lettre*" that thrived on private money creation based on interest.

41 As will be further explained in the next Chap. 3 of this book, this newly developing economic system would soon entail several pernicious emanations, such as "colonialism", "imperialism" and "slavery".

The "previous generation" of imperialist countries, in particular Spain and Portugal, had still based their colonial behavior (in the sixteenth century) to a much larger extent on a money system backed by gold and silver coins which has been one of the reasons for the historical gold and silver raids in South America.[77] The seventeenth century colonialism of the Netherlands and the United Kingdom would soon take an even bolder and more mercantile dimension, in a process where gradually the rest of the world would see itself reduced to an exploitation area for the economic interest of the leading European powers of that time.[78]

42 Once the technique described in the previous marg. 40–41 of this chapter started to take hold, the coin depositaries/debenture issuers evolved into actual bankers, i.e. institutions implementing so-called "private money creation".

A reverse side of this evolution was that any banker (depository/issuer of paper money) engaging in these credit activities by definition was no longer able to meet all and every request to exchange the paper money for coins, even though this was (still) the underlying legal obligation that such a banker had pledged to the holders of the paper money (i.e. the bearer debenture instruments).

---

mechanism where "bad" debtors (those who did not pay back their loans) could benefit from the efforts of "good" debtors (those who did pay back their loans).

The tone was hereby set for a society model that would increasingly rely on greed as a guiding principle of its socioeconomic relations. As Galbraith has put it:

> The discovery that banks could so create money came very early in the development of banking. There was that interest to be earned. Where such a reward is waiting, men have a natural instinct for innovation. (See Galbraith 1975, p. 19.)

The ethical side of this evolution will be further elaborated upon in the next Chap. 3 of this book.

[76]For further reading, see for instance Steinmetz (2015).

[77]Ferguson (2009), p. 22; Bieler (1961), p. 143; Beaud (1994), pp. 18–21 and 26 a.f.

[78]Beaud (1994), pp. 137 a.f.; Becket (2014), pp. 98 a.f.

Evidently, all of this required a great confidence[79] by the holders of the paper money in their respective banker. Such confidence had to be strong enough to deter these holders from "*en masse*" exchanging the paper money they held for the underlying coins, since their banker was by definition no longer able to meet such requirements of all the paper holders combined. On the contrary, when confronted with exchange requests for an amount greater than his stock of coins, the banker would find himself—to put it in modern terms—in a state of bankruptcy.[80]

2.3.4 Synthesis: Status of the Monetary System at the End of the Middle Ages

By the end of the late Middle Ages, the techniques described in the previous 43
margins of creating privately issued paper money had become common in several Western countries.

As a result, two distinct forms of money got in use in the countries (or territories) in which the aforementioned practice took place.

On the one hand, there was still a use of coin money. This coin money was (still) minted out of precious metals (especially silver), which in most countries (territories) could only be done by or under the auspices of a more or less central public authority.[81] These coins functioned as cash money which formed the basis for deposits with the developing bankers who were under the obligation to pay out coins against the paper money they had brought into circulation themselves.[82]

On the other hand, a second type of money consisted of privately issued paper money.

---

[79]The primary element of trust on which this form of money use relied, is also evident from the definition "fiduciary" paper money, as opposed to the notion of "representative" paper money which refers to cases whereby a sufficient amount of underlying coins (or bars of precious metal) are at hand (see *e.g.* Byttebier 2001, p. 32, no 34, a.o. referring to Bank of England (2000), 1; Bogaert 1988, p. 43; Fase and Vleminckx 1995, pp. 16–17).

Historically, paper money has gradually evolved away from being "representative" and became (more and more) "fiduciary".

[80]See *e.g.* Martin (2013), p. 104:

> In the same year [1321] the Catalonian authorities revised their 1300 order that failed bankers be forced to live on bread and water until all their clients were reimbursed. Henceforth, any banker who failed to meet his clients' demands was to be publicly denounced and then summarily beheaded in front of his bank. It was no idle threat, as the hapless Barcelona banker Francesch Castello discovered in 1360. Under such uncompromising regulatory regimes, domestic banking really was a risky business.

[81]Yet for some time the population in various territories was allowed to supply the raw precious metals for minting by the authorized public authority. The latter however had (often) the sole power to actually mint the coins and insert the required marks, which usually included the picture of the sovereign.

[82]Crump (1981), p. 17; Nussbaum (1950), pp. 32 a.f.

The choice for paper was a consequence of the fact that it was physically based on originally handwritten, and later printed documents which were created as debt instruments (in the sense used in civil law). These debt instruments got more and more issued to bearer and for rounded amounts. As the general public started to hand them to other parties to pay off debts (in classic terms of civil law: "transfer in lieu of payment"), they evolved into a second form of "paper money". Said paper money was a form of money put into circulation by private institutions, initially without any government involvement. Hence, for some time, no legal rules or restrictions regarding the issuing of this privately issued paper money prevailed.

This second type of money was "privately issued" and as it was exchangeable against coins, it could be considered as an early form of "representative" (later: "fiduciary") paper money.

2.3.5 *Evaluation of the (Late) Medieval Money Creation*

2.3.5.1 Advantages of the New Money Creation System

44 It is needless to say that the late medieval development described at marg. 38 a.f. of this chapter has been of paramount importance from both a general societal and socioeconomic point of view.

45 First, the creation of paper money got more and more detached from chance discoveries of silver and gold ore, which had become the metals most often used for coinage.[83] As a result, the privately created paper money, issued by "private circulation banks,"[84] could be issued much more abundantly than coins, as the latter required an increase in the supply of the relevant precious metals.

On the contrary, the only restriction on the issuing of (private) paper money was the need to keep a sufficient cash stock of coins in order to be able to honor the agreed upon obligation to pay back coins against bank notes upon the simple request of the holder of the latter.

For obvious reason, this new money creation mechanism had an important leverage effect on economic growth.[85]

---

[83]Pdoa-Schioppa (2011), pp. 51–73, especially 58.

[84]Bogaert, Kuran-van Hentenryk and Van der Wee (2000), p. 246.

[85]Galbraith (1975), p. 28 has phrased this as follows:

> The miracle of money creation by a bank (...) could stimulate industry and trade, give almost everyone a warm feeling of well-being.

but adding to this the question:

> How to have the wonder without the reckoning?

Compare to a more recent observation by Oxfam (see Oxfam 2016, p. 8):

As a result, money also started to play a more and more important role in government and in society in general than it had in the ages before. For instance, medieval governments ceased to rely on the old feudal levy to raise armies, which through tradition and precedent was more and more considered to be too circumscribed and inflexible, and instead started to supply and pay troops in cash money. Feudal tenants themselves started to commute their labor services into cash rents, while their lords started relying more on such cash payments or on exploiting their estates to produce surpluses which were saleable against money.[86]

In this way, the increase money supply through the private banking sector also contributed to the decline of the medieval feudal system to the advantage of a pre-capitalist society model.[87]

Second, the "new money creation system" was also an extremely liberal system, as the private market players themselves were able to determine the amount of paper money they put into circulation, solely based on their proper experience. **46**

However, in some areas, the private money creation produced an ongoing conflict with local authorities, which often tried to get a solid grip on the private banking system. Such authorities were usually eager to request credit, but not always very diligent in paying it back. In some cases, this even resulted in a dramatic outcome, with as an early historical example the sad fate of the "Templars" (see above, at marg. 24 of this chapter).[88]

Third, the aforementioned evolution (re)introduced the private initiative at the monetary level, i.e. a larger participation by the population of the national economies. As a result, issuers of private paper money got involved in the process of money creation by either honoring or not honoring requests for credit from members of their economy. **47**

Ever since, such private money issuing institutions have kept on playing this role and have, in modern-day economic terminology, become full-fledged "bankers". Needless to say that their particular role in the money supply and creation granted them a key role in the emerging capitalist economies.

Today, bankers still play this role, in particular when they grant credit to other economic agents. However, where during the Middle Ages this process of creating money by granting credit consisted in the issuing of new private paper money exceeding the value of the underlying cash reserve (coins), today's money creation

---

The size of the global economy has more than doubled over the past 30 years. In 2014, its value reached nearly $78 trillion. As production and output continue to grow, there have been absolute increases in gross domestic product (GDP)—one of the main indicators of economic prosperity—in every region of the world over this period. In South Asia, combined GDP in 2014 was more than five times what it was in 1985.

[86]Eagleton and Williams (2007), p. 83.

[87]Eagleton and Williams (2007), p. 83.

[88]Martin (2013), p. 115. See also Bogaert, Kuran-van Hentenryk and Van der Wee (2000), p. 103; Galbraith (1987), p. 143.

For further examples of defaulting worldly authorities causing severe banking problems, see Eagleton and Williams (2007), p. 82.

by banks through the granting of credit usually takes place through a booking on a bank account (leading to a so-called creation of "scriptural money"[89]) for amounts exceeding the cash reserve a bank holds (presently usually under the form of coins and bank notes). (See furthermore, under Sect. 2.4.5.)

48 Finally, the particular characteristic described under the previous marg. 47 of this chapter, moreover, once again highlights the essentially conventional nature of money, especially given the fact that it was people themselves who started to "accept" the private debt instruments issued as a means of proof of coin deposits, as a new form of money, hence as a means of payment for other commodities and services offered within the commercial field.

Otherwise put may also this evolution be considered within the larger social contract on how a society gets organized, especially vis-à-vis the societal consensus about what is accepted as money, or about what money "is."

2.3.5.2 Precarious Nature of the New Money Creation System

49 A major drawback of the (private) money creating system that was shaped during the late Middle Ages, was its inherently precarious nature (which Galbraith correctly refers to as money creation mainly based on cycles of euphoria and panic[90], a characteristic of the money creation processes which has largely remained in force since then).

50 Under the system described in the previous marg. 38 a.f. of this chapter, it did indeed not take much to get a banker into trouble. By definition, this could happen each time when such a banker would meet requests for reimbursements exceeding the amount of his coin cash reserve.

Hence, a crisis of trust, whatever the cause, was sufficient to tackle a banker and could *de facto* result in a destruction of money. This could result in a loss of purchasing power of the collectivity of bearers/owners of the privately issued paper money (which, when occurring, would amount to the difference between the total amount of paper money issued by this banker minus the value of his coin cash reserve).[91]

As bankers started to make investments in each other's paper money, the problems experienced by one banker could, furthermore, very easily create a cascade of similar problems with other bankers and hence for the whole banking sector. History has shown ample proof of this.[92]

51 It can hereby not be underlined enough that the practice of issuing paper notes was inherently based on an underlying conventional mechanism. Especially the bankers themselves were bound by obligations contained in the very paper notes

[89]Martin (2013), p. 13.

[90]Galbraith (1975), p. 21.

[91]Galbraith (1975), p. 21.

[92]Galbraith (1990), p. 20.

themselves. According to these obligations, a banker was obliged to pay out coins for the value mentioned on the notes he had issued.

This system was inherently precarious, as each banker would issue notes representing amounts (far) exceeding his cash reserve. By definition, no banker was ever able to comply with exchange requests for the total value of the bank notes he had issued.

This late medieval mechanism of private money creation by the banking system thus had a strong "fiduciary" nature and required a consistent trust of the population in the paper money, in particular, in the fact that paper money would continue to play its role as a generally accepted payment instrument, i.e. as money.

On a psychological level, this required the population of an area in which private paper money was brought into circulation to remain confident that the issuing banker would be able to comply at all times with any request to exchange paper notes for coins.

It is obvious that such a form of trust inherently had an irrational nature, as is the case with so many economic processes. Objectively, the said required trust made little sense, since, as bankers issued paper money for far larger amounts then their cash reserve of coins, by definition, it was impossible to comply with exchange requests for all the private notes issued by any particular banker.

This very dimension of extreme irrationality characterizes the conventional basis of money (as part of the social contract organizing society) and demonstrates that money is but that which the population of a given economy "believes" or "accepts" that it is money, putting their acceptance in something that intrinsically[93] is not (expected to be) of much value at all.[94]

A further striking characteristic of the banking system that emerged during the 52
late Middle Ages has been that any breach in trust could fairly easily crash the entire fiduciary monetary system of a given region.

For instance, a certain part of the population might suddenly lose its confidence in paper money while keeping confidence in coins, hence deciding to exchange their paper money for coins.

This might happen without or with a rational motive. An example of the latter could, for instance, have been the case when a competitor of a given banker massively collected bank notes issued by this particular banker and requested them to be repaid all at once, knowing that the banker in question would not have been able to honor such a request.

At the moment that a banker having issued paper money had spent all the coins of his cash reserve to comply with exchange requests, he was no longer be able to honor any further requests. He then effectively defaulted on his contractual obligations, since he was no longer able to honor his basic contractual commitment to exchange bank notes for coins. Such a banker found himself in a state of failure and literally had to close his doors.

---

[93]Harari (2014), pp. 202–203.

[94]Galbraith (1987), pp. 65–66. See also Ferguson (2009), p. 28.

In such cases, there rarely has been an easy way to remedy such a situation as the clients of the banker were no longer willing to keep on holding their deposits of coins. To put it in modern terminology, the banker in question went bankrupt.

53 Such bankruptcies of bankers occurred from the very beginning of the modern banking profession and had often dramatic consequences for the monetary system.[95]

In several cases whereby a private banker went bankrupt, the population did not just lose confidence in the paper money of the banker in question[96], but often in paper money in general, including that issued by other bankers.

Bankrupt bankers would furthermore be excluded from commercial trade. Hence, the paper money they had issued no longer represented any underlying commitment and became effectively worthless. This meant that the bearers, in particular those who had not managed to exchange even part of their paper money for coins, lost all the purchasing power previously contained in the paper money.

This might even lead to economic cascade effects. For instance, bearers of paper money who were themselves debtor to third parties, found themselves no longer able to pay their own debts. Manufacturers and merchants would as a result be confronted with impecunious clients, which in turn resulted in proper cash flow difficulties.

It comes as no surprise that such an abrupt loss of the purchasing power of fiduciary paper money could have dramatic societal and socioeconomic consequences, and in the worst cases even disrupted the very society model itself.

54 Society in general, and its public authorities in particular, obviously became eager to avoid such disruptions of the (new) monetary system, and aimed at techniques of avoiding and remedying them.[97]

As *e.g.* a massive number of private bankers went bankrupt in the sixteenth to seventeenth century[98], this would lead to various radical government interventions and in many countries even to the establishment of a (new) government monopoly on the creation of paper money (which will described in more detail in Sect. 2.4).

2.3.5.3 (Preliminary) Ethical Perception of the New System of Money Creation

55 There was obviously also an "ethical" downside of the (late) medieval "new system of paper money creation".

---

[95]For an overview of some financial crisis moments, see Schemmann (2013), pp. 22 a.f.; Galbraith (1990).

[96]While the latter might even lose his head; see above, at footnote 80 of Chap. 1 of this book.

[97]In present day terms, this topic a.o. translates as the moral hazard question of "bail outs of banks" (see especially Stiglitz 2010, p. 200).

[98]Bogaert, Kuran-van Hentenryk and Van der Wee (2000), p. 249.

As will be further elaborated upon in more detail in the next Chap. 3 of this book, the technique of private paper money creation based upon credits which private bankers provided to other economic agents and which generated interests, would open the doors for a society model increasingly characterized by greed and egoism (which would later on in history become known under the names "capitalism" and, subsequently, "the free market system").[99]

In this way, it could even be correctly argued that the industrial revolution of the nineteenth century was to a large extent preceded by a financial revolution of the seventeenth century which has made the industrial revolution possible.[100]

2.4 Genesis of the Central Banking System as a Reaction to Financial Crises

2.4.1 Banking Crises as Triggers for Government Intervention

As a result of the difficulties referred to under the marg. 52 a.f. of this chapter, the **56**
"newly" created European private banking system would find itself under increasing pressure, especially as of the seventeenth century.[101]

In view of the aforementioned characteristics of the late medieval banking system, it is no surprise that there were frequent crises of confidence, sometimes with disastrous effects, such as massive bankruptcies.[102]

In many cases, these crises of confidence turned out to be the result of excessively reckless and greedy behavior of the bankers themselves. Driven by an increasing desire for profit, bankers were more and more prepared to take increasingly big risks, in particular when granting credit to market players who were insufficiently creditworthy. The main reason of this evolution was that the said credits yielded interest—sometimes disguised as "fees" with other names—at a

[99]As will be elaborated upon in more detail in the third chapter of this book, private bankers, given their unbridled search for profits, started granting ever more credit to a.o. manufacturers (in addition to other economic agents). As a consequence, the latter were themselves driven to enhance production both in order to be able to pay back these credits (including the agreed upon interests) as for making ever more profits themselves (an evolution which led to the present-day "production for production's sake"). As economic production itself can only thrive when consumption also increases, consumers themselves were increasingly invited to start to "consume for consumption's sake", a.o. manipulated by marketing techniques which even led to so-called "created wants". Finally, within this societal model, public authorities themselves got increasingly manned by people more and more looking out for their own interests, instead of for the general good of the communities they are suppose to lead.

[100]Ferguson (2009), pp. 53–54.

[101]Galbraith (1975), pp. 21 a.f.; Schemmann (2013), pp. 29 a.f.

[102]See *e.g.* Galbraith (1990).

time when the aforementioned classic church prohibition on charging interest was gradually losing its grip on society. As a result, bankers saw opportunities to become rich quickly without much personal effort, simply by creating, out of nothing, excessive amounts of private paper money.

As a result, the amount of paper money brought into circulation by the private bankers expanded while the quantity of (underlying) coin money remained relatively stable.

It needs not much explanation that in a banking system where the obligations (to exchange paper money against coins) of the bankers kept increasing, while the number of the underlying coins economically remained virtually the same, sooner or later problems were to be expected

Moreover, this reckless behavior of bankers resulted in credit being granted to parties that were not sufficiently creditworthy, among which even worldly sovereigns and church authorities. An especially risky situation occurred when public authorities started relying on borrowed money to finance wars, per definition a completely counterproductive activity hardly ever to be made profitable for society as a whole[103]. The problems that arose when such credits would not be paid back would often lead to cascade effects.[104]

2.4.2 Genesis of (an Early) Central Banking System

57 In view of the often disastrous consequences of massive bank failures, governments saw themselves forced to intervene. From the late seventeenth century on, this resulted in various sorts of policy gradually shaping the basis for a central banking system. The latter would in many countries become characterized by (*i*) a (public) monopoly on issuing bank notes, and (*ii*) a task set to support private banks (ultimately giving rise to the creation of the *lender of last resort*-function still in vigor today).[105]

58 Once again, one must observe that there has never been a preconceived "blueprint" to shape the central banking system in any Western European country, its genesis rather also having been the result of a process of trial and (a lot of) error (see also above, footnote 9 of this chapter), sometimes inspired by foreign examples while at the same time taking local particularities into consideration.

Consequently, government measures drafted to support the private banking system (and in particular to protect it from the pitfalls of pernicious banker

[103]Albeit obviously very profitable for certain interest groups, such as arms producers and other members of the leading classes.

[104]Galbraith (1987), p. 143.

[105]Schemmann (2013), pp. 33 a.f.; Bogaert, Kuran-van Hentenryk and Van der Wee (2000), pp. 249 a.f.; Galbraith (1975), pp. 32 a.f.; Eagleton and Williams (2007), pp. 179 a.f.; Ferguson (2009), pp. 50 a.f.

behavior) came into being as a reaction to the occurrence of practical problems, in a gradual "*trial and error*" process. In many countries, it hereby took several consecutive measures to keep the private banking system afloat and/or on the right course. During a process of ongoing legislative interventions, the model was continually tinkered with, often even abolishing previous measures that had proven to be ineffective.

In hindsight, one can observe that during the eighteenth and the nineteenth centuries, the measures in question crystallized into a central banking system based upon the following pillars: **59**

1) the founding of "a central bank" (in some cases government was its only shareholder; in other cases government was its main shareholder, while other shares got in private hands; there even have been cases where the government shareholding was limited or non-existent, and central bank shares got mainly or entirely in private hands);
2) the granting of special, often exclusive competences to this central bank, the most far reaching being an exclusive competence to issue (fiduciary) paper money;
3) a task description of "general good"; in particular the central bank got the assignment to supply other (private) banks with necessary paper money, based on a system of lending against collateral; the central bank hereby started acting as a "*lender of last resort*" of paper money (potentially newly issued for this very purpose); in such cases, the private bank acted as borrower under an obligation to pay back the amount of the loan to which interest was added.[106]

Henceforward, the private banker had to generate sufficient funds from the services rendered to his clients in order to pay back the money borrowed from the central bank, plus interest. The private bankers became themselves the ones putting into circulation the paper money issued by the central bank when granting credit to their clients, the private bankers.

2.4.3 Genesis of a Central Bank Policy

As part of the evolving monetary policy referred to in the previous marg. 58 of this chapter, private banks were more and more encouraged to satisfy their financing needs among each other. For instance, a private bank with a cash surplus (coins and bank notes, the latter issued by the central bank) might "invest" this surplus by loaning it out to a bank with a cash shortage (i.e. not having enough banknotes and coins in stock to be able to pay its short-term obligations towards its own co-contractors). **60**

[106]Bogaert, Kuran-van Hentenryk and Van der Wee (2000), p. 275.

Borrowing money from the central bank hereby became a "*last resort*" mechanism. The central bank discouraged this by means of its interest rates, thus further motivating private banks to borrow (already existing) money from each other.[107]

61 Gradually, the practice referred to under the marg. 59 of this chapter evolved into a so-called "(central) interest rate policy". Hence, the central bank started positioning its central interest rate for loans to private banks systematically (a little) higher than the market interest rates, in order to discourage the private banks from knocking at its door.

This furthermore allowed the central bank to implement a policy for controlling the quantity of money that was put into circulation in function of the needs of the economy. Initially this concerned only paper money, but later it included a new form of privately issued money, namely the so-called "scriptural money" or "book money"; see further, at Sect. 2.5).

For instance, when economic growth needed to be stimulated, the central bank could lower its interest rates, thus encouraging private banks to borrow from the central bank in order to offer cheap loans to their own clients (thus putting into circulation more newly created paper money). When there was a threat of inflation, the central bank might raise its interest rates in order to confine borrowing (and the purchasing and investment behavior based on it).

62 In this way, central bank policy resulted in various countries in a strong mutual interweaving of private banks (on the so-called "interbank lending market"), but at the same time in a mechanism of steering the economy.

In this process, private bankers gradually started organizing themselves in so-called "*clearing houses*" in order to settle their mutual obligations. Initially, these clearing houses were physical spaces where the (representatives of the) bankers, on regular moments, gathered in order to settle their mutual obligations. Later on, the notion "clearing (house)" more generally started to refer to the practice of settling mutual positions between bankers (also in a virtual way).

Moreover, this system facilitated the financial soundness of private bankers and hence the upscaling of the private banking system. As they could no longer issue private paper money themselves but had to turn to their central bank in order to obtain (new) paper money, said private banks were (purportedly) moved to a more prudent behavior. As long as they respected the government directives (including those regarding their investment behavior), private bankers were in this way fairly sure they would be able to keep up with their financing needs (= the ability to comply with their obligations towards their clients).

Gradually, central banks themselves started to issue guidelines which were more and more detailed (often as part of their lending conditions) which purportedly encouraged the private banks to control their risk behavior even more.

63 The fact that the private banking system thus became *de facto* subjected to central bank supervision also allowed upscaling and professionalization.

[107]Bogaert, Kuran-van Hentenryk and Van der Wee (2000), pp. 275 a.f.

As a result, in many Western countries, small local banks grew into national market players (in Europe: also into European market players) that played an increasingly important role in various sectors of economic life.

Perhaps without having realized it explicitly, the banking system was thus being prepared for its role as the financial motor of the industrial revolution of the nineteenth century.[108] In this regard, as has been mentioned before (see above, at marg. 55 of this chapter), the industrial revolution of the nineteenth century was preceded by a financial revolution starting at the end of the seventeenth century which has made the industrial revolution possible.[109]

2.4.4 *Impact of the Aforementioned Evolutions on the Monetary System*

At this particular point in the genesis history of the "modern" banking system, there now were still two types of "cash money" in play, albeit the nature of one of these had changed. **64**

There still were the coins minted by the government, which would for a long time continue to be made out of precious metals.

On top of that, there now was also cash "paper money" issued by the central bank (which often had a monopoly on issuing it).

Both forms of money functioned as full-fledged money, fulfilling all the functions usually attributed to money. Both forms of money could, for instance, be used in payment transactions, but also fulfilled a savings and credit function. Economic residents with a savings surplus could, for instance, deposit coins or paper money (or a combination of both) with a bank and expect to be repaid (upon request) in both forms of money.

To the degree that both forms of money were issued by a government (sometimes the same), the system would even get further rationalized in many countries. In this evolution, gold and silver coins got gradually taken out of circulation and melted down to gold and silver bars which were kept by the central banks as a monetary reserve to cover their obligations.[110]

Furthermore, instead of precious metal, metals or alloys of a far lower value (for instance copper and nickel) got used for the making of coin money. In many cases, the nominal value of these copper or nickel coins was significantly higher than the intrinsic value of the metal they were made of. The issuing government often also abolished the liberty of minting and melting coins.

---

[108] Bogaert, Kuran-van Hentenryk and Van der Wee (2000), p. 292.

[109] Ferguson (2009), pp. 53–54.

[110] This was furthermore a consequence of the collateral mechanism that lay at the base of the central bank's lending policy.

While (central) governments, for practical reasons, even limited the purchasing power of coin money, coins evolved from "token mints" (minting and melting of which became the prerogative of the government) to so-called "token money" (which could only be used for payments of limited amounts).

On top of that, a new form of private money creation entered the banking and monetary system, namely the so-called "scriptural money" (also: "book money").

For reasons of clarity, the latter will be further dealt with under Sect. 2.5.

65 Further on, appropriate legislative interventions were implemented to take gold and silver coins out of circulation and melt them into bars to be used as monetary reserves.

This evolved to a system of gold coverage of the paper money issued by central banks. In some countries, legislation hereby obliged central banks to hold a sufficient reserve of gold (bars) to match the nominal value of the banknotes in circulation. In other words, the banknotes had to be "covered" by underlying gold (so-called "*gold coverage*").[111]

In many countries, central banks themselves accumulated a major part of the national gold reserves to serve as such a monetary reserve. At that point, silver was in most cases taken out of the monetary scene.

At the same time, the exchange obligations of the central bank gradually became more flexible, for instance by applying the coverage rules only to large amounts. As a result, only those economic players that held banknotes amounting to the value of a certain (large) quantity of gold (for instance a gold bar with a certain standard weight) were henceforward allowed to submit an exchange request.

66 The United Kingdom would take a leading role in the processes described in the previous margins and eventually ended up at the head of a (*de facto*) "gold (bar) standard" monetary system, allegedly the first truly international monetary system in which the central banks of the participating countries subjected themselves to a strict monetary discipline characterized by the fact that the quantity of the banknotes in circulation had to correspond to a determined amount of underlying gold (bar) reserves.[112]

From an ethical point of view, it has to be observed that already from the start, this system was intrinsically "unjust", since under this "gold standard system", the money supply within a given economy, and hence its growth potential, depended on the amount of gold the country in question had managed to build up in the past (in most cases by having robbed other territories).[113] As a consequence, countries that

---

[111] Bogaert, Kuran-van Hentenryk and Van der Wee (2000), p. 270.

[112] Weatherford (1997), p. 164; Bogaert, Kuran-van Hentenryk and Van der Wee (2000), pp. 267 a.f.

[113] This is probably why Keynes himself would dismiss the gold standard as a "barbarous relic". (See Ferguson 2009, p. 59.)

had shown the strongest drive for conquest and war, were also the ones most likely to maintain and even expand their wealth.[114]

Poorer countries were often unable to participate in the gold (bar) standard, or had to resort to "tricks", such as maintaining monetary reserves in banknotes issued by countries that themselves managed to follow the rigorous discipline of the gold (bar) standard. For the latter countries, a parallel gold exchange standard emerged, based upon central bank monetary reserves consisting of, for instance, Pound Sterling. This in turn tended to further strengthen the currency of the "strong" countries (with the Pound Sterling evolving into a so-called "strong currency").[115]

Needless to mention that the inherent unjustness of the gold standard monetary system still leaves traces today, mainly as a result of the unfair distribution of the world's wealth it has caused.

2.4.5 Further Crystallization of the Monetary System in the Nineteenth Century

As a consequence of the aforementioned genesis of the central banking system, the commercial banking system, and hence the mone(tar)y system itself, to some degree returned under state control. 67

This process started hesitatingly in the seventeenth century (for instance in Sweden and England[116]), and spread all over Europe in the course of the eighteenth and nineteenth centuries[117].

As the central bank in many (European) countries often obtained a monopoly on issuing bank notes, money creation once again ended up in the hands (or at least under the auspices) of governments.

Coin minting, on the other hand, had in most countries remained in government hands for centuries and had itself hardly or not been affected by the rise of the medieval banking system.

As a result, both paper money and coin money now had a "public" character. However, this would merely be a temporary situation, as gradually a new form of private money creation was about to manifest, namely the creation of "scriptural money" (which, at present, is by far the most important form of money).

The evolution which led to the technique of scriptural money creation will be further dealt with in a more detailed way in Sect. 2.5.

---

[114]It has, for instance, not been a coincidence that Great Britain, which had absorbed a large part of the world into the so-called "*British Empire*" (in particular between the sixteenth and the eighteenth centuries) was the leading country under this gold standard system (see Weatherford 1997, p. 162).

[115]For further reading, see Schuker (2003), pp. 77–93; Drummond (1987); Eichengreen (1985).

[116]Flandreau and Ugolini (2011), p. 47.

[117]Galbraith (1975), pp. 31 a.f.; Bogaert, Kuran-van Hentenryk and Van der Wee (2000), p. 275.

68 The further historical evolution of cash money would witness an escalating "demonetization" of precious metals.[118]

Also this development has not been sudden and/or thoroughly meditated upon, but has rather been a gradual process by which the central banks of more and more countries would systematically lower the coverage ratio of the paper money they issued, until the obligation to "cover" paper money with precious metals eventually got completely abolished in most countries (albeit the central banks of some countries would continue to hold on to their reserves of precious metals as so-called "monetary reserves").

At that moment in time, cash paper money also became entirely "conventional". Its value was no longer determined by the fact that it represented precious metals against which it could be exchanged, but instead now depended on a simple government ratified agreement between economic agents who "accepted" (or: "agreed") to consider paper money as money.[119]

69 This gradual "demonetization" of precious metal coins and the gradual evolution of paper money from "representative" to entirely "conventional" even prompted an economic scientific debate about what exactly constitutes the value of paper money.

This debate was prominent in nineteenth century England[120], which is not coincidental given the fact that this was the leading economic (and hence also monetary) power of the time.[121]

In this debate, there were two main currents, namely "metalism" (which held that the value of paper money lies in the underlying precious metal coins or bars) and "nominalism" (which held that the value of paper money is not based on any underlying commodity, but is of an intrinsic nature based on a convention between economic agents).[122]

Eventually, the nominalism current would come out as the victor of this debate.

This would by the end of the twentieth century result in an uncontrollable—and hence uncontrolled—growth of the money supply, characterized by the fact that, worldwide, numerous economic agents, including governments, have found themselves sucked into an ever more unrestrained credit behavior, with as sole winners

---

[118]Pdoa-Schioppa (2011), pp. 51–73.

[119]Nussbaum (1950), pp. 5–9; Fase, and Vleminckx (1995), p. 17.
See also Bank of England (2000), p. 1.

[120]Graeber (2012), pp. 46 a.f.; Galbraith (1975), pp. 36 a.f.
According to Galbraith, this debate is indistinct, albeit wholly recognizable, still continuing to the present day. It concerns the basic question where economic change originates, either with those who are responsible for money creation (in our economy, mainly private banks providing credit to other economic agents), or with those who produce. Otherwise put, the question is if money (should) influence(s) economy, or if money should respond to the economy. (See Galbraith 1975, p. 36.)

[121]Galbraith (1975), p. 36.

[122]For further reading, see Bogaert, Kuran-van Hentenryk and Van der Wee (2000), p. 363; Berend (2006), p. 193; Nussbaum (1950), pp. 28 a.f.; Hirschberg (1976), pp. 53 a.f.

of this evolution private banks themselves (see further Sect. 2.6.3 and Sect. 3.4.5 of Chap. 3 of this book).

2.5 Scriptural Money as the New Privately Created Money

2.5.1 Background

In the evolutionary processes described in the previous Sect. 2.4, the commercial banking system—and hence private initiative in general—for a brief period of time, appeared to have lost its participation in the money creation process, as the latter had become to a large extent under the control of central banks which came into existence as of the seventeenth century.[123] **70**

Yet it would not take long for private banks to discover new opportunities to participate in money creation, this time by developing so-called "scriptural money".[124]

2.5.2 Deposits and Money Substitution

To put it simply, the creation of scriptural money starts with the deposit of cash money (which at the point in history we have reached in the previous margins consisted of both coins and publically issued bank notes). **71**

In its elementary form, such a deposit of cash money is the legal action by which an economic agent (the depositor) hands over a certain sum of cash money to his bank. The latter, by way of proof, opens an account indicating the deposit and as a result becomes obliged to immediately repay this sum of money at the simple request of the depositor.[125]

It should be observed that this legal technique of deposit forming was almost identical to the medieval custom of economic agents entrusting their coin money to a financial institution such as a goldsmith or money changer, who supplied them with a debt instrument as proof of his repayment obligation. As explained above, it were precisely these (late) medieval debt instruments that had evolved into privately issued paper money. **72**

---

[123]See for instance, as regards the Bank of England, Galbraith (1975), p. 34.

[124]Today, private banks still hold a central position in the process of creating "scriptural money" to the extent that, in most countries, the quantity of scriptural money is much larger than the quantity of chartal money, as a result of which scriptural (hence: privately created) money has become the primary form of money.

[125]See for instance Treyvaud (1972), p. 166.

There were some differences, though. The aforementioned deposit custom of the Middle Ages initially only pertained to coins, whereas the practice of deposits emerging in the seventeenth to eighteenth century pertained both to coins and to (publically issued) bank notes. Another difference was that the medieval practice involved issuing debt instruments, whereas the deposit mechanism of the seventeenth and the eighteenth century involved the opening of a deposit account.

73 From a legal point of view, such a deposit entails a legal action resulting in a contract between the depositor and the bank in question, regulating the obligation to repay the deposit in cash money (coins or banknotes). Furthermore, the contracting parties usually agree upon other ways of using the deposit and the deposit account, in particular with regard to various payment facilities offered by the bank (initially: checks, later: bank transfers and eventually: electronic and internet based payment techniques).

Moreover, as a result of such an initial deposit of cash money, a conversion of cash money into scriptural money occurs for the amount of cash money deposited.

Henceforward, cash money could be defined as money with a physical existence and which owes its value as a generally accepted payment instrument to a government decision. Scriptural money is then a debt instrument expressing a receivable of a depositor towards his banker, including the right of reimbursement of the deposit in cash.

This conversion process is the so-called "money substitution" which does not result in the creation of new money, but in a process whereby existing cash money is "converted" into scriptural money.

Reclaiming the deposit then causes an "inverse money substitution effect".

2.5.3 Creating New Scriptural Money Through Commercial Bank Lending

74 The further historical evolution of commercial banks creating new scriptural money "*ex nihilo*" has been quite similar to the process of, *on the one hand*, displacement of the standard coin money by the token coin and, *on the other hand*, the origination of paper money (firstly "representative"; subsequently "fiduciary"; and eventually completely "conventional") as an alternative money form to precious metal coins.

The historical origination of both privately issued paper money and scriptural money illustrates that when the government tries to monopolize the monetary system, private market players will look for alternative money forms, usually motivated by an unrestrained desire for profits (see further Chap. 3 of this book, in particular Sects. 3.2–3.4 for further details).

75 The way in which the private banking system started creating new scriptural money once again was based on the practical experiences of (commercial) bankers.

Initially, the latter got involved in the process of converting cash money into scriptural money, which, as described earlier, is a form of "money substitution". As explained before, this happened at a time when, due to legal restrictions, said bankers were no longer able to issue banknotes, as this had in most countries become the privilege of the central bank.

Just as in the (medieval) origination of privately issued paper money as an alternative to precious metal coins, bankers would soon, once again, observe that the whole of depositors would at a given moment in time only convert a fraction of the sum of all deposited amounts (coins and banknotes) back into cash.

This empirical observation soon motivated the private bankers to engage in so-called "scriptural obligations" without having received a cash deposit, in particular in the context of their credit activities.

The process of creating (new) scriptural money became common practice in the **76**
nineteenth century[126], and once again the English banking system has played a crucial role[127].

Nevertheless, its historical origins go back much further. For instance, the renowned "*Amsterdamse Wisselbank*" (which could be freely translated as the "*Exchange Bank of Amsterdam*") already performed scriptural transactions in the seventeenth century,[128] thus performing an as yet unequaled creation of (private) money through the granting of credit, which even became one of the motors of the Dutch economy during Holland's "golden age."[129]

Private banks were hereby able to engage in scriptural obligations for an amount **77**
exceeding their cash liquidity (= cash reserve), based on the observation that, at any given moment in time, only a fraction of the scriptural credit was converted back into cash by the original depositors.

As a result, engaging in scriptural obligations above the amount of his cash reserves became part of the credit policy of banks towards their diverse clients.

Based on their stash of cash money, banks started to calculate the maximum amount of liabilities they could engage in without ending up short of liquid assets and hereby avoid becoming unable to comply with a depositor's request for exchange. Such calculations were based on their daily experience: the amount requested by the depositors to be converted from scriptural credit into cash money at any given time.

As a result, the scriptural liabilities of the banks became much larger than their cash reserve, which implied the creation of new (scriptural) money.

To this day, the cash reserve held by banks is still one the foundations of the **78**
prudent policy that private banks are supposed to adopt.[130]

A bank which receives a deposit from a client must at all times be able to repay this deposit *ad nutum* in cash at a simple request (at least for the classic type of

---

[126]Korteweg (1970), p. 45.

[127]Bogaert, Kuran-van Hentenryk and Van der Wee (2000), p. 274; Middelkoop (2014), p. 54.

[128]Bogaert, Kuran-van Hentenryk and Van der Wee (2000), pp. 196 a.f.; Galbraith (1975), p. 19.

[129]Harari (2014), pp. 355–356; Galbraith (1987), p. 141; Ferguson (2009), p. 49; Van Houtte (1953), pp. 89 a.f.

[130]Deweirdt et al. (1997), pp. 43 a.f.

deposit). Moreover, a bank that has granted a credit through a booking on an account is even so committed to pay out his amount at the (simple) request of the holder of such an account.[131] This obligation to pay out in cash the amounts that a bank account shows is more precisely the basic object of the deposit agreement, and it is in various legal systems even qualified as a "performance" obligation. It is hereby obvious that such a bank must adopt an investment policy which allows it to comply at any given time with a depositor's request for repayment.[132]

79 As a result of the evolutions described in the previous margins, already in the nineteenth century the banking system had largely crystallized into the form that it still has today.

Its further evolution in the nineteenth, twentieth and twenty-first century consisted at the very most of some emphasis shifts which hereafter, in the next marg. 80 of this chapter, will only be mentioned in a general way.

80 The most important of these emphasis shifts was probably the fact that "lending" (or "the granting of credit") evolved into the most characterizing banking activity through which (private) banks got involved in the process of private money creation twice in history, the first time when they commenced issuing private paper money and the second time when they started creating scriptural money.

Throughout the second half of the twentieth century, deposit banks became furthermore more and more daring in developing all sorts of high tech investment techniques.[133] *On one hand*, this allowed them to supply the necessary appropriations to the developing capitalist economy. *On the other hand*, banks at the same time developed an increasingly risky speculation behavior, mainly motivated by greed[134].

This evolution will be further dealt with in Chap. 3 of this book.

Another emphasis shift in the wake of this evolution has been an increasing specialization of the banking institutions which resulted in the genesis of several varieties of the "modern" bank.

---

[131] Albeit other means of use are also usually agreed upon, such as access to scriptural payment techniques.

[132] Harari (2014), p. 343.

[133] These will here not be summed up in detail, as they are basically all based upon some elementary basic principles of banking. As has been remarked by Galbraith:

> The rule is that financial operations do not lend themselves to innovation. What is recurrently so described and celebrated is, without exception, a small variation on an established design, one that owes its distinctive character to the aforementioned brevity of the financial memory. The world of finance hails the invention of the wheel over and over again, often in a slightly more unstable version. All financial innovation involves, in one form or another, the creation of debt secured in greater or lesser adequacy by real assets. (See Galbraith 1990, p. 19.)

[134] De Grauwe (2012).

As a result, alongside the classical deposit banks emerged several other banking institutions, such as business banks (which deal less with deposits), all sorts of investment institutions, etc.[135]

2.6 Further Aspects of the Modern Banking and Money System

2.6.1 General Characteristics of the Modern Banking System

Today's deposit banking model and the monetary system based upon it are the outcome of the aforementioned evolution, which started in the Middle Ages and crystallized throughout the nineteenth century. **81**

It must therefore be once more observed that the current banking and monetary system is not at all the result of a deliberate and calculated process. Instead, the prevailing banking and monetary system basically came into being through "trial and error," with the interaction between private and government initiative as general "leitmotiv". More precisely, governments often had to intervene to put an end to malpractices of commercial bankers, especially in cases when, usually motivated by excessive greed, the latter had put themselves and society at too much risk.

In particular, the founding of a central banking system was aimed at disciplining commercial bankers, mainly by removing their capacity for (paper) money creation. This initially also put a major brake on the profits that commercial banks could draw from lending and other investments, but, as explained before, said bankers would soon circumvent this prohibition by scriptural money creation through the granting of credit.

As a result, and as will be dealt with further in the this book, the efforts of disciplining private money creation by means of establishing central banks even seem to have had the reverse effect of giving private banks ever more economic influence and general societal power (see more in detail in Chap. 3 of this Book).

Also, the emphasis shifts of the second half of the twentieth century have **82**
furthermore raised the question whether the current banking model is compatible with the excessively risky behavior of today's bankers, who are merely driven by an ever increasing drive for profits.

---

[135]Banks and the banking groups they eventually formed, hereby became also more and more dexterous in applying company law techniques in order to expand, in many cases even on a global scale. Banks for instance got specialized in dividing their various activities into subsidiaries. Shares of the latter were sometimes even made available to the clients of the bank who, in many cases, were hardly aware that an investment product offered by their bank constituted a risky participation in a branched-off (special purpose) investment vehicle.

This essentially moral question will also be covered more in detail in Chap. 3 of this book.

83 By way of summary, the deposit banking model as we know it today, in headlines functions as follows:

- Deposit banks manifest themselves within the economy as the collectors of the savings surplus of the economic players. In some jurisdictions, banks even have a legal monopoly in this regard. Such an initial deposit of cash money (= "coins" and (publically emitted) "banknotes") results in a process of so-called money substitution, "converting" the deposited cash money into a scriptural claim for repayment or for use in scriptural transactions.
- Within the bank itself, the cash money collected from the deposits functions as a so-called "cash reserve." As a result, the latter is no longer taken into account when calculating the amount of cash money in circulation among the public.
- Based upon its practical experience, the bank discovers what the size of its cash reserve must be in relation to its liabilities. Based upon this information, bankers work out their scriptural money creation whereby they engage in scriptural obligations representing an amount of money exceeding their cash reserve.[136]
- The process of creating scriptural money (which is the method of private money creation by banks currently in use) forms more precisely part of the credit activity of said (deposit) banks.[137]

  From an economic point of view, the granting of credit by a bank is thus an activity of a peculiar nature, as it results in the creation of additional (scriptural) money.[138]

  Within Western and Western-inspired economies, the creation of scriptural money has evolved to be the most important method of money creation, which according to some authors to a large degree falls outside the influence of the monetary authorities.[139]

  As a result, most of the money in circulation does not emerge from the creation of "chartal" money by the central banks (or other (government) institutions), but rather from scriptural money creation by the private banking sector. According to some estimations, the latter amounts to at the very least 90% (and probably far more) of the total money supply (see further, at marg. 88 of this chapter and Chap. 4 of this book).

  Needless to say that this provides private banks with an almost unlimited economic and political influence which in present-day societies is hardly counterbalanced by anyone or anything else.
- Based on the diverse agreements with each of its depositors, the deposit bank is subject to "restitution obligations" towards these depositors.

[136] See further Friedman (2002), p. 47.

[137] For a general description of the bank lending mechanism, see *e.g.* Hughes (2006), pp. 9 a.f.

[138] Deweirdt et al. (1997), p. 30.

[139] Deweirdt et al. (1997), p. 44. See also Pettifor (2014).

The latter basically obliges the deposit bank to pay out a scriptural claim in cash when the holder of the claim so requests, yet the agreements between the bank and its depositors may include some extra stipulations. For instance, the bank is usually also obliged to perform so-called scriptural money transactions at the request of the depositors (mainly transfers between different bank accounts).

- As a result, the granting of credit by deposit banks plays a key role in Western and Western-inspired economies, since it supplies economic agents with (new) money for investment needs (all sorts of investment lending) and consumer needs (for instance construction loans and consumer credit).
- Hence, whenever a banker grants a credit, it should be a key moment of reflection as to the creditworthiness of the borrower. Otherwise it could be a case of too frivolous money creation, where the beneficiary does not contribute to the economic development, which could *de facto* result in economic "*free riding*" (see also further, under Sect. 2.6.3).
- Precisely on account of their role within the economy (the gathering of deposits and private money creation through the granting of credit), banks have over time been submitted to regulations motivating them to more "careful" or "prudent" behavior. The creation of such "prudential" regulation has moreover in a lot of countries formed a response to the major banking crises of the late 1920s and early 1930s.[140]
- In order to avoid banking crises, the commercial deposit banking system has, furthermore, been embedded in a monetary system, as a result of which, in most countries, a private bank can turn to a (usually, albeit not in all cases, government founded) central bank for additional funds when its cash reserve is not sufficient to meet the restitution requests of its depositors (and when it cannot get cash elsewhere, for instance through a loan from a colleague banker on the "interbank lending market").
- As a result, the banking system is typically monitored in two ways: (*i*) the monetary authorities provide direction through their "*lender of last resort*" function and (*ii*) banks are moreover subject to a "prudential" legal framework, which in most countries subjects bankers' activities to rigorous legal rules, the compliance of which is monitored by a supervisory authority.
- In most (Western) countries, a central bank which is in charge of cash creation has a so-called emission privilege for banknotes, and sometimes also for coins. In other countries minting coins is the competence of other authorities, often some organ of the executive power.

  Hence, the central bank, by definition, can always create new cash money by either minting coins and/or printing banknotes.

  Its interventions, however, will be part of its monetary policy, such as an interest policy with respect to commercial banks, aimed at monitoring the solidity of commercial banks requesting an intervention or at safeguarding the value (hence: "the purchase power") of money. Hence a commercial (deposit)

---

[140]Bogaert, Kuran-van Hentenryk and Van der Wee (2000), pp. 343 a.f.

bank cannot unlimitedly request for new cash money from the central bank. Needless to say that a commercial deposit bank that loses the support of its central bank, is in dire straits and is usually headed for bankruptcy (unless in cases when it is "bailed out" by its government).

- In this monetary and financial system, the central bank ultimately controls the money supply, at least in theory.

  Since the central bank, at least within a given territory, exclusively supplies the commercial banks with newly created cash, it is also, at least in theory, able to put a brake on the growth of the scriptural money amount. It is hereby understood that commercial banks which have restricted access to new cash money will become more prudent in creating private money, in order to avoid the risk of not being able to comply with exchange requests from depositors. The central interest rate policy is one of the mechanisms used by the central banks to keep the scriptural money growth within reasonable limits (or, inversely, to try to stimulate it).

2.6.2 The Continuous Conventional Nature of Modern Forms of Money

84 The aforementioned overview also demonstrates that, throughout the ages, money has kept its essentially conventional nature from antiquity till now.

In most current Western and Western-inspired economies, cash money (= "coins" and "banknotes") and scriptural money (= banking liabilities) together constitute "money" which the population within a national economy accepts as a universal payment instrument for commercial commodities and services.

85 The social contract that shapes money is hereby based on numerous regulatory texts, but also on various agreements between bankers worldwide and their clients (such as depositors and borrowers) and with other bankers (*e.g.* to establish arrangements prevailing on the so-called "interbank lending market" and to set up "*clearing and settlement*"-mechanisms).

Albeit the social contract concerning the use of money is, hence, to a large degree shaped in legal texts and various "agreements," acceptance of the common forms of money remains also evident by the population's behavior.

A clear (recent) illustration of this was a call by former football/soccer player Eric Cantona in 2010 (which was picked up by a French movement called "*StopBanque*" which used *Facebook*[141] and other means to publish its announcements). Cantona urged Europeans to massively reclaim their deposits in order to crash, or at least seriously hurt the banking system, as a way of protesting against the bankers' (mis)conduct which had caused the 2008 banking crisis. If this call had

[141] https://www.facebook.com/pages/StopBanque/119038221489346 (last consulted on October 21st 2014).

been successful, it would have been a sign of collective mistrust in the commercial banking system and the scriptural money it creates. The fact that this call was not successful enough to affect the solidity of the scriptural money system, illustrates the so-far still prevailing acceptance of this money form within the European economies.[142]

2.6.3 *Credit as Money*

From the foregoing, it has become obvious that in the prevailing inherently precarious system of money creation, a large degree of prudence and caution is expected from the antagonists in the process of money creation, namely the commercial bankers operating under the auspices of a central bank.[143] **86**

Any commercial deposit bank participating in the process of money creation must be aware that when it lends out money—be it to individuals, families, enterprises or governments—and hereby engages in scriptural liabilities exceeding its cash reserve, it is creating new money *ex nihilo*.[144]

As a result, it becomes crucial for the bank to monitor the creditworthiness (including the solvency) of its borrowers, even more so than for other market players who grant credit based upon their own (existing) funds.

New scriptural money created by the bank through the granting of credit is moreover immediately full-fledged money, which the borrower can spend as desired, respecting the conditions and modalities agreed upon with the lender. The borrower hereby instantly acquires purchasing power to make payments within the economy.

In other words, such types of credit are expected to stimulate economic growth, since an increase in purchasing power is expected to stimulate consumption and hence production (unless in case prices of goods and services are rising).

However, it also must be observed that if such a credit is not paid back and the legal system is too tolerant in its mechanism for absolving debts, one ends up with „easy money“. The latter is of no benefit to the economy, since the credit that has been made available to the borrower is economically not „earned back“ in case of a default of the latter. This situation may even be referred to as a form of economic „free riding“.

Hence, the (present-day) social contract underlying the creation of scriptural **87**
money by commercial banks granting credit is (and, under the capitalist system, should remain to be) based on the premise that the borrower will effectively be able to pay back the credit he has received. Otherwise put, within capitalism, the prevailing monetary system is to a large extent founded on the underlying

[142] Willsher (2010).

[143] Galbraith (1977), pp. 166–167.

[144] Ingham (2005), p. xix. See also Ingham (1984).

credibility of the collectivity of borrowers' ability to repay the credits through which (privately created) money is brought into circulation.[145]

As a result, through his own efforts within the economy, the borrower of a credit must succeed in acquiring enough income in order to repay the credit to the borrowing bank (usually increased with an agreed upon interest charge). This is usually the basic obligation stipulated in any credit agreement.[146]

The banker, in turn, must check that the borrower will effectively be able to meet his reimbursement and interest obligations. At the very least, said banker is expected to perform a preliminary investigation as to the creditworthiness of a candidate borrower before a credit is effectively granted. If the candidate borrower turns out not to be creditworthy, the requested credit should not be granted. Furthermore, said banker must also perform some (elementary form of) "permanent" supervision during the duration of the credit agreement.[147]

88 Especially within the doctrine of "capitalist thinking" itself, any credit that is not paid back has pernicious economic consequences.[148]

Some of these consequences are:

- The borrower of a non-reimbursed credit initially received purchasing power (or put otherwise: money), yet does not contribute proportionally to economic development.

  By definition, such a borrower has performed a form of *free riding*, at the cost of the rest of the economy. This may even constitute parasitic behavior, since the borrower received (newly created) money, *ergo* purchasing power, but did not perform proportional efforts for the benefit of the economy. Too many borrowers ending up in a state of default may hence affect the economic structure in a negative way.
- The bank/lender of a non-reimbursed credit loses an (active) asset.

  Initially the bank-lender will try to compensate this loss with the profits of the credits that are diligently paid back.

  Once again, this shows that diligent payers may become the victims of bad payers, who enrich themselves at the expense of the former. Ultimately this may affect all of society, to the degree that its members acquire their money from the mechanism of private money creation based on bank lending. As a result, lending banks must include the risk of defaults in the price they charge for granting credit (i.e. in the interest it charged to borrowers). Hence, an increase in credit defaults may increase the total cost of credit.

  Massive defaults may even endanger the very existence of the bank/lender.

  There is indeed for any economic player a crucial point where the deficits resulting from an excessive number of defaults of its debtors can no longer be

[145]Ferguson (2009), p. 31.

[146]Hughes (2006), p. 10.

[147]Byttebier (1994), pp. 1497–1574, especially p. 1518, no 29 a.f.

[148]See also Galbraith (1990), p. 19.

compensated by the payments from its diligent debtors. When in case of a bank this point is reached, the bank will face own difficulties in repaying its own creditors (including the central bank which supplies cash money through specific lending techniques). In extreme cases, in particular when the central bank loses trust in a bank with too many poor payers, this can result in the bankruptcy of such a bank.

- Banks threatened by bankruptcy as a consequence of too many "defaulters", create a particular paradigm for the economy.

  The balance of a bank is essentially made up of a set of debt claims (resulting from credit and other related forms of investment) on the active side of the bank balance and the sum of its debts towards its own creditors (obviously in addition to its capital) on the passive side of its balance.

  The main categories of creditors of a bank are: (*i*) the depositors who have entrusted the bank with their savings surplus in the form of a deposit (which creates the initial cash reserve of the bank); (*ii*) professional creditors who offer bridging loans to banks facing a cash shortage; (usually these are competitors on the so-called "interlending banking market") and (*iii*) the central bank as the *lender of last resort.*

  As always, the bankruptcy of a commercial bank will mainly affect its creditors.

  Practice hereby shows that the depositors are among the most vulnerable of the bank creditors. The reason hereof is that, being non-professional counterparties of the bank, such depositors do in most cases not enjoy any guarantees for the reimbursement of their deposit.[149]

  The bankruptcy of a bank can also cause a cascade effect vis-à-vis other banks/creditors, which can end up in a difficult position if they cannot cash their claim on the bankrupt bank. Due to the interweaving on the interlending banking market, this may even lead to their own bankruptcy.

  Even the central bank, which usually makes sure it has enough guarantees (often collateral from the capital resources of the bank/creditor) may lose its investments, which in turn might affect the value of the currency issued by the central bank in question.

  Hence, the bankruptcy of a bank may have a major disrupting economic effect. Depositors lose their savings; depositors of other banks may lose their trust in the banking sector and may reclaim their deposits and masse; other

---

[149]In some jurisdictions, legislators have made it mandatory to establish some elementary deposit guarantee mechanism; see for instance "Directive 94/19/EC of the European Parliament and of the Council of 30 May 1994 on deposit-guarantee schemes" (*OJ L 135*, 31/05/1994, pp. 0005–0014), as in the aftermath of the financial crisis of 2008 amended by "Directive 2009/14/EC of the European Parliament and of the Council of 11 March 2009 amending Directive 94/19/EC on deposit-guarantee schemes as regards the coverage level and the payout delay" (*OJ L 68*, 13.3.2009, p. 3–7).

For an overview of the European policy, see http://ec.europa.eu/finance/bank/guarantee/index_en.htm#maincontentSec2 (last consulted on April 13th 2016).

bankers run the risk of ending up in trouble too (including the bankers who have lent money on the interlending banking market and those confronted with massive reimbursement claims based on a lack of trust in the banking sector); in extreme cases the mone(tar)y system itself may be disrupted.

The events of 2008 on the global financial markets are a poignant illustration of this.

- Based on their past experiences with banks going bankrupt, the governments of many Western and Western inspired nations view this as a doom scenario to be avoided at all costs, especially as regards large banks.

  This concern is expressed as the "*too big to fail*" paradigm (or better: "*too specific and big to fail*"). Or, as Sheila Bair, former chair of the US "*Financial Stability Board*" has put it: the "*too interconnected to fail*" paradigm[150].

  This paradigm explains why governments of many countries have in the past not hesitated to help banks in trouble; much more readily than when confronted with requests for assistance by other enterprises facing financial difficulties.

  Such "state aids" to banks in distress can be accomplished in various ways: through capital injections in the equity capital of such a bank; through government guarantees to cover the obligations of the bank to its creditors; by taking over bad investments (often incorporated in a separate "*bad bank*" branch), etc., and have in the past usually been referred to as so-called "*bailout*" operations.[151]

  A side effect of governments' readiness to provide the banking sector with extended non-market-conform safety nets, is an even more reckless behavior by bankers. The latter sarcastically reason that "their" government will not allow them to go bankrupt. In this way, banks are sometimes even supported in and rewarded for their past misconduct, which is another reflection of the *too big to fail* paradigm (but also of the further in this book elaborated upon "*socialization of losses*"-principle).
- The government intervention methods to help bankers in trouble can have a very negative impact on government finances.

  Since the government of Western and Western financed countries, ultimately funds itself by withdrawing money (and hence purchasing power) from the general population (individuals, families and enterprises) by means of taxes and similar contributions (see also further, under Sect. 3.4.6 of Chap. 3 of this

---

[150]Sorkin (2010); Smithers (2013), p. 87; Claerhout (2014), pp. 36–38 (containing an interview with Sheila Bair, former chair of the US "*Financial Stability Board*"), especially p. 38.

[151]Schemmann (2013), mentioning several examples thereof.

See also Galbraith (1992), pp. 48–49:

> Similarly, support to failing financial institutions—the great savings and loans rescue and later that of the commercial banks—is a fully defended function of the government, however evident the financial extravagance and extensive and visible larceny that made it necessary. Were the appropriations for these rescue operations applied instead to government expenditures for welfare, they would be deemed burdensome and otherwise wholly intolerable.

book), even global prosperity within a particular national economy may be negatively affected.

The "*free riding*" of defaulting borrowers (or more generally: debtors of bank investments) thus may become a problem for society at large. When the behavior of the poor payers requires government intervention, the complete economic system may be affected.

The situation in several European countries which helped their banking sector in the wake of the 2008 banking crisis, once again presents a poignant illustration of this paradigm.[152]

2.6.4 Further Monetary Issues Within a Credit Economy

From the foregoing, it should, among others, be clear to what extent private banking **89**
is of a very peculiar nature, especially given the role of private bankers in (privately) creating new money.

In a gradual process which, throughout the ages, first got tolerated and later validated by the governments and population of most world countries, the commercial banking sector has in this way become responsible for a major part of money creation.

It is estimated that, in some countries, privately created money amounts for, at the very least more than 90% (and probably even far more) of the total money supply.[153]

Otherwise put, it is in most countries private commercial banks that decide **90**
whether the residents of a particular national economy (individuals and families, enterprises...), and even governments themselves, get access to "newly created money" to finance their activities and/or their various expenses.

Moreover, the commercial banking system also plays an important role in intermediating in the process of channeling existing savings surpluses within a national economy by using a vast set of methods that allow holders of savings surpluses to make these available to those who need new funds (again: individuals, families, enterprises, governments,. . .).

This can take various legal forms, going from shares to various types of debt instruments.

In many countries, the commercial banking sector, furthermore, supplies a variety of services to directly allocate existing savings surpluses to those in need of capital or credit (for instance: organizing financial markets; intermediating on these financial markets; providing support for financial markets entry; providing

---

[152] As regards the Belgian situation, see *e.g.* Michielsen and Sephina (2009), pp. 187 a.f.; Peersman and Schoors (2012), pp. 68 a.f.; see also Commissie voor het Bank-, Financie- en Assurantiewezen, *Jaarverslag 2008–2009*.

[153] Martin (2013), p. 13.

support for share issues; providing services for handling purchase and sales of financial instruments;. . .).

Otherwise put, within (national) economies based on capitalist principles, the commercial banking sector holds numerous key functions concerning the availability and the circulation of money.

91 It is, furthermore, a very striking aspect of the present-day monetary systems prevailing in the world that in most cases no economic agents other than commercial banks themselves can turn directly to monetary authorities (i.e. central banks) to obtain newly publically created (or so-called "chartal") money.

Hence, anyone other than banks (be it individuals, families, enterprises or governments) who is in need of new money to finance a new project has only the following two choices:

- *Either* try to find existing money in the private market, where it can be available in the form of other economic agents' saving surpluses.

  The money "requester" hereby has access to several legal procedures to try and convince the "(potential) supplier" to make his "saved" money available to the former.

  The choice of the legal procedure hereby often determines the risks for the supplier (*e.g.* an investment in the capital of a limited liability company will generally be more risky than a credit (instrument)), the yield to be expected (a share in the profits in case of capital investment *versus* fixed yield in case of a credit), the agreements regarding repayment; etc.

  As said, throughout the centuries, financial institutions have developed a great number of intermediate services to facilitate matching the demand and supply of existing money.[154] They have for instance set up specialized financial markets (formerly: "stock markets"), services for intermediation, specialized savings and investment products, etc.

  Through these various techniques, existing savings surpluses find their way to those who need new funds without resort to the creation of new money.
- *Or* they turn to a commercial bank in order to obtain a credit, hence access to newly privately created money.

  The commercial bank honoring such a request by granting a credit that is made available in an account of the borrower, hereby creates new scriptural money.

It should be clear that, although the public attention is often strongly drawn to the first of the aforementioned functions of the banking system, namely the intermediary function which makes it possible that existing saving surpluses are invested in all types of endeavors, it is above all the second of the mentioned

[154] In recent times, one may for instance witness the emergence of "new" techniques of making the supply and demand for credits match without intervenience from specialized financial institutions, such as, for instance, technique(s) of "crowd funding". (See *e.g.* De Buysere et al. 2012; Willermain 2015, p. 3; Levy Morelle 2015, p. 302; Raes 2015; Lewalle 2012, p. 224; Belleflamme and Lambert 2014, p. 288.)

functions, namely the power to create new money, which distinguishes banks from all other types of enterprises.[155]

It should be clear that, as a result of the foregoing, private banks currently possess a powerful set of instruments to steer the money and capital markets, not in the least by their role in scriptural money creation. **92**

The most important restriction on money creation that commercial banks hereby face is the set of legal and conventional banker guidelines which regulate the assets of other economic agents vis-a-vis commercial banks.

When they grant credit, commercial banks literally create (new) scriptural money *ex nihilo*. By definition, as explained before, their cash reserve will as a result not suffice to honor all their pending scriptural liabilities, among which the obligations resulting from the credit they grant themselves. Yet banks are at the same time bound by the very obligation to honor, without delay, any request for repayment in cash money of any scriptural liability—including the scriptural obligations resulting from the credit they have granted—by its titular.

This creates a remarkable "paradox" in the banking institution as, by definition, a (ny) banker accepts obligations for larger amounts than the amount of the cash reserves he holds. Moreover, this paradox has characterized the Western banks ever since the Middle Ages.

As already explained before, central banks offer a way out of this paradox by granting commercial banks access to new chartal (cash) money they need, be it at a price. **93**

By organizing this so-called "lender of last resort"-function, such a central bank finds itself in a situation whereby it can supervise the money supply and, at least in theory, can put brakes on the growth of the total money supply, for instance by raising the price for supplying new cash money. The latter is supposed to motivate commercial banks, in turn, to be more prudent in granting new credits, *ergo* in creating new scriptural money.

In other words, in the capitalist economies, the money supply process has two layers. In a first layer, the economic agents other than private banks themselves mainly depend on private money creation by the commercial banking sector, whereby, obviously, a private bank cannot grant a credit to itself for its own needs. The second level of money creation is that of cash money creation by the monetary authorities, to which only commercial banks have a direct access.

Since the total scriptural money supply is much larger than the cash money supply, the system is inherently vulnerable, which has throughout the ages motivated governments (but also monetary authorities) to work out mechanisms of supervising the liquidity and solvency of commercial banks.

This explains a.o.:

- The enormous attention in Western (and Western inspired) legal systems going to so-called "prudential regulation" (including, for instance, setting up deposit

[155]For further reading, see especially Galbraith (1992) and Galbraith (1990).

guaranties), used by the regulators of most (Western and Western inspired) countries to instill a high level of "prudential behavior" in the commercial banking sector.

Since it is often the very private sector that prepares this type of regulations—see for instance the activities of the Basel committee(s)[156]—this approach can be characterized to a large extent as a system of self-regulation and has so far mainly appeared to be inherently unworkable in times of real crisis.

- The readiness of governments of most Western (and Western inspired) countries to go very far to help commercial banks in trouble (so-called "*bailout*") in order to avoid bank failures (the so-called "*too big*"—or "*too important*", "*too specific*" of "*too interconnected*"—*to fail* paradigm).

  This will be dealt with further in the text in more detail.

94 As a result, and as has been proven throughout history, the current social contract regarding money creation resembles a true "hostage drama" (see also further, at marg. 112 of this chapter).

Historically, commercial banks have assumed a key role for themselves in the process of money creation. Hence, the money supply process within capitalist economies has largely gotten in their hands, not only as a result of their intermediary role in the money and capital markets (= matching supply and demand of existing savings surpluses), but in particular also because they have to a large degree assumed the process of money creation.

All of this explains why, while commercial banks behave as the most aggressive market players in their quest for the greatest possible profits, society must at the same provide disproportionate efforts (often at great cost) to support them.

For example, as of the seventeenth century, so-called "central banks" had to be established which were primarily designed for the comfort of the commercial banking system. Furthermore, in the course of the twentieth century, complex prudential regulation had to be promulgated and a stable banking supervision had to be organized, with all its inherent societal costs, among which the fact that during moments of banking crises, costly bailout measures have to be taken (leading to a "*socialization of (bank) losses*").

95 It may already be obvious that interweaving money creation, which is (or should be) essentially a public function, and private commercial banking, which is entirely based on capitalist principles, is inherently unhealthy.

For this reason, it will be proposed in the Chaps. 4 and 5 of this book (see especially, at marg. 24 a.f. of Chap. 4 of this book) to resolutely withdraw money creation from the commercial banking system in the belief that money is (or again should become) a so-called "public good", hence that the processes to create it do not belong in private hands.

A further proposal will be that, henceforward, private commercial banks would only be allowed to provide intermediation services as regards the demand for and

---

[156]See https://www.bis.org/bcbs/.

the offering of existing surplus savings, but would no longer be involved with the processes that lead to the creation of money themselves.

2.7 The Monetary and Banking System in a Globalized Context

2.7.1 *Interplay Between International Trade and International Payment Transactions*

The workings of the international money and capital markets in an increasingly "globalized context"[157] merely accentuates some of the inherent problems of the monetary system, without changing its inherently conventional nature. 96

In the present-day world, it is the so-called principle of "national sovereignty" that prevails in monetary and financial matters.[158] 97

This principle of national sovereignty implies that every state may determine in a sovereign way the classic functions of the currency that is used as money within its economic system.[159] Indeed, the so-called "*ius cudendae monetae*" is considered as one of the fundamental attributes of State sovereignty, which enables the State to issue money in defined units of accounts; to regulate its use as currency within the territory of the State, and in particular the conditions, including (exchange) rates, of its exchange for foreign currencies.[160] Furthermore, the monetary sovereignty principle also applies to money as a (generally accepted) payment instrument, as a value indicator, and as a savings and credit instrument (see also further, at Sect. 3.2.2 of Chap. 3).

Each state can in this regard freely set and apply rules (including, if so desired, restrictions), in order to regulate these (classical) functions of money.[161]

---

[157]See for instance Steger (2013), p. 15; see also Bruckner (2002), p. 36.

[158]Shuster (1973), pp. 1 a.f.; Hollenberg (1942), p. 103.

For critical reflections on the "national character" of money, see Pdoa-Schioppa (2011), pp. 51–73, especially pp. 57–58:

> Under the influence of deep-seated forces ranging from technology to the rise of the nation state and to the growing political influence wielded by the masses, the creation of money was freed from the blind influence of gold discoveries and entrusted to human discretion. This permitted greater progress toward more rational policies, but also to surrender to the temptations of nationalism and demagogue. New risks arose, in the form of instability at the domestic and the international levels.

[159]Such as, specifically in the international sphere, *inter alia*: (1) currency valuation (exchange rate mechanism); (2) exchange restrictions; (3) correction of balance of payments disequilibria and (4) international liquidity. (See Shuster 1973, p. 1.)

[160]Shuster (1973), pp. 1–3.

[161]About these "classic" functions of money, see also Sect. 3.1 of Chap. 3 of this book.

In most countries, a chosen "national" currency fulfills the aforementioned traditional functions of money, although there are countries that have chosen another system (for instance the countries participating in the so-called "Eurozone" where the euro is used as one common currency).

98 As a consequence, since the advent of the modern (nation) states,[162] in most countries only the currency put into circulation by (or under the auspices of) the State qualifies as a legal payment instrument for goods and/or services and performances within the national boundaries of such a country. Otherwise put may only this chosen currency fulfill the function of money as a generally accepted payment instrument.[163]

Due to the principle of national sovereignty, the use of a currency created by a particular state as a generally accepted payment instrument (hence as money) becomes by definition geographically limited, since the currency of one state will not be generally accepted as payment instrument within the territory of other states. In light of the principle of national sovereignty, these other states will have created their own currencies which, on their own turn, within their respective territories, will function as the (only) generally accepted exchange instrument.

As a result, the currency a country has created does, in principle, not fulfill monetary functions outside its territory. Hence, the money of one state will not be considered as money in other states, but rather as a regular commodity which may (or due to legal restrictions: may not) be purchased by the residents of these other states against payment of their own currency.[164]

Inversely, as a result of the national sovereignty rule, foreign currencies—i.e. currencies created by other states—do not fulfill the role of money within the territory of a given state, where they are not to be considered as legal payment instruments, but merely as a commodity that can be acquired by paying a certain sum of the own currency.[165]

99 Obviously, the aforementioned principle of monetary national sovereignty has important repercussions on international payment transactions and, hence, on international commercial and capital transactions.

100 During the twentieth century, the world economy has witnessed an increased internationalization of (international) trade and payment transactions.[166]

Steger mentions that, during the post WWII era, the total value of global trade "exploded" from 57 billion USD in 1947 to a staggering 14,900 billion USD in 2010. In the latter year, China was reported to be the world's biggest commodity

---

[162] Mackenzie (2014), pp. 55–65, especially 58; van Caenegem (1977), p. 383 p.; Harari (2014), pp. 407–408.

[163] Hollenberg (1942), p. 103.

[164] De Grauwe (1994), pp. 1116–1117.

[165] Fase and Vleminckx (1995), pp. 57 a.f.

[166] Steger (2013), pp. 41 a.f.

producer[167], accounting for 11% of the total world export, while the USA, the then most voracious consumer country in the world, accounted for 13% of the global import.[168]

This increase in world trade went hand in hand with (and was to a large extent made possible by) an escalating liberalization of international trade (for instance by the WTO[169]) and international payment transactions (for instance through efforts of the IMF). Key elements of the latter have been the deregulation of interest rates, the abolition of credit checks, the development of international (electronic) payment and clearing systems and the privatization of government banks, all having attributed to an explosive growth of business and investment banks.[170]

As a result of this "globalization" of trade and finance, the financial markets have on a global scale been heavily integrated with numerous financial institutions currently operating outside their national territories on a massive scale, which makes supervising them extremely difficult. In many cases, financial institutions have evolved into true "trans- or multinational" enterprises that escape any true supervision by national authorities.[171]

This extreme internationalization of the financial system has, *on the one hand*, offered perspectives for enormous profits, but, *on the other hand*, made the financial sector also extremely vulnerable for all types of risks.

As a result, the failure of such a financial institution that functions in a globalized context may affect the stability of the financial markets in the various countries where it is active (possibly worldwide), and even in countries where counterparty financial institutions are active.

This has already been poignantly illustrated by the financial crisis of 2008.

The further question arises what the impact of this internationalization or **101**
globalization of the financial system has been on money and its use.

In order to answer this question, a general knowledge in how international trade works is needed.[172]

At the risk of generalizing too much (in particular from an economic point of view): within the scope of international commercial trade, the residents of a given state (hence the entire national economy of such a state) acquire goods and/or

---

[167] Van der Borght (2014), p. 2, mentioning that in 2014 China became the world's biggest economy.

[168] Steger (2013), p. 41. See also De Grauwe (2007); De Grauwe (2014).

[169] Referred to by Chomsky as the result of the exportation of American values (as those especially took shape under the Reagan-administration) (see Chomsky 1999, pp. 68 a.f.).

[170] Stiglitz (2006), pp. 7 a.f.; Khor (2008), pp. 215–259, especially pp. 216 a.f.; Steger (2013), pp. 41–43; Sono and Kanda (2010), pp. 506–516; Berend (2006), pp. 263 a.f.; Chomsky (1999), pp. 65 a.f.

For further considerations on this topic, see also further, at marg. 172 a.f. of Chap. 3 of this book.

[171] Sono and Kanda (2010), pp. 506–516, especially 511; Khor (2008), pp. 215–259, especially 216 a.f.

[172] For a more profound description, see Krugman (1992), pp. 45 a.f.

See also Hume (1985), pp. 39–48.

services produced outside the territory of this state—i.e. "abroad"—either because these goods or services are not (as easily) available[173] within their own national territory, or because they are considered to be of a different quality.

In such cases, the residents of the state in question will be inclined to "import" the goods or services in question from abroad, hence by acquiring them out of the hands of residents of another state.

The former state is sometimes referred to as "import(ing) country" (or "import (ing) state") and the latter one as "export(ing) country" (or "export(ing) state"). However, these concepts are not entirely accurate as it is usually not the countries or states themselves that import or export the goods or services, but rather their respective residents (so that the use of the terms "import" and "export state" rather refers to the trade activity of the collectivity of inhabitants of these states).

Reversely, the residents of a given state may also sell their goods or services abroad in case the residents of another state wish to acquire these goods or services for reasons similar to the aforementioned ones. In that case, the residents of the former state "export" their goods and/or services.

102 As explained above, such cross-border trade (import and export) may be hindered by the fact that, on account of the national sovereignty principle, the respective currencies of the states involved cannot be used as "money" in each other's territory.

103 Hence, an importer will face the need to exchange his own currency for the currency of the state of the exporter (= the export(ing) country) in order to be able to pay for the import operation to the exporter.

Practically, this implies that the foreign currency from the export(ing) country should be freely purchasable in the import(ing) country (where by definition it does not function as money, but rather as a simple commodity) against payment in the own currency of that import country.

104 Among others[174], in order to insure the freedom of the so-called (money) exchange (for payment transactions within the scope of international trade), in

[173]An important factor determining the "easiness" of such availability may be the cost of production. In a globalized economy, probably all goods thinkable can be produced on any place on earth, however not at the same cost. As a result of several factors, among which especially the cost of labor, producing goods in one country may be a lot cheaper than producing the same goods of a same quality in another country. Taken into account the impact of transactions costs (among which the cost of transporting the goods), production is in such a case likely to shift to the country where it will be the cheapest. As a result, the impact of production costs, among which particularly the cost of labor, may have an enormous impact on the international trade flows, which has especially become clear during the last decades (especially since the liberalization of world trade by several treaties, among which especially the WTO-treaty). (See also Chomsky 1999, pp. 68 a.f.)

[174]On the sources of international law on money and monetary transactions, see Shuster (1973), pp. 3 a.f.

On the types of international agreements on money from a historical perspective, see Shuster (1973), pp. 11 a.f.

1944, the IMF-treaty was concluded (see especially the so-called "*Articles of Agreement of the International Monetary Fund*"[175]).

Within a free market economy, making foreign currencies available for international payments ultimately has become the responsibility of the monetary and financial institutions of the countries whose inhabitants are active as importers and/or exporters. **105**

This currency exchange activity has, among others, led to the trading of currencies between financial institutions (usually using foreign "correspondents" established in the export(ing) countries) and to the building up of international reserves (based on past export) which may be used to perform payments within the international scope.

In this way, the amount of international reserves that a country possesses basically reflects the purchasing power such a country has acquired by past export, which the country in question can spend abroad to finance its own future import.

It is hereby to be observed that in the current monetary systems where money has a purely conventional character (whereby even former underlying gold backing obligations have been abandoned), international trade has mainly come to rely on a huge mutual trust of (the residents of) countries in each other's currencies. **106**

This is to be explained by the fact that in exchange for exported goods and/or services, a so-called "export(ing) country" (= the country the residents of which export more goods and/or services than they import) ultimately "only" acquires money issued by the import(ing) country.

The reason for this is that, although the exporter (for instance an enterprise producing goods or services and selling them to a foreign importer) himself will generally require payment in his own currency, the mechanism of international exchange ultimately results in (the monetary authority of) the export(ing) country building up monetary reserves consisting of money issued by (the monetary authority of) the import(ing) country.

In other words, from a "collective" perspective, international trade results in the fact that the national economy of the export(ing) country will produce real goods (and/or services) and transfer them to the national economy of the import country. The latter merely substitutes these with a sum of its own created money, i.e. a fictitious product with no (significant) intrinsic value whatsoever.

---

[175] http://www.imf.org/external/pubs/ft/aa/index.htm (last consulted on October 29th 2014). See also Shuster (1973), pp. 5–6.

One of the key stipulations of this treaty with regard to the freedom of payments is its Article VIII, Section 2:

> Section 2. Avoidance of restrictions on current payments:
>
> (a) Subject to the provisions of Article VII, Section 3(b) and Article XIV, Section 2, no member shall, without the approval of the Fund, impose restrictions on the making of payments and transfers for current international transactions.
>
> (b) Exchange contracts which involve the currency of any member and which are contrary to the exchange control regulations of that member maintained or imposed consistently with this Agreement shall be unenforceable in the territories of any member. In addition, members may, by mutual accord, cooperate in measures for the purpose of making the exchange control regulations of either member more effective, provided that such measures and regulations are consistent with this Agreement.

107 Ultimately in such an import-export system, the national economy of the export country will put a lot of effort (resources, intellectual and physical labor, energy, transportation...) into producing goods and/or services, in exchange for the fictitious entity of (foreign) money issued by the import country.

108 Although from a rational approach, the effect described in the previous marg. 106–107 of this chapter may seem somewhat astonishing, this effect of international payments does not essentially differ from any other exchange based on the use of money.

Since the very introduction of money, inherent to the very money mechanism, transactions have taken place whereby goods (or services) representing a real intrinsic value are exchanged for something with hardly any intrinsic value at all, be it "sea shells" (which historically were one of the first forms of money in many areas), "precious metal coins" (the principle form of money since the Ancient Greeks until the late Middle Ages) or our current "nickel coins", "paper (central) banknotes" or "electronic bits" which represent a bank liability.

Such an astonishing mechanism can only be put into use to the degree that the seller of goods and/or services retains sufficient faith in the (permanent) purchasing power of money, the "fictional entity" one receives in exchange for his real goods and/or services. This is as much true for our prehistoric ancestor who "sold" part of his kill after a successful hunt to a less fortunate tribe member, as within our "modern" economies, where an export economy considered as a whole sells part of its painstakingly manufactured production to a foreign economy against the mere payment of money which originated in the latter.[176]

109 Within the context of international exchange, this premise of sufficient faith has been "*collectivized*" to the faith that the national economy of the export(ing) country (through its monetary or other authority responsible for managing its currency reserves) puts in the currency issued by the national economy of the import(ing) country (under the auspices of its own monetary authority).

110 Still, within the context of such international trade and payment transactions, the presumed faith has moreover been "*personalized*" to a level never seen before in history.

Since the abolition of the "gold standard" (and later the dollar-standard *de facto* functioning as a "gold exchange standard" which was in force during the first decades of the IMF, i.e. the period from 1944 to 1971[177]), the value of a country's money is no longer based on (partial) gold backing.[178]

As a result, present-day currency reserves (held abroad) merely represent a claim on the national economy of the country that issued them.

In this way, the present international payment systems differ vastly from the former, historical international monetary systems, in force well into the twentieth century.

---

[176]Ferguson (2009), p. 31.

[177]Mertens de Wilmars and Lucas (1973), pp. 145–165, especially p. 150.

[178]For further reading, see *e.g.* Buckley (2008), pp. 5 a.f.; Flandreau (2003), pp. 17–50.

When money used to consist out of precious metal coins (in national economies with a coin standard), as a result of "international trade", the national economy of an exporter of goods and services still acquired coins issued by another region in exchange for its exported goods or services. Although these coins represented, as such, no valid currency in its own region, when the faith in the national economy of the import(ing) region disappeared (for instance because the expectations regarding productivity and export of the import(ing) region in question were not met), the national economy of the export(ing) region at least could melt down its stash of coins issued by the import(ing) region and mint them into new own coins. In this way, the income obtained from a country's export activities could serve to increase the own money supply of the export(ing) country (consisting of newly minted precious metal coins) and to finance import from third regions.

In essence, this same mechanism would continue to apply to international payment systems in later times, namely within economies based on paper money backed by precious metal (usually gold) (so-called: "representative paper money").[179] The latter was backed by gold and could be converted back to it, usually on further account of treaty agreements. In case a national economy of an export(ing) country lost its faith in the purchasing power of its reserve of paper money from the import(ing) country (hence in the future productivity and export of the national economy of the import(ing) country), it might still exchange its foreign paper money reserve into gold with the monetary authority of the import(ing) country. In this context, the export(ing) country would still acquire gold for its past production, while the import(ing) country would see its gold supply decrease as a result of not meeting production and export expectancy. Consequently, the export (ing) country could use the thus acquired gold to purchase currency of a third country and thus obtain purchasing power in the latter country.[180]

When the USA abolished the convertibility of the dollar for gold in 1971[181] (in this way unilaterally revoking various parts of the IMF treaty)[182], this mechanism came to an end.

Ever since, world trade and international payments have been based entirely on mutual faith and trust. A national economy exporting goods and/or services to another country, merely does so with the (more or less justified) expectation that the currency of the import(ing) country (of which it is building up a reserve) will (continue to) represent purchasing power in said import(ing) country—and solely in that country—for acquiring goods and services (to be) produced by the national economy of the import(ing) country.

---

[179]Often, this conversion possibility was governed by bilateral treaties between the countries involved.

[180]For further reading, see Tew (1977).

[181]As publically announced by then president Nixon in a famous television discourse on 15 August 1971 (see https://www.youtube.com/watch?v=iRzr1QU6K1o; last consulted on January 22nd 2016).

[182]Mertens de Wilmars and Lucas (1973), pp. 145–165, especially p. 150.

111 For instance, the enormous monetary reserves held worldwide in USD by monetary authorities of countries the residents of which export goods to the USA, (merely) represent purchasing power which (ultimately) can only be spent in the USA, unless the national economy of a third country would also accept payment in USD for its own export.

In the latter case, this third country will in its own turn build up its own reserve of USD which ultimately can only be spent in the USA as well.

Otherwise put, a country the currency of which is used as monetary reserve in other (export(ing)) countries (such as the USA in the example above) faces the challenge of realizing a level of future production (and export) that allows the foreign purchasing power to be effectively spent within its territories.

In the present-day globalized world economy, international trade and in particular international payments are, because of this mechanism, to a large extent based on this supposed faith in balanced trade streams which are spread out over time.[183]

Hence, it needs not surprise that the same premise continues to lie at the base of the systems for monetary aid stipulated in the IMF Treaty.

Serious dents in this faith can disrupt the international payments system. For instance, the value of the currency of the import(ing) country may plummet on the exchange markets so that the import(ing) country can no longer afford any future import. Also the export(ing) country may lose the currency reserve it built up with its (real) past production and export, hence, its formerly acquired purchasing power abroad (even in a third country). This situation occurs when a foreign national economy with such a currency reserve can no longer trust that the currency in question (of the import(ing) country) represents any purchasing power.

112 As a result of the abovementioned, within the context of the international relations between export(ing) and import(ing) countries, a rather irrational hostage situation is taking place in an almost chronical way.

In particular when the international trade flows are out of balance for an extended period of time, causing a country to systematically be an export(ing) country vis-à-vis another country (which reversely becomes a systematic import (ing) country), sooner or later a breach of faith in the future production and export capacity of such a systematic import country may arise.

---

[183]One may wonder whether the USD itself has not somehow escaped the applicability of this way of reasoning. As pointed out by Emmanuel Todd, for a long time, the general acceptance of the American dollar as monetary reserve has been in contradiction with its weak export position during the same time periods. (See Todd 2003, p. 88; Todd 2002, pp. 106–107, having pointed out that

> the American dollar has remained fairly strong despite having the largest deficit in world history. Why? Because the world's money has tended to flow to the United States. Everywhere, companies, banks and institutional as well as private investors decided to buy dollars thus keeping its value high. In this context these dollars do not serve to purchase consumer goods; instead, they allow direct investment in the United States or indirect investment through treasury bonds, as well as corporate stocks and bonds.)

In the latter case, the question will be how long the export(ing) country (which sees its reserve of currency from the import(ing) country ever increasing) will be willing to wait for a corresponding production and export of the import(ing) country.[184]

2.7.2 Legal Premises and Systems for Smooth International Payments

From the aforementioned, the basic outlines of the premises for a smooth international payments system can be derived as follows: **113**

- free international payments require the possibility in the import(ing) country to freely purchase the currency of the export(ing) country against payment of the own currency of the import(ing) country; the currencies of the import(ing) and export(ing) states hence have to be freely exchangeable or "convertible" (this is the premise of "*convertibility*").[185]
- the free convertibility premise in turn requires the availability of the foreign currency in the import(ing) country, *either* as the result of earlier trade relations (export), *or* on account of credit positions; in other words, international reserves must be available in the import(ing) country;
- a balanced system of international payments implies a medium-term equilibrium between import and export of goods and/or services, so that the foreign currency is available for payment abroad, or that prior credit positions in the foreign currency can be paid back; if this condition would not be fulfilled, the import (ing) country may face a chronic shortage of international reserve (which is the case for numerous developing countries (in IMF terminology also called "*Heavily Indebted Poor Countries* (HIPC)"[186];)
- When a country systematically exports more than it imports, it will gradually build up monetary reserves. A country that systematically imports more than it exports, will gradually become an indebted country; in order to finance further imports, such a latter country will have to rely more and more on the goodwill of its credit providers, be they other countries, private credit institutions or supranational institutions such as the IMF or the World Bank.

---

[184]The IMF disposes of mechanisms for tackling these problems, a fact which, in recent times, in some cases seems to have made the monetary and financial problems the world is facing even worse (as may for instance, be illustrated by the notorious example of the financial and monetary problems Greece has been facing in the aftermath of the severe financial crisis of 2008).

[185]Several treaties exist according to which the member states have agreed upon the convertibility of their currency, among which the IMF-treaty itself.

[186]See *e.g.* http://www.imf.org/external/np/exr/facts/hipc.htm (last consulted on October 24th 2014).

See also Cohen (2008), pp. 150–179, especially p. 167.

114 It is no surprise that the IMF treaty tries to realize the aforementioned principles within the context of the international payment system through various rules and mechanisms (see already above, at marg. 104 of this chapter).[187]

Agreements between different countries may even go beyond the scope of the IMF; for instance, countries may go as far as creating a so-called "monetary union" (such as the well-known "European Monetary Union"). As a result, for instance among the member states of the EMU[188], money creation and supervision is mainly entrusted to the so-called European Central Bank (ECB).[189] Even within the scope of the IMF itself, the participating member states have yielded certain competences to the central IMF organs.[190]

115 Nevertheless, the basic premises on the "conventional" nature of money and the monetary system—and hence their intrinsic modifiability—remain valid even within the context of such an international mone(tar)y systems embedded in treaty law.

A particular illustration of this is the inherent modifiability of such international treaties themselves. For instance, the IMF treaty has over the years been modified and supplemented several times, leading to several so-called amendments, which in some cases resulted in major changes.

The genesis of the EMU also offers a typical illustration of the essential modifiability of international monetary treaties. Before the creation of the EMU, several other "conventional" systems of monetary cooperation between European member states prevailed. Hence, the implementation of the EMU (and the Eurozone) could even be considered to be the outcome of a lengthy process of gradually ever more further-reaching monetary law agreements.

2.7.3 Disruptions Occurring Within International Payment Transactions

116 In spite of the aforementioned international treaty law systems, the past quarter century has seen some major disruptions in the international financial markets.[191]

117 In particular in the 1980s and 1990s, world trade got strongly liberalized.

[187] Restrictive and protectionist practices of which many were contrary to the principles referred to at marg. 134 adopted in the 1930s hereby served as an important source of inspiration for the IMF treaty.

[188] See https://www.ecb.europa.eu/ecb/history/emu/html/index.nl.html; last consulted on November 27th 2014.

[189] For further reading, see Zilioli and Selmayr (2001).

[190] See http://www.imf.org/external/about/govstruct.htm; last consulted on November 27th 2014. See also Bergsten (1998).

[191] Khor (2008), pp. 215–259, especially pp. 220 a.f.; Stiglitz (2006), pp. 7 a.f.

This process of liberalization was even further enhanced by the quasi disappearance of communism as an economic model, which up till the late 1980s and the early 1990s had represented a certain "counterbalance" to the since then all-prevailing capitalist market model.[192] (See also further, under Sect. 3.4.3.2 of Chap. 3 of this book.)

However, this liberalization did not put the various countries in the world on an equal social and fiscal footing. As a result, among the world's countries, the free market game has since then been deployed on totally unequal playing fields.

Especially within the scope of industrial production (and the consequent export of goods), countries with a large, often poor, population were able to rise, in particular thanks to their flexible fiscal regulation and the low interference level of the labor and social law systems.[193] The price of this has been an increasing degree of deindustrialization in various Western countries (including several European countries).[194]

In such "poor(er)" countries meeting the aforementioned characteristics (among which various Asian and South-American countries)—sometimes also referred to as "cheap labor countries"—the industrial production soared, mainly due to the fact that in these countries, the cost of labor was relatively much lower than in the countries with more strict labor, social and fiscal laws.[195]

As of the 1990s, many of these countries emerged as strong export(ing) countries whose corporate sector was able to enter the liberalized world markets with far cheaper products than those of the in foreign competitors in (traditionally richer) countries with a much stronger social and fiscal structure.

The latter countries as a result had to face an increasing deindustrialization (see also further, under Sect. 3.4.3.2 of Chap. 3 of this book).

It is needless to say that the aforementioned displacement of production and the 118
build-up of a strong export position by countries which previously had been far less present in international trade, also had an enormous impact on the global monetary system.[196]

As a result of the mechanisms described earlier (see Sect. 2.7.1), strong export (ing) countries build up monetary reserve positions (and their residents also dispose

---

[192]Eyskens s.d., p. 107; Menasse (2012), p. 78.

[193]See furthermore Foucault (2008), pp. 199–200:

> There is [equally] an effect on international competition, inasmuch as the existence of different social security regimes in different countries means that international competition is distorted, and distorted to the detriment of countries with the most comprehensive social insurance cover for risks. That is to say, here again there is a source of increasing unemployment. Finally, and still due to this increase in the cost of labor, there will be a speeding-up of industrial concentration, and the development of social security has obvious economic consequences.

[194]Michielsen (2014), p. 1. See also Menasse (2012), pp. 78–79.

[195]Stiglitz (2006), p. 67. See also Michielsen (2014), p. 1.

[196]Khor (2008), pp. 215–259.

of larger quantities of money), while import(ing) countries risk evolving into debtor countries.

As a result of the abovementioned liberalization of world trade, a seeming paradox has emerged whereby the traditionally rich countries (*e.g.* the USA and various European countries) have built up large debt positions (also to foreign creditors) in spite of the relative high prosperity of their population, while traditionally poor countries (*e.g.* China and India) saw their supply of international currencies increase in the past years (albeit that in most of these countries, a major part of the population still lives in poverty).[197]

Stiglitz mentions the extreme example of Venezuela (referring to the situation back in 2006), a country receiving enormous income through the export of oil, while a large part of the population lives in extreme poverty.[198] This testifies to the paradox that countries with large natural resources (and hence also large monetary reserves) often have a poor population.[199] Obviously, and as will be explained in more detail in the next Chap. 3 of this book, this is one of the consequences of the capitalist mechanisms of socioeconomic planning (essentially: "*laissez faire, laissez passer*") as devised and promoted by the liberal and neo-liberal economic schools.[200]

As mentioned earlier (see above, at marg. 112 of this chapter), the abovementioned evolution has resulted in the international monetary situation bearing witness of a "hostage drama:" a group of now richer countries (albeit often with a poor population) holds large currency supplies which can only be spent to the degree that the debtor countries manage to increase their export position. This requires the latter to implement a more competitive production system, which is hindered by the social protection and fiscal redistribution mechanisms prevailing in these countries.[201]

119 To use a metaphor coined by Tom Ronse, the foreign currencies handled as monetary reserves have started to go around in a circle (or better put: an endless, long stretched, downward spiral). The USA and Europe have in recent times relatively consumed more than they have produced, having allowed certain new export(ing) economies—such as China and other Asian countries—to build up enormous dollar and euro reserves, which they loan out to the USA and the European countries so that the latter can finance their balance of payments deficit (*ergo* their import from the export(ing)—and credit supplying—countries).[202]

---

[197] Stiglitz (2006), p. 8. See also Piketty (2014), p. 685.

[198] Stiglitz (2006), p. 134.

[199] Stiglitz (2006), p. 134.

[200] Pesendorfer (2012), pp. 414–434, especially p. 418.

See however Rand (1992), p. 37. See also Foucault (2008), p. 247, arguing about the differences between economic liberalism and economic neo-liberalism that the latter propagates a far more steering approach towards economic processes.

[201] See also Eichengreen (2008), pp. 210 a.f.

[202] Ronse (1992), p. 77.

It is questionable if this can be regarded as the "rational economic behavior" allegedly underpinning the ideas of the (neo)liberal schools.

Once could put it even more bluntly. The question then becomes who behaves in the most idiotic way. The (formerly rich) import(ing) countries which are not willing to drastically adapt their expenses, but prefer to maintain their consumption level and finance it increasingly with foreign debt? Or the (formerly poor) export (ing) countries which are willing to produce cheaply (maintaining low wages for the laborers working within their territory) in order to supply their products relatively cheaply to the (formerly rich) import(ing) countries in exchange for foreign currency, which is under the inherent threat of losing its value on account of the law of supply and demand in the currency exchange markets?

This situation has led to a major pessimism as to the potential outcome of the **120**
inherent deadlock.

Possible outcomes hereof may be:

- *Either* the traditionally rich countries manage to again implement a competitive production.

  If they want to maintain their current prosperity level, this will require finding new comparative advantages, for instance by using an increasingly more specialized labor potential to create innovative products. Yet this will only increase their industrialization level and their export position if (*i*) the currently strong export(ing) countries do not manage to also attract such innovating production themselves and (*ii*) at the same time, there is a sufficient foreign interest to acquire these "new" products, especially from the current export(ing) countries.

  It remains unsure whether US and especially European companies will ever be able to sufficiently meet these challenges, which put great hope in the innovating power of research in various scientific domains (such as technology, biologic science, biomedical and biochemical science) (see the so-called "*fourth industrial revolution*", allegedly in progress).[203]
- *Or* the aforementioned traditionally rich countries do not rise up to the challenge in a sufficient way, which is more and more to be feared.[204]

  If these countries continue to function according to capitalist rules, there might be a further implosion of their economic structure, and even of the global economy (to the degree that the population of these countries keeps acquiring large quantities of products manufactured in the currently strong export(ing) countries).

  The currency issued by the current import(ing) countries might at some point lose so much of its value that these countries will have trouble financing further

[203]The question thus becomes how many "*Apples*" our planet can assimilate, or even generate and, on top of that, if these ever will be able to supply the world with new, high-tech products at an ever increasing frequency.

[204]Sassen (2014), pp. 35 a.f.

import. This in turn could depreciate the monetary reserves of the current export (ing) countries.

- *Or* the traditionally rich countries could start reducing the social rights established in the past (including systems of labor protection and social care mechanisms) in order to become more competitive with the countries where such social rights are mostly lacking.[205]

  As will be explained in more detail in the next Chap. 3 of this book, this course of action is what the neo-liberal doctrines increasingly aim at.

  During the past decade, said neo-liberal doctrines have moreover been very strongly supported by the media (which are in many cases owned by the most fervent adherents of neo-liberal thinking), through which neo-liberal thinking has in many countries subtly managed to convince the minds of the middle classes and even members of the lower classes[206], in addition to these of policy makers.

  As a result, the powers of the free market more and more force Western countries to phase out painstakingly established social rights in a process which may be referred to as a true "*race to the bottom*."

  As will be further described in Sect. 3.4 of Chap. 3 of this book, as a result of this evolution, the world is at the risk of being completely forced into the fabric dictated by unrestricted "economic neo-liberalism", whereby a very small rich elite subordinates (and even "enslaves") the rest of mankind to its hunger for ever more money.[207]

- *Or* a new global economic policy will be adopted, which at the very least will favor (*i*) a global convergence of labor protection mechanisms, including mechanisms of social care, (*ii*) a global standardization of fiscal policies and (iii) a new monetary system in which money is reshaped into a public good.

  Such an alternative model will be formulated in the Chaps. 4 and 5 of this book.

[205]This is certainly the solution defended by economic neo-liberalism. (See already Foucault 2008, p. 199.)

[206]For these, adherence of neo-liberal ideas can be considered of being completely detrimental, as the implementation of the neo-liberal thought good is completely opposite to the interests of the poor classes.

[207]It has already been argued by others that such a world shaped in accordance with neo-liberal ideas lies not all that far from the society model described by Aldous Huxley in his timeless novel "*Brave New World*" (1932). (See Ongenae 2014, pp. 44–45, especially p. 44.)

2.8 Preliminary Conclusion

The general description of the history of the (Western) money system in this chapter clearly shows that the money and monetary systems in vigor worldwide today, are essentially conventional models based on an underlying social contract, in which society at large expresses what exactly it accepts as money. **121**

Moreover, this conventional model has rather been shaped as the result of much trial and even much more error, than as the result of a well-elaborated thinking process.

This intrinsically "conventional" nature of money (and of the mone(tar)y system) also implies its essentially "modifiable" nature, since an agreement in force today may be modified tomorrow.

One could even argue that history has witnessed a continuous, often arbitrary genesis and evolution of money and the monetary system(s).

Hence, the money and monetary system(s) that mankind knows today may be considered more as the outcome of a process of organic growth, than as that of a premeditated and calculated system, with all its intrinsic shortcomings as a result.

This means that there is no reason whatsoever why the current money and mone(tar)y system should remain in force forever.

This chapter has also clearly shown that certain private market players, among which private commercial banks, have given themselves an overly important role in the process of money creation, while this has never been given a lot of premeditation, and over the centuries it has never been the subject of a wide public debate. **122**

This explains why private commercial banks play a crucial role in the process of creating (scriptural) money within the current national economies. One could even argue that the situation strongly resembles a modern hostage drama and that the time has come to question whether this system is still legitimate.

It can at the very least hardly still be argued that the current mechanisms of money creation serve the public interest. On the contrary, as will be further explored in Chap. 3 of this book, the globally widespread spirit of economic (neo)liberalism has above all resulted in a monetary system that primarily achieves an unrestricted money accumulation by a small financial elite at the cost of a lot of suffering and misery for the rest of mankind.

If the mechanisms of money creation that are currently in force, would be the subject to a wide public debate among a properly informed public, it is quite unlikely that they would be approved of by the global world population.

Based on the opinion that money is or at the very least should again become a "public good," it will hereafter be demonstrated why the mechanisms of money creation should no longer be surrendered to the blind forces of the (neo-)Smithian **123** "invisible hand", but should on the contrary be brought back to the more visible hands of the public arena.[208]

124 The latter brings us to the subject of the next Chap. 3 of this book which will explore a number of ethical doctrines that have pondered on the issue of unrestricted money and wealth accumulation, which is inherently possible in the prevailing monetary and financial system(s).

Based upon these "moral" insights, a proposal on how to bring money creation back into the public arena will be further described in the subsequent Chaps. 4 and 5 of this book.

References

Achterhuis H (2011) De utopie van de vrije markt. Lemniscaat, Rotterdam

Alexander K, Dhumale R (eds) (2012) Research handbook on international financial regulation. Edward Elgar, Cheltenham

Alvard R (2013) Follow the money. The money trail through history. Wordbridge Publishing

Bank of England (2000) Factsheet – bank notes, London

Barber M (1978) The trial of the templars. Cambridge University Press, Cambridge

Beaud M (1994) Geschiedenis van het kapitalisme van 1500 tot heden. Het Spectrum (Aula), Utrecht

Becket S (2014) Empire of cotton. A global history. New York, Vintage Books

Belleflamme P, Lambert T (2014) Crowdfunding: some empirical findings and microeconomic underpinnings. In: BankFin.R. 2014 (no 4)

Berend I (2006) An economic history of twentieth-century Europe. Cambridge University Press, Cambridge

Bergsten F (1998) Weak dollar, strong euro? The international impact of EMU. The Centre for European Reform, London

de Bettignies HC, Lépineux F (eds) (2009) Finance for a better world: the shift toward sustainability. Palgrave Macmillan, Basingstoke

Bieler A (1961) La pensée économique et sociale de Calvin. Librairie de l'Université, Genève

Bleaney M, Greenaway D (1996) A guide to modern economics. Routledge, London

Boatright JR (2010) Ethics in finance. Wiley, New Jersey

Boccara F, Le Héron E, Plihon D (2011) Pour un système de financement émancipé des marchés financiers. In: Les Économistes atterés, Changer d'économie! Nos propositions pour 2012. In: Les liens qui libèrent, Paris, pp 207–221

Bogaert R (1988) Deposito, Krediet and Geldhandel door de eeuwen heen. Lannoo, Tielt

Bogaert R, Brion R, Kuran-Van Hentenryk G, Moreau LJ, Van Der Wee H (2000) A history of European banking. Mercatorfonds and European Investment Bank, Antwerp (also: Bogaert R, Kuran-Van Hentenryk G, Van Der Wee H (1991) De Bank in Europa. 25 eeuwen Bankgeschiedenis. Mercatorfonds, Antwerp; Bogaert R, Kuran-Van Hentenryk G, Van Der Wee H (1991) La banque and Occident. Mercatorfonds, Antwerp)

[208]Boccara et al. (2011), pp. 207–221, especially p. 213; Ingham (2005), p. xxii.
See also Ingham (2005), pp. 222–224, especially p. 237:

> Money's transformation from, in Simmel's terms, "substance" (commodity) to pure "function" as an acknowledgment of debt (promise to pay) expressed in a money of account and issued by states and banks involved the realization that money was itself a social relation.

Boorman J, Icard A (eds) (2011) Reform of the international monetary system – the Palais Royal Initiative. Sage, Los Angeles
Breasted JH. (s.d.) De Romeinen. Servire, Den Haag
Brimo A (1968) Les grands courants de la philosophie du droit et de l'État. Éditions A. Pedone, Paris
Brook Y, Watkins D (2012) Free market revolution – how Ayn Rand's ideas can end big government. Palgrave Macmillan, New York
Bruckner P (2002) Misère de la prospérité – la religion marchande et ses ennemis. Bernard Grasset, Paris
Buckley R (2008) International financial system. Kluwer Law International, Alphen aan de Rijn
Byttebier K (1994) Ondernemingsfinanciering door kredietinstellingen. *TPR* 1994, p. 1497–1574
Byttebier K (2001) Handboek financieel recht. Kluwer Rechtswetenschappen, Antwerp
Byttebier K, Flamée M (2012) Het vraagstuk van ethisch financieren toegepast op de interestheffing mede vanuit een elementair rechtshistorisch perspectief. Stof voor een morele uitweg uit een wereld in (financiële) crisis? In: De Ruysscher D, De Hert P, De Metsenaere M (eds) Een leven van inzet. Liber amicorum Michel Magits. Kluwer, Mechelen
Byttebier K, Wera T a.o. (2016) Handboek Handels- en Ondernemingsrecht. Die Keure, Brugge
van Caenegem RC (1977) Over koningen and bureaucraten – Oorsprong and ontwikkeling van de hedendaagse staatsinstellingen. Elsevier, Amsterdam
Chérot JY, Frydman B (eds) (2012) La science du droit dans la globalisation. Bruylant, Brussels
Chomsky N (1999) Profit over people. Neoliberalism and global order. New York, Seven Stories Press
Claerhout P (2014) Enkel voldoende kapitaal kan een bank redden. Trends, 27 November 2014
Cohen D (2008) Towards a new modus operandi of the international financial system. In: Serra N, Stiglitz JE (eds) The Washington consensus reconsidered. Oxford University Press, Oxford
Commissie voor het Bank.-, Financie- en Assurantiewezen, Jaarverslag 2008–2009
Crockett A (1981) Money. Theory, policy and institutions. Nelson House, Surrey
Crump T (1981) The phenomenon of money. Routledge, London
Davies G (2002) A history of money from ancient times to the present day. University of Wales Press, Cardiff
De Buysere K, Gajda O, Kleverlaan R, Maron D (2012) A framework for European crowdfunding. http://eurocrowd.winball2.de/wp-content/blogs.dir/sites/85/2013/06/FRAMEWORK_EU_CROWDFUNDING.pdf. Last consulted 27 Mar 2017
De Grauwe P (1994) Komt er een nieuw Bretton Woods? E.S.B., 7 December 1994, pp 1116–1117
De Grauwe P (2007) De onvoltooide globalisering. Een verkenning van een nieuwe wereld. Lanno, Tielt
De Grauwe P (2012) Bankenhervorming? Veel geluk ermee, meneer Di Rupo. De Morgen, 6 September 2012
De Grauwe P (2014) De limieten van de markt. De slinger tussen overheid en kapitalisme. Lannoo, Tielt
Delisle L (1975) Mémoire sur les opérations financières des templiers. Slatkine, Genève
Deweirdt E, Van Poeck A, Annaert J (1997) Monetaire theorie en politiek. Garant, Leuven-Apeldoorn
Drummond I (1987) The gold standard and the international monetary system 1900–1939. Macmillan Education Ltd., London
Eagleton C, Williams J (2007) Money – a history. The British Museum Press, London
Eichengreen B (ed) (1985) The gold standard in theory and history. Methuen, New York
Eichengreen B (2008) Globalizing capital. A history of the international monetary system. Princeton University Press, Princeton/Oxford
Engelen E (a.o.) (2011) After the great complacence. Oxford University Press, Oxford
Eyskens M (s.d.) Is verandering vooruitgang? De maatschappelijke gevolgen van de derde industriële revolutie. Davidsfonds, Leuven
Fase M, Vleminckx A (1995) Geld in veelvoud. Inleiding monetaire economie. Uitgeverij, Utrecht

Ferguson N (1998) The house of Rothschild. Penguin Books, New York
Ferguson N (2009) The ascent of money. A financial history of the world. London, Penguin Books
Flandreau M (2003) Caveat emptor: coping with sovereign risk under the international gold standard, 1871–1913. In: Flandreau M, Holtfrerich C-L, James H (eds) International financial history in the twentieth century – system and anarchy. Cambridge University Press, Cambridge
Flandreau M, Ugolini S (2011) Where it all began: lending of last resort and the Bank of England during the Overend-Gurney panic of 1866. Working paper Norges Bank 2011/03, Norges Bank. Bicentenary Project, Oslo
Flandreau M, Holtfrerich CL, James H (eds) (2003) International financial history in the twentieth century – system and anarchy. Cambridge University Press, Cambridge
Foucault M (2008) The birth of biopolitics – lectures at the Collège de France 1978–1979 (trans: Burchell G). Palgrave Macmillan, New York
Friedman M (ed) (2002) Capitalism and freedom. The University of Chicago Press, Chicago
Galbraith JK (1975) Money. Whence it came, where it went. Houghton Mifflin Company, Boston
Galbraith JK (1977) The age of uncertainty. Houghton Mifflin Company, Boston
Galbraith JK (1987) Economics in perspective – a critical history. Houghton Mifflin Company, Boston
Galbraith JK (1990) A short history of financial euphoria. Whittle Books in association with Penguin Books, New York
Galbraith JK (1992) The culture of contentment. Houghton Mifflin Company, Boston
Giovanoli M, Devos D (eds) (2010) International monetary and financial law: the global crisis. Oxford University Press, Oxford
Graeber D (2012) Debt. The first 5000 years. Melville House, Brooklyn
Graff M, Kenwood A, Lougheed A (2014) Growth of the international economy 1820–2015. Routledge, London
Hamblin WJ, Seely DR (2007) De Tempel van Salomo. Mythe and geschiedenis. Altamira-Becht, Haarlem
Harari YN (2014) Sapiens – a brief history of humankind. Penguin Random House UK, London
Harvey D (2010) The enigma of capital: and the crises of capitalism. Profile Books, London
Hirschberg E (1976) The impact of inflation and devaluation on private legal obligations – legal aspects of contemporary monetary problems. Bar-Ilan University, Ramat-Gan
Hollenberg A (1942) De corporatieve organisatie der maatschappij. Standaard Boekhandel, Antwerp
Hughes M (2006) Legal principles in banking and structured finance. Haywards Heath, West Sussex
Hume D (1985) On the balance of trade. In: Eichengreen B (ed) The gold standard in theory and history. Methuen, New York
Ingham G (1984) Capitalism divided? The city and industry in British social development. McMillan Education Ltd., London
Ingham G (2005) Concepts of money. Edward Elgar Publications Ltd., Cheltenham
Kerste M, Rosenboom N, Slikken BJ, Wedak J (eds) (2011) Financing sustainability: insights for investors, corporate executives, and policymakers. VU University Press, Amsterdam
Khor M (2008) The world trading system and development concerns. In: Serra N, Stiglitz JE (eds) The Washington consensus reconsidered. Oxford University Press, Oxford
Kirton J, Larionova M, Savona P (2010) Making global economic governance effective: hard and soft law institutions in a crowded world. Ashgate, Farnham
Kleinpeter MA (2000) Sources et mécanismes de la création de monnaie dans le cadre de l'Eurosystème. Bulletin de la Banque de France, January 2000, no 73, pp 59–64
Korteweg S (1970) Het moderne geldwezen. B.V. Noord-Hollandsche Uitgeversmaatschappij, Amsterdam
Krugman P (1992) The age of diminished expectations. U.S. economic policy in the 1990s. The MIT Press, Cambridge

Leader S, David M (2011) Global project finance, human rights and sustainable development. Cambridge University Press, Cambridge
Les Économistes atterés (2011) Changer d'économie! Nos propositions pour 2012. Les liens qui libèrent, Paris
Levy Morelle F (2015) Le crowdfunding – outil de financement innovant. In: RBF 2015 (no 4)
Lewalle C (2012) Publication, par la FSMA, de deux communications relatives au 'crowdfunding. In: Bank Fin.R. 2012 (no III–IV)
Mackenzie D (2014) Een wereld zonder grenzen. New Scientist, November 2014, pp 55–65
Mandel E (1962) Traité d'économie Marxiste. Julliard, Paris
Mankiw G (2011) Principles of macroeconomics. Cengage Learning, Boston
Martin F (2013) Money. The unauthorised biography. The Bodley Head Random House, London
Menasse R (2012) De Europese koerier. De woede van de burger en de vrede van Europa. Een prachtig en prikkelend pleidooi pro Europa. De Arbeiderspers, Utrecht
Mertens de Wilmars J, Lucas S (1973) Het internationaal monetair fonds en de flexibiliteit van de wisselkoersverhoudingen. In: liber amicorum prof. dr. Gaston Eyskens, Universitaire Pers Leuven, Leuven
Michielsen T (2014) Slimme fabrieken moeten Vlaamse industrie redden. De Tijd, 19 November 2014, pp 13–14
Michielsen S, Sephina M (2009) Bankroet – hoe Fortis al zijn krediet verspeelde. Lannoo, Tielt
Middelkoop W (2009) Overleef de kredietcrisis. Nieuw Amsterdam Uitgevers, Amsterdam
Middelkoop W (2014) The big reset – war on gold and the financial endgame. AUP, Amsterdam
Mishkin FS (ed) (2012) The economics of money, banking and financial markets. Pearson Education, New Jersey
Nussbaum A (1950) Money in the law. National and international. A comparative study in the borderline of law and economics. The Foundation Press, Inc., Brooklyn
Ongenae C (2014) Antropoloog Rik Pinxten roept op tot verzet – Het oude kastendenken is terug. Knack, 26 November 2014, pp 44–45
Oxfam (2016) An economy for the 1%. How privilege and power in the economy drive extreme inequality and how this can be stopped. Oxfam briefing paper, 18 January 2016. https://www.oxfam.org/sites/www.oxfam.org/files/file_attachments/bp210-economy-one-percent-tax-havens-180116-en_0.pdf
Pagliari S (ed) (2012) Making good financial regulation – towards a policy response to regulatory capture. Grosvenor House, Guildford
Pdoa-Schioppa T (2011) The ghost of bancor: the economic crisis and global monetary disorder. In: Boorman J, Icard A (eds) Reform of the international monetary system – the Palais Royal Initiative. Sage, Los Angeles
Peersman L, Schoors K (2012) De perfecte storm. Hoe de economische crisis de wereld overviel en vooral: hoe we eruit geraken. Borgerhoff & Lamberigts, Ghent
Peil J, Van Staveren I (eds) (2009) Handbook of economics and ethics. Edward Elgar, Cheltenham
Pesendorfer D (2012) Goodbye neo-liberalism? Contested policy responses to uncertain consequences of the 2007–09 financial crisis. In: Alexander K, Dhumale R (eds) Research handbook on international financial regulation. Edward Elgar, Cheltenham
Pettifor A (2014) The power to 'create money out of thin air'. https://www.opendemocracy.net/ourkingdom/ann-pettifor/power-to-create-money-out-of-thin-air. Last consulted 18 Nov 2014
Pfister K (1941) Ondergang van het Romeinsche Imperium. Uitgeverij Roskam, Amsterdam
Piketty T (2014) Capital in the twenty-first century. Belknap Press, Cambridge
Pinxten R, De Munter K (2006) De culturele eeuw. Houtekiet, Antwerp
Plato (1987) The Republic (trans: Lee D). Penguin Books, London
Popper K (1940) What is dialectic? In: Mind
Raes D (2015) Etat des lieux en matière de crowdfunding: Seul chemin parcouru et quelles perspectives d'évolution ? In: Le financement des PME, documentation provided by Vanham & Vanham, Seminar of December 10th 2015, Brussels

Rand A (1992) The virtue of selfishness. New American Library (a division of Penguin Group), New York
Rolland R (1940) de levende gedachten van Rousseau. Servire, Den Haag
Ronse T (1992) Rambo op lemen voeten – Amerika in de jaren negentig. Kritak, Leuven
Rousseau (2001) Du contrat social. GF Flammarion, Paris
Sassen S (2014) Expulsions. Brutality and complexity in the global economy. Massachusetts, Cambridge
Schemmann M (2013) Money – breakdown and breakthrough. The history and remedy of financial crises and bank failures. IICPA Publications
Schuker S (2003) The gold-exchange standard: a reinterpretation. In: Flandreau M, Holtfrerich CL, James H (eds) International financial history in the twentieth century – system and anarchy. Cambridge University Press, Cambridge
Sedlacek T (2011) Economics of good and evil: the quest for economic meaning from Gilgamesh to Wall Street. Oxford University Press, Oxford
Shaxson N (2012) Treasure islands: uncovering the damage of offshore banking and tax havens. Palgrave Macmillan, New York
Shuster MR (1973) The public international law of money. Oxford University Press, London
Smithers A (2013) The road to recovery. Wiley, Chichester
Sono K, Kanda H (2010) In search of order in the world monetary system: state intervention after the decline of the lex monetae. In: Giovanoli M, Devos D (eds) International monetary and financial law: the global crisis. Oxford University Press, Oxford
Sorkin A (2010) Too big to fail. Penguin, London
Steger M (2013) Globalization. A very short introduction. Oxford University Press, Oxford
Steinmetz G (2015) The richest man who ever lived: the life and times of Jacob Fugger. Simon & Schuster, New York
Stiglitz J (2006) Making globalization work. Penguin Books, London
Stiglitz J (2010) Freefall. Free markets and the sinking of global economy. London. Allan Lane an imprint of Penguin Books
Tew B (1977) The evolution of the international monetary system 1945–77. Hutchinson of London, London
Todd E (2002) Après l'Empire – Essai sur la decomposition du système américain. Gallimard, Paris
Todd E (2003) After the empire – the breakdown of the American order (trans: Delogu J). Constable, London
Treyvaud PA (1972) Le contrat de dépôt bancaire. Imprimierie E. Ruckstuhl S.A, Lausanne
Van der Borght K (2014) China: de rechtsorde zoals we ze kennen? Intersentia, Antwerp
Van Houtte JA (1942) Economische geschiedenis – de historische wording van de hedendaagsche wereldeconomie. De Haan, Utrecht
Van Houtte JA (a.o.) (eds) (1953) Algemene geschiedenis der Nederlanden. Standaard Boekhandel. Utrecht, W. De Haan and Antwerp, t.VI
Vandewalle G (1976) De geschiedenis van het economisch denken. Kluwer, Deventer/Antwerp
Weatherford J (1997) The history of money. Random House, New York
Willermain D (2015) Le crowdfunding ou financement participative. In: Modes actuels de financement des PME, documentation provided by Vanham & Vanham. Seminar of December 10th 2015, Brussels
Willsher K (2010) Eric Cantona's call for bank protest sparks online campaign – thousands of French protesters have taken up the former Man United footballer's call for a mass cash withdrawal. In: the Observer, 21 November 2010. http://www.theguardian.com/world/2010/nov/20/eric-cantona-bank-protest-campaign. Last consulted 21 Oct 2014
Zilioli C, Selmayr M (2001) The law of the European Central Bank. Portland Oregon, Oxford

Chapter 3
The Debate About the Ethics of Money Pursuit

3.1 General Goal of This Chapter

1 The third chapter of this book deals with the impact the idea that people should above all strive for ever more money and wealth has had on society (ies), especially at two levels, namely:

- the level of an ever increasing greed money use has led to (despite attempts by key historical figures in philosophy and religion to avoid this),
  and,
- the level of the true meaning of ideologies, especially "economic liberalism" and "economic neo-liberalism" which have attempted to justify this kind of unbridled greed (and which have in this way mainly contributed to a globally spread model of society wherein egoism prevails).

3.2 Functions of Money

3.2.1 Classic Functions of Money in General

2 Already from what has been exposed in Chap. 2 of this book, the so-called "primary function" of money can be derived, namely that, within an economic system underpinned by a so-called "indirect barter trade", money forms the generally accepted means of payment which provides access to all other goods and services (on the market).[1]

[1]Harari (2014), p. 199; Ferguson (2009), p. 24; Hirschberg (1976), pp. 77 a.f.; see also Hollenberg (1942), p. 88.

K. Byttebier, *Towards a New International Monetary Order*,
Economic and Financial Law & Policy – Shifting Insights & Values 1,
DOI 10.1007/978-3-319-52518-1_3

In addition, classic economic doctrine[2] identifies several other functions of money,[3] for instance the fact that money functions as the most general measure of value; that money fulfils the role of spare purchasing power (in other words: it enables "saving", i.e. the "postponement of consumption") thus offering the possibility of (unbridled) wealth accumulation; that money enables lending and, stemming from its previous functions, that money enables modern money and capital transactions.[4]

3 Ever since the use of money started to determine economic transactions (otherwise said, from the moment when "direct barter economies" started to evolve into "indirect barter economies"), the advantages of initiating a generally accepted means of exchange turned out to be enormous.

Up to now, these advantages have lost none of their importance.

The most important of these advantages resulting from the payment function of money are the facts that:

- Any economic agent who has money, meaning the generally accepted means of exchange prevailing within his economy, at his disposal has per definition access to practically all produced goods, services and other man's labor in a (relatively) simple and quick way.[5]
- Given the fact that barter based on the use of money is facilitated, a breeding ground for the division and specialization of labor, both of which are conditions for economic growth and development, is created.[6]

4 Stemming from (and based on) the primary payment function of money, money also acts as a means to express the value of the goods, services and labor which can be acquired with it.

In this way, money acts as a "general value indicator" for the goods, services or other man's labor being traded,[7] a function which, *on the one hand*, results from its general payment function (since the appreciation of goods and services is mainly useful when a person is about to acquire them, or to transfer them to another person), and, *on the other hand*, imposes in itself a favorable impact on trade (since trade is facilitated because the appreciation of the traded goods and services may happen in a more transparent manner).[8]

5 The emergence of money as a generally accepted means of payment has also allowed the creation of a professional credit and savings system (hence also of specialized money- and capital market, which in traditional economic doctrines are considered among the main drivers of economic growth).

---

[2]These insights date back to Aristotle; see Aristotle (1996), p. 124, verses 1133 b 11 a.f.

[3]See *e.g.* Poindexter and Jones (1980), p. 50.

[4]See *e.g.* Deweirdt et al. (1997), pp. 24 a.f.

[5]See further Crockett (1981), p. 7.

[6]Crockett (1981), p. 8.

[7]See Korteweg (1970), pp. 10 and 14; Fase and Vleminckx (1995), pp. 15–16.

[8]See *e.g.* Nussbaum (1950), p. 12.

It may be clear that through the use of money, an almost unlimited possibility to acquire purchasing power (= sums of money received in return for the transfer of goods, services or other labor) arises, and, as a further result, the possibility to use this purchasing power at a later stage. 6

In other words, the use of money as a generally accepted means of payment allows the systematic "hoarding" of purchasing power. Indeed, a sum of money received in return for a transfer of goods, services and other labor does not necessarily need to be spent immediately; on the contrary, such spending can be deferred to an unspecified moment in the future. This is at least valid to the extent that the selected "form" of money is "durable" (which has been increasingly the case throughout history since the goods which have been chosen to fulfill a role as money mostly got chosen because of their durability, hence for their ability to facilitate the "hoarding" or "saving" function).[9]

In this way, money allows economic agents, in a systematic way, to "keep" the sums of money received for an undetermined period: otherwise put, money acts as an ideal instrument of (even unlimited) wealth accumulation, in other words for "saving".

The awareness that money allows saving soon created a crucial monetary principle which since the beginning of money use still underpins monetary thinking (and action) up to the present day. 7

This principle implies that holding onto money as a method of wealth creation will only take place to the extent that economic agents (can) have enough confidence in (the future purchasing power of) the chosen form of money: in other words to the extent that they (can) expect, in a justified way, that the money will not lose its value in future (when the decision to spend it will be taken) especially in comparison with the price of goods, services and other labor which can be acquired in the presence. In other words, in order to "save" (money), one has to be confident (enough) that money will retain its purchasing power throughout time.[10]

This basic principle of money use has caused the aim of safeguarding the purchasing power of money to become part of the underlying social contract on which money and the use of money are based. Hence, economic agents, being part of a certain economy, will only be willing to save money in light of the (justified) expectation that money will retain its value (an expectation which in most present-

---

[9]Harari (2014), p. 200:

> Ideal types of money enable people not merely to turn one thing into another, but to store wealth as well. Many valuables cannot be stored – such as time or beauty. Some things can be stored only for a short time, such as strawberries. Other things are more durable, but take up a lot of space and require expensive facilities and care. Grain, for example, can be stored for years, but to do so you need to build huge storehouses and guard against rats, mould, water, fire and thieves. Money, whether paper, computer bits or cowry shells, solves these problems. Cowry shells don't rot, are unpalatable to rats, can survive fires and are compact enough to be locked up in a safe.

[10]Harari (2014), pp. 200 a.f.

day countries translates into a similar (basic) objective of monetary policy embedded in monetary norms and regulations).

8 In the same way that money allows an economic agent to "save" current purchasing power in order to be able to spend it in the future, an economic agent can also, at least in an economic system based on the use of money, choose, or be forced by circumstances, to acquire goods, services or other labor at a certain moment in time, without disposing of the purchasing power required at that moment.

Such economic agent (lacking purchasing power to satisfy an immediate need), will therefore attempt to enter into an agreement with another economic agent who has an excess of purchasing power at that time (i.e. a "saver"; see above, at marg. 5–6 of this chapter), or with an institution which is authorized to create new money (in most prevailing Western legal systems: a private bank or a similar financial institution; see above, Chap. 2 of this book).

In other words, a similar economic agent, aiming to finance actual needs without the necessary purchasing power to satisfy them at his disposal, will (try to) "obtain credit".

9 The emergence of money as a generally accepted means of payment has in this way created the conditions for obtaining credit at an institutional level at two levels:

- *on one hand*, the use of money allows those who generate an excess of purchasing power in a systematic way, to "save" and to use the saved amounts in order to lend them out to other economic agents (who are in need of credit);[11]
- *on the other hand*, the use of money has created the climate for the emergence of an institutionalized banking sector, i.e. the emergence of institutions (intermediate by definition) which collect savings held in the form of money in a systematic way (= so-called "deposits gathering"; see already Chap. 2), aimed at spending these saving surpluses represented by credits to third parties and which, in the course of history, furthermore have led to credit mechanisms that entail the (private) creation of new money.

Especially under the emergence of capitalism as the world leading economic system, it would soon prove to be the case that the provision of credit would become one of the central activities of this (private) banking system (see above, under Sect. 2.3 of Chap. 2 of this book, dealing with the emergence of the Western banking system), at such levels that private credit provision, at different times throughout history, would result in private money creation mechanisms governing whole economies (see Sects. 2.3.3 and 2.5 of Chap. 2 of this book).

10 The use of money has similarly created the framework for the emergence of more sophisticated money- and capital markets (where specialized savings- and credit products are brought into circulation and traded). In this way, the use of money has led to the emergence of new forms of transactions, i.e. "transactions in the financial sphere".[12]

---

[11]Korteweg (1970), p. 7.

[12]Korteweg (1970), p. 17.

3.2.2 *Money as a System of Unlimited Wealth Accumulation and Its Interaction with Self-centered and Altruistic Thinking: A General Introduction*

From an historical perspective, the revolutionary character of the saving and credit functions resulting from the payment function of money cannot be emphasized enough. **11**

Partly as a result of the introduction of the use of money as a payment method, and alongside this, of the saving and credit functions of money, it became possible for previously small-scale (and often nomadic) societies to develop into large-scale societies and, from an economic perspective, into types of societies based on (more and more specialized) agriculture and trade[13], and later industry and specialized service provisioning, as we know them today.

However, alongside these obvious positive effects of the payment, savings and credit functions of money, significant negative effects also arose. **12**

Given that money offers a breeding ground for unlimited saving (and, because of this, hence also for unlimited wealth accumulation), money also became the corner stone of "greed" and "selfishness" as determining values of human society (ies), as we know them, virtually worldwide, today.[14]

Already in the 1950s, this insight brought Fromm to the awareness that, while during the Middle Ages capital (and more particularly: economic processes) were believed to serve mankind, in capitalist societies "capital" (hence economic processes) has (have) come to rule mankind[15], an awareness that defines the very scope of capitalist economies to the very present day, and probably, at present, under the influence of economic neoliberalism, even more than ever before in history (see also further, under Sect. 3.4).

Where, as a consequence, it is strongly suspected that in (historical) economies relying on direct barter trade (with by definition a smaller scale character) a spirit of collaboration and collectivism formed a prerequisite for a well-functioning society, it can been determined that the use of money has led to, amongst other things, institutionalized savings and credit, and thus also to an increasing abandonment of society models based on collectivism.[16]

---

[13]Harari (2014), pp. 110 a.f.

[14]Kasser (2002), p. 149.

[15]Fromm (1990), p. 84.

[16]Fromm (1955), pp. 76 a.f.

For example on the rise of capitalism, Fromm has argued as follows:

> As opposed to the social stability in the medieval system, an unheard of social mobility developed, in which everybody was struggling for the best places, even though only a few were chosen to attain them. In this scramble for success, the social an moral rules of human society broke down; the importance of life was in being first in a competitive race. (Fromm 1955, pp. 84–85)

Instead, society became largely based on a substantial degree of individualism (and even egoism)[17] which has today reached such proportions that it threatens to affect the stability of the Western civilization, in addition to the actual well-being of the planet as an eco-system able to sustain (human) life itself.[18]

13 In the choice of certain of their starting assumptions (see further, under Sect. 3.4), certain of the leading movements within economy (as a scientific discipline), among which especially "economic liberalism" and "economic neo-liberalism", have played a major role in confirming the evolutionary process towards an ever increasing self-centered economy (as a practical system), to such an extent that, especially within economic science, demands that in the past have been voiced in support of other values (other than unlimited money gain) within society in general and within economic science more specifically, have until recent times hardly been taken serious.

14 As said, it was mainly the so-called "(economic) liberalism" (in the eighteenth and nineteenth centuries) and the so-called "(economic) neo-liberalism" (in the twentieth and twenty-first centuries) which have introduced self-centeredness, egoism and greed as leading values within the economy (a belief that in neo-liberal thinking has even been expressed in a modern-day credo: "*Greed is good*"[19]).

It is more precisely in both these (closely related) doctrines held that the selfish pursuit of an individual's personal needs best serves the interests of the global economy, as such self-centeredness guarantees that every person participates actively in the production process and avoids individuals "*taking advantage of the efforts of others*" (an attitude which, according to neo-liberalism, best benefits societies as a whole).[20]

15 Conversely, (economic) neo-liberalism has also argued that the value which is the most opposite to self-centeredness, i.e. "altruism", is in fact a vice which should be combatted with all force.

---

[17]See also Fromm (1990), p. 84 (also: Fromm, p. 64), pointing out how economic individualism has caused loneliness and alienation of Western man.

[18]Lloyd (2012), pp. 375–377.

[19]Brook and Watkins (2012), pp. 37 and 175.

[20]Described by Ayn Rand as follows:

> The moral justification of capitalism is man's right to exist for his own sake, neither sacrificing himself to others nor sacrificing others to himself; it is the recognition that man – every man – is an end in himself, not a means to the ends of others, not a sacrificial animal serving anyone's need. (See Rand 1982, p. 91.)

In this primarily neo-liberal way of thinking, people advocating altruism—albeit it can be argued that within current economies altruism itself has considerably weakened down to the level of social care mechanisms as a (somehow poor) replacement for actual altruism[21]—aim to "deprive" "the rich and prosperous" of their legitimate earnings.[22]

In an extreme expression of this (neo)-liberal approach, it has even been held, at the very least implicitly, that historical advocates of a (radical) altruistic attitude towards life, and by extension of modern economists either advocating a softening of full-blooded capitalism, or having attempted to propose alternatives for capitalism, are no more than "rioters" who only encourage depriving the "capable" of their "legitimate earnings".[23]

In this way, classical philosophers such as Plato and Aristotle (who for example pointed to the levy of interest as an unnatural way of creating wealth, and usury as a form of "unfair profit gain"; see further, under Sects. 3.3.2.1 and 3.3.3.2.1.3), religious leaders such as Jesus Christ Himself (calling upon the rich to sell their goods and donate the proceeds of such sale to the poor; see further, at marg. 37 of this chapter), Marxist economists such as Karl Marx and Friedrich Engels (1820–1895) and even world famous contemporary economists, in neo-liberal thinking stereotyped as "liberals", should then be seen as such "rioters".[24]

As a result, (economic) neo-liberalism has also led to a fundamentally distorted value picture, in addition to the inverse value perception that egoism is the true virtue and altruism is a dangerous vice, for example also including: **16**

- *on one hand*, an increasing degree of economic "hubris"[25], more specifically, the (mis)judgment that wealth is "merely" the result of one's own merit, excellence,

[21]In his book "*A journey through economic time. A firsthand view*" John Kenneth Galbraith has pointed out that this may have been a consequence of industrialization itself:

> The need for protection of the old and the unemployed is inescapably allied with industrial development and had for long been so recognized. An agricultural society has its own inbuilt system of social security. The farms or peasant holdings pass on to offspring, and the latter often by rigorously enforced custom, look after their elders. A major reason for rural population increase in much of the world is the need to be assured of sons who will do the work in the fields and the responsible for their parents in their old age. As to unemployment compensation, there is the stolid fact that there is no real unemployment on a farm. (...) It is with industry and urbanization that both old age pensions and unemployment compensation become socially essential. It is then that, with a much-loosened family structure, the old have no support, the unemployed have no income. (see Galbraith 1994, p. 93).

[22]Ayn Rand has expressed this as follows:

> altruïsm seeks to rob intelligence of its rewards, by asserting that the moral duty of the competent is to serve the incompetent and sacrifice themselves to anyone's need (Rand 2008, p. 23).

See also Rand (1982), pp. 79 a.f.

[23]See also Galbraith (1987), p. 21.

[24]Galbraith (1987), p. 21.

[25]Galbraith (1992), p. 157.

competence and efforts, without taking into account factors such as life chances—*inter alia* by birth—hereditary talents, the incorporation of any human project into the whole of society and even coincidence or luck[26], where it can be noted that, for instance, the way the financial sector is organized and functioning, ever since it took shape in the (late) Middle Ages, forms an extraordinary example of this "hubris" model and,
- *on the other hand*, an increasing "intolerance" with regard to the ideals of enlightenment, among which "freedom", "brotherhood" (or "solidarity") and "equality".[27]

Otherwise put, within "economic neo-liberalism" as an economic doctrine, but also within the self-centered economies having implemented the ideas of economic neo-liberalism into daily practice (which, at present, is unfortunately the case for the majority of the global economic systems), it is believed that there are "competent", "less competent" and even "incompetent" people. In this (neo-liberal) belief system, it is solely due to their own "incompetence" that people are poor (which makes it hard to understand why the rest of society, the so-called "competent", should support them by, for instance, providing in a social security system).

It is exactly this way of reasoning that is responsible for an increasingly primitive vision of societies ruled by economic neo-liberal thinking, where a (very) limited elite can be seen as "*Übermenschen*" (= "the rich" or, as Rand holds: "the competent") and the rest as "*Untermenschen*" (= "the poor", or, as Rand holds: "the incompetent"), an image of the world that meanwhile, through the translation of the neo-liberal belief system into numerous laws and norms, lies at the basis of the increasing polarization between a small elite of (extremely) rich people and a (vast) majority of poor people (in different societies).[28]

17 The aforementioned understanding already caused the renowned historian Yuval Noah Harari to observe that in the neo-liberal belief system egoism has even become altruism[29], thus illustrating a perception that economic (neo)liberalism is inherently based on an inverse value perception (a striking observation which will be elaborated upon further in Sect. 3.4).[30]

18 In terms of entrepreneurship, the aforementioned can be fully demonstrated by means of the dictate of striving for (ever more) profit.

As a result of the abovementioned neo-liberal belief system, for instance within the entrepreneurial sector, the pursuit of profit dominates all other values, such as: labor, environment, respect for human rights, ethical norms ... (all of which are

[26]See also Galbraith (1992), pp. 18–19.

[27]Pinxten (2014), p. 7.

[28]Hazenberg (2013), p. 165.

[29]Harari (2014), pp. 347–348. Compare Rand (2008), p. 23.

[30]Rand (1992), p. ix-x.

considered to be subordinated to the pursuit of profits).[31] (See also further, under Sect. 3.4.3)

As a result, economic processes (including *e.g.* production) are in no way run with concern for their "usefulness" to society in general, or with the intention of making the majority of mankind prosperous or happy, but only for the profitability of investments made by a select group of capital providers.[32]

In addition to certain convention-based efforts, only the legislation of some national states, albeit slightly, has aimed to counter the unendless pursuit of money of the (in many cases globally organized) entrepreneurial world, including the financial sector (especially private banking, but also different other categories of specialized financial institutions which, throughout history, have emerged from, and in addition to, private banks). **19**

It is indeed via certain sectoral forms of legislation that (some) states still (albeit in many cases to an ever lesser degree) attempt to protect other interests than those of the (big) enterprises, such as social, environmental, cultural and cultural heritage interests, from the limitless pursuit of money determining the economic game.

However, especially during the past decades, these efforts have become extremely difficult, particularly in a global(ized) context; for instance climate evolution—and, in general, the (ongoing) powerlessness of the world community to stop the increasing pollution of the planet[33]—clearly illustrates the difficulty of introducing other values into the economy, alongside, let alone above, the unlimited pursuit of profit.[34]

To further illustrate the above, the next sections of this chapter will present a concise historical exploration of a number of historical reflection systems on one of the most basic financial mechanisms, namely the credit mechanism, which have resulted in the current economic (dis)order, with full awareness of the incredible impact that the world of ideas may have on the processes that have given the (human) world its material shape. **20**

Even though certain economic doctrines have also been taken into account during this exploration, this has mainly been done in order to bring to light their

---

[31]See *e.g.* Bakan (2005), p. 256; Galbraith (1992), p. 55; Galbraith (1967), p. 109; Simonet (1970), p. 47.

As Galbraith has phrased it:

> The market has only one message for the business firm. That is the promise of more money. (...) It must try to make money and, as a practical matter, it must try to make as much as possible. Others do. To fail to conform is to invite loss, failure and extrusion. Certainly a decision to subordinate interest in earnings to an interest in a more contented life for workers, cows or customers would, in the absence of exceptional supplementary income, mean financial disaster. Given this need to maximize revenue, the firm is thus fully subject to the authority of the market. (See Galbraith 1967, p. 109.)

[32]Fromm (1955), pp. 84–85. See also Galbraith (1967), p. 115.

[33]Stiglitz (2006), p. 17; Steger (2013), pp. 91 a.f.

[34]See *e.g.* Zuboff and Maxmin (2002), p. 458.

See also below, Further Illustration 3.11.

underlying ethics, where these are weighed against other ethical visions which have taken shape outside of the strict domain of economy.

The following analysis is therefore not meant as an exposure of the status of the science of economics, but on the contrary aims to reflect on the interaction between so-called "altruistic thinking" (as defended by several historical philosophical and religious teachings) and so-called "egoistic thinking" (as especially defended by "economic liberalism" and "economic neoliberalism") on certain socioeconomic issues, with as main purpose the appraisal of the underlying ethical values on which economic actions and thoughts themselves are based.

3.3 Historical Voices Against the Unlimited Accumulation of Wealth

3.3.1 Scope

21 Economic processes did not inherently have to lead to the currently prevailing egoistic model of society (being "capitalism" or, put in more modern terminology, the "free market system") to which centuries of unlimited wealth pursuit made possible by money use have led.

On the contrary, in the early history of Western civilization, prominent thinkers and religious leaders—who unfortunately have barely been heard—did indeed warn about the potential negative effects of an unlimited pursuit of wealth and advocated that a society should not be inspired solely by money gain, and definitely not be led by it.

22 Given the fact that human behavior is, to a significant extent, the result of the emergence of ideas (see also further, at marg. 25 of Chap. 6 of this book)—whereby it could even be argued that, just as (a school in) biology considers the human species (and any other form of life) as a mechanism through which genes continue to exist and mutate, but are also passed on and combined (see also further, under Sect. 3.6.3), from the perspective of the world of ideas, mankind could be considered as a mechanism in which ideas grow and through use, over the generations, continue to live and be passed on and combined in different ways, thus contributing to the formation of society and the material environment of mankind[35]—it is useful, in what follows, to take a brief look at some of the historical thought frameworks that shaped the Western civilization, of which the first group (particularly within philosophy and religion) has mostly been fervently opposed to the unlimited pursuit of (personal) wealth from early on in history, while, on the contrary, the second group (within the economy), almost as a reaction to the views of the first group,

[35]See *e.g.* Levinas (1988), p. 85.
This insight lies also at the basic of several hinduïstic philosophical systems; see *e.g.* Vivekananda (1989), pp. 25–118, especially pp. 30 a.f.

would define the same unlimited pursuit of wealth and money as a dominant moral value to which (as to the proverbial "Golden Calf" from the Book of Exodus of the Old Testament) all other values should be sacrificed.

Only (and mainly) this evolution in Western thinking[36] is considered here.[37] 23

It was no coincidence that the acquisition of money in early Western history (where the capitalist model currently ruling the present-day "egoistic" world economy developed and also, at least initially, fully expanded), mainly found opponents amongst certain Ancient Greek philosophers[38], and later amongst early Christian (clerical) thinking which wanted to promote a society model based on values other than those of pure materialism.

This is also the reason why the opinion about the inevitable negative consequences of unbridled money pursuit, historically, has its breeding ground in philosophical and religious value systems (still explaining why it is up to this day further elaborated upon in certain contemporary, philosophical and religious doctrines in which views about economic and monetary systems are still strongly expressed).

3.3.2 The Fundamental Incompatibility of (Institutionalized) Saving and Credit with Certain Philosophical and Religious Doctrines Which Lie at the Root of Western Civilization

3.3.2.1 Plato

To start this (elementary) exploration of philosophical and religious thinking about the unbridled pursuit of money, let us first take a brief look at the views of one of the first great philosophers of the Classical Greek Era, more specifically Plato (427–347 B.C.), whose writings have undeniably had an important influence on the development of Western culture in general, and on Western thinking in particular. 24

---

[36]Bearing in mind the observation made by another spiritual master that in our present-day world Western thinking has spread everywhere.

> Geographically, the East has disappeared. Now the whole world is Western. (see Osho 1992, p. 82).

[37]For similar evolutions in other cultures, see Graeber (2012), p. 534.

[38]This should not come as a surprise, as Ancient Greece was one of the first regions to be exposed both to the turning of nomadic societies into sedentary societies, as well as to the development of one of the first fully-pledged monetary systems (at least in the Western world).

Anyone examining Plato's "*The Republic*" ("*Politeia*")[39] can but be impressed by the unprecedented ideological and philosophical wisdom of this writing.[40]

Plato hereby considered a wide range of themes about the organization of a society, which have not lost any of their importance up to today.

25 In "*The Republic*", amongst others, some attention is paid to the question of the admissibility of a(n) (unlimited) accumulation of wealth[41], and it will probably not come as a surprise that Plato clearly drew the card of a society model based on altruism (which he calls "mutual affection") rather than on monetary gain.[42]

Plato was, in general, not very favorable to trade and manufacturing, as it is exactly the mechanisms in place in these sectors which cause the greatest gaps between the rich and the poor. As a consequence, Plato was much more in favour of an agricultural society, in which every citizen, through a lottery system, would temporarily own and cultivate an equal parcel of land.[43]

26 Let us further limit the study of Plato's viewpoints on the issue of wealth accumulation to the following quotation from one of Plato's other master works, namely "*The Laws*" ("*Nomoi*"), which speaks for itself[44]:

> But the intention of our laws was that the citizens should be as happy as may be, and as friendly as possible to one another. And men who are always at law with one another, and amongst whom there are many wrongs done, can never be friends to one another, but only those among whom crimes and lawsuits are few and slight. Therefore we say that gold and silver ought not to be allowed in the city, nor much of the vulgar sort of trade which is carried on by lending money, or rearing the meaner kinds of livestock; but only the produce of agriculture, and only so much of this as will not compel us in pursuing it to neglect that for the sake of which riches exist – I mean, soul and body, which without gymnastics, and without education, will never be worth anything; and therefore, as we have said not once but many times, the care of riches should have the last place in our thoughts. For there are in all three things about which every man has an interest; and the interest about money, when rightly regarded, is the third and lowest of them.

27 A clear message: the pursuit of money should not dominate society; circulation of gold and silver should be prohibited, interest may not be levied and possession needs to be seen continuously as a means, never as a goal. Instead, man should strive for other ideals and not pay too much attention to wealth accumulation, thus avoiding that society becomes too nasty (a.o. characterized by people fighting law suits instead of aiming at friendly relationships).

---

[39] Plato (1987).

[40] See also Galbraith (1987), p. 17.

In "*The Republic*", Plato (according to the dialectical method, in which he puts his thoughts and statements, via a fictional Socratic dialogue, into the mouth of Socrates and some other characters) tries to find the composition of the ideal state for the benefit of the happiest possible society.

[41] Albeit probably not to the extent as in Aristotle's "*The Nicomachean Ethics*"; see further, at marg. 62–66 of Chap. 3 of this book.

[42] See *e.g.* Plato (1987), pp. 58 a.f.

[43] Polak (1928), p. 88.

[44] Plato (1994–2000).

Contemporary societies could undoubtedly draw very wise lessons just by reading Plato's "The Republic" and "The laws" (even if only from reading the above extract).

28 Furthermore, it should be noted that Plato's vision about avoiding a greedy society is much in line with an approach which, more or less during about the same period as when Plato worked out his philosophical system, gained popularity in the East, where, more specifically Siddhartha Gautama Buddha (around 450 B.C. until around 370 B.C.), often called simply "Buddha", similarly stated that greed is the source of all evil and suffering and that, hence, man should avoid living a life of greed (see also further, under Sect. 3.6.2.5.3).

It goes without saying that the vision of both of these enlightened (historical) figures is in sharp contrast to the (actual) neo-liberal "greed is good"-credo which, as a result of the philosophy of economic neo-liberalism, dominates present-day economies and even societies in general on a global scale.

29 It appears, furthermore, that Plato's approach should in no way be considered as an "ivory tower statement" of an isolated philosopher: on the contrary, it appears that numerous Ancient Greek writers and philosophers shared similar opinions.

De Ley has attributed this to the fact that as a "true abstraction", during the time when Plato lived, money had breached the (natural) limits of agricultural society and had made living in cities possible. Many critical minds have inevitably approached the phenomenon which was emerging and overrunning the societies they lived in by "moralizing": hence the numerous tirades where money was stigmatized as the source of all evil by authors such as Soloon, Alkaios, Sophocles and Aristophanes, as well as Plato himself.[45]

As a further illustration, we may refer to the following quotation from Sophocles (496 BC–406 BC), in the play "*Antigone*" (verses 330–336)[46], undoubtedly one of the masterpieces of classical literature:

> No thing in use by man,
> for power of ill,
> can equal money.
> This lays cities low,
> this drives men forth from quiet dwelling-place,
> this warps and changes minds of worthiest stamp,
> to turn to deeds of baseness,
> teaching men all shifts of cunning,
> and to know the guilt
> of every impious deed.[47]

---

[45]De Ley (2008).

[46]Part of Creon's dialogue.

[47]Quotation based upon the edition of "*The Harvard Classics*" 1909–14 (http://www.bartleby.com/8/6/1.html).

Compare, as regards the prevailing Catholic doctrine, 1 Tim 6:10:

> For the love of money is the root of all evils; it is through this craving that some have wandered away from the faith. (See furthermore Pontifical Council for Justice and Peace 2005, no 328.)

30 Also the works of another giant of Ancient Greek philosophy, namely Aristotle (384 BC–322 BC), show clear signs of a similar resistance to the unlimited pursuit of wealth and money, albeit focusing mainly on the levying of interest (to which we will refer further when discussing the so-called medieval "interest debate") (see further, at marg. 62–66 of this chapter).

3.3.2.2 The Religious-Ethical Teachings of Jesus Christ

3.3.2.2.1 Jesus Christ's Radical Rejection of Fortune Gathering Behaviour

31 An approach similar to Plato's can be found in certain parts of the teachings of Jesus Christ[48], whose (probable) year of birth has been chosen, not by accident, as the beginning of our era, as He lies at the foundation of the largest religious system known to Western societies, i.e. the different Christian religion(s)) which have in turn, for centuries and in different spheres of social life (including law (systems), state organizations, trade in a broad sense of the word, etc.) helped to shape the (Western and Western inspired) models of society.[49]

32 Given the perception that Western countries, even those which have roots in historical Christianity, strongly apply monetary gain as a central value, it may appear surprising that Jesus Christ Himself, in very clear words, has been opposed against a society model that would put the acquisition of money at its heart.

33 In the (embryonic) economic views of Jesus Christ, as far as they can be inferred from certain verses of the Gospel, every individual is faced with the fundamental life choice between "God" and the "mammon" (a concept that could be translated as the "money devil").[50]

It is (evidently) the intention that man should choose a life in the service of God and not in the service of the mammon, whilst it is impossible to choose both (see Matthew, 6:24).

Surprisingly in line with the views of modern anthropologists and psychologists (such as Tim Kasser, quoted hereunder), the reason for the unlimited pursuit of money (and conclusively of greed) is mentioned in the very next Gospel verse

[48]Isbouts (2012), p. 368; Sullivan (2010), p. 14.

Furthermore Goguel (1950), p. 429; Renan (1949), p. 429; Nissin (1960), p. 415; Dunkerley (1962), p. 253; Stauffer (1957), p. 176; Duquesne (1994), p. 362.

[49]Lloyd (2012), pp. 256–267; Tanner (2008), p. 198; Evans (2007), p. 202; Chadwick (1995), pp. 130 a.f.; Mcmanners (1990), pp. 92 a.f.

[50]Wikipedia (last consulted on September 11th 2014) defines the term "Mammon" as follows:

> Mammon in the New Testament of the Bible, is material wealth or greed, most often personified as a deity, and sometimes included in the seven princes of Hell.

(namely Matthew, 6:25[51]; see also Luke, 12:22), more specifically, the fear for an uncertain future.

Other verses of the New Testament warn, in a similar way, against greed and materialism, so for instance the verses Luke, 3: 10–14,[52] in addition to, for instance, 1 Tim. 6:10 (holding that the love of money is the root of all evil). **34**

In a similar way, in the renowned "Sermon on the Mount", Jesus Christ furthermore held that man shall not gather treasures on earth, where they will decay from worms and moth, or be stolen by thieves, but that on the contrary, man should gather treasures in heaven (see Matthew, 6:19).[53]

As a consequence, a correct (religious) attitude to life consists of not allowing the aforementioned fear and concern for one's own insecure future to take hold, thus avoiding the need for a life led by egoism in general and the pursuit of money and wealth in particular (i.e. focused only on satisfying materialistic values), and that, on the contrary, human life should be focused on achieving the Kingdom of God.[54] **35**

---

[51]See Matthew, 6:25:

> Behold the fowls of the air: for they sow not, neither do they reap, nor gather into barns; yet your heavenly Father feedeth them. Are ye not much better than they? (Authorized King James Version; https://www.lds.org/).

See further Wright (2012c), pp. 64 a.f.

[52]Luke, 3:10–14:

> And the people asked him, saying, What shall we do then? He answereth and saith unto them, He that hath two coats, let him impart to him that hath none; and he that hath meat, let him do likewise. Then came also publicans to be baptized, and said unto him, Master, what shall we do? And he said unto them, Exact no more than that which is appointed you. And the soldiers likewise demanded of him, saying, And what shall we do? And he said unto them, Do violence to no man, neither accuse any falsely; and be content with your wages. (https://www.biblegateway.com/passage/?search=Luke+3%2C+10-14&version=AKJV).

See also Beaumont (2010), p. 70.

[53]See also Beaumont (2010), pp. 46–47.

[54]Lloyd (2012), p. 202; Van Bruggen (2014), p. 96.

Jesus Christ even warned against the consequences of a life guided by greed (see Luke, 12:15–21):

> And he said unto them, Take heed, and beware of covetousness: for a man's life consisteth not in the abundance of the things which he possesseth. And he spake a parable unto them, saying, The ground of a certain rich man brought forth plentifully: And he thought within himself, saying, What shall I do, because I have no room where to bestow my fruits? And he said, This will I do: I will pull down my barns, and build greater; and there will I bestow all my fruits and my goods. And I will say to my soul, Soul, thou hast much goods laid up for many years; take thine ease, eat, drink, and be merry. But God said unto him, Thou fool, this night thy soul shall be required of thee: then whose shall those things be, which thou hast provided? So is he that layeth up treasure for himself, and is not rich toward God. (Authorized King James Version; https://www.lds.org/).

Further Illustration 3.1: The High Price of Materialism (Tim Kasser)
It is striking how, 2000 years later, the findings of modern human sciences have reached almost the same conclusions as the ones to be found in the abovementioned Gospel verses.

For instance, Tim Kasser, in his book "*The High Price of Materialism*"[55], has demonstrated that mainly "insecurity" and "fear", but also other factors (such as low self-esteem[56], a breakdown in social contacts,...) cause materialism.[57] Kasser has reached this conclusion by applying modern scientific methods (including "co-research" in foreign countries and cultures).[58] ***"From this perspective, materialistic values are both a symptom of underlying insecurity and a coping strategy (albeit a relatively ineffective one) some people use in an attempt to alleviate their anxieties."***[59]

Furthermore, the author depicts very precisely the negative effects of a society built on the unlimited acquisition of wealth and money: ***"Even the successful pursuit of materialistic ideals typically turns out to be empty and unsatisfying"***[60].

36 Consequently, it is not a coincidence that also in the already quoted Oxfam study "*Even it up*" (2014) the struggle against growing economic inequality is conducted in order to establish a world which is "*free from fear*".[61]

In this contemporary approach towards, in principle, the same fundamental aspects of life as those referred to in the aforementioned Gospel verses, it becomes the (at least moral) responsibility of society in general, and of its policy makers in particular, to establish a society which is free of fear, thus removing the breeding ground for unlimited egoism.

Needless to say that present-day societies which, mainly under the influence of "economic neo-liberalism" (see further, under Sect. 3.4.2.3), are more and more dominated by an "egoistic" economy, lie very far from this ideal.

37 In the radical life vision of Jesus Christ, there is no room for the practice of unlimited accumulation of wealth, savings or hoarding (and for those who find this terminology too strong, it can be pointed out that even Galbraith speaks about "*the unbridled pursuit of wealth accumulation*")[62], let alone for a world dominated by an

---

[55]Kasser (2002), p. 149 p.

[56]Kasser (2002), p. 43.

[57]Ruyver (1969), p. 28.

[58]Kasser (2002), pp. 6 a.f.

[59]Kasser (2002), p. 29.

[60]Kasser (2002), p. 42.

[61]Oxfam (2014), pp. 20 and 101 a.f.

[62]Galbraith (1992), pp. 96–97.

institutionalized savings and credit system (or, otherwise put: "the financial system").

Jesus Christ left little room for misinterpretation on how a true altruistic attitude towards life should look like when He holds that those who have "too much"[63] must be willing to donate this freely to those who do not have enough.

In Christ's teachings, such donating of excess of purchasing power may not (even) occur in the form of "lending" (free or not), but needs to be done without expecting to get the donation back (or to obtain anything in its place).

This viewpoint can, for example, be concluded from Jesus Christ's reply to the question of the rich young man about what to do "*to become part of eternal life*" (Luke, 18:18; Mark, 10:17). Christ's answer to this question was: "*Sell all that you have and distribute it to the poor, then you shall have treasure in heaven; and come follow me*" (Luke, 18:22; see also Mark, 10:21)[64], which, in the then prevailing Jewish society explaining wealth as a gift of God, was according to Bahr hardly in line with the then prevailing Jewish religious doctrine.[65]

A similar illustration of Christ's social economic viewpoint can be found in a phrase from the Gospel of Luke already quoted above, where Christ said, amongst other things: "*Whoever has two coats should share with those who have none, and whoever has food, should do likewise*" (Luke, 3:11).

The fact that the teachings of Christ do not offer any breeding ground for an institutionalized saving and credit system, let alone the consequent accumulation of unlimited wealth, is even more obvious from Luke, 6:35, where Christ again explicitly clarified that those who lend and loan money should do this without expecting anything back, including the re-payment of the amount loaned itself.[66]

At other points in the Gospel, it is further narrated how Jesus Christ expels **38**
(in addition to the merchants) the (money) changers, i.e. the predecessors of the

---

[63]In financial terms: those having an "excess of purchasing power" or having "savings".

[64]Beaumont (2010), p. 49; Wright (2012c), pp. 47 a.f.; Wright (2012b), p. 133; Isbouts (2012), p. 216.

[65]Bahr (2010), p. 37. See also Beaumont (2010), p. 49. While Judaism had no problem with wealth (as, after all, Abraham was wealthy), by Jesus' day poverty had become a huge problem, with only a small sector of society being wealthy. This explains why Judaism encouraged the rich to give alms to the poor, something Jesus also encouraged (see *e.g.* Matthew 6:2–4). However, Jesus also said that wealth could be an enormous hindrance to entering God's kingdom, hereby underlining the foolishness of an unsatiable desire for ever more (Beaumont 2010, p. 49).

Traces of this attitude found in Judaïsm whereby richess are seen as a reward of God, can still be found in present-day Catholic doctrine; see for instance Pontifical Council for Justice and Peace (2005), no 323.

[66]Luke, 6:34–35:

> And if ye lend to them of whom ye hope to receive, what thank have ye? For sinners also lend to sinners, to receive as much again. But love ye your enemies, and do good, and lend, hoping for nothing again; and your reward shall be great, and ye shall be the children of the Highest: for he is kind unto the unthankful and to the evil. (King James Version; http://biblehub.com/kjv/luke/6-34.htm; last consulted on February 26th 2016).

See further Graeber (2012), p. 283.

current bankers (see above, Chap. 2. of this book), from the temple, as they had turned it into a "*den of thieves*" (see Matthew, 21:12–13).[67]

It is hereby of further significance that the Gospel of Mark describes that, after this expulsion from the temple, the high priests and scribes who had witnessed this happening, began planning how to murder Christ (Mark, 11: 18).

This raises the question whether this religious story, in addition to its literal meaning, does not also suggest, in a metaphorical way, that the power of "Supreme Love" (which in socioeconomic relations translates into "altruism") which Jesus Christ embodies, wishes to expel the opposing powers of "egoism" and "greed", as embodied by the characters of the merchants and the money changers, i.e. the predecessors of the bankers (both ancient professions in which the pursuit of greed takes the largest form; see before also Plato's similar teachings, quoted at marg. 25 of this chapter).

Galbraith has commented on this behaviour of Christ as follows[68]:

> The example was that of Jesus, the son of an artisan, who showed that there was no divine right of the privileged; power could be with people who worked with their hands. Accompanied by disciples who were mostly of similar humble background, Jesus challenged the Herodian establishment and therewith the greatly more majestic power of Rome. That one person or one small group from such origins could gain such influence, distinction and authority was an example to be cited, an influence to be felt, for the next two thousand years. Those who in later times entered a protest against the established economic order would be called rabble-rousers, and it would be part of their defense that in His assault on the Jerusalem establishment – in denigrative terms, the moneychangers and usurers from the Temple – Jesus was their ultimate role model. To a far greater extent than many conservative Christians have liked to think, He legitimized revolt against evil or oppressive economic power.

As an aside, it could be furthermore mentioned that also in Buddhism, both "desire" and "lust", such as the craving for ever more riches, are part of the legions of Mara which need to be resisted in order to reach the state of enlightenment[69].

39 Two millennia of increasingly unlimited greed later, it is not surprising that the aforementioned expulsion of the merchants and money changers from the temple, at least as testified in the four Gospels, has been the only time that Jesus Christ expressed so much anger.

Christ did not express similar anger towards the adulterous woman who, in order to test Him, was brought to Him by the scribes and the Pharisees asking Him what to do with her; on the contrary, His reply was that he who is without sin should cast the

---

[67] Walker (2009), p. 136; see also Walker (2007), p. 136.

[68] See Galbraith (1987), pp. 20–21. Compare Walker (2009), p. 236.

[69] http://homepage.ntlworld.com/pesala/Pandita/html/mara.html (last consulted on November 26th 2014).

See also Harari (2014), pp. 249 a.f.; Thich Nhat Hanh (2009), pp. 112 a.f.

first stone, after which, when everybody else had left (the eldest first), he told the adulterous woman to go and sin no more (John, 8: 3–11).[70]

Nor did Christ lose His temper when a Roman centurion, representing the occupying force of Judea, Galilea and Palestine at the time, asked Him to cure his seriously ill slave, a request which Christ met without hesitation (Luke, 7: 1–10; Matthew, 8: 5–13; John, 4: 46–54).[71]

Even when arrested in the Garden of Olives, He showed but great mercy to Malchus, the servant of the high priest, whose right ear was cut off by the apostle Simon Peter (according to the Gospel of John)—or by "one of the apostles" (according to the other Gospels)[72]—with his sword, whereby only the Gospel of Luke mentions how Christ touched the ear of the High Priest's servant and cured him (see Luke, 22: 50–51; compare Matthew, 26: 51–52; Mark, 14: 47 and John, 18: 10–11, who do not mention this miraculous healing).[73]

Finally, even in His hour of death when hanging at the cross, Christ showed but mercy to the criminal who was crucified with Him and who expressed his repentance, when saying that he would be in paradise with Him the very same day (see Luke, 23:40).

Towards an adulterous woman and her prosecutors, towards a Roman occupier, towards those who arrested Him, and, in His hour of death, even towards a crucified criminal, Christ essentially expressed no anger, on the contrary, only mercy, making the anger He expressed towards merchants and (money) changers (i.e. bankers) thus the more striking.[74]

One can, moreover, highlight the parable of the Good Samaritan, whose care for **40**
a seriously injured man was declared by Christ to be a (typical) example (of altruistic behaviour) compared to the (improper, egoistic) behaviour of the priest and the Levite who, in spite (or even because) of their higher social and

---

[70]See furthermore Beaumont (2010), p. 45.

Remark the remarkable contradiction of the way Jesus Christ dealt with this issue and the way a large part of the American (purportedly "Christian") public usually responds to comparable present-day cases in which issues of sexual moral are at hand, with as notorious example the so-called "Lewinsky scandal" former US president Bill Clinton has been faced with during his presidency.

[71]Wright (2012a), pp. 78 a.f.

[72]Wright (2012b), pp. 196 a.f.

[73]Ortberg (2014), p. 126.

[74]Galbraith (1987), p. 21.

religious standing had walked past the same man earlier and had ignored him (Luke, 10:30–37).[75]

The story of the Good Samaritan is thus the more striking given the fact that Christ's time was dominated by a mutual hate, which had existed for centuries, between the Jews and the Samaritans, which has been explained by Ann Marie B. Bahr as a consequence of the fact that the Samaritans were an apostate sect honouring God on the Mount "Gerizim" instead of in Jerusalem, which was unacceptable to orthodox Jews[76], and which—according to Tom Wright—continues to our times in the form of the ongoing conflict between Israel and the Palestinians.[77]

It is very notable in this parable that the Good Samaritan did not expect any compensation for his help to the aforementioned seriously injured man, on the contrary, he paid the innkeeper into whose care he had given the injured man, with his own money in advance announcing that, if the sum provided would not be enough to completely cover the cost of the treatment, the Samaritan would pay the balance on his way back (see Luke, 10:35).

It is hard to envision a sharper contrast to the ideal of the (neo-)Smithian egoist (one could speak of the (modern) "*homo (neo)liberalis*"), particularly since Adam Smith has mastered socioeconomic thinking, including in sectors such as medical care[78] (see further, under Sect. 3.4).

---

[75]Isbouts (2012), pp. 214–216.

See also All it needs is love. Capitalism's reputation has been damaged by the bankers. http://www.economist.com/news/finance-and-economics/21632602-capitalisms-reputation-has-been-damaged-bankers-all-it-needs-love?fsrc=scn/tw/te/pe/ed/allitneedsislove. Last consulted on February 28th 2016:

> Nor does capitalism relate easily to the Christian ethic which still permeates Western societies. Jesus did not celebrate bankers; he turned the moneychangers out of the temple. His advice to a rich man was "sell all you have and give to the poor". The role model is the good Samaritan, who selflessly helps others, rather than himself. When we raise our children, we emphasise principles of sharing and fairness; we dole out food and presents equally to each child, regardless of how well they have "performed" during the year. The most reliable complaint of any child is that a decision is "not fair". It is hardly surprising then that in adulthood, some people see the great riches accumulated by a few and feel that is not fair either. Inequality is seen as a major problem by 56% of people in rich countries, according to the pollsters.

[76]Bahr (2010), p. 37. Walker (2009), pp. 82 a.f.

[77]Wright (2012a), pp. 126 a.f. See also Beaumont (2010), p. 65, pointing out that the parable would have been much more acceptable if it had been about a good Jew helping a Samaritan in need, but that that was a twist that Jesus was not prepared to give it.

[78]Verhaeghe (2011), pp. 26–29.

Further Illustration 3.2: Health Care Within the Christian Tradition
John Ortberg mentions the willingness to provide health care, more specifically the care for contagious diseases, as one of the greatest breakthroughs that Christianity has brought to the (Western) world.[79]

Around 165 AD, a very contagious disease (probably smallpox) broke out in Rome. Less than a century later, a second similar epidemic followed, killing up to 5000 people on some days (and that was just within the city walls of Rome itself). In both cases, the Roman population reacted in the same way as had been done before in Ancient Greece (see the writings of the Greek historian Thucydides (about. 460 to about. 395 BC)), i.e. either by completely ignoring the sick (by leaving them to their fate, followed obviously by mass deaths), or, in an attempt to avoid further contamination, by expelling them, or by throwing them out on the streets (alive). Against this background, one community in the Roman Empire began to conduct itself in a different way, more specifically the Christians, who had learned from their spiritual Master Christ how, one and a half centuries earlier, He Himself had cared for the lepers (see *e.g.* Matthew, 8: 1–4; Luke, 5: 12–16).[80] As a result, Christians started to administer health care in an organized way, often at the risk of contamination (and causing the death of many Christian care providers)[81], and appeared as the first organized care providers within Roman Society.[82]

Ortberg further mentions how later in history Gregory of Nyssa (335–394) (the younger brother of Basil the Great, who is further referred to as one of the religious scholars who opposed the charging of interest; see further, at marg. 75 of this chapter) was the first to raise funds to open a care home for lepers. As a result, he established what is believed to be the first hospital in Western history.[83]

Shortly thereafter, the council of Nicaea (325) (where it was also decided to introduce the prohibition of interest for clergy) (see further, at marg. 77 of this chapter) would decide that wherever a cathedral was built, there should also be a "hospice".[84]

(continued)

[79]Ortberg (2014), p. 49. See also Beaumont (2010), p. 69, pointing out that Christians have always been at the forefront of caring for the needy (a fact which, according to Beaumont, has often been antagonized atheistic authorities).

[80]Wright (2012c), pp. 81 a.f.; Wright (2012a), pp. 55 a.f.

[81]Ortberg (2014), pp. 49–50.

[82]Ortberg (2014), pp. 49–50.

[83]Ortberg (2014), p. 51.

[84]Ortberg (2014), p. 51.

Further Illustration 3.2 (continued)

Further historical examples of the inspirational power of the teachings of Jesus Christ in the health care sector are: (i) the establishment of the Red Cross by Jean Henri Dunant (1828–1910) who did so after having witnessed how on the day after the "Battle of Solferino" (June 1859) during the Second Italian Independence war (between certain Italian regions depending on the support of France *on one side*, and Habsburg Austria *on the other*), over 38,000 wounded soldiers were left to their fate on the battle field, and because he could no longer endure their cries, decided to dedicate the rest of his life to the care of wounded soldiers in the name of Jesus Christ, which explains the choice of the (red) cross as a symbol of the organization he founded; (ii) Theodor Fliedner (1800–1864) who, out of his conviction as a Lutheran predecessor, and in a period where most German cities did not have hospitals, started training young German (peasant) women to become nurses, which resulted in the creation of a chain of hospitals all over Europe; a little later (iii) Florence Nightingale (1820–1910) aspired to a life dedicated to the care of the sick and wounded; as a result, she would establish the first secular nursing school in the world (attached to "St. Thomas' Hospital" in London)); at her death and at her explicit request, she was buried in an anonymous grave only marked by a cross[85], and (iv) Father Damian (also: "Holy Damian of Molokai"[86]) (1840–1889) who dedicated his life to the care of lepers and who would himself die of leprosy.[87]

We can clearly also add, from recent history, Mother Teresa (also known as: "Saint Teresa of Calcutta") (1910–1997) (born as Agnes Gonxha Bojaxhiu), who turned the care of the sick and weak in society into her life work (for which she received the Nobel Peace Prize in 1979). To do this, she obtained permission from the Vatican in 1950 to start a new religious order, the "Missionaries of Charity", aimed at caring for "*the hungry, the naked, the homeless, the crippled, the blind, the lepers, and any person feeling unwanted, unloved, or neglected by society, people who are considered to be a burden on society and avoided by others*". In 1952, Mother Teresa opened her first "Home for The Dying" in Calcutta, in an abandoned Hindu temple, and shortly after that an orphanage and a shelter for lepers. Thanks to donations and new members, at the start of the sixties of the twentieth century, the order had several hospices, orphanages and shelters for lepers at its disposal. During the seventies of the twentieth century, the growth of the order brought it to every continent. At the time of Mother Theresa's death, the

(continued)

[85]Sullivan (2010), p. 62.

[86]He was canonized by the Catholic Church on October 11th 2009.

[87]Ortberg (2014), p. 52.

Further Illustration 3.2 (continued)

Missionaries of Charity employed over 4000 sisters, 500 brothers (in an allied brotherhood) and over 100,000 lay volunteers working in 610 missions in 123 countries. For this, she was canonized by the Catholic Church on September 4th 2016.[88]

It should be clear from the foregoing that in Christ's radical (religious) life tenure, there is no room for wealth accumulation (= savings behaviour) and enrichment through lending (let alone for the specialized financial products which later in history have been derived from the basic credit mechanism).[89] 41

In fact, within a society based on the radical religious life tenure preached by Christ, nobody should have to surrender to an unlimited accumulation of wealth, nor should one choose for the pursuit of unlimited money and profit gain as one's life purpose (where it needs to be said that particularly early Christian societies have effectively attempted to achieve this goal; see further, under Sect. 3.3.2.2.2).

In addition, in such an evangelical (religious) society, the needs of the deprived should, by definition, automatically be met. Anyone having "too much" should indeed be willing to share with those who have "too little", and the deprived will in this way be assured that their needs will be met (so that nobody should live in fear of an uncertain material future).

In such a society model, the earth's resources would automatically serve the collectivity of mankind without leaving much room for the large distortions which nowadays characterize the distribution of wealth on a global scale (see furthermore, under Sect. 3.4.8).

To conclude this brief exploration on the ethical attitude towards wealth accumulation in Jesus Christ's teachings, it is particularly striking that both the religious-ethical life tenure of Jesus Christ[90], and the philosophical-ethical teachings of Plato[91], had already early on in the history of Western civilization reached the very similar conclusion that the unbridled pursuit of wealth, especially at the expense of others, is ethically reprehensible. 42

It is therefore thus the more remarkable that during the centuries that followed, and particularly in the economic sphere, Western societies would clearly dissociate themselves from these ethical insights, and, on the contrary, gradually develop a basic new set of ethics which is in direct contrast to the ethical principles of Plato, Aristotle and Christianity, namely the doctrines propagated by "economic liberalism" and, later on in history, "economic neo-liberalism".

---

[88]See also Dowley (2009), p. 153; Sullivan (2010), p. 20; Beaumont (2010), p. 117.

[89]Galbraith (1990), 19.

[90]Which, as stated by Levinas, formed the basis for Western religion(s).

[91]Which, as stated by the same Levinas—be it along with the similar ethical vision of Aristotle (see further, at Sect. 3.3.3.2.1.3)—formed the basis for Western thinking.

3.3.2.2.2 Attitude Towards Money Gathering in the Early Christian Societies

43 Although, under the influence of the already mentioned liberal and neoliberal economic doctrines, the present-day world economies are governed by principles which are completely opposite to the ideals of Christ, Early Christian societies have nevertheless effectively attempted to put into daily practice the evangelical value of a society based on altruism, at least as witnessed in the "Acts" of the New Testament.[92]

In the New Testament book "Acts", a picture is drawn of an early Christian society where, initially under the leadership of some of the apostles of Christ, rich Christians, as He had taught them, sold their goods, in order—and here a first difference in the actual practice of Jesus Christ's message compared to His words can already be found[93]—not to donate the proceeds of such sales to the poor, but rather to make them available collectively, so that no member of the Christian society should suffer any shortage.[94]

A similar image of early Christian "mutual solidarity" (which is one of the meanings of the concept "koinônia" as used by Saint Paul) appears from the different letters of Saint Paul (*e.g.* in Romans, 15: 25–32; 1 Corinthians, 16: 1–4; 2 Corinthians, 8–9 and Galatians, 2: 10), where he, for example, calls for donations to finance the churches (of Jerusalem), but also as a means of achieving a redistribution of wealth among the Christians in order to achieve the greatest possible

---

[92]See *e.g.* in the book "Acts" of the New Testament:

- Acts, 2: 44–45 (Authorized King James Version; https://www.lds.org/):

> And all that believed were together, and had all things common; And sold their possessions and goods, and parted them to all men, as every man had need.

- Acts, 4: 32–35 (Authorized King James Version; https://www.lds.org/):

> And the multitude of them that believed were of one heart and of one soul: neither said any of them that ought of the things which he possessed was his own; but they had all things common. And with great power gave the apostles witness of the resurrection of the Lord Jesus: and great grace was upon them all. Neither was there any among them that lacked: for as many as were possessors of lands or houses sold them, and brought the prices of the things that were sold, And laid them down at the apostles' feet: and distribution was made unto every man according as he had need.

See also Wright (2012d), pp. 43 a.f. and pp. 73 a.f.; Beaumont (2010), p. 56.

This attitude has in recent times been criticized by the spiritual master Osho who has pointed out that present-day Christianity does not convert because of its higher values, greater truth or deeper insights, but by providing food and care for the hungry and needy (referred to as conversion with "*the Holy Bible in one hand and a loaf of bread in another*"). (See Osho 2013, pp. 24–25.)

[93]It is striking that Saint Francis, when confronted with the behavior of a new disciple who had acted in a similar way by donating his fortune to his family rather than to the poor, severely reacted by refusing this person as his follower until he had managed to set this wrong right.

[94]Jones (2011), p. 162.

fairness.[95] On this occasion, Saint Paul clarified the reasons for such a system, among which the fact that love and charity assume that people provide practical help and support to one another (see 1 Thessalonians, 4:9–10).[96]

Notwithstanding the extent of mutual solidarity which the early Christian soci- **44**
eties thus demonstrated, a thorough reading of the New Testament nevertheless reveals, already from the beginning, a degree of dilution of the message of Christ Himself.

Where Christ Himself, in an above quoted verse of the Gospels (see above, at marg. 37 of this chapter) had invited a rich young man to sell all his property and to distribute the proceeds of such sale to the poor, in early Christian society, practices evolved differently: indeed, the rich were asked to sell their possessions, but on the understanding that the proceeds of these sales were re-used for the establishment of the Christian community, in other words, to divide among those who were part of the Christian community itself.

It seems that Saint Paul was well aware of the risk of Christ's words thus getting distorted, leading him to emphasize, in his various writings, the principle of "economic self-sufficiency" or "economic self-reliance": Christians were to strive, through their labor, to enable themselves to lead a generous life (compare to the similarly encouraged "generous behavior" of Aristotle), in such a way that they could (also) "give" without expecting to be paid back (see 1 Thessalonians, 4: 11–12). Saint Paul's ideal seems to have been for a world of Christian communities to emerge where no-one was in need, and where the desire to do good, would increasingly be passed on to the world outside of the Church.[97]

Nevertheless, it should further be noted that the way of fulfilling (in daily **45**
practice) the aforementioned words of Christ by Saint Francis of Assisi in the thirteenth century (see further, under Sect. 3.3.2.2.3), witnesses a much purer experience of the aforementioned "religious message".

As will be further on in the text elaborated upon in more detail, Saint Francis also wanted his followers to give up their prize possessions and sell them, but in his case, the profit was explicitly not intended to create a collective wealth, but rather for distribution to (other) poor people. It hereby seems that Saint Francis of Assisi realized very well that Christ, through His teachings, had not only called for a life of "poverty" and "solidarity", but also one of labor, where a person needs to cover his day-to-day living expenses through daily labor in exchange for daily food requirements (or other vital needs), and where there was no room for wealth accumulation,

---

[95]Jones (2011), pp. 162–163.

[96]Hoet (2008), p. 95.

[97]Jones (2011), p. 164; Hoet (2008), p. 140.

be it in a collective way, and particularly not from fear of an uncertain future (compare Matthew, 6: 25–31)[98].

46 Nonetheless, early Christian societies initially demonstrated a degree of "mutual solidarity" in a rigorous way not seen in history since then[99].

From "2 Thessalonians, 3:6–12", it is hereby clear that the principle of *"practical mutuality"* was a ruling principle in the socioeconomic relations between and within the Christian communities.[100]

At the same time, as said before, Saint Paul also-called for every Christian to provide for themselves through labor and not depend on anyone else, so that a Christian would be a "*benefactor*" and not a "*protégé*" (see 1 Thessalonians, 2: 1–12 and 4: 9–11).[101]

Soon this rigidity would however vanish.

As the expected establishment of God's Kingdom on earth was taking too long, the original, harsh attitude of the leading clerical figures towards the rich became more and more lenient. For instance, it soon was no longer necessary to distance oneself from "all" of one's possessions to be allowed to join the Christian community: on the contrary, a "partial" renunciation was deemed sufficient. When later the number of rich Christians grew exponentially, the organization of early Christian societies would also develop into a true hierarchy, which created the starting point for the subsequent institutionalized Church (where accumulation of wealth found a place again, something which is confirmed by the many treasures the Church has gathered throughout the centuries[102], significantly contrasting with the message of poverty and simplicity for which Christ Himself had called).[103]

Later on, certain parts of the Church would themselves become part of certain (pre)capitalist practices relying on the exploitation of serfs (*e.g*. the "grangia" of the

[98]Matthew, 6: 25–31:

> 25 Therefore I tell you, do not worry about your life, what you will eat or drink; or about your body, what you will wear. Is not life more than food, and the body more than clothes? 26 Look at the birds of the air; they do not sow or reap or store away in barns, and yet your heavenly Father feeds them. Are you not much more valuable than they? 27 Can any one of you by worrying add a single hour to your life ? 28 "And why do you worry about clothes? See how the flowers of the field grow. They do not labor or spin. 29 Yet I tell you that not even Solomon in all his splendor was dressed like one of these. 30 If that is how God clothes the grass of the field, which is here today and tomorrow is thrown into the fire, will he not much more clothe you—you of little faith? 31 So do not worry, saying, 'What shall we eat?' or 'What shall we drink?' or 'What shall we wear?'

See also Van Bruggen (2014), p. 96.

[99]Jones (2011), p. 162.

[100]Jones (2011), p. 163.

[101]Jones (2011), pp. 115–116.

[102]Even having resulted in the fact that the Catholic church, in its several components, is presently one of the richest institutions on earth albeit that, due to a total lack of transparency, it is impossible to measure the extent of its worldwide wealth.

[103]Praag (1954), pp. 161–179, especially pp. 172–173.

Cistercian Abbeys, referred to by Gimpel as the first "modern factories" in European history).[104]

3.3.2.2.3 The Allegorical Marriage Between Francis of Assisi and Lady Poverty

Some of the abovementioned developments did not stop some leading Catholic **47**
figures, who apparently better understood the basic teachings of Jesus Christ, from rising through the course of later Western (church) history.

A noteworthy example of such a figure has without any doubt been Saint Francis of Assisi (1181/1182–1226) who, in word and deed attempted to lead a life in (literal) accordance with the words of Jesus Christ.[105]

Saint Francis (born as "Giovanni di Pietro Bernardone"[106]) witnessed the reve- **48**
lation of God's will while, on February 24th 1208, he was celebrating mass in the chapel of Portiuncula (nearby Assisi)[107], and during mass heard (the reading of) the following evangelic words of Jesus Christ when sending out the apostles: *'"Do not get any gold or silver or copper to take with you in your belts— no bag for the journey or extra shirt or sandals or a staff, for the worker is worth his keep. Whatever town or village you enter, search there for some worthy person and stay at their house until you leave. As you enter the home, give it your greeting. If the home is deserving, let your peace rest on it; if it is not, let your peace return to you"'* (Matthew, 10: 9–12; see also Luke, 9: 1–17).[108]

After having heard these verses from the Gospel, Saint Francis concluded that he should put these words into daily practice, especially by postulating the "literal"[109] translation of three passages from the Gospel: (*i*) the sale of all earthly possessions in order to donate the profits to the poor (Matthew, 19:21); (*ii*) take nothing when you travel: possess no staff, no bread or gold, nor two coats (Matthew, 10: 9–10); and (*iii*) in order to follow Jesus Christ, deny oneself and take up one's cross (Luke, 9:23).[110]

For a long period, these evangelical verses were the only three rules of the (early) order of Saint Francis, while Saint Francis himself entered into a metaphorical/

---

[104]Gimpel (1976), p. 47.

[105]Bower (2009), pp. 107 a.f.

[106]Brugmans (1942), p. 208; Dowley (2009), p. 70.

[107]A church which Saint Francis was then (literally) restoring.

[108]Wright (2012a), pp. 105 a.f.; Armstrong and Brady (1982), p. 3; Englebert (1998), pp. 30 a.f. See also Schnürer (1949), p. 352; Englebert (1998), pp. 72–73; J. Pelikan (1987), p. 154.

[109]Russell (1948), p. 408.

[110]Bahr (2010), p. 186; Englebert (1998), p. 73.

allegorical marriage with religious poverty ("Lady Poverty") (as described in an early anonymous text "*Sacrum Commercium*").[111]

49 Saint Francis considered the literal compliance with the three aforementioned evangelical teachings to be a direct order from God (in the same way as a serf was supposed to obey his feudal lord).[112]

As more and more disciples joined Saint Francis's movement, he himself started to refer to them as "*minores*" (= the "least", or the "less important") who originally were not allowed to have a life in society, and who furthermore were not allowed to have any kind of possession, not even in a collective manner (and not even of houses to live in or of churches).[113]

On the contrary, the "*fratres minores*" needed to provide for their daily life needs (in accordance with Matthew, 10:10, implying that every laborer should be worthy of his hire) without being allowed to accept any money. When necessary, they could beg for grain (like ordinary poor people at that time), but not for money[114], while Saint Francis always served as the best example for this severe evangelical life attitude himself.[115]

By the same token, the "*minores*" were not allowed to occupy a fixed residence, but were to remain dependent on temporary shelter provided in return for their daily labor (compare the concept of "*homelessness*" in Buddhism).[116]

50 As to monetary use and gain, it is remarkable (and no less radical than in the earlier quoted Gospel verses; see above, at marg. 33–34 and 37–40 of this chapter) that in the first version of the later on more established central rules of the Order of the Friars Minor attributed to Saint Francis himself[117], it goes as follows[118]:

> Therefore, a friar is not permitted,
> Wherever he is or goes,
> In no way to take along, receive or make receivable money or coins,
> Not for clothes or books, nor as payment for a job
> In short, in no case,
> Except in case of clear need of sick friars,
> as we are not permitted to expect more profit from money and coins
> Than from stones.
> And the devil will dazzle those who desire it or find more value in it than in stones.

---

[111]Schnürer (1949), p. 352; Pelikan (1987), p. 157; Fülöp-Miller (1991), p. 182; Russell (1948), p. 408; Bahr (2010), pp. 190–191.
See further Englebert (1998), pp. 121 a.f.

[112]Schnürer (1949), p. 352. See also Freeman et al. (2004), especially p. 14; Armstrong and Brady (1982), p. 4.

[113]Russell (1948), p. 408.

[114]Schnürer (1949), p. 355. See also Pelikan (1987), pp. 160–161; Russell (1948), p. 408.

[115]De Wit and Steenvoorde (2008), p. 71; Fülöp-Miller (1991), p. 193.

[116]Russell (1948), p. 408; Bahr (2010), p. 191; Backhouse (2011), p. 95.

[117]Sweeney (2015), p. 206.

[118]See Chapter VIII ("*The brothers may not accept money*"), Verses 3–6 of the "*Rules of the fratres minores*" in the (Dutch) translation of Freeman et al. (2004), p. especially 51.
Compare Sweeney (2015), p. 213.

> We, who leave everything behind
> Have to watch out not to lose
> The kingdom of Heaven
> For such a worthless thing.
> And if we find coins somewhere
> We are to worry about it just as little as about the dust that we walk upon
> For 'vanity of vanities and all is vanity'. (Pr I,2)

According to Fülöp-Miller, this attitude towards money was thus the more remarkable in a time when money, which had just been reintroduced as the main standard of exchange in trade and commerce, was more and more considered as the essence of all values, a thing which was to be acquired and accumulated above anything else. A person who owned money and gave it away, who refused to accept a coin that was offered to him, was a fool if there ever was one.[119]

Even though, without any doubt, Franciscan teachings also offered a (clerical) reaction to another, be it spiritual, movement stigmatized as pagan, which in those days aspired to introduce evangelical values into daily society, namely "Catharism"[120], it does not prejudice the great achievements of Saint Francis and his followers, amongst whom, in addition to his female counterpart Saint Clara of Assisi[121], was the similarly soon very popular Saint Anthony of Padua[122]. **51**

---

[119]Fülöp-Miller (1991), pp. 187–188.

[120]See the works of Emmanuel Le Roy Ladurie, among which "*Montaillou, village occitan de 1294 à 1324*", Gallimard, 1975; revised edition 1982.

[121]Backhouse (2011), p. 95; Schnürer (1949), p. 359; Brugmans (1942), p. 209; Bahr (2010), p. 191; Englebert (1998), pp. 141 a.f.; Fülöp-Miller (1991), pp. 217 a.f.

[122]See Hardick (1989), pp. 39–40.

Saint Anthony's attacks on social injustice and social disorder did not spring from an aspiration to gain an enthusiastic reaction, but from an uncompromising honesty that felt obligated to the Gospel only (Hardick 1989, p. 39). Saint Anthony hereby stressed three Christian virtues, namely chastity, poverty and humility (see Spilsbury 2013, p. 240) and three capital sins for excoriation: pride, greed and lust (see Jarmak 2013, p. 223).

Saint Anthony severely opposed the in his lifetime emerging practices of "usury". (See Jarmak 2013, p. 222.)

Some of his sayings were as follows:

> The accursed usurers become great and strong on the earth. Their teeth are like the teeth of lions. The lion is distinguished by two qualities: a neck that will not bend since it is made of but one bone, and an evil-smelling mouth. Similarly, the neck of the usurer is unbending since he neither fears God nor respects his fellow human beings. His mouth smells evil because he puts nothing into it except filthy money and its dirty profit. His teeth are like those of a young lion (Joel 1:6), for he swallows and consumes the property of the poor, the orphans, and the widows. (See Hardick 1989, p. 39.)

> Anyone who strangles another person takes from that person both his voice and his life. The poor person's property is his life. As life lives from blood, so the poor person must live from his property. If you take his meager possessions from the poor person, you strangle that person; and in the end, you yourself will be strangled by the devil. (See Hardick 1989, pp. 39–40.)

Despite all this, even the teachings of Saint Francis, notwithstanding the fact that his direct followers attempted to adopt them[123], would all in all find very limited response and not succeed in weakening the dominance of the emerging pre-capitalist, Middle Age trade system, and the pursuit of profits on which this was based. A possible explanation for this is that Saint Francis was in no way an (early) socialist or revolutionary. On the contrary, the means he employed to adjust the social and socio-political evils of his day was the mutual adjustment of wealth and poverty, of power and submission, and the equalization of master and servant, and of lord and vassal on a personal basis.[124]

52 Schnürer[125] nevertheless mentions that Saint Francis and his movement indicated a beneficial reaction to the immoderate greed for money which was, because

> One who wishes to lord it over others uses gold and silver money as a security at the curia, giving it to porters and notaries, for such people well understand how to milk a cow. They suck out the blood of the poor and lighten the purses of the wealthy and give the money to their nephews and nieces, and often to their sons and daughters. They write out receipts for the money requested from them, and desire to receive great sums of gold and silver in payment. They strip their fellow human beings of everything, taking even their clothing. Even the people living in the cities are driven to complain, and the souls of those who are oppressed cry out to the Lord. But God leaves nothing unpaid. If they have acted against the light of their better insights, they will lose the light of grace and of the church. (See Hardick 1989, p. 40.)

> The Lord punishes avaricious people, permitting them to be afflicted with need and want, since in their estimation, they think they always need some more. He punishes them with a fever and envy at the good fortune of others, with a cold shiver of losing what they have accumulated, with burning heat to acquire more, with the hunger of gluttony, with the foul air of a bad reputation, and with the rust of lust. (See Jarmak 2013, p. 223.)

> Damned money! Alas! How many religious did it blind! How many cloistered religious dit it deceive! Money is the 'droppings of birds' that blinded the eyes of Tobit. (See Jarmak 2013, p. 223.)

Furthermore, Saint Anthony held that although the bodily situation of humanity is marked by the effects of sin, this nevertheless should lead people to honesty: ***"Our body is poor. For it enters this land of exile naked, blind and miserable. And it will leave this foreign land naked, blind and crying... It is subjected to need and cold, it is plagued with sickness... Of what, then, are you proud, o poor, unfortunate man? Of what can you boast? Whatever you cannot take with you later does not belong to you."*** Hardich in this regard has pointed out that his is not to be considered the opionion of an overly zealous, popular missionary, but, strictly speaking, a paraphrase of the words of the Sacred Scripture; ***"We brought nothing into the world, and we cannot take anything out of the world. But if we have food and clothing, let us be content with these. But those who desire to be rich fall into temptation, into a snare, into many senseless and hurful desireds that plunge people into ruin and destruction. For the love of money is the root of all evils"*** (1 Tim 6:7–10). (See Hardick 1989, pp. 177–178.)

[123]See *e.g.* Wintz (2012), pp. 6–7.

[124]Maloney (1931), p. 74.

[125]Schnürer (1949), p. 359. See also Pelikan (1987), p. 161.

of the revival of trade, consuming Italy at that time. Hence, Saint Francis' life and work formed a "social blessing" and a call for "spiritual elevation", particularly towards the church itself, as a counterweight to the increasing hunger for wealth, power and splendor that was taking control of all layers of society, including the clergy itself.

A sharper contrast between the teachings of Saint Francis and current neo-liberal teaching (unless perhaps with the message of Christ Himself, which in substance, was the same as that of Saint Francis, as the latter aimed at applying some of Christ's words literally) may be hard to imagine.

Who, for instance, could imagine that Saint Francis of Assisi, the allegorical husband of Lady Poverty would, instead of, based on the evangelical message that the laborer needs to be worthy of his livelihood, working every day for a meal (or for a similar need), for instance, be the CEO of a large company and be its main shareholder, in order to, by using (and exploiting) the labor of others as much as possible, and by selling his products and services at the highest possible price, get as rich as possible, for which purpose he would occasionally meet with his accountant, auditor or lawyer, in a relentless attempt to set up mechanisms that would enable him to pay the least possible amount of taxes (and for this purpose would be willing to put pressure—or have others put pressure for him—on politicians), in order to avoid contributing to the organization of society in its widest sense?

By way of a concluding remark, reference can be made to the fact that under prevailing Church doctrine, the ideal of Saint Francis is still upheld, albeit it is considered as an ideal which is not in reach for everyone, but only for those who seek poverty "*with a religious attitude*", whereby it is said that such "*poverty opens one to recognizing and accepting the order of creation*".[126]

Further Illustration 3.3: Brother Sun, Sister Moon (Franco Zeffirelli)

The movie "*Brother Sun, Sister Moon*" (1972) by Franco Zeffirelli, draws a romanticized version of the life (and especially spiritual awakening and spiritual growth) of Saint Francis of Assisi.

One of the scenes in the movie dealing with the early spiritual awakening of this great Saint in the catholic tradition (who also enjoys the status of doctor of the Church) is definitively also an indictment of the emerging (pre) capitalism in Northern-Italian regions in the twelfth and thirteenth century.

(continued)

[126]See Pontifical Council for Justice and Peace (2005), no 324:

> In this perspective, the "rich man" is the one who places his trust in his possessions rather than in God, he is the man who makes himself strong by the works of his own hands and trusts only in his own strength. Poverty takes on the status of a moral value when it becomes an attitude of humble availability and openness to God, of trust in him. This attitude makes it possible for people to recognize the relativity of economic goods and to treat them as divine gifts to be administered and shared, because God is the first owner of all goods.

Further Illustration 3.3 (continued)

In the disputed scene, the young Saint Francis ends up in one of the textile workshops of his father Pietro di Bernardone (performed in the movie by Lee Montague) (who in the previous scene had shown Francis his treasure room which the young Saint had silently witnessed in great wonder, clearly demonstrating that he did not see his purpose in life as accumulating *that* kind of treasures), where laborers (including children and youngsters), are, *inter alia*, weaving fabrics in appalling conditions (among which the condition of the workshop itself, which looks like a dark cavern).

The sight of the miserable conditions of the laborers makes such a great impression on the young Saint Francis, that he cannot hold back from inciting them to stop working and from taking them outside into the sunlight.

In the movie, the metaphors in particular are very strong: not only is the scene played in complete silence, as Saint Francis, since spiritually awakening (earlier in the movie), has not yet uttered a single word, but besides that, the image of Saint Francis leading the textile laborers working in miserable circumstances into the sunlight, is clearly to be understood metaphorically as the image of the Christian Saint leading his flock into "the Light".

In a later scene of the movie, the viewer can witness a new confrontation of two colliding ranges of thought (which have determined the current shape of socioeconomic world order), more specifically the evangelical values, adhered to by Saint Francis in all purity, as opposed to the aim of unlimited wealth accumulation which consumes his father Pietro di Bernardone. In the relevant scene, Saint Francis, moved by great compassion, is returning home from the textile workshop, where his father, driven by an unbridled selfish pursuit of riches (and this throughout the whole movie), erupts in anger. When shortly later, Saint Francis also throws his father's robes and fine fabrics out of the window, (as such kind of wealth cannot bring happiness), the father (literally) drags his son to the bishop of Assisi, Guido, hoping that the latter would be able to bring Saint Francis to "his senses". These attempts however are pointless as the confrontation with bishop Guido of Assisi causes the final breakthrough in Saint Francis's spiritual awakening, whereby he literally gives up his fine clothes (and with this, in a symbolic way, the paternal authority, as well as his heritage), and places them in front of the bishop in order finally to start his life of poverty, which will turn him into one of the most inspiring Saints ever in Catholic history.[127]

[127]See furthermore Fülöp-Miller (1991), pp. 176–177; Russell (1948), p. 407; Zwaenepoel (2011), p. 127; Freeman et al. (2004), especially p. 14.

3.3.2.2.4 The Waning Influence of Jesus Christ's Radical Teachings About Wealth Accumulation in Later Christian Societies

It is self-evident that, even on a global scale, the current socioeconomic model of capitalism, lies as far from the aforementioned ideal evangelical image as possible. **53**

Notwithstanding the fact that the Roman Empire itself and, from the early Middle Ages on, the different European Regions (later: countries), were one by one "christianized"[128], the radical "economic" vision of Christ would be barely of any real influence in the organization of these Western (and Western inspired) society (ies) and their prevailing economic system, namely (emerging) capitalism.

On the contrary, to phrase it in said evangelical terms, the evolution of Western economies rather has been characterized by an ever increasing submission to "the mammon" (rather than to God), where even Church teachers, to some extent already in Roman times, were increasingly prepared to make (extensive) compromises to validate developments in trade (and later in industry), with Protestantism eventually resulting in clerical teachings themselves being more and more sympathetic towards (pre-)capitalist practices and, as a consequence, hardly being still in line with the teachings of Christ Himself.[129]

According to Praag[130], the spirit of early religious Christianity has nowadays completely disappeared in almost all purportedly Christian countries, even within the Catholic and other Christian churches themselves. **54**

According to this author, instead of Jesus Christ, the Son of Man who had no stone to rest His weary head upon (Matthew, 20: 8), a new type of Emperor came to Rome, living in a showy palace which is guarded by even more showy soldiers, under whose watch the experience of the evangelical values gradually got reduced to a mere lip service to rigid rituals.[131]

Already from the third and fourth centuries on, the Christian Church hence strived for accumulating more and more wealth, for instance by convincing rich Christians to invest in churches and monasteries (rather than investing in community projects) in this way in its own merit contributing to the decline of the Roman empire.[132]

On a more socioeconomic level, the diminishing of evangelical Christianity can even to a further extent be demonstrated by the evolution of the Christian viewpoints on the question of wealth accumulation through means of the credit mechanism. **55**

[128]Lloyd (2012), p. 257.

[129]Todd (2015), pp. 31 a.f.; also Todd (2015), p. 47.

[130]Praag (1954), pp. 161–179, especially p. 175. See also Pelikan (1987), p. 157.

[131]Praag (1954), pp. 161–179, especially p. 175.

[132]Eagleton and Williams (2007), p. 61.

From the fourth century on, until far into the Middle Ages, clerical thinking about how the accumulation of wealth relates to the basic evangelical values, hereby focused more and more on the so-called "(clerical) interest debate", whereby the new economic teachings of the Church of that time (see further in the text, under Sect. 3.3.3.3) got already early on in history based on a fundamental weakening of the teachings of Christ Himself.

In other words, the clerical position regarding the question of (unbridled) wealth accumulation would, over the ages, increasingly start to demonstrate an ever growing tolerance towards the practices which lie at the foundation of capitalism, among which the levying of interest as a method of unlimited enrichment; as a result, since the late Middle Ages, Christian philosophy itself would ultimately contribute to the breeding ground for capitalist economic thinking to which especially the teachings of the spiritual fathers of Protestantism, Martin Luther (1483–1546) and John Calvin (1509–1564) strongly bear witness (see further, under Sect. 3.3.3.6.2).[133]

56 Since, from an historical angle, the so-called "clerical interest debate" concerns one of the most important teachings in which the issue of the acceptability of uncontrolled individual accumulation of wealth has been so profoundly covered[134], the development of this teaching will (thoroughly) be analyzed in Sect. 3.3.3.

[133]Compare Galbraith (1987), p. 22.

Already during the second half of the Middle Ages, the Catholic Church itself would not hesitate to participate in certain commercial and financial practices which were inherently inconsistent with the message of Jesus Christ.

A historical example is without any doubt the practice of the trade of (church) "permits" (purportedly diminishing the time a sinner has to spend in purgatory), which would later on be highly contested by Luther, causing a clerical schism that resulted in the establishment of the so-called protestant churches. Some of these protestant churches have, in an almost paradoxical way, developed teachings of unbridled savings behavior put forward as central ethical values (Graeber 2012, pp. 321 a.f.; see also Vivekananda 1989, pp. 25–118, especially p. 32; Bruckner 2016, pp. 36 a.f.).

Also the techniques, still applied today, of accounting undervaluation of the immeasurable (cultural) treasures of the Catholic Church in general, and of the Vatican more specifically, in order to hide the real value of these treasures from the outside world, reflect the similar craving for ever more wealth that is not shared with others that was criticized by Christ. Most probably, the leading forces of the Vatican could, without any doubt, respond to the appeal of Christ and sell many of these treasures and by doing this remove a great deal of suffering from the poor and needy. Furthermore, the Vatican even created its own bank, the "*Istituto per le Opere di Religione*" ("*Institution for the Works of Religion/IOR*"), which enables its customers to invest, offering payment transfer services and which, as many of its "secular" counterparts, has repeatedly been discredited in the past (https://www.ior.va/; last consulted on December 10th 2014; see also Bruckner 2016, p. 37).

[134]See also Bernstein (2004), p. 19.

3.3.3 *The Middle Ages Clerical Interest Debate*[135]

3.3.3.1 The Weakening of Christian Teaching Towards the So-Called Interest Debate

Although, as mentioned before, from early on in Western history[136], Christianity became the dominant religion[137], Catholic doctrine would quite quickly[138] undergo a gradual, albeit fundamental weakening of the radical vision of Christ on the issue of wealth accumulation. **57**

A.o. based upon the writings of the Ancient Greek philosopher Aristotle[139], the aversion towards unrestrained wealth accumulation was gradually reduced to a ban (with a much more limited scope) on setting a price for the lending out of money (as a substitute for giving away one's riches). This resulted into a centuries-long battle of ideas about whether or not the charging of interest could be justified in light of Christian doctrine.

In hindsight, one can but wonder whether or not said evolution implied, already from an early point in the history of Christianity, an important concession to "the mammon" which, in its own turn, paved the way for the development of a social and economic model presently prevailing in Western societies in which money and monetary gain gradually became the central (economic) value. **58**

Instead of, as still had been attempted in most early Christian societies (see above, under Sect. 3.3.2.2.2), clinging radically to the vision of Christ Himself which implied that those who have "too much", should be willing to donate to the poor without any expectancy of being refunded—an approach which is, of course, intrinsically inconsistent with the development of an institutionalized savings and credit behavior, as the latter is by definition based on the practice of wealth accumulation and on loans implying a promise of reimbursement—already during Roman times, a weakened church teaching developed which considered savings and credit behavior acceptable, provided that no (extra) charge for credit lending occurred.

The religious commitment to altruism as preached by Christ thus very soon diminished to a permission "*to lend (out) with the expectation of being reimbursed*", provided that there was no additional motive for enrichment.

---

[135]For this part of the text, there has been built further on Byttebier and Flamée (2012), pp. 2–40.

[136]Harari (2014), pp. 265 a.f.; Lloyd (2012), p. 203.

[137]In many Western regions and countries, Christianity reached the status of state religion, and in some cases even of the only religion that (public) authorities allowed.

[138]Despite the examples of (later) historical figures such as Saint Francis of Assisi and of his followers, among who Saint Anthony of Padua, who tried to put into practice the ideal religious image of a life of poverty. (See above under Sect. 3.3.2.2.3.)

[139]Vandewalle (1976), p. 6; Bahr (2010), p. 180.

In other words, this already by the end of the Roman empire newly developing church teaching allowed someone to accumulate wealth, and to keep such wealth entirely for one's self without being obliged to share this accumulated wealth with people less fortunate, provided that such wealth did on itself not become a means of generating more wealth. As a result, it became acceptable to lend out a surplus of wealth to someone who is less fortunate, provided that the lender does not charge interest on such a loan and, on the contrary, the borrower only has to pay back what he borrowed, without being submitted to any additional payments.

Although this concession regarding the message of Christ may at first glance seem innocent, it nevertheless implied a radical turnover of Christ's basic teachings (see especially at Matthew, 6:24[140]) as it would pave the way to the creation of society in which the rich could get ever more rich at the expense of the poor and the needy, ultimately leading into capitalism becoming the dominant societal model in which, completely opposed to the teachings of Christ, money gain, rather than the service to God, became the central life theme.

59 A closer examination furthermore indicates that the ethical messages of the main religious teachings which lived on in the Western world, namely Judaism, Christianity and Islam, all have, from an historical point of view, adopted very outspoken positions in the interest debate, and, given the great inspiration that these teachings have brought to the development of the (Western) national economies, it is useful to take a closer look at said teachings.

During this examination of the ethical approach to the issue of charging interest in the abovementioned religious systems, the main focus from here on will be on the examination of the Judeo–Christian approach, as it is the most ingrained in Western culture. Another reason for this choice is the personal familiarity (and access to sources) with and to this Judeo-Christian approach.[141]

3.3.3.2 Main Sources of Inspiration in the Clerical Interest Debate

3.3.3.2.1 Sources from Classical Antiquity

3.3.3.2.1.1 Scope

60 The developers of the abovementioned "new" church approach on the issue of wealth accumulation who reduced the previously discussed religious message of

---

[140]Matthew, 6:24 (King James Bible):

> No man can serve two masters: for either he will hate the one, and love the other; or else he will hold to the one, and despise the other. Ye cannot serve God and mammon.

[141]See however Schwartz (2009), pp. 409–430; Visser and McIntosch (1998), pp. 175–189. See also Shafee (2016).

Christ Himself to the so-called "clerical interest prohibition" considered themselves backed in their stance, *on one hand* by different Biblical sources—among which, of course the New Testament, but even more so the Old Testament (bringing a beneficial working of the Judaic teachings regarding interest charging; see further, under Sect. 3.3.3.2.2)—but *on the other hand* also in the approach from classical antiquity of philosophers such as Aristotle.[142]

3.3.3.2.1.2 Charging Interest in Ancient Societies

As has already been pointed out before (see above, under Sect. 3.3.2.1), already during classical antiquity, philosophers and other thinkers had struggled with moral annotations regarding the use of money. **61**

Loans, with their associated forms of compensation, are reported to go back to the Neolithic age.[143]

From the way in which these (presumed) oldest forms of loans were dealt with, their ethical approach resorts implicitly. Sumerians[144] for instance used the word "*mas*" to indicate interest, as well as "calf", and the hieroglyphic "*mess*" means both "interest" and "birth". Also the Greek word "*tolos*" has the double meaning of "birth" (what is produced) and "profit".[145]

In the "Codex Hammurabi", creditors were asked to wait to reclaim their loan until after the harvest, and in case of a failed harvest, the interest on leased land did not need to be paid.[146]

In other words, it appears from early organized societies which increasingly started to rely on indirect barter trade (characterized by the use of money), that the social admissibility of charging interest, albeit present from the beginning, was in some cases conditioned by ethical considerations of social perpetuation.

3.3.3.2.1.3 The Teachings of Aristotle

Aristotle, who, according to Galbraith, was one of the few authors from Classical Antiquity who has really dealt with economic issues[147], and who, in doing so, *inter alia* provided a philosophical-economic interpretation of the problems related to the **62**

---

[142]Graeber (2012), pp. 298 a.f.; Polak (1928), p. 90.

[143]Bogaert et al. (2000), pp. 14 a.f.

[144]Harari (2014), pp. 200 a.f.

[145]van Liedekerke (1993), pp. 17–25.

The Dutch language also shows traces of this approach, through the word "*kroos*" (meaning "interest") and the word "kroost" (meaning "offspring"). The Dutch dictionary Van Dale (in its 14th reviewed edition) also mentions in the definition of "kroost" the Old French word "*croist*" (from which the word "kroost" itself is derived), in addition to the Old French "*croistre*" (meaning "to grow").

[146]Graeber (2012), pp. 216–217; Bogaert et al. (2000), p. 16; Ferguson (2009), p. 32.

[147]Galbraith (1987), p. 10.

charging of interest[148], found that the charging of interest was a widely used practice, but stated that it was both an "unnatural" method of enrichment, as well as a form of "unjustified" use of money (as money is meant to facilitate barter trade and not to create new money on itself).[149]

63 For instance, Aristotle's "*Politica*" (v.1258a38) mentions that the charging of interest is the most unnatural way of doing business:

> There are two sorts of wealth-getting, as I have said; one is a part of household management, the other is retail trade: the former necessary and honorable, while that which consists in exchange is justly censured; for it is unnatural, and a mode by which men gain from one another. The most hated sort, and with the greatest reason, is usury, which makes a gain out of money itself, and not from the natural object of it. For money was intended to be used in exchange, but not to increase at interest. And this term interest, which means the birth of money from money, is applied to the breeding of money because the offspring resembles the parent. Wherefore of all modes of getting wealth this is the most unnatural.[150]

It has by some been indicated that Aristotle's views about the pursuit of money, the charging of interest and practices of usury cannot be seen as isolated statements, but are part of an exhaustive philosophical system reflecting on an ideal social and political order. In this Aristotelian image of society, manual labor is regarded as a low form of occupation for people with no sense and is therefore only fit for slaves, or for those who are willing to be reduced to slaves. Aristotle's view of pursuit of money fits his vision that only citizens who have free time may engage in governmental matters and, furthermore, that merchants and bankers should be considered as being part of the slave class. It is in this (somewhat elitist) vision that trade and usury practices are pointed out as "unnatural" (because money is not a living creature which can have offspring). This also may explain Aristotle's further statement that discussing about financial issues is not unworthy of philosophy, but involvement in financial issues and the pursuit of money is.[151]

64 In the context of the interest debate, one usually quotes the verse "1122a" from Aristotle's "*Ethica Nicomachea*"[152], but it may be of interest to quote the entire section of the "*Ethica Nicomachea*" containing these verses.

The aforementioned verses (known under "n° 1122a" of the "*Ethica Nicomachea*") are part of a Chapter of the "*Ethica Nicomachea*" dedicated to the so-called "moral virtues" of man, and more specifically of a subdivision about "wrong attitudes".

---

[148]Which, over the centuries, would form an significant inspiration for later ethical approaches, more specifically because of the inspiring effect that Aristotle's works had on the attitude of the Catholic Church during the early Middle Ages; see further, at marg. 66.

[149]Polak (1928), p. 89.

[150]http://classics.mit.edu/Aristotle/politics.mb.txt (last consulted on June 25th 2015). See also Aristotle (1992), p. 87.

[151]See Durant (1949), p. 99; Polak (1928), p. 90.

[152]Aristotle (1996).

Aristotle calls these "wrong attitudes" on one hand "prodigality" and on the other hand "meanness"; Aristotle's rejection of the practice of usury is hereby situated under the description of "meanness".

To understand this fully, let us quote the complete section of the "*Eticha Nicomachea*" dedicated to "meanness" (verses 1121b14 to 1122a15[153]):

> Meanness on the contrary is incurable; for we see that it can be caused by old age or any form of weakness. Also it is more ingrained in man's nature than prodigality; the mass of mankind are avaricious rather than openhanded. Moreover meanness is a far-reaching vice, and one of varied aspect: it appears to take several shapes. For as it consists in two things, deficiency in giving and excess in getting, it is not found in its entirety in every case, but sometimes the two forms occur separately, some men going too far in getting, while others fall short in giving. The characters described by such names as niggardly, close-fisted, and stingy all fall short in giving, but they do not covet the goods of others nor wish to take them. With some of them this is due to an honorable motive of a sort, namely a shrinking from base conduct – since some persons are thought, or at all events process, to be careful of their money because they wish to avoid being forced at some time or other to do something base; to this class belong the skinflint and similar characters, who get their names from an excessive reluctance to give. But some keep their hands off their neighbors' goods from fear; they calculate that it is not easy to take what belongs to others without others taking what belongs to oneself, and so they 'prefer (as they say) neither to take nor to give'. The other sort of people are those who exceed in respect of getting, taking from every source and all they can; such are those who follow degrading trades, brothel-keepers and all people of that sort, and petty usurers who lend money in small sums at a high rate of interest; all these take from wrong sources, and more than their due. The common characteristic of all these seems to be sordid greed, since they all endure reproach for gain, and for a small gain. Those who make improper gains from improper sources on a great scale, for instance princes who sack cities and rob temples, are not termed mean, but rather wicked of impious or unjust. But the dicer and the footpad or brigand are to be classed as mean, as showing sordid greed, the robber risking his life for plunder, and the dicer making gains out of his friends, to whom one ought to give; hence both are guilty of sordid greed, trying as they do to get gain from wrong sources. And all similar modes of getting wealth are mean for the same reasons.

Usury in this approach is seen as a form of meanness, whereby someone "gets" too much, i.e. what does not belong to him, or more than can be considered acceptable.

The usurer is in this regard mentioned in the same context as the brothel-keeper, the gambler, the robber and the thief.

It can already be pointed out that the uncontrolled desire for money and **65**
wealth—which under the eighteenth and nineteenth centuries "(economic) liberalism" and the twentieth- and twenty-first-century "(economic) neo-liberalism" would be raised to an absolute virtue—had in Aristotle's writings definitely the character of a "vice", namely the vice of "dishonorable profit gain".

---

[153] Aristotle (1996), pp. 89–90.

It is hereby remarkable how well "economic liberalism" and, later on, "economic neo-liberalism" have succeeded in completely turning around classical ethical thinking which, during the preceding centuries, had introduced "altruism" as the guiding ideal(s) within society (see also further, under Sect. 3.4).

As a result, the profile of the (vicious) greedy person drawn by Aristotle, especially the type of man who takes too much (or: takes more than is acceptable), may be perfectly consistent with the (neo)liberal ideal image of the "*homo (neo) liberalis*", i.e. the man devoted to appropriating as much as possible (and at any cost) from economic transactions. The characteristics have remained the same, what has changed in a fundamental way is the moral perception by society. In Aristotle's teachings, such a "greedy" or "mean" person is (acting) vicious(ly), while, within liberal and neo-liberal teachings, a similar "*homo neo-liberalis*" sets the standard for an ideal economic behavior.

66 The aforementioned viewpoints of Aristotle would, within the Catholic Church, turn out to have a substantial impact on the Middle Ages' interest debate.

As mentioned before, Plato had also protested against the charging of interest (albeit that, in a broader sense, his teachings protested against any form of unbridled wealth accumulation and even against money in general[154]; see above, under Sect. 3.3.2.1), but it have mainly been the teachings of Aristotle which, after being recovered from (historical) oblivion by especially the medieval "scholastics" (among who the renowned Thomas Aquinas), would gain general recognition during (the second part of) the Middle Ages.[155]

3.3.3.2.1.4 The Legal Approach to Interest Charging in Antiquity

67 From a legistic point of view, the announcement of a formal ban on interest had during the Classical antiquity been a rather exceptional measure.

For instance, in Ancient Greece, it seems that in most times a freedom to charge interest has prevailed, which, depending on the identity of the debtor, on the time and the era, and/or on the economic cycle at that moment, led to a variety of interest rates.[156]

In Roman law, it became more common to have measures in place whereby qualified authority (ies) imposed a maximum interest rate. These maxima could even be quite high. There is, for example, a mention of a maximum of 12% in a senate decision of 51 BC (and probably no lower under the so-called "*Leges XII Tabularum*"). In the Byzantine empire, under emperor Justinian (reg. 527–565 AD),

[154]See especially Plato (1934), p. 125, arguing that

> whereas a man who will spend on honourable objects and only make gains from honest sources, will not find it easy to become either remarkably wealthy or exceedingly poor.

[155]Schnürer (1949), p. 399; Brugmans (1942), p. 212.

[156]Bogaert et al. (2000), pp. 31–32.

this maximum was significantly reduced (4% for persons of high birth; 8% for merchants, and 6% in all other cases).[157]

Nevertheless, reference can also be made to the so-called "*Lex Genucia*" (342 BC) that contained an absolute ban on the interest clause.

3.3.3.2.2 Biblical Sources for the Prohibition of Clerical Interest

As is generally known, the teachings of Christ Himself built further on Judaism (see Matthew, 5: 17–19[158]), and, up until the present date, an important interdependence between Jewish and Christian thinking has to be acknowledged (an awareness which, for example, is clearly present in the writings of the French-Jewish philosopher Emmanuel Levinas).[159] **68**

It is therefore no great surprise that Jewish faith itself has also explicitly dealt with the question of how far society should accept "behavior of fortune gathering", albeit without reaching the same radical conclusions as Christ.

On the contrary, Jewish teachings strongly focused on the topic of interest charging (and especially on the topic of too high interest, also referred to as "usury"),[160] especially in the mutual relationship between Jews.

It therefore does not need to surprise that in the medieval (clerical) debate on interest charging, whereby the radical teachings of Jesus Christ were reduced to a ban on interest, an important source of inspiration was derived from traditional, Jewish sources, which were much more in line with a prohibition on interest charging than the far more radical teachings of Jesus Christ Himself (see above, under Sect. 3.3.2.2.1), the latter being opposed to any form of unbridled wealth accumulation and, moreover, expecting more effective action (namely "giving away") from the rich than the mere providing of free loans.

When reading the Old Testament (O.T.), one can, already in the first book "Genesis", find an implicit approach to the problem of wealth accumulation (which during the Middle Ages set the tone for the subsequent treatment of several **69**

[157]See De Katholieke Encyclopaedie (1937). N.V. Uitgeversmij Joost v.d. Vondel, Amsterdam, under "rente"; see also Temin s.d.

[158]See Matthew, 5:17–19 (King James Bible):

> Think not that I am come to destroy the law, or the prophets: I am not come to destroy, but to fulfill. For verily I say unto you, Till heaven and earth pass, one jot or one tittle shall in no wise pass from the law, till all be fulfilled. Whosoever therefore shall break one of these least commandments, and shall teach men so, he shall be called the least in the kingdom of heaven: but whosoever shall do and teach them, the same shall be called great in the kingdom of heaven.

See also Beaumont (2010), p. 47.

[159]Duyndam and Poorthuis (2003), p. 49.

[160]Elliott (1902), p. 300; Graeber (2012), pp. 282 a.f.; Jansen (1988), p. 366. See also http://www.gutenberg.org/files/21623/21623-h/21623-h.htm.

ethical questions of a socioeconomic nature; see for instance the teachings of Saint Thomas Aquinas (1225–1274) and of the other Scholastics).

For instance, the book of Genesis mentions the story of Creation, including the creation of the first mythical human couple ("Adam and Eve"), and also the "fall" (in sin) of that first couple (see Genesis, 1–3). After this fall, a clear divine mission is given to this first human couple, namely (besides the famous "procreation mission"), the assignment that *"In sweat you will work for your bread, until you return to the dust from which you have been taken (...)"* (Genesis, 3:19).[161]

70 Otherwise put, the story of man's creation in the Book of Genesis holds that one of the first assignments of (the Judeo-Christian) God to man is that he needs to work for his existence. In other words, at man's creation, God is not giving him a capital which he can invest, but rather the assignment to work for his existence "by the sweat of his brow".[162]

This immediately illustrates how, in the thirteenth century, the abovementioned aspiration of Saint Francis of Assisi to truly and practically experience the evangelical (religious) values (see above, under Sect. 3.3.2.2.3), is far more in line with this first assignment which God gave to man, after the original sin fall, namely the assignment to work for his existence through his own labor (and, on the contrary, not by other means, among which unlimited fortune gathering which, in elsewhere explained Aristotelian terms, leads to "too much taking" (see also further, under Sect. 3.6.2.2) and in too much suffering for others, a lawfulness to which capitalism itself constantly testifies).[163]

71 In other parts of the Old Testament, this approach is further refined and many ethical rules of conduct are expressed which demonstrate an aversion towards earning money in other ways than through one's own work (labor), more specifically, by interest charging, for example:

---

[161]Koorevaar and Marlowe (2013), pp. 221–255, especially p. 226.
Compare Pontifical Council for Justice and Peace (2005), no 323.

[162]Van Bruggen (2014), p. 99.
See also John Paul II (1981).

[163]It needs further not surprise that the interpretation of the concept of "*karma*" within Hinduism, more specifically the ideal image of working in a completely "unselfish" way, demonstrates a very similar religious starting point.
See *e.g.* Vivekananda (1989), pp. 32 a.f.:

> But we have to begin from the beginning, to take up the works as they come to us and slowly make ourselves more unselfish every day. We must do the work and find out the motive power that prompts us; and, almost without exception, in the first years, we shall find that our motives are always selfish; but gradually this selfishness will melt by persistence, till at last will come the time when we shall be able to do really unselfish work. We may all hope that some day or other, as we struggle through the paths of life, there will come a time when we shall become perfectly unselfish; and the moment we attain to that, all our powers will be concentrated, and the knowledge which is ours will be manifest. (Vivekananda 1989, pp. 34–35).

- a phrase in Exodus (Exodus, 22: 24–25. "If you lend to someone of my people, to a person in need in your neighborhood, do not behave as a lender. You shall not demand interest from him");
- In the Book of Deuteronomy (Book of Deuteronomy, 23: 20–21. "You cannot demand interest from your brother, not of money, not of food or of any other thing that you lend. You can ask interest from a foreigner, but not from your brother.")[164];
- With Isaiah (Isaiah, 3: 12. "My people are exploited by usurers and ruled by extortionists");
- In the Book of Proverbs (Book of Proverbs 28: 8. "He who increases his possessions through interest and usury, is collecting it for the one who has pity for the poor.").
- ...

3.3.3.3 Formal Announcement of the Clerical Interest Prohibition by the Church

3.3.3.3.1 Early Advocates of the Clerical Interest Prohibition

Stemming from the aforementioned Old Testament sources, but from certain of the earlier quoted verses of the Gospels as well, in the early history of Christianity (from the Roman era and the early Middle Ages on), church elders such as Basil (The Great), Gregory Of Nyssa, John Chrysostom, Ambrose and Augustine commenced advocating a formal ban on the practice of charging interest on loans.[165] **72**

For instance Saint Ambrose (339–397) generally praised poverty and despised wealth, without however preaching hatred towards or conflict with the rich (and in this sense his opinions do not differ much from those of the contemporary church). However, based on considerations of justice, his works demonstrate a disdain for money and certainly for the pursuit of money through conducting business ("*He who does this, lowers his mind.*"). Furthermore, Saint Ambrose stated that the rich may not claim a right to their wealth, but should rather consider it as a duty to help the poor. Saint Ambrose held also that the rich are not allowed to use their wealth as a means to acquire (more) earthly goods, but rather as a method—by stepping back from their excesses—of ensuring the pleasure of heavenly goods. In that sense, the poor man himself becomes a "*debtor to the salvation of the rich*", as the very existence of the poor challenges the rich to use their wealth in a way benefiting the poor. Saint Ambrose did however consider working for a modest land ownership **73**

[164]Ferguson (2009), p. 37, explaining that, based upon these verses, in the Middle Ages money lending came to a large extent in Jewish hands, as the quoted verses were interpreted as allowing Jews to loan out money to Christian and thereby charging interest. (See further, at marg. 84 of this chapter.)

[165]Graeber (2012), pp. 284 a.f.

justified. In this way, he intended not to justify possession as such, but rather as a means of honouring the labor that it requires.[166]

However, Saint Ambrose also fiercely turned against the unjustified grain trade at the time, more specifically the "grain usury", which he stigmatized as a cancer in the economic life of the Roman Empire. More in general, Saint Ambrose identified a vast amount of injustice and deceit in commerce. As a consequence, he showed himself to be very sympathetic towards debtors who (in line with the former Roman judicial orders) were imprisoned when they could not pay their debts. He expressed his point of view about charging interest in the form of a question: *"Would it not be Godless to demand a larger sum of money, in the name of humanity, from someone who is not able to pay back even a small sum of money*?"[167]

74 Saint Augustine of Hippo (354–430) recognized the right to earthly possessions, and even to acquiring wealth. He hereby considered wealth to be one of the gifts of God which however needs to be used in a proper way.[168] A Christian is nevertheless not allowed to become devoted to possession, nor to be mean or greedy. Most of all, a Christian must avoid pride which indeed very often results from wealth.[169]

Furthermore, Saint Augustine did not condemn (commercial) trade as such, but he did condemn the so-called "unjustified pursuit of profit". Saint Augustine hereby expected merchants to do business in a fair way. This implied inter alia: not to sell at a higher price than acceptable, and to avoid lies and perjury. Saint Augustine also condemned the charging of interest as an "art of madness" and as an "objectionable expression of greed", and he showed himself to be a proponent of a prohibition of interest charging in favour of the poor. Rather than having the rich giving alms to the poor, Saint Augustine held that they should provide them interest free loans.[170]

75 van Liedekerke[171] quotes, furthermore, the importance of the sermon "*About usury*" by Saint Basil The Great of Caesarea (330–379), who therein stated that from interest, only misery and suffering is born.[172]

3.3.3.3.2 The Decision-Making Process Leading to a Formal Ban on Interest Charging

76 After a process of decision-making in different "councils" having taken place during the early Middle Ages, the clerical prohibition of interest on loans became

[166]Schnürer (1949), pp. 34–35.

[167]Schnürer (1949), pp. 34–35.

[168]These teachings of Saint Augustine still reflect in the present-day social doctrine of the Catholic church (see Pontifical Council for Justice and Peace 2005, no 323).

[169]Schnürer (1949), p. 79

[170]Schnürer (1949), p. 83.

[171]van Liedekerke (1993), p. 20.

[172]See also Graeber (2012), p. 284.

accepted over time in a more or less general way in Western-European countries/ regions.[173]

For instance, already the council of Nicaea (from June 19th until August 25th 325)[174] adopted a general ban on interest charging for the clergy. 77

At the council of Orleans (511), such a ban was announced for deacons and higher clergy lending money in return for interest. During this council of Orleans, it was also generally prohibited to pursue "filthy lucre".

At the council of Mâcon (585), it was in a general way decided that he who deprived the poor of their possessions through violence or deceit, should be excommunicated.

During a council of Clichy (626–627), a general prohibition of interest was provided for laymen, but it was never explicitly implemented.[175]

In 789 (as part of his "*Admonitio Generalis*"), Charlemagne (also known as "Charles the Great") (747 or 748–814) announced that a ban on interest was generally applicable to loans among laymen (which makes it plausible to assume that, up until then, under the aforementioned church teachings themselves, laymen had been allowed to charge interest) (= the so-called "*decree of Aachen*").[176] 78

In 806, Charlemagne started to provide a (very) broad definition of "usury" as the receipt of any capital higher than the capital initially loaned. This measure took the form of a so-called "*capitularium*"[177], more specifically the "*capitularium missorum*" of Nijmegen (806) which, furthermore, aimed at making a distinction in a general sense between "unfair trade" and "sordid profit".[178]

Louis The Pious (787–840) would further expand these edicts of his father, but at the same time stated in a temporary decree that Jews were subject to their own laws (and thus not affected by the Christian prohibition on charging interest).[179] 79

Through these council decisions and royal decrees, already at the start of the ninth century, the Catholic Church had succeeded in announcing (and in some cases 80

---

[173] Heck (2006), pp. 23 a.f.

As explained, these were based on the aforementioned Biblical texts, as well as on the authority of the aforementioned church elders.

[174] See Canon 17: "*Clerics are forbidden to lend at interest.*" (at: http://www.rkdocumenten.nl/rkdocs/index.php?mi=650&dos=222; last consulted on February 20th 2012).

[175] Van Straaten (2002), p. 21; Schnürer (1949), p. 210.

[176] Spiegel (1991), p. 64; Wood (2002), p. 160. See also Knowles (1967), p. 196.

[177] De Ruysscher (2011), pp. 77–78, no 110.

[178] See Heck (2006), p. 27, quoting the clause 11 hereof as follows:

> Clause 11. Usury consists of claiming back more than you give. For instance, if you have given ten solidi and ask for more back, or if you give a hogshead of wheat and then demand one extra.

See furthermore Spiegel (1991), p. 64; Wood (2002), p. 160; Schnürer (1949), p. 389; Van Straaten (2002), p. 23.

[179] Heck (2006), p. 27.

enforcing) a general interest prohibition through the clerical courts, which furthermore was supported by worldly (albeit catholic) monarchs throughout Europe.[180]

3.3.3.4 Further Theoretical Foundation of the Clerical Interest Prohibition

81 During the twelfth century, the clerical interest prohibition on loans would be (even) more theoretically grounded thanks to the contributions of the scholastics, among who Saint Thomas Aquinas (1125–1274)[181], the greatest of the scholastic philosophers[182], who (mainly inspired by the aforementioned teachings of Aristotle[183]; see above, at marg. 62–66 of this chapter) raised religious-moral, as well as economic objections to the practice of interest charging.[184]

In the approach of the scholastics, only labour, in its pure form, is to be rewarded.[185] This caused Saint Thomas Aquinas to develop the theory of "the justified (or: fair) wage" (holding that, in addition to merchants, craftsmen as well as workers are allowed to account for their costs in the wage they receive for the work they perform).[186]

In the context of the interest debate, Saint Thomas Aquinas strongly referred to the Aristotelian doctrine: money, as a consumable, may not produce benefits; consequently, it is not allowed to charge interest for credit.[187]

After Saint Thomas Aquinas, many other so-called "scholars" would formulate similar comments on this topic.[188]

82 The idealistic thoughts of scholars about the clerical prohibition of interest can, in a nutshell (and translated into a more contemporary framework), be read as the intention to limit the power that lenders could have over borrowers.

Destitution in the Middle Ages was very great among large sections of the population[189], *inter alia* because of the lack of a social security system, making loans in a lot of cases the only possible way to escape from poverty, and resulting in a great vulnerability of borrowers to usury practices. It were especially the poor and the farmers who had a great need for loans to provide for their livelihood in times of crisis.

---

180 Pirenne s.d., p. 19.

181 Laporta (1966), pp. 294–301.

182 Russell (1948), p. 410.

183 Schnürer (1949), pp. 399 a.f.

184 Galbraith (1987), p. 25.
See further Bouckaert (1994), pp. 13–34; Rivoire (1984), pp. 10–11; Van Houtte (1942), p. 98.

185 Van Straaten (2002).

186 Galbraith (1987), p. 26; Vandewalle (1976), p. 7.

187 Vandewalle (1976), p. 7.

188 Vandewalle (1976), p. 7.

189 See Whitney Hall (2013), p. 215.

According to the concept of charity (which played an important role in the three large monotheistic religions in the West (as said before: Judaism, Christianity and Islam)), it was hereby considered to be immoral if one made (much) money from people in need.

In this way, theologians such as Saint Thomas Aquinas to some extent also defended the existing organization of society against the emerging practices of (pre-)capitalism (especially the idea and practice that capital, *in casu* a sum of money loaned out, could by itself generate money).

This made the scholars probably the last important movement in the development of "Western thinking" to strongly resist emerging (pre-)capitalist practices (in the context of which the acquisition of property became the main purpose of life and lending and borrowing against interest became, in practice, a more and more accepted method of enrichment).[190]

3.3.3.5 Further Development of the Ecclesiastical Ban on Charging Interest and First Signs of Its Phasing-Out

Mainly based on the works of Saint Thomas Aquinas, the Second Lateran Council **83**
(1139), the Third Lateran Council (1179) and the later councils of Lyon (1274) and Vienna (1311–1312)[191] would (continue to) maintain the prohibition of interest on loans.[192]

Not surprisingly, this negative attitude towards the practice of interest charging even reflects in medieval art. For instance in Dante's "*Divine Comedy*", a special part of the seventh circle of Hell was reserved for usurers (see Canto XVII of "*The Inferno*", the first book of the Divine Comedy).[193]

This negative ecclesiastical attitude towards interest charging would continue to prevail throughout the fourteenth century. Hence, in his renowned "*Treatise on the Origin, Nature Law and Alterations of Money*", Nicholas Oresme (1382) still remained very severe and clear in outing the church ideological restrictions underpinning the official church view on wealth accumulation, by holding that there were three ways in which profit may be made from money without laying it out for its natural purpose: one is the art of the moneychanger, another is usury and the third is alteration of the coinage. Oresme qualified the first of these ways as "contemptible", the second as "bad" and the third as even "worse".[194]

Nevertheless, in practice, more and more methods of circumventing the church ban on interest came to light, particularly in trade, for instance by way of new (real

[190]Vandewalle (1976), p. 7.

[191]Bogaert et al. (2000), p. 77.

[192]Ferguson (2009), p. 36, mentioning that (Christian) usurers were massively excommunicated by the Third Lateral Council in 1179.

[193]Ferguson (2009), p. 36.

[194]As quoted by Eagleton and Williams (2007), p. 82. See also Galbraith (1987), p. 28.

estate) security techniques.[195] One of the reasons thereof was that, in practice, the business of money lending against interest charging became too profitable to ignore. In this, for instance the rich renaissance-era families in Venice and Florence elbowed their way in, side-stepping theological dogma (which itself kept on holding that interest charging and certainly usury were sinful), by applying other names for interest, such as "penalties", "processing fees", "gifts" and "loss charges".[196]

84 It may be somewhat surprising that, throughout the Middle Ages, also from a Judeo-ethical perspective, the charging of interest is/was questionable, given the fact that, as is known, it was mainly Jewish lenders who in several Christian (catholic) countries triggered the rise of professional credit lending based on interest charging, since, as mentioned above, Christians themselves were (until late in the Middle Ages) faced with the aforementioned religious prohibition on interest charging.[197]

One of the explanations for this is that, going back to the cited decree of Louis the Pious (see above, at marg. 79 of this chapter), Jews living in the European regions fell outside the ecclesiastical interest ban (at least as regards loans to non-Jews), and there was, conversely, in Judaism no real impediment to charge interest to non-Jews (see the verses from the Old Testament quoted above, under Sect. 3.3.3.2.2).[198]

Because in the so-called Christian countries, due to many restrictions—for instance: bans on holding a government position, bans on possessing land, bans on becoming a member of merchants and traders guilds, etc.—Jews were, furthermore, denied access to many professional activities, in many regions, there remained not many professional options other than trading money. This has been indicated as one of the reasons why money trade, and later on credit lending (based on charging interest), got mainly handled by the Jews.[199]

85 Moreover, the fundamental ban on charging interest between Jews themselves was soon bypassed by the inclusion (in lending contracts) of the qualification "*al-pi hetter iskah*", which implied the permission to form an agreed partnership, in which interest conditions could be defined, thus making the transaction admissible.[200]

---

[195] Bogaert et al. (2000), p. 77. See also Byttebier (2005), p. 555, no 603.

[196] See Steinmetz (2015). As this author points out, it is remarkable that Islamic bankers still undergo a similar struggle in the present.

See also Eagleton and Williams (2007), p. 82.

[197] Bogaert et al. (2000), p. 77; Ferguson (2009), p. 35.

See further Evers (1999), p. 135; Wieviorka (2014), p. 24.

[198] Ferguson (2009), p. 37; Vandewalle (1976), p. 8.

[199] Evers (1999), p. 135; Wieviorka (2014), p. 24.

The Jewish community was for instance largely present in Venice where it formed the "*ghetto nuovo*" and where Jews became important money handlers (which reflects in Shakespeare's famous play "*The Merchant of Venice*") (see Ferguson 2009, p. 37).

[200] http://www.jlaw.com/Articles/venture3.html.

Later on, this practice would inspire Christians to act accordingly (see further, at marg. 86 of this chapter).

Further Illustration 3.4: The Jewish Community in Middle Age's Prague

It should however be noted that there has not been one overall trend throughout Europe regarding the development of the Jewish status in money transactions.

It seems, for instance, that from the year 1000 A.D. a large settlement of Jewish merchants located in Prague (alongside German and Italian ("Romany") merchants). This Jewish community in Prague soon enjoyed a special relationship with the rulers, because said Jewish merchants were all literate (as reading "The Book", and teaching and learning from its content, were part of Jewish religious life), and were usually considerably better at mathematics and accounting than local notables. When silver mining started in Bohemia (the Prague silver coin became a standard European currency in the sixteenth century[201]), Jews got employed to structure these mining activities. Sought after, but at the same time feared, they were soon confined to a local ghetto, but were at the same time granted protection (including access to many professional activities) by said local rulers, in return for loyal service.

In this way, a subtle balance emerged between the Jews and the local population (whereby it was, for instance, forbidden to hurt Jews or their goods, because they fell under royal protection, and were even considered as being "royal property"). Some cases nevertheless are known where the monarch, in return for services from the local population, granted a temporary permission to plunder the Jewish Ghetto.

The Jewish population group got legally emancipated under the rule of the enlightened Joseph II (1741–1790), who was also a popular protector of the Jewish community (see the name of the current Northern "quartier Jozefov"), even though the administrative practice to complete the assimilation (despised by many Jews, including Franz Kafka (1883–1924), but for other reasons)[202] with the rest of the population, would still take many years.[203]

As already pointed out at marg. 83 of this chapter, also in the mutual relationship between Christians, certain practices of emerging early capitalism[204] started to differ increasingly from the official viewpoints of the Catholic Church and its scholars on the charging of interest. 86

Such (divergent) practices (especially in trade) would gradually prove stronger than the traditional church doctrine itself.

[201]On the importance of silver coins throughout the Middle Ages, see Eagleton and Williams (2007), pp. 78 a.f.

[202]See for further reading Michel (1998), p. 448.

[203]Michel (1998), p. 448; see also Casanova (2011), p. 468.

[204]From the eleventh to twelfth century to the early fourteenth century.

As a result, numerous methods to circumvent the ecclesiastical interest prohibition emerged, among which the successful technique of (re)discounting letters of exchange: the discount the endorsed of such a letter of exchange charged to the endorser was hereby deemed to cover the risk involved (i.e. was economically equal to the charging of interest).[205]

Moreover, the exchange technique which came into use in the thirteenth and fourteenth century had as an additional feature that a refund could take place in a different location using a different currency, other than where the exchange relationship was carried out (hence the name letter of "exchange"). As regards such other currency, very often a lower exchange rate was used, which in turn also resulted in a higher amount to be reimbursed (which, therefore, again implied a disguised form of economic interest charging).[206]

Furthermore, relying on the exchange technique, a variety of payment and credit mechanisms evolved which were increasingly used by clerics (among which popes themselves) and not just by merchants.[207] In a similar way, the Church also allowed the use of the "limited partnership", which, from an economic point of view, had a similar effect as actually charging interest.[208]

Hence, it has been held that already by the second half of the fifteenth century, the clerical interest prohibition, although formally still applicable, had less and less practical impact on society in general or on trade in particular. On the contrary, clerical agencies, including certain popes, showed themselves to be more and more in favour of an increase in money supply and thus encouraged the emerging capitalist practices.

Indeed, in order to fund its countless (often megalomaniacal) projects, the Church got in need of more and more money. Therefore, church authorities increasingly turned to the (upcoming) bankers to get credit (at interest). There would even be a moment where the Curia had pawned the Papal Crown to *"the bank of the Centruioni"* in Genoa. This was later on returned when Lorenzo de Medici was good enough to settle the underlying debt.[209]

Eventually (as further explained below in more detail; see further, at marg. 90 of this chapter), it would be German bankers (such as the renowned Jacob Fugger) who, profiting from the new protestant Christian doctrines, would completely abandon church doctrine and commit themselves to bluntly lending against interest charges (and by doing so, to a large extent, eventually would replace Jewish lenders in the German territories, but also would clear the path for the breakthrough of capitalism as the leading economic system).[210]

---

[205] Bogaert et al. (2000), p. 99.
See further Van Straaten (2002), p. 30; Polak (1928), p. 101.

[206] Van Straaten (2002), p. 30.

[207] Van Straaten (2002), p. 30.

[208] Bieler (1961), p. 167.
See also Polak (1928), p. 101.

[209] Schnürer (1949), p. 298.

[210] See Steinmetz (2015).

3.3.3.6 End of the Ecclesiastical Prohibition of Interest

3.3.3.6.1 Further Challenging the Ecclesiastical Prohibition of Interest in Practice

Where initially the official classical Church doctrine continued to hold a ban on the charging of interest as such, in the later Middle Ages, as a result of the abovementioned evolving practices, a deterioration of the implementation of this church ban would occur. 87

As a further result, during the course of the fifteenth and sixteenth century, the theoretical debate itself also gradually shifted to the issue of the level of interest rates used in practice and the need for legislation to limit these.[211] Although the official church doctrine continued to condemn the charging of interest as such, many catholic organizations (for example the University of Paris) and catholic kings started to openly recognize the legitimacy of loans at (modest) interest rates.[212]

A further deterioration of the classical ecclesiastical doctrine resulted from the fact that, although usury and the expressing of any doubt about the correctness of the ban on usury, continued to be seen by the Church as a form of heresy, very often no actual prosecution policy was in place (for instance by the inquisition). 88

This resulted in a more practical approach in which those who were found guilty of such an act of heresy, could still be considered sincere religious people by literally paying for their sins by means of indulgences, such as the payment of a contribution to the poor, or to a monastery or church.[213]

Some of these practices would add to the reasons for Luther's denouncement, on the 31st of October 1517, of his doctrine which would result into a real ecclesiastical schism (shortly followed by a similar schism caused by King Henry VIII of England), which in its turn would create a further breeding ground for emerging capitalism. 89

3.3.3.6.2 Challenging the Ecclesiastical Prohibition of Interest in Rising Protestantism

In protestant Europe, a crucial turn-around was caused[214] by the ideas of Martin Luther (1483–1546) and, even more of John Calvin (1509–1564). The impact of 90

---

211 Van Straaten (2002), pp. 48 a.f.

212 Bieler (1961), p. 167.

213 Backhouse (2011), p. 128.

See further Van Straaten (2002), pp. 30–31; Downley (1979), pp. 360 and 362; Dowley (2009), p. 106.

The authors of these diluted doctrines clearly missed the irony with which these doctrines are to be seen in light of the radical principles which Christ, according to the Gospels, had set out Himself.

214 Wykes (2003), pp. 27–51.

their teachings may even be considered extreme in light of the economic growth in (certain regions of the current) Germany (sixteenth century)[215] and The Netherlands (seventeenth century, also known as "the golden age (of Holland)".)[216]

91 Luther stated that the organization of a society based on the aforementioned words of Jesus Christ (see above, at Sect. 3.3.2.2) was illusory.[217] In particular, as regards the interest-debate, Luther held that there is a need for a governmental power making the repayment of credit enforceable (even when a real Christian is not allowed to expect such repayment).

Graeber[218] illustrates this approach by Luther with a very notable quote from one of Luther's sermons from 1524 (entitled: "*Von Kaufhandlung und Wucher*"):

> Christians are rare in this world; therefore the world needs a strict, hard, temporal government that will compel and constrain the wicked not to rob and to return what they borrow, even though a Christian ought not to demand it, or even hope to get it back. This is necessary in order that the world not become a desert, peace may not perish, and trade and society not be utterly destroyed; all of which would happen if we were to rule the world according to the Gospel and not drive and compel the wicked by laws and the use of force, to do what is right. (...) Let no one think that the world can be ruled without blood; the sword of the ruler must be red and bloody; for the world will and must be evil, and the sword is God's rod and vengeance upon it.

These are obviously harsh words illustrating a complete reversal of Christ's own association of "merchants" and "(money) changers" (= the later bankers) with "robbers" (see Matthew, 21:12–13). Even more, there is no longer any mention of the "poor" and of "people in need", but they are now called "the wicked".[219]

This demeaning attitude towards the poor already to be observed in the teachings of Luther is at present, and more than ever, reflected in certain contemporary neo-liberal writings, for example those of Ayn Rand who has described the poor in terms such as "incompetents" who are out to rob the competent (ergo the rich) of their rightfully earned wealth (see further, at marg. 123 and 165 of this chapter), for instance by means of tax systems to finance what she calls useless purposes, such as public education and health and general social care.[220] Especially in her book "*The virtue of Selfishness*" Ayn Rand has magnified the abovementioned, in comparison

---

[215]For instance, the renowned German banker Fugger was among the first to apply practices of usury on a large scale, which made him one of the most rich and influential bankers of all times. (See Steinmetz 2015.)

[216]Bell (1996), pp. 287 a.f.; Galbraith (1987), p. 22.

[217]Compare Beaumont (2010), p. 47, pointing out that this approach came dangerously close to allowing people to choosing which parts of the message of Christ they want to obey.

[218]Graeber (2012), p. 321.

[219]The new Lutheran doctrine would, furthermore, no longer encourage to hide the sword, as those who turn to the sword will be killed by it (see Matthew, 26: 52), but, on the contrary, stated that the sword of the ruler should be red and bloody.

[220]Notwithstanding this utterly demeaning attitude towards, for instance, public health care systems, when she got terminally ill herself, Ayn Rand, purportedly under the name of Ann O'Connor, did not hesitate for a moment to make use of these "useless" public health care systems, thus in her proper actions completely denouncing the content of the teachings she had spread

still far more modest considerations of Luther, resulting in a complete inverse value perception whereby absolute selfishness has been proclaimed to best serve the general good.[221]

Questioning to what extent these Lutheran views can still be considered "Christian" is a topic further left to the domain of theological debate.[222]

Luther, who through his doctrines had closed behind him the door of the Catholic Church, would at the same time open a new door in the world of ideas, especially, through his opinion that the ideals of Christ (at an economic level) are not feasible, making it possible to develop a doctrine which no longer was based on a literal reading of the Gospels. This certainly contributed to the emergence of capitalism, and moreover of economic doctrines presenting themselves as part of a new and independent science freed from ecclesiastical dogma defending it.

For the sake of completeness, it needs however also to be mentioned that Luther occasionally also took a stand against the greed of the rich, for instance against the German banking family Fugger[223], but also against the mechanism of the charging of interest in general.[224] For that same reason, Tawney has argued that Luther's statements were often but temporary expressions of anger, and that it is very difficult to recognize in them a truly coherent social economic doctrine.[225]

Although Lutheran doctrine is by some considered revolutionary (or at least: 92
"reformatory"), this was definitely not (at least not always) the case for Luther's view on credit lending in general.

On the contrary, Luther's views on loans and interest rather bear witness of an extensive degree of conformism with the practices of the rich and powerful, and moreover those who by means of (pre-)capitalist mechanisms, aimed to get richer and more powerful (this, for instance, in strong contradiction to the doctrines defended by Saint Thomas Aquinas, and definitely by Saint Francis of Assisi, each of whom had, two centuries earlier, in their own way, still attempted to shield Christian society from the devastating influences of the emerging (pre)capitalism of their time).

---

during her life time (see http://boingboing.net/2011/01/28/ayn-rand-took-govern.html). As Michael Ford has put it:

> In the end, Miss Rand was a hypocrite but she could never be faulted for failing to act in her own self-interest. (See Ford 2010–2011.)

[221]On Ayn Rand, see also Ricard (2014), pp. 381 a.f.

[222]For instance, Vivekananda has argued that Protestantism has been characterized by a decline of the spiritual dimension of the Christian belief, whereby the distinction between Protestants and those following Auguste Comte or the agnostics who preach ethics without any religious dimension, has almost completely disappeared. (See Vivekananda 1989, pp. 29–100, especially p. 61.)

[223]Tawney (1944), pp. 82–83.

[224]Tawney (1944), p. 95.

[225]Tawney (1944), p. 88.

Needless to say that in today's context, the approach displayed by Luther is much in line with the one of "economic neo-liberalism" which similarly only focuses on the interests of the rich and the powerful.

93 Shortly later, Calvin would completely reject the ecclesiastical prohibition of interest, although he did advocate "moderate" interest rates (first of 5%, later of 6.667%)[226] anticipating (from a social angle) on the potential detrimental effects of credit lending and interest charging. At the same time, Calvin preached that the accumulation of wealth was indeed allowed for those who worked hard and zealously, provided that such saved wealth would be reinvested in economic growth and not be used for luxurious (meaning "sinful") expenditure.[227]

Over time, the Protestant Churches would come to an agreement that the charging of a "reasonable" interest (of 5%) was acceptable (and not sinful).[228]

94 Given the content of the teachings of Luther and Calvin, it is no coincidence that early capitalism first manifested within small sectarian communities supporting their teachings[229], and later, on a larger scale, in territories which provided the best breeding ground for protestant thinking, including certain German regions (sixteenth century, under the influence of Luther), then Holland (seventeenth century, as said also known as "the golden age of Holland", under the influence of Calvin) and finally the United Kingdom, where a proper "protestant" doctrine, namely Anglicism, was introduced by King Henry VIII.

Nor is it a coincidence that it was largely these regions/countries which, from that moment on, started to develop into colonial powers in a pursuit to turn the rest of the world (including all its wealth and people) into their economic exploration areas. Later on, also the United States of America (originally as a vassal area of the European powers, but after the American Independence (1775–1783), on its own merit) would adopt these capitalist-protestant concepts.

Soon, under the influence of these protestant doctrines[230], said pre-capitalist practices would degenerate into one of the largest humanitarian dramas of the (recent) history of the West, namely the re-introduction in the Western world of slavery (see also further, at marg. 157 of this chapter).[231] According to certain sources, already in the seventeenth century, slavery thus already met general acceptance among certain early Protestant-Christian groupings (such as the "Quakers" and the "Mennonites"[232]).

[226]Tawney (1944), pp. 81 a.f. and p. 120.
See further Bieler (1961), p. 168; Beaud (1994), p. 19.

[227]Bell (1996), p. 289; Weber (1967), p. 209.

[228]Graeber (2012), p. 322.

[229]Bell (1996), p. 290.

[230]See *e.g.* Stackhouse (2014), pp. 307–336.

[231]For further reading, see Van Houtte (1953), pp. 147 a.f.; Van der Heijden (1926), pp. 260–262; Jacobs (1996), pp. 31–46; Sée (1952), pp. 33, 55–56 and 63; Beaud (1994), p. 30; Van Houtte (1942), p. 129.

[232]http://nl.wikipedia.org/wiki/Slavernij#Koloniale_en_postkoloniale_slavernij (last consulted on November 25th 2014); van Oudheusden (2012), p. 16.

In this way, capitalism as an idea got first introduced through Protestantism, albeit it would soon be emancipated from its "Christian" roots and in (secular) economic liberalism meet a new ideological foundation even more fervently defending its interests.

3.3.3.6.3 Erosion of the Religious Prohibition of Interest in the Official Catholic Doctrine

As has been mentioned before, probably under the influence of their protestant counterparts, around 1600, Catholic scholars also started to accept more and more the notion of a "legitimate interest": a low interest rate became gradually accepted in cases where it was regarded as a compensation for the risk to the creditor and provided that pricing was righteous, amongst others, in light of fair competition.[233] **95**

For instance in the Netherlands, Leonard Lessius (1554–1623) caused a reversal by highlighting the businessman as an acceptable person and by introducing the concept of the *"fair lending contract"*. Lessius a.o. held that, in some cases, the charging of interest can be justified (because of "damage" suffered by the lender due to the non-availability of his capital, profit loss and risk assessment).[234]

3.3.3.6.4 Further Erosion of the Ecclesiastical Interest Prohibition in Modern Times

During the course of the seventeenth century, the debate regarding the charging of interest would increasingly be taken out of its ethical-religious context, which allowed forerunners of "economy" as an independent human science to raise their voices ever more loudly.[235] **96**

This in its own turn led to an even further erosion of the ecclesiastical debate on interest and opened new opportunities for regions and countries that had remained "catholic" to approach the charging of interest as an approved method of enrichment (whereas the former religious-ethical objections to this method of making the rich richer "to the detriment of the poor" gradually faded out).

As a result, in commercial practice and faced with the pressures of economic development, the interest clause would increasingly become more commonplace even in Catholic regions, "usurious interest" however would not[236]. **97**

---

[233]Van Straaten (2002), pp. 40 a.f.

[234]van Liedekerke (1993), pp. 22–24.

In the context of this argument, it should however be noted that in case of a credit lending stemming from money creation (a technique which emerged in this period), this argument hardly makes sense (albeit the argument could imply that the lender concerned may be faced with the necessity to take out credit himself in order to pay own outstanding debts, and will need to pay a price for this).

[235]Jadlow (s.d.), pp. 1195–1200.

[236]Van Straaten (2002), pp. 59 a.f.

Ultimately, in the era of the French Revolution, this evolution resulted in many countries into legislation proclaiming the freedom of the interest clause (see, for instance, in France already certain "revolutionary" legislation itself, such as a Decree of the Constituent Assembly of the 3th and the 12th October 1789, and later a Law of April 11th 1793).[237]

The French Code Civil of 1804 eventually copied this principle of freedom from the interim law, but took into account possible limitations through secondary legislation.[238]

98 In most Western countries, such legal measures on the charging of interest would, in the course of the nineteenth century, slowly disappear, resulting in a complete liberalization of interest and credit.

Following the opportunities that already had been created by Protestantism, this would contribute to the full development of an economic system based on capitalist principles regarding loans (or credit) and interest charging. As a result, economic processes got largely emancipated from classic-ethical concepts of Ancient Greece, as well as those contained in the Gospels, which for centuries had managed to keep said economic processes within reasonable boundaries.

It was a Scotsman, namely Adam Smith, who was among those who provided the theoretical basis to this evolution, thus supplying the first elements for an economic doctrine that would gradually evolve in a new global religion of "worship of the mammon" (see further, under Sect. 3.4.2).

Further Illustration 3.5: Further Development of Interest Regulation in Belgium

Driven by strong liberal ideas (with then Finance Minister Frère-Orban as one of the main actors), a complete liberalization of interest and credit in Belgian law was reached in 1865 (see the Law of May 5th 1865 concerning the loan at interest rate[239]), with a return to a (general) freedom of interest clause[240]. It should however be noted that the Belgian Penal Code kept foreseeing possible enforcement in case of abuse (for this, see article 494 of the Penal Code).[241] Since then, the article 1 of this Law of May 5th 1865 states that

(continued)

[237]Del Marmol (1943), p. 75, no 43.

[238]A (French) Law of September 3th 1807 would impose a maximum interest of 5% in civil matters, and of 6% in commercial matters (see the article 1 of this (former) Law of 3th September 1807: "*L'intérêt conventionnel ne pourra excéder, and matière civile, cinq pour cent, nu and matière de commerce, six pour cent; let out sans retenue.*"). (See also Del Marmol 1943, p. 6, no 49; De Katholieke Encyclopaedie (1937). N.V. Uitgeversmij Joost v.d. Vondel, Amsterdam, under the notion "rente"; Ripert 1951, p. 23.)

[239]*Official Gazette* May 7th 1865.

[240]Del Marmol (1943), p. 101; Van Houtte (1955), p. 231.

[241]Del Marmol (1943), pp. 101 a.f. See also De Katholieke Encyclopaedie (1937). N.V. Uitgeversmij Joost v.d. Vondel, Amsterdam, under "rente".

Further Illustration 3.5 (continued)

"*contracting parties are free to agree on the amount of the conventional interest rate.*"

In the nineteenth century, a counterbalancing trend in Belgian jurisdiction would emerge which defined conventional interest rates above moral acceptance (usury) as contrary to "good morality".[242] Under the law of May 1st 1913, this approach was in part adopted into article 1154 of the Civil Code dealing with "anatocism" (= the capitalization of interests).[243]

Later, the interest clause for certain specific credits (*e.g.* consumer credit and mortgage credit) became subject to mandatory rules still existing under Belgian law.[244]

3.3.3.7 The Last Convulsions of the Medieval Debate on Charging Interest

3.3.3.7.1 Further Evolution of the Catholic Church Doctrine During the Nineteenth Century and the First Half of the Twentieth Century

Despite the previously mentioned switch towards a general acceptance of interest charging in practice and in (secular) law, it would take the Catholic Church until 1838 to formally give up its fight against the charging of interest.[245] **99**

This did not imply that the Catholic Church would give up its view about the pursuit of wealth and money entirely, albeit this vision was reduced to a rejection **100**

[242] Del Marmol (1943), pp. 393 a.f., no 384; De Katholieke Encyclopaedie (1937). N.V. Uitgeversmij Joost v.d. Vondel, Amsterdam, under "rente".

[243] Byttebier (1995), pp. 96–107.

[244] For further reading, see Steennoot and Dejonghe (2007), p. 424, no 854.

[245] Van Straaten (2002), p. 52.

The Church would however continue to condemn "usury". In the already quoted "*Compendium of the Social Doctrine of the Church*" of 2004 (at no 341), it is still held:

> Although the quest for equitable profit is acceptable in economic and financial activity, recourse to usury is to be morally condemned: "Those whose usurious and avaricious dealings lead to the hunger and death of their brethren in the human family indirectly commit homicide, which is imputable to them". This condemnation extends also to international economic relations, especially with regard to the situation in less advanced countries, which must never be made to suffer "abusive if not usurious financial systems". More recently, the Magisterium used strong and clear words against this practice, which is still tragically widespread, describing usury as "a scourge that is also a reality in our time and that has a stranglehold on many peoples' lives". (See Pontifical Council for Justice and Peace 2005, no 341.)

(in general terms) of an "unbridled" pursuit of money (without interfering in the interest policies of banking), and more specifically of the pursuit of profits as a life goal in itself.[246]

101 In 1891, Pope Leo XIII (reg. 1878–1903) released the Papal Encyclical "*Rerum Novarum*" ("*Of/about new things*").[247]

The main purpose of this Encyclical was to defend the rights of workers and to preach a (more) righteous economic system based on Christian values (hereby basically reinvigorating certain teachings of Saint Thomas Aquinas).[248]

The Encyclical mainly focused on the situation of the working classes within capitalism and defined, through a number of principles, the (still active) social doctrine of the Catholic Church. This doctrine was later on clarified in several further papal encyclicals and, in 2004, in the "*Compendium of the Social Doctrine of the Church*" which was issued by the Pontifical Council for Justice and Peace[249].

Some of the concrete principles from the Encyclical "*Rerum novarum*" are, *inter alia*: the recognition of the right to an individual, fair wage[250], the acceptance of the right to (individual) property[251] and the principle of "solidarity" with the weak.

---

[246]For the modern day vision of the Catholic Church, see Pontifical Council for Justice and Peace (2005), no 323 a.f.

[247]Leo XIII (1891).

See also John Paul II (2005), pp. 123 a.f.; Dowley (2009), p. 151.

[248]Dowley (2009), p. 151.

[249]Explicit reference to the words of Pope Leo XIII has hence been made in the introductory letter to this Compendium of the Social Doctrine of the Church (see Pontifical Council for Justice and Peace 2005).

[250]See under no 5 of the encyclical:

> It is surely undeniable that, when a man engages in remunerative labor, the impelling reason and motive of his work is to obtain property, and thereafter to hold it as his very own. If one man hires out to another his strength or skill, he does so for the purpose of receiving in return what is necessary for the satisfaction of his needs; he therefore expressly intends to acquire a right full and real, not only to the remuneration, but also to the disposal of such remuneration, just as he pleases. Thus, if he lives sparingly, saves money, and, for greater security, invests his savings in land, the land, in such case, is only his wages under another form; and, consequently, a working man's little estate thus purchased should be as completely at his full disposal as are the wages he receives for his labor. But it is precisely in such power of disposal that ownership obtains, whether the property consist of land or chattels. Socialists, therefore, by endeavoring to transfer the possessions of individuals to the community at large, strike at the interests of every wage-earner, since they would deprive him of the liberty of disposing of his wages, and thereby of all hope and possibility of increasing his resources and of bettering his condition in life.

[251]See under no 8 of the encyclical:

> The fact that God has given the earth for the use and enjoyment of the whole human race can in no way be a bar to the owning of private property. For God has granted the earth to mankind in general, not in the sense that all without distinction can deal with it as they like, but rather that no part of it was assigned to any one in particular, and that the limits of private possession have been left to be fixed by man's own industry, and by the laws of individual races. Moreover, the earth, even though apportioned among private owners,

Special attention was given to the so-called "duties" of the (Christian) employer.[252] Furthermore, both governmental intervention[253] and the creation of employer unions[254] were mentioned as legitimate instruments to pursue these goals.

Especially when comparing the Encyclical to the content of the Gospels itself, one cannot ignore the general (somewhat superficial) wordings and its intent only to

---

ceases not thereby to minister to the needs of all, inasmuch as there is not one who does not sustain life from what the land produces. Those who do not possess the soil contribute their labor; hence, it may truly be said that all human subsistence is derived either from labor on one's own land, or from some toil, some calling, which is paid for either in the produce of the land itself, or in that which is exchanged for what the land brings forth.

[252] See under no 20 of the encyclical:

> The following duties bind the wealthy owner and the employer: not to look upon their work people as their bondsmen, but to respect in every man his dignity as a person ennobled by Christian character. They are reminded that, according to natural reason and Christian philosophy, working for gain is creditable, not shameful, to a man, since it enables him to earn an honorable livelihood; but to misuse men as though they were things in the pursuit of gain, or to value them solely for their physical powers – that is truly shameful and inhuman. Again justice demands that, in dealing with the working man, religion and the good of his soul must be kept in mind. Hence, the employer is bound to see that the worker has time for his religious duties; that he be not exposed to corrupting influences and dangerous occasions; and that he be not led away to neglect his home and family, or to squander his earnings. Furthermore, the employer must never tax his work people beyond their strength, or employ them in work unsuited to their sex and age. His great and principal duty is to give everyone what is just. Doubtless, before deciding whether wages axe fair, many things have to be considered; but wealthy owners and all masters of labor should be mindful of this – that to exercise pressure upon the indigent and the destitute for the sake of gain, and to gather one's profit out of the need of another, is condemned by all laws, human and divine. To defraud any one of wages that are his due is a great crime which cries to the avenging anger of Heaven. "Behold, the hire of the laborers... which by fraud has been kept back by you, crieth; and the cry of them hath entered into the ears of the Lord of Sabaoth." Lastly, the rich must religiously refrain from cutting down the workmen's earnings, whether by force, by fraud, or by usurious dealing; and with all the greater reason because the laboring man is, as a rule, weak and unprotected, and because his slender means should in proportion to their scantiness be accounted sacred. Were these precepts carefully obeyed and followed out, would they not be sufficient of themselves to keep under all strife and all its causes?

[253] See under no 32 of the encyclical:

> The foremost duty, therefore, of the rulers of the State should be to make sure that the laws and institutions, the general character and administration of the commonwealth, shall be such as of themselves to realize public well-being and private prosperity. This is the proper scope of wise statesmanship and is the work of the rulers.

[254] See under no 57 of the encyclical:

> We may lay it down as a general and lasting law that working men's associations should be so organized and governed as to furnish the best and most suitable means for attaining what is aimed at, that is to say, for helping each individual member to better his condition to the utmost in body, soul, and property.

soften the rough edges of capitalism, without aiming at replacing capitalism by a system which would put the words of Jesus Christ truly in practice.

Later on, Pope Pius XI (ruling 1922–1939 AD) would also assert the rights of the working classes while attempting to encourage catholic social principles, in an effort to overcome an alleged threat posed by communism. His fear of communism, however, would at the same time blind him for the emergence of fascism in Germany and Italy.[255]

102 In 1930, the Catholic theologian Potters[256] phrased the (Catholic) view on capitalism as follows (freely translated from Dutch):

> The vast effects of greed on society were very clearly initiated by the liberal mind, which has inspired economy since the French revolution. Society has been completely disrupted by the materialistic pursuit of profit, which rules the production and distribution of goods without restriction. Since the last century, many things have improved (. . .), but today we are still far from being free from that mammonistic spirit. There is nothing wrong in the profit motive playing a role in the practice of national economy: God Himself has bestowed selfishness upon human nature; if this self-interest is kept within acceptable limits, then it has great potential to increase people's prosperity. It is however exactly this limitation which currently still leaves much to be desired. Instead of focusing on the general prosperity of the people, their general wellbeing, economy has focused on profit for profit's sake. (. . .) In a word: nowadays limitless greed has caused society to fail in fulfilling the calling which was given to it by God: i.e. to create general prosperity for the people as a means for individuals to determine their final destination.

It is remarkable that in this vision of Potters, *on one hand*, it is clearly confirmed that the unbridled pursuit of money and profit (= by Potters described as "the mammonistic spirit"), can have a positive impact on the functioning of society[257], but, *on the other hand*, that the radical doctrine of Christ Himself seems to have been tempered as a consequence of the Smithian view of economy (see further, under Sect. 3.4.2). It has even been held that a catholic is allowed to be selfish to a certain degree, because this is how God created human nature, as long as the consequent greed is not unlimited. A similar "acceptable degree of selfishness" is even considered to be beneficial to global economic progress.

Clearly this ecclesiastical treatise reflects some of the writings of Adam Smith, with as unanswered (and probably rhetorical) question whether this approach would have found grace in the eyes of Jesus Christ Himself.

In this regard, further reference can, for instance, be made to Pope John XXIII's encyclical "*Pacem in Terris*"[258] (of April 11th 1963), in which it has been held that (under its point no 11): "*Man has the right to live. He has the right to bodily integrity and to the means necessary for the proper development of life, particularly food, clothing, shelter, medical care, rest, and, finally, the necessary social services. In consequence, he has the right to be looked after in the event of illhealth; disability*

[255] Dowley (2009), p. 151.

[256] Potters (1930), pp. 27–28.

[257] Bakan (2005), p. 259; Verhaeghe (2011), p. 52.

[258] John XIII (1963).

stemming from his work; widowhood; old age; enforced unemployment; or whenever through no fault of his own he is deprived of the means of livelihood." On the socioeconomic level, it is thus recognized that man has the right be to given the opportunity to work, to take personal initiative, to private property, to just remuneration for work effort, and to emigrate (see point no 18 a.f. of the said encyclical). Taken together, this list of rights linked to reciprocal duties—and cemented together by solidarity—lays out the preconditions for human flourishing.[259]

Over the years, this ecclesiastical view on the pursuit of wealth and its social implications would be generalized even more (see further, under Sect. 3.6.2.5.2).

Nevertheless, a remarkable viewpoint about social justice from about the same **103**
period can be found in the Anglican world, more specifically with Charles Gore (1853–1932), a renowned Anglican theologian (and bishop of his time).[260]

Based on an orthodox reading of the creed and on a literal interpretation of the New Testament, Charles Gore came to the view that a Christian should above all devote himself to "social justice" (which is clearly asserted in the written version of one of Gore's "Essex Hall"-speeches "*Christianity applied to the life of men and of nations*"[261] dating from 1920).[262]

In "*Christianity applied to the life of men and of nations*", Charles Gore advocated a fundamental reconsideration of different basic Christian values, including charity, stemming from the conviction that Christ's doctrine, above all, provides guidance for every-day life (a belief that Gore expressed in the opinion that "*religion, as Jesus sets it before men, is indisputably a manner of life – 'a way.*'"). Gore blamed modern society for not having striven to bring the word of God truly to life, and that it even has accepted a widely spread violation of true justice, for example by having agreed to the exploitation of the poor and by approving "*monstrous and unfounded*" property rights which allow people to ignore the wellbeing of society and to focus more on personal possessions than on other people. Gore also blamed society for the fact that the systems it created, such as housing and employment and education politics, in a fundamental way ignore Christian ideals[263]. Hence, Gore argued for a fundamental turn-around in society, where both the principles of capitalism, as well as those of socialism, were

[259]Sachs et al. (2016), especially p. 13.

[260]Crosse (1932).
See further De Wit and Steenvoorde (2008), p. 239.

[261]See Gore (1920).

[262]De Wit and Steenvoorde (2008), p. 239.

[263] On the largest scale we have 'made the word of God of no effect by our tradition'; (. . .)we have acquiesced in a widespread ignoring of the real meaning of justice; (. . .) we have countenanced the exploitation of the weak, and a monstrous and groundless theory of the rights of property which enabled men to ignore the welfare of the community, and to care for property more than persons; and (. . .) our systems of housing, employment, and education have ignored the indisputably Christian principle that every soul has in the sight of God and of the church (when right-minded) an equal value, and the same really divine claim to equal consideration.

to be ignored. On the contrary, charity should become the leading principle of societal organization[264].

In his speech, Gore also took a stand against nationalism, racism and the disregard for the position of women in society, viewpoints which are obviously all still relevant to the present day.[265]

3.3.3.7.2 Outside of the Church

104 In the twentieth century (at least in Western and Western-inspired countries), the trend of secularization of the economy in general and of the ethical reflection about economic processes more specifically, has even furthermore continued. In this evolution, the debate (or what was left of it) about the acceptability of (usurious) interest mainly moved to the domain of economic science.

In the context of (pure theoretical) economic research, the central question became whether interest is a natural or an economic category. In other words, the question became whether interest plays a necessary role in every human society, or whether it is tied to the capitalist economic models (implying that there is a possibility that it may disappear in a future "non-capitalist" or in a "different capitalist" society).[266]

105 Throughout this debate which henceforth became increasingly theoretical and barely concerned the practice of (banking) interest (mechanisms) itself, the ethical approach remained still to some extent in place.

106 Those who came to the conclusion that interest is a necessary economic function were mainly economists who, following Eugen von Böhm-Bawerk (1851–1914) who thoroughly researched this topic[267], have assumed that the reason explaining "interest" is the fact that a higher value is given to goods today ("actual goods") than to goods in the future ("future-goods"). This doctrine however admits that, by accepting this, no answer is given to the question to whom the interest should go. In this doctrine (be it on efficiency grounds), it is not to be excluded that society itself would claim the interest, thus avoiding the emergence of a separate class of capitalists.[268]

---

[264] Let it make 'the old commandment' to love one another once again 'a new commandment,' and let us give all men to understand that Christianity is a life before it is a theology'.

See also De Wit and Steenvoorde (2008), pp. 240–241.

[265] Gore (1920).

[266] De Katholieke Encyclopaedie (1937). N.V. Uitgeversmij Joost v.d. Vondel, Amsterdam, under "rente".

[267] See especially von Böhm-Bawerk (1912).
See also Vandewalle (1976), p. 116.

[268] De Katholieke Encyclopaedie (1937). N.V. Uitgeversmij Joost v.d. Vondel, Amsterdam, under "rente".

Recently, this latter approach has started to resonate again in, for instance, the (recent) debate advocating that income from capital (including income in the form of interest) should be taxed (more highly). A similar taxability would indeed come down to a method of allowing the community represented by the government to acquire this income for itself (see especially the so-called "Tobin-tax" debate[269]).

In the course of the further twentieth century, economists only sporadically discussed the ethical problems of interest charging, albeit not with any less enthusiasm. **107**

J.M. Keynes for example[270] made the following poignant statement:

> the disquisitions of the schoolmen (on usury) were directed towards elucidation of a formula which should allow the schedule of the marginal efficiency to be high, whilst using rule and custom and the moral law to keep down the rate of interest, so that a wise Government is concerned to curb it by statute and custom and even by invoking the sanctions of the Moral Law.

J.K. Galbraith[271] expressed a similar idea:

> Now, in the age of contentment, what economists call macroeconomic policy has come to centre not on tax policy but on monetary policy – the mediating actions of the central bank, in the United States the Federal Reserve System. Higher interest rates, it is hoped, will curb inflation, in any case, they will not threaten men and women of good fortune. Those with money to lend, the economically well-endowed rentier class, will thus be rewarded.

Even more, up until today, some philosophers and organizations (such as the Canadian "*Committee on monetary and economic reform*") have outed themselves as strong opponents of charging interest. Reference can also be mate to, for instance, Margrit Kennedy, a professor in Hanover who published her study "*Interest and Inflation Free Money*" in 1995[272] in which she expresses her support for a money compensation mechanism other than interest.[273] **108**

3.3.3.8 Contemporary Lessons from the (Ecclesiastical) Interest Debate

The decline of the historical (clerical) interest debate nevertheless does not preclude us, within the modern context, from drawing important lessons from the aforementioned historical perspective.[274] **109**

In his aforementioned study "*The interest debate in the West*"[275], van Liedekerke sums up three types of argument against interest which, on further reflection, already were brought up by the quoted ecclesiastical scholars:

---

269 Schmidt (1999), pp. 105–114.

270 In: Keynes (1935), p. 351.

271 Galbraith (1992), p. 43.

272 Kennedy (1995), p. 144.

273 http://kennedy-bibliothek.info/data/bibo/media/GeldbuchEnglisch.pdf.

274 See also Stiglitz (2003), p. 81.

275 van Liedekerke (1993), pp. 20–22.

i. Arguments of a "metaphysical" nature: the fact that money generates interest is an unnatural phenomenon and a deterioration of an order of being created by God (the divine order);
ii. The usurer exploits the needs of others and is therefore possessed of a sinful virtue; judgment of the person leads to judgment of the practice (= the person without virtue);
iii. Usury does not fit in terms of commutative justice (the unjust contract).

110 Other arguments stemming from the ancient debate on the charging of interest[276] standing out (more than ever) in the contemporary context are:

i. Interest as unearned (or not earned through labor or efforts) income, is reprehensible as a pursuit per se (see council of Laterans of 1515);
   It is remarkable that in his biography of Keynes, Skidelsky[277] has stated the psycho-political dimension of this argument in Keynes's works as follows:

> Keynes's sense that, at some level too deep to be captured by mathematics, "love of money" as an end, not a means, is at the root of the world's economic problem.

ii. Interest as an unjust redistribution of wealth: the rich get richer and the poor get continuously poorer (see the earlier mentioned calculated examples by M. Kennedy);
   Empirical research from the past years seems increasingly to confirm this observation (see further, under Sect. 3.4.8).
iii. Interest as a cause of economic instability;
   Keynes[278] himself stated on this matter:

> The rate of interest is not self-adjusting at the level best suited to the social advantage but constantly tends to rise too high.

iv. Interest as a discounting of the future;
   As an example, when it comes to the use of resources, a higher discounting of the actual value (based on a high interest rate), will generate overconsumption.[279]
   A further interesting consideration in this context is the fact that the financial economy relates to the development of nature as compound interest does to simple interest: a standing crop that is not harvested, will not necessarily generate more harvest the following year.
   Basically this last argument also blames an (essentially very unjust) breach of the intergenerational solidarity which, as discussed further in the text, in the context of the Czech phenomenological school (see further, at marg. 261 of this chapter) resulting in Patocka's writings, may be among the most essential ethical achievements that Europe has offered the world since Plato and of

[276]Visser and McIntosch (1998), especially pp. 181–186.
[277]Skidelsky (1992), p. 454.
[278]Keynes (1935), p. 350.
[279]Pearce and Turner (1990).

which the ongoing effects of the severe financial crisis of 2008 forms a striking illustration.

Finally, Keynes showed himself to be a proponent of a general charging of low interest in order (a) to enable debtors to pay their debts, (b) to ensure stability of the economic agents and (c) to install a climate of economic activity.[280] 111

Keynes also indicated that low interest rates should be implemented in the private and public sector, thus not only in the form of low interest rates which central banks grant to private banks.[281]

3.4 Doctrines in Favour of Uncontrolled Wealth Accumulation

3.4.1 The Decline of Altruism as an Underlying Ideal Within Economic Doctrines

The altruistic viewpoints opposing uncontrolled wealth accumulation which are expressed in the Gospel(s) of Christ (see above, at marg. 33–34 and 37–40 of this chapter) no longer have a decisive influence on trade or finance in the present-day secularized (Western) world. 112

To some degree, this may even be considered ironic. 113

Instead of ensuring that the teachings of Christ got applied in economic practice by developing society models where wealth accumulation would, at least to some extent, be kept within certain reasonable boundaries, and where the rich would be encouraged to share their wealth as much as possible with less fortunate people, Western (and Western-inspired) economies have over time taken a complete opposite course, in spite of the Christian roots they are (or pretend to be) rooted in.

Although, as has been explained before (see under Sect. 3.3.3), during certain periods in history, the Catholic Church attempted to somehow reduce uncontrolled wealth accumulation of the richer classes (originally: nobility and clergy, later on: traders and bankers[282], and even more later on: industrialists and specialized service providers) by means of the historical ecclesiastical doctrine which prohibited the charging of interest, even this doctrine, notwithstanding the fact that it was far less radical than the radical teachings of Christ Himself, has not been able to avoid the pressure of an ever (and differently) changing practice in economic life, whereby wealth accumulation gradually evolved into the leading societal principle.

---

[280]Pettifor (2014).

[281]Pettifor (2014).

[282]Ferguson (1998), p. 17.

114 As a result of this evolution, the dictate of uncontrolled selfishness which lies at the basis of the capitalist economic system and which has driven a large part of mankind towards unbridled greed nowadays prevails worldwide; on a global scale, nearly every society model is exposed to its several devastating effects.

Paraphrasing Christ's own words, capitalism thus presents itself mainly as an orgiastic worship of the mammon[283], rather than as an attempt to establish the Kingdom of God on earth.

Otherwise put, capitalism does not at all aim to establish a reasonable level of prosperity for all of mankind (so that all people have the opportunity to develop their true destiny, which is, in Christian doctrine, subservience to God), but instead is based on economic methods by means of which the "strong" within society (i.e. those whose behaviour best mirrors the ideal capitalist image of an uncontrolled egoism) can enrich themselves unlimitedly to the detriment of the greater masses (i.e. those who agree less with the capitalist ideal of applying such unbridled egoism).

Hereafter, it will be briefly explored how economic doctrine(s) originating form the seventeenth century on has (have) succeeded in achieving this goal.

3.4.2 *Ideological Foundation of the Selfish Economy*

3.4.2.1 Economic Liberalism

3.4.2.1.1 Ethics of Liberal and Neo-liberal Thinking in General

115 It may be somewhat surprising that the aforementioned evolution towards a society determined by an unbridled (socioeconomic) egoism, especially characterized by an unlimited pursuit of wealth, found its first thorough ideological foundation in some of the works of (enlightened) philosophers of the seventeenth and the eighteenth centuries. Their doctrines did not only justify the ever more dominating (economic and societal) processes which allowed a small part of mankind to acquire huge wealth at the detriment of the rest of mankind, but moreover succeeded to lift the principle of unbridled wealth accumulation to the level of the prevailing moral target *per se*.[284]

---

[283]Zuboff and Maxmin (2002), p. 33.

[284]Galbraith (1987), pp. 57 a.f.

See further Brook and Watkins (2012), p. 77:

> All of this implies that money is a value only under certain circumstances. The same reasons that lead a profit seeker to love earned money lead him to spurn unearned money, money won in defiance of the need to produce. Whether the money is looted from unsuspecting investors or mooched from overly generous relatives, the money does not represent a productive achievement and does not go to fuel further productive achievements.

During this process of replacing (a.o. Christ's) altruistic ideals by their opposite principles of greed and egoism, the initial aim had been to apply the technique of "rational thinking" to economic processes in an attempt to determine "natural laws" explaining them.[285] **116**

This search for a "rational" theory explaining economic phenomena would, after taking some detours alongside economic doctrines such as "anti-mercantilism" (*e.g.* Nicholas Barbon (1640–1698) and Sir Dudley North (1641–1691)), "neo-mercantilism" (*e.g.* John Law (1671–1739) who advocated, *inter alia*, an extension of the supply of money in order to combat high interest rates, and who therefore, to a certain extent, could be considered as one of the first "monetarists" *avant la lettre*), "cantillonism" (more specifically Richard Cantillon (1680–1734)) and "the physiocrats" (*e.g.* François Quesnay (1694–1774), the founder of the theory of economic circulation), finally resulted in the doctrine of "economic liberalism".[286]

The impact of "economic liberalism" on the ethics of economy itself, can hardly be underestimated. **117**

The reason hereof is that, since the emergence of economic liberalism, the pursuit of uncontrolled wealth at any cost has become accepted to be "morally correct" and even as the guiding principle of social, economic and overall societal life itself.[287]

In this development, dating back to Adam Smith himself, people behaving in accordance with the teachings of "economic liberalism" (and later on: "economic neo-liberalism") are believed not to become rich by "stealing" from others, but by increasing the size of the metaphorical *"common pie"* (of the world economy) through their exceptional efforts.[288] "*And*", to quote Harari's (ironic) description of the liberal and neo-liberal doctrines, "*when the pie grows, everyone benefits. The rich are accordingly the most useful and most benevolent people in society, because they turn the wheels of growth for everyone's advantage.*"[289]

Moreover, (neo-)liberal ideology also gave birth to a belief system validating the accumulation of ever more riches and power in the hands of the rich and powerful of the planet.[290]

---

[285]Fox (2013), p. 382.
See further Vandewalle (1976), p. 27; Poma (2009), p. 73.

[286]Vandewalle (1976), pp. 28–40; Beaud (1994), pp. 33 a.f.

[287]Harari (2014), pp. 348–349. See also Chomsky (1999), pp. 25 a.f.

[288]Harari (2014), pp. 348–449; see also Beaud (1994), p. 93.

[289]Harari (2014), pp. 348–349. See also Galbraith (1983), pp. 110 a.f.

[290]Galbraith has in this regard pointed out that nothing has been so important in the defence of modern enterprises and the power they represent, as the argument that their power does not exist, but is the mere expression of the play of the free market, an argument that forms one of the foundations of (neo-)liberal reasoning. By thus falsely representing economic reality, the most foul abuses of power all have become justified as a result of the way the free market works and should continue to work. And, still according to Galbraith, nothing is more serviceable to maintaining this system than the resulting (and up to the present-day relentlessly ongoing) conditioning of the young to that belief system (see Galbraith 1983, p. 120).

Further Illustration 3.6: Tested Recipes for Baking the (Neo) Liberal Pie

The French author Pascal Bruckner has convincingly argued that capitalism is mainly about what one can "take from others"[291] (especially in terms of money and goods, but even in term as intangible items, such as work/labour, job satisfaction and physical and mental health).

Also the French anthropologist Emmanuel Todd has expressed in a similar way that the extreme wealth of the rich classes of this world is basically based on systems of power, exploitation, exclusion and repression, a fact which in most Western countries is still denied by the leading classes and the political world (mainly) representing their interests.[292]

By means of some striking illustrations, capitalism has thrived by applying different "theft mechanisms", which all, at some moment in time or other, surprisingly, continue to be accepted as legitimate by the legal systems of most Western (or Western-inspired) capitalist countries.

Some of these mechanisms used to "bake the (neo)liberal pie" are as follows:

(i) "Colonialism" and "imperialism" (whereby entire countries, and even continents, and their populations have been robbed of their resources for centuries[293]);
(ii) "slavery", both in its narrow legal meaning, as well as in a wider economic sense of the word (being equal to the deprivation of the freedom and essential human dignity of large groups of people in order to provide—taking into account the liberal law of the "Iron Law of the Wages"—the cheapest possible labor forces in order to acquire the greatest possible wealth for one's self);
(iii) Pricing policy in North-South relations (i.e. a continuing type of robber behaviour during the so-called post-colonial era, whereby producers of numerous goods from poor countries are not paid a fair price for their products[294]);

(continued)

---

[291] Bruckner (2002), p. 27.

[292] See Todd (2015), p. 93 (also Todd 2015, p. 72):

> Reste que le bien-être de cette classe émane d'un système social non seulement égoïste, mais hypocrite puisque ses représentations officielles nient les relations de force, d'exploitation, d'exclusion et de répression.

See also Streeck (2015), pp. 87 a.f.

[293] Beaud (1994), pp. 137 a.f.; Lénine (1935); Pinxten and De Munter (2006), pp. 114 a.f.

[294] Stiglitz (2006), p. 15.

Further Illustration 3.6 (continued)

(iv) probably the largest and most systemically applied robber behaviour ever: the (banking) interest mechanism in the framework of creating new scriptural money based upon credit lending by private banks, whereby the remainder of the economy is continuously deprived of a major part of its created wealth in favour of the financial system (and the few people on the planet controlling it), thus contributing to significant difficulties (including poverty) for many economic agents and even entire states.

As the bank interest mechanism lies at the foundation of capitalism, it needs not surprise that, throughout the ages, the cycle of robbing the "common man" who actually enables the bank interest mechanism, has completely gotten out of proportion.

The term "common man" as used here may refer to anyone who depends on obtaining an income from labor for his subsistence and who is therefore, to quote Linguet (see further, at marg. 276 of this chapter), "*the hostage of the free market*" as, per definition, such a person does not have enough capital to be "life annuitant" and to be able to live from income from capital acquired in the past. Such a "common man" is, by definition, not part of the privileged class of "life annuitants"[295], but on the contrary has to work for the most part of his life, mainly in order to make the latter ever more rich.

Firstly, "the common man" is obviously, in his capacity of credit taker, victim of the banking interest mechanism. It is indeed the case that anyone depending on a bank credit in order to meet basic needs in a broad sense (see further, at marg. 129 of Chap. 4 of this book), *e.g.* the purchase of a house or a car (in most cases needed "to go to work"), needs to be aware that, in some cases: for the rest of his life, he will have to spend a large amount of his income on bank interests while, at least for the bank, the efforts needed to provide a bank credit probably represent the least intense labor thinkable, as a credit (as discussed exhaustively in Chap. 2 of this book) leads to the creation of money *ex nihilo*, and whereby production and other costs are extremely low compared to the potential profits.

Secondly, if such a "common man" lives in a country where the government has been drawn into financing its deficits through debt-related financing techniques (which is actually the case for the majority of the Western world, and for even a longer time, for almost all "poor countries") and where such financing mainly is provided by the private financial sector, then this person will also note that a substantial part of the tax skimming (of his income)

(continued)

295 Compare Galbraith (1992), pp. 95–96.

Further Illustration 3.6 (continued)

which he has to undergo for the majority of his life, is used to finance the interests his country owes to the banking sector.

Thirdly, those who—especially in the post 2008 era—are young, will also have to suffer and intergenerational disadvantage, due to the fact that taxes paid today are to a large extent needed to cover the settlement of financial debts made by governments from an earlier time period (both in capital, as in interest).

After the (mega) bail-out efforts of 2008–2009 (but also previously in history) that were required from governments worldwide in order to (referring to the neo-liberal law of "*privatization of gains and socialization of losses*"), take over the burden of the "catharsis" of the by "hubris" driven banking sector, there are further more the (enormous) financial debts which governments were forced to make for this purpose (for instance, in Belgium, this is deemed to account for an estimated 15% of the existing government debt).

By some, it has even been assumed that, on a global scale, governmental debts have become so huge that it will probably be impossible to ever pay them back, while in the meantime the interests of such debts continue to burden the financial accounts of the countries concerned. (See further, under Sect. 3.4.6.)

Fourthly, the "common man" is also victim of the robbing behaviour of banks in his daily expenditure, since the interests owed by enterprises (producing goods and services) for their own bank credit are part of production costs, and therefore calculated into the sales prices the companies charge for the goods or services they offer within economy.

And we have not yet considered the reduction in various social achievements which, under the rule of the doctrine of "economic neo-liberalism", is taking place at high speed since decades already and which particularly impacts the younger generation much more than the older.

The worst part is that the banking sector and the policy makers of this world seem to have been aware for a very long time of the inherently perverse effects of the capitalist banking interest mechanism (and hence the capitalist money creation mechanism), especially given the quotes referred to in marg. 3 of Chap. 1 of this book and in marg. 29 of Chap. 4 of this book, implying that, if the quotes are entirely accurate, the capitalist banking system could to some extent even be considered as an inexcusable, maliciously driven robbery plan.

Taking these elements into consideration, one must be inclined to believe that the philosophers quoted earlier in this book, such as Plato and Aristotle, certain historical church elders, such as the Saints Ambrose and Augustine, as well as the medieval Scholastics, such as Saint Thomas Aquinas, apparently

(continued)

Further Illustration 3.6 (continued)

knew very well what they were doing when, through their writings and in their sermons, they fought their historical battle against interest charging and usury. (See above, under Sect. 3.3.3.)

After centuries of uncontrolled private banking greed, one can but wonder whether the tide of this financial greed and its detrimental effects on the global economy and society in general, can still be turned. Nevertheless, in the Chaps. 4 and 5 of this book, an attempt to do so will still be undertaken.

As mentioned before, the insight that economic (neo-)liberalism is based on an **118** inverse (ethical) value perception inevitably leads to the further realization that the modern "*homo neo-liberalis*" adhering to this doctrine is not only led by motives which are completely opposite to those of, for instance, Jesus Christ (namely by an "unbridled selfishness" instead of a "radical altruism"), but at the same time perfectly matches the type of person described by Aristotle as a virtueless "greedy person" who is greedy because he takes more than is reasonable from others (see above, at marg. 64–65 of this chapter), and is, by definition, in doing so, attributing to the creation of an "unjust" world (see further, at marg. 271–272 of this chapter).

When, as will be attempted hereafter, evaluating economic liberal and neo-liberal thinking, one should hence, above all, keep in mind that these doctrines of economic liberalism and economic neo-liberalism have succeeded in raising to an absolute virtue precisely what is inherently "virtueless" in Aristotelian thinking, but, for instance, also in the Christian and the Buddhist tradition, namely "selfishness", "greed", and "avarice".

In this process of turning around basic life values, "economic liberalism" (which **119** later on in history evolved into "economic neo-liberalism") has, over time, become much more than a simple economic doctrine, but has turned into an overall ideology—some have even stated: a new religion—dictating how people should behave, how they should raise their children and even how they should think.[296]

In this way, the (neo-)liberal belief system increasingly has shaped the (development of) mankind's identity; in addition, it has determined man's relation towards others and to the planet he lives on to become ever more influenced by egoism, greed and selfishness.[297]

---

[296]Harari (2014), p. 351; Galbraith (1987), p. 64; Geysels (2014), p. 13.

See also the reflections of Mark Carney, Governor of the Bank of England, in Oxfam (2014), p. 55:

> Capitalism loses its sense of moderation when the belief in the power of the market enters the realm of faith. Market fundamentalism – in the form of light-touch regulation, the belief that bubbles cannot be identified and that markets always clear – contributed directly to the financial crisis and the associated erosion of social capital.

[297]Verhaeghe (2011), p. 20.

In this, the principle of economic growth is set to be the greatest good in a religious system where justice, freedom and even happiness are, on a macro level, all supposed to depend on such economic growth, and, on a micro-level, on individual wealth accumulation and personal greed.[298]

120 The ideological system originating from these (originally: "liberal" and later on: "neo-liberal") doctrines also laid the foundation for the large expansion of capitalism in the course of the eighteenth, nineteenth and twentieth centuries, whereby merchants and industrialists, being the new privileged classes who were taking over from the old nobility and clergy, later also the governments of countries adopting capitalist economic thinking, and finally, often against its own interests, even the general public of entire nations, have all, in their ever increasing unlimited pursuit of money, been backed by economic (and in general social) theories based on this attitude to life.[299]

---

[298]Harari (2014), p. 351. Compare Rand (2008).

Such a life vision could not be more contra-Christian—or should we say: "more contra-Christ"—and "contra-Aristotelian" and, as will be indicated later, more contra-Buddhist (see further, at marg. 289 a.f. of this chapter). It is therefore not a coincidence that, for instance, a refined modern-day philosopher like Emmanuel Levinas has made his purpose in life the creation of a philosophical system that turns the (neo-)liberal value scale around (with as a further merit that this is accomplished in an abstract way and, keeping in mind the premises of the concerned philosophical doctrine, without the need to spend much time explaining which particular doctrines his own teachings are a reaction to) (see further, under Sect. 3.6.4.2.2).

[299]In his masterpiece the novel "*The Magic Mountain*" (originally written in German, under the title "*Der Zauberberg*", and first published in 1924), widely recognized as one of the most influential works of twentieth century German literature, Thomas Mann has explored this theme in an unparalleled manner, especially in the notorious dialogues between Leo Naphta (loosely based on the philosopher George Lukács and hence mainly representing end defending the ideas of Hegelian Marxism), and Lodovico Settembrini (mainly representing and defending the ideals of the Schools of Enlightenment and of the values of the traditional Western society shaped by it). Both characters' opinions help shaping the world view of the antagonist character Hans Castorp and hence, through Mann's repeated invitation to learn from what Castorp experiences throughout the novel, (hopefully) also that of the reader (compare https://en.wikipedia.org/wiki/The_Magic_Mountain; last consulted on April 7th 2016).

In general, the novel "*The Magic Mountain*" bears witness of Thomas Mann's (pessimistic) re-examination of European bourgeois society and its values (as this society model has emerged from the so-called "liberal" revolutions of the eighteenth and nineteenth century, including the sources of the willful, perverse destructiveness displayed by the majority of civilized humanity) (see https://en.wikipedia.org/wiki/The_Magic_Mountain; last consulted on April 7th 2016), especially under the influence of the since then dominating economic system, namely capitalism (or in present-day terminology: the free market system), and the ideologies which have assisted in shaping it (especially "economic liberalism" and "economic neo-liberalism").

3.4.2.1.2 The Writings of Adam Smith, David Ricardo, Thomas Malthus and John Stuart Mill

3.4.2.1.2.1 Inverse Value Perception as a Leading Principle in Adam Smith's Writings

The altruistically inspired economic vision of Christ would for the first time in history (of the West) encounter a solidly based counterpart in the writings of the Scottish moral philosopher Adam Smith (1723–1790).[300] **121**

In spite of starting, as Christ Himself, with a keen insight into human nature on the question whether or not unbridled wealth accumulation should be deemed permissible, Adam Smith preached a moral vision of life that is completely opposite to the radical-altruistic vision of Christ.

In the approach of Adam Smith[301], it is stated, on different occasions and almost in a paradoxical manner, that society's interests are not best served by adhering to an altruistic way of life, but rather by the development of an essentially selfish lifestyle.

This doctrine holds that each individual (and by expansion: each "economic agent") should mainly (if not only) pursuit his own selfish interest(s), without even questioning the impact of his behaviour on others. In the long term, and as if it were guided by an "invisible hand"[302], a society where every individual mainly looks after himself is believed to evolve into a prosperous society which will optimally accommodate the interests of all those who are part of it.[303]

In this way of reversing moral values, the pursuit of selfishness even became synonymous to serving the general good.[304]

This "invisible hand"-process is in this belief system even considered to be a "law of nature" which is held to be the same in all times and places.[305]

For the sake of comprehensiveness, it may be remarked that some authors have indicated that the writings of Adam Smith himself are not as decisive on this "value reversion" as is generally believed. It is hereby argued that mainly later authors (in particular the neo-liberal authors mentioned below; see further, under Sect. 3.4.2.3) based themselves on a number of paragraphs from Adam Smith's works in **122**

---

[300] See also Harari (2014), pp. 346–348, proclaiming the book "The Wealth of Nations" as ***"probably the most important economics manifesto of all time"***. See further Berend (2006), p. 13; Whitney Hall (2013), p. 364.

[301] Or at least credited to him; see about this issue Achterhuis (2011), pp. 177 a.f.

[302] Which is why Smith's doctrine is often referred to as the "invisible hand" theory.

[303] Compare Galbraith (1987), p. 64.

[304] See Galbraith (1983), p. 112.

> The rich and the affluent do not speak in defense of their own good fortune; they speak as the benign servitors of the common good. Some may even be embarrassed as to their worldly reward, but they suffer it, nonetheless, as a service to the general well-being. (see Galbraith 1996, p. 62).

[305] Vandewalle (1976), p. 40; Polak (1928), p. 239.

order to elaborate on a new doctrine, namely "economic neo-liberalism", which holds that it is the greatest possible selfish economic behaviour that drives society to the highest possible prosperity for everyone.[306]

123 Yuval Noah Harari has nevertheless remarked that the doctrine of Adam Smith (and of his later adepts, especially the neo-liberals) may nowadays not seem very original anymore, as in the meantime, we all have been living in a capitalist world for such a long time and, as a consequence, we have become used to this kind of reasoning, but that nevertheless, the teachings of Adam Smith that the fulfilment of one's selfish human urges best serves the interests of society as a whole is to be considered as one of the most revolutionary ideas in human history.

Adam Smith in fact claimed that "greed" is a good thing, which in the actual context of neo-liberal thinking translates into the so-called "*greed is good*" credo, in other words into the idea that "selfishness" is good and that altruism is detrimental.

It need therefore not surprise that the fervent neo-liberal author Ayn Rand explicitly claims altruism to be "vicious", and for example in her book "*The virtue of Selfishness*", she has exacerbated this discourse on the turn-around of values to its fullest extent.[307]

Mankind owes to this (neo-)liberal doctrine the opinion that the unbridled selfish pursuit of wealth not only favours the individual who accumulates more wealth, but everyone. This belief system lies hence at the very basis of the so-called "*trickle-down economics*"[308], an approach which above all aims at "rationalizing" and therefore justifying selfishness.

It does not come as a surprise that this belief system is not very different from the way of reasoning by which, already during the lifetime of Adam Smith himself, colonialism had before in history been justified by the colonial powers: these colonial powers claimed that their empires were not enormous systems of exploitation, but rather altruistic projects set up to raise the rest of the world to the level of "civilization" obtained in Europe (an idea that, for instance, has been elaborated by

[306] Achterhuis (2011), pp. 177 a.f.

See also Brook and Watkins (2012), pp. 9 a.f.

[307] Ayn Rand has for instance argued that

> altruism holds death as its ultimate goal and standard of value – and it is logical that renunciation, resignation, self-denial, and every other form of suffering, including self-destruction are the virtues it advocates. (Rand 1992, p. 38).

According to this author, a so-called "altruistic" person shows the following characteristics: (*1*) a low self-esteem; (*2*) a lack of esteem for other human beings; (*3*) a perception of life as being a nightmare, i.e. a hostile happening where disasters occur all the time, and (*4*) a complete lack of ethics (see Rand 1992, p. 49).

See also Rand (2008), p. 19; Rand (1982), p. 27; compare Szalavitz (2012), who herself has observed that

> to claim, as Rand does, that "altruistic morality" is a "disease" is to misrepresent reality.

[308] Bruckner (2002), p. 26.

Rudyard Kipling in his famous poem "*The White Man's Burden: The United States and The Philippine Islands*") (1899).

It may be clear that this attempt to present a positive image to colonialism is nevertheless in clear contradiction to all facts[309] as is also the case for the present-day (neo-)liberal belief systems themselves.

The legitimate critique of Galbraith against one of the main axioms of the **124**
Smithian doctrine, namely the theory of the "invisible hand", is that it is not really empirically founded, but rather is "a tenure" and, consequently, basically a moral system on its own, which—in a few words—indicates that nothing which happens in the short term can be in conflict with the long term benefit, thus does not need any steering or supporting hand from the government.[310]

This blind faith in the invisible powers of the free market is therefore also known as the "*laissez faire, laissez passer*"-doctrine.[311] The continued adherence to this idea, albeit its detrimental effects on the wellbeing of mankind and of the planet, may moreover be explained by the fact that the freedom of industrialists and enterprises to blindly pursue their own interests has in this belief system become a matter of social principle.[312] However, still according to Galbraith, this blind faith in the powers of the free market can never contribute to maximizing efficiency within society, but rather results in a dominance of processes whereby pointless desires are created or stimulated, so that they can be satisfied later on (= the so-called "production for production's sake" and/or "consumption for consumption's sake"[313]). In this way, under capitalism, he who controls human lust (satisfaction) also accumulates and gets to control wealth and power.[314]

---

309 Harari (2014), pp. 336–337.

310 Galbraith (1992), p. 51.

Unless, again according to Galbraith, in case of the need for a bailout of a failing bank, or when national defense is at stake, both being among the few situations in which economic liberalism and economic neo-liberalism accept state intervention.

311 Galbraith (1992), pp. 51–52; Galbraith (1987), pp. 64 a.f.; Chomsky (1999), pp. 34 a.f. See also Rand (1992), p. 37.

312 Galbraith (1983), p. 117.

313 Galbraith (1970), p. 109.

Karl Marx has been one of the first to fight this intrinsic quality of capitalism. According to Marx, the aim of society cannot be the production of things as an aim itself. What has been neglected by even left-wing political parties such as socialist and communist parties, is that for Marx, maximum production and maximum consumption should not be the unquestionable aims of society. Society should be about the conquest of poverty and about putting an end to unjust levels on inequality, not about production and consumption as a supreme end. (See Fromm 2013, p. 31.)

314 Galbraith's insight is remarkably in accordance with certain religious teachings.

For example, in Hinduism, it is believed that man is entrapped in the material world of sense gratification which keeps him away from his reunion with God. The renowned spiritual leader Prabhupada has expressed this as follows:

> Therefore, this lust is the symbol of ignorance by which the living entity is kept within the material world. While one enjoys sense gratification, it may be that there is some feeling of happiness, but actually that so-called feeling of happiness is the ultimate enemy of the sense enjoyer (see Bhaktivedanta Swami Prabhupada 1983, p. 186).

Already in 1992, Galbraith expressed his concern that, under the wings of (neo) liberal doctrine, mechanisms were developing (in particular on the financial markets) which not only "shape" the market, but also "afflict" and threaten to "destroy" it (as one of the expressions of the so-called inherent self-destructive nature of capitalism).[315]

3.4.2.1.2.2 Basic Dogmas of Adam Smith on the Issue of Wealth Accumulation as Stated in Certain of His Works

125 Already in his (early) work "*The Theory of Moral Sentiments*" (1759)[316], Adam Smith expressed some of his aforementioned viewpoints, a.o. when he is writing about a selfish land owner who, led by the invisible hand, and despite the self-interest he aims for, ultimately still divides the harvest between the people he employs:

> It is to no purpose, that the proud and unfeeling landlord views his extensive fields, and without a thought for the wants of his brethren, in imagination consumes himself the whole harvest that grows upon them. The homely and vulgar proverb, that the eye is larger than the belly, never was more fully verified than with regard to him. The capacity of his stomach bears no proportion to the immensity of his desires, and will receive no more than that of the meanest peasant. The rest he is obliged to distribute among those, who prepare, in the nicest manner, that little which he himself makes use of, among those who fit up the palace in which this little is to be consumed, among those who provide and keep in order all the different baubles and trinkets, which are employed in the economy of greatness; all of whom thus derive from his luxury and caprice, that share of the necessaries of life, which they would in vain have expected from his humanity or his justice. The produce of the soil maintains at all times nearly that number of inhabitants which it is capable of maintaining. The rich only select from the heap what is most precious and agreeable. They consume little more than the poor, and in spite of their natural selfishness and rapacity, though they mean only their own convenience, though the sole end which they propose from the labours of all the thousands whom they employ, be the gratification of their own vain and insatiable desires, they divide with the poor the produce of all their improvements. They are led by an invisible hand to make nearly the same distribution of the necessaries of life, which would have been made, had the earth been divided into equal portions among all its inhabitants, and thus without intending it, without knowing it, advance the interest of the society, and afford means to the multiplication of the species. When Providence divided the earth among a few lordly masters, it neither forgot nor abandoned those who seemed to have been left out in the partition. These last two enjoy their share of all that it produces. In what constitutes the real happiness of human life, they are in no respect inferior to those who would seem so much above them. In ease of body and peace of mind, all the different ranks of life are nearly upon a level, and the beggar, who suns himself by the side of the highway, possesses that security which kings are fighting for.

---

[315]Galbraith (1992), pp. 61 a.f.

[316]Part IV, Chapter 1, number 10 (see http://www.econlib.org/library/Smith/smMS4.html; 18th December 2014; see also Smith (2005), p. 164.

In other words, in this view (on which the theory of the "trickle-down-economics" is based), there is no need for a fair division of wealth as, in their efforts to improve themselves, the rich are bound to set up systems which will divide the necessary goods of life amongst the rest of the people. This process would in no way be better if land would at the very start be divided in a fair way, implying that out of self-interest, the rich will still contribute to the advancement of the global society.[317]

A similar, well known passage, often quoted by neo-liberal authors, is from Book I, Chapter II, paragraph 2 of Adam Smith's most famous book "*The Wealth of Nations*" (1776)[318]: **126**

> It is not from the benevolence of the butcher, the brewer or the baker, that we expect our dinner, but from their regard to their own interest. We address ourselves, not to their humanity but to their self-love, and never talk to them of our own necessities but of their advantages. Nobody but a beggar chooses to depend chiefly upon the benevolence of his fellow-citizens. Even a beggar does not depend on it entirely. The charity of well- disposed people, indeed, supplies him with all the necessaries of life which he has occasion for, it neither does nor can provide him with them as he has occasion for them. The greater part of his occasional wants are supplied in the same manner as those of other people, by treaty, by barter, and by purchase. With the money which one man gives him he purchases food. The old cloaths which another bestows upon him he exchanges for other old cloaths which suit him better, or for lodging, or for food, or for money, with which he can buy either food, cloaths, or lodging, as he has occasion.

In addition, in various of the other books of "*The Wealth of Nations*" (1776), the aforementioned idea is described in more detail, for example in Book I, Chapter 7, titled: "*of the natural market price of commodities*",[319] where Smith explains how market mechanisms channel the greed of the individual into a system benefiting everyone. **127**

In Book IV, Chapter II, paragraph 5 of the same work, Smith further explains that "*every individual endeavours to employ his capital as near home as he can, and consequently as much as he can in the support of domestic industry*"[320] and that such a preference works as an invisible benevolent hand for the benefit of the entire society and from which, at the same time, all individuals benefit.

---

[317]Needless to say what sheer nonsense this starting point of the Smithian doctrine is, especially in comparison with elaborated philosophical systems (such as those of Ancient Greek philosophers). The success of this doctrine is therefore not to be attributed to its intrinsic coherence, but mainly to the fact that it especially appealed to the rich and powerful within society who saw in it a confirmation of their selfish behavior (in sharp contrast to, for instance, the classical catholic doctrine of the ages before). Chomsky has in this regard argued that capitalism is based on (the) bad ideas (of Adam Smith) which flourish because they are in the interest of powerful groups (Chomsky 1999, p. 25).

[318]Smith (1979), pp. 26–27.
See also Galbraith (1987), p. 64.

[319]Smith (1979), pp. 72–81.

[320]Smith (1979), p. 454.

In paragraph 9 of the same Book IV, Chapter II[321] of "*The Wealth of Nations*", it is furthermore stated that:

> By preferring the support of domestic to that of foreign industry, he intends only his own security; and by directing that industry in such a manner as its produce may be of the greatest value, he intends only his own gain, and he is in this, as in many other cases, led by an invisible hand to promote an end which was no part of his intention. Nor is it always the worse for the society that it was not part of it. By pursuing his own interest he frequently promotes that of the society more effectually than when he really intends to promote it. I have never known much good done by those who affected to trade for the public good. It is an affectation, indeed, not very common among merchants, and very few words need be employed in dissuading them from it.

128 In this way, economic motivation for Adam Smith centers on the role of self-interest of the individual. It is, hence, especially the private and competitive pursuit of once's individual interests that causes economic welfare, thus best serving the public good, rather than systems of collectivism.[322]

Adam Smith also had his own ideas on the interest mechanism[323], whereby he described interest as a barometer for the profitability of business. This approach states that only a (very) profitable enterprise will be willing to pay high interest rates. This accordingly makes interest rates a suitable method to measure the strength of the economy. This viewpoint of Smith's is deemed to be a reaction to the mercantilists[324] who had claimed the opposite, namely that it is the steering of the amount of money which should determine interest rates.[325]

It is, furthermore, not surprising that Adam Smith was also a strong advocate of capital accumulation. In the Smithian philosophy, capital accumulation favours production, increasing the rate of employment and, consequently, global economic prosperity.[326]

3.4.2.1.2.3 Evaluation of the Legacy of Adam Smith

129 Having addressed this topic before (see above, at marg. 122 of this chapter)[327], we will leave the question open to what extent the aforementioned thoughts of Adam

[321]Smith (1979), p. 456.

[322]See however Galbraith (1987), p. 64, further quoting Smith's saying that

> I have never known much good done by those who affected to trade for the public good. It is an affectation, indeed, not very common among merchants, and very few words need be employed in dissuading them from it.

[323]Smith (1979), p. 72.

[324]Galbraith (1987), p. 37.

[325]Vandewalle (1976), p. 42.

[326]See *e.g.* Book I, Chapter IX of "*The Wealth of Nations*" (Smith 1979, pp. 105 a.f.); see further Vandewalle (1976), p. 43.

[327]Under reference to Achterhuis (2011), pp. 177 a.f.

Smith are or are not detailed enough to be considered as an independent economic doctrine on their own.[328]

Whatever the outcome of the (ongoing) discussion (referred to at the previous marg. 129 of this chapter) may be, Adam Smith can at the very least be considered as one of the pioneers of economic theory having clearly elaborated a set of theories about economic processes which were not determined by religious reasoning (unless, as is argued at marg. 148 of this chapter, one would define Smith's own doctrine and the one of his later followers as a religion in themselves); as a result, Smith's theories have over time had a significant impact on the development of capitalist economy (ies), and have, furthermore, undoubtedly contributed to the genesis of economy as an independent science.[329] **130**

As a result, Smith, to a large extent, also contributed to the ever-declining impact of the teachings of the Catholic Church on economic processes and, by extension, on reflecting about such processes. **131**

More than a century earlier, Luther and Calvin had already cleared the path for the rise of an economy less and less impacted by the radical altruism defended in the words of Jesus Christ (see above, under Sect. 3.3.2), however with the application of their doctrine being limited to certain protestant regions.[330]

Smith would complete this process of abandoning altruism as a guiding principle of life by, in contrast to Luther and Calvin, developing a doctrine where there was no longer any attempt at all to make it sound "Christian", but where, on the contrary, the choice of subjugation to "the mammon" (without using the word) was proposed as a new ethical aspiration, ultimately resulting in the aforementioned "greed is good"-principle becoming the new creed in the modern neo-liberal variant of the Smithian doctrine.

This high level of secularization of the message of Smith clearly made it sound very universal which probably helps explaining its global appeal.

Erich Fromm in this regard has pointed out the high level of "caesura" that has manifested in society as a result. In medieval (religious) thinking, wealth was never seen as a purpose in itself, but rather as a means to accomplish one's life goal. The purpose was life itself or, as the Catholic Church had put it, the salvation of man. In this, economic actions, albeit considered "necessary", were to be seen as mere "external activities" which only made sense and only had value to the point where they promoted life and life's aim, namely human salvation.[331]

---

[328]See also Galbraith (1987), p. 62:

> Wealth of nations is a vast, disorderly treatise, rich in amusement and written in admirable prose but, with the Bible and Marx's Capital, one of the three books that the questionably literate feel that they are allowed to cite without having read.

[329]See Stiglitz (2006), p. 68, qualifying the world of Adam Smith as "*mythical*".
See further Polak (1928), p. 237.

[330]Fromm (1990), p. 83 (also: Fromm, p. 62).
See also Bell (1996), pp. 289–290.

[331]Fromm (1990), p. 83 (also: Fromm, pp. 60 a.f.).

Fromm has in this way also pointed out that the perception of economic activity and the pursuit of profit as a target in itself would have been as inappropriate to the medieval thinker as the lack of such a perception would be to the contemporary (neo-)liberal thinker.

According to de Jouvenel, this insight furthermore offers a striking contrast between the clerical intelligentsia of the Middle Ages and the liberal intelligentsia as of the eighteenth century (as revived by modern-day economic neoliberalism). Medieval church thinkers centered their attention and their works on the poor and the unfortunate. The Church was hereby deemed to be the protector of the poor and to perform the functions which, at least in the Western world, after WO II, would devolve on the welfare state: feeding the destitute, healing the sick, educating the general public... All these services were free, provided out of the wealth shunted to the Church through church taxes and huge gifts (often vigorously pressed for). While the Church was forever thrusting the condition of the poor before the eyes of the rich, it was also forever scolding the latter. The rich were not only urged to give, but also urged to desist from their search for ever more wealth.

Still according to de Jouvenel, this negative, albeit somehow ambiguous attitude towards the rich would drastically change after Smith. As a consequence of his works, liberal scholars would take a far more favourable attitude towards worldly riches. The pursuit of wealth became for them even the most noble of undertakings.[332]

In a similar way, Galbraith has argued that, on a broader economic and societal plane, Adam Smith has thus succeeded in identifying the pursuit of economic self-interest with the public good. According to Galbraith, Smith's way of presenting self-interest as a motivating force has thus been one of the most serviceable to advocate industrial power and that no other means of justifying capitalist behaviour has served for such a long time. Henceforth, commercial and industrial people need no longer make offers to explain their selfish motives. On the contrary, virtue is in advance given to any of their actions, however selfish, sordid or inspired by personal greed their motivations and purposes are, by an overriding law of economics to which they are wholly subject (just as all other economic agents).[333]

In other words, the main value reversal caused by Smith has probably been that the pursuit of economic success, material profit and economic activities became targets in themselves. Within such a (new) kind of society, man became bound by a new duty, namely serving to contribute to the growth of the economic system, amongst other things by accumulating capital (for oneself, or in most cases; for the benefit of others, the capitalists). This also implied that man no longer had to aim to improve his own life situation or happiness, but that he only exists to serve an

[332]de Jouvenel (1954), pp. 93–123, especially pp. 106–107.

[333]Galbraith (1983), pp. 112–113.

It goes without much further saying that economic neo-liberalism has picked up on this idea, resulting in the present-day societies where the (intrinsically perverse) idea that the pursuit of selfish motivations equals serving the general good is hardly been questioned anymore.

economic system. This insight is referred to as man being reduced to a symbolic "cog in the capitalist machine".[334]

In the world's happiness report of 2016, it has in this regard (under reference to the works of Alasdair MacIntyre) been pointed out that this approach has in present-day societies resulted in a so-called "emotivist culture". The term "emotivism" hereby refers to the doctrine that all evaluative judgments, and more specifically all moral judgments, are nothing but expressions of preference, expressions of attitude or feeling, insofar as they are moral or evaluative in character. In such an "emotivist culture", it is assumed that, as people cannot agree on values, (individual) rights should have priority over the (common) good and the state must remain neutral about the ends. On a socioeconomic level, this extreme individualistic view on life fits with the character of the "*homo economicus*" who cares only about maximizing his own selfish preferences in the narrowest possible sense, and who is unmotivated by all notions of virtue, values, and purpose, but even so by the interests of others, let alone the common good itself[335]. It also fits with the idea that social relationships become manipulative as people show a preference for extrinsic goods like money, power, and fame over intrinsic goods that are sought for their own sake. This attitude towards life fits with a consumerist mentality without an acquisitive ceiling, where desires can be molded, and where the "goods society" replaces the "good society."[336] It furthermore fits with the reality that public debate is both rancorous and unresolved, obsessed with scandal and celebrity. And it fits with the idea that the dominant ideology of the age is self-absorbed and unreflective libertarianism.

Still according to the same world's happiness report of 2016, a further key trait of this "emotivist culture" is that it separates means from ends, and even turns means into ends. As evidence, the world's happiness report of 2016 invites to consider the premium placed by modern society on "management"—a skill that brackets all questions of purpose and value, and instead focuses exclusively on technical efficiency and effectiveness. According to the report, it is especially this mindset which helps explaining the divorce between ethics and economics. In this view, economics is supposed to be "value-neutral", which has the effect once again of turning means—efficiency, economic growth and the striving for ever more profits even if this requires sacrificing all other values, among which the preservation of society and civilization itself—into ends. In the end, politics too have above

---

[334]Fromm (1990), p. 83 (also: Fromm, pp. 60 a.f.).

Fromm has put is as follows:

> This must not, however, becloud the insight into the fact that twentieth-century as well as nineteenth-century Capitalism is based on the principle that is to be found in all class societies: the use of man by man. (...) The fact remains the same, that a man, a living human being, ceases to be an end in himself, and becomes the means for the economic interests of another man, or himself, or of an impersonal giant, the economic machine. (Fromm 1955, pp. 88–89).

[335]In an extreme version, the idea of the common good is even totally rejected, as had been done in the works of numerous neo-liberal authors, such as Ayn Rand and Milton Friedman.

[336]See Galbraith (1996).

all become about bureaucratic competence rather than about the common good[337] (a fact of which any government aiming at implementing the ideals of economic neo-liberalism bears witness).

132 As is the case with present-day neo-liberal writings, the works of Smith furthermore expressed a high level of distrust towards states to which, for example, the least possible taxes are to be given[338]; Smith himself explicitly expressed the idea that even large infrastructure works should be left to the private initiative (and should therefore not be organized by government, and not even be financed by public funds)[339]. In addition, Smith also formulated the thought that the work of civil servants (in organizing public life) is of no or little value.[340]

These opinions of Smith (which, in the nineteenth century, would, amongst other things, result in the so-called "free trade" movements which advocated the abolishment of toll systems, free competition and, more generally, a limitation of state intervention in economic life[341]), still echo up to the present day in neo-liberal thinking, in the context of which states and governments are generally perceived as a "burden"[342] (which is also expressed in the use of the denigrating word "statism"[343])[344].

This liberal/neo-liberal approach is, furthermore, without any doubt one of the main reasons why rich people and large enterprises have, on a global scale,

---

[337] Sachs et al. (2016), especially pp. 9–10.

[338] Smith (1979), p. 724.

See also Van Houtte (1942), p. 181.

[339] Smith (1979), p. 724.

See also Van Houtte (1942), p. 181.

[340] O'Rourke (2007), p. 73.

[341] Galbraith (1987), pp. 68 a.f.; Van Houtte (1942), pp. 181 a.f.

Galbraith has summarized neo-liberal thinking on the role of states by holding that, in accordance with neoliberal economic doctrine, states are only allowed to participate as follows in economic life: (*i*) by arming themselves (thus: by buying on an as large as possible scale the products of arms manufacturers); (*ii*) by subsidizing the agricultural sector, in addition to certain big enterprises, and (*iii*) by financing the mega *bailouts* of (failing) banks whenever necessary (see Galbraith 1992, p. 45).

[342] Galbraith (1992), p. 25.

[343] Rand (2008), p. 95; Rand (1992), p. 37.

This explains the repulsion neo-liberals feel for both the person and the teachings of Keynes (see Krugman 1994, p. 33).

[344] See also Friedman (1993), p. 18.

Chomsky speaks of the idea of "minimizing the state",

> that is, transferring decision-making power from the public arena to somewhere else: "to the people," in the rhetoric of power; to private tyrannies, in the real world. (See Chomsky 1999, p. 132.)

throughout the ages become more and more tax aversive and evasive[345], which, as they hold the power, in turn has escalated, worldwide, into totally unjust tax systems[346].

The same neo-liberal aversion towards states as a further example also explains the (recent) appeal of so-called "public private financial techniques" whereby the financing of infrastructure works is provided by the private sector which is willing to do so in return for the future income it will generate from exploiting that infrastructure (for example by means of a concession, or similar right). By thus imposing future generations to the cost of actual infrastructure works, public private co-operation techniques can be considered as modern expressions of the "*laissez faire*"-doctrine contained in economic (neo-)liberalism, thus also attributing to making the rich ever more rich to the detriment of the poor.

It therefore does not come as a surprise that, going back to this classical Smithian **133**
aversion towards states and governments, as of the 1980s, neo-liberal doctrine has aimed at reducing, as much as possible, the influence of the state in different areas of the socioeconomic structure, hereby even throwing the social achievements of doctrines such as "Keynesianism", as much as possible, completely over board.[347]

In the United Kingdom, the "Thatcherist" regime in the period 1979–1990[348] has probably been one of the most characteristic examples hereof, having led, amongst others, to a dismantling of different social care mechanisms (see further, under Sect. 3.4.2.3). Regretfully, since then, this example has, on a global scale, been followed by more and more other countries (and even by supra-national entities).

In the wake of these efforts to implement neo-liberal doctrine, the authority of states has world-wide been increasingly usurped by the powers of capitalism which have, for example through the financing of election campaigns[349] (often shaped by the media[350]), acquired a much greater control over the exercise of power than can be deemed legitimate from a democratic point of view (a characteristic of the neo-liberal shaped world which Sachs has described as "*corporate power translate[d] into political power through campaign financing*"[351]).

---

[345]Galbraith (1992), p. 27.

[346]Milton Friedman has further more argued:

> I say that there is a reverse invisible hand: People who intend to serve only the public interest are led by an invisible hand to serve private interest which was no part of their intention. (Friedman 1993, p. 11).

See also Stiglitz (2012), pp. 71–73.

[347]Sterdyniak (2011), pp. 21–42, especially pp. 21 a.f.; Chomsky (1999), p. 132.

[348]Engelen (2011), pp. 22 a.f. See also Chomsky (1999), pp. 66 a.f., identifying Thatcher's Britain as a good choice to illustrate "free market gospel". (Chomsky 1999, p. 67.)

[349]Ronse (1992), pp. 236–237.

[350]Ronse (1992), pp. 68 a.f.; Sachs (2011), pp. 136 a.f.

[351]Sachs (2011), p. 116.

The processes of fiscal policy-making which, for example, have been documented in detail by Oxfam[352] (but also by renowned authors such as Stiglitz and Sachs) and which are mostly initiated by undemocratic methods of "corporatocratic" policy making, are a striking example thereof (see further, at marg. 208 of this chapter) (a characteristic of present-day societies which Sachs has described as "*political power translate[d] into further wealth through tax cuts, deregulation, and sweetheart contracts between government and industry*"[353]).

Sachs mentions four sectors with the largest lobbying power (in the USA, and presumably also in the rest of the word) in this regard: (i) the defence industry[354]; (ii) the financial (services) sector (with as the most striking example the mega bailouts which this sector has obtained after the events of 2008); (iii) the oil industry, and (iv) the health industry (more specifically the large pharmaceutical companies).[355]

This criticism most certainly also applies to the (inherently very technocratic) functioning of the European Union[356], which has in this way been inventing and implementing, without any meaningful input from or consideration for its citizens, processes of so-called "liberalization" for decades. The latter has led to questionable results in several domains of economic life, with as obvious examples the financial sector (see the severe financial crisis of 2008) and the energy sector.[357] It has in this regard also been held, for instance by Stiglitz, that the monetary system of the European Union as such has "*never [been] a very democratic project [as most] of its members' governments did not seek their people's approval to turn over their monetary sovereignty to the ECB.*"[358]

134 Otherwise stated, Smith (and his later disciples) have succeeded in increasingly undermining clerical-religious authority (which was one of the dominant powers in the Middle Ages) and usurping governmental authority (which had mainly grown more important in the New Times[359]).

---

352 See especially Oxfam (2014).

353 Sachs (2011), pp. 116–117. See also Streeck (2015), p. 87.

354 See especially Stiglitz and Bilmes (2008), p. 357.

355 Sachs (2011), pp. 117–118.

356 Ash (1999), p. 367.

357 Menasse (2012), p. 82.

358 Stiglitz (2015).

See furthermore Todd (2015), p. 50 (also: Todd 2015, p. 45), having qualified the European project as a "foolish" one and as an "economic failure". Further in his book (p. 57), the author has even referred to the installation of the euro as to the poisoning of democracy:

> Le franc fort, la marche à l'euro, l'euro realise, n'en finissent pas de torturer le corps social, de gangréner la démocratie.

See also Pironet (2014), p. 3.

359 Mackenzie (2014), pp. 55–65.

In the course of the nineteenth century, the void created in this way has been filled by "large capital", which contributed to shaping a world dominated by the invisible powers of transnational and multinational corporations of all kinds.

Furthermore, an ever increasingly close association developed between those who founded and ran the large commercial and industrial enterprises and the banking and financial sector who supplied them with money for the creation or, in some periods more often, the acquisition and restructuring of those enterprises.[360]

Without considering the impact of their behaviour on the rest of mankind, large enterprises have thus gradually subordinated the ins and outs of economy (including social relations), but also the state power to organize society (ies), to the ever increasing greed of their CEOs and underlying capital providers.

In recent literature, an appropriate term has been introduced for this in literature, the so-called "Corporatocracy", which Jeffrey Sachs, in his book "*The Price of Civilization: Reawakening American Virtue and Prosperity*"[361], has defined as the government system where powerful lobby groups from the private corporate sector dominate the political agenda.[362] Similarly, Sam Pizzigati speaks of "*a government that works only for the wealthy few*", further described by this author as a textbook definition of plutocracy.[363]

Further Illustration 3.7: Alien Et Seq

In recent times, many art forms (such as literature[364] and film[365]) have tried to forecast the outlook of future societies dealing with (and suffering from) the tyranny of a corporatist, or even corporatocratic, regime where no longer democratically elected governments are in power, but the executives of large enterprises. These future societies are in some cases characterized by a disproportionate barbarism which the respective writers and movie makers

(continued)

[360]Galbraith (1983), p. 114.

[361]Sachs (2011), p. 325.

[362]See also Krugman (2008), p. 166.

[363]Pizzigati (2012), p. 325.

[364]See *e.g.* the novel "*Jennifer Government*" of Max Barry, often mentioned in one breath with "*1984*" by George Orwell and "*Brave New World*" by Aldous Huxley.

Max Barry has summarized the theme of his novel as follows:

> The world is run by American corporations; there are no taxes; employees take the last names of the companies they work for; the Police and the NRA are publicly-traded security firms; the government can only investigate crimes it can bill for. (see Barry s.d.).

[365]See *e.g.* the movies "*Blade Runner*" (1982) and "*RoboCop*" (1987), the film series "*Resident evil*" (2002–2012), as well as the Canadian tv-series "*Continuum*" (2012–present). More recent, one can also point out the movie "*Elysium*" (2013).

Further Illustration 3.7 (continued)

seem to believe may be the result of the future continuation of the underlying principles of "economic neo-liberalism".

A perhaps surprising example of this type of movies are the four main movies from the famous "Alien"-cycle, more specifically (the unrivalled) "Alien" (1979) by Ridley Scott, "Aliens" (1986) by James Cameron, "Alien 3" (1993) by David Fincher and "Alien Resurrection" (1997) by Jean-Pierre Jeunet.

In this movie cycle, especially starting from the second movie "Aliens", its leading character Ripley (who in the last-mentioned movie "Alien Resurrection" was even raised from the dead, as she dies dramatically in "Alien 3" but, through cloning technology, is revived at least as a clone in order to serve as the protagonist of this fourth movie of the cycle)—performed by Sigourney Weavor—is fighting a double battle. *On one hand*, she is fighting the known Alien(s) themselves, but, *on the other hand*, she is also fighting the destructive powers of the (actually fictitious) "Weyland-Yutani" corporation which even sees an opportunity for commercial profit in the indestructible nature of the Aliens. Throughout the movies, the corporation attempts to catch such an alien at any price (including the loss of countless human beings) in order to exploit it in a commercial way. In "Alien Resurrection", "United Systems Military"—whereby it is not entirely clear to what extent this is a successor of the "Weyland-Yutani" corporation itself, both companies being of the same kind—even launches a breeding programme, with disastrous results.

Watching these movies closely, one will have the impression to what extent it expresses a parody of the indestructible powers of the corporate pursuit of money—and consequently of neo-liberal capitalism itself.

135 Notwithstanding the foregoing, probably one of the main revolutionary strength of the works of Smith is mostly to be found in the fundamental turnaround of the ethical perception of the economic processes they have caused.

In the Middle Ages, rich merchants and bankers, on the authority of the "Holy Scripture"[366] itself[367], were still facing suspicious looks, as their wealth did not find (complete) mercy in the clerical (Catholic) doctrine, and thus in God's own eyes.

On the contrary, in the doctrine of Smith, these same merchants and bankers were suddenly granted the status of the most beneficent and driving forces within society.[368]

---

[366]But also on the authority of church elders who had dedicated themselves to its study, and of several Saints who had claimed to live according to the values of poverty and charity according to the Gospel.

[367]Galbraith (1987), p. 64; Dowley (2009), p. 31.

[368]Galbraith (1987), p. 64.

As a result, according to Galbraith, the ongoing success of Smith's ideas throughout the ages can mainly be attributed to their support of the activities, motivations and working methods of the rich and powerful within society.[369]

Most probably, this turnaround of the ethical perception of the unlimited pursuit of wealth from "virtueless" (according to Aristotle) or "sinful" (according to the medieval Catholic church) to "benevolent" or "salutary" (according to Smith and the neo-liberals), has been the most significant impact of Smithian doctrine on society, because it cleared the way for a selfish economy as it prevails today (and more specifically since the influences of economic neo-liberalism which has further extrapolated the concepts of Smith).[370]

In modern times, Smithian doctrine holding that merchants and the likes are to **136**
be considered as the most benevolent force bringing prosperity to the whole of society has, *inter alia*, been translated into the so-called "genius principle", described by Galbraith as the virtually blind adoration present-day society has for the exceptional abilities of for example CEOs (of large enterprises) who are believed to have exceptional talents of leadership and entrepreneurship.

This attitude is presently mainly found as regards CEOs of large enterprises who first succeed in admiring themselves as genial superbeings, and later on are able to convince a large enough part of society that such blind admiration is well deserved. Hence, this genius principle provides for example the foundation for the paramount differences in wages between, *on one hand*, a CEO, and, possibly, other members of the senior management of any large enterprise and, *on the other hand,* the rest of the workers such enterprise employs. It has to be remarked that this genius principle also has played a major role as one of the causes of the severe financial crisis of 2008 (see further, at marg. 224 and 231 of this chapter).[371]

3.4.2.1.2.4 Certain Other Liberal Economists

In addition to the writings of Adam Smith, those of David Ricardo (1772–1823) **137**
also played an important role in the rise of the capitalist economy.[372]

In "*The principles of political economy and taxation*" (1817)[373], Ricardo worked out a model to explain international trade by means of the theory of "comparative

---

[369]Galbraith (1983), p. 113.

[370]See Galbraith (1987), pp. 64–65:

> As the voice of Physiocracy still rings forth when farmers come together, so the beneficent self-regard of the butcher, brewer or baker and the benign guidance of the invisible hand live again when members of the United States Chamber of Commerce, the Business Roundtable or, as this is written, the Cabinet of President Ronald Reagan gather for mutual reinforcement, rhetorical and oratorical rejuvenation and the consideration of public policy and action.

[371]Galbraith (1987), p. 64.

[372]See also Galbraith (1987), pp. 74 a.f.

[373]Ricardo (1957), p. 300.

advantages". According to this doctrine, a country will always profit from specialization; for this reason, it is important for any economy to focus on creating products which it specializes in and trading these to other economies.[374]

Furthermore, Ricardo investigated the relation between the size of "wages" as a part of the cost price of a product, and the ultimate price of such a product. His findings still form the foundation for the capitalist pursuit of keeping wages for labor within restricted limits (= the so-called "*Iron Law of Wages*"[375]), in order for the return on capital investments to be maximized, an approach which, in extreme contexts, has led to systems of real slavery (as, for instance, applied in the American economy for a long period of time).[376]

Finally, Ricardo was also an important advocate of free trade.

138 The aforementioned classical pair of British economists can be completed with the names of Thomas Malthus (1766–1834) and John Stuart Mill (1806–1873).

In "*An Essay on the Principle of Population*" (1798), Malthus stated the idea that the growth of population will always be ahead of economic growth. In this doctrine, it is held that population growth is "exponential", while economic growth, more specifically food production, is believed to be "linear" (which, *inter alia*, results in the so-called "Malthusian ceiling" of maximum population growth within a given territory). Given the fact that "natural restrictions" of population growth (such as war, disease, and similar) do not form a sufficient compensation mechanism, Malthus saw "moral restraint" (more precisely refraining from reproduction) as the only solution for the threat of over-population.[377]

With some irony, Galbraith has consistently highlighted the practical method which Malthus had proposed to turn "moral restraint" into practice, namely that, during wedding ceremonies, priests should warn about the consequences of too frequent sexual intercourse.[378]

John Stuart Mill furthermore highlighted the interconnectedness of the economic theories with the importance of individual (private) property and (individual) liberties.[379]

---

[374] Galbraith (1987), p. 81; Galbraith (1977), p. 32; Berend (2006), p. 14; Vandewalle (1976), p. 58; Polak (1928), pp. 270 a.f.

[375] Allegedly thus named by Ferdinand Lassalle (1825–1864).

[376] Galbraith (1983), p. 116; Polak (1928), p. 272; Gide and Rist (1947), pp. 135 a.f.
See also Galbraith (1987), p. 84, having argued that:

> (t)his thought, as the Iron Law of the Wages, was to enter into a history extending far beyond formal economics; it established that those who worked were meant to be poor and were not to be rescued from their poverty by a compassionate state or employer or through trade unions or by other action of their own.

[377] Malthus (1968), p. 446.
See further Galbraith (1987), p. 77; Galbraith (1977), p. 32; Vandewalle (1976), p. 56; Bernstein (2004), p. 13; Graff et al. (2014), p. 31; Polak (1928), p. 256; Gide and Rist (1947), pp. 131 a.f.

[378] Galbraith (1992), p. 79.

[379] Berend (2006), p. 14; Vandewalle (1976), p. 76.

The importance Mill paid to "freedom" and "property rights" is still strongly emphasized in the writings of many neo-liberal authors (see for instance in "*The Virtue of Selfishness*" by Ayn Rand).

Mill was also one of the first authors to analyse the phenomenon of (financial) crises. Remarkably, he mainly asserts speculative behaviour and a wrong (unbridled) private banking credit policy[380] to be the main cause thereof.[381]

3.4.2.1.2.5 Further Impact of the School of "Economic Liberalism"

Thanks to the writings of (early) liberal economists such as Smith, Ricardo, Malthus and Stuart Mill, in addition to others here not further referred to, the ideological foundation was laid for the development of capitalism[382] "pur sang" (as an economic system freed from any ethical boundaries), whereby all other values systematically got sacrificed to the individual pursuit of wealth and money (hence the comparison with the adoration of the metaphorical "golden calf" referred to in the Book of Exodus from the Bible (see Exodus, 32–35)). **139**

As a result, during the nineteenth century, the world economy got gradually dominated by the ideas of "economic liberalism", which, mainly in the United Kingdom (the main economic power at that time) and later in the United States of America met extremely strong support[383], although in the twentieth century a temporary turnaround would take place, *inter alia* thanks to economists such as Marx (in a radical way) and Keynes (in a more moderate way).[384]

---

[380]Vandewalle (1976), p. 78; Gide and Rist (1947), pp. 390 a.f.

[381]Furthermore Galbraith (1975), pp. 20 a.f.

[382]Berend (2006), p. 15; Graff, Kenwood and Lougheed (2014), p. 35; Chomsky (1999), pp. 25 a.f.

As mentioned before, Chomsky has in this regard argued that capitalism is based on (the) bad ideas (of Adam Smith) which flourish because they are in the interest of powerful groups (Chomsky 1999, p. 25).

[383]Vandewalle (1976), p. 55, pointing out that in some countries doctrines emerged which resisted "(economic) liberalism", such as, in France, "utopian socialism" (see further Vandewalle 1976, pp. 65 a.f.).

[384]As has thoroughly been argued in Chap. 2 of this book and as cannot be stressed enough, it is hereby to be noted that the industrial revolution of the nineteenth century was preceded by the financial revolution which already started at the end of the seventeenth century and which has made the industrial revolution possible. As a result, up to the present day, "capitalism"—or in present-day terms: the "free market-economy"—is basically a privately created money driven economy.

The latter will further be addressed under Sect. 3.4.2.2 and under Sect. 3.4.5.

See also Ferguson (2009), pp. 53–54, quoting Smith who described the judicious operation of banking, by substituting paper in the room of a great part of gold and silver as a "wagon-way" through the air.

Further Illustration 3.8: Smith Versus Dickens, Wilde, Stowe and Douwes Dekker

It is not a coincidence that in the nineteenth century, especially in the United Kingdom where capitalism was most successful (but also in other countries, such as the United States of America and The Netherlands) important (literal) authors have, in their time, indicted the "excesses" of the capitalist model.

In so doing they were, so to speak, providing a cultural antidote for the cold selfishness advocated by early economists.

Not coincidentally, the neo-liberal author Ayn Rand has herself seen the necessity to rage against these literary giants.[385]

Obviously there are the wonderful novels of Charles Dickens (1812–1870) often developing characters representing a parody to capitalist thinking.[386]

From the numerous examples, we can call to mind Ebenezer Scrooge from Dickens' "*A Christmas Carol*", the prototype of the perfect Smithian egoist whose story is since then brought to us almost every year around Christmas, almost as an ironic reminder to the fact that society could also have been based upon a thought system totally opposed to Smithian thinking, namely the teachings of Christ Himself. Famous is the reply Scrooge made when asked to give a donation to charity, namely that he pays enough taxes to finance, amongst others, prisons, and working houses for the poor: ***"Since you ask me what I wish, gentlemen, that is my answer. I don't make merry myself at Christmas, and I can't afford to make idle people merry. I help to support the establishments I have mentioned – they cost enough; and those who are badly off must go there."***

A similar literary masterpiece (however, less known) denouncing the capitalist production processes is the fairy tale "*The Young King*" by another giant of English literature, namely Oscar Wilde (1854–1900).

In said fairy tale, a dream makes a young crown prince aware of the distressing situations caused by capitalist production processes. As a result, on his coronation day, the young prince refuses to wear the royal robes and garments which are a result of these capitalist production methods: ***"Take these things away, and hide them from me. Though it be the day of my coronation, I will not wear them. For on the loom of Sorrow, and by the white hands of Pain, has this my robe been woven. There is Blood in the heart of the ruby, and Death in the heart of the pearl."*** Instead, he shows up to his coronation ceremony dressed as a simple shepherd (***"he opened a great painted chest, and from it he took the leathern tunic and rough sheepskin cloak that he had worn when he had watched on the hillside the shaggy***

(continued)

[385]Rand (2008), p. 118.

[386]Sullivan (2010), p. 92.

Further Illustration 3.8 (continued)

goats of the goatherd. These he put on, and in his hand he took his rude shepherd's staff").

Arriving in this humble outfit at his coronation ceremony, he is severely criticized by some representatives of the (capitalist) community, not in the least the bishop leading the coronation ceremony, until at the end of the story, when the reason why the young crown prince decided to dress as he did, is revealed:

> And lo! through the painted windows came the sunlight streaming upon him, and the sunbeams wove round him a tissued robe that was fairer than the robe that had been fashioned for his pleasure. The dead staff blossomed, and bare lilies that were whiter than pearls. The dry thorn blossomed, and bare roses that were redder than rubies. Whiter than fine pearls were the lilies, and their stems were of bright silver. Redder than male rubies were the roses, and their leaves were of beaten gold.
>
> He stood there in the raiment of a king, and the gates of the jewelled shrine flew open, and from the crystal of the many-rayed monstrance shone a marvellous and mystical light. He stood there in a king's raiment, and the Glory of God filled the place, and the saints in their carven niches seemed to move. In the fair raiment of a king he stood before them, and the organ pealed out its music, and the trumpeters blew upon their trumpets, and the singing boys sang.
>
> And the people fell upon their knees in awe, and the nobles sheathed their swords and did homage, and the Bishop's face grew pale, and his hands trembled. 'A greater than I hath crowned thee,' he cried, and he knelt before him.
>
> And the young King came down from the high altar, and passed home through the midst of the people. But no man dared look upon his face, for it was like the face of an angel.

From the richness of American literature, the (timeless) masterpiece "*Uncle Tom's Cabin*" by Harriet Beecher Stowe (1811–1896) stands out, an unforgettable indictment of American slavery, but on the other hand also a plea for its abolishment. In writing "*Uncle Tom's Cabin*", its author showcased herself as a so-called "abolitionist". This caused the novel to appear as a series in 1851 and 1852 in the abolitionist paper the "National Era". Since then, the novel has again and again been (re)published (and translated in many other languages, making it a worldwide bestseller). The book mainly tells the story of the (dramatic) fate of a number of slaves on a plantation in the American State of Kentucky (starring the unforgettable Eliza Harris and, of course, Uncle Tom himself).[387]

(continued)

[387] https://en.wikipedia.org/wiki/Uncle_Tom.

Further Illustration 3.8 (continued)

At a certain point in history, The Netherlands were also a large capitalist colonial power. This led to a literary masterpiece in the Dutch language which indicted the nineteenth century capitalism that arose from colonialism, namely the Novel "*Max Havelaar of De koffieveilingen der Nederlandse Handelmaatschappij*"[388] by Eduard Douwes Dekker (1820–1887)[389], the latter being generally known under his alias "Multatuli".

Through this novel (and through the rest of his works), Multatuli profiled himself as a representative of physical scientific rationalism and of modern self-consciousness, to which he added a new dimension, namely that of a social engagement of a humanist seeking greater justice.[390]

The novel "*Max Havelaar*" is to some extent autobiographical, but also apologetic[391], and is an indictment of the colonial abuses in Dutch India (Java), which Eduard Douwes Dekker had witnessed himself and against which he had taken action in vain (among which practices whereby the local population of Lebak was forced by native chiefs to supply cattle and labor without receiving any payment in return).

That literature can indeed have a large social impact can be illustrated by the fact that the novel "*Max Havelaar*" made such an impression on the Dutch middle classes (up to that point not knowing more about India than that it was the country of "surplus balances") that it generated a movement striving for social reform. Ultimately, this caused the second ministry Horbecke to adopt major changes in Indian law in the period 1863–1866.[392]

The reason why coffee production and trade play a central role in the novel is that, based on the so-called "Cultural doctrine", the local population of Java was forced to organize itself in such a way that one fifth of the land was reserved for growing products for the European market to be exported to Europe by the "Dutch Trade Organization", such as coffee, sugar, tea and tobacco. The trade in coffee in particular generated huge profits at that time due to the fact that the end prices to be paid by consumers were kept at a very high level[393] (as is at present still the case).

The brilliant well-known story of "*Saïdja and Adinda*"[394] (a part of the novel "*Max Havelaar*" which also stands on its own) is in principle an

(continued)

[388] Spigt, pp. 69–84.

[389] See Spigt, pp. 69–84.

[390] Spigt, pp. 69–84, especially p. 77.

[391] Stapert-Eggen (1981), pp. 5–6.

[392] Van Houtte (1955), p. 248.

[393] Stapert-Eggen (1981), p. 6; Van Houtte (1955), p. 248.

[394] See in the edition Havelaar (1981), pp. 205–222.

Further Illustration 3.8 (continued)

indictment of the abuse of authority towards the population of a colonial region. Another brilliant short story contained in the novel is that of "*The Japanese Stone Cutter*", bearing a wisdom which encourages an attitude of contentment, rather than the pursuit of trying to fulfil ever-changing desires in the hope of accomplishing a better life situation. This short story which is a masterpiece of Dutch literature in its own right can, in terms of content, be placed in addition to the novel "*Siddhartha*" by Hermann Hesse (1877–1962), Nobel prize winner for Literature in 1946. The inspiration in both stories undoubtedly stems from Buddhist doctrines.

It is, however, especially the figure of coffee broker Batavus Droogstoppel[395] (who, to some extent, could be considered as the Dutch counterpart of Dickens' Scrooge) which forms an immortal caricature of the Dutch Calvinist entrepreneur scene. Throughout the novel, this character who mainly comments on the report of the events that took place in Dutch India as brought to us by Max Havelaar himself, is driven by a naive pedantic and devout (Smithian) self-interest, half naive, half cunning, but in the end indeed "knowingly" contributing to the prevailing colonial capitalist system of oppression and exploitation, while at the same time cultivating a distorted view of what is happening on the other side of the world[396].

3.4.2.2 Corrections to and a Critical Reflection on Capitalism After WW II

3.4.2.2.1 Legislation Shaping the Welfare State

In the course of the twentieth century, many Western countries aimed for a number 140
of corrections to the unbridled functioning of "pure sang" capitalism.[397]

These efforts would especially take place starting with (and in response to) the severe economic crisis at the end of the 1920s—beginning of the 1930s[398] and were brought along due to the impact of certain pressure groups (such as trade unions[399]), as well as to new ideologies, such as socialism, and new doctrines in economic

[395] Stapert-Eggen (1981), p. 6.

[396] See http://nl.wikipedia.org/wiki/Eduard_Douwes_Dekker (last consulted on November 8th 2014); Stapert-Eggen (1981), pp. 5–6.

[397] As this, to a large extent under the influence of "economic liberalism", had emerged in the eighteenth and nineteenth century.

[398] Galbraith (1987), p. 210.

[399] Turner (1973), pp. 101 a.f.; Simonet (1970), p. 41.

thinking (for instance "Keynesianism"[400]), all setting the scene for macroeconomic policy making.[401]

According to certain authors, the changes were also made out of fear of communism[402] and under pressure of the cold war.[403]

The Belgian philosopher Jaap Kruithof has argued that this evolution of correcting capitalism already came to an end in the 1970s.[404]

As a result of the abovementioned influences, over the years, in many countries a mixture of different protective legislations emerged, characterized by different accents in different countries, which were, *inter alia*, aimed at protecting certain other values (than the pursuit of money) against the impact of "pure sang" capitalism.

For several Western countries, this led to an implementation of the "welfare state"-model (at an economic level, often resulting in a so-called "mixed economy"[405]).

Some obvious examples of such protective legislation are:

- The emergence of an anti-trust or competition law aiming at enabling a minimum level of competition (thus limiting the creation of monopolies or oligopolies);
- Labor law (especially aimed at protecting those who provide their labor to the market);
- The further development, especially since the 1950s, of a social security system (especially in Western European countries) as one of the main foundations of the modern (at the time) welfare state[406];
- The setup of public education systems;
- The enactment of legislation on environmental protection;
- The enactment of different (other) legislation for the protection of public health;
- Energy law (which however in the contemporary context, especially in the European Union, to a large extent became mainly aimed at implementing the neo-liberal principles themselves, rather than at the protection of energy consumers or of the environment);

---

[400]See especially Keynes (1935). See also Skidelsky (2010), especially pp. 55 a.f.

See furthermore Galbraith (1974); Galbraith (1975), pp. 216 a.f.; Hickson (2005), p. 35; Berend (2006), pp. 42 a.f.; see also Kruithof (2000), p. 55; Eagleton and Williams (2007), p. 236.

[401]Vandewalle (1976), p. 249.

[402]Harari (2014), pp. 347 a.f. See also Berend (2006), pp. 133 a.f.

[403]See Stiglitz (2010), p. 197. See also Berend (2006), p. 233:

> One of the most effective driving forces, however, was the emerging cold war end the competition between capitalism and socialism. It was a complex confrontation, with a sharp arms race and space race, but with an equally sharp growth race and welfare race.

[404]Kruithof (2000), p. 55. Compare Pizzigati (2012), p. 315.

[405]Baeck (1972), pp. 81 a.f.; see also Eyskens (1976).

[406]Berend (2006), p. 233.

- The enactment of legislation regarding the access to information, data protection and the protection of privacy;
- ...

For the sake of completeness, it should be noted that, besides legislation aimed at protecting values other than the pursuit of money from the disastrous powers of capitalism, especially since the 1980s, also much legislation emerged aimed precisely at supporting capitalism, among which legislation on "intellectual rights"[407], as well as most legislation of the past decades aiming at "liberalizing" or "deregulating" markets.[408]

Despite such "corrective legislation", when considering the evolution of Western economies during the nineteenth century and the twentieth century, the basic assumption of capitalism that the unbridled pursuit of personal wealth which every individual is allowed to (and, under liberal and neo-liberal economic doctrines, preferably also should) surrender to, would hardly be questioned anymore in Western (and Western-inspired) countries[409], albeit thanks to the mentioned corrective legislation, capitalism temporarily became a little more "humane"[410]. **141**

One of the main consequences of the increasing globalization of the world economy having occurred during the past decades, has however been that, worldwide, this type of "corrective legislation" has come under strong pressure.[411] **142**

This has mainly been caused by the increased mobility of capital as an economic production factor, which enables large enterprises to move production units (but for instance also "service centres") in a reasonably simple way to other countries, especially to countries where the "obstacles" caused by legislation aimed at protecting other values than the unbridled pursuit of money are at their lowest (a phenomenon which can be described as "*a race to the bottom*").[412]

Some of these consequences of capitalism will be addressed in more detail later in the text (see further, under Sect. 3.4.3).

---

[407]Kruithof (2000), p. 47.

[408]Compare Stiglitz (2006), p. 78.

[409]Berend (2006), pp. 133–189; Vandewalle (1976), pp. 97 a.f.

[410]Berend (2006), p. 233; Servain-Schreiber (1973), pp. 235 a.f.

[411]Engelen (2011), p. 49; Sterdyniak (2011), pp. 21–42, especially pp. 27 a.f.; Harvey (2010), p. 131.

[412]Kruithof (2000), p. 57.

3.4.2.2.2 Critical Voices of the 1970s

143 The severe economic crisis of the 1970s (as, *inter alia*, catalysed by a sudden increase[413] in the price of certain resources, especially crude oil[414]) created some room for further reflection and for critical views on the classical Smithian doctrines.[415]

Initially mainly young people started protesting against the excesses of the capitalist society which they considered too materialistic.[416] Also, certain academics took a more critical attitude towards capitalism, followed by numerous other people who were willing to reflect more deeply on the future of the planet in general, and of the human race in particular.

This even led to "think tanks" which, amongst other things, pointed out the incompatibility of an unbridled pursuit of ever more wealth (and the unbridled economic growth it requires) with the (natural) limits of the resources of the planet. Such thinks tanks strongly warned about the effects of an economic system solely based on a unitary value (namely the unbridled pursuit of money) on general human welfare[417].

Furthermore, a stronger awareness arose about the relationship between the North and the South, as one of the effects of capitalism is (has been) that it led to an ever-increasing structural poverty in many (Southern) countries (see further, under Sect. 3.4.8).

All of these influences caused a greater awareness about the importance of other values, such as the protection of the environment and the protection of minorities (for instance immigrants)[418], albeit one could point out that this greater awareness has to a large extent remained theoretical and so far has not had a fundamental impact on the basic organization of the world economy itself.

144 A leading illustration of the abovementioned has without any doubt been the creation of the renowned (and still active) think tank "(the) Club of Rome".[419]

Founded in 1968 as an informal association of independent executives from political life, corporations and science, the Club of Rome still exist, up until today,

[413]This itself has been a process which fully takes into account the capitalist thinking of the (residents of the) petroleum producing countries, namely their own unbridled money pursuit, and not the interests of mankind as a whole. Surprisingly, traditional capitalist countries (among which the Northern American and West European countries) have been witnessed to criticize the rise of oil prices, albeit such rise has been fully in line with the premises of capitalist thinking itself.

[414]Poma (1976), pp. 23 a.f.

[415]Hoefnagels (1975), pp. 11 a.f.; Turner (1973), pp. 161 a.f.

[416]Servain-Schreiber (1973), p. 55.

[417]Johnson (2014), pp. 79–103; Hoefnagels (1975), p. 12.

[418]Krugman (2008), p. 133; see also Hoefnagels (1975), p. 16.

[419]www.clubofrome.org

as a think tank that, from a holistic view on the world, strives for a higher and sustainable well-being of the planet and mankind.[420]

Also worth mentioning has been the establishment of "Greenpeace" (1971), "*one of the largest and most well-known environmental organizations in the world which is globally and in an independent way, campaigning to change attitudes and actions and to protect the environment and promote peace*".[421]

3.4.2.3 Economic Neo-liberalism

3.4.2.3.1 The "Philosophy" of Economic Neo-liberalism

In spite of the merits of the initiatives mentioned under Sect. 3.4.2.2, and in spite of **145** the efforts of numerous renowned economists[422], philosophers[423] and "religious" ethicists[424] (see also under Sect. 3.6), who all have, at the least, called for a reduction of certain of the detrimental effects of capitalism, they would, neither nationally, nor internationally have a significant impact on the policies of (Western and Western-inspired) capitalist countries, and they certainly did not succeed in limiting the dominance of the unbridled pursuit of money on which these have remained based.

On the contrary, especially during the last decades of the twentieth century, any form of willingness towards a more critical self-reflection about the capitalist economic systems would encounter, in the neo-liberal doctrine(s), an academic, economic-philosophical and above all policy-making opponent without parallel.[425]

The main philosophy which aimed at silencing any criticism of capitalism has **146** indeed been so-called "(economic) neo-liberalism", which, especially since the 1980s (although the foundation for the neo-liberal philosophy was already built

[420]The website of the Club of Rome mentions the following mission statement:

> to identify the most crucial problems which will determine the future of humanity through integrated and forward-looking analysis; to evaluate alternative scenarios for the future and to assess risks, choices and opportunities; to develop and propose practical solutions to the challenges identified; to communicate the new insights and knowledge derived from this analysis to decision-makers in the public and private sectors and also to the general public and to stimulate public debate and effective action to improve the prospects for the future (see http://www.clubofrome.org/?p=324; last consulted on September 15th 2014).

[421]http://www.greenpeace.org/belgium/nl/wie-zijn-we/geschiedenis/ (last consulted on October 29th 2014).

[422]For instance, besides Keynes himself, one should mention John Kenneth Galbraith and, more recently, Paul Krugman and Joseph Stiglitz.

[423]For instance, in Belgium Jaap Kruithof, and in France Emmanuel Levinas and Michel Foucault.

[424]Among which the different consecutive popes, in addition to religious leaders of other spiritual traditions, such as, for instance, the (deceased) Hinduistic leader A. C. Bhaktivedanta Swami Prabhupada and the Buddhist leader the Dalai Lama.

[425]Les Économistes atterés (2011), p. 27. See also Streeck (2015), p. 92.

before), succeeded in convincing a great deal of public leaders, in addition to a large part of public opinion, that capitalism (since then usually referred to as "the free market(s)-system") should function as unhindered by state or other influences as possible.

As already mentioned before, an extreme example of this neo-liberal philosophy can be found in the writings of Ayn Rand, author of, *inter alia*, the novel "*Atlas shrugged*", but who also wrote non-fiction and whose works "*The Virtue of Selfishness*"[426] and "*Capitalism: the unknown ideal*"[427], from the 1960s on, have attempted (and, to a large extent, succeeded) at raising the worship of selfishness to an ethical system. In this way, the works of Rand strongly contributed to a turnaround in the value perception which presently rules economic thinking and acting, but to a large extent also general societal functioning.[428]

In this neo-liberal setup, "selfishness" was elevated to the leading moral objective, while at the same time altruism (which, until the late Middle Ages and especially under the influence of Catholic doctrine, had at least on a theoretical level been the dominant moral value) got degraded to a morally condemnable behaviour (as is clearly demonstrated by the content, but even by the mere title of Rand's book "*The virtue of selfishness*").[429]

---

[426]Rand (1992).

[427]Rand (2008); Rand (1982), pp. 27 a.f., where Rand has argued that altruism serves as a tool for the rationalization of all kinds of abuses, going from mass slaughters in Sovjet Russia to legalized looting in the welfare state.

[428]See *e.g.* Rand (1982), p. 27, where Rand has a.o. criticized what she calls "legalized looting in the welfare state", and Rand (1982), p. 83, where she has described altruism as the poison of death in the blood of western civilization.

As has been mentioned before, Ayn Rand did however not succeed at upholding the moral standards she had set out in her own writings. When near the end of her life, Ayn Rand got struck by cancer (purportedly) due to the fact that she was a heavy smoker throughout her life, (purportedly) under the name of Ann O'Connor, she did not hesitate for a moment to make use of these "useless" public health care systems, thus in her proper actions completely denouncing the content of the teachings she had spread during her life time (see Ford 2010–2011). As Michael Ford has put it:

> In the end, Miss Rand was a hypocrite but she could never be faulted for failing to act in her own self-interest. (Ford 2010–2011).

[429]An example of the impact of neo-liberal philosophy on economy has been the fact that the writings of Ayn Rand are believed to have strongly influenced numerous American policy makers, such as Alan Greenspan, former president of the American "Federal Reserve" with the longest period in office (see further, at marg. 147 of this chapter). (On the influence Ayn Rand had on Greenspan, but for instance also on former President Ronald Reagan; see Ricard 2014, p. 382.)

Greenspan's monetary policy (and consequently the monetary climate he created of "too-easy money creation" based on "too-easy credit lending") was strongly influenced by neo-liberal authors the likes of Rand herself, and in this sense has undoubtedly contributed to the severe financial-economic crisis of 2008. (See Krugman 2009, p. 144, who held: "***And in fact, the Fed chairman holds what I believe is a unique record among central bankers: he presided over not one but two enormous asset bubbles, first in stocks, then in housing.***" See further also Szalavitz 2012, who has pointed out that "***Atlas Shrugged counts many politicians as admirers, perhaps***

In addition, famous academic institutions, such as "*F. A. Hayek's Mont Pelerin Society*"[430], and later the "*Chicago School of Economics*"[431] established by Frank Knight (1885–1972), helped substantively shaping neo-liberal economic thinking and, moreover, succeeded in convincing an important group of economists (with, as the name suggests, a strong concentration at the University of Chicago's faculty of economy).

Amongst other things, neo-liberal thinking strongly opposed to Keynesian philosophy (but obviously also the writings of Galbraith), and above all presented itself as the advocate of the free market economy[432], extrapolating classical Smithian philosophy up to the level of practically all domains of macro-economy and societal organization.[433] **147**

A number of concrete measures the neo-liberal schools promoted (which have been implemented in the 1980s and 1990s, and later on up to the present day, by numerous neo-liberal governments), were, amongst others: the privatization of government-owned companies[434]; the deregulation of the economy[435]; the de-liberalization of trade and industry[436]; significant tax reductions favouring the rich and the powerful, in addition to the enterprises these owned; monetarist measures aimed at combatting inflation (even if they cause an increase in unemployment); strong union regulation; a reduction in public spending (including spending on social services); a reduction in the overall role of the government; an expansion of the role of international markets, and the elimination of any true monitoring of global money and capital streams.[437]

---

most notably Republican vice presidential candidate, Paul Ryan, who cites the book as one of his main inspirations for entering politics and is known to give Rand's books frequently to his interns.") On the influence of Rand on Ryan, see also Ricard (2014), p. 382.

Apparently, Ms. Rand was well aware of her influence of numerous (American) policy makers, where she for instance, spoke of the three "A's" having determined the history of Philosophy, namely Aristotle, Saint Augustine and herself... (see Ricard 2014, p. 382).

See further also Morris (2009), pp. 77 a.f.

[430]https://www.montpelerin.org/montpelerin/mpsHayek.html (last consulted on October 29th 2014).

See especially Hayek (2001) (the first edition being of 1944).

[431]See *e.g.* Friedman and Schwartz (1963), p. 860; Stigler (1961), pp. 213–225; Becker (1971), p. 178; Coase (1937), pp. 386–405; Posner (1973), p. 415.

[432]Krugman (1994), pp. 23 a.f., referring to "*the attack on Keynes*".

See also Rand (2008), p. 18.

[433]See Clune (2013); Chomsky (1999), pp. 37 a.f.

[434]Bakan (2005), p. 117.

Compare Oxfam (2014), p. 18.

[435]Krugman (2009), p. 65.

[436]Oxfam (2014), p. 55.

[437]Steger (2013), p. 42; Sterdyniak (2011), pp. 21–42, especially 28; Kruithof (2000), pp. 57 a.f.

It is hereby important to note the central focus the "Chicago School" (and similar economic theories) attributed to so-called "monetarism", *inter alia* through the works of Milton Friedman (1912–2006)[438] and Don Patinkin (1922–1995)[439] which emphasized the role of the money and capital markets in economic life. Among other things, they considered central banking as a steering mechanism within the monetary economy which should conduct a policy aimed at keeping the money supply in line with economic growth.[440] Especially as of the 1990s, this would degenerate into an era of a(n) (unbridled) credit economy, notoriously within the policy sphere of the Federal Reserve under its former President Greenspan (see also under Sect. 2.6.3 of Chap. 2 of this book, and under Sect. 3.4.5).

Based on a "destructive state philosophy"[441], these kinds of measures would in reality above all lead to a reduction and even a dismantling of states (in the implicit logic that anything that can be profitable should be taken away from the state) (= so-called "*privatization of gains*")[442], with, as mentioned earlier (see under Sect. 3.4.2.3), as earliest and probably most extreme examples of such neo-liberal regimes, the Reagan administration in the USA and the Thatcher regime in the United Kingdom (both having dominated public policy of the 1980s).

3.4.2.3.2 The Implementation of Neo-liberal Philosophy in Practice

148 It is probably not a coincidence that, already in the 1980s, the philosophy of economic neo-liberalism first was adopted by the United Kingdom (so-called "*Thatcherism*") and the United States of America (so-called "*Reaganomics*"), as both these countries, being two of the major economic powers of that time, had always been very much in favour of capitalism, at the same time showing a great reluctance to take steps in the direction of a "mixed economy".[443] As a result, the open invitation of the neo-liberal economists to purify capitalism from the (supposed) harmful effects of such a mixed economy model, was in these countries received with open arms.

Government was hereby no longer seen as the answer to social injustice, but as the main cause of declining economics, hence the perceived need to diminish its influence as much as possible.[444]

---

[438] See for instance Friedman (2002) (the first edition being of 1962).
See also Krugman (1994), pp. 34 a.f.

[439] Vandewalle (1976), p. 345.

[440] Galbraith speaks of "*the monetary illusion*" (see Galbraith 1974, pp. 187–197; see also Galbraith 1992, pp. 88 a.f.).

[441] Kruithof (2000), p. 58.

[442] Kruithof (2012), pp. 70–77, especially p. 73.

[443] Van Oudheusden (2012), p. 132; Chomsky (1999), pp. 65 a.f.

[444] Galbraith (1994), p. 215.

In both countries, this would lead to an excessive implementation of neo-liberal philosophy, which would consequently have an inspirational effect on the rest of the world. Eventually, especially during the 1990s, this caused world trade and finances (the movement of both capital and payment transactions) themselves to be aligned with neo-liberal philosophy.

As a result, the 1980s have been characterized as "*a time of accumulating problems that would become serious and painful in the following decade*"[445] and, by extension, up to the present day, of which the severe monetary and financial crisis of 2008 and its aftermath continue to bear witness.

One of the central measures of American Government under Ronald Reagan **149**
(1981–1989) has been so-called "consumerism";[446] another such central measure consisted in adopting "deregulation" and "liberalization" as the guiding principles of public (economic) policy.[447]

The implementation of the doctrine of "consumerism" in the USA especially attempted to challenge an earlier economic crisis which had particularly impacted the American economy, by stimulating demand. In order to accomplish this goal, consumerism paved the way for an excessive deregulation of the financial sector, coupled with an unprecedented boost of all kinds of (consumer) credit mechanisms.

It needs not much further proof that this policy has played a major role in the advance of the so-called "credit economy" (itself having been one of the main causes of the monetary and financial crisis of 2008).[448]

A further mechanism by which economic neo-liberalism was implemented and **150**
through which the Ronald Reagan-administration has tried to boost American economy, consisted of a substantially increase of the public expenditure on arms[449]; Galbraith has in this regard pointed out that, according to the philosophy of economic neo-liberalism, arms expenditure is one of the few areas in which a state is allowed to be active (along with subsidizing the agricultural sector, in addition to big enterprises and bailouts of large banks).[450]

---

[445]Galbraith (1994), p. 219.

[446]Krugman (1994), p. 157. See also Galbraith (1987), p. 176.

[447]Galbraith (1994), p. 196.

[448]Steger (2013), p. 40; Lloyd (2012), p. 374; Harari (2014), p. 388; Bruckner (2002), pp. 20–21; Sterdyniak (2011), pp. 21–42, especially p. 27; Pesendorfer (2012), pp. 414–434; Streeck (2015), p. 87.

[449]Galbraith (1992), p. 122.

[450]Galbraith (1992), p. 122; Galbraith (1996), pp. 50–51, where it has been brought forward that

> in the American experience certain government expenditures remain outside the public anxiety about the deficit, those for the military (...) being the impressive case. Those for the poor most definitively not.

See furthermore Van Oudheusden (2012), p. 133; Foucault (2008), p. 241. See also Foucault (2013), pp. 189 a.f.

After 4 years of Jimmy Carter's peace-loving regime (1977–1981)[451], the Reagan administration thus made its only (inconsistent) use of Keynesian philosophy (i.e. stimulating the economy through government expenditure). Needless to say, this led to a vast increase in US arms expenditure (which mainly has benefited rich arms producers).[452]

Galbraith has pointed out that since the Reagan era, arms expenses are one of the few examples of government expenditure that the American rich and middle classes agree a state may carry out[453]. The resulting large entanglement of political power and weapons industry has since then only become ever more important.[454] This most likely also helps explaining why the USA have been so eager to get involved in so many armed conflicts all over the world during the past decades.

151 Being a good student of the neo-liberal school, the Reagan administration also carried out a number of "tax- shifts" mainly benefiting the rich and the powerful in society.[455]

Further inspired by the spirit of consumerism the Reagan administration was promoting, the rich layers of the American population began an enormous and never-in-history-seen-before expenditure of the money that was saved through these tax cuts, in a movement which Tom Ronse has indicated as *"an ever growing obscene orgy of consumption"*. So-called "created wants" especially hit young people, turning them into a very vulnerable population group for marketing purposes based upon the use of any conceivable idea which any scientific discipline has to offer (see for instance the creation of worldwide "consumer communities", a technique which is often applied by the pop industry[456], and, by extension, by the entertainment industry in general[457], but also by big enterprises[458] in several other domains of economic life).[459]

Following this American trend, the entire "globalized" world would later on be more and more dragged into an unseen "hyper commercialism", an ever increasing degree of *"consumption for consumption's sake"* influenced by the media (in order

---

[451]Galbraith (1994), p. 194.

[452]Ronse (1992), p. 74. See already Galbraith (1960), p. 19, furthermore already pointing out:

> So our economy is thought to prosper only by the manufacture of instruments of destruction. Such an economy is unlikely to enjoy high prestige in the world; it is far more likely to repel than to attract. (Galbraith 1960, p. 20).

[453]Galbraith (1992), p. 25.

[454]Sachs (2011), pp. 117 a.f. See also earlier Galbraith (1992), pp. 25 a.f.

[455]See Galbraith (1992), p. 27; Galbraith (1994), p. 252.
See also Pizzigati (2012), pp. 316–317; Subhuti (2011), p. 174.

[456]Obviously, numerous examples hereof are thinkable, in many cases also illustrating the importance of social media.

[457]In some cases even having led to real "subcultures" (such as the fans of the Star Wars movies or the Star trek tv-series and movies).

[458]With typical examples in the computer and software industry.

[459]Harari (2014), p. 408.

to continue the sale of products resulting from the *"production for production's sake"*).[460]

Said fiscal deregulation of the Reagan-administration (for instance through securitization techniques; see further, at marg. 182 of this chapter) also allowed public and private debt to go viral, which by some has been indicated as one of the main causes for the severe financial crisis of 2008.[461]

Against the hope of the Reagan administration, a consequence of the developments triggered by the aforementioned neo-liberal measures has however not been that an increase in domestic production occurred which in its own turn would have stimulated (American) economy, but, on the contrary, that a substantial increase in imports took place: in the Reagan era, between 1982 and 1989, the USA are said to have consumed for a value of 800 billion USD more than they produced.[462] **152**

In the course of the next years (from the 1990s up to today), this trend has only continued (entailing disastrous consequences for the American economy, proof of which is the fact that the American national debt in 2014 stood at ±18 trillion USD, or over 104% of American GDP and in 2016, at more than 19 trillion USD; see further the Tables 3.1, 3.2, 3.3, and 3.4 "*Debts in a number of countries*", at marg. 202 of this chapter).

Another consequence of the abovementioned neo-liberal policy measures has been that all layers of society—enterprises, consumers and governments—massively started to take up credit "*as if it were never to be paid back*" '.[463] As said before, this set the scene for the contemporary still continuing "credit economy" (see also further, under Sect. 3.4.5). **153**

It has been a real disaster that the money created from these massive credit operations was not invested in new production or in infrastructure, but mainly in even further consumption, making the USA even more dependent on import[464], an effect which in the 1990s would be even more reinforced, especially after the techniques of liberalization and deregulation which, during the 1980s, had been aimed at reducing the role of government in countries like the United Kingdom and the United Stated of America themselves, were copied by many other countries and regions (including Belgium and the European Union in general), and also got implemented in the context of the new architecture of global free trade and global

---

[460] Sachs (2011), pp. 144 a.f., referring to

> the marriage between mass media and hypercommercialism.

See also De Ruyver (1969).

[461] Subhuti (2011), p. 174:

> Let's not forget Reagan's lasting gift to the American people: fiscal deregulation that allowed public and private debt to go viral, eventually triggering the worst financial crisis since the Great Depression.

[462] Ronse (1992), p. 74.

[463] Krugman (1994), p. 157; Ronse (1992), p. 74.

[464] Ronse (1992), p. 74.

free traffic of payment and capital; this has ultimately led to the USA being forced to step down from their leading position in the world economy to the benefit of China, which, according to some sources[465], has become the leading economic power as of 2014.

154 At the same time, the Reagan administration dismantled several social care systems, among which (public) education and medical care,[466] where as a side thought one may wonder whether the increasing violence in American schools (see for example the Columbine[467] and similar tragedies) and, later on, in American society in general, are not an expression of this downward spiral in the context of investments in education and similar social care mechanisms.[468]

155 In parallel with this American version of neo-liberal policy making, under the regime of Reagan's close friend and kindred soul Margaret Thatcher, in the United Kingdom of the 1980s, neo-liberal doctrines were also applied in a policy mainly aimed at reducing social care mechanisms, as well as privatizing numerous governmental institutions and services[469]. This would mainly result in a dismantling of the state in the United Kingdom (of which the effects still are felt). (See for the impact hereof further, at marg. 174 of this chapter.)

3.4.3 Further Characteristics of the "Selfish Economies" Based on (Neo) Liberal Doctrines

3.4.3.1 The Sacrifice of All Other Values to the Unbridled Pursuit of Money

3.4.3.1.1 Depreciation of Labour

3.4.3.1.1.1 The Facts

156 In a theoretical infinite world characterized by an infinite supply of means, easily available and as easily accessible to everyone (as in the mythical earth paradise on earth described in the Bible, where everything which is produced by earth is bestowed upon man (see Genesis, 1:28–30)), the theories of Smith (and his later disciples), perhaps, could make sense to some extent.[470]

However, in a world which, by definition, is limited, where, as is premised by economic science[471], any means are likewise scarce, and where, moreover, life

[465]Van der Borght (2014), p. 2.

[466]Galbraith (1992), pp. 49–50. See also Ronse (1992), pp. 154 a.f.

[467]Cullen (2009), p. 417. See also Klebold (2016).

[468]Galbraith (1992), p. 49.

[469]Krugman (1994), p. 172 a.f.

[470]Achterhuis (1988), p. 37.

[471]Mankiw (2011), p. 4.

necessities can only be obtained through (someone else's) hard labour, the application of Smithian doctrine, whether or not correctly understood, has in practice, over a period of about two centuries (and differently from its own predictions) mainly resulted in an economic order which does not inspire feelings of pride or contentment about its inherent justice, but only presents itself as a system where the "law of the jungle" prevails.

Yuval Noah Harari has rightly remarked that (neo-)Smithian doctrine may sound *"bulletproof in theory"*, but that *"in practice the bullets get through all too easily"*.[472] **157**

Harari illustrates his viewpoint with the historical example of slave trade in the period from the sixteenth to the nineteenth century, which he rightly calls a humanitarian disaster. The author convincingly argues that this slavery was not caused by the tyranny of kings or by racist ideologists, but rather by the uncontrolled implementation of the free market mechanism itself.[473]

Nonetheless, the neo-liberal credo remains "*Greed is good*", even when it can be strongly questioned that it is, as claimed by neo-liberal schools, the case for everyone. "Greed" is in the best case (sometimes) "good" for its practitioners, but seldom for their victims.[474]

In case one would be inclined to continue the debate on this topic, one should furthermore consider the disastrous impact colonialism in general, and slave trade in particular, have had on the harrowing developments on the African continent as they are at present still being felt[475], but also the continuous problems as a result of

---

[472]Harari (2014), p. 368.

[473]Harari (2014), pp. 368–369.

> From the sixteenth to the nineteenth centuries, about 10 million African slaves were imported to America. About 70 per cent of them worked on the sugar plantations. Labor conditions were abominable. Most slaves lived a short and miserable life, and millions more died during wars waged to capture slaves or during the long voyage from inner Africa to the shores of America. All this so that Europeans could enjoy their sweet tea and candy – and sugar barons enjoy huge profits. The slave trade was not controlled by any state or government. It was a purely economic enterprise, organized and financed by the free market according to the laws of supply and demand. Private slave trading companies sold shares on the Amsterdam, London and Paris stock exchanges. Middle-class Europeans looking for a good investment bought these shares. Relying on this money, the companies bought ships, hired sailors and soldiers, purchased slaves in Africa, and transported them to America. There they sold the slaves to the plantation owners, using the proceeds to purchase plantation products such as sugar, cocoa, coffee, tobacco, cotton and rum. They returned to Europe, sold the sugar and cotton for a good price, and then sailed back to Africa for another round. Throughout the eighteenth century the yield on slave-trade investments was about 6 per cent a year – they were extremely profitable, as any modern consultant would be quick to admit (Harari 2014, pp. 369–370).

[474]See the past statement of former Californian governor Gray Davis in reaction to the Enron-crisis: ***"Someone at Enron should go to jail," Davis said. "Purposely putting people's lives in jeopardy in the name of greed is inexcusable."*** " (See Leopold 2002.)

[475]Beaud (1994), pp. 137 a.f.

the ever difficult integration of the descendants of earlier African slaves within American society permits to put a serious question mark behind the aforementioned neo-liberal credo.

One should hereby furthermore bear in mind that, in spite of slavery (in its strict legal sense) having been abolished in most countries in the world, there are still numerous mechanisms of social economic slavery flourishing in many countries (see also the Further Illustrations 3.9 and 3.13), further illustrating that, although capitalist principles have evolved over time in a more and more subtle form, their basic content has to a large extent remained identical to the ones of 200 years ago.[476]

158 Harari himself has anticipated possible criticisms of his argument about slavery where he points out that one should "*remember that the Atlantic slave trade was not a single aberration in an otherwise spotless record.*"[477]

By way of a further example of the horrors of capitalist practices, Harari refers to the so-called "humanitarian" economic actions, at the end of the nineteenth century, of King Leopold II of Belgium in Congo, which are estimated by some to have resulted in over ten million lethal victims, a number far exceeding that of the Jewish victims of the Holocaust.[478]

159 In its more contemporary context, capitalism has mainly led to an unseen "deployment" (not to say: "downgrade") of human labor (force) into capitalist production and trade processes, mainly aimed at making a small minority of people extremely rich (especially the people behind big enterprises or, in terms of company law: the shareholders, the directors and the CEOs of big companies) at the detriment of the majority of other people they exploit.

Erich Fromm has linked this phenomenon to the inherent turnaround of values which has been caused by the capitalistic system: within capitalism, labor (thus: "human beings") is (are) completely subservient to capital (or: the "economic processes"). Man, a living creature, is hereby downgraded to a device with a purpose: to substantiate, in the most effective way, the unbridled pursuit of a corporation's profit (or, ultimately, the pursuit of profit by the corporations' capital providers).[479]

In hierarchical terms, capital (and its objectives) have hereby been put on a much higher level than labor (thus: "human beings themselves"),[480] an approach which meanwhile has globally determined all conceivable interhuman relations whereby

---

[476]Murray and Bonneville (2010), p. 193.

[477]Harari (2014), p. 370.

[478]Harari (2014), p. 371; Van Houtte (1955), pp. 165 a.f.

[479]Fromm (1955), pp. 88–89. See also Marcuse (1962), pp. 89 a.f.; Marcuse (1964), pp. 306 a.f. (dealing with "labor" as a commodity serving the interests of "capital").

[480]Fromm (1955), p. 90.

these two value scales, namely profit pursuit and valuing human life itself, continuously collide.[481]

At present, more than ever in history, the principle remains that any "unpleasant work" (especially so-called "hard and/or dirty labour"), is increasingly gravitated to the poorer classes of society. The idea is that the most repulsive possible work should be done by the poor at the lowest possible wages, whereby the workers performing this type of hard and/or degrading work need to be replenished over and over again.[482]

It is exactly this negative attitude towards "labour" and those performing it (determined by liberal and neo-liberal principles themselves) which, in the period after world war II, lies at the basis of the massive import of foreign labor forces into West European countries (entailing the well-known integration problems many such countries keep facing today)[483], as well as, more recently and in the context of the working of the European Union, the massive "import" of cheap labor forces from former Eastern European countries (under the pretext of the "free traffic of persons" guaranteed by the European Treaties).

In this (neo-)liberal vision, human labor has gradually been reduced mainly to a (mere) cost factor for the companies exploiting it, and consequently ensuring it is obtained as cheaply as possible[484] (in application of Ricardo's "Iron Law of the Wages"[485]). Indeed, the higher the remuneration on labour, the lower the remaining profit left for the company exploiting it (and, ultimately, for the providers of risk capital of such company).[486]

---

[481]Fromm (1955), p. 90:

> Capital, the dead past, employs labor – the living vitality and power of the present. In the capitalistic hierarchy of values, capital stands higher than labor, amassed things higher than the manifestation of life. Capital employs labor, and not labor capital. The person who owns capital commands the person who "only" owns his life, human skill, vitality and creative productivity. "Things" are higher than men. The conflict between capital and labor is much more than the conflict between two classes, more than their fight for a greater share of the social product. It is the conflict between two principles of value: that between the world of things, and their amassment, and the world of life and its productivity.

[482]Galbraith (1992), p. 33. See also Krugman (1998), p. 15.

[483]Galbraith (1992), p. 34.

[484]See the remark of Guess (2003):

> Capitalism is not for the faint of heart. It is a system of supply and demand that reduces real workingmen and workingwomen into graphs and equations subject to "aggregate" observations devoid of any real human factors.

[485]Galbraith (1987), p. 84 a.f.

[486]Foucault (2008), p. 219 a.f. (see also Foucault 2013, p. 290).

These theoretical arguments have recently been confirmed by empirical research undertaken in a 2016-study of Oxfam entitled "*An economy for the 1%. How privilege and power in the economy drive extreme inequality and how this can be stopped*". It more precisely appears from this study that one of the key trends underlying the extremely huge concentration of wealth and incomes which has been occurring on a global scale during the past years (see further, at Sect. 3.4.8) has precisely been the increasing return to capital versus labor, hence the ever more strict application of the classic liberal " Iron Law of the Wages". The quoted study of Oxfam reports that in 2015, in

By contributing to this system (and even more, up till the present day, by continuing to do so), working classes themselves are said to have become the architects of their own misery.[487] According to Marcuse, each individual being a part of this capitalist system is thus paying the price by having to sacrifice his time, his consciousness and his dreams; moreover, civilization itself is paying by having sacrificed its own promises of liberty, justice, and peace for all.[488]

Only the awareness that "the working classes" in a broad sense of the word[489] also need some elementary level of purchasing power in order to be able to acquire the products from capitalist production, at least in some territories, causes an obstacle to reduce their (net) wages to an ever lower minimum.

According to Michel Foucault, this awareness expresses the neo-liberal idea that "*inequality is equal for all*", so that the government of a country does not need to take a role in achieving a true levelling of economic wealth. On the contrary, the only thing authorities should, in accordance with the theories of economic neo-liberalism, strive for is that a part of the over-capacity of the purchasing power available to the rich are transferred to those living in rich countries who find themselves in a situation of under-consumption (for example those permanently unfit for work, or by unforeseen circumstances unable to work). The only type of "social" policy that is, hence, considered to be acceptable under the neo-liberal approach is, otherwise put, one which contributes to economic growth on its own turn (especially by stimulating consumption).[490]

At present, this approach is in many (Western) countries, especially those suffocating under "right wing governments", translated into a public policy stimulating consumer credit (in a broad sense of the word), as this both stimulates consumption and provides for a further opportunity of making profits to the banks (and their underlying shareholders).

---

almost all rich countries and in most developing countries, the share of national income going to workers has been falling. This implies that, as predicted by the abovementioned authors criticizing economic (neo-)liberalism, on a global scale, the working classes are capturing less and less of the gains from growth, which is in sheer contradiction with the so-called "trickle-down-economics" theory upheld by economic neo-liberalism. In contrast, the owners of capital have seen their capital consistently grow (through interest payments, dividends, or retained profits) faster than the rate the economy has been growing (indicating that also the existing wealth is more and more shifting towards the rich). Tax avoidance by the owners of capital, and governments reducing taxes on capital gains are reported to have further added to these returns. (See Oxfam 2016, p. 4.)

[487] Galbraith (1983), p. 116.

Compare Marcuse (1962), p. 83:

> The economic and political incorporation of the individuals into the hierarchical system of labor is accompanied by an instinctual process in which the human objects of domination reproduce their own repression.

[488] Marcuse (1962), p. 91.

[489] Whereby this reference applies to all people who depend on providing labor to meet their life's needs, implying that also (small) independent professionals, and owners of small companies may be considered as a part of these "working classes".

[490] Foucault (2008), pp. 198 a.f. and 205 (see also Foucault 2013, pp. 192–193).

Fromm has rightly explained these characteristics of capitalism (or: "free market economies") further by arguing that the subordination (one could say: the degradation) of (personal) life as a means to reach economic targets, touches the very foundations of capitalist production, whereby the accumulation of capital and/or the distribution of profits to capital providers has become the main, not to say the only, task and target of economic activity. As a result, working classes (which form the majority of mankind) have become engaged in the capitalist production process for the benefit of (someone else's) profit, in many cases a profit which is not meant to be spent, but is meant to serve as a new capital investment (or, at present, as saving reserves to be parked in tax havens). Reinvested capital in its turn needs to generate new profits (through the use of other man's labor force). In their turn, these new profits again need to be re-invested (preferably by incorporating shareholdings in existing enterprises in tax havens) and this circular movement needs to continue infinitely (taking into account the underlying aim for the economy to grow continuously).[491]

Although Fromm acknowledges that this indeed has contributed to a certain level of material prosperity for a part of mankind (but not for all people), at the same time he points out that this has occurred at the cost of a fundamental "dehumanization" of (working) man who has thus been degraded to the status of "an eternal slave" of the capitalist machinery and who only exists to fulfil impersonal and non-personal goals, thus becoming filled with a sense of utter emptiness and meaninglessness.[492]

According to Fromm, the term "labor market" alone summarizes the entire tragedy of the fate which has befallen mankind since the rise of capitalism: just as (the capital provider of) a corporation buys resources, it (he) is also buying someone else's ability to work in order to enlist it into the economic production process of said corporation (= "labor as merchandise"[493]). This has even allowed capitalism to succeed in convincing practically every human being taking part in its processes, of the fact that humans exist only to provide labor (a reality which, in economic science, is also expressed by indicating "labour" as a so-called "production factor").[494]

The interaction between humans is in this way "reduced" (not to say: "degraded") to mere economic relations which are entirely mechanical and the result of which can only be a large degree of alienation, in a society where

---

[491] Fromm (1990), p. 87 (also: Fromm, pp. 64 a.f.).
See also Pinxten (2014), p. 13; Bruckner (2016), pp. 229 a.f.

[492] Fromm (1990), p. 87 (also: Fromm, pp. 64–65).
Compare Marcuse (1962), p. 95:

> The theory of alienation demonstrated the fact that man does not realize himself in his labor, that his life has become an instrument of labor, that his work and its products have assumed a form and power independent of him as an individual.

[493] Fromm (1955), p. 88 (speaking of "*the use of man by man*").

[494] Fromm (1955), p. 88 a.f.; Foucault (2008), p. 220.

everything can be purchased and sold, including and above all someone else's or one's own labour.[495]

In this, the implication of the so-called "free labor contract" is that as a result labor produces and perpetuates its own exploitation. Consequently; the economic forces of capitalism, left to their devices, inherently lead to enslavement, poverty and the intensity of class conflict. Hence, the truth of the freedom to enter into a labor contract results in its negation of becoming enslaved and exploited.[496]

The result of this dehumanization process is that the majority of human beings have been reduced to "hunted" and "perplexed" individuals[497], in today's (Western) society (ies) witnessed, for example, by an increasing number of depressions, burn-outs and similar pathologies resulting from the exploitation of human beings by their rich and powerful fellow human beings.[498]

In addition to Erich Fromm, other authors of (relatively) recent times have expressed similar thoughts. For instance, Herbert Marcuse has in his own works expressed the idea that capitalism implies an "*actual negation of life*", whereby the underlying motive for any economic action has taken the form of the fear for starvation of the dispossessed.[499]

160 From one's history classes, anyone will probably still remember the harrowing situation of the working classes in Europe and the USA during the nineteenth century, till far in the twentieth century.[500]

This insight brought Michel Beaud to the viewpoint that, during the nineteenth century, industrial capitalism mainly developed, both in Europe as in the USA, thanks to a cruel exploitation of the working classes in the leading industries of that period, among which the textile, metal and mining industries.[501]

---

[495]Fromm (1990), p. 92 (also: Fromm, pp. 71–72).

[496]Marcuse (1964), p. 309.

[497]Fromm (1990), p. 91 (also: Fromm, p. 72).

[498]See Ricard (2014), pp. 416 a.f.

Erich Fromm has based this insight on his understanding of the teachings of Karl Marx:

> Marx's central criticism of capitalism is not the injustice in the distribution of wealth; it is the perversion of labor into forced, alienated, meaningless labor, hence the transformation of man into a "crippled monstrosity". (Fromm 2013 (1st edition of 1961), p. 34.)

[499]Marcuse (1962), pp. 71 a.f. See also Marcuse (1964), pp. 300 a.f.

[500]Harari (2014), p. 371 and pp. 382 a.f.; Becket (2014), pp. 136 a.f.

See also Erich Fomm:

> The most characteristic element of nineteenth-century Capitalism was first of all, ruthless exploitation of the worker; it was believed to be a natural or social law that hundreds of thousands of workers were living at the point of starvation. The owner of capital was supposed to be morally right if, in the pursuit of profit, he exploited to the maximum the labor he hired. There was hardly any sense of human solidarity between the owner of capital and his workers. The law of the economic jungle was supreme. All the restrictive ideas of previous centuries were left behind. (Fromm 1955, p. 82).

See furthermore Ashton (1954), pp. 127–159.

[501]Beaud (1994), p. 131.

However, also in the modern context, the aforementioned vision on labor as a mere production factor is, at least in extreme cases, still characterized by harrowing abuses, for example the use of young children in capitalist production and trade processes[502], mostly at poverty wages, which still takes place in many countries in the world.

Even in traditionally rich countries, the "Iron Law of the Wages" is more current than ever in many a debate or reformation process presently taking place. As a result, the globalization of the world economy has an ever increasing catalyzing impact on the worldwide reduction of measures of protecting labor (and people providing labor), in addition to other social protection structures.

Further Illustration 3.9: Child Labor and Child Slavery in the Twenty-First Century

Until the present day, child labor and even slavery remain a crucial social economic problem in many poor countries.[503]

A study conducted in 1998 showed that (at that time) 95% of child labor was situated in Asia, Latin-America and Africa,[504] but also that in Europe and the United States of America (with, for example, hundreds of thousands of children engaged in agriculture), the plague of child labor and child slavery had not been exterminated at all.[505]

This study demonstrates that ***"the life of about two hundred million children all over the world (...) is ruled by the hard mechanisms of child labor. Often they are paid handouts, are exploited in a disgraceful way and are thrown away when they have no more value. Most children do not have a choice. They live in communities afflicted by poverty, they have no social security, they have unemployed parents and they cannot go to school as the government has not invested enough in education. Children – sometimes starting at the age of three to four years – perform any kind of labor: rug hooking, sewing shoes, mining, carrying stones, serve and sell. Countless children are also daily forced to work in the sex industry. Child labor is characterized by low wages, long hours and dangerous and unhealthy working conditions. Very often there is no pay or care. Thousands of children are being kidnapped and sold to spend the rest of their lives as slaves. They are continuously maltreated and abused."***[506]

The fact that, since the date of said quoted study, not much has changed can apparently be illustrated by a mixture of press releases easily to be found

(continued)

[502]See *e.g.* Hutt (1954), pp. 160–188.

[503]See Murray and Bonneville (2010), p. 193; see also Groenink et al. (1998), p. 280.

[504]Groenink et al. (1998), p. 7.

[505]Groenink et al. (1998), pp. 12–13.

[506]Groenink et al. (1998), p. 12.

Further Illustration 3.9 (continued)

on the World Wide Web, indicating that even today, shameless cases of child exploitation are still taking place.

A harrowing example thereof concerns child labor, and even contemporary forms of slavery, in the West-African cocoa cultivation (see Further Illustration 3.13).[507]

A second sector where child labor and slavery are prominent is gold mining:

> The United Nations' International Labor Organization estimates that as many a million children between ages 5 and 17 work in the small-scaled gold mines of Africa for as little as $2 a day. In the African Sahel, a semiarid region that stretches from the Atlantic Ocean to the Red Sea across parts of Mali, Ghana, Burkina Faso, and Niger, 30–50% of small-scale mine workers are children, according to ILO estimates.[508]

In addition, the modern clothing industry still actively uses capitalist practices of exploitation of cheap labor. This is indicated by a shocking press release of October 30th 2014, whereby young Cambodian women have even held that they would rather work in prostitution than in the clothing industry as the former offers them a greater chance to provide subsistence for themselves and their families.[509]

3.4.3.1.1.2 The Ethical Debate

161 Social misbehavior such as child labor and slavery, however (morally) condemnable, is nevertheless—and by some neo-liberal authors even in an explicit way—perfectly validated by the economic theories going back to Adam Smith.[510]

An entrepreneur practicing such uninhibited exploitation of other people's labor (among which child labor, slavery, the re-allocation of factories to countries with cheaper work forces,...), but also a policy maker who advocates the dismantling of legislation aimed at protecting labor or laborers, is indeed behaving as the perfect Smithian egoist (or: "*homo neo-liberalis*") who only looks for his personal interests

---

[507] See Child labor and Slavery in the Chocolate Industry. http://www.foodispower.org/slavery-chocolate/. Last consulted on February 28th 2016. See also McKenzie and Swails (2012), raising the question: ***"How many people in America know that all this chocolate they are eating – candies and all of those wonderful chocolates – is being produced by terrible child labor?"***

[508] See Price (2013).

[509] See Nog liever werken in prostitutie dan in kledingfabriek (incl. video). (http://www.zita.be/nieuws/bizar/3579765_nog-liever-werken-in-prostitutie-dan-in-kledingfabriek.html?hkey=0c771ffda5ea7807bab353fce9826df2). Last consulted on February 28th 2016.

[510] See however Rand (2008), p. 118, especially blaming nineteenth century novelists for what she describes as a misconception of reality.

and has no regard for the effect of his actions on the rest of society and especially on the poor and deprived.

In order to justify such social misconduct, classic economic liberalism has even dared to argue that it is thanks to the efforts of people who shamelessly exploit others that the latter still have jobs and, hence, receive a salary to provide for their livelihood. Even in cases in which the latter is hardly the case, such as in situations of modern-day slavery and child work, economic (neo-)liberalism nevertheless argues that it is better for such people to have a poor wage, than to have no wage at all, thus implying that people who are exploited by capitalist practices should above all be grateful for such exploitation and should stop complaining about it.

Precisely this way of reasoning lies at the very core of the so-called "trickle-down-economics" theory.

In his work "*Des embellissements de la ville de Cachemire*", the renowned French eighteenth century philosopher Voltaire (1694-1778) raised the following question[511]: 162

> Quoi! depuis que vous êtes établis en corps de peuple, vous n'avez pas encore trouvé le secret d'obliger tous les riches à faire travailler tous les pauvres!

According to Michel Beaud, the secret Voltaire is referring to is obviously the capitalist system itself, which enables the rich to force the poor to work longer, harder and more, in order to get richer themselves.[512]

It should be admitted that societies from ancient history even had a much simpler and cheaper (albeit even more inhumane) solution for the dilemma of accessing labor as cheaply as possible, namely slavery. 163

As a result, in the economies of Ancient Greece and of the Roman Empire, labor was mainly performed by slaves.[513]

Consequently, it has hardly been a coincidence that the rise of capitalism in the United States of America in the seventeenth century went hand in hand with the re-introduction of slavery, albeit the working conditions in European workshops of that time (and later: in industrial factories) were hardly any better.

Since then, the battle of ideas going on in numerous Western countries on topics such as the scale of the wages, working times, retirement age,..., often under the argument that (big) enterprises have to be able to safeguard their competitive position on the market, is to be placed in its historical perspective that whoever wants to become rich in a capitalist manner, has always aimed at doing so by, as shamelessly as possible, exploiting other people's labor power[514].

---

[511]Beuchot (1830), p. 356.

[512]Beaud (1994), p. 76.

[513]Galbraith (1987), p. 9.

[514]Fromm (2013) (1st edition of 1961), p. 47:

> The entrepreneur accedes to the most depraved fancies of his neighbor, plays the role of pander between him and his needs, awakens unhealthy appetites in him, and watches for every weakness in order, later, to claim the remuneration of this labor of love. The man who has thus become subject to his alienated needs is a "mentally and physically dehumanized being" (...).

As argued before (see above, at marg. 137 of this chapter), this translates into a classic economic law known as "the law of Ricardo on wages" or "the Iron Law of the Wages"[515].

164 By more contemporary neo-liberal authors such as, for instance, Brook and Watkins, the classic capitalist approach referred to under the previous marg. 163 of this chapter is still being defended in our times, a.o. by referring to the theory of "voluntary association", basically holding that anyone who is exploited undergoes such a fate out of his own free will:

> When Wal-Mart employees agree to work for nine dollars an hour, that is voluntary association – they are free to look for higher pay elsewhere.[516]

One should hereby bear in mind that the capital providers of "Wal-Mart"[517] are by far one of the richest families in the world (see Further Illustration 3.25, mentioning that in the Forbes ranking for 2014, Christy Walton was in 8th position, Jim Walton in 9th, and Alice Walton in 10th position; in the Forbes 2015-ranking, Christy Walton and Jim Walton managed to keep their place, albeit Alice Walton had "fallen back" to the 11th place[518]); the sum of their respective assets would, by far, put them in first place in this ranking, with an estimated joint fortune of over 115 billion USD.

When evaluating the type of argumentation developed by Brook and Watkins, one should furthermore bear in mind that, most likely dating back to the works of John Stuart Mill (see above, at marg. 138 of this chapter), neo-liberal authors consider the principles of "individual property" and "individual freedom" almost as sacred[519], and consistently try and justify all excesses of capitalism by referring to this type of abstract concepts of societal organization; for instance, Ayn Rand herself has vigorously defended the doctrine of the "voluntary association" as being the sole principle that may determine human relations.[520]

We will not offer ourselves an opinion on the question whether said neo-liberal authors would go as far as holding that the theory of "voluntary association" also applies to the phenomenon of, for instance, African child slaves.

To our opinion, in the present-day neo-liberal world which after centuries of shameless exposition to capitalist practices is characterized by vast inequalities and, consequently, also by vast unequal opportunities and where mainly the living and social conditions in which a person is born determine his chances in life, the appeal to abstract concepts such as the "voluntary association" theory makes no sense whatsoever, unless for those who consider society as no more than a gathering of

---

[515] Galbraith (1987), p. 84.

[516] Brook and Watkins (2012), p. 127.

[517] See furthermore Stiglitz (2006), p. 192.

[518] http://www.forbes.com/billionaires/list/2/#version:static; last consulted on January 22nd 2016.

[519] As explained before, this dates back to the works of the classic liberal author John Stuart Mill (see above, at marg. 138 of this chapter).

[520] See Rand (2008), p. 11; Rand (1992), p. 114.

competing selfish individualists in a process where he who is already the strongest (in terms of wealth, connections, power, prestige, etc.) to begin with, will and should always end up becoming even stronger to the detriment of the poorer and weaker.[521]

It is nevertheless this kind of unbridled selfishness and individualism which neo-liberal authors continue to outline as the leading principles of societal organization[522] (which explains, to a large extent, the disastrous outlook of the current world economy and its social order).

Ayn Rand[523] has even dared to argue that the aforementioned abuses, such as child labor, are not at all the result of processes of capitalism (but, for instance in the case of child labor, to parents forcing their children to work[524]) and that economic neo-liberalism has not caused such abuses, but has on the contrary contributed to preventing them. **165**

The same author, furthermore, has held that (at least historical) child labor has not been as problematic as pictured, using different arguments such as: the fact that it is parents who force their children to work; that the work these children do is easy work (namely: passively observing a machine, without doing anything else, except replacing a broken cable from time to time), and that, through such child labor, the prosperity of the family the children belong to increases...[525]

3.4.3.1.1.3 Illustration: Remuneration Practices of CEO's and the Likes

A further striking illustration of how the unbridled pursuit of money principle keeps challenging one's imagination and which up to day keeps prevailing within Western (and Western inspired) economies is the large difference in, *on one hand*, the remunerations that are paid to CEOs (and similar executive positions) and capital providers of (large) enterprises, and, *on the other hand*, the remuneration paid to the rest of the people employed by such enterprises ("the large working masses").[526] **166**

With regard to 2014 CEO remuneration in its broad sense (thus including, for instance, payment in shares and share options and bonuses, in addition to a fixed salary) within Europe, the United Kingdom showed itself the leading country: large corporations with a balance total of over 5 billion euro were reported to pay their CEOs on average 4.7 million euro per year. The second place in this 2014-ranking was taken by Germany, with an average of 3.1 million euro, followed, at some distance, by the Netherlands with an average of 2.5 million euro, France with an average of 2.3 million euro, and Belgium with an average of almost 2 million euro.[527]

---

[521]Compare Fromm (1955), p. 89.

[522]Rand (2008), pp. 11 a.f.

[523]Rand (2008), p. 118.

[524]Rand (2008), p. 119.

[525]Rand (2008), p. 119.

[526]See already Galbraith (1992), pp. 54 a.f.

[527]Moutton (2014), p. 48.

Figures provided by the European Banking Authority are in line with these observations. According to an EBA-report of March 30th 2016[528], the number of high earners who have been awarded 1 million euro or more annual remuneration for 2014 has increased significantly, from 3178 in 2013 to 3865 in 2014 (+21.6%). Moreover, in 2014, compared to 2013, the percentage of high earners who were identified as "bank staff" has increased significantly.[529]

Not surprisingly, as the United Kingdom is most probably the European country most adhering to the theories of economic neoliberalism, the largest population of high earners in the EU of 2926 (+ 40.27%) is located in the UK (2013: 2086; 2012: 2714).[530] In the meantime, as mentioned elsewhere in this book, the UK is also facing an ever increasing poverty among the poorer layers of its society (see further, at marg. 172 of this chapter).

During the past years, this trend seems to have deployed even further. According to the already quoted 2016-Oxfam study "*An economy for the 1%. How privilege and power in the economy drive extreme inequality and how this can be stopped*", in recent years, within the world of work, the gap between the average worker and those at the top has been reported to be rapidly widening even more. While many workers have seen their wages stagnate, there has been a huge increase in salaries for those at the top. For instance, chief executive salaries are reported to have "rocketed". CEOs at the top US firms have seen their salaries increase by more than half (by 54.3%) since 2009, while ordinary wages have barely moved. The CEO of India's top information technology firm has even been reported to make 416 times the salary of a typical employee there.[531]

These huge differences between the income of CEO's and of the working classes raise the question whether CEOs, as they like to claim in justifying these large differences, indeed show inherent qualities—such as a stronger will to work, a higher intelligence, better management skills, etc.—which make them different from other people, including those they employ.[532]

---

[528] European Banking Authority (2016).

[529] European Banking Authority (2016), p. 13, no 19.

[530] European Banking Authority (2016), p. 14, no 23.

[531] Oxfam (2016), p. 4.

[532] Galbraith (1992), p. 59, pointing out that one of the first managers having benefited from this type of self- and public adulation is Donald Trump,

> briefly and by his own effort and admission the most prestigious economic figure of the time.

See furthermore Falzani (2014).
See also Oxfam (2016), pp. 16–17:

> It would be perverse to argue that the contributions of 62 individual billionaires are worth the same as those of 3.6 billion other people. It is unimaginable that the CEO of a tobacco company in India is as productive as 439 of his employees combined, or that the owner of a UK clothing retailer can produce the same as more than 2,000 garment workers. But the gap between the richest and the rest continues to grow. The increase in the CEO-to-average pay ratio in the UK has grown even since Oxfam published its inequality report in 2014 and now stands at 183:1. For capital owners and executives the rewards continue to grow, while the average worker receives less for additional contributions as the gap between workers' productivity and workers' wages widens.

Or are these significant differences not rather caused by the lack of scruples the CEOs (and the capital providers of their companies) show to employ others for a salary which is significantly lower than the salaries and profits they attribute to themselves, hence on applying the classical economic "Iron Law of the Wages" into everyday practice.

In other words, the (probably rhetorical) question arises if the kind of people ending up in CEO positions are not among the ones mostly driven by a complete lack of conscience[533], or other altruistic characteristics, which would constrain them from paying themselves much higher remunerations than the ones they are willing to pay to others (especially the people they employ who, very often, work harder, or perform harder or more vile or dangerous work than the CEOs themselves)[534], thus best reflecting the image of the idealized "*homo (neo)liberalis*", namely the man who, in accordance with the teachings of "economic liberalism" and, later on, "economic neo-liberalism" is up to anything in his selfish and unbridled pursuit of ever more wealth and money.

Further Illustration 3.10: Capitalist Practices of Certain International Law Firms

A similar further illustration of how the aforementioned capitalist working methods of capitalism apply and that will probably (even more) appeal to the minds of any lawyer (or anyone studying law), can be detected in the manner certain big (international) law firms are organized (which is very similar to the way CEO remuneration practices are worked out in large enterprises).

The structure of this type of law firms is classical "piriform", implying that, on average, it is in the hands of a limited number of "partners" who, in many cases think that they perfectly reflect the characteristics of the so-called neo-liberal "genius principle" (see above, at marg. 136, and further, at marg. 225 and 231 of this chapter), and are at the top of the "pyramid", each of them employing an echelon of associates and trainees at the lowest possible wages.

In accordance with the capitalist working principles this type of law firms advocates, such associates and trainees are expected to work at (in line with "the Iron Law of the Wages": relatively low) monthly wages during an excessive amount of hours per week, including weekends and holidays.[535]

(continued)

[533]Reference can be made to certain research indicating that CEO's are among the professions where "psychopathy" is considered to be an advantageous characteristic. (See Holloway 2015). This same research even suggests that 4% of CEO's show psychopatic characteristics.

[534]See Raspoet (2014), pp. 51–55.

See also the observation of Sven Becket on eighteenth and nineteenth century capitalism:

> Considering their importance in forging the world of modern capitalism, the actual work of merchants seems often almost banal. Most of their time was spent writing letters, talking to suppliers and customers, traveling and making calculations. (See Becket 2014, p. 207.)

[535]See furthermore Van Eeckhoutte (2002), pp. 32–35.

Further Illustration 3.10 (continued)

From the large turnover generated by these trainees and co-workers, only a very small part is used to pay for their wages. On the contrary, as in every capitalist company, their (almost) total turnover is used to "finance the office", i.e., principally, to pay out the profits the partners are appropriating for themselves.

Anyone wanting to grow in such a firm to the level of partner, must be himself prepared to resort to an excessive exploitation of (often very talented) other young people in a so-called "up or out" or "rank or yank" logic, while, on top of that, the young trainees and associates are encouraged to adopt a killer competitive behavior between themselves.

Such an office model is completely in line with the ideal of (neo-)Smithian selfishness which the partners of this type of law firms often perfectly apply to their office structure. This also explains why this type of law firms is often very profitable (at least for the partners).

The mechanism governing such law firms (which expresses the essence of capitalism) is being applied worldwide in different types of company structures and is the main cause why a small elite of people who, mostly not limited by any moral scruples, are prepared to exercise their (neo-)Smithian selfishness to its fullest extent, become richer and richer to the detriment of the largest masses (often working much harder) whom they employ/exploit (and who are most often not characterized by such a total lack of scruples).

The extent to which any "voluntary association" of "the exploited" can be found in this, determines the size of the exploitation. Indeed, the lawyer-trainee starting in such a large (international) law firm may be expected to behave in a more empowered way (when discussing working conditions) than, for example, the poor American without any degree or education who is applying for a position with a huge American retailer, and the latter will be expected to be at least a bit more empowered than an African child slave. This does however not exclude the mechanism of exploitation being the same in the three examples; the only difference is the extent the exploitation takes. In this the level of one's education may help determine the degree of maturity which enables a person to keep the exploitation at least within certain limits.

167 In this way, neo-liberal thinking, which elevates the highest possible degree of selfishness to an absolute virtue, keeps prevailing today (probably more than ever, taking into account the massive flow of neo-liberal literature which continues to defend unbridled capitalism and/or free market(s)), with as a result that, in a global society which is characterized by an ever increasing gap between the rich and the poor, only the worst can be expected (see recently the warnings of for example Thomas Piketty, and before of Joseph Stiglitz, in addition to many others, further referred to in more detail under Sect. 3.4.8).

3.4.3.1.2 The Sacrifice of Other Values Than Labor to the Pursuit of Profits

Either way, as (neo-)Smithian (capitalist) thinking started increasingly to dominate social and economic processes[536], the (unbridled) pursuit of wealth and money would decisively come forward as the ruling value in economic thinking and action, to which, in the course of the nineteenth and twentieth centuries, almost all other values have gradually been sacrificed.[537] **168**

In addition to the idea that "capital" should shamelessly exploit (other) man's labor, another dominant feature[538] of the capitalist system as it matured in the course of the nineteenth century has been the fierce belief in competitive behavior (on the so-called "free market"), where it is not considered to be of any value to use one's own talents for the benefit of others, but on the contrary, to obtain the most dominant possible (market or more general societal) position, thereby as much as possible ensuring that others do not stand a chance within one's own market segment (but are, on the contrary, preferably "eliminated").[539] **169**

For all possible economic agents, and in our present-day world even for those involved in government policy making, the unbridled pursuit of wealth and money, gradually, and increasingly, took precedence over all other societal values and interests, such as, in addition to the aforementioned (production factor) labor[540]:

- Care for the eco-system (with consequences such as environmental pollution, having resulted in huge climate problems with inestimable dimensions[541]...);
- "Public health" (with as notorious examples: the massive use of nuclear energy, with no concern for safety issues or for the fact that the amounts of nuclear waste

---

[536]Whereby in some especially Protestant countries, especially when comparing the values of capitalist thinking to the basic values of the Gospels as referred to under Sect. 3.3.2.2, a completely incomprehensible confusion with (purportedly) "Christian" thinking has emerged.

[537]As has been explained already decades ago by the Belgian philosopher Jaap Kruithof (1929–2009) (see Kruithof 1985, pp. 56–57):

> As a result of the strong development of capitalism of 'doing' and 'having', the impact of 'being' has been weakened. The idea is cherished that in the future all 'being' could be turned into 'having'.
>
> (...)
>
> The negative consequences of this ideology are predominantly present in our culture. There is no respect for anything, except man itself, and even this is an overstatement as more than half of the world population lives in poverty and oppression. In the capitalist world, productivity rules everything and the principle that money can buy anything prevails. (...) Human interest is hereby limited to the interests of the own generation; whomever comes afterwards will have to take care of his own needs.

[538]In addition to the idea that economic activity should exclusively serve selfish needs.

[539]Kruithof (2000), p. 15.

[540]It is remarkable that in capitalist economic reasoning human labor itself is considered as a "production factor", *ergo* as a mere part of the economic processes.

[541]Stiglitz (2006), 17.
See also Kruithof (1985), p. 57.

alone have created an unmanageable problem; the way the industrial food industry (in a broad sense of the word[542]) and the pharmaceutical industry[543] function (the latter in Western countries, according to conservative estimates, for instance having caused at least 10% of the population to become addicted to antidepressants and similar "legitimate" addictive medication[544]...);

- The decreasing supply of natural resources and energy sources (such as fossil fuels and, in some regions in the world, even drinking water)[545];
- The problem of government deficits (in addition to the problem of the huge debt burden of numerous countries, one could also mention the structural problem of the excessive costs for public works, which are by means of public tenders awarded to private enterprises driven by an unbridled pursuit of profits, cost fortunes in public funds and have brought many Western countries to incur major budget deficits; one can also bear in mind the PPS- debacle in many European countries during the last decades);
- The high intergenerational conflict that in many Western countries has resulted from the collapse of pension funding[546];
- ...

The list of examples is obviously endless (and has already been discussed by in detail by various literature).

According to Herbert Marcuse (a.o. based on an analysis of the findings of Max Weber), the (neo-)liberal) approach to capitalism hence faces in itself an expression of a loss of rationality (and thus a loss of its historic roots).

Once on track, the "capitalist rationality" transforms irrationality into "ratio": ratio being the rapid development of productivity, i.e. the conquest of nature and the extension of wealth in terms of goods; irrational because the increased productivity and the control of nature and social wealth are in this way transformed into destructive powers, not only destructive in a metaphorical sense (such as sacrificing all higher values to the pursuit of personal wealth), but also literally: the battle for existence is getting more fierce and this both within separate states, as on an international scale, and the bottled-up aggression is released in legitimizing

---

[542]Wolffers (2011), p. 92; Gore (2013a), pp. 354–355 (see also Gore 2013b, p. 283).

[543]Wolffers (2011), pp. 240 a.f.

[544]Harari (2014), pp. 382 a.f.

[545]Hartwell (2014), pp. 184–211.

[546]See the Oxfam-study "*Even it up*" (Oxfam 2014, p. 19):

> Significant amounts of money that could be invested in service provision that tackles inequality are being diverted by tax breaks and public-private partnerships (PPPs). In India, numerous private hospitals have been given tax incentives to provide free treatment to poor patients, but have failed to honor their side of the bargain. Lesotho's Queen Mamohato Memorial Hospital in the capital city Maseru operates under a PPP that currently costs half of the total government health budget, with costs projected to increase. This is starving the budgets of health services in rural areas that are used by the poorest people, further widening the gap between rich and poor.

medieval cruelty (*e.g.* torture and terrorism) and in a scientifically orchestrated destruction of man and nature.[547]

It hence does not come as a surprise that already the idea has been expressed that the present-day culture of terrorism which threatens public safety in many countries is to a large extent to be considered as a manifestation of the lower classes expressing their anger towards an unjust economic, political and societal system (being capitalism).[548]

Further Illustration 3.11: The Global Climate Policy—A Story of Many Words and Few Deeds

We will suffice here with developing one of the most striking illustrations of the devastating impact of the unbridled capitalist pursuit of money on the value of protecting the environment as it has more specifically been dealt with in the so-called "climate debate"[549]

Within the so-called "climate Treaty" (= "UNFCCC"—"United Nations Framework Convention on Climate Change" of May 9th 1992), annually, a climate conference takes place aimed at debating the undesirable consequences of human behavior on climate and at preventing the (further) undesirable impact of such behavior on climate change.

Past climate conferences have however hardly been successful (the main reason having been the unwillingness of an economy driven by the neo-liberal pursuit of profits to take any concrete action, as a result of which there is a great reluctance of making economic sacrifices with regards to the capitalist production and transportation models, regardless of the disastrous impact these (continue to) have on the environment).

Hence, the somewhat "ironic" observation can be made that, periodically, busy climate conferences are organized, mostly in exotic and hence, from a touristic viewpoint, very attractive, locations, which mainly demand a great

(continued)

[547]Marcuse (1962), pp. 73 a.f. Compare Foucault (2008), p. 177.

To quote the Dutch author Jan Greshoff (1888–1971) (already in his work '*Nachtschade*' (1958)): should the European civilization ever cease to exist, it will be due to the scabies called "Americanism", due to a world view which is exclusively built on the ideas of advantage and profit.

[548]This idea has a.o. been brought forward by Emmanuel Macron (at the time "ministre de l'Économie Crédits" of France), who stated:

> Nous avons une part de responsabilité, parce que ce totalitarisme se nourrit de la défiance que nous avons laissée s'installer dans la société. Il se nourrit de cette lèpre insidieuse qui divise les esprits, et si demain nous n'y prenons pas garde, il les divisera plus encore. (See De Boni 2015).

See already (much) earlier Bonger (1916).

[549]Amesz (2012), p. 159.

Further Illustration 3.11 (continued)

effort from the transport sector, especially the use of air planes driven by kerosene (and therefore strongly polluting), without having had any concrete outcome so far.

Already in 1992 Galbraith indicated that the refusal to engage in a true climate policy is a perfect illustration of the blind faith (stemming from "*the culture of contentment*") in the (neo-)liberal "*laissez-faire*"-principle that, by doing nothing, everything will ultimately be fine.[550]

The "Copenhagen" climate conference in 2009 may to a large extent be seen as a failure because its original (modest) objectives were not met and only a partial agreement was reached, not containing any concrete objectives or binding agreements. The most important achievement of the Copenhagen climate conference was limited to a vague agreement on 100 billion USD of climate support to be provided to developing countries by 2020[551].

At the "Cancun" climate conference of 2010, certain binding agreements were made between the participating states, but still not all parts of it were as concrete as one would have hoped. It was, for instance, agreed upon that the average worldwide temperature increase should not be more than 2 degrees (in comparison to pre-industrial times); furthermore, agreements were reached on the limitation of CO2 emissions and there was some further discussion about the establishment of a fund to help developing countries tackle climate changes[552].

In 2011, the climate conference was held in "Durban". Again, it was a laborious event, though it ultimately led to a new climate agreement, once more aiming at reducing CO2 emissions. In addition to that, it was agreed

(continued)

[550]Galbraith (1992), p. 20. See in extreme terms Rand (1992), p. 37.
See furthermore Bell (1996), p. 187.

[551]See Klimaatconferentie Mexico 2010. http://www.europa-nu.nl/id/vie7ce4gamp8/klimaatconferentie_mexico. Last consulted on February 28th 2016.

[552]See Klimaatconferentie Mexico 2010. http://www.europa-nu.nl/id/vie7ce4gamp8/klimaatconferentie_mexico. Last consulted on February 28th 2016. See also Van den Broeck (2014).

Further recognizes that deep cuts in global greenhouse gas emissions are required according to science, and as documented in the Fourth Assessment Report of the Intergovernmental Panel on Climate Change, with a view to reducing global greenhouse gas emissions so as to hold the increase in global average temperature below 2 °C above preindustrial levels, and that Parties should take urgent action to meet this long-term goal, consistent with science and on the basis of equity; also recognizes the need to consider, in the context of the first review, as referred to in marg. 138 below, strengthening the long-term global goal on the basis of the best available scientific knowledge, including in relation to a global average temperature rise of 1.5 °C. (Conference of the Parties 2010).

Further Illustration 3.11 (continued)

upon that the existing Kyoto Protocol of 1997 would be extended and it was (again) decided to establish a "Green Climate Fund" which would donate 100 billion dollars per year to developing countries from 2020 on.[553]

The climate conference in "Doha" in 2012 was also not a great success, as it only resulted (at the last minute) in a (mere) agreement on the extension of the existing Kyoto-protocol which would otherwise have ended in 2012[554].

The climate conference in "Warsaw" in 2013 also did not reach the expected results, but only resulted in a partial agreement. This conference nevertheless concluded with the ambitious goal of laying the foundation for a new climate agreement which was intended to be signed in 2015 in "Paris". Following the agreement that was reached in 2013, all countries needed to indicate to what level they would reduce their CO2 emissions (making it hard to conclude how this would ultimately result in a true new agreement, ready to be signed in the course of 2015). In addition to that, a new partial agreement was reached regarding the (financial) support of the so-called prosperous countries to the developing countries in order to enable the latter to make their economy "more green"[555].

The climate conference in December 2014 in "Lima" started very promisingly, but as may already be concluded from the aforementioned precedents, it again did not result in concrete achievements. The press did indeed announce in December 2014 that the climate conference in Lima had resulted in "a blow": the only outcome of the conference has been a vague text enabling the participating countries to plead innocence for another.[556] An important cause for the failure of the Lima conference is said to be the refusal of (developing) countries such as China and India to reduce their use of fossil fuels (more specifically coal).[557]

At first glance, the climate conference of Paris 2015 seems to have been more successful. It has, for instance, been reported that the climate agreement signed at the United Nations climate summit in Paris of 2015 was "*historic,*

(continued)

[553]See Kernpunten akkoord van klimaatconferentie Durban. http://www.europa-nu.nl/9353000/1/j9vvj9idsj04xr6/viv6l635j7u5?ctx=vh7dotot4lz1. Last consulted on February 28th 2016. See also Barrez (2011).

[554]Persson (2012).

[555]See Harde afspraken blijven uit op klimaatconferentie Warschau. http://www.nieuwsblad.be/article/detail.aspx?articleid=DMF20131123_022. Last consulted on February 28th 2016; Voorzichtig compromis op klimaattop Warschau bereikt. http://www.demorgen.be/wetenschap/voorzichtig-compromis-op-klimaattop-warschau-bereikt-a1745909/. Last consulted on February 28th 2016; Posthumus (2013).

[556]Van Haver (2014a), p. 10.

[557]Van Haver (2014b), p. 10.

Further Illustration 3.11 (continued)

ground-breaking, and unprecedented". However, once the initial optimism faded away, an awareness grew that the targets laid down in said agreement of 2015 are probably too ambitious to be considered realistic. More precisely, the Paris agreement of 2015 aims to limit warming to well below 2°C above pre-industrial levels, and furthermore recognizes that avoiding 1.5°C of warming would significantly reduce the risks and impacts of climate change. However, the emissions reduction commitments made by the participating countries are far from close to sufficient to achieve these targets. Carbon budget analyses have indicated that it will be in addition to impossible to avoid the 1.5°C limit without "negative emissions", such as sucking existing carbon dioxide out of the air by using technologies that are unproven or not yet in existence. As a result, some analysts have even qualified the temperature targets in the Paris agreement of 2015 as being "the height of hypocrisy".[558]

In the meantime, it was in January 2016 decided to put the so-called "Doomsday Clock", the symbolic countdown to mankind's end, at three minutes to midnight (i.e. on the brink of the apocalypse) because of the continued existential threat posed by climate change (in addition to threats posed by nuclear war).[559]

It is at least noteworthy that it is still assumed by some that climate change can be tackled using mainly financial contributions by some Western (so-called prosperous) countries to developing countries. Meanwhile, there is still no concrete approach to combat climate change and the consequences are becoming more and more (painfully) tangible. It even seems that since former American candidate for Presidency and winner of the Nobel peace prize Al Gore, in 2006, made a significant impression with his (documentary) movie "*An inconvenient truth*"[560], not much has been achieved to reduce global warming.[561]

(continued)

[558]Donner (2015).

[559]Goldenberg (2016).

[560]See also Gore (2013a). See furthermore Gore (2013b), p. 496.

[561]See furthermore Stiglitz (2006), pp. 166 a.f. See also Hazenberg (2013), p. 137.

As troublesome is that even after his election in November (2016), (then) president-elect Donald Trump kept on referring to the theories of climate change as a hoax propagated by China in order to undermine the American industry, thus creating the concern that under his presidency the tackling of the causes for this climate change will no longer be a primary issue. It has on the contrary been reported that president-elect Donald Trump intends to withdraw the United States from the Paris climate agreement, threatening to upend a treaty that experts say does not do enough to prevent a catastrophic rise in the average temperature on Earth. (See *e.g.* Goenka 2016.)

Further Illustration 3.11 (continued)

A lot of people hereby hardly seem to realize that the (relative) success of "homo sapiens" as one of the dominant forms of life on earth has been achieved mainly by the very favorable climate conditions of the "Holocene" period (the geological era from about 11,700 years ago till now), being a (relatively mild) period where the climate became warmer than in the previous period, the last ice age, and where "homo sapiens" was able to "develop" (and "thrive" until today).[562] Put otherwise, all (positive and negative) achievements of the species "homo sapiens" have mainly been possible thanks to an historically favorable climate (in its literal sense), in which mammals, in general and "*homo sapiens*" in particular, especially during the last 10,000 years (and this is not by chance a period in which human communities have evolved from strongly "nomadic", to first "agrarian", later "industrial" and currently even "post-industrial"), have been able to develop freely, but where the question arises how mankind will cope in case of a drastic climate change (as is predicted in certain very pessimistic forecasting models).

3.4.3.1.3 Provisional Conclusion

To conclude, one can safely put that in the worldwide prevailing (neo-)liberal **170**
model of economic organization, the unbridled accumulation of wealth seems, taking into account the aforementioned observations and illustrations, not so much reserved for those who work hard themselves (or better: those who are employed by capitalists, at the lowest possible wages, to work as hard as possibly), but, on the contrary, for those who show little scruples about shamelessly exploiting their fellow human beings at the lowest possible salary (in accordance with

[562] Amesz (2012), p. 61.

The aforementioned success of the species "homo sapiens" is referred to here, in a (very) personal reflection, as "relative", as mankind has indeed accomplished many magnificent achievements in the field of science (*e.g.* the printing of books, modern medicine, developments in aerospace and technology, the development of personal computers and similar gadgets, etc.); religion (including historical figures like Buddha, Milarepa, Jesus Christ, Francis of Assisi, Theresia of Lisieux, etc.); art (to list just a few in music: Bach, Mozart and Beethoven (but also: Mahler, Liszt, Chopin, Pärt, Puccini, Händel, Vivaldi, Sibelius, Monteverdi, etc.); literature: Shakespeare, Fitzgerald, Mann, Hesse, James Joyce, Roland Holst, etc.; in addition to the numerous painters and sculptors, since ancient history; in short, too many to mention) as well as in certain areas of social organization (*e.g.* social care institutions and mechanisms), but also in the field of science and in many other fields, much less wonderful achievements (including: nuclear, biological and biochemical weapons of destruction, warfare, slavery, suppression, genocide and other forms of mass murder, political and other kinds of suppression, terrorism, etc.).

Ricardo's "the Iron Law of the Wages"[563]) and who, by doing so, are furthermore willing to sacrifice all other possible values (among which the respect for human rights, respect for the environment, respect for animal rights,...) to their unbridled pursuit of profits, and this mainly in order to get richer themselves.[564]

It comes as no surprise that this observation is completely in line with one of the starting points on which capitalism is based, namely the fact that one should behave in the most selfish way possible.[565] However, different from another of its starting points, namely that such behavior will generate the highest degree of general welfare thinkable, capitalism principally causes (strong) egoists to become very rich[566], while at the same time leaving a majority of the rest of mankind in ever more misery.

171 As has been observed by philosophers such as Jaap Kruithof since decades already, the underlying promise that capitalism will result in the highest possible prosperity for all, has thus, two to three centuries later, not really been fulfilled.[567]

On the contrary, according to some, the capitalist economic order in today's world has all the characteristics of a contemporary feudal system[568] and has thus caused a fundamental breach with the enlightened concepts of "freedom", "equality" and "fraternity/solidarity"[569], all concepts on which liberal thinking was historically based (see also further, at marg. 19 of Chap. 6 of this book).

---

[563]Compare Bruckner (2002), p. 26; Fromm (1955), pp. 84–85.

[564]Loizou (2012), p. 32.
See also the earlier quoted findings of Erich Fromm and Herbert Marcuse.

[565]See already Adam Smith himself:

> Every man is rich or poor according to the degree in which he can afford to enjoy the necessaries, conveniences, and amusements of human life. But after the division of labor has once thoroughly taken place, it is but a very small part of these wit which a man's own labor can supply him. The far greater part of them he must derive from the quantity of that labor which he can command, or which he can afford to purchase. The value of any commodity, therefore, to the person who possesses it, and who means not to use or consume it himself, but to exchange it for other commodities, is equal to the quantity of labor which it enables him to purchase or to command. Labour, therefore, is the real measure of the exchangeable value of all commodities. (see Smith 1979, p. 47).

See furthermore Berend (2006), p. 14; Bruckner (2002), p. 26; Fromm (1955), pp. 84–85.

[566]Loizou (2012), p. 32.

[567]See especially Kruithof (1985). See also Bruckner (2002), p. 20; Fromm (1955), p. 85.
See furthermore Harari (2014), pp. 346 a.f.

[568]Bruckner (2002), p. 26.

[569]Pinxten (2014), pp. 7 a.f. See also Ongenae (2014), pp. 44–45, especially p. 44.

3.4.3.2 A Further Look at Some (Negative) Aspects of Capitalism in a Globalized Context

In the context of the contemporary globalized world economy, the aforementioned disastrous consequences of "pur sang" capitalism have only been further accentuated and magnified to extreme proportions. **172**

The "neo-liberal order" that would emerge under the influence of the aforementioned neo-liberal doctrines in the 1980s would soon, namely in the period 1989–1991, get further enhanced through the then occurring collapse of the communist system in Eastern Europe and in the Soviet Union.[570] **173**

This caused the end of any resistance, especially on an economic and political level, to the power of capitalism.[571]

Since then, the collapse of communist economies has often been used as a further argument for the statement that there are no alternatives to the free market.[572]

As a result, the belief in the free market became more and more fanatic, causing free markets to be seen as an absolute condition for a free society and for both individual and collective progress.

In the 1990s, the aforementioned influences paved the way for an unseen "globalization" of the world economy, to be understood as an continuously increasing level of inter-connectedness between countries at an economic level, a.o. characterized by an increase in the international traffic of goods, services, capital and labour.[573]

The so-called principles of "liberalization" and "deregulation" became hereby the leading principles of public policy.

According to Steger, as a consequence of this increasing globalization, the world economic order has witnessed three crucial developments, more specifically[574]:

- An increasing internationalization and liberalization of commerce and finance;
- A growing power of transnational companies[575] and large (investment) banks;
- An increasing role of international economic organizations, such as the IMF, the World Bank and the WTO.

---

[570] Steger (2013), p. 41; Galbraith (1994), pp. 220 a.f.

[571] With as a possible exception China, one of the few communist countries that has remained of economic and political significance, albeit one can but wonder if China's adherence to communism is but a matter of semantics, as economically speaking China and Chinese companies act as the best servants of the capitalist ideals.

See however also Galbraith (1994), p. 228, pointing out some of the problems capitalism was facing at the beginning of the 1990s.

[572] *E.g.* Rand (2008), p. 26.

[573] Stiglitz (2006), 4. See also Chomsky (1999), pp. 68 a.f.; Streeck (2015), pp. 107 a.f.

[574] Steger (2013), p. 41; Lloyd (2012), p. 370 a.f.; Berend (2006), pp. 263 a.f.

[575] Berend (2006), pp. 269 a.f.

See before Turner (1973), p. 231 p.

174 Due to this increasing globalization, the manifest imbalances which already before characterized the post-colonial, capitalist era, have taken on unprecedented proportions[576].

Striking examples hereof are:

- The traditional North-South relations, with all its known suffering, such as famine which has been present for decades in many Southern countries.

Further Illustration 3.12: The "Hunger Paradox"

The so-called "hunger paradox" (also known under the name "food paradox")[577] presents a harrowing illustration of how capitalism operates, especially of the mechanism of enrichment based on someone else's suffering.

While there is enough food available in the world to feed every human being in a decent way, even in 2016, the way capitalism functions is still causing hundreds of millions of people to be hungry.

The following figures, published on the occasion of the world food day of October 16th 2014 speak for themselves[578]:

- On the quoted date, there were about seven billion people in the world. According to certain forecasts, this amount will increase by 50% in less than a century. The question is whether the earth is capable of providing food for everyone. Recent research has shown that this is the case.
- Nevertheless, on the quoted date, worldwide, approximately 805 million people were suffering from hunger.[579] Although this number has decreased over the last decade by 11%, it remains an unacceptably large part of the world's population.
- 11.11.11 emphasized the fact that there are large regional differences, causing people in certain regions to be hungrier than before in history: ***"The recipe for a successful policy against hunger is the support of small local farmers combined with social protection".***
- The United Nations estimated that the world's population will amount to about 10.95 billion people by 2100. This is a much higher figure than previously assumed. An important explanation for this is the increase of the population in Sub Saharan Africa.
- Worldwide, about 33% of food is wasted before it enters the consumption cycle. In the South, this waste is generally due to poor stocking facilities. In the North, this is due to consumers' and retailers' behavior. According to UN estimates, this global waste amounts to 2.6 billion USD per year.

(continued)

[576]Steger (2013), p. 31.

[577]Habets and Gloudemans (2013), p. 196 .

[578]Van Erp (2014).

[579]According to figures from the Food and Agriculture organization of the United Nations (FAO).

Further Illustration 3.12 (continued)

- The FAO estimated that in 2014, all farmers worldwide harvested 2512 billion tons of food. If this figure is correct, this would be the most successful year ever in terms of food production.
- The average number of food calories available per person per day was in 2011 (the year in which this figure was apparently for the last time measured) 2868. This number is increasing slightly every year. In 1990, the number amounted to 2619 available food calories per person per day. This growth is remarkable taking into account the population growth over that period. In other words, there is indeed enough food on the planet to feed all its inhabitants.
- According to further calculations by the Dutch foundation "*Stichting Werelddelen*", which are based on numbers published by the FAO, when effecting a fair distribution of the current world food production, the following quantities of food would be available per person per day in the world[580]: 264 g of wheat; 269 g of rice; 268 g of corn; 60 g of barley; 68 g of other cereals; 145 g of potatoes; 313 g of carrot and root crops; 25 g of pulses; 303 g of vegetables; 212 g of fruit; 50 g of raw sugar; 260 g of milk; 57 g of fish; 50 g of (kitchen) oil.

In other words, hunger is not a problem of the earth's food producing capacity, but a problem stemming from the socioeconomic organization of agriculture and trade, in other words, a problem created and supported by capitalism.

- There is, moreover, not only hunger in Southern countries.

  Even traditionally prosperous (albeit "neo-liberalized") countries, such as the United Kingdom and the United States of America (with a so called "affluent society"), are increasingly faced with hunger.
- A press release of the beginning of December 2014 reported that in the United Kingdom, at that moment, 913,138 British people regularly attended the "Trussell Trust" food bank. It was hereby also reported that the main cause for this has been the failure of the British social security system, which, since the neo-liberal regime of Margaret Thatcher (see above, at marg. 148 a.f. of this chapter), and afterwards of David Cameron (from 2010 till 2016), has gradually been dismantled.[581]

[580]http://www.beleven.org/feest/wereld_voedseldag (last consulted on October 16th 2014).

[581]McSmith (2014); see also Hunger has not vanished from our affluent, even overweight, society—as Archbishop Welby has pointed out. http://www.independent.co.uk/voices/editorials/hunger-has-not-vanished-from-our-affluent-even-overweight-society--as-archbishop-welby-has-pointed-out-9909189.html. Last consulted on February 28th 2016.

When evaluating this fact, one should bear in mind that the aforementioned illustration is most likely the metaphorical tip of the iceberg and that, in post-Thatcher United Kingdom, this type of "food banks" are most probably all over the country experiencing an increasing growth of people becoming dependent on them.

More in general, it has been furthermore reported in a recent Belgian press column[582] that the implementation of economic neo-liberalism by conservative policy makers in the United Kingdom has reached such an extent that the United Kingdom no longer qualifies as a welfare state.

Some consequences of this neo-liberal policy of destroying the welfare state speak for themselves.

One such striking example of the mentioned consequences of implementing economic neo-liberalism is that no less than 20% of the population of the United Kingdom can no longer afford to attend a private dentist and has to take its dental health care into own hands. This goes as far as resorting to repairing one's own teeth instead of having it done by a dentist and even to removing one's own teeth with pliers (or have it done by a friend or relative). As a result, thousands of people across Britain are reported using "DIY dentistry sets" which can be easily purchased on the market to replace loose fillings, caps and crowns. It consequently hardly comes as a surprise that, by the age of seventy, poor Brits have on average eight teeth less than their richer countrymen.

The same press column furthermore reports that under the government of David Cameron, as of 2010, the general budget for public services was diminished from 45% of the Gross National Product to less than 40%, and it is estimated that by 2020 this percentage will be even more lowered to 36%. In the meantime, more than a million government jobs have been abolished and the budgets of local governments have been cut in half. All over the United Kingdom, public shelters, dayrooms and nursing homes are systematically closed. Psychiatric patients become wanderers, while handicapped children have to remain indoors all the time as they have no longer any place to go to.

Neo-liberal government policy hereby also aims at replacing police offices by private security services: it has been reported that, in recent times, about 17,000 police jobs were cancelled, while in the coming years more than 20,000 further police jobs will face the same destiny.

More in general, all kinds of mechanisms protecting laborers and poor people are systematically abandoned in the United Kingdom, turning the former welfare state into a state based upon the (neo-) liberal principle that each man has to take care of his own. Teachers are even reported to pay themselves for breakfasts for the poor children in their classroom.

Shortly, by implementing the neo-liberal thought good, the United Kingdom is enhancing poverty, is evermore widening the gap between the poor and the rich classes and is systematically releasing its care function, abandoning it more

---

[582] Van Bekhoven (2016), p. 26.

and more into the hands of either the markets (hence only to be afforded by the rich) or to volunteers providing charity.[583]

- Also in the United States of America, still one of the most prosperous capitalist countries in the world, hunger and hence the need for food banks is growing at an alarming rate.

  According to the website of the food bank "Feeding America" (www.feedingamerica.org), a worrying number of one in six inhabitants of the USA is said to depend on such food help.

  Still according to this same website, in 2012, 46.5 million Americans (15% of the American population) were living in poverty (amongst which 16.1 million (or 22%) children under eighteen). This is, furthermore, reported to be the highest number in over 50 years.[584] In that same year, about 49 million American inhabitants were living in so-called "food insecure families" (including about 16 million children).[585]

  According to the findings of a similar study of 2014, 72% of families calling upon the services of the food bank "Feeding America" then lived below the official (federal) poverty line[586], at a time when their median income was 9175 USD per year. According to the same study, the food bank "Feeding America", supplied food help to 46.5 million people, including 12 million children and 7 million elderly (through a network of 58,000 food centres).[587]

  In this 2014 study conducted by "Feeding America", it has furthermore been stated that the great recession of 2008 (caused by the failure of the financial system at that time) has been one of the main causes of poverty and hunger in the USA today.[588]

  It is not a coincidence that the demise of the welfare state is particularly happening in the United Kingdom and the United States of America, both countries which have been among the first Western countries to adopt economic

[583]Van Bekhoven (2016), p. 26.

[584]Poverty and Hunger in America. http://www.feedingamerica.org/hunger-in-america/impact-of-hunger/hunger-and-poverty/. Last consulted on February 28th 2016.

[585]Poverty and Hunger in America. http://www.feedingamerica.org/hunger-in-america/impact-of-hunger/hunger-and-poverty/. Last consulted on February 28th 2016.

[586]The "federal poverty line" can be consulted on http://aspe.hhs.gov/poverty/14poverty.cfm

[587]Feeding America (2014).

[588] Unemployment and poverty rates have remained high since the Great Recession of 2008, and the number of households receiving nutrition assistance from the federal government's Supplemental Nutrition Assistance Program has increased by approximately 50 percent between 2009 and 2013. Demand for charitable food assistance has also expanded. HIA 2014 finds an increased number of individuals relying on charitable assistance to access nutritious foods for themselves and their families. (Feeding America 2014, p. 1).

The economy has experienced an unusually slow recovery since the deep recession in 2008 and 2009. The nation's poverty rate reached 15.1 percent in 2010, the highest rate since 1993. The poverty rate remained at 15 percent in 2012 with 46.5 million people living in poverty. This is the largest number living in poverty since statistics were first published more than 50 years ago. (Feeding America 2014, p. 3).

neo-liberalism in order to purify capitalism of the characteristics (which, in neo-liberal doctrine, were assumed to be devastating) of the mixed economy (see above, under Sect. 3.4.2.3).

- The traditional relationships between North and South, with, as a second illustration, the problem of the low pricing policies of products manufactured in Southern countries (among which numerous agricultural products).[589]

  Often, enterprises of Northern sphere countries purchase such (agricultural) products at (extreme) low prices in order to sell them in Northern countries at much higher prices.

  In this process, the income of the original producers (especially the farmers located in the Southern countries) usually remains extremely low, albeit the consumers in the home countries of said importers/distributors pay, in general, very high prices. Consequently, it is especially the profit margins of the large importers/distributors that are very high (while all this is justified by the personal, individualistic profit pursuit by said importers/distributors).[590]

  It speaks for itself that, as a consequence, poverty in the poor(er) countries prevails, and within capitalism (i.e. taking into account its starting premises), it is hard to see how this will ever be dealt with in a fair and just way (since capitalist mechanisms are in themselves the main cause for this poverty).

  Stiglitz has in this regard remarked that the world is characterized by an ever intensifying race between the growth of the world population and the growth of poverty, and that poverty is winning.[591]

  As a consequence, especially the African continent is increasingly characterized by ever increasing and deepening rifts between the rich and the poor, whereby some press has described (most) African cities as "*small islands of high wealth surrounded by oceans of shantytowns*", where people are fighting for basic necessities such as clean drinking water and for an elementary sewer system.[592]

  Already in 1992, Galbraith made a similar observation about what he called the "golden ghettos" in the largely poverty-stricken city of Manila in The Philippines, leaving the open question whether American and European[593] cities

---

[589] Food and Agriculture Organization of the United Nations (FAO) (2014); see also Lloyd (2012), p. 374; Stiglitz and Chariton (2005), p. 315 .

[590] The economic pie of 2014 is far larger than the pie of 1500, but is distributed so unevenly that many African peasants and Indonesian labourers return home after a hard day's work with less food than did their ancestors 500 years ago. Much like the Agricultural Revolution, so too the growth of the modern economy might turn out to be a colossal fraud. The human species and the global economy may well keep growing, but many more individuals may live in hunger and want. (Harari 2014, p. 372).

[591] Stiglitz (2006), p. 10.

[592] Meredith (2014), pp. 100–103, especially 103.

[593] See even the remark of the American Republican politician Donald Trump that Brussels has been turned into a hell hole. (See *e.g.* CDC 2016; Campbell 2016.)

will also, in the future, align to this model as well (or in many cases: even more than is already the case).[594]

Further Illustration 3.13: Cocoa Versus Chocolate
On October 24th 2014, a CNN money-report was dedicated to a donation which the chocolate industry had given of (a mere) 600,000 USD to finance the fight against "Ebola".[595]

The same report stated that the total turnover of the chocolate industry was estimated at 67 billion USD in 2014, of which 10 billion USD were company profits. The CNN-report hereby indicated that from the selling price of any (finished) chocolate product, about 70% goes to the (generally Western) chocolate producers and only about 6% to Southern cocoa farmers.

In 2014, the income of an average cocoa farmer was less than 2 USD per day.[596] As a consequence, there is a massive need for child labor in order for the production of cocoa to be economically viable to some extent.[597]

Up till today the worldwide sale of chocolate under the fair trade label only amounts to only 0.5% of total cocoa production.[598]

- Increasing poverty within the European Union in general, illustrated by recent reports that one out of five children within the European Union grows up in households struck by poverty.[599]
- To conclude, the following (recent) figures on world poverty in 2014 speak for themselves.[600]
  - 2.2 billion people were living in or on the edge of multidimensional poverty.
  - 80% of the world population was not covered by any type of social protection.
  - 12% (or 842 million people) were chronically hungry.
  - Worldwide, 1.5 billion people were working without any formal employment contract or any similar protective regulation.
- The worldwide ever growing economic inequality, which, *inter alia*, is expressed in an unequal income distribution (especially between those dependent on income from labor versus capital).

594 Galbraith (1992), p. 169.

595 Trafecante (2014).

596 Child labor and Slavery in the Chocolate Industry. http://www.foodispower.org/slavery-chocolate/. Last consulted on February 28th 2016.

597 Child labor and Slavery in the Chocolate Industry. http://www.foodispower.org/slavery-chocolate/. Last consulted on February 28th 2016.

598 The Chocolate industry. http://www.icco.org/about-cocoa/chocolate-industry.html. Last consulted on February 28th 2016.

599 Pironet (2014), p. 3.

600 United Nations Development Programme (UNDP) (2014), p. 3.

It has already been argued since decades that the modern market economy accords wealth and distributes income in a highly unequal, socially adverse and inherently functionally damaging fashion.[601]

The Oxfam study "*Even it up*", mentioned earlier, describes this as follows[602]:

> Since 1990, income from labor has made up a declining share of GDP across low-, middle- and high-income countries alike. Around the world, ordinary workers are taking home an ever-dwindling slice of the pie, while those at the top take more and more.
>
> In 2014, the UK top 100 executives took home 131 times as much as their average employee, yet only 15 of these companies have committed to pay their employees a living wage. In South Africa, a platinum miner would need to work for 93 years just to earn the average CEO's annual bonus. Meanwhile, the International Trade Union Confederation estimates that 40 percent of workers are trapped in the informal sector, where there are no minimum wages and workers' rights are ignored.

This issue will be dealt with in more detail further in the text as a separate topic (see under Sect. 3.4.8).

- The position of a small group of countries, which, by mere coincidence, dispose of a huge natural wealth (for instance certain resources, energy,. . .) that can be exploited at a (relatively) low cost and through (relatively) low efforts, but which is sold at very high prices.

  Obvious examples hereof are clearly (crude) oil (and other fossil fuels).[603]

  Some of these countries with such natural resources have (especially in the post-colonial era) been able to develop into strong export(ing) countries, which has helped them to build unusually large monetary reserves and/or enabled some of their privileged inhabitants to build unusually large reserves of foreign currency.

  On the other hand, the "consumer countries" of this type of commodity have, especially since the 1970s, increasingly become debtor-countries.[604]
- The emergence of countries, where, due to a large surplus population, linked to the absence of protective social legislation, the production factor "labour" can be used at relatively low cost, enabling enterprises with company branches in these countries to manufacture numerous goods at much cheaper prices than competitors in countries where the labor production factor has remained much more expensive.

  As a result, the globalized world increasingly witnesses an almost paradoxical situation, whereby a multitude of social protection legislation of a given country has more and more become a threat to the general wellbeing of its

[601] See Galbraith (1996), 60.

[602] Oxfam (2014), p. 15.

[603] See *e.g.* Pisani (2014).

[604] Romero-Barrutieta et al. (2011) (WP/11/157), p. 6.

inhabitants, rather than an added value. (See already the analysis under Sect. 2.7 of Chap. 2 of this book.)

Indeed, enterprises of countries where, due to a highly developed social protection policy, the cost of labor is far more expensive in comparison to other countries where no social protection prevails, in a globalized economy and in many sectors, face an important competitive disadvantage.

This has caused production more and more to shift to these countries where protective social legislation is less rigorous and/or where labor costs have remained lower. An effect of this phenomenon has been that the economies (especially the so-called "(manual) manufacturing industry") of countries with strong social legislation have systematically decreased over the past decades (a phenomenon which is also referred to as "deindustrialization") to the benefit of a rise of the economies of countries where the labor production factor has remained cheap due to a lack of comparable protective social legislation.[605]

A certain equilibrium has so far remained in place for certain sectors of industry where there is a higher need for labor forces with a higher level of specialization, given that in countries with a weaker protective social legislation the degree of schooling and education is usually also lower, but also here, the latter countries are catching up at a fast pace.[606]

Consequently, an evolution is taking place where:

- Traditionally strong Western economies are losing grip, partially as in these countries with historically strong models of social protection, the production of a growing number of products (and services) becomes less and less competitive;
- A number of economies (especially in Asian and South American countries) have been growing rapidly, where the weakness of the social protection models in those countries is translated into a larger potential for competitive production in several economic sectors;
- At the monetary level, the first group of countries is developing increasingly into "debtor countries", while the latter increasingly builds up monetary reserves, without (a large part of) the population of this group improving their life situation to a significant degree.
- In both groups of countries, the gaps between the rich and the poor are growing.

  In the traditional "rich" countries, this is mainly due to the fact that their governments, in order to enhance the competitivity of the enterprises of said countries on the global markets, have under the impulse of economic neo-liberalism been inclined to diminish the social protective mechanisms in place. In addition to this, these traditional countries are, as said, facing an ongoing deindustrialization due to the behaviour of their (big) enterprises

[605]Todd (2015), pp. 85–86 (also: Todd 2015, p. 67), pointing out how in Europe, this has been caused by the forces underlying the European unification which sacrificed the interests of industry to those of a relentless financial system, mainly having resulted in a "Europe of unequal nations".

[606]See *e.g.* OECD (2014).

which, more and more, relocate production to countries where the cost of wages is even lower.

In the traditional "poorer" countries, the widening of the gaps between the rich and the poor is due to the fact that capitalism is being developed without at the same time putting social protective measures in place.

175 These are, obviously, just a few examples of some manifest imbalances to which capitalist principles are driving the global economy, at a global (or better: globalized) level.

For more detailed illustrations of this, reference can be made to more specialized economic literature sources.[607]

3.4.3.3 Grim Prognoses for the Future

176 Modern research increasingly confirms classic critiques of capitalism[608], and has further indicated that the high level of liberalization of (international) traffic of trade and of capital and payment transactions, but also the free traffic of people (which, in fact, comes down to a free traffic of (cheap) labour), has mainly led to an increased mobility of business life, whereby enterprises increasingly settle in countries where the cost of labor is kept at the lowest level (*inter alia* because the social protective legislation there is also at the lowest level).[609]

This causes capitalism to develop even more into an economic system where, inherent of its principle that the "stronger" players in economic life are allowed, or even supposed, to take advantage of the "weaker" ones—in the current context: those controlling the production factor "capital" are able to take advantage of people "merely" providing labor—production is shifting more and more to countries where the labor production factor is the cheapest, namely countries where the social protective legislation has remained at its weakest.[610]

In the countries with strong social protective models, production is more and more in danger of being gradually dismantled (in a process which is, meanwhile, also referred to as "deindustrialization"). As a result, in these countries, the economic fabric gets increasingly eroded (as a capitalist economy, based on the principle of private money creation by private banks, cannot function purely by providing services).[611]

---

[607] Such as the works of John Kenneth Galbraith and, in later times, those of Joseph Stiglitz and Paul Krugman, all renowned economists who, in their (numerous) writings, have brought some of the excesses of capitalism to the attention of the general public, albeit one can but observe that even these renowned economists have not succeeded in convincing policy makers to basically alter the course of the economy.

[608] As, for instance, already in the 1970s strongly expressed by the earlier quoted "Club of Rome".

[609] Steger (2013), p. 31.

[610] Stiglitz (2006), p. 67.

[611] Michielsen (2014), pp. 13–14.

In the wake of this "deindustrialization" which is in progress in many Western countries (including at a disturbingly high level: Western Europe), there is in parallel a dismantling of the legislation protecting labor and of social care mechanisms, in a development which (as has been the case regarding fiscal policy making) can be more and more be described as a true *"race to the bottom"*.[612]

Further Illustration 3.14: Deindustrialization in Belgium

According to certain press releases, in the period from 2001–2011, the turnover of the industry sector in Belgium has been reduced by a shocking 15%.[613]

In 2014, the (service) sectors "banking and insurance", "marketing", "maintenance services", "transportation and logistics" and "research and development", together accounted for over half of Belgian added value, whereby it has been noted that, under capitalism, these service sectors can only survive in as far as they keep servicing "manufacturing industry".

In the same year, about 26% of the Belgian economy was made up of independent services, such as "health", "education", "administration", "catering", "food service", "art", and "media", all sectors mainly financed by the government (in other words, from tax income which is generated by other sectors).

Also in 2014, the "manufacturing industry" represented only 14% of the Belgian economic fabric. The sectors "construction", "resources", and "utility companies" together accounted for 8% of Belgian economy, and the agricultural sector only for 1%.[614]

This gradual disappearance of the "manufacturing sector" in Belgium is mainly impacting medium skilled labor, causing employees with a higher education to apply for positions where a lower grade of schooling would suffice, thus forcing employees to apply for positions requiring a lower level of schooling out of the labor market. This effect is even strengthened by the increasing level of technological developments, whereby labor positions which are disappearing due to technical evolutions, are not proportionally replaced (causing an increasing overflow of cheap labor forces).[615]

It needs to be noticed that this process is entirely in line with the impact of globalization, especially (albeit *inter alia*) on the level of the shift of labor requiring lower schooling), which for example Stiglitz already described in detail in 2006.[616]

---

[612]Stiglitz (2006), 67.

[613]Michielsen (2014), pp. 13–14.

[614]Michielsen (2014), pp. 13–14.

[615]Michielsen (2014), pp. 13–14; see also Technologie lost beloftes niet in. In: Trends December 11th (2014), pp. 28–31.

[616]Stiglitz (2006), pp. 67–68.

As a result of this shift of production from European countries (and to some extent, also the USA, where labor is still cheaper than in many (West) European countries[617]) towards mainly Asian countries, a worldwide erosion of social correction mechanisms as a result of the unbridled impact of capitalism is taking place (providing an additional indication that (neo-)liberal capitalism does not fulfil its underlying promise of achieving the highest possible wealth and welfare for the majority of people).

177 Taking into account the current globalized world economy (including its monetary system) and especially taking into account this process of "deindustrialization" which is ongoing in many Western countries, the future of Western countries within a globalized capitalist economy does not look very bright.[618]

The reason for this pessimism is that, within a globalized capitalist economy, only "manufacturing" industry can generate significant export (of manufactured products). It is, for example, much more difficult to export services abroad than to export goods (except in exceptional cases, such as the Indian call centres, in addition to tourism).

In other words, many (West) European countries, such as Belgium, witnessing a high degree of "deindustrialization", are increasingly threatened with a decrease of their export position (and, consequently, with deficits on the current account of their balance of payments).[619]

Moreover, such countries at the same time risk becoming more dependent on import, which (as discussed above; see above, under Sect. 2.7 of Chap. 2 of this book) is likely to result in a foreign debt position.

The question then becomes how long such a situation can last, as there is, moreover, a growing awareness that the preservation of the current (European and global) monetary system, leads to an even further increase of the (already in progress) dismantling of social protection mechanisms (among which legislation on the protection of labor and social care mechanisms).[620]

178 More than ever, the moment in history seems ripe to provide a new ethical foundation to (and for the correction of) the free market economy, at least based on following pillars (*i*) turning money creation into a "public tool"; (*ii*) the development of a worldwide harmonization of social protection and (*iii*) of a worldwide decisive alignment of fiscal and para-fiscal governmental policies.

---

[617]Social protection in the USA has traditionally been far lower than in most (West) European countries.

[618]Stiglitz (2006), p. 68.

[619]It hereby needs to be further taken into consideration that such countries, in as far as they are part of the Eurozone, no longer have the legal power to devalue their own currency (see *e.g.* Cohen 2008a, pp. 37–53, especially p. 38), depriving them of the possibility to "boost" their export position in that way.

[620]Jan Blommaert mentions in this context a true "divide" with the model of "social democratic consensus" which had emerged in Western Europe after the Second World War, and states that this is mainly due to the effect of the ideological choices which characterize neo-liberalism; see Blommaert (2014).

Only in this way, a sufficient level playing field will emerge whereby the world economy could be directed to a higher level of general wellbeing (instead of the current free market system which mainly leads to an (unbridled) accumulation of wealth for the benefit of a few extremely rich people) and will a further dismantling of the social protective systems to the disadvantage of the middle class and poor (er) classes be avoided.

The latter issue will be treated in more detail in the Chaps. 4 and 5 of this book.

3.4.4 The Development of the Financial System Under the Doctrine of Economic Neo-liberalism

In addition to the abovementioned more general socioeconomic impact of **179**
implementing the neo-liberal ideology into daily practice, the latter has for many (Western and Western inspired) capitalist countries also offered the theoretical framework, as well as the ethical foundation, for some major restructurings of the financial and banking sector from the second half of the 1980s on.[621]

These restructurings were based on an unbridled upscaling, often encouraged by the political world[622], which went hand in hand with a far stretching degree of "liberalization" and "deregulation" of the financial sector.[623]

The liberalization of the financial sector was to a large extent driven by regulatory impulses (for instance the policy of the Reagan-administration in the 1980s, see above, at marg. 148 a.f. of this chapter) and led to an even further increasing level of globalization, making a lot of banks, which up till then were substantially only, or mainly, active on a national level, to become more active on foreign markets, often in very distant regions and (company) cultures with which the headquarters of such banks had little or no real feeling. In this, these banks operative in other countries continued more and more to focus on the development of an ever more differentiated array of products and services under the (neo-) Smithian "Leitmotiv" of the pursuit of ever more and bigger profits.

In this way, the international financial sector got more and more characterized by **180**
the fact that a large part of the money flows were no longer used for the purpose of productive investments, such as the setup of production units (for example factories

[621]Krugman (2009), pp. 65 a.f.

[622]In Europe, the wave of mergers and acquisitions in the financial sector of the late 1980s, early 1990s was to a large extent initiated by the European preparatory works of creating an internal market for financial services, especially the so-called "White Paper on completing the internal market which was adopted by the Milan European Council of 28th June 1985" [COM/85/0310], as well as several European banking directives of a later date.

[623]Steger (2013), pp. 48–49.

with machines), or the consolidation of raw materials and labor forces in order to generate sellable products.[624]

On the contrary, a large part of the financial growth appeared in the form of high risk "hedge funds", as well as other merely monetary currency markets and markets in financial instruments (where, for instance, rights to profits from future production, or to other financial products, got traded). Financial markets got hereby more and more driven by speculation based on "not-in-the-real-world-existing" economic values.[625]

Said evolutions resulted in what has been called a real "financialization" of the world economy.[626]

Furthermore, globally operating speculators started to anticipate the deficiencies of these financial markets (among which poor regulation); this for example allowed for the making of excessive profits in the emerging financial markets of formerly developing countries (such as some Asian financial markets). As international money and capital flows could change direction very quickly, they were able to create artificial cycles of growth and decline which endangered the social welfare of entire regions.[627]

Consequently, it is of no surprise that some of these actions are deemed to have attributed to the most severe financial crisis of the post WWII era[628], namely the financial crisis of 2008.

181 Partially as a consequence of the aforementioned developments, many Western banks, from the 1980s and 1990s onwards, would undergo a true metamorphosis.

For instance, the model of the "classic deposit bank" which was embedded in a national territory and which mainly focused on the (local) collection of deposits and credit lending, was no longer considered to be a sufficiently competitive business model. Instead, furthermore as a result of an unseen wave of mergers and acquisitions[629], large banking groups, among which so called "financial conglomerates" (with subsidiaries active in other domains than banking, including insurance and stock broker activities) arose, and within these financial groups, deposit banks more and more started to resemble and to behave as true investment banks.[630]

In other words, "mixed" banks (an/or bank groups) developed, with, in addition to their classic activities of deposit collection and credit lending, a very diversified array of products and services, among which a wide array of investment and stock exchange related products and services, which however, very often, contained much higher risks (than mere credit lending to national economic residents).

---

[624] Harvey (2010), p. 29 a.f.

[625] Steger (2013), pp. 43–46; Loizou (2012), p. 176; Gore (2013a), pp. 14 and 119 (also: Gore 2013b, p. 59).

[626] Harvey (2010), p. 29. See also Streeck (2015), p. 88.

[627] Steger (2013), pp. 43–46.

[628] Steger (2013), pp. 43–46; Engelen (2011), p. 281.

[629] Stiglitz (2003), p. 162; Steger (2013), pp. 48–49, 162; Zuboff and Maxmin (2002) (1st ed.: 2002), p. 205.

[630] Smithers (2013), p. 96.

In this evolution, classic banking principles of caution were albeit completely abandoned. The classical "*know thy customer*"-principle (which, in the past, had guaranteed a cautious credit policy) had principally to make way for larger scale investment policies mainly supported by written documentation (often generated in foreign countries and based upon foreign legislation). As a result, investments by banks got more and more based on an albeit blind trust in the (often vague) validation of underlying investment values (for example claims towards ultimate debtors) by, *inter alia*, professional rating-agencies (which themselves based their validation policies mainly on mathematical models, rather than on a true knowledge of the individual debtors of the underlying credit or similar positions).[631]

This new type of financial products and services presented (in the short term) previously unknown sources of profits, while at the same time blinding the banks for the severe risks they represented.[632]

The inventivity of the banking sector, to a large extent unhindered by any regulatory prohibitions, to come up with ever more complex financial products and services (in order to make as much profit possible) was unseen before in history.[633]

In the wake of this diversification and internationalization (or: globalization) process, for example so-called "securitization"-techniques emerged, whereby a bank that became (relatively) aware of the high risk of some of its past transactions (for example loans it had provided), would consolidate these in a separate corporate vehicle which was created for that purpose only.[634] **182**

The shares of these corporate vehicles were then sold to other bank customers as so-called "interesting investments".

The banks "selling" such investments, often made huge short term profits, while, at the same time, the risks the underlying debts imposed, were (without any shame) shifted to an often unsuspicious large public of savers or to a (foreign) institutional investors public (which, in some cases, even could count on credit lending from the bank selling its investment, in order to finance the participation in these new corporate vehicles which were presented as new investment products).

Other innovative financial products, such as hedge funds based upon credit speculation, were furthermore feeding a wide variety of speculative activities.[635]

Furthermore, the use of these kinds of techniques caused a cascading effect as banks, which started to understand that they could quite easily remove high risk investments from their investment portfolio, became more careless in making initial investments (with as an obvious example banking behaviour regarding mortgage credits). Such high risk receivables positions could, thanks to securitization techniques, afterwards relatively easily be transferred to a specialized investment

---

[631] Klok and van Uffelen (2009), pp. 31 a.f.

[632] Karmel (2010), pp. 823–845.

[633] Smithers (2013), p. 90.

[634] Klok and van Uffelen (2009), pp. 32–33.

[635] Steger (2013), p. 49. See also Krugman (2012), p. 79; Mallaby (2011) (1st ed. 2010), p. 482.

vehicle which was financed with the savings surpluses of other economic agents, often residing in other countries.[636]

183 At least until the financial crisis of 2008, central banks of the leading Western countries would not impose any real objections towards these types of operations, but, on the contrary, would often support them through their central interest rate policy.[637]

Under the argument that there was a swift need for cheap money to stimulate the economy, from the 1990s on, central bank interest rates were hence kept at a very low level, causing the private banking sector even more willing to provide (cheaper and cheaper) credit to other economic agents (families and enterprises, but also governments of countries).

The credit rating limits were continuously decreased, which surprisingly did not prevent banks from providing such credits to "bad" borrowers, as the claims (towards bad borrowers) resulting from this were, as explained before, afterwards often shifted to separate vehicles which were financed by investments based upon savings surpluses of other economic agents (especially private individuals and families, in some cases even from foreign countries).[638]

184 At the monetary level, this type of "easy credit lending" would result into a high increase of (private) money creation, an evolution which, oddly enough, was not limited, but on the contrary encouraged by central banks. As a result, more and more money was brought into circulation and this to such excessive levels that the total amount of money became no longer measurable.[639]

3.4.5 The Fate of Money in a Credit Economy

185 The "easy money climate" which was generated through and in the wake of the aforementioned developments in the financial sector started already in the 1980s[640] and would have an enormous impact on the economic system of many Western (and Western-inspired) countries.

---

[636] Verhaeghe (2011), p. 40.

[637] McLean and Nocera (2011). See also Smithers (2013) pp. 88–89:

> It is also widely believed that banks were responsible for the financial crisis. My own view is that the crisis would not have occurred if central banks and particularly the Federal Reserve had not fueled the rises in debt and asset prices by foolish policies.

[638] Steger (2013), p. 49.

[639] Smithers (2013), p. 89.

[640] Indeed, many social analysts agree that capitalism changed significantly around 1980, most probably as a result of the then occurring changes as a result of the implementation of the neo-liberal economic doctrines (See Kotz and McDonough 2010, p. 93.)

The economy of these countries turned more and more into a "credit economy" which gradually started to determine the outlook of all parts of society.[641]

It has by some been held that in the present "major" economies, banking assets (that is mainly loans) are equivalent to around 150% of those countries' combined GDP.[642]

In 2006, global banking assets were reported to equal around USD 29 trillion, roughly 63% of the (then) world GDP.[643]

Even after the financial crisis, it has been reported that, on a global scale, the total outstanding bank debt is still far too big in comparison to the growth of the economy. According to figures provided by the Financial Stability Board[644], in 1990 the outstanding bank credit granted by the world's ten largest banks alone amounted to 16% of the world GDP. In 2008, this figure amounted to 40% of the world GDP and in March 2016 still to 35% of the world GDP (or to an amount of 26,000 billion USD).[645]

Otherwise put, over the past decades, in addition to governments and enterprises, also private individuals and households have increasingly been encouraged (even by fiscal stimuli) and prepared to take up credit for a diversity of expenditures, leading to the development of consumer credits for different types of utilities, student loans, first, second,... mortgages[646] (sometimes financing more than one house for the same family), etc.

"Consumer credits" (in the broad sense of the word) were even increasingly granted for all types of (intrinsically useless) luxury spending[647].

---

[641] Middelkoop (2014), p. 88, speaking of "*a planet of debt*"; Stiglitz (2006), p. 211. See also Ronse (1992), p. 75.

[642] Ferguson (2009), p. 63.

[643] Ferguson (2009), p. 63.

[644] It has however also been indicated that regulatory changes which have been made since the financial crisis of 2008 have had some impact. Although the 11 banks that most perturb the Financial Stability Board have not really shrunk, they have at least stopped growing. As a result, there has been a marked change since the pre-crisis period: in 1990 the world's ten biggest banks had just USD 3.6 trillion of assets (USD 6.6 trillion in today's prices)—equivalent to 16% of global GDP. By 2008 they had assets of USD 25 trillion (40% of global GDP). In 2016, they had assets of USD 26 trillion, or 35% of global GDP. (See Chop chop. Why haven't banking giants got a lot smaller?. http://www.economist.com/news/finance-and-economics/21689636-why-havent-banking-giants-got-lot-smaller-chop-chop. Last consulted on February 28th 2016.)

[645] Bauwens (2016).

[646] As regards the Belgian situation, see Claerhout (2014a), pp. 15–19.

[647] See on the theory of the "created wants", *e.g.* Bakan (2005), p. 174:

> The ideal is to have individuals who are totally disassociated from one another, who don't care about anyone else. My sense of value is just how many created wants I can satisfy. And how deeply can I go into debt and still get away with satisfying created wants. If you can create a society in which the unit, the smallest unit, is a person in a tube and no connections to people, that would be ideal.

For an explanation how capitalism steers consumer credit behavior, see Zuboff and Maxmin 2004 (1st edition: 2002), p. 458.

Some figures, albeit not easily obtainable (especially for a non-economist), speak for themselves.

As regards for example Belgium, according to the November 2014[648] monthly report of the National Bank of Belgium, there were then more open credits to individuals than inhabitants of the Kingdom, namely 11.37 million (of which 8,542,047 consumer credits and 2,827,992 mortgage credits), spread over 6,231,144 million individuals (being the number of individuals with at least one credit contract). Of these, 350,645 individuals were registered for late payment for at least one credit, and in total 522,231 credit contracts were registered for late payment. At the end of November 2014, the total number of delayed payments for all these individuals together amounted to 3.092130 billion euro, or on average 8800 euro per person having a payment delay. This meant an increase in payment delay compared to the end of November 2013, which was at that moment 2.950435 billion euro (mentioning as main cause the financial crisis since 2008[649]).

In 2015, there were in Belgium in total 11,248,748 credit agreements outstanding in Belgium, which was a slight decrease in comparison with 2014 of 0.7%. However, consumer credits and mortgage credits showed an increase with 4%, respectively 1.9%. In the same year, there were in total 173,417 registered late payments.[650]

According to numbers released by the think tank "Bruegel", in 2013, the total amount of mortgage credits (for house purchase) within the entire Eurozone was estimated to amount to 3800 billion euro (or 3.8 trillion euro).[651]

The explanation for this excessive consumer credit behavior, is that the modern capitalist economy needs to continuously grow in order to remain sustainable (as Harari puts it: in the same way as a shark needs to continuously swim, or else it suffocates).[652] Where there is production, there must also be consumption (if not, producers go bankrupt),[653] causing the economy to become a system of "*production for production's sake*", but at the same time a system of "*consumption for consumption's sake*", as all produced goods need to find a buyer.[654] In this way, capitalism had to evolve into an economic system serving no other purpose than

---

[648]http://www.nbb.be/DOC/CR/CCP/Publications/Kerncijfers_CKP_NL.pdf (last consulted on December 12th 2014).

[649]Centrale voor kredieten aan particulieren (NBB) (2013), p. 9.

[650]For further details, see https://www.nbb.be/doc/cr/ccp/publications/bro_ckpstat2015n_20012016.pdf; last consulted on January 22nd 2016.

[651]Altomonte and Bussoli (2014). See also Claerhout (2014b), pp. 28–30, especially p. 29.

[652]Harari (2014), p. 388.

[653]Harari (2014), p. 388.

[654]This criticism already goes back to Karl Marx (see Beaud 1994, p. 150), and has later on been further developed by John Kenneth Galbraith, for instance and especially in his book "*The Affluent Society*" which appeared in 1958 (see Galbraith 1974).

the production and the thereof resulting consumption of ever more goods[655], or, otherwise put, into a system determined to ever more "grow". This main goal of capitalism lies at the base of, *on one side*, the earlier mentioned "(hyper)consumerism" (which under impulse of neo-liberal schools "exploded" since the Reagan-era), and of, *on the other side*, the expansion of (consumer) credit in order to keep this economic production and consumption machine going.[656]

Since the 1980s, also the threshold for enterprises to take up credit has continuously been lowered, a trend which was strongly supported by "neo-liberal" doctrines (such as "monetarism").[657] **186**

According to figures made available by the think tank "Bruegel", the total amount of bank credits to the business sector (other than financial institutions themselves) within the Eurozone alone amounted in 2013 to 4200 billion euro (or 4.2 trillion euro).[658]

In this climate of (regulatory) liberalization and increasing expansionist behavior, the banking sector itself showed to be very willing to meet this large demand for credit. **187**

This launched an era where, previously unseen in world history, (banking) credits (hence private money creation) took place on an enormous scale and in an extreme careless way, whereby average borrowers did no longer show any reluctance to take up credit for, on itself, unnecessary spending (including so-called "created wants").[659]

Finally, also the governments of numerous (Western and Western-inspired) countries themselves increasingly started financing their deficits through credit, both from the banking sector, as well as from the broad savings public, but also from, for example, foreign central banks (with a surplus of currency reserves) and private investors (who often invested income surpluses in debt instruments issued by foreign (Western) governments).[660] **188**

---

[655]This insight is one of the central themes in the books of John K. Galbraith's, especially so in the book "*The affluent society*". In the latter book, the author explains how anxiety for an uncertain future has made mankind the victim of the capitalist production methods that create artificial needs in order to meet such needs by enhancing production. This has resulted in a global economic system relying on the principle of a continuous and maximal production and of an ongoing exploitation of labor. As a result, there is hardly no (free) time left to deal with other issues (such as enjoying life, fighting poverty, etc.). (See Galbraith 1974; see furthermore Galbraith 2012, p. 101.)

See also Bruckner (2002), pp. 20–21.

[656]Sachs (2011), pp. 144 a.f. Compare Ronse (1992), pp. 74–75.

[657]Such as, for instance, the theory on leverage-effects which are supposed to occur in case of credit based financing of business risks.

[658]Altomonte and Bussoli (2014). See also Claerhout (2014b), pp. 28–30, especially p. 29.

[659]Compare Fromm (2013) (1st edition of 1961), p. 47.

These processes were enhanced by systems of easy credit relief, both by legislative evolutions as by evolutions in jurisprudence, even further attributing to the an easy money-climate. (Compare Smithers 2013, p. 89.)

[660]See further Stiglitz (2006), p. 216.

This specific problem of debt financing by governments within this "modern credit economy" will be dealt with further on in the text (see further, under Sect. 3.4.6).

189 The striving for unbridled growth in numerous sectors, among which the banking sector itself, in combination with an unseen increase of bank credit, hence private money creation, in order to make this growth possible, resulted in an economic system which more and more relied on credit financing[661].

This extreme dependency on bank credit would ultimately attribute to the severe financial crisis of 2008, which, according to Stiglitz, has resulted in a true recession ("the great recession").[662]

Up to the present day, especially Western (and Western inspired) countries are indeed still experiencing the further impact of said financial crisis of 2008 (as, furthermore, the underlying causes of this financial crisis, among which the excessive credit behavior of numerous economic players, have still not been tackled and continue to challenge policy-makers on an almost global scale).[663]

In the meantime, notwithstanding the detrimental impact of the huge financial crisis of 2008, the financial sector has since then (again) been reported as one of the most rapidly growing on the planet.[664]

---

[661]Schemmann (2013), pp. 143 a.f.; see *e.g.* also Reality check: Eurozone Debt Looks Unsustainable. In: The economist, October 16th 2014 (also at http://www.businessinsider.com/reality-check-euro-zone-debt-looks-unsustainable-2014–10. Last consulted on February 28th 2016).

[662]See also Todd (2015), pp. 33–34; also Todd (2015), p. 35.

[663]Van Oudheusden (2012), p. 167.

[664]See Oxfam (2016), p. 23, (grimly) reporting:

> The financial sector has grown rapidly in recent decades, driven in particular by the growth of large banks and other financial companies in the US, Canada and Europe. The sector now accounts for an estimated 15 percent of global GDP. It has also created some of the biggest and most profitable companies in the world, including 437 of the world's 2,000 largest companies in 2014, according to the Forbes Global 2000 rankings; financial companies in this group have assets five times larger on average than non-financial companies. Globally the sector has provided more people than ever before with access to financial services: 62 percent of the world's adult population now have an account, up from 51 percent in 2011. It has also helped create vast wealth for individuals, with 20 percent of all dollar billionaires in the world in 2014 being listed as having interests or activities relating to the finance and insurance sectors.
>
> Since the 1980s, the activities of the financial sector have extended beyond providing financial services for citizens and business. They now include a sophisticated set of tools and processes designed to create value from transactions, speculation and asset prices, which are unrelated to value addition, output or productivity in the real economy, but which now dominate the sector. This has been facilitated by the deregulation of the financial sector in the past 30 years. The shadow banking sector (i.e. non-bank financial intermediaries who are not subject to regulatory oversight) now dominates the activities of the financial sector, as shown in Figure 7. In the US, the financial industry now accounts for about 30 percent of all operating profits, double its share in the 1980s;139 but is responsible for less than 10 percent of value-added in the economy. At the individual level, it has been estimated that roughly 30–50 percent of the earnings of financial sector employees is over and above what they add in value.

It has hereby been reported that the outstanding "bad credit" in Europe alone has skyrocketed in the aftermath of the financial crisis of 2008.

It has, for instance, been estimated that the European banking sector has outstanding loans to so-called emerging (or developing) countries for a total amount of 9000 billion (or 9 trillion) euro, and that it is to be feared that a lot of these loans will default (which obviously causes a huge risk for the European banking sector). A typical example hereof is the banking sector of Italy with outstanding bad loans for an estimated amount of 330 billion euro (or 17% of the Italian GDP).[665]

At the end of 2014, the IMF furthermore estimated that the total of outstanding bad credits of the European banks to its residents amounted to 1000 billion (or 1 trillion) euro. According to other estimations, this figure may even amount to 3000 billion (or 3 trillion) euro, while Diederik Schmull has suggested that the figure could even amount to 5000 billion (or 5 trillion) euro, a figure equal to 1/3 of the European GDP.[666]

With hindsight, it is surprising to see how easily during the last three to four **190**
decades the collective economy has been falling into the same traps into which it has already fallen numerous times before throughout history.

The aforementioned developments and the financial crisis of 2008 which they caused[667], are indeed very similar to similar developments (and other moments of financial crisis) in banking history of, for instance, the sixteenth to seventeenth century.[668]

In both cases, private banks increasingly led society in the trap of unlimited private money creation, based on allocating bank credit too easily (respectively, in the sixteenth and seventeenth century: by too easily issuing privately issued banking paper, and during the last decades of the twentieth century and the first decade of the new millennium: by too easily creating private scriptural money) to different economic agents, including governments.

In both cases, from the perspective of the banking sector itself, the main drive behind the mistake of such easy (private) money creation has been practically identical, namely the unbridled pursuit of profit which stimulated bankers to take too great risks.

An important difference between the two crises has however been that, while in the sixteenth and seventeenth centuries, banks were hardly subject to any regulation[669], on the contrary in 2008, (private) banking was very much subject to different types of government regulation (including, in different countries, so called

---

[665]Bauwens (2016).

[666]Bauwens (2016).

[667]As, at least to a certain degree, had been "forecasted" in 2006 by Stiglitz (see Stiglitz 2006, p. 215).

[668]Once more, further reference can be made to Galbraith (1990).

[669]Private banks were at that time not subject to any type of government regulation, nor did they operate under the auspices of a central monetary institution.

"prudential law regulations") and, moreover, in most countries, operated under the auspices of a central banking system[670].

Taken into consideration the severe financial crisis of 2008, it has in this regard to be observed that the aforementioned mechanisms of governmental supervision of private banking, have basically failed.

In a similar sense, it can also be observed that in several countries (or other types of economic regions), central banks themselves, clearly having neglected their historic origin and reason for existence, have to a large degree supported and incited the said excessive private money creation since the 1980s (for example, through a central interest policy which attributed to the overall credit-based economy)[671], thus also bearing a great responsibility for the financial crisis of 2008.

191 In this regard, both the banking sector and the policy authorities which are supposed to supervise it, seem to have forgotten the warnings formulated by even the most classic, liberal economists, such as John Stuart Mill[672], that one should deal in an as prudent way as possible with credit (hence with private money creation).

A credit position—no matter who the lender or borrower is—imposes by definition a (high) risk.

From the borrower's point of view, a credit position causes a debt position.

Such a borrower is, by definition, forced to generate in the future (from the starting date of the debt position on) an income which should at least be sufficient to repay the credit taken up (where appropriate, increased with the agreed upon interest). This implies that such a borrower, through labor or other efforts, will need to generate enough income to be able to repay the credit (increased with, where appropriate, the agreed upon interest).

Moreover, upon entering into the credit position, the borrower will also have to be able to provide sufficient certainty that through this future economic activity—or, in case the borrower is a government: through a sufficient degree of skimming off, by means of taxes or similar systems, the incomes of other economic agents—he will be able to repay the credit.

This implies that credit assumes a future economic production which will generate (at least) enough income to pay it back (either directly, if the borrower is, for instance, an enterprise, or, indirectly, if the borrower is, for instance, either an employee of a company generating income from a salary which needs to be created out of the economic proceeds of the company, or a government which gets its income from taxing enterprises and individuals).[673]

Hence, an excessive credit behavior that occurs among a large part of the members of a given society, is at the same time the expression of a strange paradox.

---

[670]As explained in more detail in Chap. 2 of this book, this had as of the end of the seventeenth century precisely been created in order to limit the unbridled growth of private money.

[671]See especially Greenspan (2008), p. 563 .

[672]Vandewalle (1976), p. 78.

[673]Compare Harari (2014), p. 335, speaking of the belief that ***"the entire global pie can grow"***.

The economy of such a society has in the past proven not to have generated enough income in order to finance its (past) spending behavior; otherwise it would not have been in need of credit financing. Hence, by taking up ever more credit, such a (credit) economy expresses a very optimistic vision of the future, namely that its further income will be sufficiently high to pay back its actual debts plus interests (on top of the income it will need for its future spending behavior itself).

Otherwise put, it should be clear that in normal circumstances, an individual banker who grants a credit should do this under the expectation that his borrower will be able to pay back the credit. On a collective level, a high number of bankers granting credit to several entities taking up credit are supposed to be doing the same with the expectation that this collectivity of credit takers—in a "credit economy", per definition these amount to a very large number—will be able to pay back their respective credit positions. **192**

In this way, bank credits put an extremely high pressure on the economy: *on one hand*, new (deposit) money is being brought into circulation which is immediately spendable on the products and services the economy generates (in the same way as already pre-existing money which has been gained or saved by economic agents), hence implying that enough goods and services are made available to be purchased out of the newly created money and, *on the other hand*, there is the expectation that all of the borrowers, through their future activities, will generate enough income (generally plus interest) to repay the debts resulting from these credits, hence that there will originate enough economic activity to earn back all of the outstanding credit.

In addition, given the premises of capitalism, these borrowers, in their attempt to generate enough income to pay back their debts, are each other's competitors who all are attempting to extract income from a closed economic system or a multitude of such systems (ultimately the world as it functions economically).[674]

It should be clear that a climate of unbridled credit lending (or, otherwise put, of unbridled private money creation) inherently creates bubbles which cannot endlessly be expanded.[675] **193**

Yuval Harari has phrased this as follows[676]:

> Over the last few years, banks and governments have been frenziedly printing money. Everyone is terrified that the current economic crisis may stop the growth of the economy. So they are creating trillions of dollars, euros and yen out of thin air, pumping cheap credit into the system, and hoping that the scientists, technicians and engineers will manage to come up with something really big, before the bubble bursts. Everything depends on the people in the labs. New discoveries in fields such as biotechnology and nanotechnology could create entire new industries, whose profits could back the trillions of make-believe

---

[674]Concerning the fact that capitalism has turned people into competitors in all of their activities, including the looking out for employment, see Fromm (1955), p. 84.

[675]Sorkin (2010), p. 542; Krugman (2009), pp. 144 a.f.; Fujii and Kwai (2012), pp. 259–284, especially p. 261. See also Morris (2009), p. 77; Middelkoop (2009), p. 53.

[676]Harari (2014), p. 352.

money that the banks and governments have created since 2008. If the labs do not fulfil these expectations before the bubble bursts, we are heading towards very rough times.

Such a credit economy is almost joining the domain of science fiction,[677] where the expectation is implied that mankind will transcend the limits of planet earth itself and will colonize space (and so potentially other uninhabited planets[678]), whereby the thought immediately comes to mind that, at a moment where it is almost a small miracle for an unmanned space vehicle to land, let alone function in an elementary way, on a nearby uninhabited planet or asteroid[679], the moment where the colonization of space (aimed at transcending the physical limits of the planet earth) becomes a reality, still seems very far away.

It is furthermore as questionable whether further industrial or other revolutions[680] will themselves be able to meet the expectations of past money creation.[681]

194 Hence, the question becomes when the current world economy will reach its growth limit and when, as a result, the bubble created by the current prevailing mechanisms of excessive money supply, will burst.

Phrased in another way, the question becomes on what moment in time too many "entities" (individuals, households, enterprises and governments, in addition to other public authorities) will have become debtors of the private banking system to such an extent that it will be impossible to generate enough income from the economy to pay back all of the outstanding credit (increased with the agreed upon interests).[682]

For Yuval Harari, a continued faith in the current money creation model, thus in the myth of unbridled economic growth, is opposite to "*almost all known phenomena in universe*"[683]. As put by Jean-Pierre Chevalier, the question is hence not if there will be a next (huge) banking crisis, but when it will occur.[684]

195 In other words[685], there is a huge risk that the prevailing unbridled credit economy, mainly driven by an as unlimited pursuit of profit, thus by greed, will sooner or later reach the limits drawn by the underlying economic reality, whereby

---

677 Compare Rand (2008), p. 19.

678 In the way described by in science fiction literature, such as the works of Isaac Asimov (for instance his Foundation-cycle) or those of Frank Herbert (see his Dune-cycle).

679 Baan (2014), pp. 50–53.

680 Such as the purportedly at present occurring so-called "fourth industrial revolution" whereby industrial production is increasingly controlled by so-called "smart" computers;

681 Michielsen (2014), pp. 13–14.

Critical in this regard: Debruyne and Claerhout (2014), pp. 88–91, especially p. 91.

682 Harari (2014), p. 352, expresses this as follows:

> A society of wolves would be extremely foolish to believe that the supply of sheep would keep on growing indefinitely.

See also Middelkoop (2009), p. 53.

683 Harari (2014), pp. 351–352.

684 Chevalier (2016); Bauwens (2016).

685 As has, for instance, been warned about by the Club of Rome from the 1970s on.

the blind faith in an ever increasing economic growth (able to bear the magnitude of banking credit, so of newly created money) will prove not to be realistic.[686]

As pointed out before, already John Stuart Mill, albeit a classical liberal author, has pointed out that speculative banking behavior and a wrong (unbridled) credit policy of private banking are among the most important causes for any (financial) crisis.[687] **196**

Nevertheless, both the banking sector itself, as public policymakers which are supposed to supervise it, are up till this very day, and even after the events of 2008, to a large extent, still refusing to accept these basic economic truths, as the banking sector has since then again taken up its business as usual and public supervisors have hardly taken any measures to counteract this traditional banking behavior.

3.4.6 The Issue of Government Financing

Over the past years, the aforementioned (adverse) characteristics of the capitalist monetary and financial system have, as already mentioned before, been further highlighted by the development of debt funding by a variety of countries and their respective governments. **197**

Under capitalism, the (central) governments of most countries in the world are basically financed by systems of tax and similar charges.[688] **198**

From an economic point of view, such a system of financing governments through taxation comes down to a periodical appropriation, through the central state authority, of a part of the economic tissue (generally: the proceeds of the national economy), in order to use this income for different (government) spending (purportedly considered to serve the "public good").[689]

By nature, such a system causes individuals, households and enterprises (but, somewhat paradoxically, sometimes also other public authorities, for example local governments) to hand over a part of their financial income (and, in some countries, fixed amounts in function of certain asset values) to the (central) government which re-spends the money thus received within the economy.

---

[686]This has also been referred to as to the "monetary illusion" (see Ugeux 2010, p. 23.) Ugeux has described this as follows:

> The financial system is a myth that is kept alive by those who gain from it, sometimes in a criminal way. (Ugeux 2010, p. 21).

[687]Vandewalle (1976), p. 78.

[688]For instance in Belgium, in addition to the actual taxes, there are different so-called "social security charges" which, economically have the same effect as taxes themselves, making of the Belgian population one of the most highly taxed in the world.

Compare Kruithof (2012), pp. 70–77, especially p. 76.

[689]Compare Baeck (1972), p. 82.

199 It is hereby self-evident that the income of (the government of) a given country will in such a system of government financing be(come) very dependent on the strength of its underlying economy.[690]

Indeed, governments of countries with a strong economy—generally expressed as a "high gross domestic product"—will be able to access a higher level of underlying economic tissue for their fiscal (and "para"-fiscal) "skimming", while countries with a weaker economy (otherwise put, with a low gross domestic product) will dispose of a much smaller underlying mass for their fiscal (and para-fiscal) skimming activities.[691]

It can already be remarked that, on a global scale, this already by itself demonstrates an inherently unjust system of government financing, which, already for many decades, is responsible for the traditional gaps between rich and poor countries in North-South relations.[692]

200 Moreover, under the current capitalist economic system, all countries determine in a (more or less) sovereign way their (government) spending behavior.[693]

Hence, guided by a diversity of policy considerations (often based on political and ideological thinking), there are countries with a traditional strong(er) role for the government (in other words: countries where the "public good" or the "general interest" is defined in a broad sense)[694], but there are also countries with governments having a traditional weak(er) role[695].

In the first group of countries, there is, in general, a huge so-called government expenditure, as a result of which the population undergoes a(n) (extremely) high tax burden (and pressure due to other similar charges), while in the other group of countries, this is less the case.

In addition to this, in the first group of countries, the government is usually (a little) more concerned with the redistribution of the gross economic income, especially among the middle and poor(er) classes mutually (but from which the rich are increasingly exempted).

---

[690] Hallerberg and Bridwell (2008), pp. 69–86, especially p. 74.

[691] This is a problem that in the past has hindered all attempts by the Belgian governments to even its financial accounts (see *e.g.* Moerman 2014, p. 18).

[692] See Oxfam (2014), pp. 16 a.f., mentioning "*the great tax failure*", with as a consequence:

> due to the disproportionate influence of rich corporations and individuals, and an intentional lack of global coordination and transparency in tax matters, tax systems are failing to tackle poverty and inequality (Oxfam 2014, p. 16).

[693] Fritz-Krockow and Ramlogan (2007), pp. 38 a.f.

[694] For example: different "Western" countries, where in the past government has to a large extent been influenced by socialist thinking, among which many European countries (for example Belgium, France, the Scandinavian countries,...)

[695] Such countries either usually have governments which strongly support capitalism in its pure form (with as typical examples: the United States of America and, especially in the post-Thatcher era, the United Kingdom), or are relying on a small economic structure as a result of which the government is forced (due to a lack of funds) to play a (more) modest role, which is usually the case for the so-called "poor countries".

As a result, the latter group of countries may face the disadvantage of having a negative pressure on individual initiative, especially in cases that the reward for labor or economic productivity is hardly any different from the replacement income provided for by the government.

Within the capitalist economic system, the tax pressure (and the pressure from similar charging systems, such as mandatory contributions to social security systems) will, in other words, be a function of the objectives the government is setting; moreover, in countries having a strong economy, it will be possible to keep the tax and other charging rates relatively low in order to generate a sufficient government income. **201**

Furthermore, the tax pressure (and other pressure due to other government charges) will in itself also impact the strength of the economy. A heavy tax pressure (and pressure due to other charges imposed by government) can indeed have a negative impact on the production costs of enterprises and, through this, negatively influence their competitive position compared to the enterprises of other countries themselves characterized by a less heavy tax pressure (and pressure from other charges).

A too heavy tax pressure (or pressure due to other government charges) may also undermine the purchasing power of the population (and in this way cause a negative impact on the demand curves within economy). A too long period of such heavy taxation may, on top of that, also cause an attitude of fatalism (for instance the idea not to be able to enjoy the benefits of one's own efforts; the idea that being economically active or not does not make a big difference in income, given the redistribution strategies of the government; the loss of faith in investments; . . .).

Fiscal and social policies are thus undoubtedly characterized by a high degree of complexity which challenges economic and political minds worldwide, whereby ideological and similar convictions continuously spice the debate.

The complexity of government financing has only increased during the past decades, especially each time, as for instance (harrowingly) in 2001 and in 2008[696], a moment or a period of economic or financial crisis presents itself. **202**

As regards the period after WWII in general, especially countries with a traditionally important government role found out that, as a consequence of the cascade of crises since the 1980s, their income from tax charges and other similar charging systems, (relatively) decreased in comparison to their spending pattern, making traditional taxes and similar charges in many cases insufficient to cover government expenditure.[697]

As a consequence, during the past decades (especially from the 1970s on), these types of countries (among which many Western and Western-inspired countries) have massively sought salvation in taking up credit, either by their own inhabitants (including local financial institutions, but in some cases also other private savers

---

[696] Stiglitz indicates this as the start of what he calls "*the Great Recession*" (see Stiglitz 2012, p. 210).

[697] See within Europe especially the situation of Greece.
See http://www.imf.org/external/country/grc/index.htm (last consulted on October 23th 2014).

and investors, often through the issue of government securities—or in later times: dematerialized financial instruments—on financial markets), by foreign private credit lenders, or even by supranational organizations (such as the IMF and the World Bank).[698]

As a result, many Western (and Western inspired) countries, including countries with a formerly traditional surplus in government finances such as the USA, have increasingly been faced with increasing government shortages[699] and, as a result, have become (chronically) dependent on debt financing themselves.

In addition to this, countries with a (historically) weak economic fabric, especially since WWII,[700] have also become increasingly dependent on taking up credit to cover essential government spending.[701]

As a result, it has been argued that states have become increasingly "monetized" and in the recent past even "privatized" .[702]

The problem of the debt of developing countries as well as the debt of deteriorating Western (and Western- inspired) countries is probably one of the most severe economic problems of our times.[703]

The numbers speak for themselves.

According to the website http://www.nationaldebtclocks.org/, on December 15th 2014, the global debt (= of all countries together), amounted to over 60.793 trillion USD. The USA on its own hereby accounted for almost 1/3rd of this global world debt, for an amount of over 17.3 trillion USD. According the same website, on March 31st 2016, the global world debt amounted to a sum of 60.070 trillion USD (with the USA accounting for 18.006 trillion USD). (See Tables 3.1 and 3.2.) Still according to the same website, on October 21st 2016, the global world debt amounted to a sum of 62.066 trillion USD (with the USA accounting for 18.060 trillion USD). (See Tables 3.3 and 3.4.)

According to another source and also as regards the situation in 2014, only five countries/regions in the world were reported not to have any debt at all: the "British Virgin Islands", Brunei, Macao, Liechtenstein and Palau.[704]

---

698 Brook and Watkins (2012), p. 33, speaking of the ***"natural disease of all Governments"***.
See also Krugman (1992), pp. 143 a.f.; James (1996), pp. 347 a.f.; Streeck (2015), pp. 138 a.f.

699 Stiglitz (2012), pp. 208 a.f. (investigating the causes thereof).

700 For a historical overview, see Ingham (1984), p. 48.

701 This is especially the case for the so-called "poor" or "developing" countries (in IMF terms: "Heavily Indebted Poor Countries (HIPC)"), whose debt in many cases has become a chronic problem (see http://www.imf.org/external/np/exr/facts/hipc.htm) (last consulted on October 23th 2014); Cohen (2008b), pp. 150–179, especially pp. 167 a.f.
See before Van Meerhaeghe (1985), p. 97.

702 Harvey (2010), pp. 48–49.

703 See Piketty (2014), especially Ch. XVI. *The question of public debt*, pp. 540–570.
See also James (1996), pp. 388 a.f.

704 Mathers (2014).
These countries are, apparently, all notorious "tax havens".

The main question is if, and at what speed, the world economy will allow these combined countries "in debt" to "skim" over ±60 trillion of USD on tax income in order to be able to repay this tremendous amount of debt. When taking this question into consideration, one should furthermore be aware that every delay in payment, as a consequence of the running interest rates (mainly benefiting private banks and other institutional investors), increases this amount of debt (while at the same time making the rich of the planet, through their shareholdings in financial institutions, ever more rich).

Moreover, the 60 trillion USD debt (in 2014) (see Table 3.1), or the 60.070 trillion USD debt (in March 2016) (see Table 3.3), or the 62.066 trillion USD debt (in October 2016), of national states are not the only debts burdening the world economy (and which, therefore, will need to be "earned back" from economic growth). On the contrary, as explained before, many other economic agents (individuals, families and enterprises) are also burdened with huge debts (which, likewise, all will need to be "earned back" from economic growth).

There is an increasing recognition by renowned economists (and other human sciences specialists) that the expectation that all that debt will ever be repayable may be utopian, while in the meantime, private banks and other institutional investors are the ones benefiting most from this ever increasing debt load (through the interest mechanism).

Nevertheless, in many countries, government policy keeps focusing on strategies of repaying these debts (which, in many countries, has resulted in a so called "rationalization policy" based on neo-liberal principles, with as a typical example the budgeting discipline the European Union subjects its member states to, but whereby many countries face great difficulties in fulfilling the requirements).

Table 3.1 Debt in some countries (in USD) (figures of December 15th 2014)

Country	Total debt in million USD	Total debt per head in USD	Total debt compared to GDP	Interest/year, in million USD	Interest/year compared to debt (own calculation)
Australia	323,610	13,780	21.82%	10,402	3.21%
Austria	325,753	38,583	75.30%	7953	2.44%
Belgium	527,610	47,270	108.27%	15,535	2.94%
Brazil	1,344,647	6631	53.09%	138,251	10.28%
Bulgaria	10,664	1464	19.49%	430	4.03%
Canada	577,490	16,339	32.84%	14,126	2.45%
China	5,157,907	3807	62.56%	174,667	3.39%
Columbia	139,210	2968	38.49%	9374	6.73%
Cyprus	26,019	30,050	115.77%	1504	5.78%
Czech Republic	91,285	8681	44.77%	2662	2.92%
Denmark	154,379	27,555	45.85%	3622	2.35%
Germany	2,990,177	36,576	80.58%	70,146	2.35%
Greece	476,234	43,049	213.83%	34,308	7.20%

(continued)

Table 3.1 (continued)

Country	Total debt in million USD	Total debt per head in USD	Total debt compared to GDP	Interest/year, in million USD	Interest/year compared to debt (own calculation)
Estonia	2582	1949	10.45%	75	2.90%
Finland	153,532	28,292	58.73%	3748	2.44%
France	2,682,351	40,869	93.54%	73,137	2.73%
Hong Kong	112,198	14,674	39.17%	2435	2.17%
Hungary	112,160	11,319	80.93%	6363	5.67%
Ireland	254,898	55,520	114.18%	12,160	4.77%
India	949,071	748	51.36%	68,454	7.21%
Israel	222,902	27,898	77.05%	9568	4.29%
Italy	2,907,162	47,799	137.37%	134,881	4.64%
Japan	10,073,728	79,171	198.26%	129,753	1.29%
Latvia	12,655	6253	39.40%	604	4.77%
Lithuania	19,346	6510	41.72%	745	3.85%
Luxemburg	14,738	27,444	24.12%	402	2.73%
Malaysia	173,324	5836	54.42%	6354	3.67%
Malta	7461	17,707	74.66%	362	4.85%
Mexico	533,599	4627	42.14%	35,559	6.66%
New Zealand	73,011	16,109	38.53%	3538	4.85%
Norway	115,388	22,843	22.77%	3278	2.84%
Pakistan	55,407	314	24.18%	5412	9.77%
Poland	320,466	8317	57.60%	15,289	4.77%
Portugal	300,928	28,695	130.91%	10,190	3.39%
Romania	75,170	3755	39.85%	4264	5.67%
Russia	234,018	1633	11.06%	14,937	6.38%
Singapore	308,495	57,134	102.55%	6621	2.15%
Slovakia	56,859	10,508	58.26%	2609	4.59%
Slovenia	36,087	17,511	73.49%	1722	4.77%
South Africa	140,646	2785	42.27%	9225	6.56%
South Korea	516,699	10,380	37.28%	22,725	4.40%
Spain	1,100,541	23,564	96.10%	52,517	4.77%
Sweden	232,773	24,359	40.95%	5648	2.43%
Switzerland	127,360	15,843	20.46%	1890	1.48%
Thailand	145,539	2097	38.86%	5875	4.04%
The Netherlands	628,233	37,440	75.71%	15,337	2.44%
Turkey	334,911	4582	40.84%	27,742	8.28%
United Kingdom	2,563,657	39,624	90.24%	72,465	2.83%
United States	18,006,159	56,621	104.12%	521,977	2.90%

Table 3.2 Debt in some countries (conversion into euro; figures and exchange rate of December 15th 2014)

Country	Total debt in million Euro	Total debt per head in Euro	Total debt compared to GDP	Interest/year, in million Euro	Interest/year compared to debt (own calculation)
Australia	259,928	11,068	21.82%	8355	3.21%
Austria	261,649	30,990	75.30%	6388	2.44%
Belgium	423,783	37,968	108.27%	12,478	2.94%
Brazil	1,080,038	5326	53.09%	111,045	10.28%
Bulgaria	8565	1176	19.49%	345	4.03%
Canada	463,847	13,124	32.84%	11,346	2.45%
China	4,142,897	3058	62.56%	140,295	3.39%
Columbia	111,815	2384	38.49%	7529	6.73%
Cyprus	20,899	24,137	115.77%	1208	5.78%
Czech Republic	73,321	6973	44.77%	2138	2.92%
Denmark	123,999	22,133	45.85%	2909	2.35%
Estonia	2074	1565	10.45%	60	2.90%
Finland	123,319	22,724	58.73%	3010	2.44%
France	2,154,499	32,827	93.54%	58,745	2.73%
Germany	2,401,749	29,378	80.58%	56,342	2.35%
Greece	382,517	34,578	213.83%	27,557	7.20%
Hong Kong	90,119	11,786	39.17%	1956	2.17%
Hungary	90,088	9092	80.93%	5111	5.67%
India	762,306	601	51.36%	54,983	7.21%
Ireland	204,737	44,594	114.18%	9767	4.77%
Israel	179,038	22,408	77.05%	7685	4.29%
Italy	2,335,070	38,393	137.37%	108,338	4.64%
Japan	8,091,348	63,591	198.26%	104,219	1.29%
Latvia	10,165	5022	39.40%	485	4.77%
Lithuania	15,539	5229	41.72%	598	3.85%
Luxemburg	11,838	22,043	24.12%	323	2.73%
Malaysia	139,216	4688	54.42%	5104	3.67%
Malta	5993	14,222	74.66%	291	4.85%
Mexico	428,594	3716	42.14%	28,561	6.66%
New Zealand	58,643	12,939	38.53%	2842	4.85%
Norway	92,681	18,348	22.77%	2633	2.84%
Pakistan	44,504	252	24.18%	4347	9.77%
Poland	257,402	6680	57.60%	12,280	4.77%
Portugal	241,709	23,048	130.91%	8185	3.39%
Romania	60,378	3016	39.85%	3425	5.67%
Russia	187,966	1312	11.06%	11,998	6.38%
Singapore	247,787	45,891	102.55%	5318	2.15%
Slovakia	45,670	8440	58.26%	2096	4.59%

(continued)

Table 3.2 (continued)

Country	Total debt in million Euro	Total debt per head in Euro	Total debt compared to GDP	Interest/year, in million Euro	Interest/year compared to debt (own calculation)
Slovenia	28,986	14,065	73.49%	1383	4.77%
South Africa	112,969	2237	42.27%	7410	6.56%
South Korea	415,019	8337	37.28%	18,253	4.40%
Spain	883,969	18,927	96.10%	42,182	4.77%
Sweden	186,966	19,565	40.95%	4537	2.43%
Switzerland	102,297	12,725	20.46%	1518	1.48%
Thailand	116,899	1684	38.86%	4719	4.04%
The Netherlands	504,605	30,072	75.71%	12,319	2.44%
Turkey	269,005	3680	40.84%	22,283	8.28%
United Kingdom	2,059,162	31,827	90.24%	58,205	2.83%
United States	14,462,779	45,479	104.12%	419,259	2.90%

Table 3.3 Debt in some countries (in USD) (figures of April 1st 2016)

Country	Total debt in million USD	Total debt per head in USD	Total debt compared to GDP	Interest/year, in million USD	Interest/year compared to debt (own calculation)
Australia	343,485	14,443	21.13%	11,207	3.26%
Austria	315,397	36,743	86.98%	7738	2.45%
Belgium	433,273	38,484	109.02%	12,932	2.98%
Brazil	681,774	3297	26.92%	71,056	10.42%
Bulgaria	13,689	1901	30.08%	557	4.07%
Canada	794,900	22,089	55.37%	19,625	2.47%
China	5,384,281	3974	65.30%	174,667	3.24%
Columbia	1652	35	0.44%	114	6.90%
Cyprus	20,851	24,617	111.25%	1214	5.82%
Czech Republic	67,003	6355	37.00%	1980	2.96%
Denmark	122,630	21,620	39.90%	2884	2.35%
Estonia	2203	1677	9.30%	64	2.91%
Finland	140,623	25,700	61.56%	3450	2.45%
France	2,289,370	34,618	97.23%	56,518	2.47%
Germany	2,349,165	28,049	73.43%	55,371	2.36%

(continued)

Table 3.3 (continued)

Country	Total debt in million USD	Total debt per head in USD	Total debt compared to GDP	Interest/year, in million USD	Interest/year compared to debt (own calculation)
Greece	394,346	36,471	208.94%	22,309	5.66%
Hong Kong	103,495	14,181	33.96%	2251	2.17%
Hungary	91,351	9376	79.89%	5299	5.80%
India	832,774	643	40.64%	54,363	6.53%
Ireland	227,762	49,245	101.36%	10,971	4.82%
Israel	189,148	23,294	59.80%	8863	4.69%
Italy	2,417,892	39,771	139.02%	94,773	3.92%
Japan	8,939,495	70,257	217.22%	115,453	1.29%
Latvia	9501	4695	36.38%	463	4.87%
Lithuania	15,272	5139	37.83%	592	3.88%
Luxembourg	12,221	21,709	21.41%	335	2.74%
Malaysia	146,622	4730	55.34%	5450	3.72%
Malta	6318	14,717	68.74%	304	4.81%
Mexico	435,109	3874	41.44%	29,403	6.76%
Netherlands	493,059	29,174	68.72%	12,097	2.45%
New Zealand	79,011	16,994	47.55%	3791	4.80%
Norway	54,306	10,512	15.42%	1563	2.88%
Pakistan	58,567	314	52.55%	5838	9.97%
Poland	238,425	6194	51.72%	11,485	4.82%
Portugal	250,820	24,177	130.72%	8551	3.41%
Romania	65,248	3285	38.24%	3744	5.74%
Russia	145,151	992	14.56%	9541	6.57%
Singapore	292,383	52,820	105.32%	7532	2.58%
Slovakia	46,359	8550	52.92%	2147	4.63%
Slovenia	34,162	16,577	82.12%	1645	4.82%
South Africa	138,550	2542	39.85%	8067	5.82%
South Korea	491,316	9707	36.45%	21,541	4.38%
Spain	1,160,604	24,850	98.34%	55,491	4.78%
Sweden	213,178	21,870	44.06%	5230	2.45%
Switzerland	101,363	12,306	15.66%	1508	1.49%
Thailand	136,590	1968	36.28%	5617	4.11%
Turkey	230,782	3157	34.48%	20,300	8.80%
United Kingdom	2,254,616	34,811	82.86%	56,131	2.49%
United States	19,150,866	59,331	106.04%	478,217	2.50%

Table 3.4 Debt in some countries (conversion into euro; figures and exchange rate of April 1st 2016)

Country	Total debt in million Euro	Total debt per head in Euro	Total debt compared to GDP	Interest/year, in million Euro	Interest/year compared to debt (own calculation)
Australia	300,459	12,634	27.30%	9803	3.25%
Austria	275,890	32,140	86.62%	6769	2.46%
Belgium	379,000	33,663	106.70%	11,312	2.98%
Brazil	596,373	2884	26.45%	62,155	10.61%
Bulgaria	11,974	1663	29.88%	487	4.10%
Canada	695,329	19,322	55.81%	17,167	2.49%
China	4,709,833	3476	64.95%	152,788	3.26%
Columbia	1445	31	0.43%	100	6.98%
Cyprus	18,239	1062	110.17%	21,533	5.88%
Czech Republic	58,610	1732	36.81%	5559	2.97%
Denmark	107,269	2523	39.74%	18,912	2.37%
Estonia	1927	56	9.25%	1467	2.92%
Finland	123,008	3018	61.31%	22,481	2.46%
France	2,002,598	49,438	96.83%	30,282	2.48%
Germany	2,054,903	48,435	73.14%	24,536	2.37%
Greece	344,949	19,515	210.31%	31,903	5.63%
Hong Kong	90,531	1969	33.84%	12,405	2.18%
Hungary	79,908	4635	79.13%	8202	5.79%
India	728,459	47,553	40.20%	562	6.60%
Ireland	199,232	9597	100.55%	43,076	4.86%
Israel	165,455	7753	59.33%	20,376	4.72%
Italy	2,115,021	82,902	138.11%	34,789	3.95%
Japan	7,819,712	100,991	216.75%	61,456	1.29%
Latvia	8311	405	36.08%	4107	5.01%
Lithuania	13,359	518	37.58%	4495	3.90%
Luxembourg	10,690	293	21.31%	18,990	2.75%
Malaysia	128,256	4767	54.99%	4138	3.74%
Malta	5527	266	68.18%	12,874	4.85%
Mexico	380,606	25,720	40.98%	3389	6.83%
Netherlands	431,297	10,582	68.44%	25,520	2.46%
New Zealand	69,114	3316	47.16%	14,865	4.84%
Norway	47,503	1367	15.35%	9195	2.89%
Pakistan	51,231	5107	51.68%	275	10.14%
Poland	208,559	10,046	51.31%	5418	4.86%
Portugal	219,402	7480	129.98%	21,149	3.43%
Romania	57,075	3275	37.87%	2874	5.79%
Russia	126,969	8346	14.40%	868	6.65%
Singapore	255,758	6589	104.87%	46,204	2.59%

(continued)

Table 3.4 (continued)

Country	Total debt in million Euro	Total debt per head in Euro	Total debt compared to GDP	Interest/year, in million Euro	Interest/year compared to debt (own calculation)
Slovakia	40,552	1878	52.51%	7479	4.67%
Slovenia	29,883	1439	82.45%	14,501	4.85%
South Africa	121,195	7057	39.46%	2224	5.88%
South Korea	429,773	18,843	36.18%	8491	4.42%
Spain	1,015,224	48,540	97.56%	21,737	4.82%
Sweden	186,475	4575	43.88%	19,131	2.46%
Switzerland	88,666	1319	15.62%	10,765	1.49%
Thailand	119,480	4913	36.03%	1721	4.14%
Turkey	201,874	17,757	33.97%	2762	8.93%
United Kingdom	1,972,197	49,100	80.91%	30,450	2.49%
United States	16,751,982	418,314	104.51%	51,899	2.89%

Based on the aforementioned website http://www.nationaldebtclocks.org/, the tables above represent a number of (indicative) figures regarding the debt situation of a selection of countries

It needs hereby to be noted that, for someone who is not a professional economist (but a lawyer) (as is the case for the author of this book), it is not always easy to obtain exact figures about the subjects discussed in this book. More often than not, different sources report different figures (whereby, astoundingly, a billion more or less does not seem to be very relevant any more)

Several sources are available about the size of the debts of the different countries in the world including, among which the aforementioned website http://www.nationaldebtclocks.org/ (on which the previous tables are based) [in addition to, for instance, even smartphone applications (For example https://itunes.apple.com/nl/app/staatsschuld-schuld-van-180+/id455810046?mt=8. Last consulted on December 15th 2014.)]. A comparison of the figures provided by such different sources confirms the aforementioned remark about the lack of consistency between those sources Nevertheless, this type of easily accessible sources provide a good impression of the speed at which the debts of the different countries are growing (with thousands, even tens of thousands ... USD or Euro per second). This however makes it, per definition, very hard to provide a "snapshot" of the debt situation of a country at a precise moment in time: even while consulting the quoted sources, the debt of any given country will in most cases have increased—or, more rarely, decreased as a result of a reimbursement made by a given country—considerably a few seconds later.

The Tables 3.1, 3.2, 3.3, and 3.4 nevertheless give a clear, albeit rough picture of the excessive debt of different European countries and the USA, and moreover provide an indication about which part of the debt is interest (assumingly mainly to the benefit of private banks and other institutional investors)

Unfortunately, from the quoted sources, it is not clear who *precisely* are the creditors of the different debts. To the extent that (as may be assumed and feared), the creditors of most countries, including European countries and the USA, are private banks, this again gives an illustration of the extremely perverted effect of the capitalist mechanism of (private) money creation, given that Western countries, more than previously in history, are forced to borrow from private banks and are obliged to pay immense amounts of interest for this.

The fifth columns of the tables give an estimation of the amount of interests in November 2014 and in April 2016 (on the government debt) of each of the countries mentioned, or, in other words, what the gain in interest has been (most likely: for the banking sector), which, ultimately, is forced upon the tax payer.

(continued)

Table 3.4 (continued)

This mechanism has mainly as effect that a huge part of the riches of any given economy flow back to the banking sector, and ultimately to its shareholders (which has been described as a system of "*privatization of gains*") and which helps declaring why those with important shareholdings in banks are in the hands of the richest people on the planet.
See Oxfam (2015) for instance at p. 5:
In 2014 there were 1,645 people listed by Forbes as being billionaires. This group of people is far from being globally representative. Almost 30% of them (492 people) are citizens of the USA. Over one-third of billionaires started from a position of wealth, with 34% of them having inherited some or all of their riches. This group is predominately male and greying; with 85%7 of these people aged over 50 years and 90% of them male.
There are a few important economic sectors that have contributed to the accumulation of wealth of these billionaires. In March 2014, 20% of them (321) were listed as having interests or activities in, or relating to, the financial and insurance sectors, the most commonly cited source of wealth for billionaires on this list. Since March 2013, there have been 37 new billionaires from these sectors, and six have dropped off the list. The accumulated wealth of billionaires from these sectors has increased from $1.01tn to $1.16tn in a single year; a nominal increase of $150bn, or 15%.
Furthermore, as a result of how the free market mechanism works, the interest rates differ largely per country. Very often, countries with a weak economy (for example a low GDP) are "punished" with high(er) interest rates, which, in general, often makes their recovery policy even more difficult and whereby lenders themselves take the largest profits from the countries facing the greatest difficulties or, when the risks involved become too high, have the loans refinanced by (supranational) public institutions (such as the IMF). Needless to say that assessments carried out by external credit raters play an important role in credit pricing of these countries (see further, at marg. 203 of this chapter).
It finally needs to be clearly understood that the taking up of debt has in many countries, to an ever greater extent, become necessary in order to finance the mega bailout efforts which have been necessary in order to save failing financial institutions in 2008 (and afterwards), whereby, ironically, the repayment of the debt burden is increasingly becoming harder in the context of a recession which, to a large extent, has precisely been triggered by the same bank failures, while on the same time, private banks are more than ever competing to obtain fiscal advantages in order to avoid being taxed on their since then newly made profits (Oxfam 2015, pp. 7 a.f.).
It is, among others, on this understanding that this book (in Chaps. 4 and 5) later on proposes a new model of money creation which would be more beneficial to governments (and whereby there would be no further room for the accumulation of interests to solely or mainly benefiting private banks or other private market players, thus, ultimately, their shareholders).

203 As a result of the aforementioned developments, *on one hand,* the classic "poor" countries and, *on the other hand,* a growing group of (formerly) "rich" Western (and Western inspired) countries have increasingly become (chronically) dependable on credit.

As mentioned earlier (see above, at marg. 202 of this chapter), although credit is also taken up from certain international public institutions (such as the IMF and the World Bank), within the capitalist economies, the (national) governments of countries in debt mostly turn to private financial institutions. Through this, the dependency of numerous countries on financing provided by the (private) banking sector has increased to such an extent that exact data on the total amount of the debt of all countries in the world to the private banking sector, are (apparently) no longer to be found.[705]

[705]At least not by the author of this book. Whoever would be in possession of such data is welcome to provide them to said author.

The high credit dependency of many countries also explains the great importance of their so-called "credit rating" (which, according to some sources, is currently estimated to be even more important than the presence of natural resources). Such a credit rating does offer a (so-called "independent") indication of the probability that a country[706] will be able to pay back its debts (providing credit rating agencies with an enormous power which sometimes co-determines the prosperity of the monitored countries).[707] It is hereby further to be noted that the credit rating of a country, for example, helps determining the interest rates which private banks charge for lending to such a country, putting the capitalist "principle of anti-solidarity" even more in place: countries already facing financial difficulties usually get a lower credit rating, making them subject to higher interest ratings than those applied to (more) prosperous countries, which often makes it for the former countries even more difficult to overcome their financial problems.[708]

It is already in itself a serious concern[709] that (national) governments of the majority of the countries in the world all have become so dependent on a small niche of private market players, namely the financial institutions. 204

In time, this concern has been more and more enhanced due to the fact that both legal and economic control over private banks has increasingly ended up in the hands of a small (financial) elite of people (namely the capital providers and managers of the private banks)[710], which, in this way[711], (be it together with the capital providers and managers of enterprises of other sectors of the economy) has obtained much more (economic) power than would be acceptable in societies which would truly be democratic.

On the internet (see for instance the earlier quoted website http://www.nationaldebtclocks.org/), one can find overviews of the total outstanding debt of several countries and, moreover, comparisons between this total debt per country and its GDP.

[706]But evidently also (huge) private enterprises, as the private sector is also "monitored" by rating agencies.

[707]Harari (2014), pp. 365–366.

See also Coffey (2012):

> That means the real power to control the world lies with four companies: McGraw-Hill, which owns Standard & Poor's, Northwestern Mutual, which owns Russell Investments, the index arm of which runs the benchmark Russell 1,000 and Russell 3,000, CME Group which owns 90% of Dow Jones Indexes, and Barclay's, which took over Lehman Brothers and its Lehman Aggregate Bond Index, the dominant world bond fund index. Together, these four firms dominate the world of indexing. And in turn, that means they hold real sway over the world's money.

[708]Skidelsky (2010), p. 25.

[709]This concern was already expressed by Plato. (See Plato 1987, pp. 305 a.f.) Plato called this the turning of "Timarchy" into "Oligarchy", "***a society where it is "wealth" that counts (...) and in which political power is in the hands of the rich and the poor have no share of it.***"

[710]History is full of irony, as may illustrated by the fact that, in Ancient Greece, the bankers profession was deemed to be an occupation for (freed) slaves (see Bogaert et al. 2000, p. 37). This facts also helps to understand Aristotle's contempt for the banking profession (see above, at marg. 63 of this chapter).

[711]For instance by means of lobbying and similar techniques of influencing governments.

This helps explaining why the (political) power structure of capitalism has, in recent literature, been described as a "Corporatocracy" which can be considered as a modern day form of "oligarchy".[712]

In this way, "capitalism" (or "free marketism") is intrinsically an undemocratic economic system, basically not dealing with the interests of the large masses, but only with these of the rich and the powerful within society.

205 As a result, the system of government financing by private banking credit inherently strengthens the fact that capitalism causes a very small group of people within society, ultimately the said capital providers and managers of private banks, to accumulate large fortunes to the detriment of the rest of society. Indeed, each time a government takes up a credit from the private banking sector, the result is that a large part of its income (mainly from taxes) will have to be spent on paying the agreed upon banking interest (see above, at marg. 202 of this chapter, the fifth column in the mentioned tables there).[713]

Galbraith has indicated this system of government financing as symptomatical for "*the culture of contentment*" characterizing (Western) societies, which has led them (through their governments) to increasingly behave in a very neglectful manner, whereby, in general, short term solutions based upon procrastination are preferred above the development of any durable long term economic strategy. The reasoning behind such an approach is that (neo-)liberal "*laissez-faire*"-thinking will

---

[712]See especially the works of Charles Wright Mills (1916–1962) one of the first to acknowledge this phenomenon (see http://www.cwrightmills.org/. Last consulted on November 25th 2014).

Present day governments are therefore to be considered rather as "oligarchies" or even "aristocracies", rather than as "democracies" as, worldwide, governments are largely controlled by the rich ("large capital"). (See *e.g.* Sachs 2011, pp. 116 a.f.; see also Kruithof 2000, p. 14.)

See before already Plato (1987), pp. 295 a.f., in his description of so-called "imperfect societies"; see *e.g.* at p. 305:

> The accumulation of wealth in private hands is what destroys timarchy. The men find ways to become extravagant, and for this reason pervert the law and disobey it, and the women follow their example.

See also Oxfam (2014), p. 21:

> To successfully combat runaway economic inequality, governments must be forced to listen to the people, not the plutocrats. As history has shown, this requires mass public mobilization. The good news is that despite the dominance of political influence by wealthy elites and the repression of citizens in many countries, people around the world are demanding change. The majority of the hundreds of thousands who took to the streets in recent protests were frustrated by a lack of services and a lack of voice, and opinion polls confirm this feeling of discontent around the world." and further: "History shows that the stranglehold of elites can be broken by the actions of ordinary people and the widespread demand for progressive policies.

Furthermore Oxfam (2015); Oxfam (2016), p. 4.

[713]See Oxfam (2015). See also Streeck (2015), p. 121, mentioning that for those who, on the free market and/or through control of taxation policy, are the victors of the struggle for the division of money, the victory is but complete when they succeed to reinvest the money they took from governments and societies in a tax exempt manner.

make sure that, in the long run, market mechanisms will by themselves straighten everything out.[714]

Precisely this mindset explains the continuing willingness of many countries to resort to credit financing on such a large scale.

However, when, as has been the case in recent history (especially following the financial crisis of 2008), national governments need to bail out banks operating within their jurisdiction, resulting in government expenditure which, in some countries, will be burdening government budgets for decades to come[715], then the skimming by private banks of the economic wealth truly takes tremendous proportions.

It need therefore not surprise that renowned economists have righteously commented that economic neo-liberalism, especially when applied to the financial sector, is characterized by "*a privatization of gains and (a) socialization of losses*"[716], referred to by Stiglitz as one of the most stringent "*moral hazard*"--dilemmas of our time.[717]

Governments which, in case of budget shortages are driven to take credit from the (private) market(s), have, over the past years, when faced with problems of repaying those credits, furthermore showed little restraint in refinancing such credits by taking up new credits, thus continuously shifting the remediation of government financing forward in time. **206**

Needless to say that with each such every operation of "re-financing" a government debt, the negative characteristics of the capitalist financial system described under the previous marg. 205 of this chapter are even more strengthened. As if this is not enough, such a system of (re)financing governments through debt provided by the banking sector is, furthermore, manifestly unjust from an intergenerational

---

[714]Galbraith (1992), p. 20.

[715]As regards the impact of the bail outs of banks in 2008–2009 in Belgium, see Van Cauwelaert (2014), p. 57.

[716]Engelen (2011), p. 27.

> The technocrats and their political masters failed in their first duty as public servants, which was to protect citizens from the depredations of capitalist business which privatizes its gains to the benefits of employees and owners and socializes its losses at the expense of taxpayers and their service consumers. (Engelen 2011, pp. 28–29).

[717]Stiglitz (2006), 217.
See also Oxfam (2016), p. 24, arguing:

> The banks have been bailed out by public funds, which ordinary people will have to pay for in generations to come. As a result of the interconnectedness of global finance and economies, the costs of the protracted slowdown in growth have hit everyone. In Europe, for example, austerity measures have hit the poorest people hardest, yet in the US the richest have been the first to recover – and recover strongly – with the top 1 percent capturing 95 percent of post-crisis economic growth.

point of view, as each next generation gets burdened more with an increasing government debt created by previous generations.[718]

In such a system of government financing, the deficiencies of a previous generation (which has refused to compromise on its spending behavior), are passed on to the next generation(s), which will consequently experience a reduced chance to enjoy the same luxuries of the previous generation(s) which was (were) accountable for the huge government debts built up in the past.

In such a case, the actual income of the government obtained through current tax and similar charges, will increasingly need to be used to repay debts made before.

Not coincidentally, this problem has been characterized as one of the greatest challenges of our time, albeit that the political world (in Western and Western-inspired countries) still shows little enthusiasm to advocate truly fundamental and just solutions to solve this problem (but, under neo-liberal doctrine, usually resorts to solutions based upon taxing lower and middle classes even more, and/or cutting back on social security and similar government expenses serving the public good or general interest, among which expenses for health care and for public education).

In Chaps. 4 and 5 of this book, a number of possible solutions for this dilemma of public financing (being the result of an "out of the box thinking" exercise) will be suggested.

207 Whichever way, as is the case for any debtor, a country building up a debt burden will at one point in time also have to start to dismantle such debt.[719]

The normal scenario for reducing a debt is to repay it to the creditor, when agreed upon, heightened with interests.

For this purpose, a country with an outstanding debt—and, in principle, the situation of such a country in debt is no different from that of any other economic agent who is also a debtor—will have to generate enough income in the future to make such repayment(s).

Under the currently prevailing system of government financing of most countries, the natural source of income of a country in debt from which, in the end, the sums needed to repay the debt will have to be generated, as explained before, consists, as mentioned before (see above, at marg. 198 of this chapter), of the collection of taxes (and other similar charges).

This source of income can increase in two ways: *either* an increase of the taxable mass (especially the global income of the underlying economy of such a country[720]) occurs, implying that in case of unchanged tax tarification (as well as tarification of other charges), more income will be generated, *or*, in case of a status quo or

---

[718]See already the warnings of Jaap Kruithof already in 1985 (Kruithof 1985, p. 57), especially pointing out the inherent short termism of capitalism.

The same idea can be found in the writings of John Kenneth Galbraith who often criticized the spirit of "laissez faire" which dominates the capitalist economic system. (See for instance Galbraith 1992, p. 20. See furthermore Streeck 2015, p. 143.)

[719]See also Piketty (2014), p. 540, expressing in this regard his preference of taxation above debt financing.

[720]For instance expressed in its Gross Domestic Product.

decrease in the taxable mass, a country can also resort to higher tax rates (or rates of similar charges), or even to new taxes (or charges).

However, the past decades have shown that the latter approach (based upon the increase of taxes and other charges) may be problematic, as the pressure on the (national) economy (ies) of countries applying this method of gaining more income, tends to become too high, which, over the past decades, has caused numerous Western (and Western inspired) countries to opt for additional credit rather than for increased tax income. Hence, this has caused numerous countries to continuously postpone necessary remediation of government financing (and on the contrary, to choose for debt refinancing), making government finances ever more problematic.[721]

Moreover, the fact of hoping for continuous economic growth in order to install a larger taxable base from the economic fabric, has also shown to be an illusory strategy[722], a fact with which especially members of the European Union have been confronted with in the ongoing aftermath of the financial crisis of 2008.

Therefore, it may be clear that a system of (uncontrolled) government debt financing tends easily to bear witness of true mismanagement, showing, at the least, a lack of awareness that economic growth has its limits, and at the same wrongly estimating that an irresponsible creation of fictitious new money (in the form of credit lending by private banks), rather than drastically overhauling spending behavior, can hardly offer a solution for the problem of government shortages.[723]

This situation is deemed the worst in Europe[724], where, as a result, during recent times, many countries have fiercely (albeit in many cases seemingly fruitlessly) been putting efforts into balancing government budgets (and more specifically into reducing government debt to acceptable proportions).[725]

Piketty has described this as follows[726]:

> Europe is the most extreme case: it has both the highest level of private wealth in the world and the greatest difficulty in resolving its public debt crisis – a strange paradox.

---

[721] Piketty describes this as follows:

> The rich world is rich, but the governments of the rich world are poor. (see Piketty 2014, p. 540).

[722] Think tanks, such as the aforementioned "Club of Rome" (see above, at marg. 144 of this chapter), have already for decades been warning about this.

[723] Compare Ronse (1992), p. 79.

[724] As regards especially Europe, see Krugman (2012), p. 177 a.f.; Stiglitz (2012), p. 254. See also Dévoluy et al. (2011), p. 52.

[725] See De Boeck (2014), p. 12; Van Haver and Blomme (2014), p. 6; Haeck (2014a).

[726] Piketty (2014), p. 540.

Further Illustration 3.15: The Growth of American Government Debt in the Reagan Era and Beyond

It is not a coincidence that, as, especially from the 1980s on, American governments, especially those of a Republican signature, strongly adhered to neo-liberal economic thinking, also American government debt has strongly increased.

During the 1980s, the Reagan-governments would not succeed in offering a durable solution for the economic crisis from that period, and consequently would, in contradiction with Reagan's firm election promises, push the problem of government debts even more forward in time.[727]

According to journalist Tom Ronse, during the presidential election campaign of 1980, Ronald Reagan himself had illustrated the gravity of the then prevailing American government debt getting out of control by remarking that the total American government debt, in notes of 1000 USD, then accounted for a pile of 107 km high. His electoral promise to remediate American government debt, but, at the same time, lower taxes and increase weaponry, was already during the battle for the Republican president candidacy, by his Republican opponent Bush (senior) referred to as "voodoo-economy". Bush sr. would prove to be more right than he had wished for.[728]

According to the same Tom Ronse, under the government of Ronald Reagan, the American government debt increased by 900,000 USD per minute on average. Under the presidency of Bush senior, this increase would speed up even more, partially because of a persistent recession of the global economy, but also as a result of Bush's preferences for warfare over more diplomatic solutions to tackle foreign difficulties. At the end of the Bush (senior) government (1989–1993), American government debt was reported to have amounted to a spectacular 4000 billion USD, or 4 trillion USD, a pile of 1000 USD-notes 429 km high.[729]

According to another source, the quoted figures may even be more impressive. For instance, Bonner and Wigger have held that in 1980 (in the pre-Ronald Reagan era), the American debt amounted to slightly less than 1 trillion USD, but that this figure would, at the end of the Reagan-administration, amount to 2.7 trillion USD, and that, at the start of the Bush (junior)-administration (so after one presidential term of Bush senior (1989–1993) and two terms of Bill Clinton (1993–2001)), to 5.7 trillion USD.[730]

(continued)

[727]Subhuti (2011), p. 174. See also Veldman and Parlevliet (2003), p. 171.

[728]Ronse (1992), p. 78.

[729]Ronse (1992), p. 78. See also Van Oudheusden (2012), p. 134.

[730]Bonner and Wiggin (2006), p. 227. See also Van Oudheusden (2012), pp. 137 a.f.

Further Illustration 3.15 (continued)

Notwithstanding the fact that George W. Bush (junior) himself had turned the remediation of government financing into one of his main electoral promises, also his government would far from turn the tide. On the contrary, during his first presidential term, American government debt would increase more than it had during the entire 200 year period before.[731]

Be as it may, from the aforementioned Tables 3.1, 3.2, 3.3, and 3.4, it can be concluded that, at the beginning of 2016, American government debt had risen to an amazing 18 trillion USD, whereby it is no longer clear how high the pile of this debt in 1000-USD notes would be (as Ronald Reagan is no longer around to point this out).

In other words, the current debt of the USA is now approximately 18 times higher than at the moment Ronald Reagan came into office as president of the USA, and this despite Reagan's own fixed determination (in addition to these of all subsequent American presidents) to reduce the American government debt.

It may be clear that the capitalist model of government financing through taxation (of lower and middle classes, and whereby the rich classes and big enterprises are mostly exempt) and through debt financing by private banks (as a result of which the rich classes, especially the capital providers and managers of private banks, get richer and richer), has proven itself not to function.[732]

As said before, for this reason, an alternative model of government financing will be proposed in the Chaps. 4 and 5 of this book.

As has already been mentioned before, a further injustice of the prevailing **208**
systems of government funding is that the vulnerability to taxation (and similar charges) mainly affects laboring (lower and middle) classes of society.

Indeed, within capitalist economies, "labor" is not only the least appreciated production factor (see above, at marg. 156 a.f. of this chapter), but it is also the least mobile factor as a result of territorial limitations (for instance the fact that many types of labor need to be performed on a fixed physical location and that the persons performing this labor need to be located in its vicinities).

In practice, this also implies that income from labor is the one most easily subject to taxation (and to similar charges), and this is why, in many countries, mainly income from labor is subject to the most heavy fiscal (and "parafiscal") charges.

---

[731] Bonner and Wiggin (2006), p. 233.

[732] A concern that recently has even been expressed by the IMF itself (albeit in less harsh wordings); see International Monetary Fund (2016), p. 54.

It needs to be emphasized that, when mentioning "income from labor", this not only refers to labor performed as an employee, but for example also to labor performed as an independent worker in his own (or in a small business). Indeed, in addition to working classes in a strict sense of the word, also small independent business owners, as well as small and medium enterprises, are clearly interesting sources of income through taxation for many (Western and Western inspired) governments.

On the contrary, especially in an economy increasingly dependent on globalized capital and money markets, as is the case for the current world economy, capital is inherently far more mobile than labor. To put it bluntly, especially in a liberalized and deregulated world economy, money is indeed far more easily (and often precisely for the purpose of preventing taxation) transportable over country borders. In the same sense, financial instruments (in the end representing money which has been invested, for example either as capital or as debt of a corporation or company), are also highly mobile and therefore easily transportable over country borders.[733]

As a consequence, the levying of taxes (and of other charges) on income deriving from (large) capital in practice is far more laborious than the taxation of income from labor, whereby it can even be remarked that the larger a capital investment, the easier it gets to organize isolating it from taxation, for instance due to the fact that transaction costs for a potential re-allocation of capital become relatively more insignificant as the capital to move is larger, but also because it is easier for large enterprises to resort to big consultancy firms which provide services of fiscal optimization and to apply corporocratic mechanisms of (fiscal) policy influencing, such as lobbying and blackmail.[734]

---

[733]Stiglitz (2012), p. 73:

> The rich and superrich often use corporations to protect themselves and shelter their income, and they have worked hard to ensure that the corporate income tax rate is low and the tax code is riddled with loopholes. Some corporations make such extensive use of these provisions that they don't pay any taxes.

[734]Stiglitz (2012), pp. 73 a.f.; see also Oxfam (2014), 16.

For some examples, see Oxfam (2016), pp. 27 a.f., for instance mentioning some of the practices of Belgian beer producer "AB InBev".

> The Belgium-based Anheuser-Busch InBev (AB InBev) is the world's largest brewing company, and sells over 200 different brands of beer across Europe, Asia and America. Not only does the company dominate the market—it has a powerful political voice too. It spent $3.7m lobbying the US government in 2014, and 56 of the 141 lobbying reports it filed were on issues relating to taxation. AB InBev has used its influence to deliberately target legislation designed in the public interest, for example establishing voluntary advertising standards to avoid limitations on advertising to young people. In Brazil before the 2014 World Cup, the company was involved with FIFA in pressuring the government to change a law banning the consumption of alcohol at football matches, so that its products could be sold. Small retailers also pay a price for corporate dominance. In the US, the Justice Department is currently probing allegations that AB InBev is curbing competition by buying up distributors, making it harder for micro-breweries to get their products onto store shelves. (see Oxfam 2016, p. 28).

To quote from the earlier mentioned Oxfam study "*Even it up*"[735]: 209

> The richest individuals are also able to take advantage of the same tax loopholes and secrecy. In 2013, Oxfam estimated that the world was losing $156bn in tax revenue as a result of wealthy individuals hiding their assets in offshore tax havens. Warren Buffet has famously commented on the unfairness of a system that allowed him to pay less tax than his secretary.

In this way, on a global scale, fiscal (and parafiscal) systems are systems which 210
mainly impact the low and middle class, as well as the poor, while, at the same time, as a result of the earlier mentioned systems of credit financing, the amount of interests on government debt (which ultimately is carried by tax payers), entails a further source of substantial profits for the already (extremely) rich credit providers, mainly private banks (and their shareholders and managers).[736]

Oxfam has in this regard even argued that, at the beginning of 2016, the global system of tax avoidance to the benefit of the rich and the powerful is sucking the life out of welfare states in the rich world, for instance denying poor countries the resources they need to tackle poverty, put children in school and prevent their citizens dying from easily curable diseases.[737]

Further Illustration 3.16: Fiscal Creativity from John C. Malone
Numerous examples of (extremely) rich people above all aiming at avoiding taxes can be given.

A notorious such example is the tax evasion behavior of John C. Malone. A number of particularly relevant quotes from a press release by Jesse Druckner (Bloomberg)[738], dating from the beginning of November 2013, speak for themselves:

> Billionaire John C. Malone escaped about $200 million in taxes, and Liberty Global's U.S. shareholders together likely saved more than a billion dollars, according to data compiled by Bloomberg.
>
> Shifting the address of his Inc. from Colorado to London last year didn't just put billionaire John C. Malone in a position to reduce his company's tax bill.
>
> He also took precautions to avoid the capital-gains hit that the so-called inversion would trigger for him and other investors. The day before was announced, Malone—the company's chairman and controlling shareholder—transferred $600 million of his shares into a tax-exempt charitable trust. He avoided paying taxes on

(continued)

[735]Oxfam (2014), 16.

[736]See also Brockmans (2014), p. 26; Bernstein (2004), p. 30.

In its study "*Even it up*", Oxfam for example mentions the case of Nicaragua, where, in 2014, the poorest 20% of the population is forced to spend 31% of their income on income taxes, while the richest 20% only have to spend 13% of their income on taxes (Oxfam 2014, p. 83).

[737]Oxfam (2016), p. 5.

[738]See Drucker (2014).

Further Illustration 3.16 (continued)

his remaining stake, worth about $260 million, by exploiting IRS regulations meant to block a different loophole.

All told, Malone escaped about $200 million in personal taxes, and Liberty Global's U.S. shareholders together likely saved more than a billion dollars, according to data compiled by Bloomberg. "He's congenitally averse to paying taxes," said Robert Willens, an independent tax accounting analyst in New York City."

(. . .)

"Malone -- whose net worth is $7.5 billion, according to the Bloomberg Billionaires Index -- has a history of creative tax-avoidance tactics. Over the years, many of the 73-year-old media billionaire's biggest deals (..) have helped his companies to cut their tax bills.

Malone has at least four other charitable trusts, with more than $210 million in assets, IRS records show. Such trusts permit wealthy individuals to use the tax-exempt status of a charity to shelter income. In the past two years, he has also taken advantage of an Irish tax break to buy prime real estate in central Dublin.

Further Illustration 3.17: Of (Highly) Profitable Companies Who Spend More on CEO-Fees Than on Taxes

According to a press release of 18 November 2014[739] (stemming from a study of the "*Institute for Policy Studies*" and the "*Center for Effective Government*"), the remuneration of seven of the thirty most important American top companies was in 2013 higher than the amount which the same companies were paying in federal taxes on their company profits.

According to this same press release, the said large companies—among which aircraft manufacturer "Boeing", car producer "Ford" and the "JPMorgan bank"—paid their CEO, on average, 17.3 million USD. At the same time, the same companies made a global profit of 74.4 billion on which they paid no taxes to the American federal state, as they could benefit from fiscal deductions. The quoted press release further mentions that for example Boeing's (then) top executive James McNerney collected an income of 23.3 million USD in 2013, while his company received 82 million euro back from the tax administration.

[739] See Zeven grote Amerikaanse bedrijven betalen meer aan hun CEO dan aan de fiscus. (http://m.hln.be/hln/m/nl/942/Economie/article/detail/2124589/2014/11/18/Zeven-grote-Amerikaanse-bedrijven-betalen-meer-aan-hun-CEO-dan-aan-de-fiscus.dhtml?originatingNavigationItemId=1. Last consulted on February 28th 2016.

Further Illustration 3.18: Fiscal Creativity Set Up with the Help of Luxembourg to the Benefit of (Amongst Others) the Belgian Business Sector

Not only American (mega-)companies and their capital providers are masters in the field of tax evasion.

Also in Europe, large companies and their capital providers aim at minimizing taxes.

At a moment in time when the then newly appointed Belgian (federal) government Michel I announced numerous cost-cutting measures which, again, mainly impact lower and middle classes[740] (a phenomenon which, as mentioned before, has been appearing globally for decades[741]), at the beginning of November 2014, the Belgian press[742] highlighted a number of massively applied mechanisms of fiscal ingenuity which were clearly aimed at minimizing contributions to government financing by the rich and the powerful.

It hereby appeared that the State of Luxembourg had fully supported the setup of tax evasion mechanisms which have cost other European countries, such as Belgium, fortunes in tax income.[743]

According to the quoted press releases, complex schemes of so-called "PO box companies" were used to shift taxable income to tax havens such as Gibraltar and the British Virgin Islands. Luxembourg government and tax authorities are hereby reported to have massively, albeit in all discretion, approved of such constructions, causing Belgium (in addition to numerous other countries) to miss out on hundreds of billions of euros in tax income.[744]

The abovementioned news articles were to a large extent based upon a massive "leak" of 548 confidential tax agreements which Luxembourg had made, such as (easily obtained) confidential tax agreements and so-called "rulings" between the Luxembourg tax authorities and the companies involved (and/or their respective capital providers) during the preceding year(s). Supposedly 343 companies from all over the world, among which large multinationals such as "IKEA", "Pepsi" and "FedEx" were reported to be part of these agreements.[745]

(continued)

[740]Van de Velden (2014a), p. 3; Van de Velden (2014b), p. 3.

[741]Van Steelandt (2014), pp. 20–24.

[742]Bové (2014a).

[743]Politicians such as then Luxembourg prime minister Xavier Bettel and then Chairman of the European Commission Jean-Claude Juncker even have defended this tax system (see Buxant 2014, p. 3; see also Lage belastingen zijn legaal. In: Trends November 20th 2014, p. 11).

[744]Bové (2014a).

[745]Bové (2014a). See also Riepl (2014), pp. 10–11, especially p. 10.

Further Illustration 3.18 (continued)

The anecdotal nature of this information nevertheless raised the suspicion that, in reality, the problem of tax evasive behavior whereby mainly large enterprises and their rich shareholders and managers exempt themselves from taxation—and, thereby, from contributing to the organization of society as a whole—is much larger than is generally assumed (as, for example, Stiglitz has been claiming for a long time).[746]

The information which leaked at the beginning of November 2014 deals more concretely with tax deals which consultancy firm "PriceWaterhouseCoopers" ("PWC") had set up in the Grand Duchy of Luxembourg for its wealthy customers in the period 2002–2010, and mainly in the years 2008, 2009 and 2010 (hence, after the outbreak of the financial crisis of 2008 and its detrimental impact on government finances in many Western (and Western inspired) countries). Three research journalists of the Flemish Belgian newspaper "De Tijd" (namely Lars Bové), the francophone Belgian newspaper "*Le Soir*" (namely Xavier Counasse) and "MOmagazine" (namely Kristof Clerix), especially commented on hundreds of leaked, confidential documents about tax deals between Luxembourg authorities and Belgians and Belgian companies.[747] Furthermore, a database containing the leaked information was made publically available at www.icij.org.[748]

At a later date, namely on December 16th 2014, "De Tijd" would further report that the identity of one of the whistleblowers had been made public. This whistleblower appeared to be a certain Alain Deltour, a man in his twenties, who meanwhile is reported to be formally accused of different offences by the competent Luxembourg authorities (among which: house theft, breach of professional secrecy, breach of company secrecy, handling stolen goods, and fraudulent access to a computer data base)[749].

From the information which leaked in November 2014, it furthermore became clear that 37 tax deals were made with 26 of the richest families and largest companies of Belgium. It concerns, amongst others, the purportedly richest family in Belgium: the "de Spoelberch" family (owning AB Inbev), in addition to the telecom company "Belgacom" (whereby it is to be noted that, at that time, the majority of the shares of this company, namely 53%, was owned by the Belgian government); the Walloon lime giant "Lhoist"; the "Artal" company, which is owned by the billionaire family "Wittouck"; the

(continued)

[746]Buxant (2014), p. 3. See also Riepl (2014), pp. 10–11.

[747]Bové (2014a).

[748]Bové (2014a).

[749]See Bové (2014b), p. 6; see also Luxemburg vervolgt LuxLeaks-bron. In: De Standaard December 16th 2014 (mentioning that, according to Antoine Deltour, other persons have "leaked" to the press also).

Further Illustration 3.18 (continued)

family "Ullens de Schooten", owners of "Weight Watchers"; "Groupe Bruxelles Lambert" (owned by the richest Belgian "Albert Frère"); "Bank Degroof"; the former "Dexia" (currently: "Belfius"); the Belgian branch of "British American Tobacco"; "Unibra" and "Accent Jobs for People".[750]

In many cases, the beneficial tax constructions concerned techniques agreed upon between Luxembourg PO box companies and PO box companies located in other tax havens such as Gibraltar, Cyprus, Hong Kong and the British Virgin Islands, but also in countries having formal programs of tax evasion, such as Ireland, whereby parties allocated each other loans, payed interest and/or dividends, claimed and payed royalties, charged each other income and fiscal interesting losses,... All these techniques aimed at ensuring that, finally, only a limited amount of taxes needed to be paid, and whereby Luxembourg itself agreed to be used as a fiscal escape route to the most famous tax paradises, even far beyond Europe.[751]

In December 2014, "De Tijd" announced a second round of similar communications confirming that the aforementioned Luxembourg practices had been taking place for (at least) 10 years and that all "big four" reviser/consultancy offices, namely, in addition to "PriceWaterhouseCoopers" itself, "EY" (the former "Ernst & Young"), "Deloitte" and "KMPG", but also numerous Belgian law firms, had actively contributed to obtaining fiscally favorable regimes from Luxembourg for the benefit of their customers (mainly consisting of large corporations).[752]

A new leak during the first half of December 2014[753] more specifically revealed the existence of tax deals between Luxembourg and (at least) 35 large Belgian and foreign corporations including "Walt Disney" (one of the largest media conglomerates in the world); the "Telecom Italia Group"; "Koch Industries" (one of the largest privately owned companies of the United States of America, and also one of the most important funders of the Republican Party in the USA); the American investment group "Colony Capital" (i.a. the most important shareholder in the Carrefour department stores); "Black & Decker" and "Reckitt Benckiser" (with famous brands such as "Durex", "Vanish", "Calgon", "Dettol", "Clearasil" and "Airwick"); the Canadian train and aircraft manufacturer "Bombardier"; "Hutchison

(continued)

[750] Bové (2014a).

[751] Bové (2014a).

[752] Bové (2014c), p. 1; Bové (2014d), pp. 8–9.

[753] Bové (2014c), p. 1.

Further Illustration 3.18 (continued)

Whampoa" (a group worth billions, owning famous brands such as "ICI Paris XL" and "Kruidvat"[754]) and internet giants "eBay" and "Skype".[755]

This "new leak" of December 2014 was also found thanks to the international consortium of research journalists ICIJ whereby, in the period November-December 2014, about 80 journalists from 26 countries had further investigated a selection of 54, newly leaked tax deals.[756]

From the press release in "De Tijd" of December 10th 2014, it seems furthermore that, while the first "LuxLeaks"-leak mainly concerned tax deals from 2008–2011, the new leak was about much older practices in the Grand Duchy of Luxembourg, with tax agreements dating back to 2003. It furthermore became apparent that, in some cases, the Belgian tax administration(s) had also played a very willing role to grant tax favors to the rich and mighty. In all these cases, it is said that, through rulings and other agreements, Luxembourg had mainly closed its eyes for large corporations (and various others) in order to elaborate favorable tax structures enhancing large scale fiscal evasion of vast sums of money.

One of the tax deals reported about in the "second leak" dealt with certain operations of a Brussels-Luxembourg office of the abovementioned "Hutchison Whampoa", a Hong-Kong based group of companies which, amongst others, is active in Belgium through the retail chains "ICI Paris XL" and "Kruidvat". Although the Belgian-Luxembourg office of this group of companies only employed four people, it was reported to manage 26.3 billion euro in loans and, in 2013, to have made 429 million euro profit, on which it only paid 65,162 euro tax (which implies a less than 1% taxation tariff). It was further reported how this company, in spite of operating also in Brussels, only declared a very small fraction (namely 0.0156%) of its billions as taxable profit.[757]

The second leak also revealed other tax routes from Luxembourg to Belgium. For instance, it turned out that the Luxembourg tax office had granted permission to top companies from all over the world to collect income from Belgian investment funds in a tax free way. Telecom group "Telecom Italia" is reported to have thus invested over half a billion euros in a Belgian investment fund.[758]

(continued)

[754]See Miljoenendans via Luxemburgse postbus. In: De Tijd December 10th 2014.

[755]Bové (2014d), pp. 8–9.

[756]Bové (2014d), pp. 8–9.

[757]Bové (2014c); Bové (2014d), pp. 8–9.

[758]Bové (2014d), pp. 8–9; Telecom Italia—Luxemburg maakt Belgische winsten belastingvrij. In: De Tijd December 10th 2014.

Further Illustration 3.18 (continued)

Also the internet giant "Skype" was reported to have obtained several lucrative tax deals. For this purpose, it had even moved its head office to Luxembourg. However, in reality, this head office was reported to only consist of a small financial and a fiscal department. In exchange for this, the Luxembourg tax office granted "Skype" a tax exemption of 95% on the millions of euros it makes every year from different licenses.[759]

Entertainment giant "Walt Disney" was also reported to have been awarded several favorable tax deals. As a result, "Walt Disney" has gathered different companies with turnovers of billions in one small building (which, according to the ICIJ-investigation, was rather a house than a real office building). "Weco One", one of the Luxembourg branches of "Walt Disney", was reported to have made a profit of over 1 billion euro during the past 5 years, but to have only paid 2.8 million euro in taxes. Again, this is a tax rate of less than 1% percent. The three companies owned by "Walt Disney" in Luxembourg were reported to have generated, between 2009 and 2011, a common turnover of 2.8 billion euro, generated by one employee on their payroll.[760]

The American chemical and energy giant "Koch Industries" was also reported to be among the lucky few benefiting from Luxembourg's fiscal willingness. Through a network of branches all over the world, including Belgium, "Koch Industries" was reported to generate a yearly turnover of 115 billion dollars. Worldwide, the Koch group employs 100,000 people. According to the press articles, the brothers David and Charles Koch (who are part of the Forbes-top 10 both in 2014 and in 2015; see Further Illustration 3.25) were furthermore not only known for their large fortune, but also for their generous support of the Republican Party of the United States of America. According to a press release in "De Tijd" of December 10th 2014, the Koch-brothers were, for instance, said to have raised over 400 million USD in order to prevent president Barack Obama being re-elected as president (during his second run for office). Moreover, these election contributions are said to be made illegally through deposits from Luxembourg branches of the Koch Industry group to the Republican electoral campaigns. The press release further mentions that one of the branches of Koch Industries generated

(continued)

[759] Bové (2014d), pp. 8–9.
[760] Bové (2014d), pp. 8–9.

Further Illustration 3.18 (continued)

269 million euro of profit during the past 4 years and paid only 6.4 million euro in taxes (this way, the tax rate has been below 4.15% during all those years).[761]

In the context of this "second leak", it became clear that not only Luxembourg fiscal authorities, but Belgian fiscal authorities as well, had allowed preferential fiscal regimes to multinational groups of companies. The Belgian deals mainly imply that a large part the profit of such a multinational companies (up to 90%) gets exempted from tax. The Belgian beer brewery "AB Inbev" and "British American Tobacco" were reported to benefit from such tax exemption "deals" for a large part of their profits[762].

Some of these press reports would prompt the (then) European Commission Juncker, mid December 2014, to request for further information of the fiscal rulings benefiting multinationals from the European member states.[763]

Since then, however, not much has been heard about the topic any more, except for, *on one hand*, some general policy declarations from the European Commission, among which the policy aspiration of establishing a Fiscal Union that will deliver both fiscal sustainability and fiscal stabilization[764] (whatever this may mean), next to, *on the other hand*, the fact that in April 2016, there has been a similar press leak dealing with information of the tax haven "Panama" (known under the name "Panama papers").

Further Illustration 3.19: Tax Avoidance by Ikea and Its Founding Father

After having succeeded in avoiding the spotlights for decades, in February 2016, as a result of the publication of a study commissioned by the green fraction in the European Parliament[765], some press coverage dealt with the tax

(continued)

[761] Bové (2014d), pp. 8–9.

[762] Vanschoubroek (2014a), p. 1; Vanschoubroek (2014b), pp. 10–11; Van de Velden (2014c), p. 6.

[763] Haeck (2014b), p. 7; Haeck (2014c), p. 7.

[764] See http://ec.europa.eu/priorities/deeper-and-fairer-economic-and-monetary-union_en (last consulted on February 18th 2016); furthermore Juncker (2016), pp. 13 a.f.

[765] Auerbach (2016).

Further Illustration 3.19 (continued)

avoidance behavior of Ikea and its founding father Ingvar Kamprad (whose estimated wealth is reported to amount to more than 35 billion euro).[766]

It was hereby reported that in 2015, after returning from a 40 years-long Swiss tax exile, IKEA's founder and the purportedly 11th richest person in the world, Ingvar Kamprad, for the first time paid Swedish tax. Kamprad had more precisely in 2014 declared an income of 1.9 million euro in Sweden as a result of which he became subject to Swedish personal income tax amounting to 640,000 euro.[767]

One of the main reasons Kamprad has managed to pay so few taxes over the years is the tax avoidance he displayed since the early start of Ikea.[768]

Apparently already as soon as Ikea was founded, it began using a number of complex albeit legal tax optimization schemes, basically consisting of three elements, namely: (1) Kamprad's own moving from Sweden to Switzerland, (2) Kamprad's giving up the direct official control over the Ikea Group, and (3) a corporate organization aimed at avoiding tax as much as possible, a.o. through the establishment of foundations in tax havens.[769]

In order to avoid wealth taxes in Sweden, already in 1973 Kamprad moved from Sweden to Switzerland, from where he spent more than 40 years building the Ikea-empire. Kamprad's voluntary tax exile was motivated in light of the high tax burden in Sweden which in 1970s could reach 85% of the income of wealthy individuals, while on the contrary, in Switzerland, generally considered as a European tax haven, federal income tax does not exceed 11.5% and the wealth tax varies around 1% (depending on the Swiss canton).[770]

Also for tax avoidance reasons, Ikea's founder was willing to give up the direct legal control over the Ikea Group, as a result of which he has not been

(continued)

[766]See IKEA's Founder Paid Tax for the First Time in 42 Years. http://www.nomoretax.eu/ikeas-founder-paid-tax-for-the-first-time-in-42-years/. Last consulted on February 28th 2016.

The "Ikea multinational" is a giant enterprise with ±33.8 billion euro in annual sales, 172,000 employees, an extended global supply chain and at least 375 stores in more than 40 countries. Despite its massive size, Ikea has basically remained a privately-owned business enterprise, controlled through a complex multinational structure by Ingvar Kamprad, his three sons and their close associates (see Auerbach 2016, p. 6).

[767]IKEA's Founder Paid Tax for the First Time in 42 Years. http://www.nomoretax.eu/ikeas-founder-paid-tax-for-the-first-time-in-42-years/. Last consulted on February 28th 2016.

[768]IKEA's Founder Paid Tax for the First Time in 42 Years. http://www.nomoretax.eu/ikeas-founder-paid-tax-for-the-first-time-in-42-years/. Last consulted on February 28th 2016.

[769]IKEA's Founder Paid Tax for the First Time in 42 Years. http://www.nomoretax.eu/ikeas-founder-paid-tax-for-the-first-time-in-42-years/. Last consulted on February 28th 2016.

[770]See Auerbach (2016), p. 6. See also IKEA's Founder Paid Tax for the First Time in 42 Years. http://www.nomoretax.eu/ikeas-founder-paid-tax-for-the-first-time-in-42-years/. Last consulted on February 28th 2016.

Further Illustration 3.19 (continued)

officially declared as an owner of the Ikea Group since 1988.[771] For the same reason, Kamprad also gave up his chairman position in the Supervisory Board of Ikea in 2006.[772]

Moreover, it has been reported that IKEA's managers and founding family have constructed a convoluted corporate structure designed to facilitate profit-shifting and tax avoidance on a grand scale.[773]

Further Illustration 3.20: The Panama Papers

The "Panama Papers" refers to a set of ±11.5 million confidential documents that were leaked in early 2016 and that provide detailed information about more than 214,000 offshore companies listed by the Panamanian corporate service provider "Mossack Fonseca", including the identities of shareholders and directors of the companies. The documents especially demonstrate how (extremely) wealthy individuals, including public officials, strive at both hiding their wealth from public scrutiny and at avoiding taxation in their home countries. At the time of publication, the papers not only brought to light detailed information about wealthy private persons, but were reported to also identify five then-heads of state or government leaders from Argentina, Iceland, Saudi Arabia, Ukraine, and the United Arab Emirates, as well as government officials, close relatives, and close associates of various heads of government of more than forty other countries. The British Virgin Islands was reported to be the home to half of the companies exposed, and Hong Kong was reported to contain the most affiliated banks, law firms, and middlemen.[774]

(continued)

[771]In 1982, Kamprad transferred legal ownership of the IKEA Group's parent company, Ingka Holding BV, to a Dutch domiciled foundation, the "Stichting Ingka". However, the legal and financial documents that would allow to fully understand the financial implications of this ownership structure are under Dutch law exempt from public disclosure. Next to the Dutch "Stichting Ingka", there is a second foundation at play, namely the Liechtenstein "Interofog Foundation", both foundations apparently being controlled by members of the Kamprad family (see Auerbach 2016, p. 10; Ikea. Hoe een fiscal bouwpakket 1 miljard voordeel oplevert. Belastingparadijs met ballenbad. In: De Standaard February 13–14th 2016, pp. 18–19).

[772]IKEA's Founder Paid Tax for the First Time in 42 Years. http://www.nomoretax.eu/ikeas-founder-paid-tax-for-the-first-time-in-42-years/. Last consulted on February 28th 2016.

[773]Auerbach (2016), p. 5.

For an analysis of the group structure of Ikea, see Auerbach (2016), pp. 7 a.f.

[774]https://en.wikipedia.org/wiki/Panama_Papers (last consulted on April 14th 2016).

Further Illustration 3.20 (continued)

While it was stressed in the numerous press articles dealing with the Panama-leaks that the use of offshore business entities is as such not illegal in the jurisdictions in which said companies are registered, the reporters who have brought the Panama Papers to the attention of the general public nevertheless found that some of the shell companies may have been used for illegal purposes, including fraud, drug trafficking, and tax evasion.[775]

Given the scale of the Panama leaks, the help was enlisted of the "International Consortium of Investigative Journalists" (ICIJ) (see above, the "Further Illustration 3.18"), which distributed the documents for investigation and analysis to some 400 journalists at 107 media organizations in 76 countries. The first news reports based on the papers, and 149 of the documents themselves, were first published on April 3th 2016.[776]

"Mossack Fonseca", the Panamanian law firm whose "papers" were leaked in the Panama Papers affair, is purportedly one of the biggest in the business of setting up offshore company structures aimed at tax avoidance. Its services to its clients include incorporating and operating shell companies in friendly jurisdictions on their behalf. These services can include creating "complex shell company structures" that, while in most jurisdictions legal, also allow the firm's clients to operate behind an often impenetrable wall of secrecy. The leaked Panama papers detail some of their intricate, multi-level, and multi-national corporate structures. From the April 2016 leaks, it became clear that Mossack Fonseca has acted on behalf of more than 300,000 companies, most of them registered in financial centers which are British Overseas Territories, and has thereto worked together with some of the world's biggest financial institutions, including Deutsche Bank, HSBC, Société Générale, Credit Suisse, UBS, Commerzbank, and Nordea.[777]

In other words, in numerous countries, governments experience many difficulties in generating tax income (in addition to income from other semi-tax charges) from income of capital (as a result of which, worldwide, fiscal policy additionally helps the rich to become ever more rich and increasingly burdens the poor(er) to carry the load of government financing).[778]

211 In the aforementioned Oxfam *study* "*Even it up*", global fiscal policy has been described as follows[779]:

---

[775] https://en.wikipedia.org/wiki/Panama_Papers (last consulted on April 14th 2016).

[776] https://en.wikipedia.org/wiki/Panama_Papers (last consulted on April 14th 2016).

[777] https://en.wikipedia.org/wiki/Panama_Papers (last consulted on April 14th 2016).

[778] Kruithof (2012), pp. 70–77, especially p. 77.
See more recent Oxfam (2016), pp. 4–5.

[779] Oxfam (2014), pp. 16–17.

> Elites, in rich and poor countries alike, use their heightened political influence to curry government favors – including tax exemptions, sweetheart contracts, land concessions and subsidies – while blocking policies that strengthen the rights of the many.
>
> In Pakistan, the average net-worth of parliamentarians is $900,000, yet few of them pay any taxes.
>
> This undermines investment in sectors, such as education, healthcare and small-scale agriculture, which can play a vital role in reducing inequality and poverty.
>
> The massive lobbying power of rich corporations to bend the rules in their favor has increased the concentration of power and money in the hands of the few. Financial institutions spend more than €120 million per year on armies of lobbyists to influence EU policies in their interests.
>
> Many of the richest people made their fortunes thanks to the exclusive government concessions and privatization that come with market fundamentalism. Privatization in Russia and Ukraine after the fall of communism turned political insiders into billionaires overnight. Carlos Slim made his many billions by securing exclusive rights over Mexico's telecom sector when it was privatized in the 1990s.
>
> Market fundamentalism and political capture have worsened economic inequality, and undermined the rules and regulations that give the poorest, the most marginalized and women and girls, a fair chance.

212 It has become clear during recent years that large enterprises very actively influences governments, and in this way the outcome of the processes of political decision making, a phenomenon which, as mentioned earlier (see already above, at marg. 10 of Chap. 1 of this book and marg. 133–134 of this chapter), is also known under the term "*Corporatocracy*".

It needs furthermore not surprise that this "Corporatocracy" focuses strongly on ensuring a legislative context which validates techniques of fiscal evasion.

As a result, fiscal policy has also been described as "the great tax failure".[780]

Already two decades ago, Galbraith has pointed out the intrinsic injustice of government subsidy policy characterizing many Western countries, whereby support to and subsidies for the poor are continuously and ever more questioned—for instance under the argument that such subsidies have a negative impact on the moral and on the labor ethics of the poor—but whereby attributing large amounts of subsidies to big enterprises is hardly debated upon (see, for instance, the mega bailouts of the banks, but also the subsidies to the ailing car industry and to large farming enterprises).[781]

Comparable more present-day insights can be found with authors such as Stiglitz and Sachs who have furthermore pointed out that fiscal legislation favoring big business in many countries (including the implied possibility to build escape routes to tax havens)[782] has often been the result of lobbying by big enterprises (according to Sachs, one of the most striking expressions of "corporatocracy", hence of the failure of democracy).[783]

---

[780]See especially Sachs (2011), p. 118 a.f.
See before Turner (1973), p. 148.

[781]Galbraith (1992), pp. 14–15; Stiglitz (2003), p. 107.

[782]Sachs (2011), pp. 118 a.f.; Stiglitz (2003), pp. 106 a.f.; Bijlo (2014), p. 63.

[783]Sachs (2011), p. 118. See also Chomsky (1999), p. 132.

Stiglitz even has argued that the failure of democracy to create a fair social economic order, especially as regards the mechanisms of government financing, is one of the most important indications that capitalist financial mechanisms have failed.[784]

Finally, Michel Foucault has held that in particular the objective of big enterprises to seize political power is characteristic for the particularity of economic neo-liberalism. Where classic "economic liberalism" had been about a given economy determining a space in which the free market can grow unhindered, neo-liberalism is exactly about how the political exercise of power can be modeled to the needs of such free market economy (or, put otherwise, the selfish needs of the rich and powerful). According to Foucault, this is precisely the reason why economic neo-liberalism is much more directing than classic economic liberalism as regards market mechanisms (= neo-liberalism as so-called "*intervening liberalism*")[785], which as a result explains in more depth the tendency of economic neo-liberalism to influence politics (*inter alia*, in the field of fiscal decision making, but for example also in the field of monetary policy[786]).

Therefore, the worldwide prevailing fiscal inequalities can be considered as the **213**
direct result of the implementation of economic (neo-)liberalism, more specifically of the idea that the rich (entrepreneurs) are the driving force within society and should therefore be burdened by taxation as little as possible, so that they may continue their "noble pursuit" of striving for unbridled wealth, given the beneficial effects this has for the rest of society.

In this, thinking of economic neo-liberalism clearly goes back to the ideas of Smith, who also expressed his contempt for taxing the rich entrepreneurs as they should remain unhindered in their noble plight to bring more prosperity to the world (see above, at marg. 132 of this chapter).

As a result, such fiscal policy has, on a global scale, contributes even further to creating the huge distances between the poor and the rich[787] prevailing in present-day societies.[788] As mentioned earlier, in its research report "*Even it up*"[789], Oxfam has described this fiscal policy rightly as "*the great tax failure*".[790]

As a result, worldwide, fiscal policy has, especially in countries where public **214**
finances are highly dependent on taxes and similar charges, led to a system whereby especially lower incomes (a.o. from labor as an employee, or in the context of a

---

[784] Stiglitz (2006), pp. 269 a.f.

Compare Soros (1999), pp. 121–123; Hazenberg (2013), p. 136. See also Kruithof (2000), pp. 145 a.f.; Bijlo (2014), p. 63.

[785] Foucault (2008), pp. 247 a.f. and pp. 270 a.f. (also Foucault 2013, p. 181).

[786] So-called "*monetarism*". (See above, at marg. 147 of this chapter.)

[787] Steger (2013), p. 42.

[788] See Lipton (2014) (http://www.imf.org/external/np/speeches/2014/031314.htm; last consulted on October 23th 2014).

[789] Oxfam (2014), pp. 16 a.f.

[790] See also Sachs (2011), p. 118.

small personal business) are taxed most, while much higher incomes, for example incomes from capital, from management services or from high public functions, tend to escape such taxes to a much greater extent.

As explained earlier, this effect is even enhanced due to the fact that capital as an economic production factor is much more mobile than labor. Hence, within the context of a liberalized global economy, a policy of too high a taxation of income from capital often leads to displacing such capital from countries with high taxes to countries with more favorable tax regimes[791].

In this way, the rich and powerful easily commit to practices which may be qualified as blackmail in their ongoing pursuit of escaping taxes (hence of not contributing to the general wellbeing of society) as much as possible.

Neo-liberal fiscal policy in this way has turned into a shadow play whereby countries are competing against each other in developing the most favorable tax regimes for big business and capital. On a global scale, fiscal policy has as a result become the text book example of a classic "*race to the bottom*"[792] (in which, for instance, Belgium, in addition to many other European countries, has enthusiastically participated; see above, under Further Illustration 3.18).[793]

215 It may be clear that the current mechanisms of government financing, based upon taxation (and similar charges) of especially the poor and lower classes, supplemented with systems of debt financing, are part of a system which is at the same time "ineffective" (as worldwide national governments are faced with huge deficits), as well as intrinsically "unjust" (as the system is mainly impacting the

[791]Bijlo (2014), p. 63.

See especially the phenomenon of "tax havens". (See *e.g.* Shaxson 2011, p. 332; Shaxson 2012, p. 272; Alexeev et al. 2004, pp. 375–387; Sachs 2011, pp. 126 a.f.; Gumpert et al. 2011, p. 62; see also Kruithof 2012, pp. 70–77, especially p. 76.)

See also Oxfam (2014), p. 17:

> Ordinary people in rich and poor countries alike, lose out as a result of taks dodging. Yet tax havens are intentionally structured to facilitate this practice, offering secrecy, low tax rates and requiring no actual business activity to register a company or a bank account. A prime example of this blatant taks dodge is Ugland House in the Cayman Islands. Home to 18,857 companies, it famously prompted President Obama to call it 'either the biggest building or the biggest tax scam on record'. Tax havens allow many scams that affect developing countries, such as transfer mispricing, which causes Bangladesh to lose $310m in corporate taxes each year. This is enough to pay for almost 20 percent of the primary education budget in a country that has only one teacher for every 75 primary school-aged children.

[792]Compare Bijlo (2014), p. 63.

As explained in Oxfam's study "*Even it up*" (Oxfam 2014, p. 16):

> The race to the bottom on corporate tax collection is a large part of the problem. Multilateral agencies and finance institutions have encouraged developing countries to offer tax incentives – tax holidays, tax exemptions and free trade zones – to attract foreign direct investment. Such incentives have soared, undermining the tax base in some of the poorest countries. In 2008/09, for instance, the Rwandan government authorized tax exemptions that, if collected, could have doubled health and education spending.

[793]Vanschoubroek (2014b), pp. 10–11.

poor and (relatively) neglecting the rich, but, on the contrary, especially through banking interests on government loans, even helps the rich get ever more rich)[794].

As a result, (neo-)liberal public finances have, to a large extent, turned into a system of government financing which, *on one hand*, has confronted the governments of many (Western and Western inspired) countries with a permanent lack of funds[795], and, *on the other hand,* mainly impacts the lower and middle classes, while the true rich are not expected to show any solidarity with the rest of mankind.[796]

From a historical point of view, this observation is hardly new, although the neo-liberal reasoning behind it relatively is, given the fact that the intrinsic injustice of taxing (poor) people is probably as old as tax mechanisms themselves, and that, from a historical angle and on a global scale, it have usually been the lower classes of any given society that suffer the most from the pressure of taxes (and other charges) imposed on them by the richer elite.[797]

Hence, any attempts to justify such the present-day prevailing systems of government financing, especially to the extent that they mainly touch the welfare and wellbeing of the lower and middle classes, as leading to a fair redistribution of wealth, bear witness, to say the very least, of a very perverted form of irony (and even: hypocrisy), where indeed, in reality, the current systems of government financing, especially given their failure to involve the true high incomes in this so-called "redistribution exercise", have mostly shown to cause an opposite effect.[798]

When aspiring for a more just society characterized by more just and fair societal mechanisms of (re)distributing wealth, there is moreover not much to say in favor **216**

---

[794]This is even so in the classical meaning Aristotle has given to the term (see further, at Sect. 3.6.2.2).

[795]These observations are completely in line with the aspirations of certain neo-liberal authors; read *e.g.* M. Friedman's publication "*Why Government is the Problem*", which is basically a pamflet against too big and too highly funded governments (see Friedman 1993).

[796]See already Galbraith (1974), pp. 91 a.f.

See also Bijlo (2014), p. 63.) Furthermore Légé (2011), pp. 89–108.

See furthermore Oxfam (2016), p. 5.

[797]Bernstein (2004), p. 30, also explicitly pointing out that in the post-modern world, the weakest and poorest are the ones who are most heavily taxed.

See also the report "Even it up" of Oxfam:

> For instance, today's lopsided tax policies, lax regulatory regimes and unrepresentative institutions in countries around the world are a result of this elite capture of politics. Elites in rich and poor countries alike use their heightened political influence to benefit from government decisions, including tax exemptions, sweetheart contracts, land concessions and subsidies, while pressuring administrations to block policies that may strengthen the hand of workers or smallholder food producers, or that increase taxation to make it more progressive. In many countries, access to justice is often for sale, legally or illegally, with access to the best lawyers or the ability to cover court costs only available to a privileged few. (Oxfam 2014, p. 59).

[798]Oxfam (2014), pp. 16 a.f. See also Streeck (2015), p. 87.

of the policies of a lot of Western (and Western inspired) countries, especially within the European Union, of striving for a greater government discipline as, based upon (neo-)liberal thinking, these efforts have not succeeded in sanitizing government accounts, but seem to have had an opposite effect of creating a detrimental economic climate.

One could conclude that the neo-liberal public policy has not in any significant way contributed to installing a sound system of government financing, as it has utterly failed to truly turn the tide of the ever increasing debt financing and tax pressure—in its largest sense—on the masses (but considerably less on the richer classes).[799]

Further Illustration 3.21: Belgian Government Finances: A Story of Everlasting Remediation Amounting to Nothing...

Belgian governments of the past three to four decades have almost all promoted the slogan of remediating government spending, without these repeated efforts having led to the aspired result of healthy government finances.

In the Thatcher-era, Belgium suffered under the consecutive Martens I, II, III, IV, V, VI, VII, VIII and IX-governments which applied neo-liberal thinking in several domains of governmental activities, while the prime minister constantly told the Belgian population that "*there would be light at the end of the tunnel*".[800] However, this "light at the end of the tunnel" has obviously never been reached (and, on the contrary, the political world seems to have made the metaphorical tunnel longer and longer).

After the Martens-governments, in the period 1992–1999, came two governments led by Martens former "protégé" Dehaene. The governments Dehaene I and II resorted to different remediation operations (including "hard" savings measures, in addition to different "ingenious" accounting adjustments) in order to prepare Belgium to enter the European Monetary Union. The said governments Dehaene I and II hereby especially focused on reaching the so-called "Maastricht criteria"[801] (with a detrimental impact of the socioeconomic structure of Belgium as a result).

During the period 1999–2008, the governments Verhofstadt I and II initially enjoyed a healthier economic climate, although the severe economic problems which would severely break through in September 2008, already became evident at the beginning of the millennium. It has been reported that

(continued)

[799]For further details, see Reality check: Eurozone Debt Looks Unsustainable. In: The economist October 26th 2014 (also at http://www.businessinsider.com/reality-check-euro-zone-debt-looks-unsustainable-2014-10. Last consulted on October 27th 2014).

[800]Van der Kelen s.d., pp. 93 a.f.

[801]Van der Kelen s.d., pp. 103 a.f.

Further Illustration 3.21 (continued)

the Verhofstadt-governments nevertheless have failed to make use of the period of economic relief to truly sanitize public finances, but on the contrary resorted to trickeries, such as financial operations which only very temporarily contributed to sounder public accounts but, in the long run, rather had a reverse effect (such as "sale-and-lease-back" operations of government properties, in addition to public private co-operation techniques).[802]

The interim government Leterme I (2008) was most rudely faced with the disastrous effects of the financial crisis of 2008 (and would even be forced to resign in the aftermath of the Fortis-case)[803], and also the policy of its successors, namely the governments Van Rompuy I (2008–2009)[804], Leterme II (2009–2011), Di Rupo I (2011–2014)[805] and Michel I (2014-now) has importantly been determined by the aftermath of said financial crisis and its negative impact on government financing. To an ever increasing extent, these governments prompted all kinds of (unpopular) measures in order to remediate government finances which mainly hurt the poor and middle classes of the Belgian society (but leave the rich unhindered).

As a result, during the period when the Dutch version of this book was being finalized, namely in November-December 2014, the last mentioned government Michel I was faced with a first wave (not been seen since years) of strong challenges to its neo-liberal remediation policy in the form of different demonstrations and strikes by the poorer and working classes of the Belgian population.[806]

For those who want to see it: the impact of the doctrines of economic neo-liberalism on the Belgian society is gradually becoming crystal clear[807]: a weakening economy (i.a. characterized by an increasing trend of deindustrialization); a dismantling of government structures and public services in many domains, such as justice, army and education; a population getting more and more dissatisfied after half a century of government sanitizing; an ever increasing dismantling of the social protection structures[808] (resulting in an ever increasing poverty (especially in Belgium's larger cities)), and all of

(continued)

[802] Van der Kelen s.d., pp. 127 a.f.

[803] Van der Kelen s.d., pp. 155 a.f.

[804] Van der Kelen s.d., pp. 179 a.f.

[805] Van der Kelen s.d., pp. 191 a.f.

[806] Blomme and D'Hoore (2014), p. 1; Van de Velden and D'Hoore (2014), p. 3.

[807] See Pironet (2014), p. 3.

[808] See *e.g.* D'Hoore (2014), p. 1; see also Top sociale zekerheid luidt alarmklok over besparingen. http://www.hln.be/hln/nl/943/Consument/article/detail/2156121/2014/12/18/56-plussers-massaal-weg-bij-Belfius.dhtml. Last consulted on December 18th 2014.

Further Illustration 3.21 (continued)

this while also in Belgium, the rich classes are getting increasingly richer and are mainly specializing in the perfection of techniques of tax evasion (see Further Illustrations 3.14 and 3.26)...

217 It can be concluded that the currently (in many Western and Western-inspired countries) prevailing systems of government financing have not only proven to be highly ineffective (taking into account the chronic government deficits in many countries, which has made them even more increasingly dependent on debt financing), but have also shown to be a very inefficient method of re-distributing wealth in a fair and just manner.

As a result, the fiscal policy of many countries has over the past years attributed to an increasing distance between the rich and poor classes.[809]

218 Aspiring for the installment of a monetary structure which would be truly just and inspired by a spirit of altruism and world solidarity, the time seems more than ever ripe to reflect upon a totally different approach towards the problem of government financing, which, as mentioned before, will be attempted in the Chaps. 4 and 5 of this book.

3.4.7 The Financial Crisis Since 2008

219 The events on the monetary and financial markets of 2008, and their economic consequences in general, have been extremely intense, and, for a moment it even appeared that, worldwide, the financial and monetary system (and through this, the global world economy) was about to collapse.[810]

220 Although blaming a single financial institution for the financial crisis of 2008 would, of course, imply an incorrect and a too oversimplifying conclusion of the events of 2008 in light of the complexity of monetary and financial mechanisms[811], it still needs to be noted that, as a result of the large interconnectedness of financial and monetary institutions, the bankruptcy of the American bank "Lehman Brothers" induced a strong catalyzing effect which even, at least for some time, opened the metaphorical can of worms which, after ages of shameless capitalist financial practices, the monetary and financial system has turned into, while the

[809]Shaxson (2011), pp. 147 a.f., explaining the relationship between tax havens and poverty in the world. See also Oxfam (2016), p. 5.

See even Friedman (2002), p. 172.

[810]Middelkoop (2009), pp. 43 a.f.

[811]I.a. characterized by a profound and wide "interconnectedness" of the institutions operating on the monetary and financial markets (see further Chap. 1 of this book).

policy making world went through huge efforts in attempting to close it again (at a very high cost to society).[812]

What hence started as a liquidity crisis (the inability of certain banks to borrow on the interbank market in order to meet their current liabilities) rapidly turned into a solvency crisis (whereby an insufficiency of bank capital to cover "toxic assets" became clear)[813], thus threatening the stability of the entire (Western) monetary and financial system itself.

For further details about the causes of the financial crisis of 2008, reference can be made to the abundantly available literature on this topic.[814]

Let us nevertheless refer to some of the main causes as they have (as the careful reader will have noticed) already been discussed in the previous parts of this book, since the monetary and financial problems which arose in 2008 are, ultimately, only symptomatic of the intrinsic problematic character of the monetary and financial system based on capitalist principles itself.[815] **221**

One of the main causes for the system crisis of 2008 has undoubtedly been the "too easy" and abundant creation of money which has been the logical outcome of the monetary and financial system that has been shaped since the end of the Middle Ages.[816] **222**

In modern times, especially since, *on one hand*, the suspension of the gold dollar standard in 1971, and, *on the other hand*, the influence economic neo-liberalism had on public policy in numerous (Western and Western inspired) countries, over the past four decades, the world has witnessed an unseen growth in the amount of money.

Another factor having contributed to this increase of money creation has undoubtedly been the policy of unsoundly reacting to previous periods of crisis (where, mainly in Western countries, there had been desperately attempted to cling to previously reached levels of prosperity, which has been an important breeding ground for the flight into a credit economy and especially for the systematic taking up of credit by several Western states), next to the economic doctrines of "consumerism" and "monetarism" (see above, at marg. 149 of this chapter).

Based on the underlying (neo-liberal) principle that the economy should ever grow (whereby the implicit question arises if such an economy policy attempts to prevent reaching the "Malthusian ceiling"), monetarism[817] offered the framework in which mainly private banks (through the method of creation of scriptural money) started to supply the world economy with incredible amounts of dollars, yens, euro's, etc... at levels unseen before.

---

812 Middelkoop (2009), pp. 45 a.f.

813 Skidelsky (2010)

814 See especially Skidelsky (2010), pp. 16 a.f.; Morris (2009), p. 207.

815 See also Galbraith (1990); Galbraith (1975); Stiglitz (2003).

816 On this, see above Chap. 2 of this book.

817 For instance, the ideas of Milton Friedman, as a.o. applied in practice by the American Federal Reserve under Alan Greenspan.

As a result of this, in the Western (and Western inspired) world, credit, i.e. (newly created) money, became widely and easily available for all kinds of purposes. (See already above, under Sect. 3.4.5.)

223 During said time period, central banks themselves in general did not aim at slowing down easy credit, hence: easy money, but, on the contrary, at least in some countries, actively encouraged it (for instance through the application of very low central interest rates; see for instance the policy of the Federal Reserve under Greenspan in the period 1987–2006).[818]

As a consequence, world-wide, money creation would significantly escape from the influence of central banking, a fact which was described by Ann Pettifor as symptomatic for an economic order which has become more and more completely withdrawn from any type of state authority.[819] The "horrible truth", according to this author, is that, world-wide, central banks have since then not had any true impact on the financial markets.

One may even wonder if, by this, a deliberate objective of neo-liberal schools and financial market players influenced by their doctrine (especially private financial institutions), namely to create a world economic order that is only steered by large enterprises (among which especially private banks) and their capital providers, has been successfully met.[820]

224 A (further) factor adding to the massive money creation which increasingly fed the liberalized and deregulated world economy was that the conditions for credit lending (by private banks) were continuously lowered.

---

[818] Skidelsky (2010), p. 26; Morris (2009), p. 77.

Skidelsky however points out that there is also a serious defense of Greenspan, being that keeping money cheap in the USA was then probably the only way to hold a global recession at bay (see Skidelsky 2010, p. 27 and pp. 165 a.f.).

[819] Stiglitz (2003), pp. 56 a.f.; see also Pettifor (2014), arguing:

> This loss of a dominant role can be understood as a result of the radically changed relationship between capitalist finance and states. This in turn is an outcome of economic orthodoxy's contempt for the state; or for what Keynes called the general organisation of resources as distinct from the particular problems of production and distribution which are the province of the individual business technician and engineer.

[820] Pettifor (2014), quoting Prof. Josef Vogl as follows:

> Central banks and states have monetized the liabilities of capital markets; once 'lenders of last resort', they have become 'investors' or 'borrowers of last resort'. The debts of private banks were financed [by governments] by raising loans from private banks. Contrary processes have been installed, in which the socialization of private debts corresponds with the privatization of national debts. Financial markets became integral to the administration of public debts, accompanied by an expansion of their logic, their rules, their imperatives and interests. This implies, finally, the shifting of the reserves of sovereignty. The financialization of government structures, the mediation between public and private debts have mechanized political decisions as market-driven decisions; the markets themselves have become a sort of creditor-god, whose final authority decides the fate of currencies, social systems, public infrastructures, private savings, etc.

See also Hazenberg (2013), p. 254.

In many countries, private bankers gave up the natural caution which should characterize banking activities, causing credit (and consequently newly created money) to flow to economic agents of whom it should have been suspected that they would never be able to repay it.

As a result, enormous (monetary and financial) bubbles were injected into the economy (see also above, under Sects. 2.6.3 and 2.6.4 of Chap. 2 of this book), especially given the disastrous consequences of credit that is not been paid back within the capitalist economic system.

An obvious example hereof has been the situation on the American real estate market in the period before 2007 which would induce a catalyst impact on the financial crisis of 2008[821].

Bankers, either blind for the risks they thus created, or, in some cases, out of sheer malice, further developed mechanisms which shifted the credit risks to the investment scene. For instance, through techniques of securitization and derivative financial instruments, (bad) banking portfolios were taken out of the banks' balance sheets and shifted towards often for this purpose alone newly created investment institutions which were financed by the wider investment public.[822]

At the same time, driven by an impulse of unbridled pursuit for profits, financial institutions became more and more megalomaniac and hence also more fierce in deploying their own investment policy (often neglecting the associated risks)[823].

As a result, in the 1980s and 1990s, as well as at the beginning of the new millennium, the financial world was turned into a metaphoric, ever growing and less and less stable "house of cards".

It should not have come as too big a surprise that when the re-payment of the underlying credits[824] became problematic and, hence, the metaphorical card at the bottom of the "house of cards" was pulled, this threatened the stability of the whole card house itself, as has dramatically been demonstrated by the events of 2008. 225

Another factor which contributed to the severe problems the financial sector has been confronted with in 2008 has without any doubt been the large up scaling of financial institutions in an ever more expanding globalized context, which the 226

[821]Van Oudheusden (2012), p. 165.

[822]Burns (2012), pp. 30–41; Van Oudheusden (2012), p. 165.

It is, for instance, reported that as a result of the application of securitization and similar techniques, in 2013, in Europe alone, an amount of 1400 billion euro (or 1.4 trillion euro) of credit issued in the form of securities was still outstanding (see Claerhout 2014b, p. 29).

[823]See *e.g.* Engelen (2011), pp. 39 a.f.

With, in the Belgian context, as a remarkable example, the strategic policy of the French-Belgian financial institution "Dexia", (then) led by (the former Brussels' business lawyer) Axel Miller who was the CEO of Dexia in the turbulent period 2006–2008 and under whose leadership (but also that of his predecessors), Dexia accrued enormous financial debts, raising the ironical question to what extent this can be seen as illustrative for the reverse side of the aforementioned "genius principle" (see further, at marg. 231 of this chapter and under Further Illustration 3.23).

[824]Especially American real estate mortgages which many European Banks, indirectly, for example through the use of derivatives and securitization techniques, in addition to additional transition channels, had helped financing.

financial sector had undergone since the 1980s on. (See already above, under Sect. 3.4.4.)

In the context of a thorough liberalization and deregulation of the financial markets which took place under the impulse of economic neoliberalism, especially from the 1980s on, private banks were driven in the direction of (ever increasing) external growth (especially through mergers and acquisitions), in some cases even causing their transformation into transnational companies, or into so-called financial conglomerates characterized by a wide variety of (financial and insurance) activities.[825]

This a.o. caused financial institutions to become operational in regions which stretched far beyond the influence and knowledge of their local management, which, as mentioned earlier (see above, at marg. 181 of this chapter), led them to abandoning traditional and cautious work methods in favor of, for example, a blind belief in mathematical models based evaluation techniques. In this way, financial institutions became, for instance, more steered by the external influence of (international) rating agencies than by everyday common business sense.

As a result, the financial sector to a great extent lost touch with reality and was especially no longer guided by a clear sense of risk assessment.[826]

227 The remuneration practices set up by banks from the 1980s on and which aimed at remunerating in an adequate way the alleged "geniality" and "zeal" of bank managers and (top) personnel have shown to be a further ingredient of the cocktail of banking mechanisms which have contributed to the financial crisis of 2008.[827]

The so-called "bonus policy" (referred to Al Gore as the result of a widespread misalignment of incentives[828]) in particular helped blinding banking management and (top) staff to the huge risks to which they were exposing the banks they managed (and, given the key role private banks are playing in the field of money creation within the economy: also the rest of society). This bonus culture, inspired by the neo-liberal credo "*greed is good*"[829], mainly encouraged exposing the banking sector, but also the rest of society, to higher and higher risks.[830]

228 Put simply, a (classic) bonus policy rewards a manager, or (another) member of staff, of a given enterprise by awarding him a commission dependent on, for

[825]See Byttebier and Verroken (1995), p. 215; see also Byttebier and Verroken (Deel I) (1997), pp. 243–255 and (Deel II) (1997), pp. 401–413.

[826]An early, albeit extreme illustration of this phenomenon is formed by the events, already during the first half of the 1990s, at the British "Barings bank", where the impact of the trading activities of (derivate) trader Nick Leeson in the Far East, which were characterized by a complete circumvention of the bank's control and audit mechanisms, as well as the failure of the bank to adequately deal with its internal culture of greed and short termism, would ultimately lead to the bank's bankruptcy. (See Rawnsley 1996; Klok and van Uffelen 2009, p. 73. See furthermore Leeson's own report on the events leading to the bankruptcy of Barings bank, at Leeson 1996.)

[827]Skidelsky (2010), 23.

[828]Gore (2013a), p. 36; also Gore (2013b), p. 59.

[829]See for instance Belfort (2013a) and Belfort (2013b).

[830]Morris (2009), pp. 154–155.

example, the turnover that is obtained through his efforts, and therefore dependent on a set of debt claims (usually collectible in the future) towards customers (which arise because of the compensation for goods or services which will be delivered by the enterprise which employs the manager, or the other member of staff concerned).[831]

Such a bonus policy becomes even more dangerous when the enterprise applying it needs to be financed by means of credit (a.o. for cash payments, including the payment of bonuses to its managers and staff members), and moreover in case such an enterprise does not (or not sufficiently) have control over the quality (more specifically the liquidity and solvency) of its customers.

In such a case, the manager (or other staff member) receives his bonus before any cash flow has been generated as a result of the turnover he helped establishing, or, when applicable, through cash flows which are pre-financed by credit provided by third parties. If in such a scenario it later turns out that customers do not (or cannot) pay their debt, the company is not only burdened with a magnitude of dubious debtors, which on its own might put its existence at risk, but it can moreover be faced with the consequences of a large cash drain due to previously paid (or awarded) bonuses.

Moreover, it seems that any bonus policy (which is too much related to a company's turnover) encourages taking (extreme) risks which especially can become problematic when no effective internal or external control mechanisms are in place.

Needless to say that business models based upon (excessive) bonus system have **229** contributed too many significant bankruptcies (with as notorious earlier examples, the bankruptcies of "*Barings bank*", "*Enron*" and in Belgium, "*Lernout & Hauspie*").

It is therefore not surprising that the problems with which the banking sector was **230** faced in 2008 were, to a large extent, (co-)determined by the strong bonus culture (then) prevailing in the banking sector, as this moreover was one of the causes for the megalomaniac policy (and its inherent highly riskful nature) which the banking sector had applied the years before.[832]

The level of sarcasm of the banking sector towards the rest of society has been unlimited in the cases where banks which were virtually bankrupt and only managed to survive through costly bail out efforts of their host countries, failing management and directorship nevertheless deemed it necessary to be rewarded for its "great" and "remarkably ingenious" efforts through the validation of previously agreed exit bonuses and similar allowances, a problem which has rightly been described as symptomatic for a policy based on the principle of "*privatization of gains and socialization of losses*" (see above, at marg. 147 and 205 of this chapter).

[831]Vermeend (2008), p. 39.

[832]Morris (2009), p. 155.

Further Illustration 3.22: Reward Policies in Banking as a Striking Example of the (Neo)Smithian Unbridled Pursuit of Money
The (ongoing) debate with regards to the remuneration systems of banking staff in general, and of banking management staff more specifically, delivers an extreme illustration of the neo-liberal principle of the unbridled pursuit of money ("*greed is good*") which continues to dominate banking—and, through this, also the operation of money, as in the actual system money is mainly created by private banking efforts—but which, contrary to what economic neoliberalism claims, does not present any real advantages for the rest of society.

Even after the financial crisis of 2008, at a moment in time where many banks, worldwide, only managed to survive thanks to substantial bail out efforts financed by governments—otherwise put: based upon financial support stemming from tax money, but also, *horrible dictu*, from money which the government had to borrow itself (i.a. from (other) private banks themselves)—and, worldwide, millions of people were affected by different fraudulent banking practices, it has to be observed that the banking sector itself is still mainly concerned about its reward systems (including bonus mechanisms).[833]

Former banker Ugeux has tried to demystify the remuneration system of banks by, a.o., pointing out that banking management and banking staff very often decide upon their remuneration system themselves, and as such, are barely hindered by any type of control by the bank board of directors (and certainly not by its general meeting of shareholders)[834]:

> This personal appropriation of glory and money is based on the idea that all profits from activities are exclusively obtained thanks to the genius of the leader concerned. A wrong assumption, but one which prevails more and more in business.

This correlation between the remuneration systems of banks and the financial disaster of 2008 (and substantially of the "house of cards" construction which still characterizes the current banking and monetary sector) cannot be emphasized enough.[835]

231 Galbraith has been among the first to have elaborated further on the disastrous consequences of the so-called "genius principle" (which, a.o., strongly determines the way banks other financial institutions are managed).

---

[833]Smithers (2013), pp. 229 a.f.
See also European Banking Authority (2016).

[834]Ugeux (2010), p. 39.

[835]Stiglitz (2012), p. 79.
See also Geysels (2014), pp. 11–59, especially p. 21.

As has already been mentioned before (see above, at marg. 136 of this chapter), this "genius principle" implies that a CEO (or another leading person within a company, for instance a private bank) who has succeeded in drawing attention to his position of so-called "genius" within his sector (and often this is mainly the result of having a good couturier, of being part of a network, and/or of disposing of a good marketing system[836]) will later on barely be questioned on any matter within the organization he leads. From a mix of admiration, fear and a pursuit to reach higher levels by flattery, most members of staff will hardly dare to question any plan or objective proposed by the CEO (and this, indeed, until it really goes wrong, like, for instance, in case of a bankruptcy, or of other severe financial problems).[837] Even the board of directors of such a company adhering to the "genius principle" which, from a theoretical corporate governance-model, is supposed to monitor (and, if needed, redirect) its CEO and higher management, in practice often does not succeed in forming a sufficient counterbalance to the power of such a CEO who is deemed to be "a genius".[838]

According to Galbraith (already in 1992), a consequence of this is that the largest mistakes especially in banking are generally made by the highest ranking executives (who no-one dares to question) and moreover involve the largest amounts of money.[839]

This genius principle is, moreover, directly related to a high degree of "deresponsabilization", whereby a CEO of a bank in trouble, during the period where everything is "supposedly" going well, takes all credit on account of his geniality, but, as soon as difficulties arise, often rejects all responsibility (and blames the problems on external factors, such as failing market mechanisms or unfavorable market conditions).

When such CEO of a company which, under his "ingenious management", is heading towards bankruptcy (or, typical for the banking sector: only survives as result of a (mega)bailout) on top of that, without any shame, hangs on to previously received or agreed upon bonuses (or, without any shame, claims an earlier agreed upon exit-bonus), the neo-liberal "*privatization of profits and socialization of gains*"-principle to which banks adhere, clearly enters the dimension of the micro-economic context of the contractual relationship between such COE and the bank employing him.

In such cases where society is expected to save a similar bank through a (mega) bailout operation, it is in general the global society which pays a(n) (often very high) price for the neo-liberal "*greed is good*"-principle.

---

[836]For instance the nomination as "manager of the year" by the readers of any type of weekly or monthly (business) bulletin often gives an extra boost to this belief in the managerial capacities of such a manager.

[837]See also Loizou (2012), pp. 59 and 281 a.f.

[838]Galbraith (1992), p. 60. See also Galbraith (1960), p. 30; Galbraith (1967), p. 49 (on the shift of power within corporations from the owners of capital or shareholders to management).

[839]Galbraith (1992), p. 60.

Further Illustration 3.23: Correlation Between the Neo Liberal Genius Principle and the Financial Problems of (the "Former") Dexia

Applied to the Belgian context, the question arises to what extent the events in the financial markets of 2008, which have led to severe financial problems for numerous Belgian banks (and which have required several mega bailout-operations financed by the Belgian state), are also due to the impact of said "genius principle" with, amongst others, the role (which, according to the Belgian weekly bulletin "Trends", has not been sufficiently examined) of Axel Miller (former CEO of Dexia in the agitated period of 2006–2008 who, in accordance with the mechanisms implementing the "genius principle", had once been elected as "Manager of the year 2006" (*"Manager de l'année 2006)"* by the readers of the business magazine *"Tendances"*[840]) within the (former) Belgian bank "Dexia".[841]

Fairly soon after the establishment of the "Dexia – group" as the result of a concentration operation between the former Belgian government owned credit institution "Gemeentekrediet" and the similar French banking institution "Crédit local de France"[842], the Dexia-group aimed at becoming the world leader in the market for financing local governments.

This corporate strategy resulted in numerous (*megalomaniac*) projects, such as, in 2000, the Dexia-group's offering of 2 billion euro for the Dutch business banks "Labouchère"[843] and of 2.6 billion euro for the American "Financial Security Assurance" (FSA), after which, the Dexia-group proclaimed itself as the "*world market leader in the market of financial service provisioning to the public sector*".[844]

As a result, Dexia soon shifted away from its "*core business*" and started more and more to venture into speculative investments. As a consequence, Dexia soon acquired a balance total of over 1000 billion euro—almost three times the Belgian GDP—which however was only supported by an equity capital of a mere 20 billion euro. Constantly in need of new cash, Dexia started massively to take up short term money credit (at the interbanking markets). With this money, Dexia provided worldwide long term financing to all types of governments, i.a. by allowing credits or by buying the bonds issued by such governments.[845]

(continued)

[840]Axel Miller (Dexia) is 'Manager de l'année 2006'. http://www.express.be/sectors/nl/chemicals/axel-miller-dexia-manager-l-annee-2006/74236.htm. Last consulted on December 11th 2014.

[841]Claerhout (2014c).

[842]Byttebier and Verroken (1997), pp. 243–255.

[843]De Wit (2014).

[844]Carleer and Ramboer (2014).

[845]Carleer and Ramboer (2014).

Further Illustration 3.23 (continued)

When in 2007 the subprime crisis broke loose, Dexia CEO Axel Miller is reported to have declared that "*if others withdraw from international markets, this is creating opportunities for us.*" According to the same source, Miller stayed very stoical about the collapsing value of the Dexia companies' investments.[846] He is even reported to have referred to those as to "*accounting noise*", and to have expressed his belief firm that the market value would only become clear in case a true sale of investments was at hand. It is further reported that, as a result of this policy, between the end of 2007 and September 2008, Dexia Crédit Local (DCL) invested an additional 70 billion euro in government issued financial instruments. Dexia's risk manager would later make the following statement before an inquiry commission of the Belgian Parliament: "*Management was stoically deaf to the warnings. It continued to buy bonds without considering the fact that they could devalue.*"[847]

In the aftermath of the collapse of Lehman Brothers in September 2008, Dexia got harshly faced with the consequences of the obvious "*mismatch*" between its "active" (mainly long term credits to local governments) and "passive" (mainly short term interbanking financing). As a result of the events following the collapse of Lehman Brothers, financial markets were soon confronted with a real shortage of liquidity (especially on the interbanking market). Due to the aforementioned mismatch, it was however on that market that Dexia needed to collect money in order to be able to continue to finance its long term portfolios. Some sources have indicated that, during that period, Dexia needed about 100 billion euro per day of new cash in order to survive.[848]

Ultimately, only a (mega)bailout operation would bring some relief to the detrimental financial situation of Dexia. This bailout was a.o. based upon a collateral obligation provided by the Belgian State which allowed Dexia to lend again on the interbanking market, and upon a capital injection from France, Belgium and Dexia's historical shareholders of 6 billion euro to complement Dexia's equity capital.[849]

After the departure of Axel Miller as CEO of Dexia, the huge losses could not be resolved. According to rough estimates, the financial debts which emerged due to the past activities of (the former) Dexia amounted to over 11 billion euro in 2011[850], an additional 3 billion euro in 2012, and an

(continued)

[846]Carleer and Ramboer (2014).

[847]Carleer and Ramboer (2014).

[848]Carleer and Ramboer (2014).

[849]Carleer and Ramboer (2014).

[850]Van Overveldt (2014).

Further Illustration 3.23 (continued)

additional 950 million euro in 2013, all together good for almost 15 billion euro (and this, apart from the state guarantee that the Belgian government had to continue to provide).[851] The bailout operation moreover led to the creation of a "*bad bank*" which was (also) named Dexia (in which all high risk positions of the former Dexia group were assembled) and whereby, obviously in an attempt to clear the stain from this name, the former "Dexia" Bank itself was christened "*Belfius*".

Meanwhile, according to the weekly bulletin "*Trends*", people are wondering if the ones really responsible for the Dexia problems and their huge impact on the Belgian state finances, will ever be brought to court. The magazine "*Trends*" hereby pointed out that ex-CEO Pierre Richard is still enjoying a very generous pension at the cost of Dexia and that Axel Miller himself was rewarded with a new CEO position within the stock exchange quoted Belgian group D'Ieteren[852]; according to a communication in the Belgian financial newspaper "De Tijd" of December 13th 2014 "*he [however] has not done much yet since his appointment*".[853]

In the meantime, it seems that the banking sector (and its leaders) have hardly learned any lessons of the banking crisis of 2008, as can, for instance, be illustrated by the "return of the bonus culture" (in as far as one could even hold that this ever has been completely "gone") which presents a clear indication that the risk behavior in the banking sector has more or less remained the same (a fact which is also clear from the amount of outstanding bank assets—hence: of banking credit—as has been reported upon elsewhere in this book; see above, at marg. 185 a.f. of this chapter).

Further Illustration 3.24: The Return of the Bonus Culture

The American economist Sarah Anderson has recently studied the income of 168,000 bankers and financial analysts of Wall Street, New York. From her research, it has appeared that, in 2014, these bankers and financial analysts obtained bonuses of on average 173,000,- USD or 160,000,- euro. Hence,

(continued)

[851]Tanghe (2013).

[852]Claerhout (2014c); Voormalig Dexia-CEO Axel Miller wordt gedelegeerd bestuurder D'Ieteren. http://trends.knack.be/economie/voormalig-dexia-ceo-axel-miller-wordt-gedelegeerd-bestuurder-d-ieteren/article-normal-248865.html. Last consulted on December 11th 2014.

[853]Lambrecht (2014), p. 16.

Further Illustration 3.24 (continued)

these bonuses of 2014 were 27% higher than those of 2009. Added together, the Wall Street bonuses for 2014 amounted to 28.5 billion USD, or a figure which is the double of the total income of about 1,007,000 million Americans who only receive a minimum income. In this way, the extra income of the Wall Street financial elite is also higher than the basic income of 1.2 million Americans who are employed at the minimum hourly wage of 7.25 USD (or 6.7 euro) per hour. The bonuses awarded to the financial elite of Wall Street in 2014 would furthermore suffice to raise the wages of the 2.9 American bar attendants, or the 1.5 million American nurses, to an amount of 15 USD per hour. Anderson hereby warns that the bonuses of 2014 come close to these of 2006 (having been one of the causes of the financial crisis of 2008).[854]

With hindsight, one can observe that it has been mainly through the efforts of 232
governments (and not as a result of free market mechanisms) that in 2008–2009 the financial sector was, more or less, again stabilized, but that these governmental bail outs, *on one hand*, have not taken away the deeper root causes of the problems of the monetary and financial sector (especially the unbridled granting of credit, hence of privately creating new money), and, on the other hand (and which is worse), these governmental efforts have made the already before painful financial situation of the governments of numerous Western (and Western inspired) countries even more disastrous.

Even the European Commission[855], usually by default a fervent advocate and applier of economic neo-liberal doctrines, has admitted that the bailout efforts of 2008–2009 by European countries have cost the tax payer vast amounts of money and, as a result, even have endangered government finances of some of its member states.[856]

---

[854]See Anderson (2015a); Van Hoogstraten (2015), p. 30; Wall Street bonuses doubled income earned by all US minimum wage workers. http://rt.com/usa/241301-wall-street-bonuses-double/. Last consulted on March 20th 2015. See also Anderson (2015b).

[855]Commission Staff Working Document Impact Assessment Accompanying the document PROPOSAL FOR A DIRECTIVE OF THE EUROPEAN PARLIAMENT AND OF THE COUNCIL establishing a framework for the recovery and resolution of credit institutions and investment firms and amending Council Directives 77/91/EEC and 82/891/EC, Directives 2001/24/EC, 2002/47/EC, 2004/25/EC, 2005/56/EC, 2007/36/EC and 2011/35/EC and Regulation (EU) No 1093/2010 {COM(2012) 280 final}{SWD(2012) 167 final.

[856]According to the Working Document (p. 10) cited in the previous footnote, between October 2008 and October 2010, the European Commission has approved €3.6 trillion (equivalent to 31% of EU's GDP) of State aid measures to financial institutions, of which €1.2 trillion has been effectively used (of which €409 billion was used for capital injections and asset relief programs). The said Working Document furthermore points out that the budgetary commitments and expenditures in this range were not sustainable from a fiscal point of view, and imposed heavy burden on

233 It needs indeed to be noted that, as explained under Sect. 3.4.6 above, especially since the 1970s, governments of numerous Western countries have become strongly credit dependent (otherwise, and put more bluntly: have lived beyond their means).

This is extremely the case within the European context and has only worsened since the financial crisis of 2008.

As was already explained before, since then, under impulse of neo-liberal doctrines, severe remediation efforts to sanitize government finances have been undertaken which have required even further sacrifices from the majority of the population[857], but of which, oddly enough, big businesses, among which financial institutions themselves, are largely exempt (see above, at marg. 212–213 of this chapter, the so-called "*great tax failure*").

234 In this way, the logic of economic neo-liberalism, when applied to the monetary and financial sector, has driven the world economy into an increasingly faster moving carousel of financial problem situations, raising the question what will be the impact of a final spluttering of the motor of the financial sector in distress which until now keeps the carousel turning (and whereby the effects of centrifugal force if the motor stops, could be disastrous).[858]

Furthermore, it needs to be noted that the "neo-liberal madness" (a term used by Paul Verhaeghe) has moreover driven the world to a situation which is above all characterized by an absurd degree of socioeconomic inequality which cannot possibly be held onto for much longer, something which will be described in more detail under Sect. 3.4.8 hereafter.

3.4.8 Social Economic Inequality Resulting from Economic Neo-liberalism

3.4.8.1 Introduction

235 The deeply rooted negativity of an economy more and more driven by the ideas and principles of economic neo-liberalism, is not a mere theoretical fact, but can, on the contrary, be experienced by each of us, every day again, within the social economic reality which presents itself to many of us as a living environment in which man has above all been turned into the proverbial "wolf to (other) man".[859]

---

the present and future generations. Moreover, still according to the Working Document, the crisis which started in the financial sector plunged the EU economy in a severe recession, with the EU GDP contracting by 4.2% or €0.7 trillion in 2009.

See also Skidelsky (2010), pp. 16 a.f.

[857] See *e.g.* Pironet (2016), p. 3.

[858] Recently, even the IMF was reported to have shared its concern that the next financial crisis might be immanent. (See Elliott 2016.)

[859] See De Stoop (2012), pp. 68–71.

It even seems that the entire (Western and Western inspired) economic model in general, and its monetary and financial system more specifically, especially since the important influence these have undergone from implementing economic neo-liberalism as from the 1980s on, have become fully submitted to the unbridled pursuit of wealth and money principle.

As a result, on a global scale, societies have been established which, on a socioeconomic level, are intrinsically and manifestly unjust, not only in traditionally "hard sectors" of the economy (such as the business world itself), but increasingly also in former "soft sectors" of social economic life which are also undergoing the disastrous influence of neo-liberal thinking (such as the sector of public services, the health "industry", the academic sector, liberal professions,...).

It could nevertheless be expected from any societal model that pretends to add to **236**
civilization that it would strive for more justice and equality between people.

Obviously, (total) equality between people does not exist.

On the contrary, human existence is characterized by all kinds of inequalities.

For instance, some people are born rich, others are born poor. Furthermore, the family, and more in general, the society in which one is born, to a large extent, further determines one's life chances. People who are born rich and/or in rich countries, obviously get better and more life chances to make something out of their lives than those who are born poor (see the "*condemned to stay poor*"--principle which characterizes the neo-liberal world). Needless to say that numerous other factors create similar inequalities, such as, for instance, one's health, one's look, one's natural abilities and talents,...[860]

However, it can be expected from society that it would provide for an environment which allows people to overcome the abovementioned inequalities, whereby the numerous factors inherently creating inequalities should, as much as possible, be leveled by societal mechanisms aiming at allowing everyone to lead as decent a life as possible.[861]

Hence, one of the most severe criticism thinkable against the philosophies of "economic liberalism" and "economic neo-liberalism" is that both systems basically aim for the opposite, and have in this way proven to be destructive forces undermining human civilization.

Especially by holding that everyone should strive for the fulfillment of his own selfish needs, both philosophical systems basically aim at establishing a societal model in which inherent inequalities get ever more intensified.

The present-day societies which are aiming at implementing economic neo-liberalism to its fullest extent possible, bear witness of this fact, having shaped a socioeconomic order which is above all intrinsically unjust and, hence, in

[860] See furthermore Byttebier (2015), pp. 50 a.f.

[861] Interesting observations in this regard are further to be found with the Indian Hinduïst philosopher and religious scholar Vivekananda, especially in Chapter VIII of his book "*Karma yoga*", where he argues that although inequality is an inherent element of creation itself, the struggle to limit it as much as possible should be one of life's aspirations of each man. (See Vivekananda 1989, pp. 25–118, especially 113–115.)

complete contradiction with the abovementioned expectation that societal organization mechanisms should add to more justice and fairness.

Hence, it comes as no surprise that through the implementation of economic (neo)liberalism, one can but observe that the rich and powerful get more rich and powerful by the minute, while at the same time, life for the poor and repressed gets ever more tough and hard.[862]

Under Sects. 3.4.8.2 and 3.4.8.4, some striking illustrations of this reality will be presented.

237 In his book "*The neo liberal madness – Flexible, efficient and insane*"[863], the Belgian psychologist, author and academic Paul Verhaeghe presents a gloomy picture of a (literally) sickening performance society, where, in the Western World, an unprecedentedly large number of people copes with serious mental problems caused by the pressure of the society model driven by neo-liberal principles (whereby, as also can be read in earlier works of Erich Fromm[864], any human being has become servant to the objective of making a small financial elite as rich as possible).[865]

The situation is even worse in poor countries, where this "(neo-)liberal madness" has revealed itself already for ages in the guise of situations of (chronic) poverty and extortion.

However, as appears from several recent research (i.a. from authors such as Piketty, Sachs and Stiglitz and, before that, Galbraith, but also from organizations such as Oxfam), also in Western countries, the growing social economic inequality is continually increasing the gap between the rich and the poor[866], a striking example hereof being that, within the purportedly rich and prosperous European Union, no less than 1 out of 5 children are presently growing up in families struck by poverty,[867] albeit the situation in the purportedly as rich and prosperous United States of America is hardly any better (see already above, at marg. 174 of this chapter).

238 It should therefore not be a surprise that in recent history, prominent philosophers and economists[868], in addition to other scientists (including the previously mentioned Verhaeghe himself, but, for example, also Nobel prize winners Stiglitz

[862]Compare Pinxten (2014), p. 7.

[863]Verhaeghe (2011), p. 51 p.

[864]See Fromm (1955), pp. 89–90.

[865]De Stoop (2012), pp. 68–71. See also Bruckner (2002), p. 55.

[866]See Oxfam (2014); Kruithof (2000), p. 60.

[867]Pironet (2016), p. 3.

[868]For example:

- J. K. Gailbraith (see especially Galbraith 1974, pp. 95–96), in addition to his numerous other publications;
- Amartya Sen (see especially Sen 2009 and Sen 1977);
- Paul Krugman (see *e.g.* Krugman 2009 and Krugman 2012);
- Joseph E. Stiglitz (see *e.g.* Stiglitz 2012; see also Stiglitz 2006);
- Thomas Piketty (see *e.g.* Piketty 2014).

and Krugman, in addition to other renowned economists such as Galbraith), have reached the conclusion that a money and banking system based on (neo-)liberal principles hardly benefits society as a whole, but has mainly evolved into a mechanism—in addition to other such mechanisms (among which the since the 1980s liberalized and deregulated international trade and business sector in general)—mainly, if not exclusively, aimed at making the rich elite on the planet even richer.[869]

The rest of the world population is at the same time principally engaged in (hard) labor which, hardly taken into account any real concern for their wellbeing (see on this subject already Galbraith[870]), is also exclusively or mainly aimed at increasing the wealth of said small financial elite.[871]

Socially inspired thinkers such as Erich Fromm and Herbert Marcuse had already before reached similar conclusions in their analyses of the impact of (neo) liberal capitalism on the general welfare of human beings, in addition to other values.

Since then, given the vast impact of economic liberalism on a global scale and in as good as all sectors of social and economic life, their research has hardly lost any of its significance, although one cannot help but observing that, as a consequence of the widespread neoliberal "brainwashing" which has hit the Western world since the 1980s on, their works have somewhat been forgotten (see before, at marg. 83 of this chapter).

Depending on the degree of protection of social (and other) legislation, impor- **239**
tant differences between countries nevertheless still prevail, but it hereby needs to be considered that, due to the increasing globalization of the world economy, where for example production units (i.a. factories, but also service centers) are easily shifted to other countries where "the nuisance" caused by this type of protective legislation is lowest[872], these differences are becoming less and less outspoken.

In this way, the capitalist world-economic order has mainly (and more specifically from the 1980s on[873]) developed into a system that allows a relatively small group of people to become (extremely) rich—the wealth of certain individuals even

[869] Raspoet (2014), pp. 51–55 (containing an interview with Jos Geysels and Erik Vlaminck). See also Lipton (2014).

[870] See Galbraith (1992), pp. 115–116.

[871] Ugeux has expressed this as follow:

> We cannot longer allow ourselves to leave the governance of the financial sector to the financiers themselves. During the last decade of arrogant and cynical directorship, not only have they usurped all the financial gains thereof, but they also committed treason towards the very nature of the banking and monetary system itself. All last illusions concerning their morality melted away once it became clear to what large risks they have exposed our economy and society in general. (free translation) (see Ugeux 2010, p. 23).

[872] And conclusively also the cost of labor itself, which in the eyes of the financial elite steering the financial and business world, is only a factor restricting their unbridled desire for money.

[873] See Oxfam (2014), p. 8.

exceeds the wealth of entire nations—to the detriment of the wellbeing of mankind as a whole (and by extension, the wellbeing of the world itself).

As a result, for people not belonging to this financial elite, social and economic globalization seems therefore to have had a mainly downward leveling effect, whereby the gap between the poor and the (very) rich which was up till a few decades ago especially striking in North-South relations, gradually and increasingly manifested itself in the context of Western (and Western inspired) countries themselves.[874]

240 In 2014, Oxfam published a thorough study on poverty in the world called "Even it up".

In this study, Oxfam reached the following conclusion on the issue of the impact of economic neo-liberalism on the division of the riches of the world: ***"it is national inequality that matters most to people's lives, and this is rising rapidly almost everywhere. Seven out of ten people on the planet now live in countries where economic inequality is worse than it was 30 years ago."***[875]

This is a striking illustration of the fact that the neo-liberal belief system, holding that, driven by an invisible hand, unbridled selfishness will result in the highest possible wealth for everyone (as this belief is summarized in the earlier quoted neo-liberal credo *"greed is good"*), is not supported by reality. It is clear from the quoted Oxfam-study that rather the contrary prevails: ***"the benefits of growth have increasingly accrued to the richest members of society, pushing income inequality ever higher".***[876]

3.4.8.2 A (First) Anthology from Research on the Gap Between the Poor and the Rich

241 The insight that capitalism, especially under the influence of economic neo-liberalism, is increasingly widening the gap between the poor and the rich is certainly not new (or, as Bruckner has put it: "***We know the figures in their terrible monotony (although some people still question them***)."[877] As Pizzigati has phrased it: ***"The early twenty-first century would begin just as the previous century had begun, with astounding quantities of wealth and power concentrated at America's economic summit."***[878]

[874]Steger (2013), p. 42.

[875]Oxfam (2014), p. 30.

[876]Oxfam (2014), p. 30.

[877]Bruckner (2002), p. 21:

> On connaît les chiffres dans leur redoutable monotonie (même si certains peuvent les contester).

[878]Pizzigati (2012), p. 319.

Already in 1958, the renowned economist John Kenneth Galbraith, reported on what he described as "*the triumph of inequality*".[879] 242

Relatively "recent" data on the macro-economic context have shown that, before the start of the (modern) globalization in 1973, the balance of income between the richest and poorest countries on earth was about 44:1. 243

Twenty five years later (i.e. after the implementation, since the 1980s, of the teachings of economic neo-liberalism), the same ratio was 74:1.

Otherwise put, at the end of the previous millennium and in spite of some progress in the alleviation of world-wide poverty (*inter alia*, in the field of fighting famine), the bottom 25% of mankind had an income of less than 140 USD per year. Meanwhile, the common possessions of the top three billionaires in the world were, already then, higher than the combined GDP of the least developed countries and their 600 million inhabitants together.[880]

In other words, it can be observed that, especially within the context of the North-South relations, since the liberalization and deregulation of the world's economy as of the 1980s and 1990s, the traditional gap between North and South has not been resolved, but rather has increased and widened (which, on itself, is an additional indication of the fact that economic (neo-)liberalism is not holding up to its promise that the invisible hand of the free market will ensure that, if everyone behaves as selfishly as possible, society as a whole will improve, but rather of the contrary).

In his characteristically concise style, Christopher Lloyd has described the problem as follows[881]: 244

> At the end of 2001, the richest 2 per cent of adults in the world owned more than half of global household wealth, with the super-rich 1 per cent owning more than 40 per cent. Conversely, the bottom 40 per cent owned less than 1 per cent between them. It has been

---

[879]Galbraith (1974), pp. 95–96:

> In 1965 the one-tenth of families and unattached individuals with the lowest incomes received before taxes about 1 per cent of the total money income of the country; the tenth with the highest incomes received 28 per cent of the total, which is to say their incomes averaged 28 times as much as the lowest tenth. The half of the households with the lowest incomes received, before taxes, only 23 per cent of all money income. The half with the highest income received 77 per cent. In 1965 only about 6 per cent of all family units had incomes before taxes of more than $15,000. They received, none the less, 27 per cent of total income. At the other extreme, 25 per cent had before tax incomes of less than three thousand and received only 4 per cent of the income.

Obviously, this author has substantiated his findings with further hard data, which have not been quoted here (as, since then, much more recent data have been made available).

See also Galbraith (1994), pp. 252–253, who furthermore pointed out that

> the counterpart of this concentration of income and wealth is a damaging unreliability as to its use. (. . .) some of it, as in the 1980s, may be absorbed by functionless debt creation, such as that which financed the mergers and acquisitions and the leveraged buyouts.

[880]Steger (2013), pp. 113–115.

[881]Lloyd (2012), p. 374.

estimated that the richest 10 per cent of the world's adults now own more than 85 per cent of its total wealth. North America alone houses just 6 per cent of the world's population, but accounts for 34 per cent of all household wealth.

245 In 2014, Thomas Piketty gained much attention with his book "*Capital in the Twenty-First Century*".[882]

This book mainly contains the findings of a detailed and systematic research on the world-wide unequal division of wealth, and hereby inevitably reaches the conclusion that an evolution is taking place towards a(n) ever increasing (extremely) high level of inequality as a result of which the majority of the world's resources are increasingly being held by a small number of people.

Piketty mentions, *inter alia*, that for instance in the USA, the richest 10% own 72% of the resources of the country, and he warns that also in Europe a similar evolution is taking place. The author moreover considers the consequences of such an extreme inequality to be disastrous, as, according to him, within societies which are characterized by such fundamental inequality, there is no room for (economic) progress.[883] Piketty also demonstrated that returns for the owners of capital have grown at a faster rate than general economic growth, which implies that workers are capturing a smaller share of the gains from growth.[884]

246 Also in 2014, the aforementioned exhaustive study by Oxfam, called "*Even it up – Time to end extreme inequality*"[885] similarly demonstrated that the financial crisis of 2008 has only strengthened the said unequal distribution of the (worlds) resources.

According to this study, in 2014 there were then, worldwide, two times as many billionaires in comparison to 2009.[886]

According to the same study, the number of billionaires has increased to 1645, and their common wealth increased by 214% to an astounding 5.4 trillion USD. The study also points out that the 85 richest people in the world together owned more wealth than the poor half of the world population, a wealth which in the course of 2014 increased by 668 million USD per day.[887]

The study "*Even it up*" of 2014 further reports that, in this way, the gap between the rich and the poor is (literally) expanding by the day[888], if not by the minute,

---

[882]Piketty (2014).

[883]See also Pauli (2014), pp. 32–35.

[884]See also Oxfam (2016), p. 12.

[885]Oxfam (2014), p. 136.

[886]Oxfam (2014), pp. 8 and 32.

[887]Oxfam (2014), pp. 8 and 32.

The Oxfam-report lists a number of consequences of this growing inequality, *e.g.*:

- During the past 5 years, worldwide one million women died during labor because they lacked medical support;
- In 2014, worldwide 57 million children were unable to attend school;
- Beneath the Sahara there are 16 billionairs, but at the same time 358 million people suffer from hunger and poverty.

[888]Oxfam (2014), p. 32.

which is attributed to the fact that it is easier for capital to make new money than from labor efforts:

> Once accumulated, the wealth of the world's billionaires takes on a momentum of its own, growing much faster than the broader economy in many cases. If Bill Gates were to cash in all his wealth and spend $1m every single day, it would take him 218 years to spend all of his money. But in reality, the interest on his wealth, even in a modest savings account (with interest at 1.95 percent) would make him $4.2m each day. The average return on wealth for billionaires is approximately 5.3 percent, 156 and between March 2013 and March 2014, Bill Gates' wealth increased by 13 percent – from $67bn to $76bn. This is an increase of $24m a day, or $1m every hour.

In the beginning of 2016, Oxfam published a new similar study entitled "*An economy for the 1%. How privilege and power in the economy drive extreme inequality and how this can be stopped*"[889] which largely confirms the findings of the 2014-study "Even it up".

From the study of 2016, it appears that the situation has even gotten worse.[890]

One of the most striking findings of this 2016-study is most probably that in 2015, 62 individuals owned as much riches as the bottom half of mankind.

According to this 2016 Oxfam -study "*An economy for the 1%*":

- In 2015, just 62 individuals had the same wealth as 3.6 billion people—the bottom half of mankind.

  The study hereby mentions that this figure is down from 388 individuals as recently as 2010, illustrating the striking tempo in which the implementation of hardcore economic neoliberalism is widening the gap between the poor and the rich on the planet;
- Also in 2015, the wealth of the richest 62 people has risen by 44% in the 5 years since 2010, which implies an increase of more than half a trillion dollars (USD 542 billion), to an astounding USD 1.76 trillion.
- Meanwhile, the wealth of the bottom half of mankind fell by just over a trillion dollars in the same period, a drop of 41%.
- Since the turn of the century, the poorest half of the world's population has received just 1% of the total increase in global wealth, while half of that increase has gone to the top 1%.
- The average annual income of the poorest 10% of people in the world has risen by less than USD 3 each year in almost a quarter of a century. Their daily income has risen by less than a single cent every year.

Studies undertaken by the OECD support these conclusions.[891]

Even recent information provided by the Swiss bank "*Crédit Suisse*" (made **247**
generally public by Forbes) confirms the aforementioned.

---

[889] Oxfam (2016).

[890] See Bahree (2016).

[891] OECD (2013).

According to an article based on the findings of "*Crédit Suisse*" which was posted on the Forbes website on October 11th 2014, total world wealth at that moment was estimated at 263 trillion USD. This (huge) wealth was however distributed in a very unequal way[892], whereby:

- people with more than 1 million USD, represented only 0.7% of the world population, but owned 41% of all wealth in the world;
- 23% of the world population owned between 10,000 and 100,000 USD, together representing 14% of the worlds wealth;
- 69% of the world population owned 10,000 USD, or less, and thus accounted for less than 3% of the worlds wealth;
- An individual needs to own no more than 3650 USD (including the value of a house, if applicable) to be part of the richest half of the world's population.

According to other research undertaken by the same "*Crédit Suisse*" (and made public in its "*Credit Suisse Global Wealth Report*"), in 2014, 41% of the (USD-) millionaires of the world lived in the USA; Japan was ranked second with a "much lower" 8%. Seven percent of the worlds millionaires were reported to live in France, and six percent in both Germany and the U.K.[893] Also in 2014, 775 (USD-) billionaires were reported to live in Europe (9 more than in 2013); 609 in North-America; 650 in Asia and 40 in Africa.[894]

Figures of 2015 also brought to the public's attention by "Crédit Suisse" have confirmed and even more underlined the foregoing trends.

In its "*Global Wealth Databook 2015*"[895], "Crédit Suisse" reported that, in the course of 2015, global inequality has been even further growing, with, purportedly for the first time in history, half the world's wealth getting in the hands of just 1% of the global population.[896]

It was hereby underlined that in recent years, worldwide, middle classes have been more and more squeezed at the expense of the very rich, and that, also for the first time, there were more individuals in the middle classes in China—109 million—than the 92 million in the US.[897]

The 2015 report of "Crédit Suisse" furthermore has shown that, as regards the situation in 2015, a person needed only 3210 USD (or £2100) to be counted among the wealthiest 50% of world citizens. A personal wealth of about 68,800 USD was furthermore reported to secure a place in the top 10%, while the top 1% were reported to have a fortune of more than USD 759,900.[898] It was also reported that,

---

[892] McCarthy (2014).

[893] McCarthy (2014).

[894] McCarthy (2014).

[895] Credit Suisse Research Institute (2015).

[896] Treanor (2015).

[897] Treanor (2015).

[898] The report hereby defines "wealth" as the value of assets including property and stock market investments, but excluding debt (see Treanor 2015).

as regards 2015, about 3.4 billion people—just over 70% of the global adult population—had wealth of less than 10,000 USD, and that a further 1 billion—a fifth of the world's population—were in the 10,000–100,000 USD range.[899] Each of the remaining 383 million adults—8% of the global population—was reported to have wealth of more than 100,000 USD, whereby this number included about 34 million US dollar millionaires. About 123,800 individuals of these were reported to have wealth of more than 50 million USD, and nearly 45,000 of more than 100 million USD. The report concluded: "*Wealth inequality has continued to increase since 2008, with the top percentile of wealth holders now owning 50.4% of all household wealth.*"

A further surprising fact that has been derived from said "*Global Wealth Databook 2015*" of "Crédit Suisse" is that, measured in personal wealth (and not: "income"), there were in 2015 more poor people in America than there were in China, which is mainly due to the Western banking system being more prevailing in the USA and in Europe than in the rest of the world, as a result of which more Americans and Europeans are in debt than people elsewhere in the world (whereby such bank debt accounts for a negative factor in calculating one's personal wealth).[900] It more precisely appeared from said report that "America" (in the said study this implies both the USA and Canada) had some 10% of the poorest people in the world and also some 30% of the richest; Europe had about 20% of the world's poorest people and 35% of the richest and China had none of the world's poorest people and about 7 or 8% of the world's richest people.[901]

Further Illustration 3.25: Multi Billionaires

Forbes has reported that at the beginning of 2014, a worldwide group of 1645 (dollar) millionaires owned a common fortune of 6.4 trillion USD.[902]

From another source, it can be learned that in Europe, in 2014, there were several "multi billionaires"[903], among which, for example, the Swedish Ingvar Kamprad (the man behind "*IKEA*"), whose capital was reported to amount to an estimated 31 billion USD in 2013 (oddly enough, in the Forbes list itself, he was reported to hold "only" a 402nd position in 2014, with an estimated capital of "only" 3.9 billion USD[904]). The capital of the Swedish Stefan Persson, the founder of "*Hennes & Mauritz*" (the famous clothing corporation better known under its abbreviated name "H&M"), was that same

(continued)

[899]Treanor (2015).

[900]Worstall (2015).

[901]Worstall (2015).

[902]Dolan and Kroll (2014).

[903]See Ikea oprichter is rijkste Europeaan. http://www.z24.nl/ondernemen/ikea-oprichter-is-rijkste-europeaan. Last consulted on October 30th 2014.

[904]http://www.forbes.com/profile/ingvar-kamprad/ (last consulted on October 30th 2014).

Further Illustration 3.25 (continued)

year estimated at 30.6 billion USD[905], and the capital of the Russian Oleg Deripaska was estimated at 28 billion USD (in the Forbes list, he was at a 177th place with an estimated wealth of 7.4 billion USD).[906]

The capital of "the (most of the times) wealthiest man on earth", Bill Gates[907], has in 2014 been estimated at ±80 billion USD (which more or less equaled the GDP of Ecuador, and was, for example, higher than the GDP of Croatia).[908]

The aforementioned Forbes-list of 2014 provided a more systematic overview of the size of the wealth of the richest people on earth.

According to this Forbes ranking of 2014, as mentioned before, Bill Gates was back at number one in the beginning of 2014 as the richest person in the world (a position which he has held for 15 times during the last 20 years).[909]

According to this Forbes-list of 2014, at the beginning of 2014, the world top 10 was as following[910]:

1. Bill Gates (USA; source of wealth: Microsoft), 81.2 billion USD;
2. Carlos Slim Helu & family (Mexico; source of wealth: telecom), 79.5 billion USD;
3. Warren Buffett (USA; source of wealth: Berkshire Hathaway), 68.5 billion USD;
4. Amancio Ortega (Spain; source of wealth: retail); 58.6 billion USD;
5. Larry Ellison (USA; source of wealth: Oracle); 48.7 billion USD;
6. Charles Koch (USA; source of wealth: CEO, Koch Industries Inc.); 42.2 billion USD;
7. David Koch (USA; source of wealth: Executive Vice president, Koch Industries Inc.); 42.2 billion USD;

(continued)

[905] http://www.forbes.com/billionaires/list/#tab:overall (last consulted on October 30th 2014).

[906] There is no clear explanation for the sometimes remarkable discrepancies between the consulted sources.

[907] In the beginning of 2014, Bill Gates was reported to be, again, at the 1st place on the aforementioned Forbes list, but later in the course of 2014, he would, presumably as a consequence of his charity work, "drop" to the second place.

[908] It needs however to be noted that "*The Bill & Melinda Gates foundation*", established by Bill Gates and his wife 1997, annually donates about 4 billion USD to good causes, which made the authoritative bulletin "*The Financial Times*" observe that

> through the stroke of a pen on a cheque book, Gates probably now has the power to affect the lives and well-being of a larger number of his fellow humans than any other private individual in history. (See Baer 2014.)

[909] Dolan and Kroll (2014).

[910] http://www.forbes.com/billionaires/ (last consulted on October 30th 2014).

Further Illustration 3.25 (continued)

8. Christy Walton & family (USA; source of wealth: Wal-Mart); 37.9 billion USD;
9. Jim Walton (USA; source of wealth: Wal-Mart; also President and CEO, Arvest Bank Group, Inc.); 36.6 billion USD;
10. Alice Walton (USA; source of wealth: Wal-Mart; also President of Crystal Bridges Museum of American Art); 35.1 billion USD.

It is remarkable that, in 2014, eight out of the top ten billionaires of the Forbes-list were Americans.

Mark Zuckerberg (USA; source of wealth: Facebook) held the 14th position of said Forbes-list of 2014, with an estimated wealth of 33.4 billion USD.

The second European on the Forbes-list of 2014 (holding the 13th position) was the French Liliane Bettencourt (& family) (source of wealth: L'Oreal), with an estimated fortune of 34.9 billion USD.[911]

The first Asian, in the 15th position in the Forbes-list of 2014, was Li Ka-shing (Hong Kong), with an estimated wealth of 31.4 billion USD.[912]

Still, according to Forbes, the richest person coming from the Middle East was, in 2014, Prince Alwaleed Bin Talal Alsaud. With an estimated wealth of 21.5 billion USD, he was reported to hold the 35th position in the list.[913]

In the already quoted "*Even it up*" study of Oxfam, the list of the 10 richest people in the world in 2014 contained slightly different figures, resulting in a different ranking[914] (which is probably due to the fact that the data provided by Forbes were of a different date than the data made publically available on the Forbes website when consulted):

1. Carlos Slim, 80 billion USD;
2. Bill Gates, 79 billion USD;
3. Amancio Ortega, 63 billion USD;
4. Warren Buffett, 62 billion USD;
5. Larry Ellison, 50 billion USD;
6. Charles Koch, 41 billion USD;
7. David Koch, 41 billion USD;
8. Liliane Bettencourt, 37 billion USD;
9. Christy Walton, 37 billion USD;
10. Sheldon Adelson, 36 billion USD.[915]

(continued)

[911] http://www.forbes.com/billionaires/#tab:overall_page:2 (last consulted on October 30th 2014).

[912] http://www.forbes.com/billionaires/#tab:overall_page:2 (last consulted on October 30th 2014).

[913] http://www.forbes.com/billionaires/#tab:overall_page:2 (last consulted on October 30th 2014).

[914] Oxfam (2014), 33.

[915] Oxfam (2014), 33. These are remarkable differences, which are, honor to whom honor is due, regarding Bill Gates and Warren Buffett, presumably caused by their decision to donate (large

Further Illustration 3.25 (continued)

The Forbes -ranking for 2015 shows some slight alterations in this ranking of the richest people on earth while at the same time confirming the trend that their fortunes get bigger and bigger (to the detriment of the poorest on earth), be it with the exception of the billionaires having underwritten the so-called "giving pledge"-commitment, such as Bill Gates and Warren Buffett, the numbers 1 and 3 on the list.

According to the Forbes -website, the top 10 ranking for 2015 was as follows[916]:

1. Bill Gates (USA; source of wealth: Microsoft), 79.2 billion USD;
2. Carlos Slim Helu & family (Mexico; source of wealth: telecom), 77.1 billion USD;
3. Warren Buffett (USA; source of wealth: Berkshire Hathaway), 62.7 billion USD;
4. Amancio Ortega (Spain; source of wealth: retail); 64.5 billion USD;
5. Larry Ellison (USA; source of wealth: Oracle); 54.3 billion USD;
6. Charles Koch (USA; source of wealth: Koch Industries Inc.); 42.9 billion USD;
7. David Koch (USA; source of wealth: Koch Industries Inc.); 42.9 billion USD;
8. Christy Walton & family (USA; source of wealth: Wal-Mart); 41.7 billion USD;
9. Jim Walton (USA; source of wealth: Wal-Mart and Arvest Bank Group, Inc.); 40.6 billion USD;
10. Liliane Bettencourt (& family) (France; source of wealth: L'Oreal); 40.1 billion USD.

In 2015, Mark Zuckerberg (USA; source of wealth: Facebook) held the 16th position of said Forbes-list of 2014, with an estimated wealth of 33.4 billion USD.

Quoting from the abovementioned Oxfam-report "*An economy for the 1%.*"[917], the Forbes-website furthermore mentions that at the start of 2014, the richest 85 people on the planet owned as much as the poorest half of mankind. Between March 2013 and March 2014, these 85 people grew USD 668 million richer each day. It is moreover mentioned that if Bill Gates were to cash in all of his wealth, and spend a million dollars every single day, it

(continued)

parts) of their fortune to charity, which probably explains why they had both dropped one place in the ranking of 2014.

[916]http://www.forbes.com/billionaires/list/2/#version:static; last consulted on 22nd January 2016.

[917]Oxfam (2016).

Further Illustration 3.25 (continued)

would take him 218 years to spend it all, but that in reality, he will most likely never run out of money as even a modest return of just under 2% would make him USD 4.2 million each day in interest alone.[918]

Based upon another Oxfam-report of 2016 entitled "*An economy for the 1%. How privilege and power in the economy drive extreme inequality and how this can be stopped*"[919], in 2015, 62 individuals were reported to own as much riches as the bottom half of mankind.

Further Illustration 3.26: (Increasing) Poverty in Belgium

What happens at a global scale, is not different within the context of a small country such as Belgium.

According to a book by Geysels and Vlaminck, titled "*De schande en de keerzijde*" (a title which could be translated as "*Disgrace and its reverse side*"), in 2014, about 15% of the Belgians, or 1.5 million people, lived in poverty. The richest 10% of Belgians were reported to be 254 times richer than the poorest 10%; the top 5% was reported to own as much wealth as 75% of the rest of the population owned. The 20% richest families were reported to own 61.2% of the total wealth in Belgium. About 100,000 people in Belgium received a living wage which was below the poverty threshold, while 94,500 Belgians were reported to be euro millionaires (not including real estate). Of the 2.2 million Belgian children, 420,000 were considered to be socially disadvantaged.[920]

3.4.8.3 Some Consequences of the Growing Inequalities

The growing economic inequality is not only a hard fact, but it entails several far **248**
reaching negative consequences, such as[921]:

- It makes it very difficult to fight poverty in the world;

---

[918]The website furthermore mentions that Bill Gates and his wife, along with fellow billionaire Warren Buffet, set up "the giving pledge", an effort to get some of the wealthiest people to give away at least 50% of their wealth in their lifetime or upon their death and that other billionaires have joined in since (see Bahree 2014).

[919]Oxfam (2016).

[920]Geysels (2014), pp. 11–59, especially pp. 24–27. See also Raspoet (2014), pp. 51–55; Pannecoucke et al. (2015).

[921]Oxfam (2014), pp. 9–11 and pp. 35 a.f.; Oxfam (2016), pp. 4 a.f.

- It hinders economic growth (especially in countries characterized by high economic inequalities)[922];
- It highlights several other types of inequality, *inter alia* inequality between men and women;
- It causes unequal access to life opportunities, including the chances of a proper education and of finding a suitable job, in addition to unequal access to health and social care;
- It is one of the main hindrances for a sufficient degree of social mobility (= the "*condemned to stay poor*"-syndrome[923]);
- It contributes to an increasing degree of violence and insecurity;
- . . .[924]

One may add to this that, in his famous analysis of the 1929 financial crisis, Galbraith has pointed out the bad distribution of income (between rich and poor) of the preceding period, which, a.o., had made the economy too dependent on a high level of investments and a high level of luxury consumer spending, had been one of the main causes of the said financial crisis[925], also indicating that a high degree of economic inequality may be contributing to causing a financial crisis.

249 Verhaeghe is, in as far as possible, even more pessimistic about the increasing inequalities at a social level, especially within Western (and Western inspired) countries themselves:

> At a social level, this has troubling consequences. The middle class is disappearing and a new top group is emerging on top of a large lower class. The relations between them become more and more grim. The top group looks down at the bottom layer, because the top layer claims the bottom layer is itself to blame for its own bad (living) situation. In this

---

[922] See *e.g.* Haeck (2014d), p. 6.

[923] See also Bahree (2014):

> There is also (...) a strong correlation between extreme inequality and low social mobility. If you are born poor in a highly unequal country you will most probably die poor, and your children and grandchildren will be poor too. In Pakistan, for instance, a boy born in a rural area to a father from the poorest 20% of the population has only a 1.9% chance of ever moving to the richest 20%. In the U.S., nearly half of all children born to low-income parents will become low-income adults.

[924] One may even see a troublesome resemblance with the situation that occurred in the Roman Empire in the fourth century:

> The structure of society in the western empire had changed radically in the third and fourth centuries AD. Towns had gone into decline, and the rich retreated to their villas and estates in the countryside, seemingly turning their backs on public life and the defence of the empire. Wealth and property became increasingly concentrated in fewer hands, while the Christian Church also took a large slice of the available wealth away from the community, as rich Christians preferred to enwod churches and monasteries than to provide public buildings or monetary largesse for their fellow-citizens. The abandonment of Roman civic culture in the post-imperial kingdoms of the west (. . .) was anticipated before the actual fall of the western empire itself. (See Eagleton and Williams 2007, p. 61.)

[925] Galbraith (1992), pp. 194–195.

context, poverty is evaluated in terms of (insufficient) commitment and talent. The only occasion where the top layer is providing support is in the form of welfare and charity – in their eyes, the bottom class does not really deserve any support. In this context it is very often easy to ignore the effects of ethnicity, social class, age, illness, misfortune and even gender."[926]—(Own, free translation.)

The (Belgian) anthropologist Rik Pinxten, has in the near past, similarly, stated that the (assumed) success story of the neo-liberal model is in reality mainly leading to an increasing level of inequality, whereby the common man is moreover systematically "stripped" of everything that makes life valuable and interesting, especially his ethic, religious, esthetic and political dimensions, whereby the meaning of life itself gets evermore devaluated, and finally only the economic sphere can remain as a system in which any given individual will only be able to function as either a "producer" or "consumer-laborer".[927] According to Pinxten, everything that is happening on earth is hereby increasingly left to the hands of the free market, leading to a society almost perfectly mirroring Huxley's "*Brave New World*".[928] **250**

251 The philosophic starting premise of Smith, holding that an economic system in which every man only strives for his own personal wealth will lead to a prosperous society benefiting the whole of mankind, has thus, after a few centuries of its application in practice, proven the opposite of its original promise.

However tempting a similar starting point could sound, especially in societies that have exposed their members to this reasoning for centuries already (resulting in a blind submission to the belief that everyone, except the very rich themselves, only lives to work as hard as possible[929]), when investigating it and its impact on society in a more scrupulous way, it continues to raise more and more questions[930].

---

[926]Verhaeghe (2011), p. 24.

[927]See before, the findings of Herbert Marcuse (especially Marcuse 2002).

[928]See Pinxten (2014). See also Ongenae (2014), pp. 44–45, especially p. 44.

[929]See especially on this Fromm (1955), pp. 88 a.f.

[930]It is indeed remarkable that (said interpretation of) the teachings of Adam Smith have had such an impact on economic thinking and acting, witnessing the limited level of civilization of human societies.

In several other domains of societal life, the application of such a way of thinking would be considered unheard of. For instance, one could argue that said preposition should dominate sexual behaviour (see also further, at marg. 295–298 of this chapter), whereby it should be permittable for anyone to act out any sexual impulses on the weaker members of society and whereby said weaker members of society should be freely available to undergo the egoistic sexual acts of the stronger members of society...

It is therefore unexplicable why mankind, already during several ages, keeps on embracing the idea that the fulfilment of one's selfish impulses should be the guiding principle of economic thinking and acting, in an economic system (namely capitalism) whereby all the riches of the planet and the entire workforce of the world population should only serve the selfish interests of a happy few rich people.

Especially from an ethical perspective, as mentioned earlier, this demonstrates to what extent economic (neo-)liberalism has succeeded in turning the classic value scale prevailing in older societies completely around.

This becomes very clear when putting the value scale of economic (neo-) liberalism in addition to the one of opposing historical doctrines, such as, for example, the teachings of historical figures as Plato, Aristoteles and Jesus Christ (see above, under Sect. 3.3.2).

Nevertheless, the quoted starting premise of economic (neo-)liberal thinking has since the seventeenth century succeeded in controlling economic action and thought, although it still cannot be concluded that the capitalist economic order which has resulted from it also implies a social model which is beneficial to everyone, rather on the contrary.[931]

252 Notwithstanding the fact that, especially during the nineteenth and twentieth century, the banking sector has undoubtedly been one of the main players in the deployment of the capitalist economic system up to the excessive level at which it prevails today, as well as one of the main players in the severe financial crisis of (or since) 2008, it is (obviously) not the sole "culprit".

It can indeed not be ignored that up to the present day, the capitalist monetary and financial system is inherently based on a social contract, in other words, an underlying conventional mechanism, in the broad sense of the word, by which the population operating within a certain economy has accepted it as the main originator of money.

Otherwise put, the prevailing monetary and financial system (and, by extension, the general economic system known as "capitalism") is still the one that we, mankind, all "want" (and which is, hence, shaped by acts of regulators who are entitled to do so thanks to (more or less) democratic systems having put them in office; see also above, at marg. 7 and 17–20 of Chap. 2 of this book).

In this way, the question whether or not the prevailing capitalist monetary and financial system, including its system of money creation (as described earlier on in Chap. 2) should be preserved as it is, is, by definition, a question that concerns every human being on this planet (which raises the idea that money (creation) is in fact a "*public good*", or at the very least should again become so).[932]

---

[931]Compare the observations of Stiglitz (2006), p. 68, as well as those of Winnie Byanyima (Executive Director of Oxfam) (at Oxfam 2014):

> I have been fighting inequality my whole life. Where I grew up in Uganda, my family did not have much, but we were among the better-off in our village. My best friend and I went to school together every day. I had one pair of shoes, she walked barefoot. I did not understand why then, and I still don't now. Inequality must be fought, every step of the way. (see Oxfam 2014, p. 4).

[932]See the observations of Pettifor (2014):

> Credit, by contrast, faces no such limitation. Credit is an intangible public good, a little like clean air or water. It is based on trust in each other; trust that can be destroyed, but if bolstered by sound institutions, has infinite capacity. Because of the frailty of human nature; because of our experience of financial fraudsters and criminals, this trust must be

The Chaps. 4 and 5 of this book will further elaborate upon this question.

3.4.8.4 A (Second) Anthology of Certain Illustrations of the Gaps Between the Poor and the Rich

In spite of all the aforementioned understandings and insights, it nevertheless continues to appear that, at a point in history where the correction models of capitalism "pur sang" (including especially systems of public services and of social security) are, under the influence of the ideas of economic neoliberalism, almost worldwide wavering, the spirit of Smith more than ever lives in the heart of many people, especially the rich and the powerful, as a central driving force behind their (economic) behavior.[933] **253**

As a result, the unbridled pursuit of money (often meant to finance meaningless luxury) far from only motivates banking managers and personnel (see above, at marg. 227–230 of this chapter), but, on the contrary, has permeated practically all levels of social life. **254**

What follows is a number of randomly chosen striking illustrations, picked from press releases, dealing with:

- The unbridled pursuit of money in the entertainment-industry.

  The example of the exorbitant lifestyle of the late Michael Jackson[934] is without any doubt legendary.

> grounded in democratic public institutions, including a sound, well-managed and regulated banking system and an impartial judicial and criminal justice system. With these in place, trust manifests itself as unlimited supplies of finance for the achievement of society's goals. That is why the 'there is no money' myth pedlars are so wrong. In countries with sound monetary and banking systems, there need never be a shortage of finance. By contrast, in low-income (sic) countries without sound democratic public institutions, the banking system does not function, is not supported by regulation, or by judicial and criminal justice systems. As a result economic activity (investment and employment) is severely curtailed.

Otherwise: Rand (2008), p. 5.

[933] In this way, an old truth from the Old Testament book Ecclesiastes, stating that "*whoever loves money never has enough*" *and* "*whoever loves wealth is never satisfied with their income*" (see Ecclesiastes, 5:10) has become applicable to an ever increasing part of mankind.

[934] See Michael Jackson, Neverland Ranch and Foreclosure. http://www.totalbankruptcy.com/blog/michael-jackson-neverland-ranch-and-foreclosure/. Last consulted on February 20th 2012:

> Jackson purchased the property [i.e. Neverland ranch] in 1987 for almost $20 million. At the time, it was a working ranch, but under Jackson's care it would become a shrine to the childhood Jackson never had. The singer spent $35 million improving the property, which featured two railway lines, two helicopter pads, its own fire department, a zoo and a plethora of amusement part-style rides. The property cost an estimated $10 million a year to maintain.") See also Hartline 2008: "Michael Jackson has been reported at various times to be in financial crisis. He's also famous for outrageous spending. He purchased ten artificial intelligence Sony AIBO dog robots at $5,000 each, and it takes over $200,000 a month just to maintain and run his home. The King of Pop dazzled the American populace

As spectacular is the fact that (leading actors) in the popular television series such as "*Friends*" are said to have negotiated, at a certain point in time, a salary of one million USD per episode[935], although such out-of-proportion salaries have since then no longer been exceptional, as, for example, also the salaries of some of the actors of and "*Two and a half men*" are reported to be in line of this figure.

- The unbridled pursuit of money in the professional sports industry.

  For instance, on September 14th 2014, an article appeared in the Belgian newspaper "Het Laatste Nieuws" (copied from the British newspaper "*The Daily Mail*") stating that the renowned soccer player Cristiano Ronaldo expressed a willingness to return to his former soccer team "Manchester United", but that he demanded a salary of 630,000,- euro per week in return.[936]
- The unbridled pursuit of money by top managers in general and of CEO's more specifically.[937]
- . . .

The many examples in all these and other domains of social life are, obviously, countless.

255 Of the countless other imaginable illustrations, the following reports from a Belgian newspaper on Sunday September 28th 2014 may also be considered as striking.

The website of a (Belgian) newspaper ("*Het Laatste Nieuws*") more precisely reported on two stories, virtually put in addition to each other, *on one hand* about a Russian grandmother who had abandoned her grandson whom she had committed herself to care for, in a supermarket and who informed the authorities later on that her small pension barely allowed her to live on, let alone to support her grandson (who before already had been abandoned by his parents)[938], but, *on the other hand*, also reported that a London restaurant "*has created the most expensive cocktail in the world: the Gigi's. The drink is exclusively available for the rich of the Mayfair region, as one glass costs 8,888 GBP, or just below 11,500 euro*", furthermore

---

when he shopped away $6 million within a matter of hours on the TV documentary "Living with Michael Jackson."

[935] https://en.wikipedia.org/wiki/Friends (last consulted on November 4th 2016).

[936] Gorissen (2014).

[937] For an overview, see Pimco-topman kreeg bonus van 232 miljoen euro. http://m.hln.be/hln/m/nl/942/Economie/article/detail/2121045/2014/11/14/Pimco-topman-kreeg-bonus-van-232-miljoen-euro.dhtml?originatingNavigationItemId=1. Last consulted on November 18th 2014.

[938] See Oma dumpt kleinzoon in supermarkt: "Hij kost te veel". http://m.hln.be/hln/m/nl/39/Lekker-Eten/article/detail/2069101/2014/09/28/De-duurste-cocktail-ter-wereld-11-500-euro-per-glas.dhtml?originatingNavigationItemId=1. Last consulted on September 29th 2014.

mentioning that "*the restaurant is asking its customers (...) to pay for the drink in advance in order to avoid "embarrassing" situations*"[939].

Another news report of October 7th 2014 brought a similar story, mentioning the launch of a new "*most expensive perfume in the world*", namely a luxury version of the perfume No 1 by Clive Christian: the price of a 30 ml bottle was reported to be 182,000 euro, or 6000 euro per milliliter.[940]

Or what to think of the (probably) most expensive nail polish in the world, produced by "*Azature*"; a bottle is filled with "*267 carat worth of black diamonds and is sold at a price of about 200,000 euro*".[941]

A press release from the newspaper "*De Tijd*" of Saturday December 13th 2014, furthermore, dealt with the fact that the unbridled selfishness of the very rich has taken on the proportions of modern scavenging when reporting on the fact that numerous Greek Islands were put for sale and that mainly (extremely) rich foreigners are the keen buyers.[942]

3.4.8.5 Conclusions on the Future of Socioeconomic Relations Under Economic Neo-liberalism

While for many people, the moral awareness is gradually growing that the contin- **256**
uation of the current capitalist system, given its many excesses and its destructive impact on the lives of numerous people, as well as on the eco-system as a whole, is no longer realistic, it looks that others, especially the (very) rich, are still attempting to cultivate greed as a guiding life principle in all its extremes.

As long as the underlying mechanisms which shape the economy, among which its monetary and financial system, continue to rely on the starting premise(s) of the Scottish moral philosopher Adam Smith (as well as on those of economic (neo-) liberalism), it becomes more and more clear that a lot of the measures undertaken in an attempt to "correct" the capitalist system are often no more than a sticking-plaster solution.

It even seems that, ages after his writings, one of the doomsday images which **257**
Plato had warned about, has fully appeared[943]:

---

[939]Kintaert (2014).
See also Shaken, not stirred: Gold-infused £9k cocktail created for 007 star. http://www.express.co.uk/news/uk/515593/Gold-infused-cocktail-created-for-James-Bond-star. Last consulted on September 29th 2014, pointing out that the price of said cocktail equals the price of ***"a brand new Mitsubishi Mirage, a Rolex Submariner, or renting a private jet to fly a family of five to the Mediterranean and back".***

[940]See Duurste parfum ter wereld: 6.000 euro per milliliter. http://www.hln.be/hln/nl/40/Style/article/detail/2078435/2014/10/07/Duurste-parfum-ter-wereld-6-000-euro-per-milliliter.dhtml. Last consulted on October 8th 2014.

[941]Meijer (2014).

[942]See Superrijken kopen Griekse eilanden. In: De Tijd December 13th 2013, 11.

[943]See Plato (1987), p. 306.

> The further they go in the process of accumulating wealth, the more they value it and the less they value goodness. For aren't wealth and goodness related like two objects in a balance, so that when one rises the other must fall. (. . .) So the higher the prestige of wealth and the wealthy, the lower that of goodness and good men will be. (. . .) And so there is a transition from the ambitious, competitive type of man to the money-loving businessman, honor and admiration and office are reserved for the rich, and the poor are despised.[944]

258 Realizing all of the forgoing, we necessarily reach the understanding that it would be irresponsible to leave (future) thinking about social economic processes (especially, in general terms, about the relation between "labor" and "capital" or, in more modern-day terms, between "the rich" and "the poor"), exclusively to the domain of economy, but that looking for new answers to these (ancient) questions require a deeper, essentially more ethical reflection, whereby also findings from other areas of science, as well as (and even probably especially) from other domains of social life more than ever merit to be taken into consideration.

3.5 The Need to Extrapolate the Reflection on the Selfish Economy to Other Fields of Science and Society

259 The insight derived from the above inevitably leads every human being to face some central questions of life, namely: whether he thinks he needs money; if yes: how much, and for what purposes, and, finally, what he is prepared to do (and to sacrifice especially in terms of moral values) in order to effectively acquire this "needed" amount.

260 André Comte-Sponville[945], the author of "*Le capitalisme est-il moral*", in this regard righteously put forward the question whether any man is physically able to drive two cars at the same time, or to live in two houses at the same time.

Comte-Sponville recalls the fact that accumulating money can never be fulfilling, as the possession of money is directly linked to man's attempt to fulfill the desires which arise in his mind. However, man's imagination, especially with regards to the creation of desires, is unlimited, and so no human being will ever be able to physically accomplish all his imaginable desires within a lifetime[946].

---

[944]See also the rebuttal of neo-liberal authors such as Yaron Brook and Don Watkins:

> In Plato's Republic, Socrates declares "the more men value moneymaking, the less they value virtue." Rand's view is exactly the opposite. The value of virtues is its role in promoting your own welfare – including your economic welfare. The more men value money making, the more they value virtue. (see Brook and Watkins 2012, p. 77).

[945]Comte-Sponville (1996), pp. 25–39.

[946]Compare Bruckner (2016), p. 161.

It is somehow remarkable that this insight can, already for ages, be derived from old religious texts, such as the book Ecclesiastes from the Old Testament, stating: *"Everyone's toil is for their mouth, yet their appetite is never satisfied."* (see Ecclesiastes, 6:7; Quotation from: https://www.

Hence, depending on someone's ethics, the one person can—as already was clear to writers of ancient literature (see above, the references under Sect. 3.3.2.1)—go very far in submitting to the unbridled pursuit of ever more wealth and money[947] (by, literally, undertaking ventures such as warfare, looting, robbery, and even murder[948])—while another person (who is, per definition, less supportive of the (neo-)Smithian idea that life only serves as a means of unbridled wealth accumulation (at the detriment of others), and who, moreover, also wants to take into account the wellbeing of other individuals within society, or, by extension, other moral values), may prefer to show a more ethical attitude towards life and keep his personal selfish pursuit of money and wealth within reasonable boundaries, while at the same time also attempting to accomplish more altruistic (or other ethically inspired) goals.[949] **261**

With regards to this last point, for instance the "*Czech phenomenological school*", with renowned representatives such as Edmund Husserl and Jan Patocka[950]—in addition to Tomas Garrigue Masaryk[951] and Vaclav Havel[952] who have translated the reasoning of their colleagues and mentors into human language—have attempted to transform their ethical concepts into political reality in spite of, or maybe thanks to, the extreme conditions under which they lived and worked (namely during the Ist and IInd World War and during the Stalin dictatorship in the former Soviet-Union).

Any further reflection on this type of questions obviously goes hand in hand with "thinking" about another crucial question, namely what exactly is "needed" in order to (be able to) live the decent, responsible and useful life of a person who is willing to limit his own needs in regard to higher moral principles, such as care for others and, by extension, for the well-being of the planet itself. **262**

Realizing that by limiting once' s needs, one will probably never face shortage, while the accumulation of (too) many needs, may lead to a subjective experience of shortage, even for he who has many means (see above, the aforementioned examples at marg. 254 of this chapter), becomes in this way one of life's main challenges.[953]

---

biblegateway.com/passage/?search=Ecclesiastes+6; last consulted on October 10th 2015), and, more general, from religious systems such as Hinduism and Buddhism.

[947] Theoretically, the law is an instrument which can pose boundaries to such behaviour.

[948] See before the quote from Sophocles' "*Antigone*"; see above, at marg. 29 of this chapter.

[949] These and similar questions are profoundly dealt with in the book of Pascal Bruckner "*Misère de la prospérité – la religion marchande et ses ennemis*"; see Bruckner (2002), p. 206. See also Hoefnagels (1975), pp. 18–19.

[950] See Patocka (1999), p. 250; furthermore, about Patocka's impact in general, see Laignel-Lavastine (1998), p. 124.

[951] See Kovtun (2009), p. 194. See also Capek (1995).

[952] About the impact of Patocka on Vaclav Havel, see Picq (2000), p. 123.

[953] *E.g.* Amartya Sen has given noteworthy examples of these ethical questions in his book "*The idea of Justice*" (Sen 2009).

Such insight leads to the conclusion that "need" is by far an unambiguous concept and that it can (ultimately) be understood differently by every individual.

263 These are, of course, questions which mankind has been facing for a very long time already (and which, as a result, have for a long time formed crucial subsets of the main religious doctrines of the world, such as "Christianity" and "Buddhism", but surely also "Islam" and "Judaism", as well as (moral) philosophical schools, from Plato to Levinas).

Pondering about these questions has probably been going on as long as money has existed, so there is no reason whatsoever why these questions should merely be dealt with in a context where only an economic or legal input would prevail (as, under the impulse of economic liberalism, and later on economic neoliberalism, has become too much the case since the second half of the seventeenth century).

Hence, as history continues to dictate, the continued attention which is required about reflecting on and developing of an approach of "living towards a greater ethic conscience", even and especially within the domain of economy, ideally should be shaped and further developed within a framework where, in addition to ethics and (moral) philosophy[954], politics and law, also other domains from societal and scientific life, such as arts, religion, history, psychology, sociology and anthropology, but, for example, also medicine, biology, mathematics and other "hard" or "exact" sciences, should be able to contribute to the creation of new ethical doctrines, and to finding the answer to the question how these can potentially translate into concrete and more just societal models (especially as regards the domain of economic activities and the way they are organized, and, by extension, of the legal system which helps shape and steer them).

To leave the answer to these questions, as is preached in neo-liberal thinking, to the free market itself, can in this way not make any sense and would even be completely immoral[955], especially given the close connectedness of free market mechanisms with the neo-liberal dictate of unbridled selfishness which everyone is expected to demonstrate, and which the aforementioned ethical exploration is exactly attempting to put an end to.

---

[954]It should be pointed out that Adam Smith was himself (initially) a professor of Logic and Rhethoric, and later of Ethics (see Berend 2006, p. 13; Galbraith 1987, p. 60).

[955]Especially given the fact that economy itself seems to be more and more deprived of any moral backbone.

3.6 The Need for (Real) Change

3.6.1 The Need for a New Ethical Foundation of the Socioeconomic Order

Given the above, a further question that arises is to know if the answer to the aforementioned, essentially ethical questions, should be exclusively dealt with by every individual separately, or whether they should be answered through collective decision-making processes. **264**

A traditional—albeit, as history shows, far from satisfactory—approach, especially within our current secular (Western and Western inspired) societies[956], has, already for decades, been to exclusively direct these types of questions to the private domain of individual conscience.[957] **265**

Given the omnipresence and dominance of the capitalist economic system, such an approach obviously cannot imply anything else than the conclusion that any attempt to lead a live in accordance with another morality than sheer (neo-) Smithian (or neo-liberal) "mammonism", becomes an extremely difficult venture (unless for the rare being who decides to go and live in complete isolation, such as in the metaphorical cave in the Himalayas).

The current apparent developments in societies worldwide, which, according to some are the result of a degradation into a real "ego-culture" (see the so-called "emotivism", referred to above, at marg. 131 of this chapter), are harrowing further illustrations of this phenomenon.

In such an approach, this book could just as well end here, as there would not be much more to add to the above, except for the ongoing observation that each man remains free to go on behaving as egoistically as he wants, while, at best, at the same time observing where the collective outcome of such an attitude will further lead to (which, bottom-line, is the approach defended by neo-liberal thinking).

After more or less two to three centuries of applying the vision conceived by Adam Smith (and his successors)[958] on socioeconomic processes, which, worldwide, resulted in the current economic "ruins" (characterized by, a.o., numerous exploitation mechanisms, chronic monetary and financial and other crises, and, in general, by the sacrifice of almost all other values, including the well-being of the planet and mankind itself, to the biblical "mammon"), one may nevertheless **266**

---

[956]See Cliteur (2007), p. 295 a.f.

[957]Kruithof (1985), p. 77:

> As unacceptable is the fact that every Sunday, in many Christian churches, the tune resounds that if every individual human improves his own life, things will turn for the better.

[958]One may even wonder if both the idea that it is preferable to be selfish rather than altruistic, and the debate about this intrinsically ethical question, is not as old as economic thinking (and acting) itself.

wonder if the time is not ripe for another approach towards socioeconomic questions, which inevitably leads us to the question how an economy could be based upon a more altruistic attitude.

Realizing this, we may even reach the conclusion that the circle of about two and a half millennia of ethical exploration of the socioeconomic domain seems to be closing, which could lead back to an approach of social and economic processes which, already ages ago, was developed by classical philosophers (such as Plato and Aristotle), but also by leading figures of early Christianity[959], and which strived for a total different attitude towards socioeconomic processes, characterized by a resolute altruism, instead of an unbridled selfishness and egoism.

267 Already in September 2008, the American president Barack Obama released his book "*Change we can believe in*"[960], his program for the future of the United States of America and at the same time his commitment during his electoral campaign.

Without prejudice to the credits of the Obama-administration, noteworthy in the domain of social care (for instance the so-called "*Obamacare*"), and of its obvious commitment to world peace (for which Obama himself received the Nobel Peace Prize on October 9th 2009), it nevertheless needs to be noted that, especially within a globalized context, it is clear that even an American president motivated by the highest noble intentions, has not been able to fulfill his promise of "real change" on a socioeconomic level.

To the extent that such a real change of the social economic world order would still be possible, it will have to be driven by a true global perspective, for which the Chaps. 4 and 5 of this book will attempt to provide a blueprint, but only, under the next Sect. 3.6.2, after having first concised an overall image of the arguments stemming from some of world's leading religious, philosophical and even scientific doctrines, which offer even further ethical arguments why such a true change is more necessary than ever.

---

[959]In addition to Jesus Christ Himself, His immediate successors, the apostles and their own converts, but also later key historical figures within the catholic church, such as the renowned Saint Francis of Assisi and Saint Anthony of Padua, and leading church scholars, such as Saint Thomas Aquinas.

[960]Obama (2009), p. 304.

3.6.2 Further Interpretation of the Need for a New Ethic Substructure of the Socioeconomic Order in the Context of Certain Humanitarian, Philosophical, Religious and Scientific Doctrines

3.6.2.1 Scope

Both (different) (humanitarian, philosophical and religious) ethical doctrines, as **268**
well as findings of modern natural sciences, provide several additional ethical and other arguments for an altruistic, instead of a selfish, approach to economy in general, and to its monetary system more specifically.

In many of these reasonings, the common thread seems to be a commitment to ensure a more just living environment for all human beings.

It is obviously an impossible task in the context of this book to profoundly deal **269**
with all imaginable philosophical, religious and other systems of "thought" in its widest sense advocating more justice in the world (also, and especially, on a social economic level).

We limit ourselves here to a number of striking doctrines which at least to some extent have dealt with social and economic issues, among which (*i*) Aristotle (himself)[961]; (*ii*) certain French enlightened philosophers; (*iii*) (modern) humanism; (*iv*) Christianity and Buddhism; (*v*) certain insights of modern biology, and (*vi*) certain contemporary philosophers.

In this book, communist doctrines have as such not been considered, as com- **270**
munism can be seen as a stand-alone philosophical system of approaching social and economic processes on itself which, *on one hand*, has been subject to a very elaborate magnitude of scientific (but also popular) publications already[962] and, *on the other hand*, in practice, has not succeeded in leading to a societal model sufficiently practicable.

3.6.2.2 Aristotle

As has been pointed out before (see above, at marg. 62 a.f. of this chapter), already **271**
ages ago Aristotle provided a (relatively) simple and (probably also because of this) up till today very appealing interpretation of the concept of "injustice", which he describes as follows:

> to act unjustly meaning to assign oneself too large a share of things generally good and too small a share of things generally evil.[963]

---

[961] Even by Ayn Rand referred to as one of the greatest philosophers of all times. (See Ricard 2014, p. 382.)

[962] Reference should obviously be made to Marx 1982 and 1983 (edition in three volumes).

[963] Aristotle (1996), p. 126, verses 1134a8.

In this Aristotelian approach, a (disproportionate degree of) "inequality"—in the way it, worldwide, determines socioeconomic relations today (as described above)—is "unjust" by definition, where there is mention of "*injustice*" on the part of those who, disproportionately "have too much" of what is good and/or "have too little" of what is bad, and of "*suffering from injustice*" on the part of those who, equally disproportionately, "have not enough" of what is good and/or have too much of what is bad[964].

According to the world's happiness report of 2016, one of the main aspects of Aristotelian teaching is furthermore that the good life is inherently a life of good relationships. In this view (and contrary to the belief system of economic neoliberalism), human beings should not only strive for a good life for themselves, but for a good life for and with others. This sense of "mutual flourishing" translates in the present-day notion of "the common good", which Jesuit theologian David Hollenbach has defined as "*the good realized in the mutual relationships in and through which human beings achieve their well-being.*" Considered this way, the individual and the common good become inseparable, and the whole is greater than the parts. Hence, while "the common good" is distinguished from the good of the individual, furthering the common good in turn furthers the good of the individual.[965]

272 Based on the authority of Aristotle, one can therefore safely argue that for instance the previously developed example from Brook and Watkins (see above, at marg. 164 of this chapter) of a big retailer the capital providers of which are reckoned among the wealthiest people on earth and that makes its personnel work for minimum wages, acts in an unjust way (and that in this regard, clearly, the so-called "*voluntary association*" argument does not have a real convincing power).

Similarly, fiscal systems which are, on a world-wide scale, impacting middle and lower classes within society, in a relative sense, much more than the rich classes of society, are equally unjust because the middle and lower classes suffer too much of what is bad (i.e. taxes and para-taxes), while the richer classes are barely, or at least much less, impacted by this "bad" thing.

Probably even more unjust is that in this world 1.2 billion people have to survive on 1.25 USD/day and 2.7 billion people have to survive on less than 2.5 USD/day[966], while on the contrary, in the same world, there are individuals having gathered fortunes of billions of USD (mainly by making use of capitalist mechanisms that allow them to exploit their more deprived fellow human beings).

---

[964] Aristotle (1996), p. 127, verses 1133b30-33.

[965] Sachs et al. (2016).

In the next Chaps. 4 and 5 of this book, it will be further explored how this "common", "general" or "public" good could be revived within the context of a "New Monetary World Order".

[966] United Nations Development Programme (2014), p. 71.

3.6.2.3 Certain Enlightened Philosophers from the Era of the French Revolution

It is somehow remarkable that the same philosophical system, more specifically seventeenth century "rationalism", inspired two completely opposed social economic schools, *on the one* side the UK school of "economic liberalism" (as initiated by Smith himself), propagating the idea of selfish behavior and the unbridled pursuit of wealth and money by the rich capitalist classes, and, *on the other hand* a (mainly) French school of strongly socially inspired thinkers who were defending completely opposite views of establishing a more just social order.[967] 273

Even more remarkable is the fact that in the current context, the debates of the seventeenth and eighteenth century seem to have gone on as if nothing fundamentally has changed. Hence, by relying on almost the same arguments as were used in the debates of the seventeenth and eighteenth century, social abuses which in present societies are still prevailing, are *either* exonerated (by economic neo-liberalism), *or* contested (see the recent insights reached in many domains of science fundamentally questioning the impact of economic neo-liberalism).

A large number of the criticisms of the said French seventeenth and eighteenth century enlightened philosophers were dealing with the unfair distribution of the resources in the world, and several of their arguments developed at that time, are as valid now as then. For this reason, some of the most remarkable of these insights are hereafter quoted.

The following quote from the earlier mentioned "*Discours sur l'origine et les fondements de l'inégalité parmie les hommes*"[968] (1754) by the renowned French philosopher Jean-Jacques Rousseau (1712–1778)[969], sets the scene for the reasoning developed among the French school of enlightened philosophers (of the pre-revolutionary era)[970]: 274

> The true founder of the civil society: that was the one who was first in fencing a parcel of land and had the guts to say: "this is mine", to the one who was naive enough to believe him. How many crimes, wars, murders, suffering and atrocities would not have happened to humanity, if someone had just withdrawn the poles or had filled the ditches and had shouted to his fellow-men: "Do not listen to this imposter, you are lost if you forget that the fruits of

[967] Beaud (1994), p. 76.

[968] See http://classiques.uqac.ca/classiques/Rousseau_jj/discours_origine_inegalite/discours_inegalite.pdf (last consulted on December 1st 2012).

[969] About Rousseau in general, see Beaud (1994), pp. 72–73.

[970] In the original French version, the text is as follows:

> Le premier qui, ayant enclos un terrain, s'avisa de dire: Ceci est à moi, et trouva des gens assez simples pour le croire, fut le vrai fondateur de la société civile. Que de crimes, de guerres, de meurtres, que de misères et d'horreurs n'eût point épargnés au genre humain celui qui, arrachant les pieux ou comblant le fossé, eût crié à ses semblables: Gardez-vous d'écouter cet imposteur; vous êtes perdus, si vous oubliez que les fruits sont à tous, et que la terre n'est à personne. Mais il y a grande apparence, qu'alors les choses and étaient déjà venues au point de ne pouvoir plus durer comme elles étaient.

> the earth belong to everyone and that the earth belongs to no-one!" But apparently at that time evolution had already reached the stage where things could not remain anymore as how they were.—(free translation)

In general, Rousseau's philosophy held that society had degenerated as a consequence of so-called "civilization". According to Rousseau, this civilization has begun when human beings started to produce more than they needed and, in this way, initiated a since then ever expanding artificial stimulation of needs, beyond the level of truly natural needs. The excesses to which this led, became moreover distributed unequally and unfairly, resulting in a division between "rich" and "poor" people, or put otherwise between the "powerful" and the "powerless". In Rousseau's reasoning, all wealth and power basically come down to an "usurpation", which in itself is a consequence of angered passions. Rousseau saw two models to solve this, knowingly, *on one hand* "education" (see especially his book "*Émile, ou De l'éducation*") and, *on the other hand*, a just and fair state mechanism (see especially his book "*Le contrat social*" which has already been mentioned elsewhere in this treatise).[971]

275 Claude Adrien Helvétius (1715–1771) also protested against the vast social and economic injustices which characterized the French "*Ancien Régime*" of that time.

Helvétius held that (at that time, but his insight equally applies to our own time (see above, under Sect. 3.4.8.2)) in most countries, there were only two categories of people (left), namely, *on one hand* the (largest) group of people owing nothing, and, *on the other hand* a (minority) group of people thriving in excess, whereby the first group can (or even: in the best case) provide for its basic needs only by working extremely hard, resulting in making the other group as rich as possible. Hence, it becomes completely justified to expect from government that it would install mechanisms aiming at creating a more just and fair distribution of (societal) wealth.[972]

In the context of the increasing gaps between the rich and the poor in current societies, one cannot but help observing that these insights have (once more in history) become more valid than ever.[973]

276 In his work "*Théorie des lois civils ou principes fondamentaux de la société*" (1777–1792), Simon-Nicholas Henri Linguet (1736–1794) argued in general that greed and violence control the world, and that the concept of "ownership" is relying on one of the most outrageous forms of usurpation. This author, furthermore, held that the living conditions of the working classes (of his time) were worse than ever before in history, to such an extent that misery had *"forced the poor to their knees in front of the rich to beg for their permission to make them even more rich"* (a statement which, more and more, applies to the behavior of many a private bank or capitalist employer).[974] Also noteworthy is Linguet's statement that *"the*

---

[971] Delfgaauw (1960), p. 54; Talmon (1966), p. 56.

[972] Beaud (1994), p. 74.

[973] Compare Kruithof (2000), p. 60.

[974] Beaud (1994), p. 74.

grandiloquent language [of the rich] concerning slavery (...) is similar to the squeak of a raptor ripping apart a dove with its claws", a quote which is easily applicable to many a contemporary neo-liberal author or policy-maker.[975]

Linguet in general proved to have a strong understanding of economic liberalism, leading to the insight that mankind is being cheated by economists who promise an increase in wealth, where in reality market forces are only providing more wealth to the rich (an insight which also in the current context is experiencing a true revival among many scientists in various domains).

Significantly in contrast with the current (neo-)liberal doctrine of "*voluntary association*" (see above, at marg. 164–165 of this chapter), Linguet further stated that working classes are trapped in what the author describes as "*the trap of the free market*". Given the fact that the working classes can only offer their labor on the market (the use of which an employer can easily postpone, and which is moreover, in many cases, perfectly "fungible"[976]), laborers are forced to accept low prices (wages) for their labor[977] (as they cannot live one day themselves without food or a roof above their head and, as a result, are completely dependent on their wages for their daily living).[978]

It is therefore very significant (especially given the degree of understanding Linguet already showed in the eighteenth century), that for example also Stiglitz, in his book "*Making globalization work*", has indicated the fear "*of losing his job*" as one of the most serious economic problems of the globalized world economy[979], an understanding which is in line with another idea defended by Marcuse (describing this as the compulsion resulting from the risk of having a complete lack of facilities for themselves and for [once' s] relatives (children, spouses, eventually parents) for whom only one person is caring).[980]

Linguet who, through his opinions, presented himself as the advocate of the interests of "the fourth class" (at his time), reached the conclusion that for the working classes, there is no freedom[981], causing the poor to be, in truth, the slaves of the rich.[982]

As said, from this (and from comparable) rich and passionate debate(s) of the **277**
eighteenth century, unfortunately, there can still important lessons be drawn, given

---

[975] Beaud (1994), p. 75.

[976] As may be illustrated, in the current context, by the practice of the re-allocation of factories and other production units to other countries, as well as by the practices of importing cheap labor from other (poorer) countries.

[977] It can be observed that this insight basically concurs with the insight of for example Ricardo (see his famous "Iron law of the wages"), although the latter derived other conclusions from this insight.

[978] Beaud (1994), p. 75.

[979] Stiglitz (2006), p. 67.

[980] Marcuse (1962), pp. 91 a.f. See also Stiglitz et al. (2010), p. 84.

[981] Note that this is one of the main conditions for the aforementioned neo-liberal doctrine of "*voluntary association*" to be ever able to claim any credibility.

[982] Beaud (1994), p. 75.

the fact that, as has been pointed out in several recent studies (see above, under Sect. 3.4.8.2), the gaps between the rich and the poor have in present day world, once more in history, become deeper and wider (which, as is argued here, may mainly be attributed to the impact of economic neo-liberalism).[983]

3.6.2.4 (Modern) Humanism

278 Essentially being an ideological system premising human dignity, promoting the individual's freedom, and, furthermore, assuming that man(kind) is the measure of all things, (modern) humanism could be considered as a continuation of the ideas of rationalist thinking or, at the very least, as an expansion of those ideas.

Central values within (modern) humanism are, inter alia: reason, ethics, justice, equality, empowerment, respect for human rights, respect for nature and tolerance.[984]

279 It need not surprise that, derived from (modern) humanism, one can think of many arguments in favor of a new "social contract" on social and economic themes, including the way the monetary and financial system should be construed, that would be more just than the mechanisms prevailing in present day societies.

In this regard, neo-liberal inspired capitalism can hardly be considered respecting the basic principles of (modern) humanism, among which, in addition to the pursuit of justice itself, surely also: (*i*) the principles of equality and human dignity (as under capitalism, the rich are claimed to be more valuable than the poor); (*ii*) human rights (with as a striking example systems of slavery which prevail up till today), and (*iii*) respect for nature (a painful illustration being the problem of global climate warming and its disastrous consequences, but also the extinction of many plant and animal species, as well as the subjection of many forms of life to industrial interests—such as experiments on animals needed to test beauty products).

280 Also from humanist considerations, there is a clear need, higher than ever, for a true change of the capitalist economy in general, but more specifically of the monetary and financial system which is part of it.

---

[983] Again, an old lesson brought by the biblican book "Ecclesiastes" seems to apply, where, apparently, there is indeed nothing new under the sun (Ecclesiastes, 1:9), which however should not lead to too much pessimism, but which, on the contrary, especially given the very long timeframe of many centuries during which the majority of mankind is suffering the same intrinsic socioeconomic injustices over and over again, should stimulate striving for a more just socioeconomic order (which, as already mentioned before, is the objective of the further Chaps. 4 and 5 of the current book).

[984] Poma (2009), p. 49; de Roose (1989), pp. 51–62; Van Aken (1995), pp. 13 a.f.; De Lubac (1943), p. 384.

See also Goud (1992), p. 39; Mommen (1989), pp. 15–35.

3.6.2.5 Religion

3.6.2.5.1 General Perspective of Judaism and Christianity

Some of the basic world religions of the Western world (especially Judaism and Christianity, and to some extent Islam as well), hold that all men are children from the same "Supreme Deity" or "Heavenly Father"[985] Who has entrusted the earth to all people without any distinction of race, color, gender, sexual orientation, or any other criterion of distinction.[986] **281**

3.6.2.5.2 Catholicism

It has already been mentioned earlier in this chapter that, after abandoning the battle against the charging of interest which had been one of the central themes of the economic debate in the Western world for several ages (see above, under Sect. 3.3.3), the further position of the (catholic) Church regarding the capitalist system itself, especially in the course of the nineteenth and twentieth century, was characterized by an amazing degree of tolerance and acceptance[987] (significantly **282**

---

[985] See Galbraith (1987), p. 21:

> The principal social attitude perpetuated by Christianity supported the equality of all mankind. All being children of God, all were, in consequence, equals in brotherhood of man.

[986] This understanding is with no doubt also reflected in the aforementioned writings of a more secular nature, such as the "*Discours sur l'origine et les fondements de l'inégalité parmie les hommes*" of Rousseau (see above, at marg. 274 of this chapter), but also of the writings of, for example, Levinas, on which we will focus further in this book (see below, at marg. 301–306 of this chapter).

[987] The ambivalent nature of the Church doctrine towards capitalism may be due to the somehow twofold attitude towards economic goods and riches which can be found in many biblical sources, especially in the Old Testament itself. As explained in the "*Compendium of the Social Doctrine of the Church*", the Old Testament itself bears, *on one hand*, witness to an attitude of appreciation which sees the availability of material goods as necessary for life. Abundance — not wealth or luxury — is hereby even seen as a blessing from God. For instance, in "Wisdom Literature", poverty is described as a negative consequence of idleness and of a lack of industriousness (*cf.* Prov 10:4), but also as a natural fact (*cf.* Prov 22:2). *On the other hand*, economic goods and riches are not in themselves condemned so much as their misuse. The prophetic tradition condemns fraud, usury, exploitation and gross injustice, especially when directed against the poor (*cf.* Is 58:3-11; Jer 7:4-7; Hos 4:1-2; Am 2:6-7; Mic 2:1-2). (See Pontifical Council for Justice and Peace 2005, no 323.)

This tradition, however, although looking upon the poverty of the oppressed, the weak and the indigent as an evil, also sees in the condition of poverty a symbol of the human situation before God, from whom comes every good as a gift to be administered and shared. (See Pontifical Council for Justice and Peace 2005, no 323.)

contrasting with, for example, the strong condemnation of communist and even socialist economic doctrines and this in and since "*Rerum Novarum*"[988]).

To the present day, the Catholic Church has to a large extent maintained this friendly attitude towards capitalism, albeit on occasion warning against too strong excesses of the capitalist system[989]; however, it seems that under the pontificate of Pope Francis I (pope as of 2013), this attitude towards capitalism has become somewhat less friendly.[990]

Nevertheless, as has been pointed out in the world's happiness report of 2016, the Catholic Church has throughout the ages also been one of the few institutions that always has kept on defending the role of the "common good" as opposed

---

[988]It has hereby even been held in "*Rerum novarum*" that "socialism" is in contradiction with the Divine order:

- (no 5) ***"Socialists, therefore, by endeavoring to transfer the possessions of individuals to the community at large, strike at the interests of every wage-earner, since they would deprive him of the liberty of disposing of his wages, and thereby of all hope and possibility of increasing his resources and of bettering his condition in life."***
- (no 14) ***"The socialists, therefore, in setting aside the parent and setting up a State supervision, act against natural justice, and destroy the structure of the home."***
- (no 15) ***"Hence, it is clear that the main tenet of socialism, community of goods, must be utterly rejected, since it only injures those whom it would seem meant to benefit, is directly contrary to the natural rights of mankind, and would introduce confusion and disorder into the commonweal [sic]."***

(see Leo XIII 1891).

Pope Pius XII (1876–1958) declared in 1949 that any catholic who would adhere te communism would be excommunicated (see Les communistes sont escommuniés. In: Chroniques de l'Histoire—Jean-Paul II (1998), Jacques Legrand sa Éditions Chronique, Bassillac, p. 55).

Decades later, in his book "*Memory & Identity*", Pope John-Paul II qualified communism as "***an oppressive system imposed from the East***" (see John Paul II 2005, p. 49). Under reference to the gospel, communism is therein considered to be "*evil*" (under reference to the letter of Saint Paul to the Romans, 12:21).

[989]See *e.g.* Pontifical Council for Justice and Peace (2005), no 335:

> In the perspective of an integral and solidary development, it is possible to arrive at a proper appreciation of the moral evaluation that the Church's social doctrine offers in regard to the market economy or, more simply, of the free economy: "If by 'capitalism' is meant an economic system which recognizes the fundamental and positive role of business, the market, private property and the resulting responsibility for the means of production, as well as free human creativity in the economic sector, then the answer is certainly in the affirmative, even though it would perhaps be more appropriate to speak of a 'business economy', 'market economy' or simply 'free economy'. But if by 'capitalism' is meant a system in which freedom in the economic sector is not circumscribed within a strong juridical framework which places it at the service of human freedom in its totality, and which sees it as a particular aspect of that freedom, the core of which is ethical and religious, then the reply is certainly negative". In this way a Christian perspective is defined regarding social and political conditions of economic activity, not only its rules but also its moral quality and its meaning.

[990]Bruckner (2016), pp. 36–37.

towards the ideal of an unbridled selfishness (as defended under the doctrines of economic liberalism and economic neoliberalism).[991]

In the encyclical "*Centesimus annus*" (of May 1st 1991, hence dating from before the severe financial crisis of 2008), pope John-Paul II, in general words, criticized and condemned some of the excesses of the capitalist system, however without condemning capitalism as such[992]: **283**

> These are situations in which the rules of the earliest period of capitalism still flourish in conditions of "ruthlessness" in no way inferior to the darkest moments of the first phase of industrialization. (...) In these cases, it is still possible today, as in the days of Rerum Novarum, to speak of inhuman exploitation.

This encyclical "*Centesimus annus*", furthermore, highlighted the problematic situation of the North-South relations.[993] The free market[994], as well as the pursuit of profit[995], are nevertheless recognized as being "valuable" principles. However, pope John Paul II warned that the pursuit of profits may not be turned into the only principle controlling business life, but that other human and moral elements should be taken into consideration as well.[996]

Pope John-Paul II himself did not express stronger objections towards capitalism, although, under his pontificate, they have occasionally been upheld by other church leaders. **284**

A striking example of the latter has been Casaldàliga i Pla (also known as: Pedro Casaldáliga), former bishop of Sao Felix in the Brazilian Amazon, who, in a famous letter to pope John-Paul II of February 22nd 1986, wrote the following:

> The choice for the poor who will never exclude the rich as a person – because salvation is offered to all and the pastoral care of the church itself is obliged to be there for everyone – excludes the way how the rich live, which is an insult to the misery of the poor. it also excludes the system of money accumulation and of privileges which inevitably marginalize

[991] According to said world's happiness report of 2016, one of the pillars of Catholic social teaching is indeed the notion of the common good, under Catholic doctrine defined as "*the sum of those conditions of social life which allow social groups and their individual members relatively thorough and ready access to their own fulfillment*". Otherwise put, the common good is the good in and through which all can flourish. While the post-enlightenment tradition reduces the common good to the mere aggregation of individual goods, the Catholic doctrine has kept favoring the old idea that the individual's own good is intrinsically linked to the good of others. This for instance coheres with how Thomas Aquinas viewed the "bonum commune"—each person wills the other's well-being for the other's sake, which gives rise to a true "common" good, not reducible to the good of either taken separately or summed. There is an element of sacrifice involved as only by giving up and risking some individual good can we build something in common. (See Sachs et al. 2016, p. 11.)

[992] John Paul II (1991), no 33.

[993] John Paul II (1991), no 33.

[994] John Paul II (1991), no 34.

[995] John Paul II (1991), no 35.

[996] John Paul II (1991), no 35.

> and plunder the immeasurable majority of the human family, of populations and of entire continents.[997]

No proof of the Vatican leaders of that time supporting this remarkable position has been found, albeit, on the contrary, strong condemnations[998] against the liberation theology[999] have been expressed (which the aforementioned letter of Casaldàliga i Pla has attempted to answer)[1000].

285 According to actual church teachings, "*unjust inequalities*"[1001] impacting millions of men and women are held in contradiction with the Gospel.[1002]

Said actual church teachings, in general, hold that "labor" should obtain its rightful place within society, and that, through one's proper labor, every man should be able to build up an elementary fortune.[1003] It is hereby held that, through his labor, every man should be able to acquire humane and just living conditions. Too important economic and social inequalities between members or populations of one human community are in this regard believed to cause "irritation", and are therefore to be considered in contradiction with elementary fairness, human dignity and social and international peace itself.[1004]

---

[997]Truyman (2002), p. 145.

A German version of this letter can be found on http://www.konzilsvaeter.de/aktuell/pedro-casaldaliga/brief-an-den-papst-johannes-paul-ii/index.html (last consulted on December 4th 2014), stating:

> Erstens, weil wir die reale Armut, in der die Mehrheit unserer Menschen lebt, weder in unseren Instituten noch im privaten Leben teilen. Zweitens, weil wir dem "ungerechten Mammon" nicht mit jener Freiheit und Festigkeit entgegentreten, wie der Herr es getan hat. Die Option für die Armen, die nie die Person des Reichen ausschließen wird -da ja das Heil allen angeboten ist und der Dienst der Kirche allen gelten muss-, schließt aber sehr wohl den Lebensstil der Reichen, eine Beleidigung der Armen im Elend, aus. Sie schließt ebenso das System der Anhäufung und der Privilegien aus, welches notwendigerweise die immense Mehrheit der menschlichen Familie, ganze Völker und Kontinente, ausplündert und an den Rand drängt.

[998]Thus especially against the activities of the former archbishop of San Salvador Óscar Arnulfo Romero y Goldámez (1917–1980). (See Truyman 2002, pp. 182–183. About Romero, see also Ortberg 2014, p. 151.)

[999]Which had gained popularity during the early years of John Paul II's pontificate.

[1000]Truyman (2002), pp. 146–147.

[1001]This doctrine also seems to be inspired by Aristotle; see Aristotle (1996), pp. 124 a.f., verses 1133b30-1134a15.

[1002]Catechismus van de Katholieke kerk (2008), p. 443 (no 1938).

[1003]Brand (1966), pp. 500–505.

[1004]See Pastoral Constitution on the Church in the Modern World *"Gaudium et Spes"* promulgated by his holiness, Pope Paul VI on December 7, 1965, 29, § 3:

> Human institutions, both private and public, must labor to minister to the dignity and purpose of man. At the same time let them put up a stubborn fight against any kind of slavery, whether social or political, and safeguard the basic rights of man under every political system. Indeed human institutions themselves must be accommodated by degrees

In all this, a crucial role is reserved for the principle of "solidarity": solidarity among the poor, between the poor and the rich; among workers; between employers and employees within companies, and between nations and populations. International solidarity is in this regard seen as a moral necessity and as a condition for world peace.[1005] States are hereby expected to especially pursue the protection of the rights of the poor and of the working classes.[1006]

Finally, the principle of "distributing justice" should determine the distribution of possessions on earth. The pursuit of gathering possessions may hereby not be seen as a life goal as such, but only as a means to fulfill one's own life, which under Catholic doctrine remains finding the Kingdom of God.[1007]

In the *"Compendium of the Social Doctrine of the Church"* (2004)[1008], it is hereby explicitly mentioned that economic activity and material progress should be placed at the service of man and society.[1009] This *"Compendium of the Social Doctrine of the Church"* moreover holds that *"if people dedicate themselves to these with the faith, hope and love of Christ's disciples, even the economy and progress can be transformed into places of salvation and sanctification"*.[1010] Otherwise put, even in economic life, it is believed to be *"possible to express a love and a solidarity that are more than human, and to contribute to the growth of a new humanity that anticipates the world to come"*.[1011]

In other words, it seems that, after giving up its historical battle against the **286**
charging of interest as an unjustified method of wealth accumulation (of the rich, to the detriment of the poor), Catholic doctrine as shaped enduring the second half of the twentieth and the beginning of the twenty-first century seems no longer to have any problems with wealth accumulation as such, as well as with accepting that the rich may "preserve" and "accumulate" wealth (without it is expected of them—contrary to the teaching of Jesus Christ Himself (see above, at marg. 37 of this chapter)—to sell their possessions, in order to share the proceeds of such sale with

to the highest of all realities, spiritual ones, even though meanwhile, a long enough time will be required before they arrive at the desired goal.

See also Catechismus van de Katholieke kerk (2008), 443 (no 1938).

[1005]Catechismus van de Katholieke kerk (2008), p. 444 (no 1941). See also John-Paul II (1991), no 10.

[1006]John-Paul II (1991), no 10.

[1007]See Pontifical Council for Justice and Peace (2005), no 326; Brand (1966), p. 506.

The latter point of view is in line with the Church's classic viewpoints of the Middle Ages.

[1008]See Pontifical Council for Justice and Peace (2005).

[1009]Pontifical Council for Justice and Peace (2005), no 326.

[1010]Pontifical Council for Justice and Peace (2005), no 326.

[1011]Pontifical Council for Justice and Peace (2005), no 326.

the poor), on condition that the rich strive for some degree of solidarity with the poor, and that no "too large" distortions occur.[1012]

Modern day church teachings hereby nevertheless keep emphasizing that by living in accordance with the teachings of Christ "*a new manner of social life is made possible, in justice, brotherhood, solidarity and sharing*".[1013]

As a result, under Church doctrine, a distinction seems feasible between "permissible" wealth accumulation and "improper" wealth accumulation, the distinguishing criterion being what one does with one's richess: "*Riches fulfil their function of service to man when they are destined to produce benefits for others and for society.*"[1014]

287 Hence, the present-day position of the Catholic church has to some extent remained in in line with the relative mildness it has been showing towards capitalism since the second half of the nineteenth century (see above, at marg. 101–102 of this chapter), although under the pontificate of pope Francis I, a tendency to condemn some practices of capitalism in a more severe manner is manifesting.

Already in the "*Compendium of the Social Doctrine of the Church*" (2004), it is held that it is not acceptable to achieve economic growth at the expense of other

[1012]However, the opinion of the Church on "usury" and similar practices has remained unaltered:

> Although the quest for equitable profit is acceptable in economic and financial activity, recourse to usury is to be morally condemned: "Those whose usurious and avaricious dealings lead to the hunger and death of their brethren in the human family indirectly commit homicide, which is imputable to them". This condemnation extends also to international economic relations, especially with regard to the situation in less advanced countries, which must never be made to suffer "abusive if not usurious financial systems". More recently, the Magisterium used strong and clear words against this practice, which is still tragically widespread, describing usury as "a scourge that is also a reality in our time and that has a stranglehold on many peoples' lives". (Pontifical Council for Justice and Peace 2005, no 341).

[1013]Pontifical Council for Justice and Peace (2005), no 325.

[1014]Pontifical Council for Justice and Peace (2005), no 329:

> How could we ever do good to our neighbour," asks St. Clement of Alexandria, "if none of us possessed anything?". In the perspective of St. John Chrysostom, riches belong to some people so that they can gain merit by sharing them with others. Wealth is a good that comes from God and is to be used by its owner and made to circulate so that even the needy may enjoy it. Evil is seen in the immoderate attachment to riches and the desire to hoard. St. Basil the Great invites the wealthy to open the doors of their storehouses and he exhorts them: "A great torrent rushes, in thousands of channels, through the fertile land: thus, by a thousand different paths, make your riches reach the homes of the poor". Wealth, explains Saint Basil, is like water that issues forth from the fountain: the greater the frequency with which it is drawn, the purer it is, while it becomes foul if the fountain remains unused. The rich man — Saint Gregory the Great will later say — is only an administrator of what he possesses; giving what is required to the needy is a task that is to be performed with humility because the goods do not belong to the one who distributes them. He who retains riches only for himself is not innocent; giving to those in need means paying a debt.

human beings, let alone entire populations or social groups, condemning them to indigence.[1015]

In an more recent "open letter" of June 15th 2013 by pope Francis I to the British Prime minister David Cameron (pursuant to the G8-top which was held on June 17th and 18th 2013 in Ireland)[1016], an even more radical position was taken, probably as a result of the impact of the financial crisis of 2008 and its world-wide aftermath, albeit that, also in this letter, capitalism and/or the free market economy are not as such questioned. In this letter, Pope Francis I (again) mainly calls for an economy which serves (or would serve) the establishment of God's kingdom on earth and he is asking for special attention regarding the position of the poor within society.

In his book "*Church of mercy*" (2014), pope Francis I repeated his call to the policy makers (of the entire international community) to, above all, take into account the needs of the oppressed and the poor. Also in this book, the importance of solidarity is emphasized, in addition to a tendency to be the voice of the poor and to promoting justice.[1017]

The encyclical letter "*Laudato si'*" (2015)[1018] of pope Francis I, probably for the first time in the history of the Church, demonstrates a clearer understanding and hence a more critical attitude towards the impact of economic neo-liberalism on the general well-being of the earth and its inhabitants. As a result, this encyclical letter expresses several critical remarks on neo-liberal economic mechanisms and their

---

[1015] The growth of wealth, seen in the availability of goods and services, and the moral demands of an equitable distribution of these must inspire man and society as a whole to practise the essential virtue of solidarity, in order to combat, in a spirit of justice and charity, those "structures of sin" where ever they may be found and which generate and perpetuate poverty, underdevelopment and degradation. These structures are built and strengthened by numerous concrete acts of human selfishness. (See Pontifical Council for Justice and Peace 2005, no 332.)

[1016] See Francis (2013), a.o. stating:

> Therefore concern for the fundamental material and spiritual welfare of every human person is the starting-point for every political and economic solution and the ultimate measure of its effectiveness and its ethical validity. Moreover, the goal of economics and politics is to serve humanity, beginning with the poorest and most vulnerable wherever they may be, even in their mothers' wombs. Every economic and political theory or action must set about providing each inhabitant of the planet with the minimum wherewithal to live in dignity and freedom, with the possibility of supporting a family, educating children, praising God and developing one's own human potential. This is the main thing; in the absence of such a vision, all economic activity is meaningless. In this sense, the various grave economic and political challenges facing today's world require a courageous change of attitude that will restore to the end (the human person) and to the means (economics and politics) their proper place. Money and other political and economic means must serve, not rule, bearing in mind that, in a seemingly paradoxical way, free and disinterested solidarity is the key to the smooth functioning of the global economy.

[1017] See Francis (2014), pp. 109–118.

[1018] Francis (2015).

consequences, such as "consumerism"[1019] and irresponsible development; the letter, furthermore, laments the environmental degradation and deals with the issue of global warming, and calls mankind to take "swift and unified global action".[1020]

288 When considering Church doctrine during the past two centuries, one can but conclude how "soft" its attitude towards capitalism with all its severe excesses has been, although under pope Francis I, the tide seems somehow to be turning.

Yet, the on itself fine-sounding call to abide, on a voluntary basis, to the (vague) principle of "solidarity", remains in contrast with the much stronger expectation expressed by Christ that he who wants to follow Him should be willing to sell all his properties and to give the proceeds to the poor (see above, at marg. 37 of this chapter).

In the meantime, one may wonder if (even Christian) rich people are up to the charge of voluntarily becoming "solidar" with the poor, a question which already before has been raised by Galbraith in his book "*The affluent society*"[1021]:

> Few things have been more productive of controversy over the ages than the suggestion that the rich should, by one device or another, share their wealth with those who are not. With comparatively rare and usually eccentric exceptions[1022], the rich have been opposed. The grounds have been many and varied and have been principally noted for the rigorous exclusion of the most important reasons, which is the simple unwillingness to give up the enjoyment of what they have. The poor have generally been in favor of greater equality.

3.6.2.5.3 Buddhism

289 It seems that Buddhism has managed better to uphold the teachings of its (supposed) founder (the historical "Buddha") in practice, especially in comparison to other religions such as Christianity.

[1019]See before also the condemnation of consumerism in Pontifical Council for Justice and Peace (2005), no 360:

> The phenomenon of consumerism maintains a persistent orientation towards "having" rather than "being". This confuses the "criteria for correctly distinguishing new and higher forms of satisfying human needs from artificial new needs which hinder the formation of a mature personality". To counteract this phenomenon it is necessary to create "life- styles in which the quest for truth, beauty, goodness and communion with others for the sake of common growth are the factors which determine consumer choices, savings and investments". It is undeniable that ways of life are significantly influenced by different social contexts, for this reason the cultural challenge that consumerism poses today must be met with greater resolve, above all in consideration of future generations, who risk having to live in a natural environment that has been pillaged by an excessive and disordered consumerism.

[1020]Yardley and Goodstein (2015).

[1021]Galbraith (1974), p. 91.

[1022]See, in this regard, the charity work of Bill Gates (see Baer 2014).

This can, for instance, be illustrated by the modest lifestyle of one of Buddhism's most inspiring leaders, the "*Dalai Lama*"[1023], at least as can be perceived in the West, highly contrasting with the extreme riches of the Catholic church and its leading figures.

Within Buddhism, for over 2500 years now, it is believed that everything is "one" (hence resulting in a belief system in which another human being is perceived as being one with one's own self)[1024], which provides a standard of moral conduct applicable to all life situations, including socioeconomic relations[1025].

Another basic principle of Buddhism is the belief that limiting once's desire is one of the most basic conditions for true happiness.[1026]

In this concept, it has been held that all the troubles of the world are caused by what could called "greed"—but what could also be described as "hunger", thirst", craving" or "desiring"—in the sense of an unquenchable thirst for all possible possessions, power and sex[1027].

As is the case for a drug addict, such "thirst", when given into it, starts controlling the human mind and spirit, causing him to act blindly on these desires. As it is impossible to fulfill desires, this can only lead to an everlasting state of suffering, which is the outcome of a continuous hunt for the satisfaction of new

---

[1023]http://www.dalailama.com/biography (last consulted on December 3th 2014).

[1024]See *e.g.* Kornfield (1995), p. 48. See also De Lorenzo (1949).

[1025]A similar, more modern day approach can be encountered in the philosophical system of Emmanuel Levinas; see below, Sect. 3.6.4.2.

[1026]See *e.g.*, among many others, the following verses of the Dhammapada (Buddha):

> The craving of a thoughtless person grows like a creeper.
> That one runs from life to life,
> like a monkey seeking fruit in the forest.
> Whoever is overcome by this fierce poisonous craving
> in this world has one's sufferings increase
> like the spreading birana grass.
> Whoever overcomes this fierce craving,
> difficult to control in this world,
> sufferings fall off, like water drops from a lotus leaf.
> This beneficial word I tell you, "Do you,
> as many as are gathered here, dig up the root of craving,
> as one digs up the birana grass to find the usira root,
> so that Mara may not destroy you again and again,
> just as the river crushes the reeds."
> As a tree, even though it has been cut down,
> grows again if its root is strong and undamaged,
> similarly if the roots of craving are not destroyed,
> this suffering returns again and again.

See also Adams Beck s.d., p. 173; Epstein (2007), p. 54.

[1027]In the *Dhammapada*, it is said that "craving is the worst disease" (see Buddha), a saying that is obviously opposite to the "*Greed is good*"-principle on which economic neo-liberalism is based.

desires in order to forget the disappointment of not having succeeded in fulfilling old desires in a satisfactory way[1028].

In this way, given the fact that most forms of Buddhism adhere to a belief in reincarnation, the endless circle of rebirth in "*samsara*" can never be broken[1029] (except then by putting an end to desire and greed).

In this, it is crucial to accept that no experience which is aimed at satisfying a need or desire can ever be enough to attain a complete state of satisfaction. This ultimately must lead to the understanding that when (or as long as) desires remain unsatisfied, suffering will go on, and that when they are, albeit imperfectly, satisfied, new desires are likely to arise. Only the insight that it is better not to long for anything anymore can hence set one free.[1030]

A genuine attitude towards life needs to aim at restraining these desires, which is, obviously, completely contrary to the unbridled pursuit of money and the "*greed is good*"-principle, which (neo-)liberal doctrines have proclaimed as the main purpose in life.

Renowned contemporary Buddhist authors, such as Thich Nhat Hanh, have hereby tried to provide practical guidelines on how to achieve this "limiting of desires" in everyday (even Western) life.[1031]

3.6.2.5.4 Evaluation

290 Even when taking into account the obviously inadequate way by which religious institutions, such as, noteworthy, as regards for instance Christianity, the Catholic church itself, have implemented their basic religious beliefs into daily practice, it can nevertheless be concluded that, throughout the ages, the Western (and Western inspired) societies, especially in the field of their "socioeconomic order"[1032], have

---

[1028] Epstein (2007), p. 81.

[1029] Trainor (2012), p. 66.

[1030] Epstein (2007), p. 55.

[1031] For an overview of the books of Thich Nhat Hanh, see http://plumvillage.org/about/thich-nhat-hanh/ (last consulted on 19th January 2016).

In the same way, also Osho (formerly known as the Bhagwan Sri Rajneesh) has aimed at making the teachings of Buddhism (in addition to those of other religions) understandable for the modern man (see http://www.osho.com/; last consulted on 19th January 2016).

See also Ricard (2014).

[1032] Or perhaps better: the lack of such socioeconomic order, given the blind belief in the "*invisible hand*"-theory as a leading principle of establishing the neo-liberal ideal of a completely free (d) market which prevails in Western (and Western influenced) societies.

not only become increasingly "*contra-Christian*"[1033], but also increasingly "*contra-Buddhist*"[1034].

Western societies are, in their socioeconomic organization, "contra-Christ(ian)" to the extent that they have replaced the basic value of altruism by selfishness and egoism, but also to the extent that they have strived for an over-materialistic view towards life (instead of adhering to the belief that life's sole purpose is to find the Kingdom of God). In a similar way, Western societies are, in their socioeconomic organization, "contra-Buddhist" to the extent that they are led by greed and by the aim of fulfilling all thinkable desires (even "created wants"), instead of adhering to the insight of Buddhism that only by abandoning one's desires one can reach true happiness (or, there called: "enlightenment").

When evaluating the prevailing world social and economic order against the insights derived from the underlying belief systems of Christianity and Buddhism (but, as may be assumed, also the ones of other leading world religions, such as Judaism and Hinduism), the conclusion can but be that it is unthinkable to adhere to the prevailing social contract on the capitalist social and economic order, including its monetary and financial system[1035].

Otherwise put, the mentioned religious systems, when properly understood, call for a fundamental change of said prevailing capitalist world social and economic order.

3.6.3 *Some Insights Derived from Biology*

To (modern) biology, we owe the insight that all mankind descends from the same ancestor(s). **291**

[1033]As, as been extensively developed above, the value of the "radical altruism" as preached by Jesus Christ, especially since Adam Smith, but to some extent already before, noteworthy also in the teachings of leading Christian theologians as Luther and Calvin, has been rejected as a guiding principle of societal organization in favor of the value of "unbridled selfishness".

[1034]In this regard, one may consider, *on one hand,* especially since the Reagan-era when so-called "consumerism" was introduced as a leading economic doctrine (see *above*, at marg. 149 of this chapter), the focus on the pursuit of immediate satisfaction of all possible desires, even fictitiously created (see the so-called "*created wants*"), and, *on the other hand*, the credit economy which has been a logical outcome or companion of it. (See furthermore Bruckner (2002), p. 68, having described consumerism as

> une utopie de la diversion, l'idée à la fois ingénieuse et triste que les hommes, dès lors qu'ils échangent ou achètent, ne se font pas la guerre, détorunent leurs pulsions agressives sur l'espace du supermarché ou du grand magasin.)

[1035]Compare Galbraith (1987), p. 21.

292 For instance, the renowned biologist Richard Dawkins[1036] has demonstrated, in his work "*The Ancestor's Tale. A Pilgrimage to the Dawn of Life*", that an old enough "being" which has spawned at least one human being, must be an ancestor of all human beings. Dawkins hereby convincingly argues that, going back long enough in time, the ancestry of a specific group of descendants, such as human beings, is a question of all or nothing.[1037]

In other words, contemporary biological science seem to have proven that the entire human species descends from one common ancestor and, hence, that all human beings are (at least distant) relatives of each other. Surprisingly, one does not even need to go back very far in time to find this "common predecessor" of all mankind, apparently only a few ten thousands of years[1038], which is indeed a small number compared to the estimated age of the universe as known by us, which is reported to be about 13,798 billion years old.[1039]

Going back even more in time, it has moreover been argued that all living beings on this planet, ultimately, have one common ancestor, in other words, that any living being is a (distant) relative of every other living being.[1040]

Moreover, this same biological science, for which we, again, quote a work of Dawkins, namely his book "*The Selfish Gene*", also teaches us that all living beings, ultimately, are (merely) "survival vehicles" of genes which all living beings have in common. *"We are all surviving machines, but "we" does not just mean people. It embraces all animals, plants, bacteria, and viruses."*[1041]

In other words, just as has been the case with the above quoted religious belief systems, scientific (biological) facts also lead to the conclusion that all living beings are strongly connected and that this is even more specifically the case for the members of one race, for instance the members of the human race themselves.

293 At first sight, it could come as a surprise that, based upon these insights, arguments in favor of the establishment of a more altruist society in general (and a more altruist social and economic model, including its monetary and financial

---

[1036] The works of Dawkins are especially appealing as they are not only the result of a profound scientific research, but can also be easily understood by a layman in this field of science. In the "*Preface to first edition*" of his book "*The Selfish Gene*", Dawkins explains that one of his goals has been to make his scientific field available to laymen:

> Three imaginary readers looked over my shoulder while I was writing (...). First the general reader, the layman. For him I have avoided technical jargon almost totally, and where I have had to use specialized words I have defined them. (...) I have worked hard to try to popularize some subtle and complicated ideas in non-mathematical language, without loosing their essence. (see Dawkins 2006, p. xxi).

Moreover, many of Dawkins' works read like the most gripping novel.

[1037] Dawkins (2005), p. 40.

[1038] Dawkins (2005), p. 46.

[1039] See http://en.wikipedia.org/wiki/, under the term "Age of the Universe" (last consulted on December 4th 2012).

[1040] See also Dawkins (2011), p. 50.

[1041] Dawkins (2006), p. 21.

system more specifically) can be derived from the works of biologists such as Dawkins[1042], especially given the fact that the economic neo-liberal schools themselves are very often juggling with arguments which they, fragmentary, have borrowed from other insights of biology.

For instance the principle of "*natural selection*", in addition to the idea of "*the survival of the fittest*", as derived from the works of another famous scientist/ biologist, namely Charles Darwin[1043], and, more recently, the idea of "*the selfish gene*" taken from Dawkins himself, are concepts that have become extremely popular among neo-liberal scholars.

Nevertheless, this tactic of said neo-liberal authors becomes the less applicable knowing that Dawkins himself, in conclusion of his own insights from the research which has lied at the basis of his book "*The Selfish Gene*" (such as research material about the wild forces of nature which also spawned the genes of human beings), has held that mankind needs indeed to behave in a more altruist way.

Knowing this, it becomes important to correct an important misconception often **294**
met in human sciences writings.

For instance, the Belgian psychologist and academic Verhaeghe has pointed out that several neo-liberal ideas and practices are indeed often defended by referring to Darwin's idea of "*the survival of the fittest*"[1044] and Dawkins' idea of "*the selfish gene*".[1045]

The misuse of the teachings of biology is not a contemporary phenomenon, but is reported to date back to the end of the nineteenth century, when business tycoons, such as John Davison Rockefeller (1839–1937) and James Jerome Hill (1838–1916), already adhered to the idea of the "*survival of the fittest*", by expressing their opinions that the strongest and most efficient enterprises would automatically become market leader and, through this, would be best suited to further stimulate economic prosperity.[1046]

This way of thinking even obtained a validation in pseudo-scientific works by writers such as Herbert Spencer (1820–1903). Hence, as explained by Galbraith, one of the most ultimate cases for capitalism came into existence, namely the idea that capitalism is nothing else than the manifestation of Darwin's teachings in the social and economic order, whereby the principle of the "survival of the fittest" is applied to economic and, in general, societal interactions. The great capitalists are in this way believed to be "great" or "extra-ordinary" because they are biologically superior. The poor are poor because they are biologically inferior. Wealth is the reward of those who are inherently better and the effort to cost what cost attain it both reveals and develops this superiority. In this reasoning, even the poverty of the

---

[1042]Which, obviously, are based on research undertaken by different other scientists in his domain.

[1043]Especially with his book: "*The Origin of Species*" (1859) (see *e.g.* the modern edition in "*Collector's Library*", New York, Barnes & Noble Books).

[1044]On this topic, see *e.g.* Galbraith (1987), p. 164.

[1045]Verhaeghe (2011), p. 20.

[1046]Galbraith (1983), p. 117; Browne (2008), p. 101.

poor can but be accepted as being socially good, as it provides man with a motivation to aim to do better.[1047]

Again one can but remark that anyone abusing such ideas and insights of biology in this way to support the thoughts of economic neo-liberalism has (probably) at the very least misunderstood these.

In his book "*The Selfish Gene*", Dawkins himself has clearly anticipated such an abuse of his own scientific research, where he undeniably pronounces himself as a supporter of a civilization model based on altruist principles, instead of a societal model which would propagate a blind adhering of everyone's selfish genes.

As Dawkins himself has put it[1048]:

> I know I am in danger of being misunderstood (...). My own feeling is that a human society based simply on the gene's law of universal ruthless selfishness would be a very nasty society in which to live. (...) Be warned that if you wish, as I do, to build a society in which individuals cooperate generously and unselfishly towards a common good, you can expect little help from biological nature. Let us try to teach generosity and altruism, because we are born selfish. Let us understand what our selfish genes are up to, because we then at least have the chance to upset their designs, something that no other species has ever aspired to.

Dawkins further developed the argument, that what seems "altruistic" can also be considered "selfish", where the conviction of self-preservation (not only of the individual, but of the entire human race, and, by expansion, of life in general and even of non-living matter), itself bears witness of the only acceptable level of selfishness, namely the self -preservation of everything that "is" (in other words, of existence in its broadest meaning, of which mankind forms a part)[1049].

With the latter idea, the insights of Dawkins even come very close to the Buddhist idea that everything is "one", as it sets a high ethical standard for an individual's relationship with everything surrounding him.

295 One could further wonder why those who use the ideas of "*the survival of the fittest*" and "*the selfish gene*" to justify a social and economic system (i.e. capitalism) thriving on the notion of unbridled selfishness, should also not be inclined to apply to these other domains of human behavior, for instance sexual lust?

296 Theoretically speaking, one could indeed develop an argumentation holding that everyone should be allowed to act upon any impulses his genes drive him to, and that weaker members of society, in whatever sense, should be at hand to serve the sexual appetites of the strong ones.

It could in this context, furthermore, be interesting to know if there ever has been research undertaken that investigates a possible correlation between, *on one hand*, the support of neo-liberal thinking and, *on the other hand*, conservatism in the field of sexual morality.

[1047] Galbraith (1983), p. 117.

[1048] Dawkins (2006), p. 3.

[1049] Dawkins (2006), pp. 4–5.

Given the sometimes very strong opinions of, for instance, republican candidates for American public offices, not rarely characterized by explicit averse opinions on the use of contraceptives, abortion and homosexuality, such a correlation may very well be likely.[1050]

If such a correlation moreover would indeed be determined (preferably trough scientific methods), then neo-liberals relying on Darwin's and Dawkins' ideas in support of the neo-liberal "*greed is good*" -doctrine, while at the same time adhering to a conservative sexual morality, would in a very selective manner quote from findings of (modern) biology, to the extent that they would call to, for instance, "the survival of the fittest" and to "the working out of the selfish genes" in order to advocate an unbridled selfishness on an economic level, but would at the same time call for suppressing the actions of sexual lust, albeit these are equally driven by the same selfish genes.

Comparably, calling upon the ideas of "*the survival of the fittest*" and "*the selfish* **297**
genes" could also be questioned in the context of raising children in a completely liberal way.

Such an extreme liberal model of education could, for instance, rely on the principle that any child, from the date of its birth, should be allowed to do and act according to his impulses, or, otherwise put, by his "genes", and that even in the relation between children, the law of the "survival of the fittest" should equally apply.

Although it may seem that in a world becoming more and more without ethical values (except the "values" of selfishness and greed), (some) parents and other educators are already attempting to apply such an educational model, at least to some extent, as far as known, no-one has up till now advocated a full compliance with such an extremely "gene-driven" education model.

Nevertheless, one could be curious to the outcome of applying such an educational system, albeit the prognosis in this regard made by novelist William Golding in his famous novel "*Lord of the flies*" permits one to fear for the worst.

Both the abovementioned examples on how the application of said biological **298**
insights to other domains of societal life than economics could work out demonstrate how absurd it is to conclude from findings of biology that man is allowed to

---

[1050]See *e.g.* http://en.wikipedia.org/wiki/Conservatism_in_the_United_States (with further references) (last consulted on November 11th 2014), a.o. stating:

> President Ronald Reagan set the conservative standard in the 1980s; in the 2010s the Republican leaders typically claim fealty to it. For example most of the Republican candidates in 2012, "claimed to be standardbearers of Reagan's ideological legacy." Reagan solidified conservative Republican strength with tax cuts, a greatly increased military budget, continued deregulation, a policy of rollback of Communism (rather than just containing it), and appeals to family values and conservative morality. The 1980s and beyond became known as the "Reagan Era." Typically, conservative politicians and spokesmen in the 21st century proclaim their devotion to Reagan's ideals and policies on most social, economic and foreign policy issues. Conservative voters typically oppose abortion, gun control, and gay marriage.

For further reading, see Veldman and Parlevliet (2003).

(or even supposed to) behave in a selfish way at a socioeconomic level, because such an argumentation completely neglects the role of civilization as a determining mechanism of steering interhuman relations.

Luckily, it appears that such a use of Darwin's and Dawkins' ideas in order to advocate a completely free experience of sexual lust or a completely liberal education model, has not been taken place yet, and that even the most fervent adherents of economic neo-liberalism accept that, for instance, in the domains of sexual experience and of education, civilization is allowed and needs to apply corrections to the blind application of biological impulses.[1051]

Finally, is it not exactly this which forms the essence of a civilization, and, if this is the case, should man then not also (and mainly) within the domain of economy advocate a larger civilization model which lifts mankind to a higher level than a blind adherence to the aforementioned biological impulses?

3.6.4 Some Further Contemporary Arguments for More Altruism in Socioeconomic Relations

3.6.4.1 Context

299 In addition to the abovementioned "traditional" frameworks of religious and ethical reflection, also in the contemporary context, some voices in favor of a larger extent of altruism in the socioeconomic relations have made themselves known.

From the wide diversity of such voices, hereafter follows a limited selection (as they have particularly appealed to the author of the current book himself).

3.6.4.2 French (Moral)philosophers

3.6.4.2.1 Context

300 In France, many prominent twentieth century (moral) philosophers, such as Emmanuel Levinas and Michel Foucault, have announced themselves as advocates of a society model and/or, more in general, interhuman relationships characterized a

---

[1051] See *e.g.* Wolffers (2011), p. 99:

> Sex is not only an individual matter, notwithstanding it may seem so, but it is a societal matter whereby the boundaries of what is permissable or not are strictly drawn. (free translation)

sufficient level of altruism (both Levinas and Foucault), in addition to, already for decades, having raised arguments for a greater for the environment (Foucault).[1052]

Reference should also be made to the impressive work "*Plaidoyer pour l'altruisme. La force de la bienveillance*" of the French Buddhist monk Matthieu Ricard which was for the first time published in 2013.[1053]

3.6.4.2.2 Emmanuel Levinas

The philosophy of Emmanuel Levinas (1906–1995) not only forms an original thinking system, but it also provides a "contemporary" sharp contrast with economic neo-liberalism. **301**

In general, the doctrine of Emmanuel Levinas (1906–1995), which mainly bears witness of a fundamental respect for the fellow-man (as in "the Other", "the self" finds the reflection of the face of God), as opposed to the principle of unbridled selfishness taught by economic neoliberalism. **302**

In propagating his teachings, Levinas made reference to the term "egology"—or "me-culture"—as it has emerged since Descartes[1054] (and has, since then, been translated into "rationalist" economic doctrines, such as Adam Smith's, and later economic neo-liberal doctrine), as well as to the power of any "ontology", submitting the "self" to a universal "Being" (whereby reference seems to be made, in an abstract way, to any totalitarian system, such as "Stalinism", but also "Capitalism") and hereby erasing all individualism.[1055]

The own life experience of the Jewish Levinas, who in the 1930s had personally experienced the prosecution of the Jews, is said to be one of the main explanations for this central idea in his philosophy that man should free himself from any ontological system.[1056]

Levinas believed that "egology", nor "ontology", is able to give a sense to life. **303**

This lead Levinas to the further insight that every human being (= "the self") basically needs to acquire freedom, especially from any egological and/or ontological system imprisoning him. This leads to breaking out from the enclosure of one's own self ("*sortir de l'être*"), and to the necessity for a human being (= "the self"), mainly through his own thinking and reflection, to develop his own conscience based on his interaction with other.

[1052]See especially Foucault (2008), p. 346. (See also Foucault 2013, p. 427; Foucault 2003, p. 310.)

See also the works of Bruckner and Todd, all French authors, which should not be entirely surprising as the French schools of enlightenment historically have been far more pleading for social justice than their British counterparts.

[1053]Ricard (2014), 1022 p. See also before Ricard (2003) (384 p.).

[1054]See Descartes (1948).

[1055]Levinas (1974), p. 9. Compare Marcuse (1962), p. 105.

[1056]See Van Hove (1993), pp. 75–91, especially p. 80.

In this, "the Other" cannot just be an *"alter ego" of the self, but needs to be perceived as a real subject (= "the Other") with whom "the self" interacts and, hence, for whom it becomes responsible.*[1057] "The self" should hereby avoid to rely upon an abstract model of morality, but rather learn to experience the other as "the Other" from a first-person perspective and based upon his own interaction with this "other".[1058]

By this approach, Levinas mainly attempted to introduce "the Other" (and the very, day-to-day practical interaction with this "Other") into the domain of ethics.

Any relation with the Other should, hence, not be only, or mainly, the result of a process of abstract thinking. On the contrary, the self needs to become aimed at "experiencing" the other as "the Other", expressed by the idea that it is in the face of the Other that "the self" will experience the development of his proper ethical code of interaction with "the Other" (in analogy with the *"panim el panim"-principle derived* from the bible, a concept that could be translated as *"from face to face"*, an idea which Levinas thus also introduced to the level of interhuman relations).[1059]

One cannot help but observing the striking similarities between said Levinas' teachings (admittedly strongly rooted in Judaic doctrines[1060]) with certain catholic doctrines which were developed in the same country (France) and (more or less) the same time period, and which preached the application of a practicable "humbleness" in " day-to-day life" relations, such as the well-known *"small path"* (*"la petite voie"*) of the Saint Theresia of Lisieux (1873–1897).[1061]

304 At a more "political" and "economic level", Levinas recognized that, for instance, an unbridled pursuit of wealth (as taught by liberal and neo-liberal schools since Adam Smith) can become a threat to the Other, whereby the pursuit of money may lead to a practice of "killing" or "swallowing up" the Other in the totalization of "the self" (and especially as regards to what "the self" aspires for)[1062], in other words, to completely subject the other to once' s own selfish desires.

The conclusion of this reasoning should be that the pursuit of one's own desires should not happen in an unbridled way, but that "the self" should aspire for far more than fulfilling one's own selfish needs. Levinas described this by the notion of "the miracle of the humane" (*"le miracle de l'humain"*). This implies that the self should not "kill" the Other in his own selfish pursuit of satisfying his needs, and this by

---

[1057]Levinas (1974), pp. 3 a.f.

[1058]See Duyndam and Poorthuis (2003), p. 19.

[1059]Levinas (2014), pp. 50 a.f.; Levinas (2012), pp. 199 a.f.; Forié and Nemo (2006), pp. 177 a.f. See also van Hove (1993), especially 86; Duyndam and Poorthuis (2003), 20.

[1060]About the impact of Judaïsm on Levinas' writings and teaching, see Goud (1992), p. 17.

[1061]See Sainte Thérèse (1957), p. 237, where a letter of Theresia van Lisieux to Mère Marie de Gonzague of June 1879 is printed; in this letter, the Saint explains her so-called "little way" (*"la petite voie – la grande épreuve intérieure"*).

See also Descouvemont and Nils Loose (1991), pp. 226 a.f.; De Meester (1997), pp. 147–154; De Wit and Steenvoorde (2008), p. 220.

[1062]Duyndam and Poorthuis (2003), p. 20.

knowing that in the face of the Other, the self can see its own reflection, making "the self" truly, and even in an infinite way, "responsible" for "the Other"[1063].

As a consequence, "the Other" becomes entitled to the complete compassion and empathy of "the self". Hence, "the self" will also not abandon the Other when in need, but will, necessarily, knowing that the own hunger is "selfish", but the hunger of the Other is "sacred", express the will to support, or, otherwise put: to express altruism, including mainly a "willingness to give". It is hereby stated that the responsibility of "the self" for "the Other", is, rather than "inviting", of an "imperative" nature.[1064]

On an economic level, this understanding translates into a decisive abandonment of any form of "egology" (such as the (neo-) Smithian principle of selfishness as a guide for socioeconomic action) and into a practical understanding that one exists "*through-and-for-the-other*". The latter should at the very least be accomplished, when meeting "the Other", through a simple statement like "*me voici*" ("here I am"), or by not arriving empty-handedly, but ideally, in much more developed methods of expressing this responsibility for the Other, such as expressing hospitality, performing a service for another or performing care.[1065]

In this approach, Levinas pleads for a way of life where the ethic dimension **305**
precedes politics and economy.[1066] As a result, there cannot be such thing as a "permanent" political economic model, albeit one needs to aspire for a continuous improvement of the existing social and economic mechanisms so that the abovementioned understanding can be put into reality[1067]. This is, for instance, expressed in the idea that "*justice is necessary, but it is ultimately motivated by the face of the Other*".[1068]

In a number of answers given during an interview, Levinas stated, in addition to **306**
some practical tips to reach the abovementioned objectives concretely, that one of the main societal problems is that people exist in a multitude. This means that as soon as three or more people need to live together a necessity of "*calculation*", or "*comparison*" and, hence, of "*politics*" will arise. Given the fact that whenever more than two people are concerned, it becomes difficult to find out which relation there is between "the self", "the Other" and the third person, "giving" (in terms of love) is in danger of being reduced to "political economy".[1069]

When furthermore politics are left to themselves, there is a risk that they become totalitarian as, for instance, has happened in Stalinism, as well as in Capitalism.

[1063]Levinas (1974), p. 10.

[1064]Duyndam and Poorthuis (2003), p. 21.

[1065]Van Hove (1993), pp. 75–91, especially 87; Duyndam and Poorthuis (2003), p. 22.

[1066]Goud (1992), p. 169.

[1067]Burggraeve (1995), pp. 11–16. See also Stanford Encyclopedia of Philosophy, under "*Emmanuel Levinas*" (to be consulted at http://plato.stanford.edu/index.html; last consulted on November 29th 2011).

[1068]Goud (1992), p. 169.

[1069]Goud (1992), p. 172. See also Duyndam and Poorthuis (2003), p. 27.

According to Levinas, the solution to this dilemma is that, albeit the self remains to be there only there for the Other, exactly because there are many "others", "the self" (necessarily) must succeed in limiting this original kindness and should obtain the wisdom and justice of love.[1070]

In economic relations, this leads to the idea that "the self" should "spare" the bread from his mouth for the benefit of the Other ("*se donner le pain de sa bouche*"), which is once again a metaphor aiming at making humanism concrete, over and over again, in daily life. In this way, the inevitable understanding will grow how one should behave in a just way and in accordance with Levinas' difficult requirements, with as remaining question how to avoid that "the self" takes someone else's place, which is a concrete reality in a world where many die of hunger, and where the self can hence be blamed that it is ultimately still existing and thus taking the place of "another". This finally leads to the realization that the philosopher knows where sanctity can be found, but that this knowing does not (necessarily) lead to sainthood (on) itself.[1071]

3.6.4.3 Several Further Voices Calling for More Justice on a Socioeconomic Level

307 During the past decades, also among economists and policymakers, a further awareness has been growing that capitalism as the socioeconomic system which has emerged from the way of thinking whereby the selfish pursuit of wealth and riches has been raised to a (or: the) central moral value, should either be halted, or at the very least corrected.

In this, a growing number of authors have explicitly or implicitly opposed neo-liberal thinking in as far as this has taken the opposite viewpoint that the free market—hence the capitalist model itself[1072]—should be even more enhanced.

As regards economists who at the very least have aimed at "softening" capitalism, reference can be made to renowned authors such as John Kenneth Galbraith, Paul Krugman, Jeffrey Sachs and Joseph Sitglitz, in addition to numerous others.

Within the Belgian context, reference should be made to the strong warnings clearly expressed by Jaap Kruithof already in 1985 (and almost in a visionary way), from which the following quotation speaks for itself[1073]:

> At the end of the twentieth century, effectiveness in the context of humanity is a necessity from which there is no retreat. The neo -liberal vision is apart from naive – the projected harmonious outcome is mere an illusion – also dangerous because social, ecological and military disasters without macro society planning have become inevitable. To leave the ultimate decision to the laws of demand and offer is irresponsible; the risks are too high for this. The free market will not solve the problems but will lift them to ominous heights. As a macro

[1070]Goud (1992), p. 173.

[1071]Goud (1992), p. 176.

[1072]Indeed Galbraith has pointed out that "the free market" is just another way of denominating capitalism itself. (See *e.g*. Galbraith 1994, p. 228.)

[1073]Kruithof (1985), p. 67. See furthermore Kruithof (2000), p. 17.

social legislation system this market is dysfunctional and irrational. It is a crime to release the arms race into unlimited competition and the same goes for the emergence of the large capital, environmental pollution, tensions between rich and poor – through the effects of the free market five hundred million people are in life danger – and the pillarization of the West.

More recent, in 2014, even the Belgian economist Paul De Grauwe, although previously having been known for defending (neo-)liberal thinking, reached a similar conclusion[1074]:

It will be extraordinary difficult to avoid future catastrophes. It may already be too late. (...) There is an extremely small chance that we can avoid the downturn by conducting a reformist policy (...). But even if this does not work, we have no other choice than to, as Sisyphus did, start over every day. it is the only way to bring meaning to our existence.

If we do not take action, our grandchildren will not forgive us for not putting any effort into saving them. That alone is enough motivation to keep going.

Among the numerous figures taking leading places in international organiza- 308
tions, one can for instance refer to a (relatively) recent interview of Francine Mestrum, in which she stated that the notion of "a free market" is a myth and that free markets cannot exist in a world of inequalities, because of (inter alia) the following simple reason:

If you allow someone who is really strong to compete with someone who is small and weak, the result is clear from the beginning.[1075]

With this saying, Mestrum has implicitly expressed the idea that the neo-liberal theory of "*voluntary association*" does not make any sense as long as people are not truly equal.

Even the world leading physicist Stephen Hawking has recently shared his insight that capitalism should stand corrected. During a so-called "*Reddit Ask Me Anything*" session of October 8th 2015, Hawking predicted that economic inequality will "skyrocket" as, due to the way the free market is evolving, more jobs become automated and, due to the inherent nature of the capitalist mechanisms, the rich owners of production units (i.e. the enterprises owning the automated machines) will even further refuse to share their fast-proliferating wealth.[1076]

To quote from Hawking's own words:

If machines produce everything we need, the outcome will depend on how things are distributed. Everyone can enjoy a life of luxurious leisure if the machine-produced wealth is shared, or most people can end up miserably poor if the machine-owners successfully lobby against wealth redistribution. So far, the trend seems to be toward the second option, with technology driving ever-increasing inequality.[1077]

[1074]De Grauwe (2014), p. 232.

[1075]Habets and Gloudemans (2013), pp. 37–48, containing an interview with Francine Mestrum.

[1076]See Kaufman (2015).

[1077]See https://www.reddit.com/r/science/comments/3nyn5i/science_ama_series_stephen_hawking_ama_answers/cvsdmkv (last consulted on October 9th 2015).

3.6.4.4 The Call for More Altruism by Certain International Institutions

309 Among the numerous examples of international and supranational organizations having called for a more just socioeconomic world order, reference can obviously be made to the already quoted study of Oxfam "*Even it up*"[1078]:

> The world needs concerted action to build a fairer economic and political system that values everyone. The rules and systems that have led to today's inequality explosion must change. Urgent action is needed to level the playing field by implementing policies that redistribute money and power from wealthy elites to the majority.

Also, in the Oxfam -study of the beginning of 2016[1079], it has been similarly held:

> Our world is not short of wealth. It simply makes no economic sense – or indeed moral sense – to have so much in the hands of so few. Oxfam believes that humanity can do better than this, that we have the talent, the technology and the imagination to build a much better world. We have the chance to build a more human economy, where the interests of the majority are put first. A world where there is decent work for all, where women and men are equal, where tax havens are something people read about in history books, and where the richest pay their fair share to support a society that benefits everyone.

Further reference can also be made to the already quoted from Catholic Church's "*Compendium of the Social Doctrine of the Church*" (2004), also calling for a just and fair financial regulatory framework:

> It is therefore indispensable to introduce a normative and regulatory framework that will protect the stability of the system in all its intricate expressions, foster competition among intermediaries and ensure the greatest transparency to the benefit of investors.[1080]

and

> The more the worldwide economic-financial system reaches high levels of organizational and functional complexity, all the more priority must be given to the task of regulating these processes, directing them towards the goal of attaining the common good of the human family. There is the clear need not just for States but for the international community to take on this delicate chore with adequate and effective political and juridical instruments.
>
> It is therefore indispensable that international economic and financial institutions should be able to identify the most appropriate institutional solutions and formulate the most suitable plans of action aimed at bringing about a change that, if it were to be passively accepted and simply left to itself, would otherwise produce a dramatic situation detrimental above all to the weakest and defenseless classes of the world's population.
>
> In international agencies it is necessary that the interests of the whole human family be equally represented. It is necessary moreover that "in evaluating the consequences of their decisions, these agencies always give sufficient consideration to peoples and countries which have little weight in the international market, but which are burdened by the most

[1078]Oxfam (2014), pp. 7–8.

[1079]See Oxfam (2016), p. 6.

[1080]Pontifical Council for Justice and Peace (2005), no 369.

acute and desperate needs, and are thus more dependent on support for their development".[1081]

Even so, in the world happiness report of 2016[1082], it has been held that:

One conclusion, therefore, is that human beings have strong tendencies toward altruism—even toward strangers or in large groups. Matthieu Ricard lists two essential components of altruism—valuing the other and being concerned about his or her situation.

This altruistic attitude manifests itself as benevolence toward others and a willingness to take care of them.

Altruism does not necessarily require sacrifice, although it frequently rises to heroic dimensions. Adam Smith summed up this innate tendency toward altruism well when he wrote that "how selfish so ever man may be supposed, there are evidently some principles in his nature, which interest him in the fortune of others, and render their happiness necessary to him, though he derives nothing from it except the pleasure of seeing it."

Even a conservative (and usually "pro-capitalist") institution as the IMF, has **310**
recently come to the understanding that the monetary-financial system which is one of the main motors of the capitalist economy, needs a thorough ethic re-sourcing. For instance, in a call to a colloquium of 12 October 2014 "*The Future of Finance*", it was said that[1083]:

economists and policymakers are increasingly coming to the view that economic concerns cannot be divorced from ethical concerns.

3.6.4.5 Conclusion

The understanding that all mankind, and by extension everything else that is alive, **311**
shares a common ancestry (and even a common set of genes), regardless of such understanding stems from a philosophical or religious-ethical doctrine, or from the conclusions from modern sciences[1084], should at the very least convince everyone[1085] that capitalism, mainly a system of shamelessly exploiting one' s fellow-man deemed weaker, of (less) value and/or incompetent, is intrinsically unjust and that, at the same time, the principle of unbridled selfishness (especially in socio-economic relations) should be abandoned in favor of a more radical altruist life tenure.

[1081]Pontifical Council for Justice and Peace (2005), no 371.

[1082]Sachs et al. (2016).

[1083]http://www.imf.org/external/POS_Meetings/SeminarDetails.aspx?SeminarId=13 (last consulted on 12 oktober 2014).

[1084]Whereby the side remark can be made that for instance the earlier quoted Dawkins himself has proven to be one of the greatest opponents of any form of religiosity. (See *e.g.* his books "*The God Delusion*" and "*The Blind Watchmaker*".)

[1085]In complete (true) humility and without seeing himself, as economic neo-liberalism holds, as a kind of extremely competent "super being" which, based on a law of nature (such as "*the survival of the fittest*" or the belief that one possesses superior genes) is allowed to exploit his (deemed) lesser fellow-man.

312 Unfortunately, this plea for more altruism in macro-economic (and through this also monetary and financial) relations has up till now hardly been heard, especially not among (most of) the rich and the powerful, among which policy makers themselves, who, at present more than ever, keep adhering to the capitalist principles.

313 With the approach further developed in (the Chaps. 4 and 5 of) this book, we will nevertheless resolutely advocate for a higher level of ethics within the world economic order.[1086]

3.7 Guidelines for a More Altruistic Monetary System (Based Upon the Insights Derived from the Chap. 2 and This Chapter of This Book)

314 The question by what impulses mankind should be led, is, in principle, an ideological choice and should hence not be dealt with as a fixed axiom (as the believers of the free market want us to believe).

315 The conclusion from this finding is that, contrary to what neo-Smithian thinking has been assuming for ages already, the impulse of (unbridled) selfishness[1087] does not necessarily need to be the only motivation behind human behavior, not even in regard to the socioeconomic domain.

On the contrary, as many behavioral sciences have demonstrated[1088], man can as well show a tendency to altruism.

In other words, the policy choice that has been made by (or since) Adam Smith and whereby, especially within the context of socioeconomic thinking and acting, one is mainly advocating a life tenure towards social and economic relations which is driven by the impulse of selfishness, it is only one of the possible choices. The determining life choice could as well be, even within the domain of the economy, in favor of a radical altruism.[1089]

316 This does obviously not preclude that the path of (economic) history, especially during the past ages, has mainly been drawn with the pen of an unbridled selfishness, which has resulted in the current society model and that it would be far from easy to re-orient it in the direction of an economy based on (more) altruist principles.

[1086] Compare Kruithof (2012), pp. 70–77, especially p. 74; Kruithof (1985), pp. 67–68.

[1087] See *e.g.* Rand (2008), p. 19.

[1088] See *e.g.* Hargreaves Heap (2009), pp. 416–425 especially p. 417 a.f. See furthermore Szalavitz (2012), pointing out that evidence for altruism as a critical part of human nature is presented by several scientific disciplines, among which anthropology, in addition to other disciplines studying human and/or social behavior.

[1089] Hoefnagels (1975), p. 19. See furthermore Sen (1977), pp. 317–344; Rodriguez-Sickert (2009), pp. 223–229; Hargreaves Heap (2009), pp. 416–425; Schmidtz (1995), pp. 98 a.f.

Anyone wishing to make a different choice than the one of the (neo-)Smithian egoism will, by definition, have to row against the current. Especially since the decline of (most of) the communist empires, this has become an extremely difficult task as since then economic neo-liberalism has upheld that there are no alternatives for the free market(s).

The latter does however not mean that taking another road should be deemed **317**
completely impossible and it is at the very least conceptually possible to perform a test of reflection on what, for instance, to start at the basis of the capitalist system, a monetary and financial order based on (more) altruistic goals and principles could look like.

As has been mentioned before, the following Chaps. 4 and 5 of this book contain **318**
such an attempt of exploring how a more altruistic monetary (and financial) system *could* look like.

In this, the main objective will be to indicate how a monetary (and financial) system could look like, which no longer would be based upon the most important mechanisms of neo-Smithian "mammonism", with all of their negative consequences, such as:

(i) the domination of private money creation, causing the supply of money within economy to be at the mercy of the goals and strategies of a limited number of private market players (and especially of the unbridled pursuit of profits and money driving them)—i.e. private banks—and which, during the past centuries, has repeatedly resulted in financial and economic crises mainly caused by greed, at the same time turning (the rest of) the economy—and by extension society as a whole—into its permanent hostage;
(ii) subsequently: the magnitude of the credit economy having resulted in an amount of credit impossible to "gain back" from economic activities (as a result of which economics have turned into a system driven by short-termism and utter nervousness);
(iii) the mechanisms of "pricing" newly created money, i.e. the interests which private banks charge when they grant a(ny new) credit, which inter alia leads to the fact that (*i*) the poor within society have to pay a (high) price for the access to new money, an effect which is (ultimately) to the benefit of a limited financial elite (i.e. the capital providers of banks), which moreover—as can be learned from centuries of historical reflection—has contributed to the fact that a limited number of people is getting richer all the time to the detriment of the rest of mankind (see above, under Sect. 3.4.8.2) and (*ii*) government budgets, world-wide have completely been depleted after decades, or even ages, of suffering from having to pay interests to private bankers;
(iv) the current fiscal (and parafiscal) systems, which mainly skim the income of the poor and the middle classes, and whereby the rich themselves remain practically untouched, resulting in society models where mainly the poor and the middle classes are forced to finance government spending and the rich remain largely undisturbed (a characteristic of capitalist state financing which,

obviously, has also contributed to the ever growing gap between the rich and the poor);

(v) the mechanism of debt financing for government needs, which has further underlined the aforementioned negative characteristics of capitalism.

319 A similar exercise of reflection can obviously not claim the last word in this debate[1090]; the social stakes are obviously too high for this.

Moreover, the exercise of reflection (undertaken in the Chaps. 4 and 5 of the current book) will essentially be limited to finding an answer to the question what a monetary and financial system which would be based on goals and principles of altruism could look like.

Any such attempt obviously needs to be undertaken in a full understanding that a re-orientation of the economy in the direction of more altruism will also imply an approach in different other domains of socioeconomic life, and more in general, as regards the societal order itself, and for instance will also induce reflection on questions such as[1091]:

- Continuous attention to reducing poverty in several (socioeconomic, but also other societal) relations[1092];
- An approach to tackle the problems of the environment and the climate[1093];
- A new approach on energy policy;
- A new approach on natural resources policy;
- A new approach on social relations (for instance: a global salary and minimum wages policy, the establishment of a global equal system of social care);
- The problem of migration[1094];
- A policy of price setting (at least of essential products);
- Dealing with the issue whether or not essentially "*unaltruistic*" expenses, such as defense and weaponry expenses, should be maintained and how they should be financed;
- The question of global peace and (international) security (with policy issues such as war, weaponry and terrorism);
- . . .

320 As has the warning of organizations such as the "Club of Rome" for decades now: the problems with which mankind is currently faced are extremely large and will continue to increase as long as they are not fundamentally tackled, but also the

[1090]See already Carrel (1950), XI:

> Aucun homme moderne n'a assez d'intelligence et de courage pour attaquer les grands problèmes de la civilisation.

[1091]See also Goldin (2014), pp. 212–238; Compare Stiglitz (2008), pp. 309–323, especially pp. 318 a.f.

[1092]Oxfam (2014), p. 9.

[1093]Compare Galbraith (1996), pp. 82 a.f.

[1094]Compare Galbraith (1996), p. 89.

matters at stake, such as the future of mankind and of the planet on which it lives, are as equally important.

It is with this (in addition to the considerations of the previous Chap. 2 and this chapter of this book) in mind, that said attempt of reflecting how a more altruistically based monetary (and financial) system could look like is undertaken in the further Chaps. 4 and 5 of this book.

References

Achterhuis H (1988) Het rijk van de schaarste. Van Thomas Hobbes tot Michel Foucault. Ambo, Amsterdam

Achterhuis H (2011) De utopie van de vrije markt. Lemniscaat, Rotterdam

Adams Beck L (s.d.) Wijsheid uit het Oosten. Een overzicht van de Oosterse wijsbegeerte (trans: Limburg R). Servire, Den Haag

Alexeev M, Janeba E, Osborne S (2004) Taxation and evasion in the presence of extortion by organized crime. J Comp Econ 32(3)

Altomonte A, Bussoli P (2014) Asset-backed securities: the key to unlocking Europe's credit markets? http://www.bruegel.org/publications/publication-detail/publication/842-asset-backed-securities-the-key-to-unlocking-europes-credit-markets/. Last consulted 17 Dec 2014

Amesz B (2012) Aan de knoppen van het klimaat – Het hele verhaal over de opwarming van de aarde. Fontaine Uitgevers BV, Hilversum

Anderson S (2015a) Off the deep end: The Wall Street bonus pool and low-wage workers. http://www.ips-dc.org/deep-end-wall-street/. Last consulted 20 Mar 2015

Anderson S (2015b) Wall Street bonuses and the minimum wage. http://www.ips-dc.org/wall_street_bonuses_and_the_minimum_wage/. Last consulted 20 Mar 2015

Aristotle (1992) The politics (trans: Sinclair TA). Penguin Books, London. http://classics.mit.edu/Aristotle/politics.mb.txt. Last consulted 25 June 2015

Aristotle (1996) The Nicomachean ethics (trans: Rackham H). Wordsworth Classics of World Literature, Hertfordshire

Armstrong RJ, Brady IC (1982) Francis and Clare – the complete works. Paulist Press, New York

Ash TC (1999) Geschiedenis van het heden. Atlas, Amsterdam

Ashton T (1954) The standard of life of the workers in England, 1790–1830. In: Hayek F (ed) Capitalism and the historians. The University of Chicago Press, Chicago, pp 127–159

Auerbach M (2016) Ikea: Flat Pack Taks avoidance (a study commissioned by The Greens EFA in the European Parliament). http://www.greens-efa.eu/fileadmin/dam/Documents/TAXE_committee/Report_IKEA_tax_avoidance_Feb2016.pdf. Last consulted 18 Feb 2016

Baan M (2014) Bestemming komeet. New Scientist, November 2014

Backhouse S (2011) The compact guide to Christian history. Lion Hudson, Oxford

Baeck L (1972) Groei en onkruid in de welvaartstaat. De nederlandsche boekhandel, Antwerp

Baer D (2014) 21 insightful quotes from Bill Gates, who just turned 59. http://www.businessinsider.com/quotes-from-bill-gates-the-worlds-richest-man-2014-10. Last consulted 29 Oct 2014

Bahr AMB (2010) 2000 jaar Christendom – Geïllustreerde reisgids door 20 eeuwen Christelijk geloof. Kok, Kampen

Bahree M (2014) Who's to blame for the increasing gap between the rich and the poor? Market policies, says new report. http://www.forbes.com/sites/meghabahree/2014/11/05/whos-to-blame-for-the-increasing-gap-between-the-rich-and-the-poor-market-economy-says-new-report/. Last consulted 22 Jan 2016

Bahree M (2016) The world's richest 1% just got a lot richer, while everyone else didn't. http://www.forbes.com/sites/meghabahree/2016/01/19/the-worlds-richest-1-just-got-a-lot-richer-while-everyone-else-didnt/. Last consulted 22 Jan 2016
Bakan J (2005) The corporation. The pathological pursuit of profit and power. Constable & Robinson Ltd., London
Barrez D (2011) Laten we onszelf niets wijsmaken, Durban klimaatconferentie is mislukt.. http://www.dewereldmorgen.be/artikels/2011/12/12/laten-we-onszelf-niets-wijsmaken-durban-klimaatconferentie-mislukt
Barry M (s.d.) http://www.maxbarry.com/jennifergovernment/
Bauwens D (2016) Niet of maar wanneer krijgen we een nieuwe Europese bankencrisis? http://www.msn.com/nl-be/financien/nieuws/niet-of-maar-wanneer-krijgen-we-een-nieuwe-europese-bankencrisis/ar-BBr6W9h?ocid=spartandhp. Last consulted 31 Mar 2016
Beaud M (1994) Geschiedenis van het kapitalisme van 1500 tot heden. Utrecht, Het Spectrum (Aula)
Beaumont M (2010) The one-stop guide to Jesus. A Lion Book an Imprint of Lion Hudson plc, Oxford
Becker G (1971) The economics of discrimination. University of Chicago Press, Chicago
Becket S (2014) Empire of cotton. A global history. Vintage Books, New York
Belfort J (2013a) The wolf of Wall Street. Hodder & Stoughton General Division, London
Belfort J (2013b) Catching the wolf of Wall Street. Hodder & Stoughton General Division, London
Bell D (1996) The cultural contradictions of capitalism. Basic Books, New York
Berend I (2006) An economic history of twentieth-century Europe. Cambridge University Press, Cambridge
Bernstein WJ (2004) The birth of plenty. How the prosperity of the modern world was created. McGraw-Hill, New York
Beuchot M (1830) Oeuvres de Voltaire, tXXXIX – Mélanges tome III. Chez Lefèvre Librairie, Paris
Bhaktivedanta Swami Prabhupada AC (1983) Bhagavad-Gita as it is. The Bhaktivedanta Book Trust International Inc., Lanarkshire
Bieler A (1961) La pensée économique et sociale de Calvin. Librairie de l'Université, Genève
Bijlo E (2014) Nobelprijswinnaar Joseph Stiglitz: 'Europese landen moeten belastingen gelijktrekken'. Knack, 19 November 2014
Blommaert J (2014) Gratis bestaat niet? Oh jawel. http://jmeblommaert.wordpress.com/2014/11/19/gratis-bestaat-niet-oh-jawel/. Last consulted 24 Nov 2014
Blomme P, D'Hoore J (2014) Bonden leggen bal in kamp regering. De Tijd, 16 December 2014
Bogaert R, Kurgan-van Hentenryk G, Van Der Wee H (2000) History of European Banking. Mercatorfonds and European Investment Bank, Antwerp (also: Bogaert R, Kurgan-van Hentenryk G, and Van Der Wee H (1991) La banque en Occident. Mercatorfonds. Antwerp; Bogaert R, Brion R, Kuran-van Hentenryk G, Moreau LJ, Van der Wee H (1991) De Bank in Europa. 25 eeuwen Bankgeschiedenis. Mercatorfonds, Antwerp)
Bonger WA (1916) Criminality and economic conditions (trans: Horton HP). Little, Brown, and Company, Boston
Bonner W, Wiggin A (2006) Empire of debt – the rise of an epic financial crisis. Wiley, New Jersey
Bouckaert L (ed) (1994) Interest en cultuur. Een ethiek van het geld. Acco, Leuven
Bové L (2014a) Geheime Luxemburgse belastingdeals kosten België miljarden euro's. De Tijd, 5 November 2014
Bové L (2014b) BeLastingschandaal rond Luxemburg bereikt climax. De Tijd, 10 December 2014
Bové L (2014c) LuxLeaks-klokkenluider spreekt. De Tijd, 16 December 2014
Bové L (2014d) Nieuw datalek zet Luxemburg helemaal in zijn blootje. De Tijd, 10 December 2014
Bower S (2009) Saints. Lion Hudson, Oxford
Brand P (1966) De nieuwe katechismus. Paul Brand, Hilversum

Brockmans H (2014) Vermogenswinstbelasting treft vooral middenklasse. Trends, 27 November 2014
Brook Y, Watkins D (2012) Free market revolution – how Ayn Rand's ideas can end big government. Palgrave Macmillan, New York
Browne J (2008) Over het ontstaan van soorten van Darwin. Een biografie (trans: Ruitenberg J). Mets & Schilt, Amsterdam
Bruckner P (2002) Misère de la prospérité – la religion marchande et ses ennemis. Bernard Grasset, Paris
Bruckner P (2016) La Sagesse de l'Argent. Bernard Grasset, Paris
Brugmans H (1942) De Middeleeuwen. Wereldbibliotheek, Amsterdam
Buddha. (s.d.) The Dhammapada (trans: Beck S). http://www.sapphyr.net/buddhist/buddhist-dhammapada.htm. Last consulted 15 Sept 2015
Burggraeve R (1995) The ethical meaning of money in the thought of Emmanuel Levinas. Ethical Perspectives
Burns T (2012) The shadow banking system as a new source of financial turmoil. In: Alexander K, Dhumale R (eds) Research handbook on international financial regulation. Edward Elgar, Cheltenham, pp 30–41
Buxant M (2014) We worden afgeschilderd als crapuul. De Tijd, 19 November 2014
Byttebier K (1995) Anatocisme. T.Not
Byttebier K (2005) Voorrechten and hypotheken in hoofdlijnen, 2nd edn. Maklu, Antwerp
Byttebier K (2015) De onvrije markt. Garant, Antwerp
Byttebier K, Flamée M (2012) Het vraagstuk van ethisch financieren toegepast op de interestheffing mede vanuit een elementair rechtshistorisch perspectief. Stof voor een morele uitweg uit een wereld in (financiële) crisis? In: De Ruysscher D, De Hert P, De Metsenaere M (eds) Een leven van inzet. Liber amicorum Michel Magits, Kluwer, Mechelen
Byttebier K, Verroken A (1995) Structuring international co-operation between enterprises. Graham & Trotman/Martinus Nijhoff, London
Byttebier K, Verroken A (1997) De bi-nationale, horizontale groep Gemeentekrediet – Crédit local de France (Deel I). In: V&F; De bi-nationale, horizontale groep Gemeentekrediet – Crédit local de France (Deel II). In: V&F
Campbell C (2016) Donald Trump says Belgium's capital is 'like living in a hellhole'. http://uk.businessinsider.com/donald-trump-brussels-muslim-ban-hellhole-2016-1?r=US&IR=T. Last consulted 29 Feb 2016
Capek K (1995) Talks with T.G. Masaryk. (trans: Heim MH). Catbird Press, North Haven
Carleer D, Ramboer R (2014) De teloorgang van Dexia (2): "Hoe maak ik financiële springstof?". http://archive.ptb.be/nieuws/artikel/article/de-teloorgang-van-dexia-2-hoe-maak-ik-financiele-springstof.html. Last consulted 11 Dec 2014
Carrel A (1950) Réflexions sur la conduit de la vie. Librairie Plon Paris
Casanova P (2011) Kafka and colère. Seuil, Paris
Catechismus van de Katholieke kerk (2008) Gooi & Stict, Utrecht (Dutch version)
CDC (2016) Trump: "Brussels? It's like living in a hell hole!" http://deredactie.be/cm/vrtnieuws.english/News/1.2557064. Last consulted 29 Feb 2016
Centrale voor kredieten aan particulieren (NBB) (2013) Statistieken 2013. Nationale Bank van België, Brussels
Chadwick O (1995) A history of Christianity. Weidenfeld and Nicolson, London
Chevalier J.P. (2016) Leverage des big banks: USA / Europe (4° trimestre 2015). http://chevallier.biz/2016/02/leverage-des-big-banks-usa-europe-4%C2%B0-trimestre-2015/
Chomsky N (1999) Profit over people. Neoliberalism and global order. Seven Stories Press, New York
Claerhout P (2014a) Banken verhogen kredietmarges op hypotheken – Lage rente, hoge marge. In: Trends August 28th 2014
Claerhout P (2014b) De terugkeer van de massavernietigingswapens. In: Trends September18th 2014

Claerhout P (2014c) Dexia is te belangrijk voor electorale spelletjes. http://trends.knack.be/economie/dexia-is-te-belangrijk-voor-electorale-spelletjes/article-opinion-222271.html. Last consulted 11 Dec 2014
Cliteur P (2007) Moreel Esperanto. De Arbeiderspers, Amsterdam
Clune MW (2013) On masters of the universe: Hayek, Friedman, and the birth of neo-liberal politics (26 February 2013). http://lareviewofbooks.org/review/what-was-neo-liberalism#. Last consulted 27 Oct 2014
Coase R (1937) The nature of the firm. Economica 4(16)
Coffey B (2012) The four companies that control the 147 companies that own everything. http://www.forbes.com/sites/brendancoffey/2011/10/26/the-four-companies-that-control-the-147-companies-that-own-everything/. Last consulted 25 Nov 2014
Cohen BJ (2008a) The Euro in a global context: challenges and capacities. In: Dyson K (ed) The Euro at 10 – Europeanization, power, and convergence. Oxford University Press, Oxford
Cohen D (2008b) Towards a new modus operandi of the international financial system. In: Serra N, Stiglitz JE (eds) The Washington consensus reconsidered. Oxford University Press, Oxford
Comte-Sponville A (1996) Impromptus PUF, Paris (Vol. "Argent"
Conference of the Parties (2010) Report of the conference of the parties on its sixteenth session, held in Cancun from 29 November to December 10th 2010. http://unfccc.int/resource/docs/2010/cop16/eng/07a01.pdf#page=2
Credit Suisse Research Institute (2015) Global Wealth Databook 2015. http://publications.credit-suisse.com/tasks/render/file/index.cfm?fileid=C26E3824-E868-56E0-CCA04D4BB9B9ADD5. Last consulted 14 Oct 2015
Crockett A (1981) Money. Theory, policy and institutions. Nelson House, Walton-on-Thames, Surrey
Crosse G (1932) Charles Gore: a biographical sketch. Morehouse, Milwaukee. Re-published in Project Canterbury. http://anglicanhistory.org/gore/crosse.html. Last consulted 16 Dec 2014
Cullen D (2009) Columbine. Old Street Publishing Ltd, London
D'Hoore JD (2014) Top sociale zekerheid luid alarmklok over besparingen. De Tijd, 18 December 2014
Dawkins R (2005) The ancestor's tale. A pilgrimage to the dawn of life. Orion House London
Dawkins R (2006) The selfish gene. Oxford University Press (30th anniversary edition), Oxford
Dawkins R (2011) The magic of reality. Transworld Publishers Ltd, London (also: Dawkins R (2012) De betoverende werkelijkheid. Nieuw Amsterdam Uitgevers, Amsterdam)
De Boeck E (2014) Begrotingsbesparingen in België, Frankrijk, Nederland and Eurozone. Hoeveel al gerealiseerd, hoeveel moet nog volgen. Trends, 20 November 2014
De Boni M (2015) Terrorisme: pour Macron, la société française a une part de responsabilité. http://www.lefigaro.fr/politique/le-scan/couacs/2015/11/23/25005-20151123ARTFIG00069-terrorisme-pour-macron-la-societe-francaise-a-une-part-de-responsabilite.php. Last consulted 13 Jan 2016
De Grauwe P (2014) De limieten van de markt. De slinger tussen overheid en kapitalisme. Lannoo, Tielt
de Jouvenel B (1954) Treatment of capitalism by intellectuals. In: Hayek F (ed) Capitalism and the historians. The University of Chicago Press, Chicago
De Ley H (2008) Phusis & Polis: Aristoteles' praktische filosofie at http://www.cie.ugent.be/aristoteles/4productiewijze.htm#4.3
De Lorenzo G (1949) Het oude Boeddhisme. Wereldbibliotheek N.V, Amsterdam
De Lubac H (1943) Le Drame de l'humanisme athée. Unions Générales d'Éditions, Paris
De Meester K (1997) Op zoek naar de kleine weg. In: Thérèse van Lisieux – Leven. Leer. Milieu. Carmelitana, Ghent, pp 147–154
de Roose F (1989) Ecologisch humanisme. Dwarsdenken omtrent Jaap Kruithof. Berchem, Epo
De Ruysscher D (2011) Westers recht in ontwikkeling: privaat- and publiekrecht van Rome tot vandaag. Kluwer, Mechelen

De Stoop C (2012) Paul Verhaeghe. De neo-liberale waanzin treft ons allemaal. Knack, 22 August 2012
De Wit P (2014) Dossier. Fusie zakenbank Kempen and Dexia-dochter Labouchere in recordtijd mislukt. http://www.standaard.be/cnt/dst06122002_089. Last consulted 11 Dec 2014
De Wit A, Steenvoorde R (eds) (2008) Christendom. Lannoo, Tielt
Debruyne B, Claerhout P (2014) Bij succes komt een grote dosis geluk kijken. Trends, 18 September 2014
Del Marmol C (1943) La répression de l'usure. Imprimerie Groeninghe, Kortrijk
Delfgaauw B (1960) Beknopte geschiedenis der wijsbegeerte – II. De moderne wijsbegeerte. Het Wereldvenster, Baarn
Descartes (1948) Discours de la méthode – Les passions de l'âme. Bader-Dufour, Paris
Descouvemont P, Nils Loose H (1991) Thérèse et Lisieux. Éditions du Cerf
Dévoluy M, Lang D, Mathieu C, Mazier J, Sterdyniak H (2011) La politique économique and Europe. In: Les Économistes atterés, Changer d'économie! Nos propositions pour 2012. Les liens qui libèrent, Paris
Deweirdt E, Van Poeck A, Annaert J (1997) Monetaire theorie en politiek. Garant, Leuven and Apeldoorn
Dolan K, Kroll L (2014) Inside the 2014 Forbes billionaires list: facts and figures. http://www.forbes.com/sites/luisakroll/2014/03/03/inside-the-2014-forbes-billionaires-list-facts-and-figures/. Last consulted 30 Oct 2014
Donner S (2015) Why we need the next-to-impossible 1.5° C temperature target. http://www.theguardian.com/environment/climate-consensus-97-per-cent/2015/dec/30/why-we-need-the-next-to-impossible-15c-temperature-target. Last consulted 28 Jan 2016
Dowley T (2009) Christenen door de eeuwen heen. Ark Media, Amsterdam
Downley T (1979) Handboek van de geschiedenis van het Christendom. J.N. voorhoeve, Den Haag
Drucker J (2014) Malone gained double tax break in liberty address shift. http://mobile.bloomberg.com/news/2014-11-03/malone-gained-double-tax-break-in-liberty-address-shift.html?hootPostID=a2c6dff9021e3fc768d87efd9ff7ef8c. Last consulted 3 Nov 2014
Dunkerley R (1962) Le Christ. Éditions Gallimard, Middlesex
Duquesne J (1994) Jésus. Éditions Flammarion
Durant W (1949) Van Socrates tot Bergson. L.J.C, Boucher, Den Haag
Duyndam J, Poorthuis M (2003) Levinas. Kopstukken filosofie. Lemniscaat, Rotterdam
Eagleton C, Williams J (2007) Money – a history. The Bristish Museum Press, London
Elliott (1902) Usury, a scriptural, ethical and economic view. The Anti-Usury League, Millersburg
Elliott L (2016) IMF warns of fresh financial crisis – urgent action to sort out Eurozone banks called for in financial stability report warning market turmoil may recur, article of April 13th 2016. http://www.theguardian.com/business/2016/apr/13/imf-warns-fresh-financial-crisis-global-stability-report-eurozone-banks. Last consulted 14 Apr 2016
Engelen E (a.o.) (2011) After the great complacence. Oxford University Press, Oxford
Englebert O (1998) La vie de Saint François d'Assise. Albin Michel, Paris
Epstein M (2007) Vol verlangen. De spirituele kracht van begeerte, hartstocht and intimiteit. Asoka, Rotterdam
European Banking Authority (EBA) (2016) EBA-report: benchmarking of remuneration practices at the European Union level and data on high earners (data as of end 2014). March 30th 2016. http://www.eba.europa.eu/documents/10180/1359456/EBA+Op-2016-05++%28Report+on+Benchmarking+of+Remuneration+and+High+Earners+2014%29.pdf. Last consulted 31 Mar 2016
Evans G (2007) The church in the early Middle Ages. I.B. Tauris, London
Evers L (1999) Jodendom voor beginners. Een heldere inleiding. Forum – De Boekerij BV, Amsterdam
Eyskens M (1976) Bouwstenen van de gemengde economie (2 delen). Standaard Wetenschappelijke Uitgeverij, Antwerp

Falzani D (2014) What makes an entrepreneur – luck or skill? http://www.ft.com/cms/s/2/dcef8160-5dcc-11e4-b7a2 00144feabdc0.html#axzz3Ifv1QDDo. Last consulted 10 Nov 2014
Fase M, Vleminckx A (1995) Geld in veelvoud. Inleiding monetaire economie. Uitgeverij Lemma BV, Utrecht
Feeding America (2014) Hunger in America 2014 (national report). Feeding America, Chicago
Ferguson N (1998) The house of Rothschild. Penguin Books, New York
Ferguson N (2009) The ascent of money. A financial history of the world. Penguin Books, London
Food and Agriculture Organization of the United Nations (FAO) (2014) The State of Food and Agriculture – innovation in family farming FAO, Rome
Ford M (2010–2011) Ayn Rand and the VIP-DIPers. http://www.huffingtonpost.com/michael-ford/ayn-rand-and-the-vip-dipe_b_792184.html
Forié F, Nemo P (2006) 11 gesprekken – Emmanuel Levinas aan het woord. Ten Have, Kampen
Foucault M (2003) Society must be defended (trans: D. Macey). Allen Lane (an imprint of Penguin Books), London
Foucault M (2008) The birth of biopolitics – Lectures at the Collège de France 1978–1979 (trans: Burchell G). Palgrave Macmillan, New York (also: Foucault M (2013) De geboorte van de biopolitiek. Boom, Amsterdam)
Foucault M (2013) De geboorte van de biopolitiek. Boom, Amsterdam
Fox J (2013) The myth of the rational market. Harriman House Ltd., Hampshire
Francis (2013) Letter Of Holy Father Francis To H.E. Mr David Cameron, British Prime Minister On The Occasion Of The G8 Meeting (June 17–18th 2013). http://M.Vatican.Va/Content/Francescomobile/En/Letters/2013/Documents/Papa-Francesco_20130615_Lettera-Cameron-G8.html. Last consulted 29 Sept 2014
Francis (2014) De Kerk van Barmhartigheid. Prometheus – Bert Bakker, Amsterdam
Francis (2015) Laudato si', Encyclical letter of the Holy Father Francis on care for our common home. http://w2.vatican.va/content/francesco/en/encyclicals/documents/papa-francesco_20150524_enciclica-laudato-si.html. Last consulted 8 Oct 2015
Freeman GP, Bisschops H, Corveleyn B, Hoeberichts J, Jansen A (2004) Franciscus van Assisi – De geschriften. Franciscaanse Beweging and Uitgeverij J.H. Gottmer/H.J.W. Brecht BV, Haarlem
Friedman M (1993) Why government is the problem. Hoover Institution on War, Revolution and Peace, Stanford University
Friedman M (ed) (2002) Capitalism and freedom. The University of Chicago Press, Chicago
Friedman M, Schwartz A (1963) A monetary history of the United States 1867–1960. Princeton University Press, Princeton
Fritz-Krockow B, Ramlogan P (eds) (2007) International monetary fund handbook. Its functions, policies and operations. International Monetary Fund
Fromm E (1955) The sane society. A Fawcett Premier Book, Greenwich
Fromm E (1990) Die Furcht vor der Freiheit. Deutscher Taschenbuch Verlag, München (also: Fromm E (s.d.) Escape from Freedom. Open Road, Integrated Media, New York)
Fromm E (2013) Marx's concept of man. Bloomsbury, London
Fujii M, Kwai M (2012) Lessons from Japan's banking crisis – 1991 to 2005. In: Alexander K, Dhumale R (eds) Research handbook on international financial regulation. Edward Elgar, Cheltenham
Fülöp-Miller R (1991) The Saints that moved the world. Ayer Company, Publishers, Inc., New Hampshire
Galbraith JK (1960) The liberal hour. The Riverside Press, Cambridge
Galbraith JK (1967) The new industrial state. Houghton Mifflin Company, Boston
Galbraith JK (1970) American capitalism. Penguin Books, Middlesex, England (first edition of 1952)
Galbraith JK (1974) The affluent Society. Penguin Books, Middlesex (first edition of 1958)
Galbraith JK (1975) Money. Whence it came, where it went. Boston, Houghton Mifflin Company
Galbraith JK (1977) The age of uncertainty. Houghton Mifflin Company, Boston

Galbraith JK (1983) The anatomy of power. Houghton Mifflin Company, Boston
Galbraith JK (1987) Economics in perspective – a critical history. Houghton Mifflin Company, Boston
Galbraith JK (1990) A short history of financial euphoria. Whittle Books in association with Penguin Books, New York
Galbraith JK (1992) The culture of contentment. Houghton Mifflin Company, Boston
Galbraith JK (1994) A journey through economic time – a firsthand view. Houghton Mifflin Company, Boston
Galbraith JK (1996) The good society – the Humane agenda. Houghton Mifflin Company, Boston
Galbraith JK (2012) American capitalism. The concept of countervailing power. Martino Publishing, Mansfield Centre CT
Geysels J (2014) De Schande. In: Geysels J, Vlaminck E (eds) De Schande en de Keerzijde. Van Halewyck, Leuven, pp 11–59
Gide C, Rist C (1947) Histoire des doctrines économiques tI. Recueil Sirey, Paris
Gimpel J (1976) The Medieval machine – the industrial revolution of the Middle Ages. Holt, New York
Goenka H (2016) Donald Trump's policies will worsen climate change, China holds steady on commitments. http://www.ibtimes.com/donald-trumps-policies-will-worsen-climate-change-china-holds-steady-commitments-2449688. Last consulted 22 Nov 2016
Goguel M (1950) Jésus. Payot, Paris
Goldenberg S (2016) Doomsday Clock stuck near midnight due to climate change and nuclear war. http://www.theguardian.com/environment/2016/jan/26/doomsday-clock-three-minutes-to-midnight-climate-change-nuclear-war. Last consulted 28 Jan 2016
Goldin I (ed) (2014) Is the planet full? Oxford University Press, Oxford
Gore C (1920) Christianity applied to the life of men and of nations. The Lindsey Press, London. http://anglicanhistory.org/gore/christianity1920.html. Last consulted 16 Dec 2014
Gore A (2013a) Onze toekomst. Spectrum, Antwerp
Gore A (2013b) The future – six drivers of global change. Random House, New York
Gorissen W (2014) Ronaldo wil weeksalaris van 630.000 euro bij United. http://m.hln.be/hln/m/nl/950/Buitenlands-Voetbal/article/detail/2050060/2014/09/14/Ronaldo-wil-weeksalaris-van-630-000-euro-bij-United.dhtml?originatingNavigationItemId=1. Last consulted 16 Sept 2014
Goud J (1992) God als raadsel. Peilingen in het spoor van Levinas. Kok Agora, Kampen
Graeber D (2012) Debt. The first 5000 years. Brooklyn and London
Graff M, Kenwood A, Lougheed A (2014) Growth of the international economy 1820–2015. Routledge, London
Greenspan A (2008) The age of turbulence. Penguin Books, London
Groenink E, Holtwijk I, Van Straaten F (1998) Slotenmakers en gangstermeisjes – Kinderarbeid wereldwijd. Uitgeverij Jan Mets, Amsterdam
Guess S (2003) General introduction. In: Keynes JM (ed) The general theory of employment, interest and money. http://gutenberg.net.au/ebooks03/0300071h/printall.html
Gumpert A, Hines JR, Schnitzer M (2011) The use of tax havens in exemption regimes. Deutsche Bundesbank. Economic Research Group, Frankfurt am Main
Habets J, Gloudemans H (2013) De voedselparadox. Over grootschalige honger in een wereld die (meer dan) genoeg voedsel produceert. Stichting Werelddelen, Tilburg
Haeck B (2014a Ook begrotingsalarm in Frankrijk and Italië. De Tijd, 29 November 2014
Haeck B (2014b) EU vraagt alle taxrulings van voorbije drie jaar op. De Tijd, 18 December 2014
Haeck B (2014c) De spotlights schijnen breder. De Tijd, 18 December 2014
Haeck B (2014d) Ongelijkheid kost België een tiende groei. De Tijd, 9 December 2014
Hallerberg M, Bridwell J (2008) Fiscal policy coordination and discipline: the stability and growth pact and domestic fiscal regimes. In: Dyson K (ed) The Euro at 10 – Europeanization, power, and convergence. Oxford University Press, Oxford
Harari YN (2014) Sapiens – a brief history of humankind. Penguin Random House UK, London

Hardick L (1989) He came to you so that you might come to him. Franciscan Herald Press, Chicago

Hargreaves Heap S (2009) Rationality. In: Peil J, Van Staveren I (eds) Handbook of economics and ethics. Edward Elgar, Cheltenham

Hartline K (2008) How celebrities go bankrupt. http://www.legalzoom.com/money-matters/bankruptcy/how-celebrities-go-bankrupt

Hartwell A (2014) Sourcing mineral resources – problems and solutions. In: Goldin I (ed) Is the planet full? Oxford University Press, Oxford

Harvey D (2010) The enigma of capital and the crises of capitalism. Profile Books, London

Havelaar M (1981) Max Havelaar. Amstelpaperback, Uitgeverij L.J. Veen B.V., Utrecht and Antwerp

Hayek F (2001) The road to selfdom. Routledge, London (first edition of 1944)

Hazenberg J (2013) De machteloze staat. Hoe globalisering en individualisering de overheid uithollen. De Geus, Breda

Heck GW (2006) Charlemagne, Muhammad, and the Arab Roots of Capitalism. Walter de Gruyter, Berlin

Hickson K (2005) The IMF crisis of 1976 and British politics in International Library of Political Studies 3.Tauris Academic Studies, London

Hirschberg E (1976) The impact of inflation and devaluation on private legal obligations – legal aspects of contemporary monetary problems. Bar-Ilan University, Ramat-Gan

Hoefnagels H, a.o. (1975) de toekomst staat op het spel. Kapellen, De Nederlandsche boekhandel

Hoet H (2008) De weg van Paulus. Lannoo, Tielt

Hollenberg A (1942) De corporatieve organisatie der maatschappij. Standaard Boekhandel, Antwerp

Holloway K (2015) 10 careers with the most psychopaths per capita.. http://www.salon.com/2015/06/23/10_careers_with_the_most_psychopaths_per_capita_partner/

Hutt W (1954) The factory system of the early nineteenth century. In: Hayek F (ed) Capitalism and the historians. The University of Chicago Press, Chicago

Ingham G (1984) Capitalism divided? The city and industry in British social development. McMillan Education Ltd., London

International Monetary Fund (2016) Global financial stability report – potent policies for a successful normalization. International Monetary Fund, April 2016

Isbouts JP (2012) In the footsteps of Jesus. A chronicle of his life and the origins of Christianity. National Geographic, Washington DC

Jacobs EM (1996) De grootste multinational van de zeventiende eeuw. In: Dreschsel W (ed) Varen naar de Oost, Elmar, Rijswijk

Jadlow JM (s.d.) Adam Smith on usury laws. J Fin 32(4)

James H (ed) (1996) International monetary cooperation since Bretton Woods, Washington D.-C. International Monetary Fund, Oxford University Press, New York and Oxford

Jansen H (1988) Geschiedenis van de middeleeuwen. Het Spectrum B.V, Utrecht

Jarmak C (2013) If you seek miracles. Reflections of Saint Anthony of Padua. Edizioni Messaggero Padova, Padova

John XIII (1963) Pacem in Terris. http://w2.vatican.va/content/john-xxiii/en/encyclicals/documents/hf_j-xxiii_enc_11041963_pacem.html

John Paul II (1981) Laborem exercens. http://www.vatican.va/holy_father/john_paul_ii/encyclicals/documents/hf_jp-ii_enc_14091981_laborem-exercens_en.html

John Paul II (1991) Encyclical letter: Centesimus annus

John Paul II (2005) Memory & identity. Personal reflections. Hachette, UK

Johnson I (2014) Towards a contemporary understanding of the limits to growth. In: Goldin I (ed) Is the planet full? Oxford University Press, Oxford

Jones S (2011) De wereld van de vroege Kerk. Boekencentrum, Zoetermeer

Juncker CJ (2016) Completing Europe's Economic and Monetary Union. http://ec.europa.eu/priorities/sites/beta-political/files/5-presidents-report_en.pdf. Last consulted 18 Feb 2016

Karmel RS (2010) The controversy over systemic risk regulation. Brooklyn J Int Law 35(3)
Kasser T (2002) The high price of materialism. A Bradford Book and The MIT Press, Cambridge and London
Kaufman AC (2015) Stephen Hawking says we should really be scared of capitalism, not robots. http://www.huffingtonpost.com/entry/stephen-hawking-capitalism-robots_5616c20ce4b0dbb8000d9f15. Last consulted 9 Oct 2015
Kennedy M (1995) Interest and inflation free money: creating an exchange medium that works for everybody and protects the earth. New Society Publishers, Gabriola Island
Keynes JM (1935) The general theory of employment, interest and money
Kintaert T (2014) De duurste cocktail ter wereld: 11.500 euro per glas. http://m.hln.be/hln/m/nl/39/Lekker-Eten/article/detail/2069101/2014/09/28/De-duurste-cocktail-ter-wereld-11-500-euro-per-glas.dhtml?originatingNavigationItemId=1. Last consulted 29 Sept 2014
Klebold S (2016) A mother's reckoning: living in the aftermath of the Columbine tragedy. WH Allen
Klok P, van Uffelen X (2009) Bonus! Waarom bankiers de grote winnaars zijn van deze crisis. J.M. Meulenhoff B.V, Amsterdam
Knowles MD (1967) Geschiedenis van de kerk. Deel IV. De kerk in de Middeleeuwen, tII. Uitgeverij Paul Brad, Hilversum
Koorevaar H, Marlowe C (2013) De zonde: oorsprong en verwoesting, genezing en overwinning. In: Koorevaar H, Paul M (eds) Theologie van het Oude Testament – De blijvende boodschap van de Hebreeuwse Bijbel. Boekencentrum, Zoetermeer
Kornfield J (1995) De leringen van Boeddha. Altamira, Heemstede
Korteweg S (1970) Het moderne geldwezen. B.V. Noord-Hollandsche Uitgeversmaatschappij, Amsterdam
Kotz DM, McDonough T (2010) Global neoliberalism and the contemporary social structure of accumulation. In: McDonough T, Reich M, Kotz DM (eds) Contemporary capitalism and its crises. Cambridge University Press, Cambridge
Kovtun G (2009) Masaryk and America, testimony of a relationship. http://lcweb2.loc.gov/service/gdc/scd0001/2009/20090709004ma/20090709004ma.pdf
Krugman P (1992) The age of diminished expectations. U.S. Economic Policy in the 1990s. The MIT Press, Cambridge
Krugman P (1994) Peddling prosperity. W.W. Norton & Company, New York
Krugman P (1998) The accidental theorist and other dispatches from the dismal science. W.W. Norton & Company, New York
Krugman P (2008) The conscience of a liberal: reclaiming America from the right. Allen Lane, London
Krugman P (2009) The return of depression economics and the crisis of 2008. W.W. Norton & Company, New York
Krugman P (2012) End this depression now! W.W. Norton & Company, New York
Kruithof J (1985) De mens aan de grens. Over religiositeit, godsdienst en antropocentrisme. EPO, Antwerp
Kruithof J (2000) Het neoliberalisme. EPO, Antwerp
Kruithof J (2012) Het algemeen belang en de overheid. In: Jaap Kruithof – Teksten voor de toekomst. EPO, Berchem
Laignel-Lavastine A, Patocka J (1998) l'Esprit de Dissidence. Michalon, Paris
Lambrecht K (2014) Axel Miller, de onzichtbare topman. De Tijd, 13 December 2014
Laporta J (1966) Het einddoel van de mens in de filosofie van Thomas van Aquino. Tijdschrift voor wijsbegeerte 5(6):294–301
Leeson N (1996) Rogue trader: how I brought down barings bank and shook the financial world. Little Brown and Company
Légé P (2011) Pour une nouvelle fiscalité. In: Les Économistes atterés Changer d'économie! Nos propositions pour 2012. Les liens qui libèrent, Paris

Lénine V (1935) L'impérialisme, stade suprême du capitalisme. Éditions sociales internationales, Paris

Leo XIII (1891) Rerum Novarum. http://www.vatican.va/holy_father/leo_xiii/encyclicals/documents/hf_l-xiii_enc_15051891_rerum-novarum_en.html

Leopold J (2002) Enron linked to California blackouts. http://www.marketwatch.com/story/enron-caused-california-blackouts-traders-say

Les Économistes atterés (2011) Changer d'économie! Nos propositions pour 2012. Les liens qui libèrent, Paris

Levinas E (1974) Autrement qu'être ou au-delà de l'essence. Martinus Nijhoff, Den Haag

Levinas E (1988) In de tijd van de volkeren. Garant, Leuven

Levinas E (2012) Totaliteit en oneindigheid. Boom, Amsterdam

Levinas E (2014) Humanisme de l'autre homme. Le Livre de Poche – Fata Morgana, Paris

Lipton D. (2014) Fiscal Policy and Income Inequality (speech of March 13th 2014). http://www.imf.org/external/np/speeches/2014/031314.htm. Last consulted 23 Oct 2014

Lloyd C (2012) What on earth happened? The complete story of the planet, life & people from the big bang to the present day. Bloomsbury, London

Loizou A (2012) Het duivelspact. Een insiderverhaal over hoe het grote geld wordt verdiend. Zuidnederlandse uitgeverij, Aartselaar

Mackenzie D (2014) Een wereld zonder grenzen. New Scientist, November 2014

Mallaby S (2011) More money than God. Hedge funds and the making of a new elite. Bloomsbury, London

Maloney R (1931) Anthony of Padua. Saint, Apostle and wonderworker. The Anthonian Press, Dublin

Malthus T (1968) Principles of political economy considered with a view to their practical application. Kelley Publishers, New York

Mankiw G (2011) Principles of macroeconomics. Cengage Learning, Boston

Marcuse H (1962) Eros and civilization – a philosophical inquiry into freud. Vintage Books (A division of Random House), New York

Marcuse H (1964) Reason and revolution. Beacon Hill, Boston

Marcuse H (2002) One-dimensional man: studies in the ideology of advanced industrial society. Routledge Classics, London

Marx K (1982/1983) Das Kapital – Kritik der politischen öconomie (edition in three volumes). Dietz Verlag Berlin, Berlin

Mathers D (2014) The only 5 countries in the world living debt free. http://www.therichest.com/rich-list/rich-countries/the-only-5-countries-in-the-world-living-debt-free/?view=all. Last consulted 15 Dec 2014

McCarthy N (2014) There are more billionaires in the world than ever. http://www.statista.com/chart/2750/there-are-more-billionaires-in-the-world-than-ever/. Last consulted 10 Nov 2014

McKenzie D, Swails B (2012) Child slavery and chocolate: all too easy to find, CNN – January 19 th 2012. http://thecnnfreedomproject.blogs.cnn.com/2012/01/19/child-slavery-and-chocolate-all-too-easy-to-find/. Last consulted 24 Oct 2014

McLean B, Nocera J (2011) All the devils are here. The hidden history of the financial crisis. Penguin, London

Mcmanners J (ed) (1990) The Oxford illustrated history of Christianity. Oxford University Press, Oxford

McSmith A (2014) Food banks: Archbishop of Canterbury Justin Welby urges politicians to face up to Britain's hunger, 8 December 2014. http://www.independent.co.uk/news/uk/politics/food-banks-archbishop-of-canterbury-urges-politicians-to-face-up-to-britains-hunger-9909324.html. Last consulted 13 Dec 2014

Meijer S (2014) Duurste nagellak kost 200.000 euro. http://www.nu.nl/lifestyle/2874724/duurste-nagellak-kost-200000-euro.html. Last consulted 17 Oct 2014

Menasse R (2012) De Europese koerier. De woede van de burger en de vrede van Europa. Een prachtig en prikkelend pleidooi pro Europa. De Arbeiderspers, Utrecht

Meredith M (2014) Alle rijkdom verdwijnt. Knack, 26 November 2014, pp 100–103
Michel B (1998) Histoire de Prague. Fayard, Paris
Michielsen T (2014) Slimme fabrieken moeten Vlaamse industrie redden. De Tijd, 19 November 2014, pp 13–14
Middelkoop W (2009) Overleef de kredietcrisis. Nieuw Amsterdam Uitgevers, Amsterdam
Middelkoop W (2014) The big reset – war on gold and the financial endgame. AUP, Amsterdam
Moerman B (2014) Regering moet vijf miljard extra besparen. De Standaard, 6 December 2014
Mommen A (1989) Het humanistisch liberalisme van Condorcet en de rechten van de mens. In: Denkers van het Licht – Opstellen over verlichting, Revolutie and Moderniciteit samengesteld door Koen Raes. Masereelfonds, Ghent
Morris C (2009) De meltdown van 2 biljoen dollar. Uitgeverij Business contact, Amsterdam
Moutton A (2014) Zin and onzin van het maximumloon. Trends, 18 September 2014
Murray K, Bonneville P (2010) Wall of honor – 100 organizations keeping the world together. Patrick Bonneville Society, Quebec
Nissin A (1960) Histoire de Jésus. Éditions du Seuil, Paris
Nussbaum A (1950) Money in the law. National and international. A comparative study in the borderline of law and economics. The Foundation Press, Inc., Brooklyn
O'Rourke PJ (2007) The wealth of nations van Adam Smith. Mets & Schilt, Amsterdam
Obama B (2009) Change we can believe. In: Barack Obama's plan to renew America's promise. Canongate Books, Edinburgh
OECD (2013) Crisis squeezes income and puts pressure on inequality and poverty. OECD
OECD (2014) Country note on Belgium. http://www.oecd.org/edu/Belgium-EAG2014-Country-Note.pdf
Ongenae C (2014) Antropoloog Rik Pinxten roept op tot verzet – Het oude kastendenken is terug. Knack, 26 November 2014, pp 44–45
Ortberg J (2014) Impact – Jezus. Geen mens heeft de wereld zo ingrijpend veranderd. Ark Media, Amsterdam
Osho (1992) Meditation. The first and last freedom. A practical guide to medidation. The Rebel Publishing House GmbH, Cologne
Osho (2013) Speak to us of love. Reflections on Kahlil Gibran's the Prophet. Osho International Foundation, New York a.o.
Oxfam (2014) Even it up – time to end extreme inequality. Oxfam GB, Oxford
Oxfam (2015) Wealth: having it all and wanting more, study of January 2015. www.oxfam.org
Oxfam (2016) An economy for the 1%. How privilege and power in the economy drive extreme inequality and how this can be stopped. Oxfam briefing paper. https://www.oxfam.org/sites/www.oxfam.org/files/file_attachments/bp210-economy-one-percent-tax-havens-180116-en_0.pdf. Last consulted 18 Jan 2016
Pannecoucke I, Lahaye W, Vranken J, Van Rossem R (eds) (2015) Armoede in België – Jaarboek. Academia Press, Ghent
Patocka J (1999) Essais Hérétiques sur la philosophie de l'Histoire. Verdier
Pauli W (2014) De kloof in de democratie – Het historische belang van Thomas Piketty. Knack, 10 December 2014
Pearce DW, Turner RK (1990) Economics of natural resources and the environment. Harvester Wheatsheaf, London
Pelikan J (1987) Jezus door de eeuwen heen – Zijn plaats in de cultuurgeschiedenis. Kok Agora, Kampen
Persson M (2012) Klimaattop eindigt in grote teleurstelling. http://www.demorgen.be/wetenschap/klimaattop-eindigt-in-grote-teleurstelling-a1546395/
Pesendorfer D (2012) Goodbye neo-liberalism? Contested policy responses to uncertain consequences of the 2007–09 financial crisis. In: Alexander K, Dhumale R (eds) Research handbook on international financial regulation. Edward Elgar, Cheltenham
Pettifor A (2014) The power to 'create money out of thin air'. https://www.opendemocracy.net/ourkingdom/ann-pettifor/power-to-create-money-out-of-thin-air. Last consulted 18 Nov 2014

Picq J, Havel V (2000) La Force des sans-pouvoir. Michalon, Paris
Piketty T (2014) Capital in the twenty-first century. Belknap Press, Cambridge
Pinxten R (2014) Schoon protest (want er is wel een alternatief). EPO Berchem
Pinxten R, De Munter K (2006) De culturele eeuw. Houtekiet, Antwerp
Pirenne H (s.d.; 2nd edition) De Middeleeuwen (original title: "Histoire du Moyen-Age"). L.J. Veen's Uitgeversmij N.V., Amsterdam
Pironet E (2014) Uit het pluche. Knack, 26 November 2014, p 3
Pironet E (2016) Vluchtelingen splijten de EU. Knack, 27 January 2016
Pisani B (2014) Look what lower oil prices do to company profits. http://www.cnbc.com/id/102113748. Last consulted 29 Oct 2014
Pizzigati S (2012) The rich don't always win. The forgotten triumph over plutocracy that created the American middle class, 1900–1970. Seven Stories Press, New York
Plato (1934) The Laws (Nomoi) (trans: Taylor A). J.M. Dent & Sons Ltd., London
Plato (1987) The republic (trans: Lee D). Penguin Books, London
Plato (1994–2000) The laws (Nomoi) (trans: Jowett B). http://classics.mit.edu/Plato/laws.mb.txt
Poindexter J, Jones C (1980) Money. Financial markets and the economy. West Publishing Co., Minnesota
Polak S (1928) Beknopte Geschiedenis der Staatshuishoudkunde. Maatschappij voor goede en goedkope lectuur, Amsterdam
Poma K (1976) Energie en democratie – Waar het om gaat. De Nederlandsche Boekhandel, Antwerp
Poma K (2009) De verlichting – Pijler van onze beschaving. Garant, Antwerp
Pontifical Council for Justice and Peace (2005) Compendium of the Social Doctrine of the Church (to His Holiness Pope John Paul II Master of Social Doctrine and Evangelical Witness to Justice and Peace). Bloomsbury, London. http://www.vatican.va/roman_curia/pontifical_councils/justpeace/documents/rc_pc_justpeace_doc_20060526_compendio-dott-soc_en.html
Posner R (1973) Economic analysis of law. Little Brown & Company, Boston
Posthumus N (2013) http://www.nrc.nl/nieuws/2013/11/22/klimaatconferentie-lijkt-af-te-lopen-zonder-duidelijke-doelen/
Potters P (1930) Verklaring van den Katechismus der Nederlandsche bisdommen. Teulings' Uitgeversmaatschappij, 1930 (3de revised edition), tV, 's Hertogenbosch
Praag M (1954) Humanisme and Evangelie – II. Jezus van Nazareth. Mens and Kosmos (1):161–179
Price L, (2013) One million children labor in Africa's goldmines, PBS 10th July 2013. http://www.pbs.org/newshour/updates/world-july-dec13-burkinafaso_07-10/. Last consulted 24 Oct 2014
Rand A (1982) Philosophy: who needs it. New American Library (a division of Penguin Group), New York
Rand A (1992) The virtue of selfishness. New American Library (a division of Penguin Group), New York
Rand A (2008) Capitalism: the unknown ideal. New American Library (a division of Penguin Group), New York
Raspoet E (2014) Steuntrekkers zijn luieriken, zeggen ze. Maar overleven in armoede is keihard werken. Knack, 22 October 2014
Rawnsley J (1996) Total risk: Nick Leeson and the fall of Barings Bank. Harpercollins, London
Renan E (1949) Vie de Jésus. Calmann-Lévy, Paris
Ricard M (2003) Plaidoyer pour le bonheur. NiL éditions, Paris
Ricard M (2014) Plaidoyer pour l'altruisme. NiL éditions, Paris
Ricardo D (1957) The principles of political economy and taxation. J.M. Dent & Sons Ltd, London
Riepl W (2014) Martus Kohl, De fiscale held van Luxemburg – Monsieur Ruling. Trends, 13 November 2014
Ripert G (1951) Aspects juridiques du capitalisme modern. Librairie Générale de droit de de jurisprudence, Paris
Rivoire J (1984) Que sais je? Histoire de la banque. Presses universitaires de France, Paris

Rodriguez-Sickert (2009) Homo economicus. In: Peil J, Van Staveren I (eds) Handbook of economics and ethics. Edward Elgar, Cheltenham, pp 223–229
Romero-Barrutieta AL, Bulir A, Rodriguez-Delgado JD (2011) The dynamic implications of debt relief for low-income countries. IMF Working Paper (WP/11/157). IMF Institute
Ronse T (1992) Rambo op lemen voeten – Amerika in de jaren negentig. Kritak, Leuven
Russell B (1948) Geschiedenis der westerse Filosofie in verband met politieke en sociale omstandigheden van de oudste tijden tot heden (trans: Limburg R). Servire, Den Haag
Ruyver R (1969) Éloge de la société de consommation. Calmann-Lévy, Paris
Sachs J (2011) The price of civilization: reawakening American virtue and prosperity. Random House, New York
Sachs J, Becchetti L, Annett A (2016) World Happiness Report 2016, Special Rome Edition (Vol. II). Sustainable Development Solutions Network, New York. http://worldhappiness.report/wp-content/uploads/sites/2/2016/03/HR-V2Ch2_web.pdf. Last consulted 30 Mar 2016
Sainte Thérèse de l'Enfant Jésus (1957) Manuscrits autobiographiques. Lisieux, Office central de Lisieux
Schemmann M (2013) Money – breakdown and breakthrough. The history and remedy of Financial crises and Bank Failures. IICPA Publications
Schmidt R (1999) Een belasting op internationale kapitaalbewegingen: van theorie naar praktijk. In: De Meyer R, Vervliet E (eds) Klinkende munt – De bokkensprongen van het grote geld. In: Noord-Zuid-Cahier, Year 24, n° 3, September 1999, pp 105–114
Schmidtz D (1995) Rational choice and moral agency. Princeton University Press, Princeton
Schnürer G (1949) Kerk en beschaving in de Middeleeuwen tII. N.V. Drukkerij De Spaarnestad, Haarlem
Schwartz NP (2009) The prohibition of usury (Riba), a moral-ethical perspective of Islamic financial and banking law: a comparative study between the Islamic and the conventional model. Shariah J 17(2):409–430. http://docs.docstoc.com/pdf/4107922/aca5adfc-4f88-474b-8230-ccc44cb8cf49.pdf
Sée H (1952) Ontstaan and ontwikkeling van het moderne kapitalisme. Wereldbibliotheek, Amsterdam
Sen A (1977) Rational fools: A critique of the behavioral foundations of economic theory. Philos Public Affairs 6(4):317–344
Sen A (2009) The idea of justice. Allen Lane, London
Servain-Schreiber JL (1973) L'entrerpise à visage humain. Éditions Robert Laffont
Shafee K (2016) The role of Central Bank on credit control in Islamic Banking: case of Palestine. Phd defended at the "Vrije Universiteit Brussel" on February 15th 2016, Brussels
Shaxson N (2011) Treasure islands. Tax havens and the men who stole the world. Vintage books, London
Shaxson N (2012) The life offshore. The human factor. In: Treasure Islands: uncovering the damage of offshore banking and tax havens. Palgrave Maxmillan, New York
Simonet H (1970) La gauche et la société industrielle. Éditions Gérard & Co, Verviers
Skidelsky R (1992) John Maynard Keynes: The Economist as Saviour, 1920–1937. Macmillan, London
Skidelsky R (2010) Keynes. The return of the master. PublicAffairs, New York
Smith A (1979) An inquiry into the nature and causes of the wealth of nations, as republished by Campbell RH, Skinner A, Todd WB (eds). Clarendon Press, Oxford
Smith A (2005) The theory of moral sentiments, Sixth edition. MetaLibri, Sao Paolo. Available at http://www.ibiblio.org/ml/libri/s/SmithA_MoralSentiments_p.pdf. Last consulted 18 Dec 2014
Smithers A (2013) The road to recovery. Wiley, Chichester
Sorkin A (2010) Too big to fail. Penguin, London
Soros G (1999) Het liberale fundamentalisme bedreigt de democratie. In: De Meyer R, Vervliet E (eds) Klinkende munt – De bokkensprongen van het grote geld Year 24, n° 3. Noord-Zuid-Cahier

Spiegel HW (1991) The growth of economic thought. Spiegel HW, USA
Spigt P (s.d.) Multuli, 'n bevrijder. In: Bevrijdend denken. Gedenkbundel ter gelegenheid van het honderdjarig bestaan van de Vrijdenkersbeweging De Dageraad. Wereld-bibliotheek, Amsterdam
Spilsbury, P (2013) Saint Anthony of Padua. His life and writings. Edizioni Pessaggero Padova, Padova
Stackhouse M (2014) Weber, theology, and economics. In: Oslington P (ed) The Oxford handbook of Christianity and Economics. Oxford University Press, New York
Stapert-Eggen M (1981) "Inleiding" tot de editie van Max Havelaar van Amstelpaperback. Uitgeverij L.J. Veen B.V, Utrecht and Antwerp
Stauffer E (1957) Jesus Gestalt und Geschichte. Francke Verlag, Bern
Steennoot R, Dejonghe S (2007) Handboek consumentenbescherming en handelspraktijk. In: Reeks Instituut Financieel Recht, Intersentia, Antwerp
Steger M (2013) Globalization. A very short introduction. Oxford University Press, Oxford
Steinmetz G (2015) The richest man who ever lived: the life and times of Jacob Fugger. Simon & Schuster, New York
Sterdyniak H (2011) Quelle politique économique? Morts et renaissances du keynésianisme. In: Les Économistes atterés Changer d'économie! Nos propositions pour 2012, Les liens qui libèrent, Paris
Stigler G (1961) The economics of information. J Polit Econ 69(3)
Stiglitz J (2003) Globalization and its discontents. W.W. Norton & Company, New York
Stiglitz J (2006) Making globalization work. Penguin Books, London
Stiglitz J (2008) The future of global governance. In: Serra N, Stiglitz J (eds) The Washington consensus reconsidered. Oxford University Press, Oxford, pp 309–323
Stiglitz J (2012) The price of inequality. Allen Lane (an imprint of Penguin Books), London
Stiglitz J (2015) Europe's Attack on Greek Democracy. Opinion of July 29th 2015. http://www.project-syndicate.org/commentary/greece-referendum-troika-eurozone-by-joseph-e--stiglitz-2015-06. Last consulted 16 Oct 2015
Stiglitz J, Bilmes L (2008) The three trillion dollar war. The true cost of the Iraq conflict. Penguin Books, London
Stiglitz J, Chariton A (2005) Fair trade for all – how trade can promote development. Oxford University Press, Oxford
Stiglitz J, Sen A, Titoussi JP (2010) Mismeasuring our lives. Why GDP doesn't add up. The New Press, New York
Streeck W (2015) Gekochte tijd. De uitgestelde crisis van het democratisch kapitalisme (trans: Hemelrijk W). Leesmagazijn n° 21
Subhuti A (2011) My dance with a madman. Tales by a British journalist about his life with a controversioal Indian mystic. Perfect Publishers Ltd., Cambridge
Sullivan R (ed) (2010) Life – 100 people who changed the world. Time Inc. Home Entertainment, New York
Sweeney J (2015) The complete Francis of Assisi. His life, the complete writings and the little flowers. Paraclete Press, Brewster
Szalavitz M (2012) Is human nature fundamentally selfish or altruistic? Time, 8 Oct 2012. http://healthland.time.com/2012/10/08/is-human-nature-fundamentally-selfish-or-altruistic/. Last consulted 15 Oct 2015
Talmon JL (1966) Les origines de la démocratie totalitaire. Calmann-Lévy, Paris
Tanghe N (2013) De bodemloze put Dexia. http://www.standaard.be/cnt/dmf20130221_00479136. Last consulted 11 Dec 2014
Tanner N (2008) The church in the later Middle Ages. I.B. Tauris, London
Tawney RH (1944) Religion and the rise of capitalism. John Murray, London
Temin P (s.d.) Financial intermediation in the early Roman Empire. http://www.histecon.magd.cam.ac.uk/docs/temin.pdf.
Thich Nhat Hanh (2009) Boeddha leeft, Christus leeft. Asoka, Rotterdam

Todd E (2015) Qui est Charlie? Sociologie d'une crise religieuse. Éditions du Seuil, Paris (also: Todd E (2015) Wie is Charlie. Xenofobie en de nieuwe middenklasse. De Bezige Bij, Amsterdam and Antwerp)

Trafecante K (2014) Big chocolate goes small on Ebola donations. http://money.cnn.com/video/news/2014/10/23/big-chocolate-goes-small-on-ebola-donations.cnnmoney. Last consulted 24 Oct 2014

Trainor K (2012) Boeddhisme. Librero, Kerkdriel

Treanor J (2015) Half of world's wealth now in hands of 1% of population – report. The Guardian. http://www.theguardian.com/money/2015/oct/13/half-world-wealth-in-hands-population-inequality-report. Last consulted 14 Oct 2015

Truyman A (2002) Johannes Paulus II de onfeilbare. Van Halewyck, Leuven

Turner L (1973) Onzichtbare wereldmachten – multinationale ondernemingen en de wereld van nu. Boekenuitgeverij Keesing, Amsterdam

Ugeux G (2010) Het verraad van de financiële wereld. Lannoo, Tielt

United Nations Development Programme (UNDP) (2014) Human Development Report 2014. UNDP, New York

Van Aken P (1995) Niemand te hoog. Humanisme, Vrijzinnigheid and Vlaamse literatuur. VUBPRESS, Brussels

van Bekhoven L (2016) Eén op de vijf Britten trekt zelf tanden. De conservatieve regering van David Cameron schrapt ettelijke publieke voorzieningen en schroeft de zorgstaat steeds meer terug. Zelfs doe-het-zelftandheelkunde zit in de lift. Knack, 13 January 2016

Van Bruggen J (2014) De bergrede – Reisgids voor Christenen. Uitgeverij Kok, Utrecht

Van Cauwelaert R (2014) De schuldfactuur van de banken. De Tijd, 29 November 2014

Van de Velden W (2014a) Het gaat niet goed met de regering-Michel. De Tijd, 17 December 2014

Van de Velden W (2014b) Met de hervormingen creëert deze regering 200.000 banen. De Tijd, 17 December 2014

van de Velden W (2014c) Heisa over fiscale achterkamertjes in België. De Tijd, 9 December 2014

Van de Velden W, D'Hoore J (2014) Van sociaal conflict naar compromis? De Tijd, 16 December 2014

Van den Broeck S (2014) U vraagt Paul De Grauwe, econoom – Deze regering denkt vooral aan de ondernemers. Knack, 22 October 2014, p 21 (containing an interview with P. De Grauwe)

Van der Borght K (2014) China: de rechtsorde zoals we ze kennen? Intersentia, Antwerp

Van der Heijden E (1926–1927) De feestuitgave der Broederschap. In: NV 1926-'27

Van der Kelen L (s.d.) Koning Albert II and zijn vijf premiers – Een leven in de Wetstraat – Memoires van een commentator. Manteau, Antwerp

Van Eeckhoutte W (2002) Statuut stagiairs en medewerkers vrije beroepers. Acc Tax 1:32–35

Van Erp A (2014) Wereldvoedseldag: Er is voldoende voedsel beschikbaar, niemand zou honger moeten lijden. http://m.knack.be/nieuws/planet-earth/wereldvoedseldag-er-is-voldoende-voedsel-beschikbaar-niemand-zou-honger-moeten-lijden/article-normal-443595.html. Last consulted 16 Oct 2014

Van Haver K (2014a) Processierups. De Tijd, 16 December 2014

Van Haver K (2014b) Kloof arm-rijk bedreigt mondiaal klimaatakkoord. De Tijd, 16 December 2014

Van Haver K, Blomme P (2014) Europees knipperlicht voor Belgische begroting. De Tijd, 29 November 2014

Van Hoogstraten D (2015) Amerikaanse ongelijkheid blijft toenemen. Bonus-bonanza door beurssucces. De Standaard, 20 March 2015, p 30

Van Houtte JA (1942) Economische geschiedenis – de historische wording van de hedendaagsche wereldeconomie. De Haan, Utrecht

Van Houtte JA (a.o.) (eds) (1953) Algemene geschiedenis der Nederlanden t.VI. Standaard Boekhandel, Utrecht, W. De Haan and Antwerp

Van Houtte JA (a.o.) (eds) (1955) Algemene geschiedenis der Nederlanden t.X. Standaard Boekhandel, Utrecht, W. De Haan and Antwerp

van Hove RJ (1993) Emmanuel Levinas. De existentie van het subject and de ander. In: Woldring HES (ed) Moderne Franse filosofen. Kok Agora, Kampen
van Liedekerke L (1993) Het interestdebat in het Westen. In: Ethische Perspectieven 3
Van Meerhaeghe MAG (1985) Museum of grootmacht. De identiteitscrisis van Europa. Lannoo, Tielt
Van Oudheusden J (2012) Een kleine geschiedenis van Amerika. Bert Bakker, Amsterdam
Van Overveldt J (2014) Dexia is onze financiële Fukushima. http://www.knack.be/nieuws/dexia-is-ons-financiele-fukushima/article-opinion-44360.html. Last consulted 11 Dec 2014
Van Steelandt A (2014) Het zombiesysteem. Trends, 20 November 2014
Van Straaten AJ (2002) Woeker en het verbod op rente. Een verkenning naar drie wereldgodsdiensten gedurende drie millennia. Boom, Amsterdam
Vandewalle G (1976) De geschiedenis van het economisch denken. Kluwer, Deventer
Vanschoubroek C (2014a) België sloot zestig geheime belastingdeals. De Standaard, 11 December 2014
Vanschoubroek C (2014b) België speelt al jaren mee in fiscale ratrace. De Standaard, 11 December 2014
Veldman H, Parlevliet P (2003) Spierballentaal en cowboylaarzen. Reagan, Bush I en Bush II in de context van het Amerikaanse conservatisme. Uitgeverij Aspekt, Soesterberg
Verhaeghe P (2011) De neoliberale waanzin – Flexibel, efficiënt en... gestoord. Uitgeverij VUBPRESS, Brussels
Vermeend W (2008) De kredietcrisis. Lebowski, Amsterdam
Visser AMW, McIntosch A (1998) A short review of the historical critique of usury. Acc Bus Financ History 8(2)
Vivekananda (1989) Karma yoga. In: The complete works of Swami Vivekanda (Mayavati Memorial Edition), Advaita Ashrama, Kolkata, Volume I
von Böhm-Bawerk E (1912) Positive Theorie des Kapitales. Verlag der Wagner'schen Universitäts-Buchhandlung, Innsbrück
Walker P (2007) In het voetspoor van Jezus. Een geïllustreerde gids voor de plaatsen van het Heilige land. Ark Boeken, Amsterdam
Walker P (2009) In the steps of Jesus. Lion Books an Imprint of Lion Hudson plc, Oxford
Weber M (1967) L'éthique protestante et l'esprit du capitalisme. Plon, Paris
Whitney Hall J (ed) (2013) History of the world. Earliest time to the Present Day. World publications Group, East Bridgewater
Wieviorka M (2014) Het antisemitisme uitgelegd aan jongeren. De Bezige Bij, Amsterdam
Wintz J (2012) Saint Anthony of Padua. Franciscan Media, Cincinnati
Wolffers I (2011) Gezond. Over de mens, zijn gezondheid en de gezondheidszorg. Nieuw Amsterdam Uitgevers, Amsterdam
Wood D (2002) Medieval economic thought. CUP, Cambridge
Worstall T (2015) Credit Suisse Wealth Report: there are more poor people in America than China, Forbes, 14 October 2015. http://www.forbes.com/sites/timworstall/2015/10/14/credit-suisse-wealth-report-there-are-more-poor-people-in-america-than-china/. Last consulted 14 Oct 2015
Wright T (2012a) Luke for everyone. For Everyone Commentary Library Edition, London
Wright T (2012b) Mark for everyone. For Everyone Commentary Library Edition, London
Wright T (2012c) Matthew for everyone. For Everyone Commentary Library Edition, London
Wright T (2012d) Acts for everyone. For Everyone Commentary Library Edition, London
Wykes M (2003) Devaluing the scholastics: Calvin's ethics of usury. Calvin Theological J 38 (2003)
Yardley J, Goodstein L (2015) Pope Francis, in Sweeping Encyclical, Calls for Swift Action on Climate Change. The New York Times, 18 June 2015
Zuboff S, Maxmin J (2002) The support economy (why corporations are failing individuals and the next episode of capitalism). Penguin Books, London
Zuboff S, Maxmin J (2004) The support economy (first edition: 2002). Penguin Books, New York, p 33
Zwaenepoel T (2011) Een jaar met Johannes Paulus II. Lannoo, Tielt

Chapter 4
Building Stones for a New Monetary World Order

4.1 Introduction: Towards a New Monetary World Order Based on Five Pillars

As has been mentioned before, in this chapter of the current book, an attempt will be made to establish what a monetary system which would relinquish the principles of (neo-)Smithian selfishness and would, on the contrary, aim at establishing a more just (and more altruistic) economic order, could look like. 1

This attempt is inherently based on one of the crucial characteristics of money (and the prevailing monetary system), namely that money is but a conventional system that is inherently variable. 2

As has been explained in more detail in the previous chapters of this book, money and money creation are indeed based on the fact that an economy (or several interactive "economies") accept "something" as money and is (are) moreover willing to fully (and by all conceivable means, such as the law system itself) support the use of money in all economic and financial transactions.

It could hereby even be held that the monetary system is itself based on, or embedded in, a "social contract" through means of several types of mechanisms and procedures (such as (international) law, including treaties establishing a monetary order and/or the free movement of money and capital; state organization itself; all types of conventional systems between financial institutions and other market players,...) (see above, especially at marg. 7 and 17–20 of Chap. 2 of this book).

The major characteristics of these mechanisms and procedures have been dealt with in detail (and also illustrated) in Chap. 2 of this book, whereby it has also been indicated that the inherently "conventional" nature of money also implies that it is intrinsically subject to changes.

Indeed, the history (of the financial and monetary system) has effectively witnessed several such changes, even to the extent that money, as we know it today, could be basically considered as the result of a continuous (fine)tuning

K. Byttebier, *Towards a New International Monetary Order*,
Economic and Financial Law & Policy – Shifting Insights & Values 1,
DOI 10.1007/978-3-319-52518-1_4

during a long evolutionary process. (See above, at marg. 10 of Chap. 2. of this book.)

The "conventional" (and through this, also essentially "variable") nature of money, furthermore, implies that the mechanisms of money creation and distribution themselves are also subject to changes, on condition that the powers which are shaping the underlying social contract (of which money and money creation are a part), and ultimately this is the whole of mankind itself, would become sufficiently in favor of such a change.[1]

3 Based upon the further basic insight that money is "a public good"[2], or at least should become so again (see further, at marg. 24 a.f. of this chapter), in this chapter of this book, an attempt is undertaken to describe how a new, more just monetary system, which would be based on altruism rather than on egoism, could look like.

This attempt is furthermore based on the realization that the continuation of the current monetary system, given its starting premises (as described in detail in Chap. 3 of this book), will very probably on itself never be able to lead to a more just social and economic order (but, on the contrary, threatens to bring closer the ruin of mankind and the planet it inhabits).

This attempt is, moreover, the result of an exercise in deliberate "*out of the box* – thinking", knowing that, up till now, many (sometimes very) critical reflections have been made regarding the capitalist economic system as such, but that barely any alternatives have been offered for the current monetary and banking system as it is based upon said capitalist starting premises.[3]

It is hereafter more precisely proposed to establish a "New Monetary World Order" that would be based on five "pillars", namely:

- *Pillar I*: a global monetary system;
- *Pillar II*: a monetary system fulfilling altruistic policy aims;
- *Pillar III*: a monetary system which no longer relies on private money creation;
- *Pillar IV*: a monetary system which is based upon a differentiated price setting for newly created money;
- *Pillar V*: a monetary system in which a central global institute (the to-be-created "New Monetary World Institute") would become responsible for all levels of new money creation.

---

[1] Ann Pettifor has phrased this as the necessity for a willingness:

> [to] move on beyond Adam Smith towards a fuller understanding of the public good that is credit. (See Pettifor 2014)

[2] See *e.g.* Ingham (2005a), p. xxii; Ingham (2005b), pp. 222–224, especially p. 237.

It needs no further saying that this approach is opposed to the principles of economic neo-liberalism which, on the contrary, holds that there is no such thing as "a general good" (or, by extension, as "public goods") (see Rand 2008, p. 12).

[3] Compare Van Steelandt (2014), pp. 20–24, especially 20.

The outlook of each of these five "pillars" will hereafter be dealt with (albeit in a general way).[4]

4.2 Pillar I. A Global Monetary System

The new monetary system which is considered in the present chapter and Chap. 5 of this book stems from the idea that mankind should no longer adhere to the essentially "national" nature of money. 4

As has already been explained before, so far, (cash) money has to a high extent a "national character", which is a consequence of the fact that money creation is deemed to be part of the so-called "sovereign state authority" of national states (see above, at marg. 97 of Chap. 2 of this book). 5

This implies that, up till today, in principle, any sovereign state may determine itself what it considers to be money within its own frontiers.

However, taking into account the numerous transnational human practices (going from traveling outside one's own country borders to any types of international trade), it has turned out over time that, notwithstanding the basically national nature of money, there is also a need for convention-based, international agreements in order to streamline foreign currency exchange—i.e. the exchange of national money for other national money—as well as the international traffic of payments and capital. 6

It goes indeed without saying that, in the "globalized" world as we know it today, no country operates as an isolated entity, but (almost) all countries have more and more become part of a globalized "ensemble" which, in economic terms, is characterized by an almost continuous stream of transnational transactions, including transactions of payments and capital, but also of people (i.e. so-called "human resources").[5]

The need for international agreements dealing with monetary issues has, especially in the course of the twentieth century, led to a number of extensive convention-based monetary systems, among which obviously the IMF and the EMU.[6]

Probably the most extensive convention-based mechanism in the field of monetary law and economics, is indeed the so-called "monetary union", which 7

[4]In case mankind would ever be willing to consider implementing the ideas brought forward in these present chapter and Chap. 5 of this book, it will obviously be necessary to work said ideas out in more detail (for instance in the treaty (ies) and other rules and regulations dealing with the to-be-established "New Monetary World Order").

[5]Recently, this has even led to the questioning of the national state model itself (*e.g.* in the works of John Breuilly of the "*London School of Economics*"); see furthermore Mackenzie (2014), pp. 55–65.

On the interaction between the national state model and the issue of (social and economic) globalization, see especially Stiglitz (2006), p. 19.

[6]See *e.g.* Umbach and Wessels (2008), pp. 54–68.

(in general terms) could be described as the (convention-based agreed upon) system whereby, within a certain geographical area—in general a group of countries—one common currency is (at least) functioning as a generally accepted means of payment (in addition to fulfilling the other classical functions of money).

Countries constituting such a monetary union are in other words setting aside their own national currency and join a (monetary) system in which one single currency is used instead.[7]

The most remarkable example of such a monetary union is, without any doubt, the aforementioned EMU.[8]

8 A new monetary system which aims to be more just and altruistic should be of a similar essentially "international", or even: "supranational" nature (whereby, on a global scale—or at least among the countries taking part in such "New Monetary Order"—there will exist a willingness to create one global monetary union).[9]

9 In such a monetary system which would aim at finally omitting the starting premises of the (neo-)Smithian or (neo-)liberal selfishness currently determining the monetary and financial world, the assumed advantages of national monetary systems can indeed no longer prevail.[10]

For instance, by re-directing the monetary (and hence economic) order towards a system based upon altruism, the economic and political aspiration of accumulating as much of another country's currency as monetary reserves as possible (which is, presently, the result of the fierce competitive battle between economic agents of different countries that is prevailing under the economic neo-liberal system)[11], will no longer make sense.

Nor will it be longer of any importance for large financial institutions[12] and (other) transnational enterprises (with high cash reserves in different currencies) to continue to trade currency as a method to make quick profits (or losses).[13]

In a monetary (and hence economic) system based on altruism, neither will there be much further need for a central interest rate policy to offer a levy which causes a

---

[7]A similar result as reached by means of a monetary union can be obtained when a country starts using the currency of another country. The IMF qualifies both systems as so-called "*exchange arrangements with no separate legal tender*". (See *e.g.* International Monetary Fund 1999, p. 164.)

See furthermore Fase and Vleminckx (1995), p. 156; Healey and Levine (1993), pp. 371–386, especially p. 372.

[8]About the "genesis" of the EMU, see *e.g.* Bertaut and Iyigun (1999), pp. 655–666; Louis (1993), pp. 285–299; Bonneau (1999), p. 16, no 26 ; see also De economische en monetaire unie en België. In: Trefpunt Economie, (1999), pp. 3–5.

[9]Compare Galbraith (1996), p. 128; Mateos y Lago et al. (2011), pp. 91–116.

[10]Compare Stiglitz (2006), p. 21, and this author's further arguments about the problematic nature of acquiring monetary reserves (at pp. 148–149 of the quoted book).

[11]On the disastrous effects of an economy which is too much based on competition, see also Oxfam (2016), p. 16.

[12]Financial institutions are among the most important players on the (international) exchange markets often practicing so-called "*proprietary trading*" (for their own account) (see Loizou 2012, p. 165).

[13]Loizou (2012), p. 161 a.f., pointing out that at the time when he wrote his book, the daily trade of currencies, on average, amounted to 4 trillion USD ("4 biljoen USD").

country's own national interests to prevail above (and to the detriment of) the wellbeing of (the population of) other countries, let alone to constitute mechanisms by which a few privileged entities (especially the shareholders and top-executives of private banks), through all types of financial techniques, can go on accumulating wealth to the detriment of the rest of society.

Hence, the new monetary system which is proposed here—under the proposed practical working name "the New Monetary World Order" (in short: "NMWO") (albeit, of course, any other similar denomination could be thought off)—will inherently need to be based on a convention (-based system), whereby all participating member states would adopt one new (international) currency and would hereby also, in a definitive way, be willing to give up their own national currency, as well as their national monetary sovereignty. **10**

For the sake of completeness, it needs to be remarked that in the more or less recent past similar voices advocating the introduction of a new world-wide monetary system have already been heard. **11**

One of the advocates of such a new global monetary order has, for instance, been economics professor Robert Mundell (Columbia) who, in a speech dating from 2005 entitled "*The case for a world currency*", has pleaded for a similar world-wide monetary system[14]:

> My approach is rather to start out with arrangements for stabilizing exchange rates, and move from there to a global currency. It would start off from the situation as it is at present and gradually move it toward the desired solution. We could start off with the three big currencies in the world, the dollar, euro, and yen, and with specified weights, make a basket of them into a unit that could be called the DEY," (...) "The DEY[15] could then become the platform on which to build a global currency, which I shall call the INTOR[16].

In his research of the 1990s, Mundell mentioned as advantages of a global monetary union mainly the favorable effect such a monetary system would have on price setting and price transparency, which would furthermore smoothen international trade (and thus would, ultimately, contribute to higher economic growth and prosperity).

In the past, some central bankers have defended similar statements.[17]

Similarly, (also) within the IMF, the position has been taken that SDRs should be developed into a fully-fledged world currency (see further, at marg. 62 of this chapter).

---

[14]Quoted by Newman (2010).

See also Mundell (1996), pp. 74–81; Mundell (2000), pp. 57–84; Pdoa-Schioppa (2011), pp. 51–73, especially p. 61.

[15]DEY hereby stands for "*dollar-euro-yen*".

[16]The word "INTOR" is formed by a contraction of the words "international" and "or", the latter itself being the French word for "gold".

[17]See Newman (2010). See also Stevenson (2009).

4.3 Pillar II. A Monetary System Based on "Altruistic" Objectives

12 Secondly, the New Monetary (World) Order should be based on a clear understanding of the true sense of money.[18]

13 For (textual) clarity sake, we will from now on also refer to the new type of money to be used in the context of the New Monetary Order, i.e. an international currency which will henceforth be the sole type of currency for, and in, all participating member states, in a uniform way, provisionally adopting as such new working name the term "the New World Currency" (in short: "NWC") (but, again, any other similar term could be thought off).

14 Money, hence in the case of the New Monetary (World) Order: the "New World Currency", constitutes per definition a receivable towards the streams of goods and services produced by the economy, in case of the New Monetary Order: the entire world economy[19] (or put otherwise: the combined economies of all participating member states of this New Monetary World Order).

In this, and contrary to one of the basic working premises of capitalism itself, it will be necessary that mankind would become more and more willing to accept that the economic streams of goods and services cannot be infinitely subject to further growth.[20]

By definition, the supply of resources (including energy resources) of the planet is limited[21] and the operational techniques to obtain them entail many types of (severe) problems (environment related and other), many of which are not (at least not in the short term) in a simple way solvable.[22]

Hence, in addition to the aim of developing a more just and altruistic monetary system, the consideration to deal with the resources of the planet with more care and consideration than capitalism (inherently based upon one of its starting premises, namely the sacrifice of all values to the unbridled pursuit of money; see above, under Sect. 3.4.3.1 of Chap. 3 of this book) has done for the past two/three centuries, should be a further motivation in the development of the New Monetary Order.[23]

15 Otherwise put, in an altruistic view towards human society in general and towards its economy more specifically which should lie at the basis of the here proposed New Monetary World Order, it should no longer matter to any individual to, at any cost and without any significant attention to the impact of one's own behavior on others, accumulate as much money as possible[24], under the false

---

[18]Pettifor (2014), deriving further arguments from the works of Keynes.

[19]Such a global New Monetary Order will, of course, also imply free trade and free capital and free payment traffic.

[20]Johnson (2014), pp. 79–103.

[21]See also Johnson (2014), pp. 79–103, especially p. 87.

[22]Johnson (2014), pp. 79–103, especially p. 87.

[23]Harari (2014), pp. 372–373.

[24]Per definition: to accumulate the largest possible receivable position towards the flow of goods and services produced by the world economy.

assumption that such a selfish pursuit of money and wealth would allegedly best serve the general interest[25], but on the contrary, it will be expected from everyone to contribute to a world where *all* human beings, and not only the top 1% of the planet, can build up a humane existence and where enough attention is given to values other than the selfish satisfaction of one's own (unbridled) needs, such as the conservation of the planet and its eco-system(s).

Indeed, a true altruism can (evidently) not imply that only the interest of a few **16**
individuals are served (as is the case under capitalism), or even those of mankind in general, but will need to take into consideration the interests of the totality of everything that is (hence the eco-system "earth" and its surrounding area).[26]

In the New Monetary World Order, the basic guideline for human (economic) behavior can hence no longer be the one that, since the works of the Scottish moral philosopher Adam Smith[27], has prevailed under capitalism, namely adhering to an unbridled selfishness[28] or, otherwise put, to the idea that "*greed is good*".

---

[25]See the statement of, for instance, Ayn Rand that there exists no such thing as "the general good" (see Rand 2008, p. 12).

[26]Dawkins (2006), pp. 9–10 has stated this as follows:

> Recently there has been a reaction against racialism and patriotism, and a tendency to substitute the whole human species as the object of our fellow feeling. This humanist broadening of the target of our altruism has an interesting corollary, which again seems to buttress the 'good of the species' idea in evolution. The politically liberal, who are normally the most convinced spokesmen of the species ethic, now often have the greatest scorn for those who have gone a little further in widening their altruism, so that it includes other species. If I say that I am more interested in preventing the slaughter of large whales than I am in improving housing conditions for people, I am likely to shock some of my friends.
> (...)
> The muddle in human ethics over the level at which altruism is desirable – family, nation, race, species, or all living things – is mirrored by a parallel muddle in biology over the level at which altruism is to be expected according to the theory of evolution.

[27]It is here not further explored to what extent this presentation of Smith's works is based on a fully correct interpretation of all of these works (see above, at marg. 122 of Chap. 3 of this book). What matters more is how his works have influenced and inspired ages of capitalist practices, and how these themselves have shaped the world into the detrimental state it finds itself in today.

[28]Defending the policy choice for selfishness and egoism has been explained in a so-called "rationalized" way, which comes as no surprise as, historically speaking, economic liberalism has itself emerged from the schools of enlightenment who aimed to explain all human behavior, including economic transactions, as the result of rational processes (see above, at Sect. 3.4.2 of Chap. 3 of this book) (compare Rand 2008, p. 19).

Given the way the world looks like after only a few ages of such "rational" behavior while at the same time realizing that it already exist for ±4.5 billion years, having based human sciences on this extreme rationalization idea may have proven one of the biggest mistakes in the history of mankind.

Moreover, under further reference to, for instance, Herbert Marcuse, one can even wonder whether the policy choices made under impulse of economic liberalism and economic neo-liberalism deserve to be qualified as truly "rational" given their detrimental consequences (see above, at marg. 169 of Chap. 3 of this book).

Instead, the New Monetary Order will need to be based on a clear understanding that the endless cycle of selfish pursuing individual needs to be breached for the benefit of advocating general interest, not only of all other human beings, but also of the planet as a whole.[29]

17 Therefore, the altruism which is referred to in the current book obviously needs also to be seen as the force (present in human nature itself) which is opposed to selfishness.

Otherwise put, as already mentioned earlier in this book (see for instance above, at marg. 118–119 of Chap. 3 of this book), unbridled selfishness and radical altruism are clearly to understood as opposed forces which are (both) present in (human) nature, and a clear policy choice for one of these opposite forces, namely altruism, is at stake.[30]

It needs moreover not surprise that this approach is, in essence, not different from the position of most neo-liberal authors who, albeit with a different outcome of said policy choice, have confirmed that the moral meaning of the principle of the free market is opposed to the teachings of altruism which, by them, have been stigmatized as "*vicious*".[31]

18 Phrased otherwise, when setting out the objectives of the New Monetary (World) Order, one of the essential points will be to determine what is to become the decisive (underlying and structural) force inspiring this new monetary system: the one defended by economic neo-liberalism, namely complete selfishness, or rather that of a radical altruism, as throughout the ages defended by a vast set of philosophical and religious doctrines (see the overview hereof under Chap. 3 of this book).

To use one of the basic metaphors of Christianity, the question is if we ("mankind") want(s) (the preservation of) a society where the selfish behavior of the Levite and the priest from the parable of the Good Samaritan (see above, at marg. 40 of Chap. 3 of this book), who both, driven by self-interest, chose to leave a seriously injured fellow man to his fate, is seen as normal, and even as virtuous, or do we want (to grow towards) a society in which the expectation will increasingly prevail that people will behave as the Good Samaritan from the same story who,

[29]A further motivation for this can be borrowed from the works of the Belgian moral philosopher Jaap Kruithof, in his plea for an ethical world policy which would abandon "anthropocentrism" and would instead prioritize the care for the global eco-system (in an ultimate sense, this is earth with all its surroundings) (see in general Kruithof 1985), or also from the works of Emanuel Levinas, from which we can rephrase that "the self" does not only need to recognize the needs of "the Other" but, based upon an understanding of being responsible for "the Other", also effectively needs to prioritize these needs (even above his own selfish needs; see above, under Sect. 3.6.4.2.2 of Chap. 3 of this book).

[30]This insight is supported by the findings of (modern) biology itself:

> An entity, such as a baboon, is said to be altruistic if it behaves in such a way as to increase another such entity's welfare at the expense of its own. Selfish behaviour has exactly the opposite effect. 'Welfare' is defined as 'chances of survival', even if the effect on actual life and death prospects is so small as to be negligible. (Dawkins 2006. pp. 9–10).

[31]Rand (2008), p. 19.

while neglecting any personal interest, recognized the suffering of his fellow man and above all wanted to try to help him in his hour of need. Even so in terms derived from the Gospels, the said policy choice is basically the one between serving the "Kingdom of God", namely at the very least establishing a society in which love for one's neighbor prevails above anything else (see Mark, 12:31) and certainly above one's own selfish needs, or, otherwise put, above serving the "mammon" (i.e. the money devil) as is the expectancy under the capitalist economic system.

In terms of Buddhist doctrine, the question becomes if we truly want (the preservation of) a world (monetary order) where everyone increasingly continues to surrender to the so-called "*armies of Mara*"[32], in other words, chooses for a life that is solely aimed at pursuing, at any cost, the immediate satisfaction (in the modern world: pre-financed with consumer credits which mainly help to get the rich of the planet ever more richer) of any thinkable physical or other need, i.e. a life serving "evil" (= "*samsara*").[33]

Through this approach, the choice for the guiding principle within society and 19
within economics (and its monetary system) becomes reduced to the classical choice between "altruism" (as historically defended by figures such as Plato, Aristotle, Jesus Christ,. . .) or "selfishness" (as has, especially within economic thinking, already early in history been defended by "Christian" thinkers such as Luther and Calvin, and later by Adam Smith and his successors, currently mainly the neo-liberal economists).[34]

In this classical metaphysical sense, the choice whether or not to aspire for a New Monetary Order which the world community faces, basically becomes the one between what is (basically) "good" (altruism) and what is (basically) "evil" (selfishness/"*greed*"), whereby these concepts are to be comprehended in accordance with the mentioned classic philosophical and religious doctrines, and whereby it needs to be noted that the new religion of economic (neo-)liberalism itself has clearly attempted to turn around this most classical value scale by—in some cases even literally (see *e.g.* Ayn Rand)—arguing that "evil" (selfishness) is good and "good" (altruism) is evil.[35]

---

[32]According to Wikipedia (https://en.wikipedia.org/wiki/Mara_%28demon%29; last consulted on October 15th 2015), in Buddhism, Mara is the demon that tempted Gautama Buddha by trying to seduce him with the vision of beautiful women who, in various legends, are often said to be Mara's daughters. In Buddhist cosmology, Mara personifies unwholesome impulses, unskillfulness, and the "death" of the spiritual life. Mara is hence a tempter, distracting humans from practicing the spiritual life by making mundane things alluring, or by making the negative seem positive.

It does not need to surprise that this theme lies at the basis of masterpieces of world literature exploring the so-called "Faust"-theme, such as obviously Goethe's "*Faust*" itself, in addition to, for instance, Thomas Mann's masterwork "*Doctor Faustus*".

Compare these insights of Buddhism to the findings of Tim Kasser in his earlier quoted book "*The high price of materialism*". (See above, Further Illustration 3.1 in Chap. 3 of this book.)

[33]See also Harari (2014), pp. 250–251.

[34]About this question, see Habets and Gloudemans (2013), p. 23.

[35]What Ayn Rand has basically upheld is, in biblical terms, that, faced with the choice between worshipping God or worshipping the mammon (see Luke 16, 13), man should choose for worshipping the mammon.

20 To the extent necessary, it is furthermore emphasized once more that in the current book, the choice for a new (monetary, economic and fiscal[36]) world order which should develop towards a higher degree of altruism is definitely advocated, having as its objective the creation of a more just world.[37]

21 The second pillar of the New Monetary World Order, namely the aim of pursuing altruism translated into concrete (monetary) objectives, can moreover be considered as an extension of the first pillar, namely, as mentioned earlier (see above, at marg. 4–11 of this chapter), its essentially international character (and *vice versa*).

The choice for a decisive altruism as a starting premise for the New Monetary World Order (which, consequently, will also have to constitute its underlying policy guideline)[38] is, indeed, by definition, not compatible with maintaining nationalist reflexes whereby the economic well-being of a certain population (or of a certain race, or races) or a given economic household (such as the inhabitants of a certain state) would be put above the general well-being of the whole of mankind.

Assuming that all people are born in order to develop themselves, and that every person should have the same rights and life chances as others, or at least this should become the case in a near future (see the insight derived from various philosophical and religious doctrines, as referred to above, under Sect. 3.6.2 of Chap. 3 of this book), a new world economic and monetary order will have to create a climate that supports this objective.

See furthermore Rand (1982), pp. 27 a.f., where Ayn Rand has argued that altruism serves as a tool for the rationalization of all kinds of abuses, going from mass slaughters in Sovjet Russia, the legalized looting in the welfare state, the power lust of politicians seeking to serve the common good, the concept of common good itself, etc.

See furthermore Rand (1982), p. 83, where Rand describes altruism as "the poison of death in the blood of western civilization".

[36]On the interaction between fiscal and monetary policies, see *e.g.* Galbraith (1973), pp. 38–39.

[37]Even in the classical "Aristotelian" sense of the word, to be read as a world where no-one takes more, or receives less, of what is good than what is his ethical part (see above, at marg. 271–272 of Chap. 3 of this book).

[38]One should also take into consideration the possible impact of a complete economic and financial failure in case mankind would continue to adhere to the opposite choice as has been made since the seventeenth century, namely the choice for an unbridled selfishness as the guiding principle of economy, which has also increasingly determined the operation of the current IMF over the past decades (albeit greed and selfishness had already earlier on in history determined economic choices, a fact against which prominent philosophers and religious leaders like Plato, Aristotle and Jesus Christ, had strongly protested).

See furthermore Krugman (2004), p. 454; Stiglitz (2003), p. 196.

Stiglitz has described the policy choices of the IMF as follows:

> We have an obvious problem: a public institution created to address certain failures in the market but currently run by economists who have both a high level of confidence in markets and little confidence in public institutions. (Stiglitz 2003, p. 196). See also Harvey (2010), p. 55.

Regardless the economic and financial interests national frontiers, which in the past have often been drawn in an artificial way, may serve in the context of the current economic and monetary order, such frontiers can no longer be allowed to support a socioeconomic system characterized by inequality[39], as this prevails today.

4.4 Summary of Pillars I and II

In summary: the first pillar of the New Monetary World Order will assume that the participating countries come to an international (convention-based) agreement whereby they abandon their national sovereignty at the monetary level to the benefit of a new world organization which will, from then on, be responsible for money creation on a global scale.[40] **22**

As has been done in regard to the notions "New Monetary World Order" and "New World Currency", we will here also choose a working name for this new "central monetary institution" thus proposing as such a working name: "the New Monetary World Institute" (in short "NMWI") (but, again, any similar, alternative name could serve the same purpose).

The second pillar of the New Monetary World Order presupposes that (neo-) Smithian selfishness as one of the main underlying monetary policy objectives would even so be abandoned, and that, instead, a mixture of altruistic values would be proposed as guiding monetary policy goals, such as (in general terms): the common good of the entire world and its inhabitants. **23**

4.5 Pillar III. Money as a "Public Good": Towards a Monetary System Excluding Private Money Creation

4.5.1 Key Aspects of the Currently Prevailing System of (Private) Money Creation

The implementation of the here proposed "New Monetary World Order" would furthermore put a resolute end to one of the presently most prevailing systems of private money creation, namely the scriptural money creation which occurs each time a private (deposit) bank provides credit to its customers for total amounts higher than its cash reserve. **24**

[39]Especially also in terms of life chances; see for this the so-called "*condemned to stay poor*"-syndrome.

[40]Compare Stiglitz's appeal for stronger international institutions; see Stiglitz (2006), p. 21.

25 As has been explained more in detail in the previous Chaps. 2 and 3 of this book, within the prevailing monetary order, private (deposit) banks indeed play a key role in the process(es) of money creation every time they provide credit to other economic agents (individuals, families, enterprises, but also public authorities) on top of the cash reserves (usually issued by the central monetary institution) which they hold.

Within this system, the global amount of money which is circulating in a certain economy at a given time, is basically (and considered from a legal point of view) made up of two components, *on one hand*, the amount of "chartal" or "cash" money (i.e. the number of banknotes and coins issued by a public authority, in many countries, at least for an important part, the central bank)[41], and, *on the other hand*, the amount of "scriptural" money consisting of the claims towards the banking sector[42].

In most countries, the central monetary institution is usually, ultimately, responsible for controlling the global amount of money within its economy (both by guarding the amounts of "chartal" or cash money it issues itself, as by guarding, especially through its "lender of last resort"-policy, the amount of scriptural money brought into circulation).

The amount of "chartal" or cash money is hereby managed "directly" by the central monetary institution, as the latter itself determines how many bank notes it brings into circulation (and in some countries: also coins, albeit in other countries/ monetary systems, coinage is still performed by other public authorities).

Guarding the amount of scriptural money is managed "indirectly" through the so-called "lender of last resort-task" of the central monetary institution. In very general terms, this "lender of last resort"-task implies that, as private banks are obliged to pay out their scriptural obligations when the holder of a banking account[43] requires so, they need to have a sufficient amount of "chartal" or "cash" money at their disposal in order to fulfill such payment requests of the account holders and for which they are ultimately dependent on the intervention of the central bank (which in theory has access to an unlimited supply of "chartal" or cash money, as it may legally and literally "produce" it). This process is in practice controlled by the central monetary institution through different monetary mechanisms, such as several methods of credit lending (against interest charging) by the

[41]Whereby the cash reserves retained by the market players who are authorized to create private money, mainly private banks, normally is not taken into account when calculating the total amount of "chartal" or "cash" money that has been issued by the central monetary institution.

[42]I.e. the total of claims on private banks, regardless of the fact that such claims are generated either as a counterclaim for an original cash deposit or for a scriptural payment transaction, or as the result of a commitment from a private bank to grant a credit.

[43]And hence of a claim towards the bank such an account represents (which, from a contract law point of view, forms the counterpart of the scriptural obligation of the bank itself).

central bank to the private (deposit) banks which are using its services.[44] (See, for more details, above, under Chap. 2 of this book.)

Harari mentions that in 2006, there was, world-wide, a total amount of money for a value of ±473 trillion USD in circulation, of which "chartal" or "cash" money (coins and bank notes) for an estimated value of 47 trillion USD[45] (so about ten percent of the total amount of money). **26**

More recent detailed data on the size of the "total global amount of money" in general, and of the global amount of scriptural money more specifically, seem to be no longer available (at least are they not (easily) accessible), although it is believed by some authors that the scriptural money supply by the private banking sector keeps representing an ever bigger multiple of the banknotes (and coins) in circulation.[46]

There are however partial data available on the amount of money in a number of (important) economic regions/countries. **27**

As an illustration, the following data regarding the money quantities in some economic zones in 2013 and 2014 are quoted:

- According to data provided by the ECB, there were, at the end of 2013, *on one hand*, 17 billion euro bank notes circulating, representing a total value of 956 billion euro (or 0.956 trillion euro), and, *on the other hand,* 106 billion euro and eurocent coins, representing a total value of 28 billion euro.[47]
  Also according to data provided by the ECB, in October 2014, the total "narrow amount of money" (in macroeconomic terms also expressed as the amount of "M1" money) consisting of, *on one hand,* "chartal" or cash money, and, *on the other hand*, the non-cash money in the form of so-called "overnight deposits"

[44]See *e.g.* De Grauwe (2014), p. 190.

It should be pointed out that in classical economic writings, money forms have been further classified dependent on their long or short term convertibility into cash ("chartal") money. However, from a more legal approach, the basic distinction is the one between "chartal" money (i.e. the cash money created by a central bank or similar (governmental) institution) and "scriptural" money (i.e. money created by a private bank or similar financial institution when it grants a private credit).

[45]Harari (2014), pp. 198–199.

[46]Martin has put this as follows:

> The vast majority of our national money – around 90 per cent in the US, for example, and 97 per cent in the UK – has no physical existence at all. It consists merely of our account balances at our banks. The only tangible apparatus employed in most monetary payments today is a plastic card and a keypad. (See Martin 2013, p. 13.)

See also Deweirdt a.o. who explain the historical evolution of scriptural money creation in Belgium. These authors point out that scriptural money has steadily grown during the second half of the twentieth century. In the 1950s, scriptural money accounted for ±40% of the total amount of money in Belgium, a percentage which has in the 1990s already risen to ±70% (see Deweirdt et al. 1997, p. 33).

[47]http://www.ecb.europa.eu/euro/banknotes/circulation/html/index.nl.html (last consulted on September 23th 2014).

(i.e. mainly deposit accounts), amounted to 5747 billion euro (=5.747 trillion Euro) for the entire euro area.

According to the same source, of the aforementioned "narrow amount of money", 13.5%, or 949 billion euro consisted of "chartal" or cash money, and 83.5%, or 4797 billion euro (=4.797 trillion euro), of non-cash or scriptural money.[48]

Also in October 2014, the total "broad amount of money" (in macroeconomic terms also expressed as the amount of money "M3"), which, inter alia, also includes longer term deposit accounts and shares, amounted to 10,134 billion euro (=10.134 trillion euro) for the entire euro area.[49]

It is furthermore mentioned that within the Eurozone a relative decline in the share of cash money (estimated at hardly 9%) in the total amount of money is taking place[50], which is a further illustration of the ever increasing (not to say dominating) role of non-cash money (i.e. private money created out of credit lending by private banks).

- According to similar data provided by the American "Federal Reserve", in October 2014, the total so-called "seasonally adjusted" "narrow amount of money" M1 within the USA amounted to 2854.3 billion or 2.8543 trillion USD.[51]

  According to the same source, of this total narrow amount of money, 43.1%, i.e. 1230.2 billion or 1.2302 trillion USD, consisted of cash money (illustrating that, in the USA, cash is far more used than in the Eurozone); 0.1%, or 3 billion USD consisted of travelers checks from nonbank issuers; 40.0%, i.e. 1140.9 billion or 1.1409 trillion USD consisted of directly claimable credits with commercial banks (with explicit exclusion of the amounts held by depository institutions, the U.S. government, and foreign banks and official institutions), and 16.8%, i.e. 480.1 billion or 0.4801 trillion consisted of other checkable deposits (OCDs).

  Since March 23th 2006, the "Federal Reserve" has not published figures on the "broad amount of money" M3.[52] The last known "broad amount of money" M3 figure of the United States of America was announced on March 16th 2006 and then amounted to 10,294.3 billion or 10.2943 trillion USD (figures of February 2006).[53]

  Meanwhile, in October 2014, the "intermediate amount of Money" (in macroeconomic terms also expressed as the amount of money "M2") had in the USA risen to a formidable 11,511.3 billion or 11.5113 trillion USD[54]

[48]http://www.ecb.europa.eu/press/pdf/md/md1410.pdf (last consulted on November 27th 2014).

[49]http://www.ecb.europa.eu/press/pdf/md/md1410.pdf (last consulted on November 27th 2014).

[50]http://www.ecb.europa.eu/press/pdf/md/md1410.pdf (last consulted on November 27th 2014).

[51]http://www.federalreserve.gov/releases/h6/current/#t3tg1f3; last consulted on December 10th 2014.

[52]http://www.federalreserve.gov/Releases/h6/discm3.htm; last consulted on December 10th 2014.

[53]http://www.federalreserve.gov/releases/h6/20060316/; last consulted on December 10th 2014.

[54]http://www.federalreserve.gov/releases/h6/current/; last consulted on December 10th 2014.

(even though this is still considerably less than the government debt of the USA of the same year; see above, at marg. 202 of Chap. 3 of this book).

- According to data provided by the Bank of Japan, in November 2014, the total "narrow amount of money" in Japan amounted to 593.9 trillion Yen. According to the same source, of this aforementioned amount of money, 14%, or 83.3 trillion Yen, consisted of cash money and 86%, or 510.6 trillion Yen consisted of non-cash or scriptural money.[55]

  In November 2014, the total "broad amount of money" M3 of Japan amounted to 1199.7 trillion Yen.[56]

Comparable figures of February 2016 confirm these trends:

- Again according to data provided by the ECB, there were in February 2016, *on one hand* 18.2 billion euro bank notes circulating, representing a total value of 1063 billion euro or 1.063 trillion euro, and *on the other hand,* 116 billion euro coins representing a total value of 25.8 billion euro.[57]

  Also according to data provided by the ECB, in February 2016, the total "narrow amount of money" "M1" amounted to 6716 billion Euro (=6.716 trillion Euro) for the entire euro area.

  According to the same source, of the aforementioned "narrow amount of money", 15.6%, or 1047 billion Euro consisted of cash money, and 84.4%, or 5669 billion Euro (=5.669 trillion euro), of non-cash or scriptural money.[58]

  In February 2016, the total "broad amount of money" "M3" amounted to 10,968 billion Euro (= 10.968 trillion Euro) for the entire euro area.[59]

  It was again mentioned that, within the Eurozone, the relative decline in the share of cash money (to hardly 9%) in the total amount of money was a continuing trend.[60]

- According to data provided by the American "Federal Reserve", in February 2016, the total so-called "seasonally adjusted" "narrow amount of money" M1[61] within the USA amounted to 3101.6 billion or 3.1016 trillion USD.

  According to the same source, of this total narrow amount of money, 43.5%, i.e. 1349.9 billion or 1.3499 trillion USD, consisted of cash money; 0.08%, or 2.4 billion USD consisted of travelers checks from nonbank issuers; 39.7%, i.e. 1231.1 billion or 1.2311 trillion USD consisted of demand deposits at domestically chartered commercial banks, and 16.7%, i.e. 518.1 billion or 0.5181 trillion consisted of other checkable deposits (OCDs).

---

[55] http://www.boj.or.jp/en/statistics/money/ms/ms1411.pdf; last consulted on December 10th 2014.

[56] http://www.boj.or.jp/en/statistics/money/ms/ms1411.pdf; last consulted on December 10th 2014.

[57] http://www.ecb.europa.eu/stats/money/euro/circulation/html/index.en.html (last consulted on April 1st, 2016).

[58] https://www.ecb.europa.eu/press/pdf/md/md1602.pdf (last consulted on April 1st, 2016).

[59] https://www.ecb.europa.eu/press/pdf/md/md1602.pdf (last consulted on April 1st, 2016).

[60] https://www.ecb.europa.eu/press/pdf/md/md1602.pdf (last consulted on April 1st, 2016).

[61] http://www.federalreserve.gov/releases/h6/current/#t5tg1f1 (last consulted on April 1st, 2016).

Meanwhile, in February 2016, the "intermediate amount of Money" "M2" had in the USA further risen to 12,472.2 billion or 12.4722 trillion USD.[62]

- According to data provided by the Bank of Japan, in February 2016, the total "narrow amount of money" in Japan amounted to 630.9 trillion Yen. According to the same source, of this aforementioned amount of money, 14.3%, or 90.3 trillion Yen, consisted of cash money and 85.7%, or 540.6 trillion Yen consisted of non-cash or scriptural money.[63]

  In February 2016, the total "broad amount of money" "M3" of Japan amounted to 1237.7 trillion Yen.[64]

Further Illustration 4.1: Available Amount of Money Related to the Capital of the "Multi Billionaires"

When compared to the vast wealth of the extremely rich "multi-billionaires" (see above, Further Illustration 3.25), the aforementioned figures on the available amount of (cash and scriptural) money within, for instance, the Eurozone are, as such, quite revealing about the unjust character of global wealth distribution.

A person having a wealth of for instance 5 billion euro has by himself a fortune which is worth ±1/200th of the amount of cash money which has been put into circulation in the entire Eurozone.

If, as a further example, one would take the sum of the amounts of the (estimated) wealth of the "top 10" richest people on the Forbes—list of 2014, this would lead to a figure of ±530.5 billion USD. When converting this amount to euro (by applying the exchange rates of December 3th 2014), the said figure equals ±431 billion euro, implying that the combined wealth of this "Forbes-top 10", would cover ±45% of the total amount of cash money circulating in the Eurozone in November 2014.

This further implies that, in the same example, if the "members" of the "Forbes top 10" all would convert their fortunes into "cash" money[65], subsequently would place these cash deposits with banks in the Eurozone and eventually would decide to withdraw these deposits in cash (so-called

(continued)

[62]http://www.federalreserve.gov/releases/h6/current/#t5tg1f1 (last consulted on April 1st, 2016).

[63]http://www.boj.or.jp/en/statistics/money/ms/ms1602.pdf (last consulted on April 1st, 2016).

[64]http://www.boj.or.jp/en/statistics/money/ms/ms1602.pdf (last consulted on April 1st, 2016).

[65]Of course, it is rather uncertain that such a hypothetical situation would actually occur. It needs, for instance, to be taken into consideration that the large fortunes of the "Forbes-top 10" members, are most probably not easily convertible in cash as they most probably consist of all kinds of goods not easily to be sold, and certainly not on the same moment, such as, spread over many countries, different types of tangible assets (real estate, all kinds of consumer goods, art, etc.), in addition to all types of financial instruments, among which shares held in the big enterprises the rich of the planet control, and probably also huge amounts of cash money and/or immediately available bank deposits. Needless to say that a (speedy) conversion of such fortunes would not be an easy task.

Further Illustration 4.1 (continued)

"inverse money substitution"), this would mean that an equivalent of ±45% of the amount of cash euro's currently in circulation would come into the hands of but 10 people of the world.

This is evidently only a rough comparison (and the mentioned calculations could undoubtedly be done in a much more precise way, for instance if we would have had better access to the required data and if we could rely on precise figures of the exact same dates). Ideally, the comparison should (also and mainly) be made taking into account the available cash reserves of the private banks in the Eurozone themselves, in order to be able to relate the magnitude of the fictitious request for payment from the previous example to the available cash reserves of the private banking sector within the Eurozone itself.

However, in the context of the given example, one could furthermore assume that the private banks of the Eurozone would probably not have enough cash reserves at their disposal to immediately meet the hypothetical request for re-payment of the "Forbes-top 10" (not even by withdrawing these from colleagues and competitors on the so-called "interbank market"), causing, in a similar hypothetical case, the private banks to be faced with such large conversion requests that they would probably be forced to take out massive short term credits with the ECB (and the ECB itself would, probably, itself be forced to create masses of additional bank notes, which, in the aforementioned fictitious example, would, most probably, result in an increase of the total amount of cash money by a little less than half of the actual amount of cash circulating). As a consequence, after such a massive hypothetical conversion request, most likely a little less than one third of the total amount of cash of the Eurozone would come in the hands of 10 people (and, hence, the other two thirds of the available cash money, in the hands of (according to data from Eurostat) the at the time of our given example then other 334,570,678 people living in the Eurozone).

Taking into account that, in 2014, according to the quoted Eurostat data, the number of people within the Eurozone (then consisting of 18 countries) came to 334,570,678[66], a further (rough) calculation points out that an average inhabitant of the Eurozone then had ±2836 euro of cash available. In the aforementioned example, the Forbes-top 10 people, would, compared to this, together have about 431 billion euro in cash at their disposal, or, an average of ±43.1 billion euro per person, i.e. each 15 million times more cash

(continued)

[66]http://epp.eurostat.ec.europa.eu/tgm/table.do?tab=table&init=1&language=en&pcode=tps00001&plugin=1 (last consulted on December 4th 2014).

Further Illustration 4.1 (continued)

than the average European, be it, as said before, in the hypothesis that the (other) Europeans would themselves not have converted their assets into cash (whereby it needs to be pointed out that the comparison between the two groups of people would only be fully relevant if we could rely on figures of a hypothetical conversion into cash of the assets of all the (other) residents of the Eurozone as well, which would result in a more subtle image).

In a further hypothetical example whereby the "members" of the "Forbes-top 10" only would convert half of their respective fortunes into cash and through a so-called "inverse money substitution", would "convert" this cash fully into Euro's, this still would cause the total amount of cash, through the additional creation of bank notes in order to meet the conversion requests involved, to increase by a percentage of $\pm 23\%$. In this example, the Forbes-top 10 would then all together hold an amount of about 215 billion euro in cash, or an average of 21.5 billion per person, i.e. 7.5 million times more cash each than the average European has at his disposal.

Notwithstanding the rough nature of the aforementioned examples (which could be calculated in a more refined way if more precise data were available), the aforementioned comparisons nevertheless give (at least) a good idea of the (incredible) size of the fortunes of the 10 richest people in the world, compared to the cash which, be it in one of the richest territories of the planet, is available to the "average person" to cover his daily needs.

4.5.2 *Putting an End to Private Money Creation*

4.5.2.1 General Motivation for the Proposal of Ending Private Money Creation

28 If the abovementioned figures, especially in light of the huge financial crisis of 2008, demonstrate one thing, it is that the processes of (scriptural) money creation by the private banking sector over the past decades have been conducted in an extremely undisciplined way, which in turn has led to a seemingly unbridled growth in the total money supply, with a disruptive effect on the real economy as a result.

Also earlier financial crises in history were of a similar nature, whereby one could even speak of a "repetitive pattern"[67] (referred to by Galbraith as cycles of "cycles of euphoria and panic")[68].

[67]See furthermore Galbraith (1990).

[68]Galbraith (1975), p. 21.

From this, it can be concluded that the unbridled pursuit of profit which dominates the behavior of private market players in general, among who private bankers and other private money creating institutions more specifically, has proven to be incompatible with the aim of a disciplined and reliable growth of the amounts of money put available to a given economy.[69] As a result, private money creation by the banking sector has proven a poor mechanism for steering economic growth in a way respecting the capacity of the planet and aiming at the general well-being of mankind.

On the contrary, private money creation has basically turned into a mechanism only serving the interest of a limited elite of (very) rich people on the planet who, in general, show little consideration for anything else than their own private interests and have, again and again, proven to be willing to sacrifice all other values to their own greed.[70]

The earlier mentioned "*privatization of profits and socialization of losses*"--phenomenon is but the manifestation hereof in recent history.

For this reason, it is here proposed that within the "New Monetary World Order", by way of its "third pillar", private market players would henceforth no longer be allowed to participate in the processes of money creation at all, a task which, on the contrary, would in the future completely be assigned to the monetary authority (ies) themselves, in other words, to the newly (to be) established "New Monetary World Institute" (and to its components within the countries participating in the New Monetary World Order).

The abovementioned proposal, however radical, is partially in line with posi- **29**
tions which earlier on in history were taken by prominent policy makers, in addition to certain renowned economists, as well as with certain, more recent concerns expressed by certain (central) bankers themselves.

In (relatively) recent times, for instance Karl Marx was one of the renowned economists who have argued that money creation should entirely become a government task: Marx hereby considered the seizure of the credit system (hence of private money creation) by a central (public) authority as one of the possible solutions of preventing the collapse of the capitalist economic system.[71]

However, for those who would consider that quoting Marx is synonymous to defending the systems of communism which have been prevailing in the twentieth century, further reference can also be made to a number of (in essence not very different) statements by various prominent statesmen from the American scene.

---

[69]See one of the main objectives of the I.M.F. laid down in article I. (ii) of the Articles of Agreement: "*to facilitate the expansion and balanced growth of international trade, and to contribute thereby to the promotion and maintenance of high levels of employment and real income and to the development of the productive resources of all members as primary objectives of economic policy*" (at https://www.imf.org/external/pubs/ft/aa/#art1; last consulted on March 30th 2016).

[70]Who still would doubt this is advised to read Luyendijk (2015).

[71]Vandewalle (1976), p. 101.

On the Marxist ideas about money, see Mandel (1962), tII, pp. 252 a.f.

To start with, reference can be made to one of the founding fathers of the (former) American Union, more precisely Thomas Jefferson (1743–1826) who is reported to have expressed his concern that:

> If the American people ever allow private banks to control the issue of their currency, first by inflation, then by deflation, the banks (. . .) will deprive the people of all property until their children wake-up homeless on the continent their fathers conquered (. . .). The issuing power should be taken from the banks and restored to the people, to whom it properly belongs. – Thomas Jefferson in the context of the debate on the "Re-charter of the Bank Bill" (1809)".[72]

James Madison (1751–1836) is also reported to have stated in a very similar way that

> history records that the money changers have used every form of abuse, intrigue, deceit, and violent means possible to maintain their control over governments by controlling money and its issuance.[73]

Abraham Lincoln (1809–1865) shared a similar insight, which can be demonstrated by the following quote holding that

> the Government should create, issue, and circulate all the currency and credits needed to satisfy the spending power of the Government and the buying power of consumers. By the adoption of these principles, the taxpayers will be saved immense sums of interest. Money will cease to be master and become the servant of humanity.[74]

The long list of statesmen having realized that money is (or needs to be) a public (ly created) good and not a mechanism controlled by private banks continues in the twentieth century with Theodore Roosevelt (1858–1919) who is reported to have held that the

> issue of currency should be lodged with the government and be protected from domination by Wall Street. We are opposed to (. . .) provisions [which] would place our currency and credit system in private hands.[75]

Woodrow Wilson (1856–1924) is mentioned to have stated, only a few years after he had announced the *Federal Reserve Act* (1913) (leading to the establishment of the American "Federal Reserve" which, from the beginning, has been dominated by the private banking sector) the following:

> I am a most unhappy man. I have unwillingly ruined my country. A great industrial nation is controlled by its system of credit. Our system of credit is concentrated. The growth of the nation, therefore, and all our activities are in the hands of a few men. We have come to be

---

[72] http://www.themoneymasters.com/the-money-masters/famous-quotations-on-banking/ (last consulted on November 28th 2014).

[73] http://www.themoneymasters.com/the-money-masters/famous-quotations-on-banking/ (last consulted on November 28th 2014).

[74] http://www.themoneymasters.com/the-money-masters/famous-quotations-on-banking/ (last consulted on November 28th 2014).

[75] http://www.themoneymasters.com/the-money-masters/famous-quotations-on-banking/ (last consulted on November 28th 2014).

> one of the worst ruled, one of the most completely controlled and dominated Governments in the civilized world no longer a Government by free opinion, no longer a Government by conviction and the vote of the majority, but a Government by the opinion and duress of a small group of dominant men. [76]

It is somehow bewildering that all these prominent American Statesmen, in some cases already centuries ago, reached the (correct) conclusion that money (and money creation) need(s) to be a public good and should not be controlled by a private sector (namely the private banking sector), but that, nevertheless, up till today (and, under the impulse of "economic neoliberalism", even more than ever), the processes of money creation continue to be left in the hands of the private banking sector, and, hence, delivered to its unbridled pursuit of money (the detrimental consequences of which the world has suffered from for a long time already, as once more in history has been demonstrated by the events of and since 2008). **30**

This is undoubtedly the clearest illustration of the inability of democracies to resist the powers of capitalism (referred to, inter alia, by Stiglitz as an expression of the failure of democracy).

Furthermore, also renowned economist such as Keynes and Galbraith have kept on indicating that, because of the special nature of (bank) credit lending leading to (private) money creation, the (cost) price hereof mainly consisting of (bank) interests, is totally different from the cost price of any other product, or any other service within the economy. **31**

According to these authors, the price setting for newly created money should hence not be left to the (invisible hand of the) law of supply and demand (as is currently to a too large extent the case under the prevailing capitalist money creation systems).

On the contrary, money creation and its price setting mechanisms should be dealt with as a "social construct".[77]

In this view (relating to Keynes himself), the thought clearly arises that money is "a public good", or at least needs to be become such a public good again. It should, in this regard, be further noted that Keynes, in his role as one of the notorious architects of the IMF-treaty, had effectively advocated the introduction of a global system of public money creation (as an alternative for the systems of monetary aids between IMF countries), which however was eventually not adopted in the IMF treaty of 1944–1945, but which, in 1969, would lead to the introduction of the so-called "SDRs" (as a less extreme variant for a system of effective international money creation by a supra-national organization itself) (see further, at marg. 61–62 of this chapter).

The fact that, up till this present day, no further attempts have been made to introduce a global monetary system which would completely be based on public money creation (and that even no true dialogue on the subject has been attempted)

---

[76] http://www.themoneymasters.com/the-money-masters/famous-quotations-on-banking/ (last consulted on November 28th 2014).

[77] Pettifor (2014).

is, furthermore, a striking illustration of the power of big enterprises in general (see the earlier mentioned "corporatocracy"), and of private banks more specifically (to the extent that one could even speak of a "bankocracy").

32 It is furthermore worth mentioning that, in the recent past, even the Bank of England, which can hardly be qualified as one of the more progressive monetary institutions of the world, at the beginning of October 2014, announced that it wanted to have more authority to impact the mortgage market (this probably means: the mortgage credit lending market), including influencing the maximum values of mortgage credit, in order to attempt to avoid further disruptions on the financial markets.[78]

33 It goes without saying that in the here put forward proposals for a New Monetary World Order, the processes of money creation should, henceforth, reflect the (correct) viewpoint that money is to be considered as a "public good", the creation of which cannot be left in the hands of the private sector, but needs to come under the direct and exclusive authority of a supra-national public organization (hereafter referred to as "the New Monetary World Institute"), to be formed and governed by democratic principles and mechanisms.

4.5.2.2 Further Motivation of the Proposal to End Private Money Creation

34 From the foregoing, it may be clear that within the current monetary and financial system, it is mainly the private (deposit) banks (in addition to similar financial institutions who may differ from country to country) who decide upon credit requests made by other economic agents (namely individuals, families, enterprises and even the public sector), and hence have the power to create new (private) money.

In other words, it is also (private) banks that decide (*i*) who is sufficiently creditworthy in order to be eligible for a credit (and thus for being granted newly created scriptural money), and (*ii*) under what conditions—especially conditions and modalities on the repayment of the credit and on the payment of interests—such credit can be obtained (and through this: under what conditions private money creation takes place).

35 In the current context, this process of private money creation has evolved into an important source of income for the private banking sector, a phenomenon which during the last centuries (especially since the decline of the historical clerical interest prohibition) has been an important factor leading to the wide gaps between the rich and the poor which have occurred world-wide (see above, under Sect. 3.4.8 of Chap. 3 of this book), but also to the huge government shortages which countries all over the world are facing (see above, under Sect. 3.4.6 of Chap. 3 of this book).

[78]Treanor (2014).

Rather than what economic neo-liberalism wants us to believe, such an economy driven by private money creation (which is one of the main foundations of capitalism) has however not led to an increased well-being for all mankind[79], but has, on the contrary, on a global scale, contributed to a continuous increase of wealth for a small elite of people, especially those holding the shares issued by financial institutions themselves (and those of other big businesses enterprises) and the CEO's and higher staff employed by them, in addition to, *on one hand* a devastating poverty for a vast portion of the world population (of poor(er) countries) and, *on the other hand* a modest level of prosperity for the rest of the world population (especially the lower and middle classes of the rich(er) countries).

Through the different capitalist mechanisms, among which the mechanism of private money creation by the private banking sector, a vast majority of mankind has thus basically been condemned to a status of "contemporary slavery" being forced to lead a life exclusively aimed at providing labor in order to make the modern "feudal lords", namely the extreme rich, ever more rich.[80]

Hence, it should be clear that the prevailing mechanism of private money **36**
creation is mainly an instrument of (unbridled) pursuit of profits for private banks (and their shareholders, as well as their (management) staff), whereby all related risks are shamelessly passed on to the rest of society (especially the lower and middle classes), and this without any concern for the general interest (among which the general well-being of all of mankind).[81]

In fact, when things go wrong, as has for instance been the case during the recent severe financial crisis of 2008, and when the extremely high risks which are inherently part of the mechanisms created (and deliberately wanted) by the private banking sector are manifesting, eventually even in the form of a loss of trust by the rest of the population (and, as a result, the underlying social contract by the grace of which the existing monetary system exists, even gets undermined), then the

---

[79]This is the (false) promise of the so-called "trickle down-economics".

[80]One of the first economists to have pointed this out was John Kenneth Galbraith (see especially Galbraith 1974, 295 p.; see furthermore Lipton 2014).

Galbraith has in this regard also pointed out that, because of this, modern man barely does not dispose of any real free time for doing anything else than providing labor to capital.

As elaborated before (see above, under Sects. 3.4.4 and 3.4.5 of Chap. 3 of this book), banking discipline has furthermore almost disappeared over the past years, also and especially at the level of private money creation, which was favored, particularly from the end of 1980s, both by the liberalization and the de-regularization of the credit and financial system, as well as by implementing new financial techniques, such as securitization of claims and comparable techniques, which have allowed banks to divest their credit portfolio's into separate vehicles the financing of which is left to third party depositors and/or investors (and, because of this, the estimated solvency of the borrowers has become secondary for banks, as under these conditions the credit risk is ultimately passed on to third parties).

[81]One may, furthermore, refer to a saying of William Paterson (1658–1719), one of the founders of the "*Bank of England*" in 1694: ***"The bank hath benefit of interest on all moneys which it creates out of nothing."*** (See http://www.themoneymasters.com/the-money-masters/famous-quotations-on-banking/ (last consulted on November 28th 2014.)

banking sector will, without any shame, call upon (national) public authorities to get very generous (to an extent of which other private market players can only dream) non market conform subsidies, so that the banking sector can be kept alive in an artificial way, under reference to its role in the processes of private money creation and therefore the underlying basis of trust which supports the economy.[82]

Each time when the banking sector needs to be sustained in such a way—i.e. ultimately with financial means obtained by national authorities through taxes imposed on the lower and middle classes—the population of an economy where this occurs, becomes once more the victim of the banking sector's excessive greed.

It may hence be clear that this "victimization" of the general public to the benefit of the (extremely) wealthy of the planet occurs on several levels[83]:

- *firstly:* on the level of the price for the privately created money (i.e. the interests charged on credit);
- *secondly*: by, for instance in the context of securitization and other similar operations, being burdened with the risks related to private money creation (after the banks have skimmed the profits first);
- *thirdly*: in the context of *bail out*-operations, when tax money (especially paid by the lower and middle classes and from which the rich are to a large extent exempt) needs to be spent in order to maintain this inherently unfair money creation mechanism;
- and, *horribile dictu,* even a fourth time, due to the interests which private banks make on the ever growing debts of many countries, whereby in numerous countries this debt burden has severely increased as a result of said bailout operations.

This is precisely why recent literature has described this inherently ambiguous attitude of the private banking system as "*a privatization of gains and a socialization of losses*" (whereby it can even be pointed out that the banking sector seems to have been aware of this for a long time; see above, at marg. 3 of Chap. 3 of this book, the earlier mentioned quote of the Rothschild-brothers).

37 As throughout history, it has repeatedly been demonstrated that the private banking sector is incapable of (and probably even unwilling to) show(ing) a more healthy monetary discipline (whereby further reference can be made to the numerous bankruptcies of banks which have repeatedly occurred throughout history[84]), presumably for the main reason that, supported (and encouraged by) the teachings of economic (neo-)liberalism, this private banking sector is too much concerned with making profits, instead of with correctly estimating the risks related to credit lending and money creation in a sound way.

All this has been extensively examined in Chaps. 2 and 3 above, to which further reference can be made.

---

[82]See Luyendijk (2015).

[83]As has already been pointed out before; see above, Further Illustration 3.6.

[84]Once again, reference can be made to Galbraith (1990).

To paraphrase the Belgian ethical philosopher Jaap Kruithof: how much longer will mankind bear to stand by this societal model where all values are sacrificed to the short term financial interests of a few individuals, while all other values, among which the general well-being of mankind and a proper care for the planet and its resources, are continuously compromised.[85] 38

In order to truly change this, the New Monetary World Order proposed in this book should, as argued before, also at the level of money creation itself, choose for altruistic underlying policy aims, namely, in addition to the (general) well-being of the whole of mankind, a spirit of respect for the (limits) of the capacity of the planet (see the above proposed "Pillar II" for the New Monetary World Order, at marg. 12 a.f. of this chapter).[86] 39

It is very obvious that the fulfillment of these objectives cannot be left in the hands of private market players, but should be turned over to a public institution, namely the newly to be established New Monetary World Institute.

4.5.2.3 General Outlook of the "Third Pillar" of the New Monetary World Order

Hence, as a third basic starting point or "pillar", the New Monetary World Order should make the clear policy choice that money should become a "public good" (once again) and, consequently, that in the process(es) of money creation, there can be no further room for any participation of private market players.[87] 40

---

[85]Kruithof (1985), p. 84.

And in case one would be inclined to doubt the vision of Kruithof, reference can even be made to the quotes mentioned earlier in this treatise of, for instance, Henry Ford and the Rothschild-brothers (see above, at marg. 3 of Chap. 3 of this book), in addition to the similar views shared by the most diverse historical figures, such as Karl Marx and some of the "founding fathers" and early presidents of the USA itself (see above, at marg. 29 of this chapter).

Pettifor (2014) has phrased this concern as follows:

> The challenge now facing the world is this: can democratic states regain control over "the fate of currencies, social systems, public infrastructures, private savings etc." – or are we forever beholden and victim to unseen and unaccountable 'creditor-gods'?
>
> Are the world's people, their social and political organisations, their small and large businesses going to tolerate regular financial and economic crises, in which the 'creditor-gods' make all the gains, raid the balance sheets of taxpayer-backed central banks, while real incomes of taxpayers fall, governments remain supine, opportunities for this and future generations diminish, and social and political breakdown threaten? Or is it inevitable that people will mobilise – behind reactionary as well as democratic political organisations – to resist such onslaughts on their taxes and living standards?
>
> Given the challenge posed to Haute Finance by right-wing and fascist political parties in for example the Euro area, and given the weakness of more progressive political organisations, my own prognosis is pessimistic.

[86]See already Hoefnagels (1975), pp. 12 a.f.

[87]See furthermore Gore (2013a), p. 37 (also: Gore 2013b, p. 59).

41 It could indeed be expected from a modern civilization that it would start to draw, in a more resolute way, lessons from the past than it has been willing to do so far.

If anything can be learned from the ± past four to five centuries of (Western) monetary history, it is definitely the fact that the methods of private money creation (by private bankers), again and again in history, have turned out to be the perfect recipe for all types of distortions and financial crises, which moreover have above all allowed a (financial) elite to accumulate ever more (extreme) wealth at the expense of much suffering and distress for a large part of the rest of mankind.[88]

A second subsequent lesson which can be drawn from (recent) monetary and financial history entails the fact that as long as profits continue to pour in, the financial sector monopolizes them without much hesitation and for the exclusive benefit of a small elite group of bank owners and bank employees (especially the shareholders and (other) capital providers, as well as the members of the banks' board of directors and the banks' top management) (i.e. a so-called "*privatization of gains*"), but as soon as the risks which are generated by capitalist banking mechanisms become apparent in the form of losses, the same banks will, without shame[89], pass these losses on to the rest of society (such as the consumers of the banking products and services, or the states which need to help the ailing banks, mostly through bail out procedures[90] funded by tax money) (i.e. so-called "*socialization of losses*").

Given the central role played by private banking in the creation and circulation of money, the currently prevailing capitalist economic system hereby often leaves society no other choice than to bear the consequences of such a shift (given the risk, as the example of Lehman Brothers in recent history has shown[91], that when the losses are left to the bank in question, this can have a disrupting and even destabilizing effect on the financial and monetary system, and hence on the entire economy, a paradigm which has also been described as the "*too big to fail*"-paradigm).[92]

It speaks for itself that such an inherently fundamental imbalance in dividing profits and losses created by the private banking system can no longer be tolerated in the context of a new, altruistically inspired monetary system.

---

[88]See especially Galbraith (1990).

[89]And moreover based upon an ideology (namely "economic neo-liberalism") which opposes any kind of support to the benefit of the poor and the deprived, under the argument that such support would stimulate laziness.

[90]A.o. by having bought bank shares and by simultaneously having bought, guaranteed or insured toxic banks assets (see Skidelsky 2010, p. 17).

[91]See McDonald and Robinson (2009), p. 308; see also Smithers (2013), p. 87; Krugman (2012), p. 114.

[92]Engelen (2011), pp. 28–29. See also Geysels (2014), pp. 11–59, especially pp. 20–21; Streeck (2015), p. 85.

Hence can such a New Monetary World Order, as aforementioned, not entail much other benefit from a continued participation in the processes of money creation by the private banking system which clearly has shown that it is solely inspired by an unbridled pursuit of profit of its underlying shareholders, or otherwise put, by the greed of the latter.

The proposed "second" and "third" pillars of the New Monetary World Order **42**
should, obviously, go hand in hand.

It is clear from past experiences that the current private banking system, as driven by the unbridled pursuit of profits by its underlying shareholders, has proven not to be fit for the purpose of keeping the amount of money (an hence the pressure it creates on the world economy and the worlds resources) within reasonable boundaries, and neither for the purpose of establishing an elementary fairness as regards the distribution of wealth within societies.

Also for this reason, in a (more) altruistic and just monetary system, the control on money growth (and therefore of the burden which money imposes on the planet and its resources) can no longer be left to private financial institutions.

The elimination of private banks as participants in the money creation process **43**
will, obviously, need to be accompanied by a re-orientation of their role within the economy.

Indeed, a monetary model where there will no longer be room for private money creation by private banks will also need to be based on the principle that some forms of credit lending can no longer be left to private banking.

Within the New Monetary World Order, money creation through credit lending could, as such, still be kept in place as a mechanism of creating new money, especially as regards the creation of new money on behalf of (other) private market players (see further, under Sect. 4.7.3), albeit that the granting of such money creation power should completely be left over to a central monetary institution, hereafter also named "the New Monetary World Institute", in addition to a set of national central banks (working closely together under the auspices of said New Monetary World Institute) who together would have as one of their main tasks to provide credit (leading to newly created money) to the general public.

As will be elaborated upon further in detail (see further, under Sect. 4.7.3), some of these credits should, in the future, moreover be provided in light of policy considerations of general well-being (instead of, as is the case under the prevailing banking system, for the sake of the individual pursuit of profits by banks and other credit lenders, mainly on behalf of their rich shareholders).

It would furthermore be proposed to require from private banks themselves that, in **44**
the future, they would finance their further activities in the same way as any other market players, in other words with on one hand equity capital (collected among capital providers and/or built up out of past profits) and on the other hand by borrowing themselves (thus through means of credit, in any form, i.e. whether incorporated into financial instruments or not, provided by other private market players).[93]

[93]Compare Claerhout (2014a), p. 6; Claerhout (2014b), pp. 36–38 (containing an interview with Sheila Bair, former president of the US "*Financial Stability Board*").

Under this system, such a private bank will then be able to spend these collected means on different types of investments, at its own choice and risk, but however without the convenience of being allowed to develop a spending behavior relying on a system of private money creation and/or the convenience of a lender of last resort.

At most, the new system could thus be developed that private banking would continue to have access to credits granted by the future (public) central banks (forming part of the aforementioned New Monetary World Order), but only to the same extent and under the same conditions as all other private business enterprises (so that, in the New Monetary World Order, private banks would no longer enjoy a preferential treatment in this regard).

Also these proposals will be further elaborated upon in this book (see further, at marg. 149–156 of this chapter).

45 Through this newly proposed system, it will also be possible to disconnect (at least to a large degree) money creation (which thus will become "a public good") from the impact of speculative behavior, and the latter will entirely be brought into the private domain (without being able to cause any interferences with the money creation function itself).[94]

The many risks which are related to the investment behavior of private banks (as has, throughout the ages, been proven again and again), will henceforth no longer be able to hold the entire economy (and, by extension, the whole society) hostage (as has been repeatedly the case during the past decades).

Otherwise put will it also be possible to classify the so-called "too big/specific/important/interconnected to fail"-paradigm, once and for all, as ancient history.

4.6 Pillar IV. A Differentiated Price Setting for Newly Created Money

46 Within the New Monetary World Order, a completely new logic could furthermore be worked out as regards the price setting for newly created money.

One of the (many) great merits of Galbraith has been that he has pointed out the important difference between credit which is taken up for personal needs (essentially aimed at living, or surviving, in a humane way), and credit which implies a production cost for enterprises (which, in essence, is aimed at ensuring that the profits generated by an enterprise as much as possible flow to the company shareholders).[95]

It is based upon this understanding that in the current proposals for a new monetary order, a fundamental distinction will be made between three levels of

[94]Compare Boccara et al. (2011), pp. 207–221, especially p. 218.

[95]Galbraith (1987), p. 12.

money creation, more specifically as regards the price to be set for such newly created money, i.e.:

i. money creation for the benefit of "governments" of the countries participating in the NMWO (in addition to certain other "public entities", such as international or supranational institutions that are in need of public funds in order to be able to operate).

   In the model for a "NMWO" which is here proposed, such governments and other public bodies will mainly (have to) continue to work for the common good.

   It is, therefore, hereafter suggested that these public entities will, henceforth, receive their operational funding entirely in the form of non-repayable allocations handed out by the NMWI (and in this way will be able to withdraw from the devastating supremacy of the financial markets, as well as from the arbitrary and intrinsically unjust methods of deriving income from taxation and similar systems at the detriment of the poor and middle classes);

ii. Money creation for the benefit of "the average person" in order to meet his basic life needs, as well as money creation for (temporarily) continuing (true) "*non-profit*-organizations".

   As regards this "second" level of money creation, it could be suggested that this will be based on free credit[96] to be handed out by the NMWI (and, by extension, by the NGSCB). Hence, the credits from this second type will no longer rely on mechanisms of interest charging, which essentially and throughout the ages, have proven to be a method to make the rich richer to the detriment of the poor(er)[97];

   and,

iii. Money creation for the benefit of (established) businesses, including private banks, for which credit lending is to be considered as a production cost in their striving for ever more profits, and for which, therefore, the charging of interest remains fully justified.

   On this third level, interest charging could continue to be an instrument of monetary policy, which could enable the monetary authorities to encourage the business sector to act in a more ethical way, whereby a relevant differentiated price setting system (of interests) could potentially encourage businesses to display a greater ethical attitude (a.o. characterized by a sense of more altruism).

A simple presentation in the form of a table may already clarify the differences aspired for between the said "three levels of money creation" (see Table 4.1). 47

[96]One could even think of credits against negative interests (i.e. basically credits which would not be reimbursable in full). This could, for instance, be the case for student loans, credits to the (very) poor, etc.

[97]See also Galbraith (1992), p. 93, who has pointed that (high) interest charging has been devastating for the modal man.

Table 4.1 Schematic representation of three levels of money creation

Target audience for money creation	Method of money creation	Conditions under which resort to newly created money can take place	Motivation
1. *Government (and other "public entities")*	Allocation ("absolutely" free money creation).	• No obligation to pay back, nor an obligation to pay interest; • Obligation to report; • Monitoring mechanisms.	• Money as a "public good"; • Financing of **general well-being**; • Decision process by the world community based upon a system of "*checks and balances*".
2. *Private individuals, for personal basic needs*	Credit (without interest) ("relative" free money creation).	• Obligation to pay back the credit; • Agreement to co-operate for smooth credit management (information provisioning and other); • No obligation to pay interest; • Mechanisms of monitoring and coaching.	• Enable everyone to live and build **a dignified or humane life**; • Enable everyone to build a basic wealth; • Money creation is no longer considered as a mechanism allowing the rich to get richer to the detriment of the poor(er).
3. *Nonprofit-sector*	Credit (without interest, or against low interest).	• Obligation to pay back the credit; • Obligation to co-operate for smooth credit management (information provisioning and other); • Interest obligation or not (depending on the exact nature of the activities of the borrower); • Mechanisms of monitoring and coaching.	• The nonprofit-organizations sector is gradually to be converted to the public domain; • Where (and as long as) nonprofit-organizations continue to exist, they will be guaranteed access to newly created money at fair conditions (according to the duties they will fulfill in society).
4. *Established Businesses*	Credit at an interest rate.	• Obligation to pay back the credit; • Obligation to co-operate for smooth credit management (information provisioning and other); • Obligation to pay interest; • Mechanisms of monitoring and coaching.	• For business enterprises aiming at making profits, money is a **production cost** • Interest charging becomes a monetary policy instrument to direct businesses in the direction of more ethical behavior.

When we shall further address the different levels of money creation, we will go deeper into the details of these various aspects (whereby a more elaborated motivation for the proposed differentiated approach regarding the price setting for newly created money will also be developed).

4.7 Pillar V. Full Control of the Monetary Authority (ies)

4.7.1 Basic Principle of the Fifth Pillar

In as far as the four aforementioned newly proposed pillars of the New Monetary World Order—namely: (*i*) a global monetary system with no further room for state sovereignty; (*ii*) the acceptance of basic underlying altruistic objectives; (*iii*) *the* effective elimination of private money creation and (*iv*) a differentiated price setting for newly created money—may sound revolutionary, this will most probably be even more the case for the here proposed fifth pillar, namely a multiplication of the processes of money creation, through and under the auspices of the New Monetary World Institute (and, by extension, the "NGSCB"), at different levels, i.e.: **48**

- A level of money creation on behalf of the operation of the NMWI/the NGSCB itself;
- A level of money creation for the benefit of the (central) national authorities (governments) of the countries participating in the New Monetary World Order;
- A level of money creation for the benefit of the "general wellbeing" of the private sector, which can be split as follows:
  - A sublevel of money creation for the benefit of private individuals in order to allow them to fulfill "basic needs" (in a sufficiently wide-ranging interpretation; see further, at marg. 129 of this chapter);
  - A sublevel of money creation for the benefit of "starters" in professional life;
  - A sublevel of money creation for the benefit of the "nonprofit-sector" (as long as this will continue to exist);
- A level of money creation for the benefit of (the further needs of) (private) business enterprises.

4.7.2 Money Creation for the Benefit of the Governments of the Countries Participating in the New Monetary World Order

4.7.2.1 Context

It has already been explained above that the (central) authorities or governments of most of the countries in the world are mainly financed by systems of taxes and similar charges, but, especially during the last decades, a growing group of countries has also become dependent on several methods of debt financing (see above, under Sect. 3.4.6 of Chap. 3). **49**

It has also been demonstrated (see above, especially at marg. 197 a.f. of Chap. 3 of this book) that the prevailing system(s) of government financing has (have) many disadvantages including, *inter alia*:

(i) the method of government financing through taxes and similar charges is not "*efficient*" (anymore); on the contrary, it has in many countries mainly become an obstacle for a solid operation of the economy, which has attributed to the fact that many of these countries, over the past decades, have resorted to an unbridled debt financing to overcome shortcomings, with all known problematic consequences;
(ii) the method is inherently "unjust" (and because of this, does not contribute at all to the general well-being of the global world population, let alone to a more just distribution of wealth in the world);
(iii) as regards government finances as such, the method does not encourage a practice of healthy "budgetary discipline";
(iv) the method has contributed to an inherent "unhealthy competition" between countries (of which the business sector eagerly takes advantage by enforcing upon national governments all types of favorable fiscal systems through all sorts of lobby mechanisms and even through blackmail, but, for instance, also by enforcing subsidies financed with public money[98], while (implicitly) threatening to relocate elsewhere in case similar demands are not met, which on a global scale has been detrimental for an optimal allocation of production resources[99]);
(v) the problem of the increasing debt burden of many countries has created a real problem of "intergenerational" injustice, even endangering the general prosperity of next generations (who, in a system of debt financing by governments, through taxes, have to increasingly pay the bills for debts which have been accumulated in the past to pay for the luxuries of previous generations);
(vi) ...

[98]In this way, government policy becomes very "paradoxal": governments that accumulate their financial means mainly through taxing the lower and middle classes, decide to use these means to reward the rich classes by subsidizing big enterprises (owned by these rich classes). As a result, it is made possible for such big enterprises to make even more profits (which are hardly taxed themselves), while, at the same time, the big enterprises threaten the subsidizing governments that in case the latter would not be willing to grant or maintain such subsidies, they will re-allocate to another country, thus harming the local economy of the country they thus would abandon even more.

[99]Stiglitz has in this regard pointed out that the future of Europe and the euro depends on whether the Eurozone's political leaders will be able combine a modicum of economic understanding with a visionary sense of, and concern for, European solidarity (based, a.o., upon a unitized tax model) (see Stiglitz 2015b).

4.7.2.2 Towards a New Model of Government Financing (Based on a System of World-Wide Money Creation)

4.7.2.2.1 Principle of (International) Money Creation for the Benefit of National Authorities

4.7.2.2.1.1 General Principle

In as far the New Monetary World Order would aim to contribute to a more just distribution of the world's wealth, it cannot possibly continue to ignore the aforementioned findings. **50**

Nevertheless, public policy of the past decades, especially as regards government financing in general (and of financing social care more specifically (see above, under Sect. 3.4.6 of Chap. 3 of this book)), has only magnified the inherently unjust nature of the capitalist economic system (also and especially from an intergenerational perspective) (where, mainly since WW II, bearing in mind the (neo-)liberal law of "*laissez faire/après nous le déluge*", problems have continuously been shifted to the next generation).[100]

Even within, for instance, the IMF, hardly to be considered as a progressive international institution, this understanding seems to be present among some, albeit it not yet determines its own policy. **51**

For instance, in a speech of March 13th 2014, the (then) "*First Deputy Managing Director*" of the IMF, David Lipton, shared the following insight regarding this topic[101]:

> Many advanced and developing economies are facing the challenge of rising inequality. Fiscal policy has played a major role in reducing inequality in the past and is the primary tool available for authorities to affect income distribution. Whether these policies help, or hurt growth, is all a matter of design. And the details matter. Thus, debates on the impact of the government's redistributive policies must go far beyond a mere discussion of tax and spending ratios. In the end, it is design that matters. And on this, the good news is that quite a lot is now known about how authorities can best address the challenges of squaring their equity and efficiency concerns, a task on which the Fund stands ready to help.

4.7.2.2.1.2 Abolition of the Possibility of Tax and Other Charges and of Debt Financing

Given the aforementioned considerations and in order to obtain a more just system of financing the governments of the countries that would participate to the New Monetary World Order—it is here proposed to principally and generally abolish the taxability (and parafiscality) of the (relatively) "low incomes" (especially income from labor). **52**

---

[100] See Stiglitz (2003), p. 55, on the impact of this attitude on government deficits.

[101] Lipton (2014).

As regards those countries that would be willing to participate to the New Monetary World Order, said (radical) proposal would imply a definitive abolition of all systems of taxes and similar charges in the broad sense of the words, on both income which is generated through labor—hence not only actual income taxes, but also, for instance, succession taxes, and regardless of the fact whether such labor is performed as an employee or on an independent basis—as on income derived from other sources, such as capital, in as far as such income would fall under certain (to be determined) parameters.[102]

Income from labor (as well as other "low" incomes, regardless of their source) would in this way be exempted from all kinds of government skimming[103] and would consequently for the first time in (recent) history, remain entirely for the benefit of the person who has provided the labor.

Further down the text, it will be discussed (in more detail) how such a tax system could concretely look like (see further, under Sect. 4.7.2.3.2).

53 In the same sense, it is here further proposed to also completely abolish all types of (common) consumer taxes (including taxes charged in the context of transactions of goods and services which are meant to enable the average person to lead a humane life, such as the purchase of food and other daily consumables, in addition to the purchase or decoration of a living house, of a vehicle, etc.).[104]

---

[102]Compare Galbraith (1979), p. 93. See also the ideas of Rudolf Goldscheid on the limits of the so-called tax state (Streeck 2015, pp. 112 a.f.).

[103]As already explained before, as governments of most (Western and Western inspired) countries are but the expression of systems of "*Corporatocracy*", such government skimming by taxing the lower and middle classes, comes, bluntly put, down to a system by which the reach steal from the poorer and middle classes. (See already Plato (1987), pp. 298 a.f.)

More recent: Oxfam (2014), p. 14; Sachs (2011), p. 118.

See also the opinion of Stiglitz that the financial and monetary problems (some member-states of) the European Union has (have) been facing during the past years, are to a large extent due to the failure of democracy:

> The rising crescendo of bickering and acrimony within Europe might seem to outsiders to be the inevitable result of the bitter endgame playing out between Greece and its creditors. In fact, European leaders are finally beginning to reveal the true nature of the ongoing debt dispute, and the answer is not pleasant: it is about power and democracy much more than money and economics.

and, furthermore:

> We should be clear: almost none of the huge amount of money loaned to Greece has actually gone there. It has gone to pay out private-sector creditors – including German and French banks. Greece has gotten but a pittance, but it has paid a high price to preserve these countries' banking systems. The IMF and the other "official" creditors do not need the money that is being demanded. Under a business-as-usual scenario, the money received would most likely just be lent out again to Greece. But, again, it's not about the money. It's about using "deadlines" to force Greece to knuckle under, and to accept the unacceptable – not only austerity measures, but other regressive and punitive policies. (See Stiglitz 2015a).

[104]Muttin (2014a), p. 13; Muttin (2014b).

It goes without saying that the proposed approach cannot be the result of a stand-alone measure (of one country or a small group of countries), but on the contrary will need to be part of a world-wide aligned public policy whereby, based on international agreements, all countries (which will participate in the New Monetary World Order) would in the same way adopt this new fiscal system (further ensuring that there will be no more room for competition between fiscal regulators and, moreover, that the existence of tax havens and similar tax escape countries will be definitely become part of history).[105] **54**

The result of such an approach should be that, world-wide (in the hypothesis that all countries in the world would be encouraged to join the suggested New Monetary World Order), the (relatively) "poorer classes", i.e. the lower and middle classes, would henceforth be fiscally (and parafiscally) spared and, for the first time in (recent) history, obtain enough breathing space to live and build a dignified life free from government taxes. Only then, it will become effectively feasible to bridge the ever-widening gaps between the poor and the rich, by putting a resolute end to the different (fiscal and other) mechanisms under which these gaps are created within the current systems of public financing.[106] **55**

The moral justice of the proposed new system is obvious, at the very least when read together with the other proposals on creating a new system of government financing made below. **56**

A true moral just system will however only be reached at the moment when such a system would be put in place for all of mankind, regardless in what country one lives.

Subsequent to the aforementioned proposals, a final proposal for a new system of government financing states would be that, in accordance with the model for a new Monetary World Order, there will no longer be room for any type of credit **57**

It appears indeed from the earlier quoted research undertaken by Oxfam that such types of indirect (consumer) taxes (including for instance the notorious VAT-systems) are to a great extent contributing to the increasing economic inequality which is currently world-wide prevailing (see Oxfam 2014, p. 83).

To illustrate this, further reference could be made to the situation in Japan, where a persistent recession has been caused by Japan's VAT-system which has been reported to undermine too much the purchasing power of the general population (and because of this: the demand within economy).

[105] Oxfam (2014), p. 16, where it has been pointed out:

> Well-meaning governments around the world are often hamstrung by rigged international tax rules and a lack of coordination. No government alone can prevent corporate giants from taking advantage of the lack of global taks cooperation.

On several other places in said Oxfam-report, it is pointed out that there is a most definite need for a globally uniformalized fiscal policy (see *e.g.* Oxfam 2014, pp. 17 and 22).

[106] Compare Galbraith (1996), p. 65, pointing out:

> The basic need, however, is to accept the principle that a more equitable distribution of income must be a fundamental tenet of modern public policy in the good society, and to this end progressive taxation is central.

financing or debt financing by states (or other public authorities), and this regardless of who the credit provider would be.

Also this proposal will be further elaborated upon hereunder.

4.7.2.2.1.3 Allocations by the NMWI as an Exclusive New Source of Financing Governments

58 The abolition of (*i*) systems of taxing the income of lower and middle classes; (*ii*) systems of taxing common transactions of goods and services (needed to lead a humane life), and (*iii*) of systems of financing governments through debt will obviously require that an alternative source of income would be offered to the (central) authorities of the countries participating in the New Monetary World Order.

Hence, the further proposal made here would imply that the (central) authorities of the countries participating in the New Monetary World Order would, henceforth, receive, on an exclusive and sufficient basis, their income directly from allocations which would periodically be provided to them by the "New Monetary World Institute".[107]

The same principle would apply to other public entities that are dependent on public funding, including supranational institutions (which would, of course, need to be defined more precisely in the treaty (ies) organizing the New Monetary World Order).

59 Otherwise put, the New Monetary World Order would, as regards government financing (in addition to the financing of other public entities, such as international and supranational organizations), imply a system of direct money creation by the monetary authority (ies) benefiting the governments of the participating countries.

Such a public financing model, whereby new money would be directly created by the monetary authority (ies) for the benefit of the (national) authorities of the countries participating in the New Monetary World Order (and, by extension: certain other public entities), would, moreover, fall under the responsibility of the world community itself (through its representation in the New Monetary World Institute).

Such a system would, furthermore, not only encourage the maintenance of a much higher level of budgetary discipline, but a similarly organized global monetary system would, moreover, allow that the processes of government financing be run in a much more transparent, just and democratic way than is the case under the prevailing (basically capitalist) systems of money creation (mainly by private banks).

However, a possible risk of such a system could be that public authorities would be inclined to create too much money on their own behalf (which could result in a

---

[107] See for further reasons why this system is here proposed Kousari (2006), pp. 35–46, pointing out that the African continent, above all, is in need of new capital and of debt relief.

devaluation of the New World Currency, and even undermine its acceptance by the general public).

Although one may wonder whether the risk of excess money creation is not even higher under the prevailing capitalist money creation systems, this aforementioned risk will probably be easily avoided given the fact that the proposed allocations of new money for the benefit of participating governments will obviously not be decided upon by the national authorities themselves and for their own individual behalf, but rather will be carried out by a newly established monetary institution (referred to before as "the New Monetary World Institute") which, under the auspices of its (ultimate) "organizing authority", namely the world community, will be able to (and will need to) advocate a fair global balance among the participating countries.

Moreover, the decision making processes in this regard could be enhanced by organizationally ensured "*checks and balances*" (which will be dealt with further on in this chapter; see further, at marg. 76 of this chapter).

Although the proposals mentioned before may indeed appear to be revolution- **60**
ary, they nevertheless are not completely original.

On the contrary, a similar system of enhancing public money creation already forms an embryonic part of the current IMF, whereby, obviously, the possibility of the IMF to grant to its Member States so-called "*Special Drawing Rights*"[108] comes to mind.

Be as it may, the proposal put forward in this treatise goes nevertheless far **61**
beyond the prevailing SDR-mechanism.

---

[108]For further reading, see *e.g.* Skidelsky (2003), pp. 125–151. See also Tew (1977), pp. 101 a.f.; James (1996).

At the approval of the original text of the IMF-(*Articles of Agreement*) in 1944, the so-called "Keynes plan" (Keynes having been one of the architects of the IMF-treaty) presuming a far reaching system of international money creation had been rejected.

However, 25 years later, in a period during which the international exchange mechanism originally agreed upon came under a lot of pressure, it became clear that the system that had been agreed upon in 1944, was too burdensome on the American dollar as it, a.o., implied a continuous deficiency in the current accounts of the American balance of payments. Hence, a strong need for a new supplemental international liquidity was felt. To accommodate this need, the IMF-Board of Governors approved, obviously taking inspiration from the Keynes plan (which, as said, had not made it in 1944–1945), on September 29th 1967, the so-called "*First Amendment of the Articles of Agreement*" (of the IMF). This amendment introduced a new kind of international liquidities, namely the "*Special Drawing Rights*" (abbreviated: "SDRs") and entered into force on July 28th 1969 (i.e. after the acceptance by three fifths of the members representing four fifths of the voting rights) (For additional details, see Devries 1976, pp. 25 a.f.)

The original goal of the first Amendment was that in case of a worldwide scarcity of international reserves, the Fund could intervene by granting newly created Special Drawing Rights to the Member States, with which the Member States could subsequently acquire currency from (an) other Member State(s). To make this possible, the SDRs were set up as an international monetary reserve deriving their value from the participating Member States' commitment to maintain and accept the SDRs on the one hand and to comply with the obligations imposed by the Fund with respect to the functioning and use of the SDRs on the other hand (see *e.g.* International Monetary Fund (IMF), Pamphlet Series No. 45, p. 1).

In accordance with the proposal made in this book, the New World Currency to be allocated to the countries participating in the New Monetary World Order, would regard actual money. Moreover, this New World Currency will become the only currency to be used for payments (and other transactions) in the real economic and financial environment.

This New World Currency allocated to the member countries of the New Monetary World Order will moreover (and differently from the current SDRs) not need to be converted into another (national) currency, as in the New Monetary World Order (at least for the participating countries), there will be only one currency left, namely said "New World Currency".

Otherwise put, the amounts of New World Currency allocated to the governments of participating countries (and if applicable, to other "public entities") will be "full" money in their own accord and will be no different from the money to be used for payments in the private sphere (such as payments for acquiring goods and services).

Otherwise put, pursuant to this first amendment, the Fund obtained the power to create new liquidities through SDR grants awarded in function of the size of the participating IMF Member States' quota (see International Monetary Fund (IMF), Pamphlet Series No. 45, p. 1).

To this end, Article XV.,- Section 1, *Articles of Agreement* provides that "*[to] meet the need, as and when it arises, for a supplement to existing reserve assets, the Fund is authorized to allocate special drawing rights to members that are participants in the Special Drawing Rights Department.*"

Any such grant comes down to a form of creation of international reserve "*ex nihilo*", as the SDRs are in fact not covered by any other monetary value. On the contrary, they come into life solely by decision of the IMF, the only "coverage" being the commitment that the participating States will, in accordance with the IMF rules, accept SDRs in exchange for (other) freely usable currencies which they themselves possess. In this sense, the SDRs can be described as an "international transferable currency" (or more accurately: a credit on account), of which only the participating countries and the prescribed holders (namely some international institutions) can make use.

Such allocation of SDRs can however, in principle, solely be made to Member States and in proportion to the quotum of the Member State concerned at the time of said allocation; the holding and use of the SDRs can however also be done by other acknowledged holders.

Any decision regarding a (new) SDR allocation depends furthermore on a collective decision of the participating countries that a global demand for such new currency exists in addition to existing reserves. Such decision requires a voting majority of at least 85% of the votes.

Given the above characteristics the SDRs is by some regarded as a conventional form of money which is nevertheless not fully valuable, as the SDRs does not fulfill one of the most important functions of money, being the one of generally accepted means of payment. (In this regard Devries 1976, pp. 180 a.f.; Fritz-Krockow and Ramlogan 2007, pp. 40 a.f.).

Although the possibility to create "SDRs" as a method aiming at providing the world economy with a new international reserve currency has been set up already in 1969, SDR creation has, in practice, remained relatively limited. According to some sources, the IMF has, from the 1970s until 2009, "only" issued SDRs for a value of 21.4 billion SDRs, i.e. about 32 billion USD (which is but a small fraction of the total money supply in circulation worldwide) (see Aiyar 2009).

Rainer Masera has argued that the failure of the SDR system has not been due to intrinsic features of the system, but rather to the fact that "*they were introduced too late in the game*". (See Masera 1996, pp. 65–73, especially p. 66.)

For the sake of completeness, it needs to be furthermore mentioned that in the past, within the IMF itself, the introduction of a global monetary system in which the current SDRs would be converted into a fully-fledged world currency, has already been advocated (albeit to a less far reaching extent than is proposed here).[109] 62

Through a declaration of (at the time) Governor Zhou, the People's Bank of China has in this regard even worked out a "road map" of how the reform of the SDR-system could look like.[110]

In conclusion: in the here proposed "New Monetary World Order", the provision of funds to the governments of the participating countries (and if applicable, to other "public entities" as well) would become the responsibility of (the representatives of) the world community through its (their) presence in the bodies of the New Monetary Institute. 63

As aforementioned, this newly proposed system should, above all, ensure that national economies, for the first time in history, at least at the level of "the working classes" (in a broad sense of the term), will be able to escape from the pressure of tax (and comparable) charges and thus obtain enough breathing space for their revival.

In order to achieve this (ambitious) goal, it should be made sure (in the legal set-up of the New Monetary World Order) that said allocations to be given by the New Monetary World Institute to each of the participating countries (and if applicable, to other "public entities"), will be the only source of income for their beneficiaries and, consequently, should suffice to cover all of the financial needs (of the latter), whereby these allocations should moreover be handed out on a sufficiently periodical, and when required (*e.g.* in case of emergencies), immediate basis.

---

[109] For instance, in a remarkable paper by the "Strategy, Policy, and Review Department" of the IMF, called "*Enhancing International Monetary Stability—A Role for the SDR?*" and dating from January 7th 2011, several proposals have been brought forward to significantly expand the current (limited) role of the SDR's, including the proposal to use them in the private sector.

See also Hu (2011), pp. 143–158.

[110] Camdessus (2011), pp. 33–43, especially pp. 39–40.

Elements of this proposed "road map" consist of:

- broadening the present basket of currencies which determine the value of the SDR, at present the USD, the euro, the yen and the pound to some further major currencies, such as the yuan, but also the Indian and Brazilian currencies (in addition to others);
- working towards an expanded use of the SDR (beyond the present official holders);
- transforming the SDR into a real currency that can also be used as a payment instrument for current (international) transactions;
- working towards the use of the SDR as a payment instrument on the private markets;
- encouraging the renewed creation of financial assets denominated in SDR's;
- facilitating the determination of the value of the SDR.

4.7.2.2.2 Need for a Profound Review (and Global Leveling) of the Role of (National) Governments

64 It goes without saying that the aforementioned revolutionary proposal(s) will imply a fundamental shift in both the thinking and the practical behavior of the leading figures of the world.

In accordance with the here proposed new system of providing money to the public sector, money creation for the benefit of national (and international) authorities should become the sole responsibility of the world community (through the newly established "New Monetary World Institute"), rather than, as is the case under the prevailing capitalist doctrines, that of the private banking sector.

Once such a revolutionary change would be acknowledged and implemented, the then newly created "New Monetary World Institute" will, obviously, periodically have to determine which are the (basic) operational funds each of the national governments of the participating countries (in addition to other "public entities", such as international organizations) is in need of and will have to provide these through its allocation decisions (leading to new money creation).

65 Such a new system of world-wide money creation for the benefit of national authorities (and other public entities) will (also) obviously and primarily require a world-wide consensus about the parameters on which such periodic allocations of New World Currency will need to be based.

It will become equally imperative to translate these parameters into clearly defined and convention-based rules and regulations governing the NMWO.

Needless to say that all of this will, at the very least, require a universal understanding on what, world-wide (or at least: among the countries participating in the New Monetary World Order), should be the role of national governments, especially as regards conceiving a sufficient level of welfare for their population. This will obviously require a global consensus about what the tasks of such national authorities (and if applicable, other "public entities") will be, for instance regarding the question to what extent any (participating) national government, or other public entity, will need to ensure certain basic needs of its citizens.[111]

66 Shifting the supply of money on behalf of the national governments (and other public entities) from the private banking sector to the newly to be created New Monetary World Institute will, furthermore, require the setting up of a level playing field between the participating countries.

(Rich) countries which currently enjoy very large budgets (and hence are able to finance a magnitude of activities, among which often luxurious projects) will under this system probably be required to do with less and, on the contrary, (poor) countries hardly having any operational funds at their disposal, will henceforth obtain more such means.

---

[111] See already the works of Galbraith advocating a sufficiently large understanding of the notion "public interest". (See *e.g.* Galbraith 1964.)

As a result, for instance a more just redistribution of the world wealth in North-South relations could occur, which at the end should enable any human being, regardless from which country in the world he originates, to be offered an equal opportunity to build up a reasonable prosperous, or at least dignified life.[112]

A similar system should result in a social and economic order which would be fundamentally just on a global scale, whereby each national government will have enough operational funds at its disposal to, when necessary, provide for all of its citizens the possibility to meet their basic life needs.

At the same time and given the abovementioned aim of setting up a monetary order which functions in respect of the limitations of the planet, a sufficient high level of financial (budgetary) discipline should be made possible (which, under the prevailing monetary and financial order, seems completely lacking at the level of the governments of many Western and Western-inspired countries). **67**

In other words, it will be expected of the national governments of the countries participating in the NMWO (but also from the other participating "public entities" which will depend on its allocations) that they will learn to operate within a budget fixed by the world community as represented in the New Monetary World Institute, without being able to rely on ever higher and more taxes and similar charges burdening the lower and middle classes, let alone on ever more expanding debt financing (ultimately similarly burdening the lower and middle classes).

4.7.2.2.3 Parameters for (International) Money Creation on Behalf of the National Governments of the Participating Countries

The extent to which the here proposed system of government financing which would be based on a system of direct global money creation by the newly to be created "New Monetary World Institute" on behalf of every country participating in the NMWO (in addition to other "public entities") will effectively succeed in contributing to a more just world, will obviously (and perhaps even mainly) depend on defining well-conceived parameters for the said periodic allocations of New World Currency to these national governments (and other "public entities"). **68**

As explained above under Sect. 3.4.6 of Chap. 3 of this book), the presently prevailing systems of financing national authorities based on tax and similar systems and on money lending on the private financial markets have indeed, *inter alia*, as a consequence that countries with (more) flourishing economies enjoy much larger operational funds than countries with a sluggish economy. **69**

Consequently, in the prevailing system of government financing, the strength of a given economy also determines the level of skimming a government can afford itself and, hence, also the operational budget which such a government has at its disposal.

---

[112] See Oxfam (2014), pp. 16 a.f.

This creates as an important side-effect that the richer an economy (of a given country) is, the richer its government is (or at least can be) and the more funds the latter will (or can) have at its disposal to cover its own needs and the needs of its citizens.

In other words, such a system threatens to become a vicious circle, which during the past decades has implied, at least to a certain degree, that in rich countries (with flourishing economies) there is likewise more prosperity for the entire population (possible) to the detriment of poorer countries (with weak economies) where there is hardly any progress to be observed.

In this way, the prevailing capitalist monetary and financial system has proven to lead to more prosperity in richer countries (albeit practically nowhere for their entire population), but hardly to offer a remedy for countries which have not succeeded in having their economy going; it is obvious that this is one of the elements which helps declaring the ever increasing accumulation of an ever growing part of the world resources in the hands of a small group of (extremely rich) individuals.

70 As an aside, one could even begin to wonder whether many, formerly "rich(er)" countries, including many Western (and Western-inspired) countries, can still be thus qualified given their ever increasing debt burden.

To put it bluntly, one could question if someone who appears rich, but has excessive debts, can truly be called rich, or at the very least for still how long.[113]

In any case, one has to observe how many Western (and Western-inspired) countries with high government debt (due to their past excessive expenditure) are, more and more, scaling down their earlier exorbitant spending pattern, which, under the doctrine of economic neo-liberalism, generally leads to the reduction of public care systems and public services financed or organized by the government (such as certain social benefits, all types of subsidies except those to ailing private banks and other big enterprises, education systems, etc.).[114]

This also in return, has contributed to even further increasing and deepening the gap between the rich and the poor.

71 It may hence be clear that the prevailing mechanisms of financing governments which are based on taxing the lower and middle classes and on public debt mechanisms (which, eventually, also weigh on the same lower and middle classes) cannot become a successful formula for contributing to a fair and just redistribution of the worlds wealth as long as there is not, on a global scale, a complete alignment of fiscal policies and on providing national governments with equal means.

72 The here proposed alternative system of government financing through periodical allocations by the NMWI could allow these "vicious circles" to be broken.

A balanced mix of parameters for future money creation (of New World Currency) on behalf of the national governments of the countries participating in the New Monetary World Order, could hereby be worked out in order to ensure that

---

[113]At least implicitly, this question has also been raised by Piketty. (See Piketty 2014, p. 540.)

[114]Engelen (2011), p. 49. Compare Stiglitz (2003), p. 107.

all participating countries will dispose of enough operational funds in order to guarantee a set of responsibilities characterized by world-wide harmonization at a global minimum level.

The parameters on which this money creation on behalf of the national governments of the participating countries (in addition to certain other "public entities") will be based will in this way—and also different from what is too much the case with the prevailing IMF-system of allocating SDR's—need no longer to be dependent on the strength of their underlying economy, but, on the contrary, merely on the answer to the following questions:

(i) which responsibilities the governments of the participating countries should fulfil,
and/or
(ii) for the fulfillment of which of its citizens' needs should such a government (be able to) be responsible globally.

Hence, the development of such a balanced mix of parameters which will take the aforementioned concerns into consideration should imply that national governments (and other "public entities") are no longer exclusively dependent on the strength of their own underlying economy (and of the lobbying and blackmailing activities of big enterprises), so that, on a global scale, national governments (and other public entities) can be transformed into institutions which are truly concerned with the wellbeing of their global population (rather than with the interests of big enterprises and their shareholders). 73

Obviously, a genuine concern for cultural and other relevant differences between the participating countries will remain necessary. The parameters for allocating funds to the participating governments (and, when applicable, other public entities) should thus, for instance, reflect the impact of objective differences, such as: the presence (or absence) of natural resources within their own territory; autonomy (or not) in the field of energy supply; climatological circumstances (including their impact on agriculture); population numbers and density; the existing level of schooling and education of the population, etc.[115]

4.7.2.2.4 Practical Working Method of (International) Money Creation for the Benefit of National Authorities

In addition to the importance of conceiving fair and balanced parameters for the abovementioned new system of world-wide money creation on behalf of the national governments of the participating countries (in addition to other relevant supra-national "public entities"), it will be of equal importance to establish equally fair and balanced allocation decision making processes. 74

[115]To some extent, the presently prevailing IMF already conducts a policy whereby such factors may be taken under consideration (see Fritz-Krockow and Ramlogan 2007, pp. 44 a.f.).

75 The starting point here could be that any decision on the allocation of operational funds to the (national) governments of the member states[116] (in addition to other relevant supra-national "public entities"), should firmly be the responsibility of the global world community.

In order to accomplish this, it will be necessary to establish fair allocation decision making processes which will ensure a system of money creation based upon the underlying principles of equality, solidarity and justice for each of the countries participating in the NMWO, and even so upon the awareness that the growth of the quantity of money (and therefore of the globally available purchasing power for the stream of goods and services) always needs to relate to the capacity of the planet (hence: to reasonable expectations with regards to the output of the production potential of mankind as a whole and as part of the planet's eco-system).

76 Concretely and based on the objective of installing decision making processes which guarantee true "checks and balances", the newly to-be-established "New Monetary World Institute" (or a division or a department of it) which will become responsible for the allocation of money on behalf of the national governments of the participating countries (and, if applicable, of other supra-national "public entities"[117]), could be organized into different panels in order to achieve the said targets.

For instance, for every participating country in need of a fund allocation, within the "New Monetary World Institute", a panel could be set up, consisting of

[116] Abstraction was made from the fact that in many countries, in addition to a central government, a lot of further local governments or other entities with public authority may prevail. In some cases, such local or decentralized authorities may even have the competence to impose taxes or to take on debt financing.

The system for a New Monetary World Order which is proposed here will, in principle, imply that the newly to be created New Monetary World Institute will decide upon allocations on behalf of the national or central governments of the participating countries, who in their own turn will be responsible for redistributing the thus obtained means to the lower authorities. Hence, when drafting its proposal to obtain an allocation of funds, a participating country will also have to bear in mind the needs of all of the authorities operative on its territory. Otherwise put, as long as the world remains artificially divided in countries (sovereign states), it seems advisory to mirror the outlook of the newly to be established "New Monetary World Order" to the ones currently in place for similar supra-national organizations (whereby membership and membership rights and obligations are for the sovereign states with exclusion of delocalized or decentralized lower authorities).

Hence, when speaking of an allocation of New World Currency to the national (or central) government of a participating country, one needs to bear in mind that such an allocation will also have to meet the needs of such lower (delocalized or decentralized) authorities as there may be: member-states of a federal state, provinces, cities, communities, in addition to decentralized public legal persons, regardless of their (international) public law denomination.

[117] As regards the latter, it could be considered to establish a separate sub-department for public money creation within the New Monetary World Institute.

representatives of—let us say (merely) as a first thought—ten different countries (but there could, of course, also be more or fewer).[118]

Alternatively, there could be a system in which "larger countries" (mainly in terms of population) would receive a greater number of representatives on the total number of panels which will decide upon the allocations to other countries in comparison with "smaller countries" (with lower population levels) which for instance could also help to avoid that smaller countries would form alliances against larger countries and which could also help ensuring that larger countries are stopped from abusing their stronger position to the detriment of smaller countries.

Furthermore, the exact composition of an individual country allocation panel could be based on an impartial draw system which would ensure that each of the participating countries forms part of the allocation panels of (at least) ten other countries (or, in case of a system of pondered representation, a different number per participating country). The draw system could be organized in an objective random way, for instance by putting the names of each of the countries participating to the "New World Monetary Institute" into the draw ten times, so that names are drawn for each individual allocation panel (as is currently done in certain national lottery systems) until the names of ten different countries have been drawn.[119]

Another rule could be that a country whose allocation needs to be determined could not be drawn as a member of its own allocation panel, but that such a country *(i)* could be made responsible for formulating the allocation proposal (according to models and budgets to be established by the New World Monetary Institute) and *(ii)* could take part, when invited by its allocation panel, in an advisory capacity, in panel meetings, for instance by being available to answer questions from the panel or to provide additional information.

As said, a "fresh lottery" could be organized for each new allocation, in such a way that an allocation panel of a given country would, over time, have a continuously changing composition, thus enhancing fairness in the allocation decisions and at the same time minimizing the risk of mutual (even informal) "alliances" whereby members would become tempted to favor each other (contrary to the general global interest).

---

[118] One could also work out a system with panels that fluctuate, so that the composition of such a panel would be different for each subsequent allocation decision, resulting in a system which guarantees that the panels may function independently and impartially over time.

[119] In case, under such a system, the name of a country would be drawn two times for the same panel, the drawing process should continue until ten different names are drawn.

In such a case, the name of a country which would be drawn more than one time, should be put back in the "drawing put" in order to ensure that all participating countries are equally (or proportionally) present in the allocation panels. In case a country would be drawn to be part of its own panel, this will of course have to be neglected and the drawing process should continue until a panel constituted of ten different countries has been selected (and whereby the name of the former country itself should also be put back in the "drawing pot" so it will become again available to be selected as a member of a panel of another country).

77 A similar approach could be, *mutatis mutandis*, considered as regards the panels for deciding upon the allocations to other, supranational, "public entities".

78 Clear convention-based rules will also need to be established regarding the periodicity of the periodic allocations to the countries participating in the New Monetary World Order (in addition to, if applicable, other supra-national "public entities") by the New Monetary World Institute.

These rules will probably best follow the logic of budget annuity, the way it is currently applied in many Western (and Western inspired) countries for the preparation of their national budgets.[120]

It may be clear that there will be a need for sufficient level of discipline and an optimal collaboration spirit between all the participating countries and the departments of the NMWI, which is a justified expectation with regard to a system that strives to introduce a just and humanitarian system of global money creation for the benefit of all participating countries (and, if applicable, other supra-national "public entities").

79 Evidently, it will also be possible that a participating country would be(come) affected by unforeseen circumstances (which were and/or could not be anticipated upon at the moment of submittal of an allocation proposal for a given (next) year).

In these circumstances, appropriate procedures could be planned whereby the New Monetary World Institute would be given the authority to assign "additional", "extra" and/or "*ad hoc*"-allocations to a country (or, if applicable, a supra-national "public entity") facing such a special need.[121]

4.7.2.3 Elements of Further Appeal of the Proposed System of (International) Money Creation on Behalf of the National Governments of the Participating Countries

4.7.2.3.1 A Simplified Government Financing

80 As already said before, the result of the aforementioned proposed new system of international money creation on behalf of the national governments of the countries participating in the New Monetary World Order would (when implemented) be that

[120]In this way, every country (or other "public entity") could, for instance, no later than on June 30th of year X, hand in its allocation proposal to the New Monetary World Institute and the latter will then have time until November 30th of that same year to decide upon the allocation for the (next) year X + 1 (whereby, if needed, the decision process could run in phases and the New Monetary World Institute could for instance already announce its decisions on certain sub-parts of the proposed allocation in order to enable the participating country to properly prepare its future policy for the spending year X + 1). If this would be deemed necessary or advisable, the moment in time to submit the allocation proposal could also be brought forward by 6 (or even more) months (e.g.: submittal by December 31th of year X − 1, decision by the New Monetary World Institute on November 30th of year X, for approval of the allocation for the year X + 1).

[121]See already, under current IMF-policy International Monetary Fund (2000).

government financing will become separated from the actual (often draconian) systems of taxation and para-fiscal taxation of the incomes of the lower and middle classes (and of certain transactions of goods and services for common needs).[122]

In addition, such a system of directly allocating (operating) funds to the national governments of the participating countries would make it possible to end the large distortions which are currently prevailing between countries. For instance, the strong dichotomy in North-South relations could thus gradually be reduced and be replaced by a system of government financing whereby, on a global scale, an equal level of government role (and public service provision) could be developed. This could, moreover, help to substantially bridge the ever increasing gaps between the rich and the poor.

On a fiscal level (and, by extension, on the level of policy making in the countries participating in the NMWO), there would be no further need for a fierce competition between countries.

On the contrary, under the here proposed system of government financing, countries participating in the NMWO will indeed no longer be depend on fiscal income (and/or income through means of similar taxes) and moreover will no longer be as dependent, at least not to the large extent as is currently the case, on the presence of large enterprises in their territories (providing for employment for the lower and middle classes). This will also imply that there will be no longer a further need for the elaboration of favorable tax concessions in order to attract large enterprises to their own territories.

Otherwise put, to the extent that the (national) governments of the participating countries will no longer be (as) dependent on income derived from taxing the lower and middle classes (see also above, at marg. 58–63 of this chapter), there will no longer be a need for an interstate competition on a fiscal (and para-fiscal) level leading to a race to the bottom.

In this approach, the New Monetary World Order could provide for a monetary and financial framework which will help building a more just world, making sure that basic needs of life—such as: a minimum basic income for every individual, (equal) access to a sufficient level of schooling and education[123], (equal) access to sufficient medical care, (equal) access to care for the disabled and the elderly, etc. (for further details on the outlook of such a globally harmonized "social care system", see further, under Sect. 4.7.2.4)—will be globally met in an equal way. In this, as aforementioned, the supply of money to the national governments of the participating countries will be(come) the responsibility of the world community which will also help ensuring that a larger financial (governmental) discipline can be introduced, bearing in mind that the natural resources of the planet are limited[124].

---

[122] On the policy goal of diminishing the gap between the rich and the poor, see Foucault (2008), p. 206.

[123] See especially Galbraith (1996), pp. 68 a.f.

[124] See once more Kruithof (1985), or more recent De Grauwe (2014).

81 As a further side-effect of this here proposed system of government financing, there could also be an enormous administrative simplification, whereby, for instance, the national tax (and similar) authorities of the countries participating in the New Monetary World Order could significantly be reduced and replaced by government services which truly care about the general wellbeing of the population (see also further, the explanation about the outlook of the administration of the NMWI and the NGSCB which, under the newly proposed system, would become responsible for the creation of money on behalf of private persons, as well as for wealth accumulation and asset planning, both referred to further in the text; see further, at marg. 46–48 of Chap. 5 of this book, respectively marg. 108 of this chapter).

4.7.2.3.2 Further Reflections on a More Just Fiscal System

4.7.2.3.2.1 Building Stones for a New and Just Fiscal System

82 The here proposed, simplified and more just fiscal system could itself be based on four pillars:

(i) "A true solidarity" (in the spirit of a universal altruism).

Under the here proposed new system of government financing, it should be avoided that "solidarity", as is, world-wide, the case in the currently prevailing fiscal (and para-fiscal) systems, would again be one which the rich classes (through so-called "corporatocracy"-mechanisms; see above, at marg. 10 of Chap. 1 of this book, and at marg. 133–134 of Chap. 3 of this book) mainly impose on the middle and poor(er) classes (and to which the rich classes form no part thanks to all kinds of types of tax evasion techniques).

On the contrary, the solidarity principle should be implemented through a system whereby mainly the rich would be encouraged to share their wealth with the less fortunate within society.[125]

This concern is more concretely expressed in the proposals formulated further on in this book, *inter alia*, when elaborating upon certain proposed mechanisms of "social cultural participation" of (future) tax payers (see further, at marg. 92 of this chapter).

(ii) A sufficient degree of "respect for individual wealth accumulation" which needs to become an achievable goal for every human being of any generation (= in an intergenerational perspective) and from anywhere in the world and, hence, not only for a select elite of (extremely) rich people.

---

[125]In the earlier mentioned study by Oxfam, "*Even it up*" 2014, it has, in this context, already been noted that if for instance estates worth 1 billion USD or more would be taxed at 1.5%, this would make enough money available to organize appropriate medical care and appropriate education in all developing countries (see Oxfam 2014, p. 9).

As under this newly proposed system of money creation on behalf of the national governments of participating countries (in addition to certain other supra-national "public entities"), authorities will no longer depend on taxes for their own spending behavior, they will, henceforth, be able to accept the fact that also the lower and middle classes would acquire a certain degree of wealth.

For this reason, the here(after) proposed tax system will mainly aspire to fulfill the objective of a mutual altruism by means of a transparent and unambiguous system of income taxes (excluding almost all other tax mechanisms, such as inheritance taxes) which will only impact those who have already been able to build a certain level of wealth (and which, by contrast, will not have an impact on anyone who will remain below these "thresholds of already acquired wealth"), in addition to transaction taxes for certain luxury expenditures (see hereafter, at marg. 99 of this chapter).

(iii) A "truly just" fiscal system which would not impact the middle and poorer classes whose income and/or wealth would remain under the abovementioned "thresholds of already acquired wealth".

(iv) A (relatively) "simple" fiscal system, whereby only a limited number of taxing techniques would prevail, namely:

(a) In addition to an income tax system for individuals whose wealth exceeds the abovementioned thresholds, which will be neutral as regards the "source" of income (whereby, consequently, any income regardless if from labor or from capital, would be taxable), and which will impact only individuals with large fortunes, there will be no other taxes or parafiscal taxes other than:

(b) the possibility of transaction taxes with regards to goods and services of either a very luxurious nature, or of an esteemed harmful nature (which would, however, not be considered of such severity that it would be deemed necessary to completely ban the transactions in question); and,

(c) a tax charge on the operational profits of legal entities (in the framework of which a fiscal policy could be pursued of focusing on employment and on a truly ethical management of big enterprises).

Needless to say that a fiscal system which would be based on said four pillars will only be achievable in a global context (whereby all countries in the world would be persuaded to implement such a system) and under the condition that the national governments of the countries participating in the NMWO will have access to sufficient funds acquired differently (more specifically: based upon the periodic allocations of the NMWI; see above, under Sect. 4.7.2.2.1) in order to cover their (own) spending needs (including the establishment of a universal social care system).

4.7.2.3.2.2 Basic Content of the Here Proposed New and More Just Global Tax System

83 Within the framework of the treaty (ies) which will shape the here proposed "New Monetary World Order", there could already be basically agreed upon the main principles, based on the four aforementioned pillars, of the new and more just global tax system, which, as said, could be based on three tax mechanisms, i.e.:

- a tax on expenditures for luxuries and (certain other) "nonessential goods" (to be categorized under the newly to establish rules and regulations implementing the New Monetary World Order)[126],
- an income tax for natural persons which would only be applicable to individuals who already have accumulated a relatively high wealth level (according to parameters also further to be defined in the rules and regulations implementing the New Monetary World Order),[127]
  and,
- an income tax regarding the (operating) profits of certain legal entities, among which especially big enterprises.

4.7.2.3.2.3 A Transaction Tax on Certain Expenditures for Luxurious and (Certain Other) "Nonessential Goods"

84 The most simple of the three aforementioned tax systems would consist of an indirect tax on expenditures for luxuries and (certain other) "nonessential goods", namely goods (and services) which are qualified as harmful (but not harmful enough to completely ban them).

Contrarily, under the newly to be established "New Monetary World Order", ordinary transactions of "common" goods and services which are necessary for leading a dignified life would become completely exempted from any indirect tax systems[128], with as policy goal to enable every human being to build up a basic wealth allowing him to live a dignified life. However, transactions regarding luxurious goods and services or goods and/or services deemed harmful (by the world community) could on the contrary be(come) the subject of (heavy) taxes.[129]

Such a discriminatory indirect tax system will obviously need to be based upon a thorough cataloguing (which could be established in more detail according to

---

[126]Kruithof (2012), pp. 70–77, especially p. 77.

[127]This would meet an "old demand" of "left" political thinking that income from capital and from capital transactions should be more taxed. In a similar way, the "New Monetary World Order" should aim at completely banning tax havens (a policy objective which, per definition, will require an international agreement between all countries participating in the NMWO). (See *e.g.* Kruithof 2012, pp. 70–77, especially p. 76.)

[128]It has already before been pointed out that indirect taxes are among the most unjust, as they weigh relatively much higher on the lower than on the richer classes as people all have to eat (and commit to other daily consumption) in order to live (see Todd 2015, p. 95).

[129]Compare Galbraith (1996), p. 29.

directives of the "NMWI" itself and/or of the NGSCB). For instance, as regards this second category of goods "of a so-called harmful nature", one could think of goods such as alcohol, tobacco, certain types of industrial food (for instance processed food; food products containing a high percentage of sugar, etc.), certain goods for leisure (for instance electronic toys), but the list can go further (depending on the policy goals to be set out by the world community).

4.7.2.3.2.4 Income Tax for Individuals Already in Possession of Great Wealth

To the extent that, under the here newly proposed New Monetary World Order, the **85**
(private) economy would otherwise (and at least for some time) continue to rely on the principles of the free market economy, a redefinition of government financing as such will by itself not fundamentally result in the free market to function in a different way.

Given human nature, the price setting on the free markets will presumably still (albeit, taking into account the incentive-mechanisms which could be built in into the treaty (ies) and the rules and regulations implementing the "New Monetary World Order") (see further, at marg. 149–156 of this chapter), hopefully to a lesser and lesser extent, continue to be driven by individual greed and the aim of pursuing money of certain of its most active market players, more specifically the professional producers and merchants.

As a result, also under the "New Monetary World Order", (relatively small) groups of the population (among which especially big entrepreneurs) will still (be able to) continue to make (huge) profits, in other words, will still be able to acquire a high income, and through this accumulate large capital.

Bearing in mind the aforementioned observations, a more just system of gov- **86**
ernment financing and of redistributing the world's wealth could consequently entail the establishment of a fiscal system which would imply a (substantial) taxation of the incomes of the wealthy.

In order to avoid a further competition between the countries participating in the New Monetary World Order, such a system should, moreover, be world-wide the same[130], hence the need for a convention-based system established in the treaty (ies) and further rules and regulations that will shape the New Monetary World Order.

Without entirely removing the incentive for (large) capital[131], such a fiscal system should have as one of its main purposes the achievement of a larger scale leveling of incomes than is currently the case, while at the same time, it should encourage the more fortunate people to actively participate in the development of

[130]Earlier, Stiglitz pleaded for a full harmonization of taxes within the context of the European Union (see Bijlo 2014, p. 63; see also Stiglitz 2015c).

[131]See before Galbraith (1974), p. 93.
Stiglitz has "demystified" this argument (see Stiglitz 2012, p. 78).

the social and cultural fabric of society (further in the text described as: "social-cultural participation"; see further, at marg. 92 of this chapter).

Moreover, such a taxation of (large) incomes of wealthy individuals could be of such a nature that it would enable global money creation to take place in a (more) ordered way (and through this, it could even produce a new means of controlling money supply).

87 This (new) taxation mechanism could, for instance, be aimed at, on a global scale, keeping income from capital within reasonable limits, especially for natural persons as capital providers (= resulting in a mechanism of taxation "*at the source*" of the money streams), and at fulfilling the underlying objective of establishing a new social contract regarding the use of money (whereby it would no longer be permitted that huge inequalities, usurping social and economic relations, would arise within the global society).

88 In this, the thresholds below which assets/income should be completely safeguarded from the fiscal (and para-fiscal) skimming behavior of governments, should not necessarily be unreasonably low, as it cannot be ignored that (correctly applying) the argument that (truly) hard work (but not: making capital "work")[132] should result in a sufficient reward (which can be significantly higher than for people solely dependent on social benefits).

89 Particularly as regards (rich) natural persons, one could for instance think of a world-wide implementation of a very simple and transparent tax system.

In this "simple tax system", *on one hand*, there would no longer be room for any type of taxes on (low) income as such[133], and neither for registration taxes and other taxes on transactions of goods and/or services[134], and, *on the other hand*[135], a (progressive) income taxation should only come into play as regards people who have succeeded in acquiring a certain (minimum) wealth enabling them to lead a "decent", but moreover sufficiently "generous"[136] life.

The thresholds of such a "progressive" income tax system should hereby be aimed at leaving the income of "the common (or moderate) man" untouched, while

---

[132]See Pascal Bruckner:

> Il s'en faut donc de beaucoup que les plus méritants touchent les émoluments les plus élevés: "Si les marchés imposaient vraiment une discipline, les personnes qui travaillent dur ne seraient pas pauvres et les spéculateurs en général ne seraient pas riches" (John Kenneth Galbraith). L'argent ne va pas au mérite mais à la puissance et au désir; quiconque capte les désirs capte aussi les ressources. (see Bruckner 2002, pp. 22–23).

[133]In its widest sense, thus including succession taxes and otherwise heritage related taxes.

[134]With exclusion of the aforementioned taxes on transactions aimed at acquiring (to-be-listed) luxurious and/or (too) harmful goods or services.

[135]Based upon an ongoing appreciation for individual property as a (human) right, which under the "New Monetary World Order" should be(come) accessible to everyone who is willing to make reasonable efforts to acquire it.

[136]In the true meaning of the word as used by, for instance, Aristotle. (See Aristotle 1996, pp. 85 a.f.)

at the same time assuring that the (really or "sufficiently") rich would be impacted most.[137]

In this way, income should not be taxed as long as a (natural) person has not acquired the goods which enable him to live a decent and sufficiently generous life, whereby the latter should be defined in a sufficiently broad sense (and, for instance, could include a living house, a car, all types of consumer goods, etc., but not luxurious goods, in addition to goods acquired for investment purposes, such as (expensive) art work, jewelry, excessively priced perfumes, financial instruments, yachts, private jets, excessively luxurious cars, etc.).

Furthermore, the "New Monetary World Order" could, in addition to the "exempted (basic) goods (needed for a decent life)", also be tolerant (even from an intergenerational perspective) towards a (modest) accumulation of (company or corporate) capital, which could be even separately taken into account for measuring a second threshold beneath one would remain free of income taxes (especially as regards the income out of capital), and so up till the point where such an acquired capital reaches a level which is acceptable within the underlying objective that "hard work must remain truly rewardable".

As a further thought, one could for instance imagine such a second "universal taxation threshold" for an additional accumulation of (company or corporate) capital to be determined at 5 million euro or USD (obviously to be expressed in terms of the New World Currency) per individual (but evidently any other amount which would deemed better serving the policy goals of the New Monetary World Order could be chosen by the world community).

The latter approach should enable everyone to have the opportunity to establish a reasonably successful business enterprise, without being hindered by tax mechanisms, up till the point where such an enterprise (regardless of its legal form) will have grown to a size where taxing the income derived from such an enterprise would be considered socially desirable.

Furthermore, the income tax (for natural persons) system could be based on the principle that any income (regardless of its source, meaning income from labor, as well as income from capital[138] or from other assets, such as real estate) will principally not be taxed up till the point where both aforementioned thresholds (i.e. (*i*) a sufficient accumulation of "basic goods of life" and (*ii*) if applicable, an

---

[137]Compare Taylor (1934), p. xxxviii:

> Economic inequalities cannot be altogether prevented, but they may be kept within reasonable bounds by a series of wise regulations.

and

> Plato proposes a similar division, the fourth, or poorest class, possessing nothing beyond their patrimony, the first or richest being allowed to own four times the annual yield of the patrimony. Any increasement of wealth beyond this upper limit will be escheated to the Treasury, or, as we should say, subject to an income-tax of one hundred per cent.

[138]In the fiscal system that is proposed here, such a distinction would hardly be of any further relevance. (Compare Crombez 2013, p. 102.)

additional (company or corporate) capital amounting to the aforementioned threshold) would be reached.

As soon as both thresholds would be reached, a (substantial) tax charge could be applied to that part of the income which leads to additional capital accumulation above the "universal taxation threshold(s)" (but where there will still be a sufficiently reasonable amount of tax free income left for financing basic life needs, including those of a family or relatives who would be dependent on the person gaining said income).

Such a taxation could furthermore evolve in a progressive way (as is currently customary in many countries which charge income tax), implying that the higher one's income, the higher the tax rate would be (and, if needed, a 100% tax rate from a certain income level on could be thought of).[139]

90 The proposed new fiscal system could for instance look as mentioned in the table hereafter (whereby the amounts are chosen purely for the exercise undertaken here) (see Table 4.2).

91 As mentioned before, as regards natural persons, no other tax and (para-fiscal) systems than the ones mentioned before would remain in force.

In this context, it will be important that, for instance, there would be no more systems of succession taxes in force so that the lower and middle classes of society will also be allowed to also accumulate some wealth, especially from an intergenerational perspective.

In this way, goods necessary to build up a humane live which have been acquired by one generation could be passed on to the next generation without states (under the impulse of the rich and the powerful) being able to prevent this, but keeping in mind that if in such a case a member of this "next generation", by inheriting assets, would reach the aforementioned "taxation thresholds" himself, such a person would, of course, immediately fall under the abovementioned income tax system (but would, on the contrary, not have to pay taxes for inheriting the assets as such).

92 Furthermore, a system of reductions on income tax which under the abovementioned system would be due by "fortunate" natural persons could be elaborated upon, whereby, for instance, donations made by such natural persons for different "social-cultural" objectives (to be summed up in the rules and regulations of the NGSCB), such as, for example, donations to cultural institutions, to education or medical institutions, for youth work, to orphanages, to international aids, etc.

Under the here proposed system, such donations could completely be deducted from the income tax due by a fortunate person (and one could even implement a principle of transferability of deductions to a next tax year).

A "fortunate person" who, by his past efforts, has already accumulated a wealth to the level of the abovementioned "taxation threshold(s)" and who furthermore has an income which would be taxable, will henceforth have the choice either to undergo the income taxation, or to actively contribute to building a better world

[139]Compare Moutton (2014), pp. 44–48, especially 46.

Table 4.2 Diagrammatic presentation of the new proposed fiscal system

Characteristics of the assets	Income	Tax rate
Accumulation of a personal fortune consisting of (certain, to be catalogued in the treaty (ies) and/or rules and regulations governing the NGSCB) "*necessary goods of life*" (such as a living house, a vehicle, consumer goods for daily *use,* leisure related goods (except luxury goods),...):	Total exemption from taxation of all types of income (from labor as well as capital) till said goods needed to lead a decent life are obtained.	–
Accumulation of a further capital needed for a business enterprise (on top of the already exempted "*necessary goods of life*"), with a value equal to or below a to be defined "universal taxation threshold" (for instance the equivalent in NWM of 5 million euro or USD).	Total exemption from taxation of all types of income (from labor as well as capital), till a level of capital equal to the said threshold has been reached.	–
As soon as the "additional capital", on top of the already exempted "*necessary goods of life*", has *been* reached:	Progressive taxation of any type of income (from labor, as well as from capital) according to the following conceivable tariffs:	• Income portion up to an equivalent in NWM of 60,000,- euro or USD per year: 0%-tariff (as its purpose is to pay for daily costs of life); • Income portion from an equivalent in NWM of 60,001,- euro or USD to 120,000 euro or USD per year: 50%-tariff; • Income portion from an equivalent in NWM of 120,001,- euro or USD to 250,000 euro or USD per year: 60%-tariff; • Income portion from an equivalent in NWM of 250,001,- euro or USD to 500,000 euro or USD per year: 70%-tariff; • Income portion from an equivalent in NWM of 500,001,- euro or USD to 1,000,000 euro or USD per year: 80%-tariff; • Income portion from an equivalent in NWM of 1,000,001,- euro or USD to 10,000,000 euro or USD per year: 90%-tariff; • Income portion from an equivalent in NWM of 10,000,001,- euro or more per year: 100%-tariff.
Acquisition of goods or services which are categorized as "luxurious" or "harmful":	A "sanctioning" tax on these transactions.	Tarification to be determined, based on the underlying policy objective.

by proactively making donations to social-cultural objectives for the amount of taxes due.[140]

93 In order to ensure a smooth co-ordination of the here proposed tax system regarding the "rich" of society, one could furthermore think of assigning to every ("tax paying") citizen a so-called "file manager for asset accumulation and asset

---

[140]Compare to the insights of Arnold Carnegie (1835–1919), one of the richest Americans of the nineteenth century who was also one of the main drives behind the then occurring American industrial revolution (having been the leader of the enormous expansion of the American steel industry in the late nineteenth century). By 1898, his corporation "Carnegie Steel Corporation" had become the largest of its kind in the world. During the last part of his life, Carnegie aspired for a societal leadership role as a philanthropist. Hence, during the last 18 years of his life, he gave away to charities, foundations, and universities about USD 350 million (in 2015 share of GDP, this would amount to USD 78.6 billion), almost 90% of his fortune. (See https://en.wikipedia.org/wiki/Andrew_Carnegie; last consulted on February 27th 2016; http://www.biography.com/people/andrew-carnegie-9238756; last consulted on February 27th 2016.)

In a 1889 article entitled "*The Gospel of Wealth*", Carnegie had called on the rich to use their wealth to improve society, an insight that he himself wanted to put into daily practice by giving away the largest part of his fortune (See https://en.wikipedia.org/wiki/Andrew_Carnegie; last consulted on February 27th 2016. See also Veldman and Parlevliet 2003, p. 53.)

Carnegie's viewpoint on money gathering was in one of his writings described as follows:

> I propose to take an income no greater than $50,000 per annum! Beyond this I need ever earn, make no effort to increase my fortune, but spend the surplus each year for benevolent purposes! Let us cast aside business forever, except for others. Let us settle in Oxford and I shall get a thorough education, making the acquaintance of literary men. I figure that this will take 3 years active work. I shall pay especial attention to speaking in public. We can settle in London and I can purchase a controlling interest in some newspaper or live review and give the general management of it attention, taking part in public matters, especially those connected with education and improvement of the poorer classes. Man must have no idol and the amassing of wealth is one of the worst species of idolatry! No idol is more debasing than the worship of money! Whatever I engage in I must push inordinately; therefore should I be careful to choose that life which will be the most elevating in its character. To continue much longer overwhelmed by business cares and with most of my thoughts wholly upon the way to make more money in the shortest time, must degrade me beyond hope of permanent recovery. I will resign business at 25, but during these ensuing 2 years I wish to spend the afternoons in receiving instruction and in reading systematically! (See https://en.wikipedia.org/wiki/Andrew_Carnegie; last consulted on February 27th 2016.)

In his article "*Wealth*", more commonly known as "*The Gospel of Wealth*" (1889), Carnegie describes the responsibility of philanthropy by the new upper class of self-made rich. Carnegie hereby argued that the best way of dealing with the new phenomenon of wealth inequality was for the wealthy to redistribute their surplus means in a responsible and thoughtful manner. This approach was in contrast with traditional bequest where wealth is handed down to one's heirs, and other forms of bequest where wealth is willed to the state for public purposes. Carnegie furthermore argued that the surplus wealth acquired by the captains of industry produces the greatest net benefit to society when it is administered carefully by the wealthy. Hence, the wealthy should administer their riches responsibly for the general good of society. (See https://en.wikipedia.org/wiki/The_Gospel_of_Wealth; last consulted on February 27th 2016. For the full text of "*The Gospel of Wealth*", see https://archive.org/stream/gospelofwealthot00carnuoft/gospelofwealthot00carnuoft_djvu.txt; last consulted on February 27th 2016.)

planning" who, for instance, would be employed by the national central bank and who would provide assistance (to the individuals assigned to him) with regard to: (*i*) asset accumulation (within the aforementioned parameters); (*ii*) income management; (*iii*) tax planning, and (*iv*) social-cultural participation (in the aforementioned meaning of the term).

As regards persons who would be borrowers from their national central bank (see further, under Sect. 4.7.3.2), this "file manager for accumulation and planning of assets" could have as an addition task to assist in the management of the credit accounts of the people assigned to him.

Otherwise put, the here proposed income tax system as regards the "fortunate" **94**
members of society could allow global citizens to actively participate in the reconstruction of the social-cultural (in a wide sense) fabric of society, which after suffering for centuries from the selfish economy of capitalism, could thus enjoy a genuine revival.

Moreover, as it should be the case from an true ethical perspective (other than selfishness as taught by economic neo-liberalism), the further principle would apply that the richer a person gets, the stronger the invitation will be to share one's wealth with others, especially by participating to the restoration of the socio-cultural fabric of society (with as an alternative being subjected to the aforementioned tax skimming).[141]

Hence, implementing such a tax system would invite everyone, but especially the rich classes, to indulge in a spirit of altruism which could, on a global level, contribute to establishing a truly equitable social economic order (instead of, as is currently the case under the impulse of economic neo-liberalism, stimulate everyone to, at all costs, accumulate the greatest possible fortune solely for one's own greedy needs).

4.7.2.3.2.5 *Tax on "Business Profits"*

In addition to the abovementioned income tax system to which the rich individuals **95**
of society would be subject, a second income tax system could be implemented dealing with the profits of legal entities (such as enterprises).

For reasons of simplicity, we will refer to such "profits" of all types of legal entities as to "business profits" (although such profits obviously could also be the result of activities other than "business" in the strict sense of the word).

Also as regards such "business profits", the to be established tax system could be based upon the observation that countries (in addition to certain other supra-

[141]For a moral ground, reference can be made to the comparison made by Jesus Christ in Luke, 21:1–4 (King James Version):

> And he looked up, and saw the rich men casting their gifts into the treasury. And he saw also a certain poor widow casting in thither two mites. And he said, Of a truth I say to you, that this poor widow has cast in more than they all: For all these have of their abundance cast in to the offerings of God: but she of her penury has cast in all the living that she had.

national legal entities) will no longer depend on income from taxes, as they would, under the here proposed system of financing countries (in addition to supra-national entities) derive all their needed income directly from allocations from the "New Monetary World Institute" (see above, at marg. 65 a.f. of this chapter).

By this, it would at the same time be ensured that countries (and other public entities) would no longer be exposed to the extortion and blackmail techniques used by big enterprises and their rich capital providers (such as the threat of business migration in case of excessive taxes on company profits).

96 Furthermore, if it would be deemed necessary to submit profits of enterprises to their own taxation system, such a system could also be held as simply as possible, for instance by installing a global equal tax rate on similarly defined (operational) business profits by any legal entity.

97 As a result, such a system of taxing "business profits" of private legal entities could be seen as an instrument which could help creating a fair market environment for all kinds of businesses, whereby one could, for instance, imagine a progressive tax rate system which would impose higher taxes on entities making bigger profits at a huge cost for the rest of society (instead of, as is currently the case, making it the more easy to avoid taxation for big enterprises than for small entrepreneurs, let alone for ordinary people not being active as businessmen).

Otherwise put, such a "differentiating" tax system could, hence, distinguish between enrichment that is socially permissible and benign and that which is at social cost.[142]

The here proposed tax system of business profits could hence fulfill a large number of policy goals, such as:

- a higher tax rate for unethical businesses;
- a lower tax rate for legal entities with deploy an ethical attitude (for instance as regards employment policy);
- a lower tax rate for legal entities who would innovate in a responsible ethical manner;
- a taxation policy with a steering impact on price setting, ensuring that enterprises will be encouraged to keep the prices for their goods and services, and thus their business profits, within reasonable limits (under the awareness that when prices would reach at a certain (too high) level, business profits will be taxed away);
- a taxation policy which would aim for a fair system of management and staff compensation, whereby, for instance, companies and other legal entities would be encouraged to pay overall fair salaries.

  The concept of "fair salaries" could, a.o., imply that excesses wages for CEO's (and other high personnel members) would be avoided, but also that lower personnel would be given acceptable wages.

[142]To paraphrase Galbraith, it is hereby expected that this differentiating tax system would assume the essential, difficult and intensely controversial task of making and making effective such (types of) differentiation. (See Galbraith 1996, p. 29.)

The latter could furthermore help ensuring that the business profits of said companies (and other legal entities) would be kept within reasonable limits, under the awareness that too high business profits (which could be the result from exploiting one's lower personal by, for instance, keeping their salaries too low) would be taxed away;

- a system of tax reduction for social-cultural participation similarly to the system described earlier (see above, at marg. 92 of this chapter);
- ...

4.7.2.3.2.6 *Allocation of the Collected Taxes*

The above proposed systems of income taxes regarding natural persons and legal entities should normally have as a result that any individual subject to taxation will prefer to spend the amounts of due taxes, in agreement with his "file manager for asset accumulation and asset planning" (see above, at marg. 92 of this chapter), to the aforementioned social-cultural participation programs. **98**

Otherwise put, anyone who would become subject to the said taxation regimes will have a free choice to either participate in such social-cultural participation programs (and thus avoid taxation), or to pay taxes.

It is here furthermore proposed that taxes thus collected (if any) would not be handed over to the national governments participating in the New Monetary World Order (or any other country organ such as a tax administration), but that they would flow back to the NGSCB itself. In this way, taxation would rather become a system for controlling the supply of money than a system of financing governments, as the charging of taxes would simply have as a result that (too) excessive money (which would moreover not have been spent in the context of an approved social-cultural participation program) would be withdrawn from circulation.

The said income tax system would, furthermore, help avoiding that the taxation policy of a given country would be used as a means of attracting big enterprises and their rich shareholders (and by this, investments), and thus also help ensuring that private investments will, henceforth, only be made on the basis of rational economic principles (such as the presence of a sufficiently specialized labor potential, of natural resources, etc.), without leaving any further room for tax policy based-distortions. **99**

Consequently, such income tax systems would help avoiding an unhealthy competition between tax regulators (so-called "*race to the bottom*"[143]).

An alternative approach could be one whereby the member states of the New Monetary World Order would still themselves receive said taxes and would, furthermore, be able to spend them. **100**

In other words, these revenues from taxes would consist of an additional source of income for these participating countries (in addition to and on top of the periodic allocations of New World Currency granted by the New Monetary World Institute).

---

[143]See Oxfam (2014), pp. 16 a.f.

101 Taking into account the objectives of the here proposed new model for a more just (and altruistic) system of money creation and of state financing, the alternative reasoning referred to in the previous marg. 100 of this chapter, would preferably not be pursued.

Indeed, if the member states, on top of the New World Currency allocations granted to them by the "New Monetary World Institute", also would continue to receive tax money themselves (and would furthermore be able to spend these themselves), a breeding ground for competition among the member states would still remain at hand, whereby such member states could still attempt to attract as much rich individual and/or big enterprises as possible to their own country.

In order to establish a true world solidarity, it would therefore be preferable that the member states of the New Monetary World Order would exclusively be dependent on allocations made by the New Monetary World Institute and that no residue of fiscal autonomy would remain in place.

Only in this way will it be possible to establish a fully level playing field between the member states of the New Monetary World Order, not only as regards their income, but also as regards their spending behavior (and, hence, also as regards the policy aim of building a world-wide system of equal social and economic prosperity).

4.7.2.4 Towards a Global Social Care System

4.7.2.4.1 Background

102 As mentioned earlier (see above, at marg. 64 a.f. of this chapter), in the here new proposed system of government financing which would be based on a system of global money creation (rather than on income derived from taxation and similar charges), also the spending pattern of the national governments of the participating countries (but also of the other supra-national legal entities which will receive allocations from the New Monetary World Institute) will need to be reviewed.

In addition to classic government spending on infrastructure works and matters such as national and international security (police force and army)[144], justice, schooling, education and training,... a central focus should in this regard also go to the establishment of a globally harmonized social care system.[145]

---

[144]However, in a more altruistically based social and economic order, the expectancy should be that societies would become less conflictual both on a national and international level, resulting in a lesser need for army and police forces. The focus in organizing society could hence shift from guarding private property (in addition to other interests of the rich classes), to the establishment of a society model which cares for all people, including the poor and the deprived. (Compare Sachs 2011, p. 204, also and for similar reasons calling for a diminishment of government expenditure on army and police forces.)

[145]The necessity of ensuring free education and free health care is one of the main themes of the earlier quoted Oxfam-report "*Even it up*" (see *e.g.* Oxfam 2014, pp. 5, 13 and 18).

Compare Galbraith (1996), p. 65.

Currently, the development of a social care system is a matter falling under the sovereignty of each country whereby hardly any international agreements are in place (in sharp contrast with the numerous treaties dealing with all kinds of economic and financial mechanisms mainly to the benefit of the rich and the powerful within societies). **103**

Hence, in the present-day world, every country decides to a large extent for itself if it wants to have a social care system for its citizens (and, occuringly, which type of social care is made available and under what conditions).

It goes without saying that in such an approach, very large distortions have occurred among the countries of the world.

4.7.2.4.2 Plea for a World-Wide Synchronized Social Care System

As has been argued before, within the framework of the here proposed New Monetary World Order, one should advocate a globally leveled system of social care (based on the principle of so-called "*universal coverage*"[146]) which should ensure that every human being, wherever in the world he is born or residing, has an equal access to a minimum of social care organized and/or financed by his government.[147] **104**

Otherwise put, on a social level, the New Monetary World Order should aim at installing an altruistic monetary system whereby money should be made accessible in order to meet the needs of the poor and deprived within society.

Hence, under the regime of the New Monetary World Order, especially the implementation of a globally equalized social care system should be put high on the agenda.[148]

In the earlier mentioned study "*Even it up*", Oxfam has similarly pleaded for a system of "*universal free social services*".[149]

---

[146]Oxfam (2014), p. 102.

[147]See *e.g.* United Nations Development Programme (UNDP) (2014), p. 85:

> Universal coverage of basic social services is not only imperative—it is also possible at early stages of development. And recent evidence shows that it can be achieved in less than a decade. Furthermore, universal provision of basic social services is better than targeting, which leads to social stigma for recipients and segmentation in the quality of services, as those who can afford to opt out of receiving public services do so.

[148]See Oxfam (2014), p. 19, furthermore arguing that

> there are (. . .) good examples from around the world of how expanding public services are helping to reduce inequality.

[149]Oxfam (2014), p. 23, furthermore mentioning that

> such social services must be universal and permanent.

105 The idea that the public sector, especially with regards to social care, should provide a "*countervailing power*" to the interests of big enterprises and their rich shareholders is obviously not new.

Amongst the many economists who have advocated such idea, reference can, for instance, be made to Galbraith (1909–2006) who advocated the role of the state as a defender of the general interest. Galbraith, for instance, stated that certain services which cannot be provided for on the free markets in an efficient way, such as the construction of living houses for the general public, medical care, urban transport, education,. . . should mainly be taken over by the government (and it will not come as a surprise that many neo-liberal authors have taken opposite viewpoints on this regard). Galbraith's opinion was that in modern societies prosperity has reached a high enough level for such collective systems of general well-being to be established.[150]

It will be no surprise that, on the other side of the spectrum, Ayn Rand, one of the most fervent "neo-liberal authors", has raged against any role for the state in sectors such as (public) education and health care. Her answer (unfortunately at present, especially in the traditional "rich" countries, well accepted by a broad public) to the central question whether states should provide for public services in sectors as schooling, health and social care, public transport, etc. is a very clear: "No".[151]

It should, furthermore, not come as a surprise that Rand's historical "mentor", Adam Smith himself, also expressed very similar opinions regarding, for instance, the question whether or not education should be financed through government means.[152]

It deserves to be mentioned (and even underlined) here that Ayn Rand, as mentioned before, did not succeed at upholding herself the theoretical purportedly "moral" standards she had set out in her own writings. When near the end of her life Ayn Rand got terminally ill, she did not hesitate for a moment to make use of the "useless" public health care systems (purportedly under the name of Ann O'Connor), thus in her proper actions completely denouncing the content of the teachings she had spread during her life time[153] and by doing so, moreover, obviously demonstrating the moral failure of said teachings.

As Michael Ford has put it[154]:

> In the end, Miss Rand was a hypocrite but she could never be faulted for failing to act in her own self-interest.

Milton Friedman also showed himself to be an advocate of governments kept to a minimum size and having only a minimum of funds (hence of tax money) at their disposal. Friedman has, furthermore, been witnessed to call for a substantial

---

[150]See Galbraith (1996); Vandewalle (1976), pp. 315–316. Compare Hollenberg (1942), pp. 205–207.

[151]Rand (2008), p. 93.

[152]See Smith (1979), p. 759.

[153]See http://boingboing.net/2011/01/28/ayn-rand-took-govern.html.

[154]See Ford (2010–2011).

diminishment of the role of governments in public life and wanted this role as much as possible left to the operation of the free market(s):

> The problem is not that government is spending too little but that it is spending too much. The problem in schooling is that government is spending too much on the wrong things. The problem in health care is that government is spending too much on the wrong things. The end result has been that government has become a self-generating monstrosity.[155]

Since then, this neo-liberal vision has become the prevailing policy vision in many Western (and Western inspired) countries, for instance reflecting in the widespread belief that the welfare state model but encourages laziness and enables an increasing number of people to survive who are deemed not worth living (see above, the observations on the "survival of the fittest"-idea, at marg. 293–294 of Chap. 3 of this book), while at the same time subsidies (and other advantages) to ailing banks and other big enterprises remain as high as conceivable.[156]

A step further to the right in this thinking pattern, it may start to sound as though the "dislocation" of people (such as immigrants), or even the "extinction" of fellow men who are seen as "inferior" or "incompetent", could be considered as a justified solution for the social problem of poverty.[157]

It will be clear that the author of this book continues to adhere to the first view (as brilliantly defended by Galbraith in many of his publications[158]) that social care (in addition to public services in general), in a spirit of altruism, needs (need) to be borne by the community as a whole and cannot be left to the powers of the free market (which, given the principles under which the free markets work, can only lead to the fact that only the rich and fortunate are able to afford these kinds of services).[159]

Oxfam has furthermore rightly argued that the aim of a new (social) world order should be the establishment of a world characterized by the absence of fear ("*freedom from fear*")[160]: **106**

> Social protection provides money or in-kind benefits (. . .) which allow people to live dignified lives, free from fear even in the worst times. Such safety nets are the mark of a caring society that is willing to come together to support the most vulnerable. Like

---

155 Friedman (1993), p. 11.

156 Browne (2008), p. 101.

157 One may in this regard refer to the way street children are treated in certain South-American countries (see Child Poverty in Brazil—Facts, Reasons, and what can be done. http://www.childrenofbahia.com/childpoverty.htm. Last consulted on December 18th 2014):

> Most street children are viewed at best as a nuisance and at worst as an infestation to be eradicated. Because they have no vote or voice there is little impetus on the politicians to work to solve the issue. Whilst there is a drive from the president's office any actions are so watered down by the time it gets to city level that they become almost useless.

158 See especially Galbraith (1996) and Galbraith (1960).

159 Reference can again be made to the illustrations made above under marg. 174 of Chap. 3 of this book.

160 Oxfam (2014), p. 20.

healthcare and education, social protection puts income into the pockets of those who need it most, counteracting today's skewed income distribution and mitigating the effects of inequality.

It needs not surprise that this "*freedom from fear*"-argument also resonates in an earlier quote from the Gospels (see above, at marg. 33 of Chap. 3 of this book) whereby Christ is reported to have said that no-one should any longer be "*anxious for [his] life, what [h]e shall eat, or what [h]e shall drink; nor yet for [his] body, what [h]e shall put on*" (see Matthew, 6: 25[161]).

107 Concretely within the context of the New Monetary World Order, one could, for instance, work towards an approach where the financing of the social care system of any country participating in it, would be (a substantial) part of the (periodic) allocations of New World Currency to be granted by the New Monetary World Institute (as described earlier on; see above, at marg. 65 a.f. of this chapter).

Again, the policy goal should be to aspire for a global social care system which will be based upon the acknowledgment of the basic needs of every human being and which should, furthermore, become independent of the strength of the national economy of the country where one is born, or where one is residing (which under the New Monetary World Order, as opposed to the current capitalist system, should no longer be of any further relevance in determining the size of the operational funds, including those for social care, to such a country).

4.7.2.4.3 The Policy Question of a Fixed Basic Income

108 As part of this to be established globally equalized system of social care (as referred to under the marg. 104 a.f. of this chapter), the question arises whether or not the minimum required care package to which every human being should become entitled under the New Monetary World Order should also contain a so-called "fixed basic income" (in other words, a basic income which would become available to anyone, regardless of a state of illness, disability, old age,. . .) which would ensure that every human being, regardless of how much luck or misfortune he encounters in life, will always have the certainty to be able to cover his or her basic needs.[162]

109 In the recent past, there have indeed been calls for such a "fixed basic income" system whereby everyone would be(come) entitled to a (modest) basic income out of public funds.[163]

---

[161]Quotation from: http://www.earlychristianwritings.com/text/matthew-asv.html (last consulted on October 21st 2015).

[162]Already, some countries are thinking of introducing such a basic income as an alternative for social security. It has, for instance, been reported that the government of Finland has committed to implement a universal basic income experiment (see Laterza 2015; see also Schiller 2016).

[163]See *e.g.* Van den Broeck (2014), p. 21 (containing an interview with Paul De Grauwe).

Within the New Monetary World Order, as it will be based on considerations of altruism, there is no apparent reason why such a fixed basic income should not be implemented, provided that the set-up of such a system would not undermine mankind's incentive of continued participation in economic production in a sufficient way (as no economic system can survive if too great a section of the population would entirely withdraw from the economic processes).[164]

A similar "basic income" system should, moreover, properly and precisely address what is to be understood by the notion "basic needs" to be covered by it, which, per definition, should be of a sufficiently modest nature. One could, for instance, think of access to only food and (collective) housing, with exclusion of products of a more "luxurious" nature, ensuring that actively participating in society would (obviously) remain to be more rewarded than not participating at all (and merely enjoying the basic income)[165]. Furthermore, the setting up of such a "(fixed) minimum basic income" system could also be accompanied by measures of awareness-raising which encourage active participation in society (including its economy).

As regards those who would not participate in the regular society (economic) processes for a longer period, one could also think of mechanisms where the preservation of the fixed basic income would become dependent on a certain degree of "activation" within society, for instance within social groups or entities where a minimum of societal dynamic and productivity is still taking place and which encourage a (minimum degree of) integration into mainstream society.[166]

---

[164]See nevertheless Galbraith (1996), p. 28:

> That some will choose not to work must be accepted. Socially compensated idleness unquestionably affronts deep-seated social attitudes; public pressure may, indeed should, be exerted to get able individuals into the work force, the exercise of such pressure being undoubtedly enjoyed by some. Starvation is not, however, a tolerable sanction. Some abuse, as it will be regarded, is inevitable in this part of the welfare system and must be tolerated.

[165]See already Plato's warning on finding the proper balance in this regard (Plato 1987, p. 129):

> So we have found two further things (. . .) which our Guardians must at all costs prevent from slipping unobserved into our state. (. . .) Wealth and poverty (. . .). One produces luxury and idleness and a desire for novelty, the other meanness and bad workmanship and the desire for revolution as well.

[166]For all clarity: there will be no need for such correction mechanisms as regards the types of replacement income under the abovementioned social care system which are granted because of obvious, objective reasons, such as disease, invalidity, old age, etc.

4.7.2.4.4 Towards a Global Alignment of the Rules and Regulations Protecting Labor

110 A further part of the social measures the New Monetary World Order should be willing to embrace, should relate to the creation of a "*level playing field*" as regards the protection of labor (in a broad sense of the word).

This would obviously imply that the treaty (ies) and further rules and regulations establishing the New Monetary World Order, would also have a "labor related" dimension, in addition to a "monetary", "fiscal" and "social" dimension.

As regards the content of social and labor protection, agreements to be established under the umbrella of the New Monetary World Order could, for instance, deal with questions such as: (*i*) minimum wage; (*ii*) working hours; (*iii*) pension age; (*iv*) labor conditions (inter alia questions on safety and health); (*v*) holiday arrangements; (*vi*) equal (gender) opportunities; (*vii*) minimum and maximum age requirements; (*vi*) pension rights;...

111 *As* mentioned before, the policy purpose of such agreements should be that a (true) "level playing field" would be established with regard to protection of labor in a broad sense of the word, not only to the benefit of the "working classes" (also to be interpreted in a broad sense of the word) themselves, but also of their employers.

As regards the latter issue, it should, for instance, be avoided that national differences in labor protection would have a detrimental effect on competitivity, a problem which under economic neo-liberalism is usually tackled by policies of diminishing labor (and social) protection in countries where a stronger protection is in place, rather than, as will be expected from the more altruistic setting of the newly to be established New Monetary World Order, enhancing labor and social protection in countries where such protection is either weaker, or even completely lacking.

Bearing in mind the "altruistic" starting points on which the New Monetary World Order will be based, the treaty (ies) and the rules and regulations implementing it, should offer a socially accepted answer to this question by, at the very least, aligning labor protection to an equal minimum level everywhere in the world. By accomplishing this policy goal, it will at the same time be feasible to reconcile such enhanced degree of labor protection in the relations between employers and employees with the objective of ensuring a sufficient degree of fair play between employers (especially those belonging to the business sector), thus ensuring a fair and true level playing field within the global markets.

4.7.2.5 Measures to be Thought of During a Transition Period

112 If the world community would ever be willing to consider the introduction of the aforementioned system (or a similar one) of direct money creation on behalf of the national governments of the countries participating to the New Monetary World Order as an alternative for the presently prevailing systems of government financing based on taxes and similar charges and of money lending on the private markets

(of which the costs are, ultimately, also borne by tax generated money), the question arises how (quickly) such a system should be implemented in practice.

The introduction of the here proposed New Monetary World Order could indeed not be a moment of creation "ex nihilo", as already a complex structure of monetary systems is currently in place, implying that the replacement of these existing systems by an entirely new system will, obviously, not be a simple operation. **113**

However, to the extent that continuing the present-day monetary system(s) may not be an option in order to truly face the huge problems the world is facing, transition difficulties regarding the introduction of the here proposed "New Monetary World Order" should as such not be considered as an obstacle against the launch of the here proposed model (or a similar one) for a more altruistic and just monetary system.

In any event, through the course of history, it has happened before that a new (convention based) monetary system was introduced whenever a previous system appeared to have failed. A recent example hereof has been the introduction, in 1944, of the currently still prevailing IMF (although the IMF system had a less significant impact than the system proposed here), in addition to, even more recently, the launch of the EMU (although the territorial impact of the latter, given the limited number of countries involved, has remained relatively limited and, moreover, the member states of the EMU are characterized by a larger degree of affinity than is present among all world countries). **114**

One of the main questions when implementing the here proposed New Monetary World Order in practice will obviously be how to deal with the existing monetary reserves (which have been accumulated under the monetary systems actually in place) and debts of countries to other countries (and/or their central banks or other, similar monetary institutions). **115**

A similar question will be how to deal with existing large private capitals and/or debt positions; some introductory reflections on the latter question will be elaborated upon when discussing the impact of the New Monetary World Order in the private domain (see also further, at marg. 14 of Chap. 6 of this book). **116**

As has been explained before, under the actual monetary systems in place, countries (or their respective central banks) acquire monetary reserves mainly because of how the international traffic in trade and payments is organized (see above, under Sect. 2.7 of Chap. 2 of this book). **117**

When for instance the residents of a certain country (massively) export goods (or services), i.e. sell them to residents of another country (or several other countries), this will, in most cases, ultimately result in a payment in the currency of the exporter (because said exporter will, in most cases, ultimately wish to obtain purchasing power within his own economy). To this purpose, the importer (buyer), as an example, could choose to "buy" the currency of the export(ing) country (on the currency exchange market(s)) in return for its own currency. As a result, the money exchanger, often a private bank or similar institution, will hence obtain currency of the import(ing) country, which will provide a basis for money creation (of new currency of the export(ing) country), for instance as such money exchanger will be able to use the foreign currency as collateral for obtaining credit from its own central bank. Otherwise put, the central bank of the export(ing) country could, at the request of such a money exchanger (in general a private bank), be willing to create a new quantity of its own currency, in exchange for the currency of the import(ing) country. In this way, (the central bank of) an export(ing) country will start to build a supply of currency consisting of currency of the import(ing) country (while more of the currency of the export(ing) country will be brought into circulation, which is logical as an increase in production and trade, even if it is partially intended for export, justifies an increase of the amount of money).

More simply put, the presently prevailing monetary system implies that export usually contributes to the building up of monetary reserves (in foreign currency) within the central bank (or within comparable institutions) of the export(ing) country (and, more generally, to an increase in the monetary base of the export (ing) country).

Therefore monetary reserves (in foreign currency)—such as any type of "savings" in the broad sense of the word—express "purchasing power" that a(n export) country, through the collective efforts of its economic residents, has been able to accumulate in the past and which is, ultimately, spendable in the country of origin of the foreign currency in question (but has, intrinsically, no purchasing power in the export country itself). In other words, the (residents of) the export(ing) country has (have) made efforts, mainly having consisted of deliveries of goods and/or services to the (residents of) the import(ing) country. The import(ing) country (or better: its residents) has (have) benefited of these goods and services, and in return has (have) only needed to give up its own currency (which in an economic context, at least from the perspective of the import(ing) country itself, requires a considerably lower effort than economic production and export). From a rational perspective, an export(ing) country will only have been willing to do this to the extent that the monetary reserves consisting of foreign currency issued by this import country effectively will (continue to) represent purchasing power, in other words, to the extent that the acquired reserves of foreign currency will, sooner or later, be spendable for the purchase of goods and services produced by (the residents of) the import(ing) country.[167]

If during this process confidence in the productivity of (the residents of) the import(ing) country would get lost, the monetary reserves (in foreign currency issued by such an import(ing) country) may tend to be considered worthless (whereby, for instance, a mass sale of said foreign currency on the currency

[167]For reasons of completeness, it should be pointed out that a transfer of monetary reserves to a third country may occur, implying that such a third country which is willing to acquire said monetary reserves in foreign currency, expresses its own belief in the purchasing power of this foreign currency, hence in the economy of the country having issued it. Otherwise put, the third country which is willing to acquire the monetary reserves (in foreign currency) of another (export (ing)) country, takes over the aforementioned legitimate expectation of the latter (export(ing)) country that this foreign currency will equal actual purchasing power in the import(ing) country's economy.

exchange market(s) would cause the exchange rate of the currency issued by the import(ing) country to collapse and could lead to a further disruption of the economy of the import(ing) country, as similarly the trust of all other countries in the currency of the import(ing) country would be imperiled, ultimately causing the import(ing) country to be unable to finance its further import).

In other words, such as any form of money (which has been "saved"[168]), monetary reserves in foreign currency (which, strictly spoken, are only money in the strict sense of the word in the country of origin of said currency) represent by definition "purchasing power", albeit purchasing power which, in most cases, is (only) spendable in the economy of the country of origin, i.e. the import(ing) country which has issued the currency.

The other way around, a chronic dependence on imports may cause a country to **118**
build up (foreign) debt.

When for instance the global import (on behalf of the residents) of a country exceeds the global export (by those same residents) of that country, a shortage on the current account of the balance of payments of that country will occur, implying that the income (in foreign currency issued by the third countries that import goods and services from said country) obtained from abroad will be smaller than the money which is spend abroad. For this reason, one could say that such a country becomes an "import(ing) country".

A similar import(ing) country may, in order to finance the shortage in its current account, first use its existing monetary reserves (which were accumulated in the past through its own export), but when these run out, the country will ultimately be forced to finance the deficit by borrowing foreign currency to finance its own imports (which will lead to an accumulation of debt expressed in foreign currency).

In this way, such an import(ing) country will build up debt positions abroad (especially with the residents,—including private banks and monetary institutions—of export(ing) countries), which as such is logical, as a country in debt has "spent" before having accumulated purchasing power (which is an alternative representation of debt accumulation).[169]

Hence, the prevailing monetary and trade systems have as a result that countries **119**
with thriving economies (usually) succeed in building of monetary reserves in foreign currency as a result of exporting goods and services to countries with less thriving economies, hence to become the creditors of the latter group of countries. Similarly, countries with less thriving economies show a tendency to become dependent on import for even their basic needs, turning them into the debtors of the more thriving (export(ing)) countries.

Otherwise put, the prevailing monetary and trade systems, being themselves an expression of the "free market"-system, intrinsically (and when remaining "incorrected") add to the gap between the rich and the poor countries, which should

---

[168]It may be clear that any period of possession of money, how short it may be, constitutes an act of saving (brief as it may), as money in hand represents future purchasing power.

[169]See also Stiglitz (2003), p. 200.

not come as a surprise as it is the case with practically all capitalist mechanisms and methods that they add to more wealth for the rich and more debt (with all its added misery and suffering) for the poor.

The question will become how to take these elements into consideration when switching from the existing monetary systems to the here proposed New Monetary World Order, as it should be avoided that the introduction of this new system would, from day zero, be chanceless due to distortions built up in the past.

120 From an ideal and fully abstracted level of global justice which would be characterized by a perfect sense of altruism, a possible solution could be to reset to zero the global counters in terms of monetary reserves as well as foreign debts.[170]

Given the purpose of achieving a perfect altruist monetary and financial system, the further objective should indeed, by definition, be that the rich (among which: "the rich countries") would be fully willing to share their wealth with the poor (hence also: "the poor countries"), and that this willingness to ultimately "share" would characterize everyone's behavior forever, implying that as long as everyone remains willing to behave according to the spirit of such a perfect altruism (instead, as is currently the case: to the spirit of a completely neo-Smithian or neo-liberal "selfishness"), no-one will ever need to fear not being able to provide for his own livelihood (which, evidently, implies that the assets of the planet and their exploitation through the collective efforts of all mankind, should (continue) to suffice in order to cover everyone's (reasonable) needs).[171]

Within such a reasoning, the (rich(er)) countries with monetary reserves in foreign currency could accept that their monetary reserves would be completely abolished in exchange for participating in the New Monetary World Order in the context of which their needs will ever be covered in the spirit of a perfect world solidarity (thus removing the need for relying on backups of earlier acquired monetary reserves in foreign currency).

One could even go a step further whereby, for instance, also (and at least) the claims of private banks (and similar financial institutions) stemming from credits provided to public authorities, would be entirely eradicated. Given the "robbing strategies" of the past which the private banking sector has, meanwhile for many centuries, deployed towards the rest of society (including national and other public authorities) (see also Further Illustration 3.6 in Chap. 3 of this book), this proposal should be seriously taken into consideration (and eventually, if applicable, its

[170] In theory, all debts worldwide could be wiped out on a Sunday afternoon. We could start from scratch with a new balance sheet the next morning. If every citizen in the world was to be credited with let's say 1000 newly designed Bancors, we could start anew in an instant. We could even write off all mortgages an nationalize all real estate, and have a system whereby we pay rent to the state. (See Middelkoop 2014, p. 167.)

[171] Otherwise put: one could deal with the issue of monetary reserves in foreign currency in the manner recommended by Jesus Christ to the rich young man in the already before quoted story from the Gospel (see marg. 37 of Chap. 3 of this book): ***"Sell everything you have and give to the poor, and you will have treasure in heaven."*** (Luke, 18: 22; quotation from: http://www.biblestudytools.com/luke/18-22.html; last consulted on October 22nd 2015).

application could be accompanied by a mechanism of compensation via a one-off allocation granted by the "New Monetary World Institute" to the benefit of said private banks in question, which could avoid a massive collapse of the banking sector, albeit under stringent commitments to a much more altruistic and ethical behavior).

However, even in case the world community would ever be willing to consider the implementation of the here proposed "New Monetary World Order" (or of a similarly altruistic monetary system), it is to be feared that especially the rich (er) countries may not respond in an overenthusiastic way to the aforementioned proposal of abolishing their existing monetary reserves and/or claim positions towards debt countries.[172] **121**

Although the switch to the New Monetary World Order should, preferably, happen as radically as possible (whereby, ideally, it should not be held of any importance, given the spirit of international solidarity which should support the introduction of this New Monetary World Order, that monetary reserves and/or claim or debt positions have been accumulated in the past), a concession towards the likely wishes of the richer countries (with existing monetary reserves) could be that the existence and the size of such existing reserves would be taken into account when calculating the first allocation of "New World Currency" by the "New Monetary World Institute" (or even: when calculating the allocations of a first set of years starting from the year of implementation of the New Monetary World Order).

However, the extent to which this would take place would then, obviously, have a delaying effect on the achievement of the objectives of a truly just and equally applied new monetary order.

The issue of the debt burden (of poor(er) countries) could, *mutatis mutandis*, be dealt with in a similar way.[173] **122**

Given the altruistic objective of achieving a monetary world order characterized by a perfect degree of solidarity, there should even so be a full willingness to eliminate the existing (foreign) debt burden of all participating countries (at least as regards debts towards other participating countries, but preferably also towards the private banking sector located within the territories of the participating countries).

To the extent that also this proposal may probably be considered too hard a pill to swallow, one could also here opt for a transition system, whereby the size of the existing debt of the participating countries would be taken into account when calculating the first allocation of New World Currency to these countries (or: will be taken into account for some time as regards the allocations of a first set of years), although, also in this regard, the extent to which such a "correction method" would be applied, a further delaying effect on the achievement of the objectives of a just and equally applied new monetary order will occur.

---

[172] Also from the rich young man appearing in the earlier mentioned story from the Gospel, it is said that, ***"when he heard this, he became very sad"*** (Luke, 18:23.A), because, according to the same Gospel verse, ***"he was a man of great wealth"*** (Luke, 18: 23.B); quotations again from: http://www.biblestudytools.com/luke/18-23.html; last consulted on October 22nd 2015.

[173] See Wolf (2014).

123 Although the aforementioned proposals to reset to zero the world-wide counters of monetary reserves and foreign debt could be a shocking thought, the reasoning on which it is based, does even in practice have some precedents.

For instance both the IMF and the World Bank already apply a policy[174] under which heavily indebted countries (with "heavy debts" towards the IMF and the World Bank) can, under strict conditions, enjoy a waiver from past debts.[175] Both institutions furthermore have been witnessed to attempt, where applicable, to involve other creditors (including commercial and private creditors) in this so-called "debt waiving policy".[176]

Further reference in this regard can, for instance, be made to "*The Multilateral Debt Relief Initiative*" (2005) which aimed at achieving a general relief of debt[177], in addition to other IMF debt relief policies (in addition to those of other global financial institutions).[178]

124 The "*Jubilee 2000*"-movement, which already for a long time has been advocating that the debt of poor countries should be relieved, also deserves to be mentioned here.[179]

4.7.3 Money Creation on Behalf of the Private Sectors of the Countries Participating to the New Monetary World Order

4.7.3.1 Principle

125 When having dealt with the "third pillar" of the New Monetary World Order (see above, under Sect. 4.5), it has been thoroughly argued that after centuries of

---

[174] See in general http://www.imf.org/external/about/lending.htm (last consulted on October 23th 2014).

[175] On the website of the IMF, this policy has been motivated as follows:

> Debt relief is one part of a much larger effort, which also includes aid flows, to address the development needs of low-income countries and make sure that debt sustainability is maintained over time. For debt reduction to have a tangible impact on poverty, the additional money needs to be spent on programs that benefit the poor. (See http://www.imf.org/external/np/exr/facts/hipc.htm (last consulted on October 23th 2014).)

[176] See http://www.imf.org/external/np/exr/facts/hipc.htm (last consulted on October 23th 2014), in this regard mentioning the following:

> Given the voluntary nature of creditor participation in the HIPC Initiative, the IMF and the World Bank will continue to use moral suasion to encourage creditors to participate in the Initiative and to deliver fully their share of HIPC Initiative debt relief.

[177] http://www.imf.org/external/np/exr/facts/mdri.htm (last consulted on October 23th 2014).

[178] See furthermore Stiglitz (2006), p. 226; Romero-Barrutieta et al. (2011); Cohen (2008), pp. 150–179, especially p. 169.

[179] See http://jubileedebt.org.uk/ (last consulted on December 6th 2014).

unbridled capitalism based upon a system of private money creation system that above all serves the private interests of a small elite of people, it should be clear that the antagonists of this private money creation system, particularly private banks themselves, have proven to be completely unwilling and unable to aim for a more just and altruistic social and economic system.

As previously explicated, this can hardly come as a surprise, given the fact that aiming for a more just and altruistic economy would in essence be in total conflict with the starting premises of capitalism which holds that, within the economic spheres, private market players should behave in the most selfish way possible.

Reaching this conclusion helps to understand why under the present monetary and financial system, it is albeit impossible to find solutions for some of the most stringent economic problems of our time, among which, in both the public and private domain, the increase of the debt burden of more and more economic players (going from states to enterprises, families and individuals) and, especially in the private domain, the increase of poverty and the growing gaps between the rich and the poor.

Hence, also as regards the domain of money creation on behalf of the private sector, the New Monetary World Order should look for other methods and mechanisms of providing private persons (going from enterprises to families and individuals) with newly created money than leaving this level of money creation into the hands of private banks.

On the contrary, within this New Monetary World Order, the domain of money creation on behalf of private persons as well should fall under the competence of the New Monetary World Institute and its representations in the countries participating in said New Monetary World Order (consisting of a network of national central banks that will operate under the direction of the New Monetary World Institute in providing local economies with newly created money when needed).

In the process of rearranging the international monetary system, the current **126**
functions of credit lending to (other) private market players which are today fulfilled by private banking could be split up into two categories:

- (A) (to be established) monetary authority (ies), namely the New Monetary World Institute surrounded by a network of central banks of the participating countries[180], should become exclusively responsible for the different types of credits to private persons (in the broad sense of the word) which lead to the creation of new money.

[180]The organizational institutional aspects of said authority (ies) (namely the already mentioned "NMWI" and, by extension, the further in the text proposed "New Global System of Central Banks" or, abbreviated, the "NGSCB") will be explained further on in more detail (see further, under Sect. 5.1 of Chap. 5 of this book).

- Private banking institutions themselves will no longer grant credits which lead to newly created money, and will henceforward function by means (generally speaking: debt and equity) that will *ex ante* be generated on private markets, without being able to rely on a system of private money creation for their credit lending behavior, nor on any form of preferential treatment by monetary authorities (= the so-called "lender(s) of last resort").

  This will be dealt with hereafter in more detail.

4.7.3.2 Levels of Money Creation on Behalf of the Private Sector

4.7.3.2.1 General Overview

127 For the sake of a clear understanding of what follows, it is advisable to bear in mind the following differentiation within the domain of money creation on which the here proposed New Monetary World Order should be based:

- Money creation on behalf of the national authorities of the countries participating in the New Monetary World Order (in addition to the NGSCB itself and, if applicable, to certain other public, supra-national entities).
  This "first" level of money creation which would technically be based on allocations of newly created money (which, per definition, would not be refundable) has already been dealt with before (see Sect. 4.7.2).
- Money creation on behalf of the private sector.
  This "second" level of money creation could continue to be based upon the technique of credit lending, albeit provided by the New Monetary World Institute in co-operation with the national central banks of the countries participating in the New Monetary World Order.

  It would consist of the following sub-levels:

- Credit lending to/money creation for the benefit of private individuals and households for basic needs of life;
- Credit lending to/money creation for the benefit of private individuals to enter into professional life;
- Credit lending to/money creation for the benefit of the nonprofit-sector (as long as this sector will still be in place);
- (Other) Credit lending to/money creation for the benefit of established businesses (and similar private entities).

Each of these (sub)levels of money creation on behalf of the private sector will be hereafter developed in a general way.

4.7.3.2.2 Credit Lending to/Money Creation for the Benefit of Private Individuals (and Households) for Basic Needs of Life

The first sub-level of money creation for the benefit of the private sector would concern money creation for the benefit of private individuals (and households) meant to cover their basic life needs. **128**

The notion "basic needs" will have to be interpreted in a sufficiently broad sense as implying all needs of an individual (or a household consisting of an individual and the family members dependent on him) which aim at leading a truly dignified life (and, therefore, not just at surviving on, or even under the edge of poverty which is how "basic life needs" are presently defined in most capitalist countries). **129**

One of the underlying objectives of the New Monetary World Order should furthermore consist of establishing a global level playing field, implying that the notion of a "truly dignified life" should for every human being, wherever born or wherever residing, have the same minimum meaning (albeit that, obviously, objective local factors, such as factors of a cultural nature, may be taken into account). **130**

Hence, the notion "basic needs" used hereafter should certainly not be limited to absolutely vital elements, such as access to food, fresh water[181], medical care and (decent) housing[182], but should be seen in a wider context, namely, *on one hand* in the area of a sufficient level of material comfort for all people (thus: not only access to the abovementioned absolutely vital elements, but, inter alia, also access to elements of basic comfort, such as transportation, communication, recreation,...) and, *on the other hand*, also in the area of certain intangible elements which are needed for a basic dignified life, such as (obviously) education and (professional) training, the ability to participate in social, religious and cultural life...

As regards these "basic life needs", it is here proposed that within the New Monetary World (Order), the mechanisms of money creation for the benefit of private individuals (and households) should ensure that every human being, worldwide, can (easily) cover these basic life needs. **131**

As mentioned before, in each of the countries partaking to the NMWO, systems of providing public services, among which social care, will also have to be established (see above, under Sect. 4.7.2.4). These public services will be moreover funded through allocations periodically handed out to each of these countries.

Needless to say that these public service mechanisms will have to be narrowly coordinated with the mechanism of private credits to meet the basic needs of life. A central question hereby will, obviously, be what fundamental needs will be met through the systems of public services (including social care) and what (other)

[181] See especially Kruithof (2000), p. 60.

[182] For further reflections on the topic of publicly subsidized shelter becoming necessary due to the fact that in no economically advanced country the market systems builds houses that the poor(est) can afford, see already Galbraith (1992), p. 44; Galbraith (1996), p. 65.

needs will be left over to the system of reimbursable credits in order to cover one's basic life needs.

132 Further down the text, there will be a practical review of a number of points of attention on how the mechanisms of money creation for the benefit of private individuals (and households) could help meeting this proposed policy aim of the New Monetary World Order (see further, under Sect. 5.2.4 of Chap. 5 of this book).

4.7.3.2.3 Credit Lending to/Money Creation for the Benefit of Private Individuals for the Start-Up of a (New) Professional Activity

133 The second sub-level of money creation for the benefit of the private sector in the framework of the here presented proposal for a New Monetary World Order would aim at offering any individual a fair chance to establish a (basic) professional activity.[183]

Otherwise put, one of the starting points of the New Monetary World (Order) would imply that every human being should, in a truly equal manner, have the possibility to deploy a professional activity of his free choice and from which a sufficient income can be generated which enables him to lead a dignified and sufficiently prosperous life.

134 As explained before, capitalism is characterized by the fact that a majority of people provides labor to another market player (for instance a company which then acts as "an employer") in return for a monetary compensation which is often, albeit with high differences from country to country, derisory, certainly in comparison with the massive company profits that often flow towards the capital providers of said companies-employers.

While some people (especially in richer countries), through no effort of their own whatsoever, are fortunate enough to get the ownership of or the control over such an existing company, which was started by others, thrown at them by mere chance (for instance through an inheritance of a parent)[184], the majority of mankind is often much less fortunate.[185]

The capitalist system undertakes no attempt to recognize this basic reality and the intrinsic inequalities within society which result from it (see also above, under Sect. 3.4.8 of Chap. 3 of this book).

---

[183]See also Ferguson (2009), p. 15, arguing that poverty is mainly the result of a lack of access to newly created money:

> Only when borrowers have access to efficient credit networks can they escape from the clutches of loan sharks, and only when savers can deposit their money in reliable banks can it be channeled from the idle to the industrious or from the rich to the poor.

[184]Pauli (2014), pp. 32–35, especially 35.

See also Geysels (2014), pp. 11–59, especially p. 25; Raspoet (2014), pp. 51–55.

[185]Galbraith (1996), p. 61.

On the contrary, it is often said and even written (mainly by fervent supporters of neo-liberal thinking) that one should not question such inequalities as everyone in the world does get equal chances in life, a statement which cannot be taken seriously at all as it is obviously completely contradicted by all objective observations.

As a result, as has been argued by Galbraith, within the capitalist system, far too much income and wealth comes with slight or no social justification and with little or no economic service on the part of the recipient.

> Inheritance is an obvious case. So also the endowments, accidents and perversions of the financial world. And the rewards that, from its personal empowerment, modern corporate management bestows on itself.[186]

One of the main consequences of this societal capitalist model is that the more fortunate people having rich(er) parents, in most cases, are able to make a head-start in (professional) life compared to less fortunate people.[187]

As a result, a global societal model prevails whereby practically all levels of **135**
social and economic life are characterized by a fundamentally unjust nepotism, not only in the business sector, but in numerous other sectors, such as:

- State and public life organization; for instance, in many countries, the role of head of state is still passed on from parent to child, whereby the entire "royal" or "imperial" family often enjoys many state funded advantages, such as free housing, generous allowances, periodical vacations, financing of all sorts of expensive hobbies, access to interesting (additional) job opportunities[188] and this, only because of their blood relationship with the head of state and often regardless of personal talent or abilities;
- the political domain, in which children, grandchildren, and other kinsmen of successful politicians are given the opportunity to start a political (or other) career with a large advantage compared to those individuals who do not have such influent relatives or friends in high places;
- the cultural sector (where it can for instance be witnessed that children of famous (movie) actors, directors or producers are, often at a very young age, given opportunities of which children of other parents can only dream);
- (also) the academic world;
- ...

The further examples are, of course, numerous.

The question how to deal with nepotism is obviously a (very) old one. **136**

Already Plato (albeit apparently fruitlessly) has given his (strong) opinions on the problem, resulting in his radical proposal for a society where children should, at birth, be taken away from their natural parents and where their education should be

[186] Galbraith (1996), p. 61.

[187] See also Oxfam (2014), p. 65.

[188] It has, for instance, been estimated that in 2014 alone, the cost of the Belgian royalty which was borne through public funding, amounted to ±38,742,000 euro (see Debels 2014, p. 192).

entrusted to specialized neutral teachers, so that, at maturity, people can be given a role in society solely in accordance with their talents and skills, rather than for purely nepotistic motives.[189]

It speaks for itself that the aforementioned ideas of Plato have met with little or no response in our present-day society (ies). On the contrary, especially as early as from the IVth century A.D. (i.e. from the moment when Christianity became one of the state religions of the Roman Empire), under the influence of Judeo-Christian thinking, Western society models (which have later on also influenced other cultures), started more and more to adhere the (niche or core) family model[190], which has only even more enriched the breeding ground for unbridled nepotism in societal life in general.

137 In certain domains in science, it will probably (or at least hopefully) be investigated in more detail whether or not nepotism is a natural phenomenon—as almost every species (of mammal) by nature always tends to favor its own offspring[191], so it need not be a surprise that man also, still a mammal[192], acts in a similar way—albeit this should not prevent that society should attempt to correct such animal impulses in as far as they cause injustice and prevent talented people of truly deploy their potential.

Money, the topic which is mainly dealt with in this book, but by extension wealth in general (the gathering of which is, to a large extent, mainly made possible by the use of money) are in themselves also but products of civilization; one could even argue that outside the scope of human civilization, there is not one single comparable mechanism which would allow a single animal to make such claims on the resources of its habitat (and to pass these on to its offspring) as is in the human world made possible by money.

---

[189] See Plato (1987), pp. 181 a.f.

Reflecting on an ideal method of upbringing and education of children is one of the main topics of Plato's "*The Republic*". Hence, in order to have a good overview of the opinions of Plato in this regard, one should (re-)read the whole work. One may nevertheless already get some idea about Plato's radical reasoning by reading this quote:

> Each generation of children will be taken by officers appointed for the purpose (. . .). They will arrange for the suckling of the children by bringing their mothers to the nursery when their breasts are still fill, taking every precaution to see that no mother recognizes her child. (Plato 1987, pp. 181–182).

See also Vandamme (1985), p. 24; Popper (1966), p. 145.

[190] Indeed, throughout history, Judeo-Christian thinking has increasingly promoted the "niche family" as being "sanctifying" (which is "literally" expressed in the fact that, for instance under the doctrine of the Catholic church, marriage is considered as a so-called "sacrament"; see Marc., 10: 2–12), and through this, the niche family has worldwide become a dominant type of living in the micro sphere. One needs, nevertheless, observe that, in our time, more and more people choose for other arrangements of living than the coercive "niche family" model.

[191] See also Dawkins (2006), p. 6 (dealing with the topic of how different types of animals care, above all, for their offspring, sometimes against their own interest or well-being).

[192] According to modern biologists, man could even be considered as "a fish" as, going back in time, one of the ancestors of "man" (and, by extension, all mammals) has been a fish (like creature) (see *e.g.* Reumer 2013, p. 46).

Therefore, to the extent that ethics are supposed to deliver the fabric of society, there should be no doubt that the social contract that underpins the monetary system (of which the mechanisms of money creation are part), should (be allowed to) impose restrictions on the accumulation of money and wealth gathering by a given single individual (also and especially from the perspective of passing wealth on to offspring).

As explained above, it is this awareness that lies at the basis of the here proposed system for a New Monetary World Order (based on the "five pillars" mentioned above), including its earlier in this book proposed global and fair taxation mechanism (see above, under Sect. 4.7.2.3.2).

Anyhow, it is still an extremely harrowing observation which testifies to the low **138**
level of civilization that has been reached so far, that up to this very day, one person, by birth, enters an environment where he will enjoy the highest possible luxury for the rest of his life (without ever having done or undertaken anything to "deserve" this)[193], while another human being, also by birth, even if he works himself (sometimes literally) to death, is born into an environment where poverty and even hunger and disease will prevail (and this, even assuming that he would ever reach an adult age, for the rest of his life).[194]

---

[193]As shamelessly exhibited on all kinds of social media; see *e.g.* http://www.huffingtonpost.com/news/rich-kids-of-instagram/ (last consulted on October 24th 2014).

See also Bruckner (2002), pp. 25–26, speaking of the "rent aristocracy":

> Pitié pour les nababs : ces derniers s'imposent comme les nouveaux rois de notre temps, se moquant des lois ordinaires, jouissant d'un pouvoir et d'un prestige démusurés, s'accommodant de tous les régimes pourvu qu'ils vivent à leur guise. Qu'ils ressortent du showbiz, du sport ou de la finance, ils forment une élite transnationale qui parle le nouvel espéranto planétaire, le wallish, l'anglais de Wall Street, et habite le royaume envoûtant de l'opulence et du divertissement de luxe. Une aisance privée inconcevable voisine avec un dénuement affligeant ou des services publics déplorables comme dans certains pays anglo-saxons. Et tout cela au nom du vieux principe utilitariste du plus grand bonheur pour le plus grand nombre, "chacun comptant (en principe) de manière égale" (Jeremy Bentham).

[194]See also Byanyima (2014), p. 4:

> A child born to a rich family, even in the poorest of countries, will go to the best school and will receive the highest quality care if they are sick. At the same time, poor families will see their children taken from them, struck down by easily preventable diseases because they do not have the money to pay for treatment. The reality is that across the world, the richest people are able to live longer, happier and healthier lives, and are able to use their wealth to see that their children do the same.

And furthermore:

> Researchers have shown that, across the 21 countries for which there is data, there is a strong correlation between extreme inequality and low social mobility. If you are born poor in a highly unequal country you will most probably die poor, and your children and grandchildren will be poor too. In Pakistan, for instance, a boy born in a rural area to a father from the poorest 20 percent of the population has only a 1.9 percent chance of ever moving to the richest 20 percent. In the USA, nearly half of all children born to low-income parents will become low-income adults. (Oxfam 2014, p. 11).

As also mentioned earlier in this book, precisely this phenomenon has by Oxfam been described as the so-called "*condemned to stay poor-syndrome*", through which, world-wide, social mobility has only deteriorated during the past decades.[195]

139 It may even be considered more remarkable that, already in 1754, Rousseau had reached this same conclusion in his "*Discours sur l'origine et les fondements de l'inégalité parmie les hommes*" which he qualified as "inconsistent" with the laws of nature (see above, at marg. 274 of Chap. 3 of this book), from which we can conclude that more than 250 years later, in essence, little has changed in the Western (so-called) model of civilization.[196]

Even more harrowing is the fact that in Western culture—given its pretensions to be influenced by the teachings of historical leading figures such as Jesus Christ, but even so by numerous similar teachings preaching a message of justice, equality and fairness, among which, in addition to numerous religious and philosophical systems, for instance also "humanism"—a social and economic doctrine continues to prevail where this fundamental injustice, although having been questioned for centuries, is tackled by theoretical arguments[197] such as: "*everyone has equal opportunities*", or "*that through hard work, everyone can reach the same level of success (in the spirit of neo-Smithian thinking: become "rich")*".[198]

---

[195] Oxfam (2014), p. 47.

[196] Quoted by Beaud (1994), p. 72.

[197] Given the further insight that, for instance, world food production is effectively more than sufficient to amply feed every citizen in the world, and that the facts that, up till today, hundreds of millions of people are still starving, and more than one billion people are living in extreme poverty, are only due to the existing social economic order, namely capitalism (see above, under Sect. 3.4.8 of Chap. 3 of this book), it can only be hoped for that whoever has ever expressed or defended such thoughts should as soon as possible come to his senses (as eventually even happened to Ebenezer Scrooge in the aforementioned famous story "*A Christmas Carol*" by Charles Dickens, albeit this first required the nightly visit of the ghost of his former partner Jacob Marley and of the three spirits of Christmas-past, Christmas-present, and Christmas-future).

[198] This argument, often quoted by neo-liberal authors, has in the Oxfam-report "*Even it up*" been qualified as a "myth":

> This myth assumes that everyone starts from a level playing field and that anyone can become wealthy if they work hard enough. The reality is that, in many countries, a person's future wealth and income is largely determined by the income of their parents. A third of the world's richest individuals amassed their wealth not through hard work, but through inheritance.
>
> This myth is also flawed in its assumption that the highest financial reward is given for the hardest amount of work. Some of the lowest paid jobs are those that require people to work the hardest, while some of the highest paid jobs are those that require people to work the least. Many of the richest collect large profits from the rent they generate on stocks, real estate and other assets. When this is taken into account, it becomes clear that those who are paid less work just as hard (or even harder) as those at the top of the wage ladder. Women spend more time on unpaid domestic and caring responsibilities than their highly paid counterparts, and are more likely than men to have multiple jobs. (see Oxfam 2014, p. 65).

Also John Kenneth Galbraith has pointed out that not people who work hard have the greatest chance to get rich (as, otherwise, a lot of people working up till 14 h/day would not be living in

The here proposed New Monetary World Order will need to be willing to acknowledge the intrinsic injustice of the current society model in the field of career possibilities and opportunities and to search for solutions to improve them.[199] **140**

At the very least, a socioeconomic climate will need to be created where everyone receives a basic fair chance of a worthy professional development. For this reason, the aspiration of this objective has been mentioned here as a "second" sub-level of money creation on behalf of the private sector, namely the (sub-)level of money creation aiming at ensuring a basic access to professional life.

As is the case for the notion "basic life needs" (see above, at marg. 129 of this chapter), also the notion "ensuring (a) basic access to professional life" will need to be interpreted in a sufficiently broad sense and could, inter alia, include: the financing of specialized (professional) training, the financing of the costs related to the start-up of a new activity (for instance a new business); etc.

A detailed review of how the mechanism of money creation on behalf of a private individual to ensure his right of developing a basic professional activity could function, will be described further in the text (see further, under Sect. 5.2.4.2.2 of Chap. 5 of this book). **141**

---

poverty), but those who, by living on investments, ultimately exploit other man's labor. (See *e.g.* Galbraith 1992, p. 30 a.f.)

See furthermore, again, the quoted Oxfam-report "*Even it up*":

> Income from work determines most people's economic status and their future chances. But the vast majority of the world's poorest people cannot escape poverty, no matter how hard they work, and far too many suffer the indignity of poverty wages. Meanwhile, the richest people have high and rapidly rising salaries and bonuses, as well as significant income from their accumulated wealth and capital. This is a recipe for accelerating economic inequality. (Oxfam 2014, p. 15).

And furthermore:

> Economic inequality also leads to huge differences in life chances: the poorest people have the odds stacked against them in terms of education and life expectancy. The latest national Demographic and Health Surveys demonstrate how poverty interacts with economic and other inequalities to create 'traps of disadvantage' that push the poorest and most marginalized people to the bottom – and keep them there. (Oxfam 2014, p. 10).

[199] In the more recent past, one can, for instance, refer to Galbraith who in his book "*The Good Society – The Humane Agenda*" has pointed out that

> in the good society, however, achievement may not be limited by factors that are remediable. There must be economic opportunity for all (...). And in preparation for life, the young must have the physical care, the discipline, let no one doubt, and especially the education that will allow them to seize and exploit that opportunity. No one, from accident of birth or economic circumstance, may be denied these things; if they are not available from parent or family, society must provide effective forms of care and guidance. (see Galbraith 1996, p. 65).

4.7.3.2.4 Credit Lending to/Money Creation for the Benefit of the Nonprofit-Sector

142 The third sub-level of money creation for the benefit of the private sector within the New Monetary World Order could involve the so-called "nonprofit-sector".

143 In many (especially Western and Western-inspired) countries, an (often very extensive) nonprofit sector is in place (including the so-called "NGO's" or "Non-governmental organizations").[200]

In order to finance their operations, the various types of (private) non-profit foundations, associations and other organizations, often rely on different types of government subsidies, in addition to contributions and gifts from their members (next to other types of donations from private persons), which does, however, not exclude that these foundations, associations and other organizations sometimes find themselves in need of credit.[201]

In a lot of countries, the non-profit foundations, associations and other organizations, furthermore, often perform different tasks and duties which closely align with the "general interest" and which, at least in principle, are not aimed at establishing a personal advantage for the stakeholders within these associations and organizations.

Other (especially "poorer") countries do not enjoy the luxury of such an extensive "non-profit-sector", often because the governments of these poorer countries do not have the means to subsidize it and, moreover, the local population itself often has much more elementary needs than participating in such non-profit foundations, associations and/or organizations (albeit that in these "poor(er)" countries, often "non-profit"-organizations from the "rich(er)" countries are active).

144 It is here proposed that, within the New Monetary World Order, public policy regarding the "nonprofit"-sector, would be such that the (public good) tasks now performed by the abovementioned non-profit foundations, associations and other organizations would, henceforth, gradually be taken over by the public sector itself (based on means made available through the above explained periodical allocations to the countries participating in this New Monetary World Order).

As explained above, the organization of the New Monetary World Order should consequently lead to new types of public authorities which, world-wide, should primarily advocate the general well-being of the entire population (while respecting the limits of the capacity of the planet).

In other words, a large part of the tasks and duties currently performed by private persons active in the non-profit-sector, should, henceforth (and at least gradually) be shifted to the public sector itself.

145 In this approach, the global (monetary) community should itself start to play a leading role by determining to what extent national authorities will still be able (or not) to (albeit temporarily) call upon the private "non-profit"-sector.[202]

---

[200]See *e.g.* Moutton (2014), pp. 22–24; Murray and Bonneville (2010), p. 257.

[201]De Ekstermolengroep (2000), pp. 32 a.f.

[202]Needless to say that the answer to this question will need a thorough study of the most cost-efficient solution (also in relation to the capacity of the planet).

To the extent that, in addition to (national) authorities which will henceforth perform all tasks deemed of general interest themselves (and would get the necessary financial means thereto through the allocations received from the New Monetary World Institute), there would still be a further (temporary) need for non-profit private organizations which will continue to fulfill tasks of general interest (or other tasks that aspire to the general well-being of the global population), the question will remain how to finance this type of "nonprofit"-organizations. **146**

Probably, if applicable, the financing of these "nonprofit"-organizations, will be able to continue to be of a mixed nature, consisting of, in addition to (*i*) government financing (which will then be considered as a compensation for outsourcing tasks which have in fact become governmental tasks[203]), also (*ii*) financing from private individuals (membership contributions and donations, which could stem from the earlier described system of social-cultural participation; see above, at marg. 92–94 of this chapter) and, occasionally, (*iii*) credit.

To the extent that these (future) non-profit organizations functioning in the New Monetary World Order, would in this way (temporarily) continue to participate in carrying out governmental tasks of general interest and/or aimed at the general well-being, it could also be held that, when applicable, their need for additional credit will, furthermore, be able to be covered by the monetary authorities themselves. **147**

Otherwise put, such "non-profit"-organizations would have access to credit lending from the national central bank, itself being a part of the network of central banks operating under the New Monetary World Institute, of the country in which they operate.

This mechanism of money creation for the benefit of the "non-profit"-sector (as long as it would continue to exist) will be described in more detail further in the text (see further, under Sect. 5.2.4.3 of Chap. 5 of this book). **148**

4.7.3.2.5 Credit Lending to/Money Creation for the Benefit of Established Businesses

The fourth sub-level of money creation for the benefit of private individuals within the New Monetary World Order will, finally, concern the established business sector. **149**

The New Monetary World Order as proposed here will obviously not be able to operate in line with the premises proposed above without a new vision about the ethics of business life itself, especially with regard to the question how to deal with the pursuit of profit as it currently dominates the entire world economy. **150**

[203]For this reason, there will also be a need for a unified policy on such outsourcing of tasks of general interest to the private non-profit sector in all countries participating in the New Monetary World Order.

This pursuit of profits should under the New Monetary World Order no longer be the overpowering value. On the contrary, the (global) business world should henceforth need to be re-oriented in such a way that other values also (such as: care for the environment; respect for the planet and its resources; a humane treatment of people employed; a true consideration for the interests and the well-being of customers; etc.) will get the same, or even a higher degree of attention as making profits.

A new legal framework should clearly set out a solid legal basis for this new approach to business ethics.

151 Within an economy which would be based on altruism rather than on the selfish pursuit of (company) profits, it should for instance no longer be the intention that capital investments will continue to remain a mechanism solely aimed at getting the rich and powerful of the planet even richer.

On the contrary, the New Monetary World Order should create a climate that mainly assures that efforts from labor are valued in such a way that every person can build a dignified life for himself (and his family), or put otherwise, that puts the interests of people performing labor above the interests of capital.[204]

In this context, it will be necessary to (at least gradually) abandon the idea that running a business (and the therefore needed capital investments) should mainly and at any cost be aimed at making enormous (business) profits which, through the operation of company law mechanisms, are mainly intended to enrich a select elite of shareholders who afterwards park their thus created wealth in tax havens in order not to have to participate in the financing of public life.

As mentioned several times before, the earlier in this text proposed new fiscal logic which should characterize the functioning of the New Monetary World Order, should play an important role in contributing to these new business ethics (see above, under Sect. 4.7.2.3.2).

152 A further underlying idea of the here proposed new business ethics should be that established businesses would, much more than happens under the current capitalist mechanisms, be encouraged to re-invest their profits in either their own operation (rather than paying out huge dividends to the shareholders and extreme huge salaries to their CEO's), or in the well-being of society in general.

Also to reach this objective, there will be a global need for rethinking the legal framework of company and company tax law. This will, henceforth, need to be based on almost opposite principles to those of the now prevailing company law systems in as far as these, in most Western (and Western inspired) countries, are mainly aimed at maximizing shareholders profits[205].

153 In order to achieve these underlying policy objectives, for instance, a fiscal skimming policy could come into play which will help to keep the level of business

[204]See earlier in the history of Christianity the ideas of Saint Paul on the importance of "social economic self-reliance" which under the New Monetary World Order should become a possibility for every human being (see above, under Sect. 3.3.2.2.2 of Chap. 3 of this book).

[205]See also Galbraith (1992), p. 54; Byttebier and François (2015), pp. 221–250.

profits within reasonable boundaries in order to serve several other policy goals, such as preventing a market player from becoming too strong or from abusing his economic power, encouraging a reasonable price setting for products and services offered (as a surplus of profits made would be taxed away anyhow), paying a truly fair compensation to staff and (smaller) suppliers, etc.

Furthermore, a policy of fiscal skimming of dividends paid to shareholders could prevent that their income would exceeds certain thresholds. For this, we refer to what has been discussed earlier in the text (see above, under Sect. 4.7.2.3.2).

In summary, the new company and fiscal law systems to be created under the **154**
umbrella of the New Monetary World Order (and by extension: by the countries participating to this NMWO) should serve to encourage business life to operate in an "ethical" correct way, thus rather serving the general well-being of the whole of mankind than the selfish pursuit of profits of a select elite of (extremely) rich people.

In such a new environment, it is furthermore to be expected that the need for **155**
(huge) credit to enterprises should decrease (as, for instance, the pursuit of leverage effects introduced with the purpose of maximizing profits for the benefit of shareholders dividends, will also no longer be a purpose on its own).

In as far (established) enterprises will continue to show a need for credit financing, it is furthermore proposed here that they will continue to primarily depend on the private markets for such credits.

This would, for instance, imply that companies with a "profit surplus" (for which it would not be sensible to re-invest it in the growth of the own company itself and which, furthermore, given the fiscal discouragement of too large dividend payments to shareholders, could neither any longer be paid out to shareholders) could use this to provide credit to other companies, possibly through the intermediate role of the (also re-oriented) private banking system (see further, under Sect. 5.4 of Chap. 5 of this book).

Nevertheless, in such a system, it could still occur that the financial means which are at a given moment in time available on the money and capital market, would not suffice to cover the credit needs of established business. For such cases, the New Monetary World Order could leave room for a system (earlier referred to "sub-level") of money creation/credit lending for the benefit of established businesses.

Again, a description of how this mechanism of money creation for the benefit of **156**
established businesses could look like, will be discussed later in the text (see further, under Sect. 5.2.4.4 of Chap. 5 of this book).

References

Aiyar S (2009) Can IMF currency replace the Dollar? http://www.cato.org/publications/commentary/can-imf-currency-replace-dollar. Last consulted 18 Nov 2014

Aristotle (1996) The Nicomachean ethics (trans: Rackham H). Wordsworth Classics of World Literature, Hertfordshire

Beaud M (1994) Geschiedenis van het kapitalisme van 1500 tot heden. Utrecht, Het Spectrum (Aula)
Bertaut C, Iyigun M (1999) The launch of the Euro. Federal Reserve Bulletin, October 1999
Bijlo E (2014) Nobelprijswinnaar Joseph Stiglitz: 'Europese landen moeten belastingen gelijktrekken'. Knack, 19 November 2014
Boccara F, Le Héron E, Plihon D (2011) Pour un système de financement émancipé des marchés financiers. In: Les Économistes atterés, Changer d'économie! Nos propositions pour 2012. Les liens qui libèrent, Paris
Bonneau T (1999) Droit bancaire. Montchrestien, Paris
Browne J (2008) Over het ontstaan van soorten van Darwin (trans: Ruitenberg J). Een biografie. Mets & Schilt, Amsterdam
Bruckner P (2002) Misère de la prospérité – la religion marchande et ses ennemis. Bernard Grasset, Paris
Byanyima W (2014) Foreword. Oxfam 2014:4–5
Byttebier K, François A (2015) For-profit or not-for-profit? That's the question. Profit maximization in company law: myth or (legal) reality? In: Cornelis L (ed) Finance and law: twins in trouble. Intersentia, Antwerp, pp 221–250
Camdessus M (2011) Towards a new international monetary system. In: Boorman J, Icard A (eds) Reform of the international monetary system – the Palais Royal Initiative. Sage, Los Angeles, pp 33–43
Carnegie A (1901) The Gospel of wealth. https://archive.org/stream/gospelofwealthot00carnuoft/gospelofwealthot00carnuoft_djvu.txt. Last consulted 27 Feb 2016
Claerhout P (2014a) Bad economics, bad leadership. Trends, 27 November 2014
Claerhout P (2014b) Enkel voldoende kapitaal kan een bank redden. Trends, 27 November 2014
Cohen D (2008) Towards a new modus operandi of the international financial system. In: Serra N, Stiglitz JE (eds) The Washington consensus reconsidered. Oxford University Press, Oxford, pp 150–179
Crombez J (2013) Zwart en Wit. Een betere toekomst zonder fraude. De Bezige Bij, Antwerp
Dawkins R (2006) The selfish gene. Oxford University Press (30th anniversary edition), Oxford
De Ekstermolengroep (2000) Don Quichote voorbij. Brussels, NCOS/11.11.11
De Grauwe P (2014) De limieten van de markt. De slinger tussen overheid en kapitalisme. Lannoo, Tielt
Debels T (2014) Vorstelijk vermogen – Het fabuleuze fortuin van de Belgische royals. Pelckmans, Kalmthout
Devries MG (ed) (1976) The International Monetary Fund – 1966–1971, vol 1. Narrative, IMF. Washington
Deweirdt E, Van Poeck A, Annaert J (1997) Monetaire theorie en politiek. Garant, Leuven
Engelen E (a.o.) (2011) After the great complacence. Oxford University Press, Oxford
Fase M, Vleminckx A (1995) Geld in veelvoud. Inleiding monetaire economie. Uitgeverij Lemma BV, Utrecht
Ferguson N (2009) The ascent of money. A financial history of the world. London, Penguin Books
Ford M (2011) Ayn Rand and the VIP-DIPers. http://www.huffingtonpost.com/michael-ford/ayn-rand-and-the-vip-dipe_b_792184.html
Foucault M (2008) The birth of biopolitics – Lectures at the Collège de France 1978–1979 (trans: Burchell G). Palgrave Macmillan, New York
Friedman M (1993) Why government is the problem. Hoover Institution on War, Revolution and Peace, Stanford University
Fritz-Krockow B, Ramlogan P (eds) (2007) International Monetary Fund handbook. Its functions, policies and operations. International Monetary Fund (IMF). http://www.imf.org/external/pubs/ft/imfhb/eng/handbook.pdf
Galbraith JK (1960) The liberal hour. The Riverside Press, Cambridge
Galbraith JK (1964) Economic development. Houghton Mifflin Company, Boston
Galbraith JK (1973) Economics and the public purpose. Penguin Books Ltd., Harmondsworth

Galbraith JK (1974) The affluent Society. Penguin Books, Middlesex (first edition of 1958)
Galbraith JK (1975) Money. Whence it came. Where it went. Houghton Mifflin Company, Boston
Galbraith JK (1979) Annals of an abiding liberal. A Meridian Book New American Library, New York
Galbraith JK (1987) Economics in perspective – a critical history. Houghton Mifflin Company, Boston
Galbraith JK (1990) A short history of financial euphoria. Whittle Books in association with Penguin Books, New York
Galbraith JK (1992) The culture of contentment. Houghton Mifflin Company, Boston
Galbraith JK (1996) The good society – the humane agenda. Houghton Mifflin Company, Boston
Geysels J (2014) De Schande. In: Geysels J, Vlaminck E (eds) De Schande en de Keerzijde. Van Halewyck, Leuven, pp 11–59
Geysels J, Vlaminck E (2014) De Schande en de Keerzijde. Van Halewyck, Leuven
Gore A (2013a) The future – six drivers of global change. Random House, New York
Gore A (2013b) Onze toekomst. Spectrum, Antwerp
Habets J, Gloudemans H (2013) De voedselparadox. Over grootschalige honger in een wereld die (meer dan) genoeg voedsel produceert. Stichting Werelddelen, Tilburg
Harari YN (2014) Sapiens – a brief history of humankind. Penguin Random House UK, London
Harvey D (2010) The enigma of capital and the crises of capitalism. Profile Books, London
Healey N, Levine P (1993) European Monetary Union or "Hard EMS"? J Reg Policy 13:371–386
Hoefnagels HJM, a.o. (1975) De toekomst staat op het spel. De Nederlandsche boekhandel, Kapellen
Hollenberg A (1942) De corporatieve organisatie der maatschappij. Standaard Boekhandel, Antwerp
Hu X (2011) Thoughts on reforming the international monetary system and enhancing the role of the SDR. In: Boorman J, Icard A (eds) Reform of the international monetary system – the Palais Royal Initiative. Sage, Los Angeles, pp 143–158
Ingham G (ed) (2005a) Concepts of money. Edward Elgar Publications Ltd., Cheltenham
Ingham G (2005b) Money is a social relation. In: Ingham (ed) Concepts of money. Edward Elgar Publications Ltd., Cheltenham
International Monetary Fund (IMF) (1999) Annual Report:1999
International Monetary Fund (IMF) (2000) Review of fund facilities—preliminary considerations (prepared by the policy development and review department in consultation with other departments, March 2, 2000). http://www.imf.org/external/np/pdr/fac/2000/faciliti.pdf. Last consulted 23 Sept 2014
International Monetary Fund (IMF) Financial Organization and Operations of the IMF, Pamphlet Series No. 45 – V SDR Department. http://www.imf.org/external/pubs/ft/pam/pam45/V/VA.htm
James H (ed) (1996) International monetary cooperation since Bretton Woods, Washington D.-C. International Monetary Fund, Oxford University Press, and New York and Oxford
Johnson I (2014) Towards a contemporary understanding of the limits to growth. In: Goldin I (ed) Is the planet full? Oxford University Press, Oxford, pp 79–103
Kasser T (2002) The high price of materialism. A Bradford Book – The MIT Press, Cambridge and London
Kousari K (2006) Interne en externe handicaps – Afrika in de wereldeconomie. In: De Meyer R, Vervliet E (eds) Gevaarlijke rijkdom – Grondstoffen in de mondiale economie year. Noord-Zuid-Cahier (31, no 2, pp 35–46)
Krugman P (2004) The great unraveling: losing our way in the new century. W. W. Norton & Company, New York
Krugman P (2012) End this depression now! W.W. Norton & Company, New York
Kruithof J (1985) De mens aan de grens. Over religiositeit, godsdienst en antropocentrisme. EPO, Antwerp
Kruithof J (2000) Het neoliberalisme. EPO, Antwerp

Kruithof J (2012) Het algemeen belang en de overheid in Jaap Kruithof – Teksten voor de toekomst. EPO, Berchem

Laterza V (2015) Finland: basic income experiment – what we know. http://www.basicincome.org/news/2015/12/finland-basic-income-experiment-what-we-know/. Last consulted 21 Jan 2016

Les Économistes atterés (2011) Changer d'économie! Nos propositions pour 2012. Les liens qui libèrent, Paris

Lipton D (2014) (First Deputy Managing Director, IMF) Fiscal Policy and Income Inequality. Speech of March 13th 2014. http://www.imf.org/external/np/speeches/2014/031314.htm. Last consulted 23 Oct 2014

Loizou A (2012) Het duivelspact. Een insiderverhaal over hoe het grote geld wordt verdiend. Zuidnederlandse uitgeverij, Aartselaar

Louis VJ (1993) L'institut monétaire européen. In: Reflets et Perspectives de la vie économique, tXXXII, pp 285–299

Luyendijk J (2015) Swimming with sharks: my journey into the world of the bankers. Guardian Faber Publishing, London

Mackenzie D (2014) Een wereld zonder grenzen. New Scientist, November 2014

Mandel E (1962) Traité d'économie Marxiste tII. Julliard, Paris

Martin F (2013) Money. The unauthorised biography. The Bodley Head Random House, London

Masera R (1996) Discussion. In: Kenen P, Papadia F, Saccomanni F (eds) The international monetary system. Cambridge University Press, New York, pp 65–73

Mateos y Lago I, Duttagupta R, Goyal R (2011) The debate on the international monetary system. In: Boorman J, Icard A (eds) Reform of the international monetary system – the Palais Royal Initiative. Sage, Los Angeles

McDonald L, Robinson P (2009) Collossal failure of common sense – the inside story of the collapse of Lehman Brothers. Three Rivers Press, New York

Middelkoop W (2014) The big reset – war on gold and the financial endgame. AUP, Amsterdam

Moutton A (2014) Gesubsidieerde banen redden arbeidsmarkt. Trends, 21 Aug 2014

Mundell R (1996) Discussion. In: Kenen P, Papadia F, Saccomanni F (eds) The international monetary system. Cambridge University Press, New York, pp 74–81

Mundell R (2000) The Euro and the stability of the international monetary system. In: Mundell R, Clesse A (eds) The Euro as stabilizer in the international economic system. Kluwer Academic Publishers, Norwell, pp 57–84

Murray K, Bonneville P (2010) Wall of honor – 100 organizations keeping the world together. Patrick Bonneville Society, Quebec

Muttin M (2014a) BTW-verhoging zet extra druk op Japanse premier – Opdoffer voor Japan. Trends, 21 Aug 2014

Muttin M (2014b) Japan sukkelt opnieuw in recessie. Trends, 20 Nov 2014

Newman A (2010) Waking up to a world currency. http://www.thenewamerican.com/economy/economics/item/4498-waking-up-to-a-world-currency. Article of September 15th 2010. Last consulted 18 Nov 2014

Oxfam (2014) Even it up – time to end extreme inequality. Oxfam GB, Oxford

Oxfam (2016) An economy for the 1%. How privilege and power in the economy drive extreme inequality and how this can be stopped, 210 Oxfam briefing paper, January 18th 2016. https://www.oxfam.org/sites/www.oxfam.org/files/file_attachments/bp210-economy-one-percent-tax-havens-180116-en_0.pdf

Pauli W (2014) De kloof in de democratie – Het historische belang van Thomas Piketty. Knack, 10 Dec 2014

Pdoa-Schioppa T (2011) The ghost of bancor: the economic crisis and global monetary disorder. In: Boorman J, Icard A (eds) Reform of the international monetary system – the Palais Royal Initiative. Sage, Los Angeles, pp 51–73

Pettifor A (2014) The power to 'create money out of thin air'. https://www.opendemocracy.net/ourkingdom/ann-pettifor/power-to-create-money-out-of-thin-air. Last consulted 18 Nov 2014

Piketty T (2014) Capital in the twenty-first century. Belknap Press, Cambridge
Plato (1987) The Republic (trans: Lee). Penguin Books, London
Popper K (1966) The open society and its enemies. Routledge, London
Rand A (1982) Philosophy: who needs it. New American Library (a division of Penguin Group), New York
Rand A (2008) Capitalism: the unknown ideal. New American Library (a division of Penguin Group), New York
Raspoet E (2014) Steuntrekkers zijn luieriken, zeggen ze. Maar overleven in armoede is keihard werken. Knack, 22 Oct 2014
Reumer J (2013) de vis die aan land kroop. Historische uitgeverij, Groningen
Romero-Barrutieta AL, Bulir A, Rodriguez-Delgado JD (2011) The dynamic implications of debt relief for low-income countries; IMF Working Paper (WP/11/157). IMF Institute
Sachs J (2011) The price of civilization: reawakening American virtue and prosperity. Random House, New York
Schiller B (2016) How Finland's exciting basic income experiment will work—and what we can learn from it. http://www.fastcoexist.com/3052595/how-finlands-exciting-basic-income-experiment-will-work-and-what-we-can-learn-from-it. Last consulted 21 Jan 2016
Skidelsky R (2003) Keynes's road to Bretton Woods: an essay in interpretation. In: Flandreau M, Holtfrerich CL, James H (eds) International financial history in the twentieth century – system and anarchy. Cambridge University Press, Cambridge
Skidelsky R (2010) Keynes. The return of the master. Public Affairs, New York
Smith A (1979) An inquiry into the nature and causes of the wealth of nations. As re-published by Campbell RH, Skinner A, Todd WB (eds) Clarendon Press, Oxford
Smithers A (2013) The road to recovery. Wiley, Chichester
Stevenson D (2009) SDRs – a new world reserve currency? http://moneyweek.com/sdrs-a-new-world-reserve-currency-43011/. Article of April 10th 2009. Last consulted 18 Nov 2014
Stiglitz J (2003) Globalization and its discontents. W. W. Norton & Company, New York
Stiglitz J (2006) Making globalization work. Penguin Books, London
Stiglitz J (2012) The price of inequality. Allen Lane London (an imprint of Penguin Books), London
Stiglitz J (2015a) Europe's Attack on Greek Democracy. Opinion of July 29th 2015. http://www.project-syndicate.org/commentary/greece-referendum-troika-eurozone-by-joseph-e--stiglitz-2015-06. Last consulted 16 Oct 2015
Stiglitz J (2015b) Greece's creditors need a dose of reality – this is no time for European disunion. http://www.theguardian.com/business/2015/jun/05/greeces-creditors-need-a-dose-of-reality-this-is-no-time-for-european-disunion. Last consulted 16 Oct 2015
Stiglitz J (2015c) Europe's economic madness cannot continue. http://www.theguardian.com/business/2015/jan/09/europe-economic-madness-cannot-continue-greece-elections. Last consulted 2 Mar 2016
Streeck W (2015) Gekochte tijd. De uitgestelde crisis van het democratisch kapitalisme (trans: Hemelrijk W). Leesmagazijn no 21
Taylor A (1934) Introduction: In Plato The Laws (Nomoi) (trans: A. Taylor). J.M. Dent & Sons Ltd., London
Tew B (1977) The evolution of the international monetary system 1945–77. Hutchinson of London, London
Todd E (2015) Qui est Charlie? Sociologie d'une crise religieuse. Éditions du Seuil, Paris (also: Todd E (2015) Wie is Charlie. Xenofobie en de nieuwe middenklasse. De Bezige Bij, Amsterdam and Antwerp)
Treanor AJ (2014) Bank of England asks for powers to intervene in housing market. In: the Guardian, October 2nd 2014. http://www.theguardian.com/business/2014/oct/02/bank-england-powers-intervene-housingmarket?utm_content=buffer99f70&utm_medium=social&utm_source=twitter.com&utm_campaign=buffer. Last consulted 2 Oct 2014

Umbach G, Wessels W (2008) The changing European Context of Economic and Monetary Union: 'Deepening', 'Widening' and stability. In: Dyson K (ed) The Euro at 10 – Europeanization, power, and convergence. Oxford University Press, Oxford, pp 54–68
United Nations Development Programme (2014) Human Development Report 2014. UNDP, New York
Van den Broeck S (2014) U vraagt Paul De Grauwe, econoom – Deze regering denkt vooral aan de ondernemers. Knack, 22 Oct 2014
Van Steelandt A (2014) Het zombiesysteem. Trends, 20 Nov 2014
Vandamme F (1985) Stromingen in de politieke wijsbegeerte 2. Communication & Cognition, Gent
Vandewalle G (1976) De geschiedenis van het economisch denken. Kluwer, Deventer
Wolf M (2014) The shifts and the shocks. What we've learned – and have still to learn – from the financial crisis. Allen Lane, London

Chapter 5
Some Further Institutional and Other Practical Aspects of the Organization of the New Monetary World Order

5.1 Institutional Organization

5.1.1 General

As mentioned in the previous Chapter (see above, especially under Sect. 4.5 of Chap. 4 of this book), when implementing the propositions developed in this book for a "New Monetary World Order", on an organizational level, it will become necessary to install a central global monetary institution, which already before in this book has been named "the New Monetary World Institute" (abbreviated: "NMWI").[1] 1

From a practical perspective, this "New Monetary World Institute" could obviously be the continuation of the current "International Monetary Fund (IMF)" provided that, obviously, some major adjustments (would) take place, both as regards its policy goals, as on a more institutional level. 2

In the framework of these adjustments, one could even go as far as considering "merging" the IMF with certain international non-government organizations, such as, *on one hand,* the World Bank (and/or other financial institutions belonging to the World Bank group) and, *on the other hand,* renowned (private and public) international charity organizations, such as Oxfam, Unicef and 11.11.11, ensuring that the "(metaphoric) heart which still pounds there" on issues of a socioeconomic nature, could henceforth also help to construct the motor from which the new "NMWI" will be able to determine and execute its policies of an altruistic nature.[2] 3

[1] Which, as mentioned earlier, is a merely a first proposed working name, whereby any other similar name could also be thought off.

[2] Whereby, preferably, not too much attention should go to the different legal qualification and further characteristics of the institutions thus to be merged.

K. Byttebier, *Towards a New International Monetary Order*,
Economic and Financial Law & Policy – Shifting Insights & Values 1,
DOI 10.1007/978-3-319-52518-1_5

4 The further proposition would be that this "New Monetary World Institute" would be the only institution within the New Monetary World Order which will be authorized to create money—be it in close cooperation with its "branches" which will operate within the national member states, i.e. the national central banks of the participating countries, to be organized in the form of a "New Global System of Central Banks" (abbreviated: "NGSCB")—with, as also has been mentioned earlier (see above, under Sect. 4.5 of Chap 4 of this book), explicit exclusion of any participation into the processes of money creation by the private (banking) sector.

5.1.2 *Supranational Level of Organization of the NMWI*

5.1.2.1 Classification of the NMWI into Departments

5 A further proposal regarding the organization of the New Monetary World Order entails that, in view of a smooth operation of money creation (and distribution) processes, within the New Monetary World Institute (NMWI), two main departments (for money creation) would be organized, each divided into further (for instance two or three) subdepartments, namely:

- A department for "public" creation of money, consisting of:
  - A subdepartment for money creation on behalf of the NMWI (and, by extension: the NGSCB) itself;
  - A subdepartment for money creation on behalf of the (national) authorities (governments) of the participating countries;
  - Possibly: a subdepartment for money creation on behalf of certain other "supranational public entities".
- A department for "private" creation of money, consisting of:
  - A subdepartment for money creation to the benefit of the private sector for "general welfare" purposes (including the needs of the nonprofit sector);
  - A subdepartment for money creation to the benefit of the private sector for the funding of "established business" (in a broad sense of the word).

6 Within the New Monetary World Order, each of these departments (and further subdepartments) should be responsible for a certain segment of the global money creation, and this based on the broader overall policy aims of the New Monetary World Order which have already been explained in the previous Chap. 4.

Hence, the department for "public" money creation should, possibly by use of two (or three) appropriate subdepartments, become responsible for money creation for the benefit of its own operation and for the benefit of (the central governments of) the participating countries (and, by extension, of certain similar supranational public organisms) (see above, under Sect. 4.7 of Chap. 4 of this book).

In a similar way, the department for "private" money creation could also be divided into two (or more) subdepartments.

A first of these subdepartments could be made responsible for money creation for purposes of general welfare, where, for instance, one could imagine money creation in order to cover for:

- "Basic life needs", implying money creation for the benefit of private individuals (and families) which is meant to cover their "basic life needs" (in the aforementioned, broad sense of the word; see above, at marg. 129 of Chap. 4 of this book), as well as money creation for the benefit of private individuals for the start-up of a (new) professional activity which (at least over time) should allow them to cover their basic life needs themselves;
- The needs of the nonprofit sector (as long as this sector would continue to exist).

Finally, the subdepartment for money creation for the established business sector could be made responsible for credit lending to established businesses (in a broad sense of the word, and therefore regardless of their legal organizational form).

As regards the level of money creation in the private sphere (hence to individuals, families, the non-profit sector and business enterprises), the same subdepartments could be installed at the level of the national, central banks of the countries which will participate to the NMWO.

5.1.2.2 Working Method of the Different Departments of the NMWI

5.1.2.2.1 Operation of the Department for Public Money Creation

With regards to the working methods of the above proposed (sub)departments of the NMWO, the operation of both "main departments" could be further characterized by an important difference. **7**

As regards the department of creation of money for the public sector, it would more precisely be the intention that this department would allow the public authorities it will fund (going from the national governments of the participating countries to the NMWI itself, in addition to other similar supranational entities) to operate by means of periodical allocations.[3] **8**

Such "allocations" will be characterized by the fact that, once an allocation decision will be made (in function of certain parameters to be worked out in the

[3]In the present monetary World order, the "*Special Drawing Rights*" which the IMF can allocate, show some resemblance to the here proposed "money allocations" on behalf of the public sector (see however above, at marg. 31 and marg. 61–62 of Chap. 4 of this book, where some differences have already been pointed out).

treaty (ies) and the rules and regulations on the functioning of the NGSCB[4]; see above, under Sect. 4.7.2.2.4 of Chap. 4 of this book), such an allocation will be definitively and without any reimbursement obligation acquired. As a result, the operation of the NGSCB itself (of which the NMWI will form a part), respectively the national governments of the participating countries, will be fully ensured.

Otherwise put, such allocations will not concern "credit" (so that there will not come any reimbursement obligation or obligation to pay interest in play), but on the contrary, definitively attributed money which will be fully acquired by the beneficiaries once an allocation decision will be made.

5.1.2.2.2 Operation of the Department for Private Money Creation

9 Contrary to the way the department for money creation on behalf of public authorities will function, the department for money creation on behalf of the private sector could still be based on the technique of providing credits which (in principle) will have to be reimbursed.[5]

Indeed, in order to prevent the world population to be encouraged to inactivity (which would be completely counterproductive both from an economic, as from a general societal perspective), it will be necessary to ensure that the department for money creation on behalf of the private sector will not provide non-refundable allocations, but rather different types of credits which, in accordance with the rules and regulations implementing the NMWO, will be reimbursable.

Otherwise put, whereas money creation on behalf of the public sector could be made entirely "free" (of any reimbursement or interest obligation) in order to make it possible for public authorities to function without having to take refugee to unjust or unfair tax systems, or to take up credit (from private banks) themselves, money creation on behalf of the private sector will still be subject to reimbursement and/or interest obligations in a way best reflecting the overall policy goals of the NMWO, among which the principle that every human being should have access to the same life chances in order to make something of his life, while at the same time being invited to contribute as much as possible to establishing a loving society.

10 In order to prevent arbitrariness, the NMWI and the national central banks of the countries participating in the NMWO, should be given the necessary regulating authority to shape their policy on credit lending to the private sector (for instance as regards loan conditions and procedures, follow up of the credit files,...) into clear,

---

[4]Obviously, the operation of the department for such "public" money creation (on behalf of public authorities) will also need to be based on conventionally agreed upon legal principles of reporting and monitoring (a.o. in connection to preparing and making the allocation decisions and to supervising the use of money thus allocated, in light of the public policy goals of the NGSCB itself).

[5]In the present monetary World order, for instance the way the European Central Bank (System) is organized (see Zilioli and Selmayr 2001), shows some resemblance to the here proposed NMWI-department for money creation for the public sector.

transparent and legally secured directives which furthermore should be easily accessible and consultable by the inhabitants of all countries participating in the NMWO.

A specific question will, of course, be whether the NMWI should be given the authority to determine a maximum threshold of "credits" to be provided to private persons per country within a certain period of time (for instance per year), or if the national central bank of each of the participating countries should be completely free to decide on the extent of the money creation on behalf of the private sector of its own economy. 11

An argument in favor of a system of maximum thresholds per country to be determined periodically (a.o. in function of prognoses to be made about the needs of the population and the economy of each of the participating countries) can be derived from the overall objective of advocating a monetary system which limits the total amounts (of money) in function of the capacity of the planet.

A specific proposal based upon this policy goal could then be that a convention-based system would be set-up, based on which, at the level of the NMWI, periodically (for instance each year) and per country, a maximum threshold of credits to be attributed to the private sector would be determined (with possible differentiations in function of the different types of credits), after which, per country, the national central banks of each of the participating countries can handle the credit demands of the own population within these limits thus set by the NMWI itself.

A possible argument against such a system could be the large degree of dirigisme such a system could have on the economies of the participating countries (which by some is said not to be workable).[6]

Hence, an alternative proposal could be that each of the national central banks of the participating countries would be allowed a sufficient degree of sovereignty in the field of credit provisioning to the private sector, albeit such a policy will need to be aligned with the objectives of the NMWI and the NGSCB, among which, for instance, a sufficiently balanced control of the growth of the amount of money, as well as the avoidance of reckless credit lending, hence money creation, so that the stupidities to be witnessed under the prevailing (capitalist) system of money creation by private banks, will under the working of the New Monetary World Order be avoided.

In the latter approach, the NMWI could for instance be given a supervisory role towards the central banks participating in the NGSCB, especially in order to prevent that credit lending (hence money creation) for the benefit of the private sector could derail in any of the countries participating in the NMWO. In case there would be a threat of such a derailment (or in case an effective derailment would occur), the NMWI could be given the authority to intervene, for instance by imposing temporary maximum thresholds of money creation on behalf of the private sector).

[6]See even Galbraith (1992), p. 88.

12 It may be evident that the processes needed to install the above proposed monetary policy in the field of credit lending, hence money creation, for the benefit of the private sectors will need to be determined in a transparent and legally secured way, which at the very least will require the installment of a solid legal framework going from (1) working out the basic principles in (an) international treaty (ies), through (2) a solid set of basic directives at the level of the NMWI itself, and (3) a set of (sufficiently detailed) concrete rules and regulations at the level (of the national central banks) of the countries participating in the NMWO.

5.1.3 National Organization Level

13 Besides the aforementioned level of supranational organization through the establishment of the "New Monetary World Institute" (or "NMWI")[7] and its several departments or subdepartments, as has already been mentioned before, a second level of organization of the NGSCB will have to be worked out at the level of each of the participating countries.[8]

14 The proposal here formulated is that every country participating in the NMWO would be under the (treaty) obligation to establish a national central (public) bank that constitutes a subdivision of the "New Global System of Central Banks" or "NGSCB".[9]

15 Given the set of tasks to be performed by these national central banks, especially in the field of implementing and executing the monetary policy of the NMWO with regard to money creation on behalf of the private sector, there will moreover be a need for a sufficient level of accessibility of each of these national central banks by the general public (consisting of the inhabitants of each of the participating countries).

For this purpose, it is here furthermore proposed that each of the national central banks which will participate to the NGSCB will (henceforth) need to dispose of a fine mazed network of (physical) branches with counter function and easily accessible to the general public.[10]

The aforementioned proposals will obviously call for a sufficient staff within each of the national central banks partaking to the NMWO, whereby one could, for instance, consider "mutating" the existing staff of the tax authorities of the participating countries for which, under the New Monetary World Order, there will be a

[7]Which, obviously, could compare to certain existing supranational institutions, such as, for instance, the IMF and the ECB/ESCB.

[8]For instance comparable to the current model of the ESCB (See Umbach and Wessels 2008, pp. 54–68, especially p. 58; Zilioli and Selmayr 2001, pp. 54 a.f.).

[9]It could obviously be the existing central banks of the participating countries which could take up this role under the NMWO, provided that the necessary changes would take place.

[10]Following the example of the current private deposit banks.

considerably lower need, as well as personnel presently employed by the private banking sector (given the fact that, within the NMWO, there will be a lesser need for private banks themselves to dispose of a multitude of physical branches with counters).

As regards the need for offices (and other "material goods" needed to set up a national central bank with sufficient physical branches throughout the territory of a given country participating in the NWMO), one could furthermore appeal to the buildings (and other material) of existing private banks, if needed by relying on expropriation techniques.[11]

Finally, the "fine mazed network" of physical branches of a given national central bank partaking to the "New Global System of Central Banks" or NGSCB will, in each country, function under the supervision of their headquarter, i.e. the national central bank itself which will in turn form a part of the overarching NGSCB lead by the NMWI.[12] 16

5.1.4 Financing the NGSCB

It goes without saying that the NGSCB, and the national central banks forming part of it, should in no way be subject to the neoliberal objective of pursuit of profit, given the basic intent of the NMWO to establish a global monetary order based on "altruistic" principles. 17

Consequently, as has also been mentioned earlier (see above, under Sect. 4.7.2.2.4 of Chap. 4 of this book), it is here proposed that the operation of the NGSCB itself would in the future be financed by periodic allocations (in New World Currency)[13] to be decided upon by the NMWI, both for its own benefit, as for the benefit of each of the national central banks participating in the NGSCB (in addition to, as mentioned earlier, certain other to be determined supranational public entities).

Given the fact that these allocations will (also) come down to an (additional) money creation to cover for the proper needs of the NGSCB, there will also here be a need for (very) strict convention-based agreements whereby, for instance, the approval of these allocations will become the (ultimate) authority of a 18

---

[11]There can hardly be any serious objection against these proposals in light of the huge sums of money public authorities have spent on bail out operations during the past years, not to mention the vast sums of interests which have been paid by public authorities to the private banking sector since decades (not to say for centuries) already, which, bottom line, had to be paid by taxing the broad population of inhabitants of such countries.

[12]As mentioned earlier, to the example of the ESCB.

See furthermore Umbach and Wessels (2008), pp. 54–68, especially p. 58; Zilioli and Selmayr (2001), pp. 53 a.f.

[13]For instance, with an equal interval as those of the decisions of granting allocations to the national authorities of the participating countries themselves.

representative body functioning within the NMWI (preferably a kind of plenary member council in which all countries participating in the NMWO will be represented).

Moreover, there will be a need for clear supervision mechanisms, aiming at avoiding that the NMWI staff and, in a broader view, the global NGSCB staff, would create for itself an elitist (financial) status (as this is, currently, too much the case within the present IMF and similar supranational institutions).

5.1.5 Composition of the Governing and Managing Bodies of the NGSCB

5.1.5.1 Organizational Aspects

19 From an ethical perspective, the question also arises how to organize the governance and management organs of the NGSCB.

For instance, at the level of the NMWI itself, one could opt for the establishment of different governance and management organs, including:

- A plenary (member) counsel;
- A Board of Directors;
- A daily management.

20 Preferably, the NWMI should have at its disposal a plenary council acting as the highest body of the NMWI. For instance, every country participating in the NMWO could hold one seat in this plenary council (implying that every such country could thus appoint one representative to the meetings of the plenary council of the NMWI).[14]

The plenary council could be vested with powers which are usually allocated to the representative bodies of already existing supranational organizations, such as: the authority to change the basic operational rules of the NGSCB (for instance through the authority to approve amendments to the basic treaty (ies) governing the NMWO); the approval of further rules and regulations governing the NGSCB and how it will operate; the approval of the annual budgets and accounts; the ratification of the decisions on financial allocations to the participating countries and to the

[14]As an alternative, one could think of a system of "pondered" representation.

If ever the world (leading) countries would be willing to work out a more altruistically based world monetary order, it may indeed be feared that especially the rich and powerful countries will favor such a system of pondered representation, whereby richer and more powerful countries would be given more seats in the decision making organs of the NMWI than the smaller and less powerful countries. In case such a model of "pondered" representation would be established, one can but hope that criteria such as population numbers per country will be given more influence than criteria such as existing economic welfare, given the overall aspiration to work out a global monetary order which would be fair, just and (as) altruistic (as possible) for the majority of mankind.

NGSCB itself; establishing the parameters according to which the creation of money for the benefit of the private sector in each of the participating countries will be organized; etc.

The Board of Directors could become the highest governance organ of the NMWI. In the treaty (ies) establishing the NMWO, one could set out how many seats the board of directors will hold and according to which system(s) these seats will be assigned (for instance, by means of a rotating system allowing every country to periodically hold a seat in this board of directors of the NMWI).

In the same treaty (ies) (possibly to be worked out in more detail in operating rules and regulations to be determined by the plenary body), also the authority and the competences of this board of directors could be worked out whereby one could, *inter alia*, think of the following powers:

- the determination of the allocations to each of the participating countries (*in globo* to be ratified by the plenary council);
- the determination of the allocations to the NGSCB (*in globo* to be ratified by the plenary council);
- the determination of the allocations to other supranational entities (*in globo* to be ratified by the plenary council);
- possibly: the determination of the parameters of money creation for the benefit of the private sector in each of the participating countries (*in globo* to be ratified by the plenary council);
- the determination of the (operational) rules and regulations of the NGSCB;
- the determination of further (global) directives with regards to the operation of the processes of money creation;
- ...

Finally, a daily management organ—which could consist of one, or a number of "general managers" (whereby, obviously, any other name could be thought of to describe their function)—could be made responsible for the day-to-day operation of the NMWI (including the management of its buildings and other possessions, in addition to its management and staff; the preparation of the decisions of the board of directors; the leadership over a global documentary and research center; etc.). 21

5.1.5.2 A New Ethics of Filling Positions and Mandates

Also as regards the filling in of the positions of member of the board of directors and of the management of the NMWI, the time is more than ripe for a thorough global reflection. 22

In today's world, the filling of such positions as directors or managers (and even, more in general, of the entire staffing) within (existing) supranational institutions is traditionally organized by the political world (hence decided upon by the leading political parties of the countries participating in such supranational institutions, which generally operate in accordance with "aristocratic" or, in modern terms "corporatocratic" principles).[15]

Through the game of politics, the concrete filling in of these types of director and management positions in supranational institutions are, in general, decided upon per country on a national level by its leading political party (ies), whereby, more often than not, the said positions are not handed out to the best qualified people, but rather to persons who have accrued the most power or influence within said political parties (or to those holding the best connections with such people in power).

As moreover can be witnessed, in many countries, present-day "central banks" (or similar monetary authorities) are often to a large extent manned by (former) bankers or people strongly connected with the private banking sector, which obviously also leads to an unhealthy entanglement between the private banking sector and said central banks (the latter being supposed to "monitor" said private banks).

These methods of handing out positions of influence within supranational institutions has already been criticized before in academic literature, whereby even the overall question has been raised to what extent one could call these processes of party politics steering society, democratic, and whereby alternative models (as an alternative for party politics) of democratic representation have been debated upon.[16]

From a higher ethic, one can but express the hope that the aforementioned traditional method of having party politics determine the mandates of supranational institutions would not be applied to the operation of the NMWI (and, by extension: the NGSCB) as well, but that, on the contrary, a representation system will be developed whereby, *on one hand,* the filling in of said mandates would increasingly take place in a truly democratic method way and, *on the other hand*, not the ones most affiliated to the political world (or even: to the private banking world itself), but rather the most skilled people who can show a thorough expertise[17] would be appointed to the (bodies of the) NMWI.

One could, for instance think, of a composition of the aforementioned bodies (and staffing) of the NMWI based on a healthy mix of representatives from the (genuine) levels of society and moreover based on objective recruitment systems, such as truly comparative selection methods (for instance: anonymous exams).

23 Similar considerations should also apply to the level of the bodies of the national central banks as a part of the NGSCB.

For each of these national central banks, one could for instance proceed to the installment of two central organs, namely a board of directors and an organ of daily

[15]See Sachs (2011), pp. 116 a.f.; Chomsky (1999), p. 132.

[16]See *e.g.* Devos et al. (2009), pp. 15–40, especially p. 23; see also Sachs (2011), p. 116 a.f.

[17]Ideally, the organs of the NMWI and the NGSCB should not only be manned with economists and monetary and financial experts, but as well with prominent other scientists, such as, for instance, experts of scientific fields examining how agricultural, industrial and commercial developments influence the eco-system of the planet earth.

management, both with appropriate tasks and authorities (including the authority to issue directives as regards money creation on behalf of the private sector at the national level).

One could further imagine the installment of a joint supervisory committee, consisting of, *on one hand*, (a minority of) members of the nationally elected parliament and, *on the other hand,* a (majority of) international observers (for instance delegated by third member states which hold a position in the allocation panel of a given country (see above, at marg. 76 of Chap. 4 of this book)).

Also here, the concern rises that the concrete filling in of positions within these representative organs would not take place in accordance with the principle of politically determined appointments, but that, on the contrary, one would strive for a system which allows to recruit based on true skills and craftsmanship.

5.2 Further Elements of Money Creation at the Proposed Levels

5.2.1 Overview

As has already (partially) been mentioned before, within the New Monetary World Order, (at least) the following (monetary) tasks should be performed by the NMWI or/and the national central banks participating in the NGSCB: **24**

a. Money creation in order to finance the operation of the NMWI and the national central banks participating in the NGSCB themselves (= public sphere; allocation, no credit);
b. Money creation for the benefit of the national governments of the participating member states (= public sphere; allocation; no credit);
c. Money creation for the benefit of certain other supranational public organisms (= public sphere; allocation; no credit);
d. Money creation for the benefit of the private sector in order to cover basic needs of life (= private sphere; general wellbeing, thus "free" credit);
e. Money creation for the benefit of private individuals for the start-up of a professional activity (= private sphere; general wellbeing, thus "free" credit);
f. Money creation for the benefit of the (private) nonprofit sector (= private sphere; (in general:) general wellbeing, thus (in principle:) "free" credit);
g. Money creation for the benefit of the (private) established business sector (in a broad sense of the word) (= private sphere; no general wellbeing, thus no free credit);
h. The collection of deposits and the organization of basic payment traffic (= private sphere; general wellbeing, thus "free" service).

Except for the task as described in the aforementioned point sub h., it has already been indicated before in Chap. 4 of this book why, within the New Monetary World **25**

Order, the aforementioned tasks should be assigned to the NMWI and/or to the national central banks participating in the NGSCB.

In addition to the justification why also the task mentioned under point h. of the previous marg. 24 of this chapter should, henceforth, preferably also be assigned to the NMWI and/or to the national central banks participating in the NGSCB, and in as far as such outlines have not yet (in a sufficient way) been proposed before in Chap. 3, we shall hereafter propose an outline of how each of the proposed tasks should (preferably) be performed.

5.2.2 *Creation of Money for Financing the Proper Operation of the NMWI and the NGSCB*

26 The here first mentioned task of the NMWI (and by extension: the NGSCB), namely the creation of money for its proper operation, has already been elaborated upon in the previous Chap. 4 of this book (see above, under Sect. 4.7.2.2 of Chap. 4 of this book).

27 In a monetary system whereby only one currency, namely "the New World Currency", will exist, it is logical to hold that the (supranational) institution which will be responsible both for its emission, as for safeguarding the (global) total amount of money, will also be able to decide upon the scale of its own operational funds.

This principle should concretely apply to the operational funds of both the New Monetary World Institute itself, as to those to be attributed to the national central banks participating in the NGSCB.

28 It should hereby be avoided that such a competence would be turned into an instrument whereby the leadership of the NMWI (and by extension: the NGSCB) would get transformed itself into a new "financial elite" (as is, currently, too much the case as regards the leadership and staff of certain existing supranational institutions, such as the European Community[18] and the IMF, of which the leaders and staff, in strong contrast with the policy work of general interest which they are supposed to pursue, as well as generous salaries and other working conditions, enjoy many fiscal and other advantages).[19]

Hence, through the organs of the newly to-be-established NMWI, the world community will need to ensure that sufficient control mechanisms are established in order to guarantee that, also in the context of allocation decisions regarding the

[18]About the high salaries of the people manning the European institutions, see *e.g.* Dohmen (1999), p. 204; Quid (2014). See also EU-parlementairen krijgen samen tot 18 miljoen euro bovenop loon. http://m.hln.be/hln/m/nl/957/Binnenland/article/detail/2088210/2014/10/13/EU-parlementairen-krijgen-samen-tot-18-miljoen-euro-bovenop-loon.dhtml?originatingNavigationItemId=1. Last consulted on October 13th 2014.

[19]See Geldverslindend europarlement aan de kaak gesteld http://www.nieuwsblad.be/cnt/dmf20130626_012. Last consulted on December 18th 2014.

proper operational funds of the NMWI (and, by extension, the NGSCB), the NMWI will be guided by the underlying objectives of the new international monetary system, especially the general wellbeing (and not the wellbeing of a limited financial elite), and furthermore taking into account the overall policy goal that the total amount of money issued by the NMWI (and by the national central banks participating in the NGSCB) will remain limited in accordance with the capacity of the planet (even more so from an intergenerational perspective).[20]

5.2.3 Money Creation for the Benefit of the National Governments of the Countries Participating in the NMWO

As has already been extensively elaborated upon earlier (see above, under Sect. **29**
4.7.2 of Chap. 4 of this book), the here proposed second task of the NMWI (and by extension: the NGSCB) will consist of the creation of money for the benefit of the countries participating in the NMWO.

Given the different intrinsic injustices which world-wide characterize the actual systems of government financing, it has earlier on in this book resolutely been proposed that, within the New Monetary World Order, taxation of (average) income and assets, in addition to regular transactions of goods and services, would be resolutely abandoned and that, on the contrary, the (national) governments of the countries participating in the New Monetary World Order would, henceforth, receive their financing directly from the NMWI itself through direct allocations for their benefit. (See already under Sect. 4.7.2.1 of Chap. 4 of this book.)

In this way, the supply of (new) money to the (national) governments of the countries participating in the New Monetary World Order (and, by extension, certain other supranational "public organisms"), will henceforth take place directly from the public creation of new money expressed in the same currency.

Such a system of government financing based upon direct allocations by the world monetary authority will obviously need to operate in a sufficiently disciplined way, whereby the specter of unbridled money creation for the benefit of the government sector will need to be avoided (further taking into consideration that

[20]Compare Galbraith (1996), pp. 82 a.f.

See also Pettifor (2014), who expressed a similar concern as follows:

> Above all our credit creation system must be managed to make it possible for society as a whole – not just a tiny financial elite – to mobilise the resources needed to achieve that which is in the interests of society (and the ecosystem) as a whole.

the government sector is, in itself, intrinsically not productive[21] in the sense of creating "hard" economic output).

30 It goes without saying that the inception of such a system of government financing based upon allocation decisions by the world monetary authority will require a world-wide understanding of what the core tasks to be performed by the national governments of the countries participating in the NMWO should be. (See already above, under Sect. 4.7.2.4 of Chap. 4 of this book.)

Indeed, as the pursuit of a more just (monetary) world (order) should be one of the underlying pillars of the NMWO (see the previous Chap. 4., especially its Sect. 4.3.), it will need to be based on a world-wide consensus about the tasks and (public) services which any world citizen can expect from his national government (and by extension, from any of the other supranational "public organisms" financed through allocations by the NMWI).

It will hereby be necessary that the currently prevailing monetary model which is basically of a capitalist nature and which is characterized by large distortions between the countries (see above, Sect. 3.4.6 of Chap. 3 of this book) will have be abandoned in favor of a globally unified model, which will be characterized by a world-wide alignment, at an equal minimum level, of access to a completely "free" package of public services which should help ensuring that every person on the planet can lead a decent life.[22]

In a financial model based upon allocations to be assigned to the countries participating in the NMWO (instead of on taxing the lower and middle classes of society), such an obviously ambitious end goal should indeed come within reach.

When working out such a world-wide "level playing field" of access to public services, central points of attention will most likely be[23]:

- Working out a world-wide level playing field regarding public works for an adequate infrastructure (taking into account national characteristics, often mainly due to purely natural factors, of each of the participating countries);
- Defining clear limits of (the compensation for) public mandates and officials (valid for all participating countries);

---

[21] It should however be pointed out that the (liberal and neoliberal) perceptive that governments are to a large extent unproductive and hence should be kept at a level which is as minimal as possible (see especially Friedman 1993) is here obviously not shared. Nevertheless, it is reminded that it is not the basic task of governments to partake in economic production, but mainly to accomplish a fair and just societal organization, a.o. by enacting systems of redistribution of wealth, of social care, of public education, of safety and justice, etc., all matters which are as important as hard economic output itself.

[22] Compare Stiglitz (2012), pp. 274 a.f.

[23] Compare Oxfam (2014), pp. 17 a.f., correctly stressing the importance of systems of (public) schooling and health care.

- Setting out a framework for a world-wide acceptable "public welfare" package, among which access to overall comprehensive social security[24];
- Working out a world-wide model of equal access to (public) schooling and education within all of the participating countries;
- Working out a world-wide model of equal access to medical[25] care systems, systems of child care and care for the sick and elderly within all of the participating countries;
- possibly: ensuring an equal basic minimum income within all of the participating countries;
- . . .

This topic has already extensively been dealt with in Chap. 4, to which we can further refer here (see above, under Sects. 4.3 and 4.7.2 of Chap. 4 of this book).

In the previously quoted before study of Oxfam "*Even it up*", equal access to 31
such public services which should moreover be "free"—implying that they should be provided by the government and funded out of government budgets without the user of the services needing to pay an additional fee—has even been referred to as a human right[26]:

> Providing clinics and classrooms, medics and medicines, can help to close the gap in life chances and give people the tools to challenge the rules that perpetuate economic inequality. Free public healthcare and education are not only human rights; they also mitigate the worst impacts of today's skewed income and wealth distribution.

The prerequisite that such public services need to be "free" (in the aforementioned significance of being freely accessible for their users) has, furthermore, been substantiated[27] as follows in the same study "*Even it up*" by Oxfam:

> When public services are not free at the point of use, millions of ordinary women and men are excluded from accessing healthcare and education. User fees were encouraged for many years by the World Bank, a mistake their president now says was ideologically driven. Yet, despite the damage they do, user fees persist. Every year, 100 million people worldwide are pushed into poverty because they have to pay out-of-pocket for healthcare. In Ghana, the poorest families will use 40 percent of their household income sending just one of their children to an Omega low-fee school. Women and girls suffer most when fees are charged for public services.[28]

---

[24]It is clear that this alone presents a sensitive and colored theme in the present ongoing debates and that the current ideological differences which now determine the outcome of these debates should make way for a unitary vision based on an equal value of every human being regardless of race, color, gender, origin, sexual preference, religious belief or non-belief, etc.

[25]Oxfam speaks of an "*universal health coverage*" (see Oxfam 2014, p. 97).

[26]Oxfam (2014), p. 18.

[27]Oxfam (2014), p. 18.

[28]This rationale is here fully recognized, albeit not in the cynical and heartless ideology of neoliberal authors such as Ayn Rand who, in her appropriate style, hence without showing any empathy or mercy for her less fortunate fellow-man, has commented on this type of questions (in the quote hereunder specifically the question whether there can be such a thing as a "human right" to education) as follows:

32 It is obvious that already merely reflecting upon a globally minimum level of access to (free) public services will be no sinecure, and that the debate about this question can only stand a chance provided that a global willingness emerges that the wellbeing of mankind and of the planet it inhabits requires a drastic shift away from the ideology of economic neo-liberalism as the main driving force within the economy, and that instead, an economic system should be developed which, above all, will be concerned with the general wellbeing (and no longer with the wellbeing of a privileged financial elite).

33 Moreover, if the NWMO were ever effectively established, in all of its decisions, including the decisions of periodically allocating funds to the (national) governments of the participating countries, the NMWI will, as has been mentioned several times before, not only need to focus on the general wellbeing of the world's population, but will also need to take into account the fact that the global amount of money needs to be limited in relation to the capacity of the planet (also from an "intergenerational" perspective).

Be that as it may, many have already reached the conclusion that the unbridled "consumerism" which currently prevails (in all levels of societal organization) can no longer be justified, given its detrimental effect on the planet.[29]

In order for the NMWO to be successful, this awareness will on a global scale need to determine the behavior of public authorities, whereby, henceforth, spending behavior should become resolutely related to the (only source of) income which will still be accessible in the NMWO, namely the allocations granted by the NMWI, with explicit exclusion of any additional taxation and/or additional borrowing on the financial markets and/or from financial institutions.

Thus, unbridled taxation (of lower and middle classes), in addition (or not) to an unbridled debt financing (ultimately also borne by the lower and middle classes) should no longer offer an alibi for the national governments of the countries participating in the New Monetary World Order not to cut in their own (over) spending behavior while at the same time their spending behavior should become focused on the true societal needs.

What must be challenged is the prevalent belief that education is some sort of "natural right" – in effect a free gift of nature. There are no such free gifts. But it is in the interest of statism to foster this delusion – in order to throw a smokescreen over the issue of whose freedom must be sacrificed to pay for such "free gifts". (See Rand 2008, p. 95. See also Veldman and Parlevliet 2003, p. 54.)

[29]See especially Kasser (2002), pp. 1 a.f.

See even the modern day viewpoints of the Catholic Church, quoted above, under Sect. 3.6.2.5.2 of Chap. 3 of this book.

5.2.4 *Money Creation for the Benefit of the Private Sector*

5.2.4.1 Task Division Between the NMWI and the National Central Banks Participating in the NGSCB

It has already earlier been proposed in this book (see above, Chap. 4., especially the description of the Pillars III. and V. of the NMWO under Sects. 4.5 and 4.6), that, within the New Monetary World Order, global money creation would become the exclusive domain of the monetary authorities to the explicit exclusion of the private (banking) sector. This principle will not only apply to money creation on behalf of public authorities (in the broad sense of the word, implying: the NMWI and the NGSCB themselves, in addition to the national governments of the countries participating in the NMWO and to certain other supranational public entities), but also to money creation on behalf of the private sector. **34**

It can hereby, obviously, not be the intention that one single central global institution, namely the NMWI, would be solely responsible for money creation on behalf of every individual world citizen. **35**

On the contrary, the working of the NMWO should become based on a clear task division between on one side the NMWI itself and on the other sides the national central banks of the countries participating in the NMWO.

Hence, the NMWI itself would be competent for making decisions about allocations for its proper functioning and that of the national central banks participating in the NMWO (see above, under Sect. 5.2.2), in addition to allocation decisions for the benefit of the (national) governments of each of the participating countries and, by extension, of certain other, supranational public organisms (see above, under Sect. 5.2.3).

On the contrary, money creation for the benefit of the private sector within each of the participating countries, should not become a (direct and exclusive) task of the NMWI itself, but should become based on a detailed task division between, *on one hand*, the NMWI itself and, *on the other hand*, a network of national central banks participating in the NGSCB (as a part of the institutional framework of the NMWO).

Thus, as regards money creation for the benefit of the private sector, it could for instance be the task of the NMWI itself to, *on one hand* set out the parameters according to which the NGSCB (and the national central banks participating to it), will concretely work out money creation for the benefit of the private individuals in each of the participating countries (possibly with inclusion of the authority to, periodically or at least in case of to-be-defined crisis situations, determine a maximum level of money creation for the benefit of the private sector per country) and, *on the other hand,* to ensure compliance with these parameters by each of the national central banks participating in the NGSCB.

Furthermore, any concrete act of money creation for the benefit of the private sector would become the task of each of the national central banks of the countries participating in the NGSCB, knowing that such a task will be performed within the parameters set out by, and under the supervision of the NMWI that in this way will bear the final responsibility for global money creation (in line with convention-based defined principles which will have to be elaborated for this purpose in the treaty (ies) establishing the NMWO).

5.2.4.2 Credit Lending/Money Creation for the Benefit of Private Individuals and Families

5.2.4.2.1 Credit Lending/Money Creation for the Benefit of Private Individuals (and Families) for Basic Needs of Life

36 As mentioned earlier, within the New Monetary World Order, any concrete money creation for the benefit of the private sector, including private individuals and families for covering their basic needs of life should (within the parameters to be defined by the NMWI) become the task of the national central bank of the country where such private individual (or family) resides.

37 In order to perform this task, it will be necessary that, in each of the countries participating in the New Monetary World Order, its national central bank will dispose of a "fine mazed" network of offices (with counters) accessible to every individual or family in order to file a request for a (private) credit (see also above, at marg. 15 of this chapter).

38 The definition of the term "basic needs of life" (see also above, at marg. 129 of Chap. 4 of this book) will hereby become the responsibility of the monetary authorities which, within the framework of the treaty (ies) establishing the NMWO, could even be given regulatory authority in this regard.[30]

The NMWI could, for instance, be granted the competence to issue an overall "directive" (or similar guideline) of what, world-wide, will be considered as "basic needs of life", according to which, subsequently, each of the national central banks participating in the New Monetary World Order could issue a more detailed "national" directive (or similar guideline) fine-tuning the NWMI-overall guidelines within the context of its own country framework.

Under marg. 129–130 of Chap. 4 of this book above, it has already been explained in detail what might constitute "basic needs of life"; practical "basic needs of life" could for instance be:

- Access to food and drinking water;
- Access to (basic) individual housing;
- Access to assets providing basic comfort (for instance: furnishing one's house);

---

[30]Similarly to the regulatory authority the ECB and the ESCB presently dispose of (see article 132 of the Consolidated version of the Treaty on the Functioning of the European Union (to be consulted at: http://eur-lex.europa.eu/legal-content/EN/TXT/?uri=CELEX:12012E/TXT; last consulted on November 17th 2015).

See also Zilioli and Selmayr (2001), pp. 83 a.f.; Byttebier (2001), pp. 253–256, marg. 316.

- Access to medical and similar care (especially to the extent that this would not be provided sufficiently through the systems of public care which each of the participating countries will have to organize anyhow; see above, under Sect. 4.7.2.4 of Chap. 4 of this book);
- The purchase of an individual private means of transport;
- The purchase of a personal computer (or similar device) ensuring the (human) right to information and communication;
- ...

In accordance with these "directives" (for instance, a general NMWI-directive, in addition to more specific directives per country), every human being should be able to determine which of his needs will be categorized as "basic needs of life", for which, when needed, an appropriate credit can be obtained from the national central bank of the country where he resides.

5.2.4.2.2 Credit Lending/Money Creation in Order to Ensure Basic Access to a Professional Activity

As regards the category of credits which will ensure access to a professional activity, there will also be a similar need to establish a clear, albeit broad enough definition of this notion (see also above, at marg. 139–140 of Chap. 4 of this book). **39**

Moreover, there will be a need for strict control mechanisms dealing with the question whether or not a specific request by a candidate-borrower is indeed justified. Such control mechanisms could, for instance, be worked out in the context of a transparent system of parameters which, i.a., should make it possible to distinguish a person starting a professional activity from an already established market player.

There will also be a need to establish a mechanism which helps determining when a person starting a professional activity will have sufficiently "grown" in order to stop his dependence on free credit lending by his national central bank, in addition to a mechanism which, in case a free credit is no longer justified, will make it possible to convert such a free credit into a credit which is subject to interest payments.

5.2.4.2.3 Further Characteristics of Credits for the Benefit of Private Individuals and Families

In order to meet the here proposed objectives of the New Monetary World Order, both of the aforementioned categories of "credits for basic needs of life" will, obviously, have to be completely "free" credits.[31] **40**

[31]See also Pettifor (2014).

The underlying reason for this is that, within a monetary system based on altruistic principles, it will no longer be a policy goal that a limited elite within society would acquire ever more personal wealth from systems designed to provide basic needs of life to the poor(er) classes.[32]

In this way, it can no longer be justified to charge interest payments for credits providing basic needs of life, albeit, especially in order to avoid the dilemma of "(too) easy money creation", it will remain necessary that these credits would still be based on the reimbursement principle.

Dependent on the policy goals of the NMWO, one could even consider cases in which "negative interests" would become applicable.[33] One could for instance think of credits which are granted to the victims of a natural disaster or to people living in areas where there is a shortage of bare necessities of life, such as drinking water and food.

41 The agreements between the national central bank providing the credit and the borrower on the reimbursement of the credits for the financing of "basic needs of life" will, furthermore, need to be aligned with the reasonable ability of the borrower to generate an income from labor or, in other words, to obtain enough income to be able to reimburse the credit and, increasingly, to cover his (or his family's) basic needs of life himself, whereby it clearly should not be the intention to create a chronic dependence on credit lending to cover basic needs of life (= see the "*principle of economic self-sustainment*" already worked out in the letters of Saint Paul, referred to above, at marg. 43–46 of Chap. 3. of this book).

This will imply that credit lending (and also the administration of the credit files of this category of borrower) will, as much as possible, need to be based on a personal approach.

Hence, a system should be worked out whereby a national central bank that grants a credit in order to meet a basic life need would assign a credit manager to each of its credit takers who, in line with the directives provided by the national central bank, with a sufficient adequacy, will be able to assess the credit taker, especially as regards his creditworthiness and reimbursement capacity. If appropriate, it should also be possible that a credit request in order to provide for a basic need of life would be refused to people who are not willing to make a proper effort to provide in these needs themselves.[34]

---

[32]See indeed Stiglitz (2012), p. 245.

Compare to the remarks of John K. Galbraith on monetarism; see Galbraith (1992), especially pp. 93–94.

[33]Such credits would imply that not the entire sum that has been loaned out, should be reimbursed. The negative interest percentage could hereby be made dependent on the policy goals aimed with a given type of credit (whereby, at least theoretically, a negative interest percentage of even 100% could be accorded, implying that such a credit equals a gift or non-refundable subsidy).

[34]In which case such persons will qualify for support under the public services systems which all countries participating in the NMWO will have to provide for (and which will be funded through the allocations to be provided by the NMWI) (see above, under Sect. 4.7.2.4 of Chap. 4 of this book).

Be that as it may, it should be clear that, within the framework of the NMWO, access to credit for financing elementary needs of life should become a true (human) right of every human being, provided that a number of basic conditions are met, namely: 42

- The filing of a formal application describing the objectives of the credit (which should be in line with the notion of covering "basic needs of life" as defined in the to be worked out NGSCB-regulations);
- (Sufficient) proof of an effective ability and willingness to reimburse such a credit (a.o. by showing a reasonable willingness to provide for an income which will make it possible to meet such reimbursement obligations).

Otherwise put, a NMWO-credit aiming at providing in a basic need of life will (effectively) remain a "credit", i.e. essentially "reimbursable".

Hence, any candidate requesting for a credit in order to meet a basic life need will need to be able to demonstrate, when applying for such a credit, that he will be able to repay the credit and that, for this purpose, he will make the necessary efforts, especially labor efforts.

The said low threshold of obtaining a credit for a basic life need should, in other words, not be allowed to become an excuse for completely abandoning labor efforts, provided that, within the New Monetary World Order, the fruits of one's labor should mainly go to the person providing it[35] (and not, as is currently too often the case, to the rich and powerful within society who, in line with the principles of capitalism, mainly aim at getting richer through an (often shameless) exploitation of other people's labor; see Ricardo's "*Iron Law of Wages*").[36]

In other words, the underlying objective of the New Monetary World Order should be that the economy will gradually evolve towards an economy where, world-wide, everyone, by means of his own "reasonable" labor efforts[37] will be able to cover his basic needs of life.

In such a "new economy", the here mentioned mechanism of credit provisioning to cover basic needs of life will, consequently, mainly serve to pre-finance certain larger expenses, such as the acquisition of a residence (*e.g.* a house or an apartment), or to overcome periods in which no sufficient income can be obtained through one's own labor efforts, albeit, in the latter case, access to public support

---

[35]Compare Pontifical Council for Justice and Peace (2005), no 336. See also the doctrine of Saint Thomas Aquinas on "the fair wage". (See above, at marg. 81 of Chap. 3. of this book.).

[36]As mentioned earlier, it is also from this reasoning that elsewhere in this book (see under Sect. 4.7.2.2 of Chap. 4. of this book) a new fiscal system has been advocated which aims at enabling also the poor(er) and middle classes to live a worthy life (a.o. by allowing them to also acquire some elementary assets).

[37]Whereby the word "reasonable" is referring to both a minimum of labor efforts which society can expect from every individual who is able to work and a maximum of labor efforts so that no human being would be the victim of exploitation mechanisms developed to make a limited elite richer and richer.

systems should make it possible to overcome at least certain objective difficult life circumstances (such as, obviously, illness).

43 In order to reconcile the objectives of, *on one hand*, establishing a level playing field of general wellbeing and, *on the other hand*, keeping in balance the global amount of money, it could be further considered that the monetary authorities would provide guidelines regarding the maximum amount of credit an individual will be able to of borrow in order to cover said basic needs of life.

Furthermore, the credit mechanism for providing basic life needs suggested here should, as mentioned earlier, not be considered as a "blank cheque". On the contrary, the mechanism should be applied in accordance with the overall policy goal of the NMWO to keep the global amount of money in control, as well as the aspiration to fulfill everyone's basic life needs, while taking into account the true reimbursement capacity of the borrower concerned, in addition to his continuous willingness to make efforts to have a sufficient income therefore by contributing to the development of society and its economy.

The guiding policy principle could hereby be that the credits for the benefit of general wellbeing will, in principle, need to be paid back effectively and in full, in light of the fact that the underlying objective of establishing a new monetary world order based upon altruism rather than on bankers' greed does not justify (too) easy money creation in its own turn implying that anyone who wants to benefit from the mechanism will in return need to make sufficient efforts to contribute to society. Such a (minimal) expectation translates into the principle that even the credits granted to individuals to meet basic life needs should effectively be reimbursed (whereby, as mentioned earlier, a discharging role of "force majeure" will only be applicable in case there is a true situation of such "force majeure", such as illness or another cause of inability to work, possibly in addition to other unfortunate circumstances which will be determined in objective NGSCB-directives and -guidelines).

44 A further element of reflection when establishing this credit system to cover for people's basic life needs could be that aiming for an absolute leveling, whereby everyone would be able to borrow the exact amount of money during the course of his life, will most probably have to be avoided.

On the contrary, it will be essential to find the correct balance for each individual between, *on one hand,* his (human) right to a decent life and, *on the other hand,* his willingness as candidate-credit taker to effectively develop his talents in a constructive way benefiting society as much as possible and from which an income can be derived that will make it possible to reimburse a credit that has been taken up.

For this reason also, the said credit mechanism will need to be based on keeping individual credit files per borrower (which, of course, will imply a large sense of responsibility by the staff of the new national central banks participating in the NGSCB; see above, at marg. 15 of this chapter).

45 A further question regarding the credits (of both categories) for provisioning basic needs of life, is whether or not they should be made revocable.

In this regard, the New Monetary World Order could, for instance, consider to establish credit monitoring and supervision mechanisms (fixed into transparent legal guidelines). These could, for instance, allow for an effective control of the agreed upon reimbursement obligation(s) which will make it possible to exercise a reasonable degree of rigor in the monitoring of the execution of the reimbursement obligations by the credit taker.

As indeed the underlying expectation of the NMWO should remain that everyone who is capable of providing labor,[38] will also demonstrate an acceptable degree of willingness to provide labor efforts in order to cover for his needs of life, this expectation should also apply to the effective reimbursement of money obtained by means of a credit granted by one's national central bank.

Sanction mechanisms could imply that those who do not succeed in doing so, other than through objective justifying factors, such as old age or health problems, would (temporarily) be banned from accessing credits to cover basic needs of life, among which the revocation or suspension of a credit that has earlier been granted.

When applicable, such persons could then have recourse to the public care system which, as mentioned before, will need to be established by the countries participating in the New Monetary World Order (see above, under Sect. 4.7.2.4 of Chap. 4 of this book). However, also as regards these public care systems, there should be a similar dynamic which will sufficiently encourage each individual to behave as a truly responsible member of society (at least as regards those individuals capable of doing so).

Nevertheless, the legal guidelines regarding (private) credits for covering basic needs of life should equally be based on a principle of (total or partial) abandonment of the reimbursement obligations in case of to-be-defined adverse life circumstances (a notion which will also need to be defined in objective terms). Hence, and differently from what is at present too much the case in the prevailing capitalist credit systems mainly provided by the private banking sector (but also by even more aggressive "loan sharks"[39]), a credit taker who gets hit by a similar unfortunate life event should as a result no longer be condemned to a life of eternal poverty (see the so-called "*condemned to stay poor*"-syndrome).

It is for these reasons that not only the granting of a credit to cover a basic life need, but also the monitoring of the credit files, will have to be based on a sufficiently personal approach. This approach should moreover find a proper balance between, *on one hand*, society's expectation that anyone, within reasonable limits, should in a productive way contribute to its development, also on an economic level, and, *on the other hand*, such person's freedom and individual preferences, as well as his "life course" (in its classical meaning of "*fortuna*").

As has been argued earlier (see above, under Sects. 4.7.3.2.2 and 4.7.3.2.3 of Chap. 4 of this book), under the regime of the NMWO, the possibility to provide **46**

[38]Taking into account (objective) factors such as age and health, in addition to other possible factors which could cause an impediment for participating as a productive member of society.

[39]See *e.g.* Loan Sharks. https://www.moneyadviceservice.org.uk/en/articles/how-to-spot-a-loan-shark. Last consulted on March 3th 2016.

"free of charge" credits to cover basic needs should preferably be the exclusive responsibility of the national central banks participating in the NGSCB.

In other words, these national central banks, operating as part of the NGSCB and therefore under the auspices of the NMWI, should be granted a "monopoly position" for granting such credits to the general public.

As has also been explained before, there hereby should preferably be assigned a credit manager among the members of the personnel of the national central bank to each citizen of any country participating in the NMWO. Said credit manager should hereby be made responsible for the granting and supervising of credits to cover basic life needs to the people assigned to him, whereby the role of such a credit manager could at the same time be one of a true "social economic life coach" (see above, at marg. 93 of Chap. 4 of this book).

47 If the here proposed system for NMWO-credits to cover for basic life needs were to be effectively installed,[40] the abovementioned "credit managers"/"life coaches" will obviously play a decisive role in the decision making processes regarding the allocation, supervision and management of the individual credits, as well as with regard to the suspension or occasional termination of said individual credits.

48 Given the fact that the "credit managers"/"social economic life coaches" (or stewards) will play a crucial role in the process of credit allocation (and through this: in the process of money creation in the global world economy), they will themselves need to be subjected to systems of accountability.

For instance, by means of appropriate systems of evaluation and supervision, accountability models could be worked out to ensure that an individual credit manager will not have a more than average acceptable number of defaulters (meaning "bad credits") in his portfolio.

5.2.4.3 Credit lending/Money Creation for the Benefit of the Nonprofit-Sector

49 As mentioned earlier (see above, under Sect. 4.7.2.2.4 of Chap. 4 of this book), a different steering role for the monetary authorities with regard to the so-called *nonprofit*-sector will also be at hand within the New Monetary World Order.

50 As explained before, it should be one of the main policy goals of the NMWO that the (national) authorities of its participating countries will, world-wide, be increasingly engaged in ensuring the general wellbeing of all their population.

Hence, the allocations in New World Currency which will periodically (for instance on a yearly basis) be granted to the (national) government of every participating country by the NMWI itself (see above, under Sect. 4.7.2 of Chap. 4 of this book), should, in principle, enable each of these governments to guarantee an

[40]Which would, obviously, imply that this would be agreed upon between the member states of the NMWO.

(internationally agreed upon) minimum of public services, among which health and other types of social care.

In such a new approach, the role of the national governments and the way these will be financed in future should normally result in a (gradual) decrease in the need for nonprofit organizations providing similar services of care, whereby it could even be expected that the existing nonprofit organizations would gradually be absorbed by the public administrations of the countries participating in the NMWO.

However, this process of "gradual" absorption by the public administrations of **51** nonprofit organizations which provide systems of care to the general public, should it ever be effectively enforced, will most probably be "a process of progressivity" whereby furthermore strong national differences are likely to occur.

Nevertheless, the proposal that is advocated here is one whereby the common thread in the overall NMWO-policy should, world-wide, be the pursuit of a mature government body in each country participating in the NMWO which will, henceforth, mainly be concerned with the general wellbeing of all humanity and which, moreover, should ensure that the need for private initiatives will gradually decrease (as these are, moreover, strongly dependent on public subsidies in many countries anyway).

As said, it is to be expected that such a process of replacing nonprofit organiza- **52** tions for general care by a mature government body which ultimately will be solely responsible for a full public services package will be a gradual process and that the (national) authorities of the participating countries in the NMWO will need to work out a time frame and thereby work out priorities.

Hence, if the re-orientation of the role of public authorities functioning within **53** the new monetary order proposed here is installed, this will not preclude the possibility that, at least during a transition period, in many countries there will remain a need for (partially) and temporarily preserving the nonprofit sector (see also above, at marg. 142–148 of Chap. 4 of this book).

As a consequence, it can be expected that general care nonprofit organizations which would, albeit temporarily, continue to exist, will continue to depend on their classical means of financing, such as government subsidies (henceforth to be attributed as a part of the new role of national governments functioning within the NMWO), private gifts or subsidies, and occasionally also credits.

Given the abovementioned considerations, it is furthermore proposed here that **54** the credit policy of the NGSCB as regards the nonprofit organizations which will (temporarily) continue to provide general care services, would, henceforth, also become one of the further tasks of the national central banks of the countries participating in the New Monetary World Order.

Also this policy should preferably be based on a transparent regulatory system, whereby, for instance, the basic policy goal(s),[41] would be laid down in the treaty (ies) governing the NMWO.

[41]Including the underlying objective that the nonprofit sector—to the extent that it is aimed at providing services contributing to the general wellbeing—would gradually be absorbed by the public administration in its renewed role.

Furthermore, the NMWI could be given the authority to design a general framework of guidelines or directives with regard to the organization and operation of the nonprofit sector in relation to the renewed role of the (national) authorities of the participating countries. Finally, the national central banks of the countries participating in the NGSCB could—in the context of their national credit lending policy—be given the authority to translate the aforementioned NMWI-guidelines or directives into practice under the form of national rules and regulations (based on the specific situation of their respective countries).

55 As is the case for the other "general wellbeing" credits mentioned before, it is furthermore proposed here that the credits to nonprofit organizations providing general care services could also, in principle, be of a "free of charge" nature, albeit a system of differentiation could be considered, whereby, for instance, the price for a credit (under the form of an interest charge) could be made dependent on the extent to which a nonprofit organization requesting for such a credit meets very basic general wellbeing needs, rather than needs of a more "luxurious" nature.

For instance, a nonprofit organization providing basic medical care could be considered to rank higher in contributing to the general wellbeing than a nonprofit organization supporting leisure activities.[42]

A concrete proposal to deal with such differentiation could be that the former organizations would be able to rely on credit from the national central bank of their country which would be completely "free of charge", whereby the latter would be given access to credit at a certain price (which could be higher for services considered to be of a more luxurious nature).

It should hereby, moreover, also be taken into consideration that, in the context of the here proposed New Monetary World Order, it is to be expected that an increasing importance should be given to the private support of socio-cultural projects through the earlier proposed system of fiscally promoted social cultural participation (see above, at marg. 92–93 of Chap. 4 of this book).

56 The further characteristics (including the so-called contract law "modalities") of the credits which the national central banks of the countries participating in the NMWO will be able to provide to specific nonprofit organizations which would continue to provide general welfare services will, in essence, not need to be different from the other types of credits for the benefit of the private sector serving objectives of general wellbeing.

Conclusively, such credits to nonprofit organizations which provide services of general wellbeing could be credits:

- which will be provided completely free of charge (or, on a case-by-case basis, at a very low interest rate[43]; see, for some further reflections on this topic, above at marg. 142–148 of Chap. 4 of this book);

---

[42]Without questioning the importance of topics such as sports, culture, youth care, etc., which can all be considered being valid ingredients of the concept "general wellbeing".

[43]Also here, negative interest rates could be thought of (for instance as regards non-profit associations handling the consequences of extraordinary events, such as a natural disaster, a famine or drought, etc.).

- which will in principle be subject to a reimbursement obligation;
- which will be subject to a sound monitoring by the national central bank providing the credit (amongst others: in order to verify if repayments are made effectively, timely and completely);
- Which, if appropriate, will be revocable in case of a breach of contract by the borrower.

For the remainder, it has not been considered relevant here to work out a fully 57
nuanced framework about the policy the NMWO should or could deploy towards the (future) nonprofit sector.

The above thoughts are only intended to offer some basic observations in this regard.

The eventual design of a more detailed public policy towards the nonprofit sector will obviously need to be part of the preparatory work in the event that the world community effectively wants to establish the New Monetary World Order (based on altruistic principles) proposed here.

5.2.4.4 Credit lending/Money Creation for the Benefit of the Business Sector (in a Broad Sense of the Word)

In the proposed New Monetary World Order, a fourth sublevel of private sector 58
money creation would consist of money creation for the benefit of so-called established businesses.

It goes without saying that a sufficiently differentiated approach towards, *on one* 59
hand, individuals who, starting from scratch, want to access to a professional activity (especially those who want to establish a new business) and, *on the other hand*, businesses who have successfully passed the growth phase, should be considered appropriate within the context of the New Monetary World Order proposed here (see also above, under Sect. 4.7.3.2.5 of Chap. 4 of this book).

An established business which successfully underwent its growing pains is indeed of a different nature than an individual wanting to start a professional activity from scratch.

For instance, such an established business will not only already occupy a part of the market, but it will, most probably, also be able to rely on, amongst others:

- a clear legal structure (for instance a company law form with, depending on the law governing it, may give access to all kinds of legal and other advantages stemming from this legal structure);
- a full staff (especially employees who are willing to work for (low) wages);
- a more or less fixed customer and supplier base;
- a high degree of knowledge and professionalism, in addition to access to appropriate legal protection mechanisms;
- ...

Furthermore, an established enterprise will, as it becomes more successful, very likely develop further into a mainly profit-driven market player itself.

Hence, it is evident that in the suggested New Monetary World Order, money creation for the benefit of such established businesses should be run in a different way than money creation for the benefit of individuals who are seeking access to a professional life (to cover their basic life needs).

60 In this context, it needs furthermore to be pointed out that, in the here proposed New Monetary World Order, so-called private banks should themselves, henceforth, also be considered as part of the (private) business sector.

Hence, when such private banks face their own (*ex ante*) credit needs, in the system proposed here, they should no longer enjoy any preferential treatment, and hence no longer be treated differently than the rest of the sector of "established (private) businesses".

Otherwise put, in the system proposed here, such private banks should no longer have access to preferential mechanisms of (*ex post*-)financing by the NGSCB to cover (temporarily self-created) deficits.

61 Credit lending by the national central banks of the countries participating in the NMWO to established enterprises could, in principle, through a widespread network of offices (see above, at marg. 15 of this chapter), be organized under the form of credits bearing interest.

The new monetary authorities could hereby even pursue a "differentiation" policy laid down in (sufficiently specific) guidelines, directives and regulations of the NGSCB, with as possible criteria:

- the size of the enterprise applying (in terms of turnover, number of staff, and other);
- its profitability;
- its market share (and the extent to which it faces competition);
- its pricing policy;
- the type of products or services it provides (and their impact on society in general);
- the extent to which the enterprise is or is not adopting certain ethical codes of conduct (for instance aimed at the correct handling of values other than the pursuit of profit on account of CEO's and shareholders);
- the actual behavior of the enterprise in practice;
- etc.

62 Also the credits to be provided to established businesses could furthermore be based on the principle that they should be applied for by the candidate-credit takers themselves.

As regards the application procedures, one could hereby moreover pursue a system (also to be embedded into guidelines, directives and regulations of the NGSCB) according to which the submission of at least applications of a more complex nature (for instance large or complex credits) should be formulated with the assistance of a private bank which thus could offer this type of assistance as a specialized service to its customers, namely other established businesses.

A further proposal could be to submit credit lending by the national central banks of the countries participating in the NMWO for the benefit of established (private) business enterprises, to conditions of an ethical nature.[44] 63

One could hereby work towards a sufficiently detailed regulatory framework (again based on a general framework of guidelines and directives issued by the NMWI, which could be further elaborated by means of executive directives from the national central bank of each of the countries participating in the NMWO) which would, hence, determine the specific conditions which an established business enterprise should fulfill in order to be eligible for a credit from its national central banking system.

These conditions should, obviously, be based on the underlying objectives of the New Monetary World Order themselves, ensuring that the private business sector itself would also gradually, albeit increasingly, become re-oriented towards a business environment primarily at the service of the general wellbeing of mankind (and of the planet), rather than mainly serving the unbridled pursuit of money of the capital providers and managers who drive it.

One could, for instance, consider some kind of "reward system" aimed at inviting the business world to voluntarily participate as much as possible in creating a more altruistic world, whereby, for instance, business enterprises which would participate to a higher extent to the objectives of the New Monetary World Order, would get access to cheaper credit than enterprises that would score lower in that domain.[45]

---

[44]Compare Pontifical Council for Justice and Peace (2005), no 338 a.f, a.o. holding:

> The Church's social doctrine has emphasized the contribution that [economic] activities make to enhance the value of work, to the growth of a sense of personal and social responsibility, a democratic life and the human values that are important for the progress of the market and of society. (Pontifical Council for Justice and Peace 2005, no 339).

[45]Again, the guidelines, directives and regulations of the NGSCB could set out the parameters to judge which business enterprises succeed best at developing an ethical behavior. It goes without saying that the working out of such parameters will have to be based on finding the right balance between the altruistic aims of the NMWO and the sustainability of the business sector itself, which will imply that the said parameters should be worked out in a sufficiently realistic way.

Accomplishing a more altruistically inspired business and economic environment will hereby, most probably, not be achieved overnight, but will rather be an end goal which will only be reached in a gradual way.

This insight again makes it very clear to what extent currently prevailing capitalism, which is mainly based on the principle of short-termism (especially on the principle that anyone should do whatever it takes to make as much possible profits for himself, regardless of the detrimental impact of his behavior on the rest of mankind, and on the wellbeing of the planet itself) and on the naïve belief that the world's problems will eventually all be solved by themselves (or, otherwise put, by the invisible hand guiding the free markets).

64 For the remainder, the credits to be provided to the established business sector should be credits:

- in which detailed reimbursement obligations are agreed upon;
- at a price (*ergo* against payment of interest);
- which are subject to a sound monitoring by the central national bank;
- Which, if appropriate, will be revocable in case of a breach of contract.

Once again, the NGSCB-directives, guidelines and regulations could provide more detailed rules on the different types of modalities and conditions these credits could be subject to.

5.3 Collection of Deposits and Organization of the Basic Payments

5.3.1 Deposit Services as a Task of the New National Central Banks

65 As explained earlier (see above, at Chap. 2), especially since the Middle Ages, the so-called "deposit function" regarding money has, first in the Western world and from there practically on a global scale, (mainly) been in the hands of private banks.

66 Roughly stated, the archetype of the "deposit function" consists of the collection, by the private banks (and similar financial institutions), of the surpluses of cash money which are not immediately spent by economic agents, in order to safe keep it.

Economic agents who dispose of cash money that they do not immediately spend for their immediate needs can deal with this in different ways.

Such economic agents can, obviously, keep their saved money themselves in a safe place, a method which, from a historical perspective entails high risks (including the risk of theft, robbery, but also: the risk of accidental destruction, for instance through a fire, a flood...); as an alternative, they can also involve a third party to hold it for them.

As has been elaborated in a more detailed way in Chap. 2 of this book, it is this latter referred to method that lies at the very basis of the "modern bank" as it has been shaped in the (late) Middle Ages.

Hence, the deposit function was, historically, in essence a service provided by a professional depository to a person who wishes to safely deposit a valuable resource (*in casu* cash money).

From an economic perspective, one could hence even expect that the person rendering this service would charge a payment for it.[46]

---

[46]This insight to some extent translates in the modern-day "negative interest"-debate.

However, throughout the ages, the deposit function has gradually evolved in such a way that, albeit its classical function of "preserving" cash money has not entirely disappeared, it has somewhat been relegated to the background. 67

Indeed, after an evolutionary process that took centuries (and of which the main steps have been dealt with in Chap. 2 of this book), the deposit function became a so-called "mixed contract". The classic aspiration of depositing cash (coins and paper money) in a safe way has in this "mixed contract" remained but one of the possible subject matters. The "modern" deposit contract usually also covers several other functions, such as the management of scriptural money (after it has emerged either from a mutation of cash money that has been deposited, from a wiring of money by a third party, or from credit lending by the bank leading to newly created scriptural money), as well as the provision of different scriptural payment methods.

As furthermore the cash reserves of a banker, at least partially, determine his capacity to create new scriptural money (in a "monetary safe way"), commercial practice has evolved in such a way that giving money in deposit has become rewardable (albeit that since the crisis of 2008 this type of compensation has generally become very low[47]).

Through this evolution, the focus of the deposit function has partially shifted from (originally) a true "deposit" (whereby it is generally agreed upon that the "depositor" will pay a fee to the "depository"[48]), to (currently) a simple method of saving or investing (whereby it is generally agreed upon that the bank owes a modest fee to the depositor), in combination with an access to organized[49] (scriptural) payment systems.

In many countries, there even exist legal measures vesting several privileges in the field of deposit collection and the organization of scriptural payments to the private banking sector; for instance, within the European Communities, the banking sector has even been given a monopoly on the general collection of deposits.[50] 68

Although precise and up-to-date numbers on this matter have not been found, one can but imagine that the organization of the prevailing deposit collecting and scriptural payment system(s) amounts to a high cost for the banking sector. 69

Indeed, the organization of the deposit and payment system plays on different levels, such as organizing a specialized and secured informatics network (through which scriptural transfers and bank payment techniques can take place); installing clearing and netting systems aimed at retaining the mutual positions (between private banks), in addition to safe cash transport in order to provide bank terminals

[47]It has to be remarked that the opinion that deposits should bear "negative interests" is gaining field. In reality, the charging of negative interests on a deposit account basically comes down to charging a price for receiving (and "safeguarding") the deposited money.

[48]It has been reported that, during the seventeenth century, "de Amsterdamse Wisselbank" played a pioneer's role in this regard; see *e.g.* Van Houtte (e.a.) (eds) (1953), p. 93; Beaud (1994), p. 30.

[49]By the collectivity of private banks, or, otherwise put, by "the banking system".

[50]See above, at marg. 83 of Chap. 2 of this book.

and offices with the needed amounts of cash (i.a. in order to meet cash withdrawals from bank depositors).

70 It is to be suspected that the willingness of the private banking sector to, up till today, continue to bear the cost of organizing the deposit and scriptural payment system can at least partly be explained by the fact that the collection of deposits leads to cash reserves, that these cash reserves themselves enable (private) banks to create scriptural money based on their credit activity, and that it is mainly through the latter activity (as well as through financial products derived from, or based upon, such credits) that private banks generate (a major part of) their profits.

71 In accordance with the proposals made in the Chap. 4 and this chapter for a new global and altruistic monetary system, the private banking sector should no longer have the possibility to privately create (scriptural) money.

On the contrary, it has been proposed to assign money creation (and the additional tasks of controlling the global amount of money brought into circulation) resolutely, and on an exclusive basis, to the (new) monetary authorities (namely the NMWI and the NGSCB), with explicit exclusion of the private (banking) sector itself.

It goes without much further saying that in such a new monetary system, the private banking sector would not gain much from retaining the deposit function. On the contrary, within the new monetary world order, this task could—in addition to the tasks of certain of the abovementioned types of credit lending—henceforth be considered as a task of general wellbeing, an observation which in its own turn leads to the conclusion that this task should also better be performed by the national central banks participating in the NGSCB.

Hence, bringing new money into circulation, as well as the organization of, *on one hand*, methods of safekeeping and managing this money, and, *on the other hand*, the main function of money, namely its payment function, would in the interest of everyone—and therefore as a so-called "*public good*"—, rightly be considered as tasks to be assigned to (a) public entity (ies) which is (are) not driven by market principles.

Only in this way will it be possible to ensure that money creation by the monetary authorities, would, henceforth, decisively be decoupled from the speculative behavior which characterizes the private banking sector.

5.3.2 Further Technical Details About the Deposit Task of the NGSCB

72 The new model of organizing deposits and basic payments proposed here will on a practical level imply that every resident of a country participating in the NMWO should be able to open one (or more) deposit account(s) with the national central bank of this country for the purpose of managing his money and basic payment

transactions. Such deposit accounts held with the national central banks should be free of charge, but should also not merit any interests.

A further proposal would be that the processes of (national) money creation by a given national central bank participating in the NGSCB for the benefit of the private sector (in accordance with the abovementioned parameters to be defined by the NMWI), would run through these (deposit) accounts opened with the central national bank, ensuring that any money creation for the private sector, whether created for the benefit of a private individual or a for an (established) business enterprise, would lead to a booking on such an account. From such an account, its holder would then have further access to basic payment transactions, amongst which, at least to the extent that (and as long as) the new monetary order keeps the concept of "physical money", the possibility of a classical cash withdrawal, in addition to the possibility of transferring money through wiring and electronic transactions.

Furthermore, the national (and other) authorities of any country participating in the NMWO should, obviously, also be given the possibility to open one or more accounts with the national central bank of their country. **73**

As a result, a basic allocation from the NMWI to a given country (see above, under Sect. 4.7.2 of Chap. 4 of this book) could, henceforth, be booked on such a central account (or a set of such accounts) held by that country.

From such a central account, there could subsequently be a further dispatching of the allocation received by a country for the benefit of its several (decentralized and/or local) authorities, to accounts held by each of these "decentralized" and/or "local" authorities; besides, the central authorities will, furthermore, be able to organize all other payments from this central account.

Otherwise put, the national governments of the countries participating in the NMWO should have equal access to the new deposit and payment systems to be organized by their respective national central banks, in a similar way as that granted to the private sector.

In addition to this basic deposit and payment system to be organized by the national central banks of the countries participating in the NMWO, there should be no impediment that also the private banking sector could continue to offer (other) deposit and payment services of a more specialized nature to its customers. **74**

Otherwise put, the national central banks participating in the NGSCB should not necessarily hold a monopoly position as regards the organization of deposit and payment mechanisms, except as regards the receiving of allocation payments by the NWMI which should at all time happen through (an) account(s) held by the participating countries with their national central banks, and as regards the payment of credits granted by a national central bank to any private person which should also happen through an account held by such a private person with the national central bank of his country.

In this way, under the deposit and payment system of the NMWO, everyone should also be able to, in addition to the account (or possibly several accounts) held with the national central bank, open one (or more) account(s) with a private bank, which could, for instance, be advisable in order to optimize specialized financial services provided by the private banking sector (such as (specialized) credits, investment services, etc.), but also to provide for more complex payment services for the private sector, especially for large enterprises and the like.

5.3.3 Parenthesis: Physical Appearance of the New Global Currency

75 Within the New Monetary World Order, there will most probably also be a need for further reflection about the physical appearance of money.

76 Throughout history, money has had the most different material appearances, from shells found on the shore, metal spits (see in classic Greece the so-called "*oboloí*") which were used to roast poultry, salt, metal coins in all possible shapes and forms, animal hides, cigarettes to, in present days, electronic bits representing a claim on a private bank or another private entity.

Today, as explained in more detail in the second Chapter of this book, in most countries, a combination prevails of so-called "cash" or "chartal" money (mostly issued by authorities in the broad sense of the word, including monetary authorities, and which (mostly) exists in the physical form of coins and/or bank notes), and so-called "scriptural" money (which consists of receivables[51] towards a private bank or another financial institution).

In the recent history of money, several variants of the aforementioned formats of money have emerged, for instance so-called "electronic money" in the shape of electronic data which allow for electronic payment transactions through plastic cards, through the internet or even through other communication devices, such as smartphones (as an alternative to coins and bank notes).

77 Hence, as regards the physical appearance of money, it needs to be observed that under the working of the NMWO, there will be no absolute need to maintain any specific form of money in its current forms.

78 Thus, the NMWI, when implementing the aforementioned concept for a new global monetary system, could work out a policy aiming at ultimately having money only on accounts, whereby, for instance, every world citizen would have a (simple) electronic device (possibly a smartphone) at his disposal, which, according to the principles of a permanent online operation, would allow all possible payment transactions.[52]

---

[51]Usually expressed in a banking account.

[52]Compare Wolman (2014), referring to Björn Ulvaeus plea for a cash-free society, especially for considerations of safety (among which the diminishing of street violence):

> The outgoing head of Sveriges Riksbank, Sweden's central bank, has argued for years that society has been cheated by cash for too long, thanks to security, transportation, and production expenses, as well as less-direct costs such as tax evasion. Meanwhile, a number of local startups are pushing new ways to pay, or otherwise bypass the need for cash. There

Otherwise put, there could be aimed for creating a global monetary order based upon fully fledged "electronic/scriptural money".

In the present era, where all imaginable mobile electronic devices which allow an endless variety of data exchange systems have conquered the world for all types of purposes (presently, bearing in mind that capitalism relies on numerous so-called "*created wants*", the most "idiotic" the first), it should be beyond doubt that the technology needed to fine-tune a similar type of device allowing all types of (electronic) money transactions can be considered of being within reach. **79**

It even appears that this technology is already available (see for instance certain developments of "*Apple*"[53]), albeit perhaps not yet available on a global scale.

Certain press reports have even indicated that for instance in Kenya, a simple and widely used electronic payment system (the so-called "M-pesa"-payment system) has in recent times already become the dominant payment system.[54]

Hence, all that seems to be needed to further develop this technology into a standardized global network enabling all (global) payment traffic to take place electronically, is the necessary (political) goodwill to make this happen.

Given the policy goals of the NMWO proposed here, this goodwill should easily take shape in the context of the NMWO, and especially as regards the deposit and payment system to be developed under its guidance.

The many advantages of a cash free society may be obvious. **80**

Money that would only exist on accounts will, by definition, be much more "traceable", which could be beneficial for many policy objectives, such as the fight

---

> is banking startup Tink, which already has more than 200,000 users and has no real-world presence. A consortium of the country's major banks launched a service called Swish that enables real-time transfer between accounts; in less than two years they have drawn 1.7 million customers. And payments service IZettle, sometimes referred to as the Square of Europe, is one of the fastest-growing companies on the continent.

[53]Higgins and Dexheimer (2014), Brustein (2014). See also Sury and Racquet (2014), p. 38.

[54]See Graeber (2014), mentioning that in Kenya electronic money has already become the dominant money form:

> It is Safaricom's version of mobile money that has become common currency in Kenya. The company grew out of Kenyan Posts & Telecommunications, the former state monopoly, and has been publicly traded since 2002. It introduced M-pesa in 2007, and people now make about 80 billion shillings in monthly M-pesa transactions and move more than 130 billion shillings in and out of the mobile system via 45,000 independent agents throughout the country.
>
> M-pesa took off almost instantly because it made it safer for Kenyans to send money home (instead of having cash carried by a cousin, say, on a bus prone to breakdowns, traffic accidents, and theft) and because M-pesa on a SIM card allowed millions of Kenyans without a bank account to become their own personal ATMs, especially appealing to farmers between harvests. If a Kenyan didn't have a phone, she could simply borrow one; all she needed was a SIM card to be in business.

against fraud, organized crime and (international) terrorism, but also the fight against (minor) offences (for instance street theft).[55]

Provided that the electronic systems on which the cashless society would be based, could be sufficiently secured, money could also be better protected against counterfeiting.

A cashless society could also serve several fiscal purposes, and, more generally, within the new monetary order proposed in this book, the objective of optimally managing the credit and assets files of the world's citizens under the operation of the NGSCB (see above, at marg. 93 of Chap. 4 of this book and marg. 47–48 of this chapter).

81 To the extent that, for instance due to a difference in the level of technological development between the countries participating in the NMWO, maybe not all countries will be ready at the same time for the introduction of the exclusive "(electronic) money on accounts" proposed here, one could consider of relying upon transitional measures.

The countries participating in the NMWO could, for instance, be temporarily divided into different zones: the exclusive system of (electronic) money on accounts could hereby immediately be introduced in the countries which will be up to the challenge of such immediate introduction, while a mixed system, characterized by a (temporary) coexistence of (electronic) money on accounts and cash money, could on a temporary basis prevail in the countries where the level of technological development would be considered to be too low to introduce overnight the exclusive system of (electronic) money on accounts. If such a temporary system of dividing the countries participating in the NMWO into two zones would be deemed necessary, there will obviously be a need for systems guiding the payment transactions between (residents of) the countries from the two types of zones.

Notwithstanding the foregoing, in the long run, one should aim at realizing one type of money (which only will exist on accounts) for the entire NMWO. Hence, it should be the intention that, when the NMWO is introduced, a (strict) time schedule to finally establish a cashless monetary system on a global scale will already have been agreed upon.

82 The plea for a complete "dematerialization" of money should, however, be read together with the other proposals made in this book regarding the overall establishment of a new monetary world order.

Indeed, if a complete dematerialization of money would already be established in the context of the current monetary landscape whereby money is mainly the product of the credit policy of the private banking sector, this would subsequently give the private banking sector even more free rein in the field of money creation (and through this, in the control of the economy), which is, obviously, not desirable at all.

[55]See Wolman (2014).

In the current monetary context, the need to dispose of sufficient amounts of cash money in order to be able to meet the demands of depositors exchanging their receivables into cash, is precisely one of the main techniques by means of which the monetary authorities (especially the central banks) can at least still exhibit some control over the total amount of money brought into circulation, and hence over the supply of money into the economy.

If, on the contrary, cash money were to be abolished in the present monetary system, otherwise put: without the processes of money creation (especially the creation of scriptural money based on credits to the private sector) being exclusively entrusted to the monetary authorities (namely, in the to be established NMWO: the NMWI and, by extension, the NGSCB), then one of the main brakes on private money creation by the banking sector would disappear, thus leaving the world economy even more at the mercy of the greed, vagaries and mismanagement of the private banking system.[56]

To summarize: taking the aforementioned elements into consideration, the plea **83**
for an integral dematerialization of money proposed here only holds to the extent that the other here proposed changes to the monetary system also take place, thus, on condition that money creation, as a "public good", is allocated to (a) public authority (ies), more precisely, under the proposals set out here, to the NMWI (and by extension the NGSCB).

5.4 Further Metamorphosis of the Private Banking Sector

5.4.1 Avoidance of Interference with the Tasks of the NMWI/NGSCB

It should be obvious that, under the "New Monetary World Order" proposed in this **84**
book, not only the (national) authorities and the national central banks of the countries participating in this NMWO should be fundamentally transformed, but also the private banking system itself.

The proposals drafted so far with regard to the New Monetary World Order **85**
would indeed imply that certain types of financial service provisioning which, on a global scale, are currently (mainly) offered by private banks, would henceforth be entrusted to bodies operating in the public sphere, namely the new to-be-established world monetary authorities (being, in addition to the NMWI itself, the national central banks participating in the NGSCB).[57]

[56]It seems hereby hardly necessary to repeat once more that during each monetary and/or financial crisis, mankind has already witnessed a small foretaste of the abuses a too uncontrolled system of unbridled money creation by the private banking sector may lead to.

[57]Compare Smithers (2013), p. 95.

This "transfer" of tasks from the private to the public (authority) sphere would particularly, in light of the previously made proposals, need to occur in:

- Primarily, the deposit function and the organization of (scriptural and/or electronic) payment systems based on it;
- Secondly, different types of credit lending to the private sector (see above, under Sect. 4.7.3 of Chap. 4 of this book).

Under the New Monetary World Order, there would, furthermore, no longer be any need for credit lending by private banks (and similar financial institutions) to governments, supranational entities or other public authorities (as, in the system proposed here, all these authorities would, henceforth, obtain their operational funds exclusively from periodic allocations from the NMWI; see above, under Sect. 4.7.2 of Chap. 4 of this book).

86 Presently, the set of tasks mentioned at marg. 85 of this chapter are in most (Western and Western inspired) countries, performed by the private banking sector, but would, under the New Monetary World Order, henceforth be assigned to the monetary authorities, more precisely to the NMWI and to the national central banks participating in the NGSCB (the latter themselves operating under the auspices of the NMWI).

87 It has already been explained earlier in this text that, as regards credit lending to the private sector for the general wellbeing, the national central banks participating in the NGSCB should in that context be granted a true monopoly position, implying that such credits (resulting in new money creation) should only be granted by these national central banks.

88 From the foregoing, it may already also be clear that as regards the deposit mechanism, the organization of payment systems (based upon the deposit mechanism) and credit lending for the benefit of private individual entities for other reasons than the general welfare, there will not be a similar need for a true monopoly of the monetary authorities of the NMWO.

89 Hence, in addition to these monetary authorities themselves (especially the national central banks of the countries participating in the NGSCB), the private banking sector could also still (be allowed to) perform deposit and payment services and to grant credits against interest (for instance: to other established business enterprises), provided that the latter credits are exclusively based upon existing funds, and not on the creation of new money. This latter requirement will help to ensure that the private banking sector will align its spending and investment behavior with true and completely "*ex ante*" valuable assets (financed through equity capital, or through credit investments by third parties in advance), in other words, without being able to rely on the possibility of new money creation (and the associated mechanisms of "*ex post*" financial support from the monetary authorities).

On the contrary, as has also been explained earlier in this book, the credits to be provided by the national central bank of a given country participating in the NMWO, will themselves be based on their competence to create new money, and this both with regard to the free credits to be granted to private individuals (or entities) for the general wellbeing, as well as the credits at interest for other purposes (for instance credits to established business enterprises) (see above, under Sect. 4.7.3 of Chap. 4 of this book and at marg. 34 a.f. of this chapter).

As a consequence, the national central bank of such a country participating in the NMWO will be able to control the amount of money (and hence the "demand side" of the economy) in a far more profound way than is possible under the current monetary system.

For instance, if a sufficient amount of money is available in the economy, a high central interest rate on non-general-welfare credits could encourage the private sector (enterprises, in addition to other organizations to whom interest will still be charged) not to take up credit from the national central bank (but rather from the private markets based upon money already available). Contrarily, should there occur a shortage of money (or a need for stimulating economic growth), a lowering of the central interest rates could encourage the private individual sector to take out interest-bearing credits from its national central bank.

Under the NMWO, these processes will obviously need to be in accord with the underlying monetary objectives of the New Monetary World Order, namely establishing a world economy which, above all, serves the general wellbeing—instead of, as is currently the case, mainly the interests of a small (financial) elite, especially the shareholders, directors and managers of private banks and other (big) enterprises—, while at the same time taking into account the (limited) capacity of the planet (considered from an intergenerational perspective) (see above, Chap. 4, under the description of the "Pillar II" of the NMWO in Sect. 4.3.).

5.4.2 Some Further Reflections on the Appearance of the Private Banking System Operating Under the NMWO

5.4.2.1 General

The complete transfer of the task of (free) credit lending to the private sector for purposes of general wellbeing, leading to the creation of new money, for the monetary authorities, will necessarily have to be accompanied by a thorough metamorphosis of the private banking sector itself (which, under the prevailing monetary system, still fulfills this task, albeit under the form of credits at interest). **90**

5.4.2.2 Consequences in the Field of the Origin of the Means of Financing of Private Banks

One of the main consequences of the transfer of the tasks referred to at marg. 87 of **91**
this chapter will be that the private banks will henceforth no longer be involved in

the processes of money creation, so consequently there will be no more need for a protective statute in order to secure this participation to money creation.

In other words,[58] under the NMWO system, private banks should no longer have the possibility to rely on credit lending (and "chartal" money creation) from their monetary authority, which in the prevailing capitalist monetary order is mainly a safeguard mechanism in order to protect their own participation in the processes of "scriptural" money creation.

On the contrary, under the NMWO, private banks will henceforth need to generate their operational funds in the same way as other private enterprises, namely by raising equity capital or obtaining credit on the private markets, and they will furthermore need to ensure (in the same way as all other private market players) that they dispose of sufficient such funds "*ex ante*", hence before making their own investment decisions.

A further advantage of the foregoing system will probably also be that it will encourage the private banks to adopt a much more careful spending behavior as, henceforth, the operation of any private bank will be based on collected funds, and not on the unbridled possibility to create new money "out of nothing".

Otherwise put: it is to be expected that the self disciplinary behavior of private banks under the NMWO would become much more in line with that of all other private market players: at an "internal" level (especially in order to secure the equity capital which has been collected through the efforts of private capital providers), as well as at an "external" level (through the supervision of third-party creditors).

5.4.2.3 Consequences as Regards the Spending and Investment Behavior of Private Banks and as Regards the Regulatory Framework Regulating this Spending and Investment Behavior

92 In addition to the change in the way private banks will have to finance their activities, there will also be a need for a thorough metamorphosis in the field of the spending and investment behavior of the private banks, hence as regards their activities and the risks related to them.

As explained above (see above, at marg. 91 of this chapter), under the NMWO, private banks (and similar financial institutions) will henceforth, in the same way as all other private enterprises within the economy, only be able to function through funds collected from (private) capital providers (= equity capital), respectively (private) credit lenders in the broad sense of the word.

In this new system, the savings surplus of the general population will no longer automatically flow to the cash reserves of the private banking system, in light of the abovementioned proposal that, under the NMWO, the general deposit function will

[58] As has been mentioned earlier (see above, the description of the "Vth Pillar" under Sect. 4.7 of Chap. 4 of this book).

no longer be fulfilled by the private banks themselves, but by the national central banks participating in the NGSCB.

Henceforth, the so-called "prudential concern" implying that the private banking sector needs to be protected by the legal system more than average, which in many Western (and Western inspired) countries lies at the basis of a complex set of (prudential) rules and regulations which a.o. aim at protecting the deposit function of the private banking system, will in this regard become fully obsolete.

Within the proposed NMWO, both the deposit function and the function of new money creation will, under the conditions explained above, "largely" be entrusted to the national central banks partaking in the NGSCB. These national central banks will perform these duties for the general wellbeing and without any motive of profit pursuit, which already in itself will help ensure that the protection of these functions will be run in a much better, more transparent and legally secured way through the rules and regulations organizing the operation of the NGSCB itself (including the NMWI and the national central banks participating in it).

In other words, under the operation of the NMWO, the aforementioned pruden- **93**
tial concern towards private banks will no longer be as relevant as it is under the prevailing monetary and financial system.

Hence, there will also no longer be a need for a strongly detailed prudential legal framework (including extensive mechanisms of private banking supervision) to which the private banking sector is subject today (as moreover, during the past decade(s), strong questions have been raised as regards the effectiveness of these prevailing prudential law systems).

Otherwise put, in a society where the unbridled pursuit of profit in general, and through this the concept of (capital) investments in return for (high) profit expectations especially, will no longer be a sanctifying dictate, there will be also a lesser need for a vast set of legal rules protecting this type of practice.

The underlying principle of the NMWO as regards capital or similar investments could in the future even become that those who still aim at becoming rich from capital or similar investments, will still have this possibility, at least, within the parameters set out by the new fiscal order of the NMWO (which, as mentioned earlier (see above, under Sect. 4.7.2.3.2 of Chap. 4 of this book), should in the future be mainly aimed at fair income distribution among all people), but henceforth only at their own risk.

Consequently, under the NMWO, private banks (and similar financial institu- **94**
tions) will be able to expand their activities, including their investment portfolios, at their own discretion and without being hindered by a complex (and barely effective) legal system of prudential and similar regulations, albeit also completely at their own risk and no longer to the detriment of society as a whole.

Moreover, provided that these private banks do not enter the domains exclusively reserved for the national central banks (among which, as explained above: the (basic) deposit function for the general public, the installation of the basic payment systems, as well as the mechanisms of credit lending leading to money creation for the general wellbeing), they will, in future, be able to offer and/or execute all (other) types of investment activities in a more lenient way than under the prevailing financial law system. As it is expected from all other participants within the economy, it will hereby also be expected from the private banks that they will in this regard act in a sufficiently self-disciplined way.

When, still guided by the spirit of (unbridled) pursuit of profit, they want to take high risks, private banks can be allowed to do so without there being a special need for complex legal systems to regulate such hazardous activities, provided that each time the risks involved effectively become manifest, they will remain entirely their own responsibility (and, ultimately, that of their capital providers and/or creditors).

95 A consequence of this new kind of reasoning regarding to banking behavior will, obviously, be that private banks would become completely subject to the principles of the free market which they already claim to adhere and of which they are themselves among the most predominant advocates (except when they are themselves in need, as is the case in times of financial crises, in which case they are among the first to shout for financial support in order to be able to survive).

Henceforth, private banks (and other financial institutions) could also be allowed to go bankrupt according to the principles of general insolvency law, by which the risks of such bankruptcies would be the ultimate responsibility of the capital providers, and where it will no longer be possible to pass these risks on to the rest of society.[59]

Otherwise put, the so-called "*too big to fail*"–paradigm which is in the prevailing private banking system—given the key role of private banks as regards the collection of deposits, the organization of payment traffic and the creation of new scriptural money—, constantly hanging above the head of society like the proverbial "sword of *Damocles*", will also forever become a thing of the past.

Under the NMWO, private banks (and similar financial institutions) could, in other words, henceforth be subjected to the purifying effects of the free market, and this in full accordance with the way in which the private banks (and similar financial institutions) adhere to the free market principles regarding their unbridled pursuit of profit.

In other words, under the NMWO, private banks will not only enjoy the principle of "*privatization of gains*", but will also become subject to the principle of "*privatization of losses*".

96 Also as regards the protection of private individual investors, the NMWO could in the same way adhere to the principle that any person who wants to build income from a capital investment should be able to continue to do this, albeit completely at his own risk.

---

[59]See also Smithers (2013), p. 88:

> As It is very important for the health of the economy that financial companies should be allowed to go bankrupt, it has become all the more important that no financial company should be "too big to fail".

Indeed, under the NMWO, there should be a shift from legally protecting capital and capital providers towards emphasizing the legal protection of labor and labor providers, as the latter is indeed the method trough which any person should be able to create a decent and dignified life. The overall aim of this labor protection should even be that there will be no more room for any mechanisms for acquiring huge personal wealth by shamelessly exploiting the labor of others.

Henceforth, under the NMWO, law as a system will mainly need to ensure that every human being, through the supply of labor, will be able to primarily establish a civilized life for himself (and his family), but should no longer provide special protection towards investment activities in general.

For those who, within the New Monetary World Order, still want to risk getting rich through saving or investing systems,[60] the law could satisfy itself by providing basic protection in a similar way to that which some countries nowadays provide to those who walk into a casino hoping to make fortune by gambling. As regards both types of practices, it could be enough to apply a policy of warning (comparable to the warning policy on the use of tobacco), and the role of the law could be limited to this.[61]

Hence, the legal systems of the countries participating in the NMWO will no longer need to call special attention to the potential devastating effects of certain forms of financial behavior, nor put their efforts into devising a complex legal system in order to regulate such financial behavior.

Otherwise put, there will no longer be a need to develop complex financial law systems (which ultimately, at a high cost to society, only serve the interests of a financial elite driven by an unbridled pursuit of money), for deploying a financial supervisory system (which, in the prevailing financial law system, is even so very expensive to society, has more often than not shown to be ineffective and which, so far, has proven in the past not to be able to detect real monetary and financial problems before their effects fully manifest themselves), nor for making available a legal system where complaints from investors who feel cheated, could be heard.

In this way, society will be provided with an enormous saving in the area of the **97**
creation of rules and regulations for the protection of financial institutions and/or the savings system in the broad sense of the word (which is mainly aimed at securing the interests of a limited financial elite), and will, on the contrary, be able to focus on legislation dealing with the organization and the operation of the national central banking system (which will serve the general welfare of the entire global population).

---

[60]For an intriguing report on how the financial sector in this regard operates, see e.g. van der Slikke (2013), p. 254.

[61]Compare Krugman (2012), p. 97.

References

Beaud M (1994) Geschiedenis van het kapitalisme van 1500 tot heden. Het Spectrum (Aula), Utrecht

Brustein J (2014) How Apple Can Make Mobile Wallets Actually Work. http://www.businessweek.com/articles/2014-09-05/how-apples-iphone-6-can-finally-make-mobile-payments-happen. Last consulted 29 Oct 2014

Byttebier K (2001) Handboek financieel recht. Kluwer Rechtswetenschappen, Antwerp

Chomsky N (1999) Profit over People. Neoliberalism and global order. Seven Stories Press, New York

De Rynck F, Verschuere B, Wayenberg E (eds) (2009) Re-thinking the state – critical perspectives on the citizen, politics and government in the 21st century. Wolters Kluwer Belgium, Mechelen

Devos A, Bouteca N, Van Lieferinge H, Lannoo S (2009) Democracy, parties and representation: a complex and dynamic triangle. In: De Rynck F, Verschuere B, Wayenberg E (eds) Re-thinking the state – critical perspectives on the citizen, politics and government in the 21st century. Wolters Kluwer Belgium, Mechelen, pp 15–40

Dohmen J (1999) Europese idealisten – Vraag niet hoe het kan, profiteer ervan. Sun, Nijmegen http://m.hln.be/hln/m/nl/957/Binnenland/article/detail/2088210/2014/10/13/EU-parlementairen-krijgen-samen-tot-18-miljoen-euro-bovenop-loon.dhtml?originatingNavigationItemId=1. Last consulted 13 Oct 2014

Friedman M (1993) Why government is the problem. Hoover institution on war, revolution and peace. Stanford University, Stanford

Galbraith JK (1992) The culture of contentment. Houghton Mifflin Company, Boston

Galbraith JK (1996) The good society – the Humane Agenda. Houghton Mifflin Company, Boston

Graeber C (2014) Ten Days in Kenya With No Cash, Only a Phone. http://www.businessweek.com/articles/2014-06-05/safaricoms-m-pesa-turns-kenya-into-a-mobile-payment-paradise. Last consulted 29 Oct 2014

Higgins T, Dexheimer E (2014) American Express and Visa Love Apple Pay. Will Consumers? http://www.businessweek.com/articles/2014-10-23/apple-pay-partners-with-american-express-visa-card-networks. Last consulted 29 Oct 2014

Kasser T (2002) The high price of materialism. A Bradford Book – The MIT Press, Cambridge

Krugman P (2012) End this depression now! W.W. Norton & Company, New York

Oxfam (2014) Even it up – time to end extreme inequality. Oxfam GB, Oxford

Pettifor A (2014) The power to 'create money out of thin air'. https://www.opendemocracy.net/ourkingdom/ann-pettifor/power-to-create-money-out-of-thin-air. Last consulted 18 Nov 2014

Pontifical Council for Justice and Peace (2005) Compendium of the Social Doctrine of the Church (to His Holiness Pope John Paul II Master of Social Doctrine and Evangelical Witness to Justice and Peace). Bloomsbury, London, New Dehli, New York and Sydney. http://www.vatican.va/roman_curia/pontifical_councils/justpeace/documents/rc_pc_justpeace_doc_20060526_compendio-dott-soc_en.html

Quid J (2014) Tom Staal trekt rioolput EU open: Straatsburg. http://www.geenstijl.nl/mt/archieven/2013/06/tom_staal_trekt_de_rioolput_eu.html. Last consulted 18 Dec 2014

Rand A (2008) Capitalism: the unknown ideal. New American Library (a division of Penguin Group), New York

Sachs J (2011) The price of civilization: reawakening American virtue and prosperity. Random House, New York

van der Slikke P (2013) Ontmaskerd. Hoe de financiële wereld echt werkt. Einstein Books, Den Haag

Smithers A (2013) The road to recovery. Wiley, Chichester

Stiglitz J (2012) The price of inequality. Allen Lane (an imprint of Penguin Books), London

Sury C, Racquet E (2014) Stop een portemonnee in uw mobieltje. De Tijd, 29 November 2014

Umbach AG, Wessels W (2008) The changing European context of economic and Monetary Union: 'Deepening', 'Widening' and 'Stability'. In: Dyson K (ed) The Euro at 10 – Europeanization, power, and convergence. Oxford University Press, Oxford, pp 54–68
Van Houtte JA (a.o.) (eds) (1953) Algemene geschiedenis der Nederlanden t.VI. Standaard Boekhandel, Utrecht and Antwerp
Veldman H, Parlevliet P (2003) Spierballentaal en cowboylaarzen. Reagan, Bush I en Bush II in de context van het Amerikaanse conservatisme. Uitgeverij Aspekt, Soesterberg
Wolman D (2014) An ABBA Star's Campaign for a 100% Cash-Free Sweden. http://www.businessweek.com/articles/2014-10-28/abbas-bj-rn-ulvaeus-does-his-part-to-make-sweden-cashless?hootPostID=d5834153339802aa0e1fb8005cb3c01d. Last consulted 29 Oct 2014
Zilioli C, Selmayr M (2001) The law of the European Central Bank. Portland Oregon, Oxford

Chapter 6
Concluding Reflections

The research undertaken in the previous Chaps. 4 and 5 as to how a new (global) monetary system based on (more) altruistic principles might look is basically, albeit limited to the monetary and financial domain,[1] also the result of a search for a better balance between the public and the private sphere. 1

Money, as the generally accepted means of payment within the global economy, should hereby be considered to be in everyone's interest, hence a true "*public good*". 2

Although this insight is far from new as, throughout history, many prominent thinkers and statesmen have expressed similar ideas, there has in recent history been no true attempt to make the necessary changes to the financial and monetary system in order to develop a money (creation) system in which money would truly function as such a "public good", hence serving the general wellbeing, instead of solely the interests of a small financial elite within the economy.

Indeed, mainly as a result of some historical developments (described in more detail in Chap. 2 of this book), the financial and monetary system has during the past centuries (and especially since the introduction of the "modern" banking system in the Middle Ages, and of the central banking system later on in history) evolved in such a way that the money creation processes, and therefore also the main technique of steering the (global) economy, to a great extent, have come under the influence of a limited number of private market players who have mainly used this money creation power for their own selfish purposes, especially the pursuit of personal gain by the capital providers and managers of the private banks, without much regard for the general wellbeing of mankind and the planet it inhabits.

In combination with the fiscal (and parafiscal) systems prevailing all over the planet, as well as the unequal playing field of social and labor protection, one could

[1]Needless to say that also in other domains of societal, political and economic life, there will be a need for similar reflection and (real) change. (See in this regard already the concluding remarks at the end of Chap. 3 of this book.)

K. Byttebier, *Towards a New International Monetary Order*,
Economic and Financial Law & Policy – Shifting Insights & Values 1,
DOI 10.1007/978-3-319-52518-1_6

even consider that the current monetary and financial system, as embedded in the philosophy of economic (neo)liberalism that the free markets should rule everything and all, is one of the most important mechanisms that have led to the contemporary socioeconomic order, above all characterized by layers upon layers of injustice (of which the recent highly commented upon unequal distribution of the world's wealth is but a symptom, albeit a very disturbing one).

One of the man conclusions of the research which led to the present book is therefore that the prevailing monetary mechanism can hardly, if not at all, be called an instrument serving the general wellbeing, which in societies claiming to be of a democratic nature, could nevertheless be considered a justified expectation.

As a consequence, there is more than ever a need for fairer and more just mechanisms of money creation than the ones that prevail now and which are, basically and literally, an invention of the Middle Ages, especially when it is further considered that these prevailing monetary mechanisms have in no way contributed to a fair global distribution of income and assets, whereby one should at the same time, above all, consider that money is but a legal instrument which provides a generally accepted means of access to the goods and services produced by the collective efforts of mankind, and that all human beings share a common interest in having access to these goods and services in a sufficiently fair and equal way.

3 From a philosophical and even spiritual point of view, every human being (and by extension: every living creature) undoubtedly comes into this world to exist and to develop in it.

Processes which have grown historically, such as the current monetary system should, at least in a (more) just and fair world, no longer be an obstacle to a human right to equal opportunities, at the very least as regards the most basic needs of life (in the broad sense as argued before; see above, at marg. 129 of Chap. 4 of this book), but preferably also as regards all that which is necessary for a decent development of any human being in all domains of life.

A (more) just and fair world should at the very least ensure such an equal access to all that is necessary to lead a humane and dignified life, and it goes without saying that the current world (economies), especially given the way its leading socioeconomic defining system, namely untempered capitalism (as based upon the principles of economic neoliberalism and which i.a. determines the monetary system), in addition to the fiscal and parafiscal policies of most countries, operate, falls well short.

4 As long as the monetary system and the supply of money within the economy remains dominated by the private interests of a small financial elite, especially given its limitless hunger for ever more money, it is hard to see how the tide can be turned.

On the contrary, one can but witness how this small financial elite, thanks to the way capitalism works, has succeeded, over the past centuries and not in a real way contributing to the creation of general prosperity[2], in acquiring an ever growing

[2]This, as demonstrated before, in contradiction with the "trickle-down-economics" theory. (See above, marg. 123 of Chap. 3 of this book.)

disproportionate large part of the planet's riches, while at the same time hardly making any noteworthy effort to share this enormous wealth with the less fortunate on the planet.

The sword to cut this "Gordian knot" which has been presented in the current **5**
book, would be to start with the development of a new monetary world order which would be based on altruistic principles.

This development of such a new monetary world order would, above all, imply that the ideas of economic (neo)liberalism dating back to Smith and on which capitalism is to a large extent based, would be abandoned, which in the monetary domain should lead to a resolute turnaround of the (financial-economic) ethics on which the current mechanisms of money creation are based.

The aforementioned fundamental turnaround of the mechanisms of money crea- **6**
tion would hereby call for an uncompromising end to the power of private banks to create (scriptural) money.

Consequently, when considering money as a true "public good", the power to create money should lie exclusively in the hands of a new global monetary authority which should have as its basic task the organization of the money supply within the economy, based on underlying principles of fairness, especially the radical altruistic insight that every human deserves a fair and equal chance to achieve a dignified life.

Such a resolute turnover of the prevailing monetary and financial system would also require clear limits on the possibility of unbridled asset and wealth accumulation provided by money (a policy goal for which, in addition to the monetary policy, fiscal and parafiscal policy should also offer the appropriate tools).

It is in any case harrowing to realize that since the introduction, in the Middle **7**
Ages, of the currently prevailing monetary and financial system, the world is completely fully (and probably even more than ever) faced with the same questions that already have been raised by ancient philosophers and religious leaders about the sense—and *a fortiori*, the underlying justice—of:

(1) a (monetary) system which allows a small (financial) elite to build up huge fortunes (enabling them to live a life of inconsequential luxury), while at the same time and in the same world, other people are forced to live a life of hunger and poverty (often weighed down by malnutrition and deadly diseases);
(2) a socioeconomic system in which the labor power of the great masses is aimed, if not exclusively, then at least mainly, at enriching the same aforementioned (financial) elite, allowing a limited group of individuals to enjoy fortunes which are a multitude of what is left of the world's resources for the rest of the world's population, the latter itself being the victim of exploitation mechanisms solely designed to make the rich of the planet even richer;
(3) a global abuse of government's power in order to sustain these intrinsically unfair systems and mechanisms, even, for instance through the operation of inherently unfair fiscal and parafiscal mechanisms, strengthening them.

As argued in this book, at least to a certain extent, an answer to these dilemmas **8**
could be offered by a fundamental re-orientation of the monetary mechanisms as proposed above, whereby, at the very least, both the mechanisms of money

creation, as well as the techniques available to control the global amounts of money, should be turned into instruments aimed at achieving a global minimum of general wellbeing for all mankind.

The here proposed approach will obviously only be sustainable provided that such an “altruistic” monetary system is paired with an equally fundamental re-orientation of the fiscal and parafiscal systems, whose main purpose should no longer be to finance the operation of the national governments (and other public authorities), but to achieve a truly fair distribution of income and assets, while, as more thoroughly explained in the Chaps. 4 and 5 of this book, state financing itself should be provided for out of the monetary mechanisms themselves.

In this fiscal new approach, it should however be avoided that productivity incentives are completely removed. People who (truly) work hard and who provide innovation for the (real) economy should indeed be rewarded for their efforts[3], provided that the worker himself enjoys the fruits of his labor, and not, as happens far too much under capitalism, others who exploit the labor of those who work hard.[4]

As explained above, fiscality should, henceforth, only serve to skim the incomes and assets which tend to grow too excessively, because, to be honest, who can (continue to) claim that he deserves or is in need of a multiple of billions, in the knowledge that, at the same time, other people are living a life of poverty and misery.

9 To reach these objectives, the monetary system as proposed in Chaps. 4 and 5 of this book has been based on a proposal to deactivate a number of historical capitalist practices which, on a global scale, have mainly affected the lower and middle classes in a negative way and which, i.a., have resulted in a socioeconomic order characterized by the fact that the riches of the planet, to a very large extent, have become concentrated in the hands of a limited elite.

Among these practices, there are, as said, *on one hand,* the mechanism of scriptural money creation by the private banking sector (which should be replaced by a differentiated mechanism of money creation by a global public monetary institution) and, *on the other hand*, the dependence of government financing in most countries on tax and parafiscal systems and on the taking up of credit from mainly

---

[3]As such, at least this idea of economic neoliberalism that those who work hard should be rewarded, bears some further consideration (see Brook and Watkins 2012, pp. 76–77 and 124).

However, the argument that those who work hard should be rewarded accordingly, should be dealt with in a fair and just way, as under prevailing capitalist mechanisms, it is not as much those who work hard themselves, but rather those who succeed in making other people work (too) hard and who seize the fruits of this labor almost exclusively to enrich themselves, who get even richer (see also Oxfam 2014, p. 65).

A good illustration of this question is whether the CEO of a company who gets wages which are a couple of hundred times larger than those of the other employees of the same company, is indeed working such a couple of hundred times harder than these other employees, or if he really is such a couple of hundred times more worth than those other employees.

[4]Compare Galbraith (1996), p. 61.

the private financial sector (which should be replaced by a system of public money creation based on allocations by the said monetary institution).

In such an alternative monetary system, financing public authorities would 10
become separated from the dictates of the national economies, and instead be linked to a realistic estimation of the needs of each country which moreover would be based on a global perspective and on a fair distribution of world resources.

As has also been explained in Chaps. 4 and 5 of this book, under the here proposed new monetary order, the providing of new money to the private sector (s) would also be organized in such a way that it would be based upon a globally defined objective of general wellbeing, while at the same time respecting the limits of the natural resources of the planet in an intergenerational perspective, and, hence, no longer be aimed at maintaining mechanisms which mainly strive to make the rich of the planet even richer (and resulting in a lot of poverty and misery for a large part of the rest of the world's population).

Otherwise put, the new monetary world order proposed here (and through this, the new monetary policies, especially in the field of new money creation) should be based on two main "altruistic" principles:

- To aspire[5] or a global level of general wellbeing everywhere in the world and for the whole of mankind;
- To establish a deeply rooted and fundamental awareness of the limits of the planet (in an intergenerational perspective).[6]

The (rest of) economy itself could (provisionally) continue to be based on the 11
principles of the free market, in the knowledge that another way of supplying the economy with money will necessarily (and especially within the guidelines and directives that will be worked out by the new monetary authorities) encourage the economic players themselves towards greater discipline and towards greater respect for the objectives underlying the new monetary order, namely the general wellbeing and a fundamental respect for the limits of the natural resources of the planet in an intergenerational perspective.

Such a new monetary system could moreover result in an important economic impulse (perhaps even comparable to the dynamic after WWII which stemmed from the Marshall-plan[7]).

For instance, given the objective to work out a more just and fair world order, it is to be expected that, at least during an initial period, in the new monetary world order, the (poorer) developing countries in particular, would dispose of more

---

[5]As has been explained in the Chaps. 4 and 5 of this book, this should become the case on all levels of money creation, both money creation on behalf of the (national and other) of the countries participating in the New Monetary World Order, as money creation on behalf of the private sector (s).

[6]To paraphrase one of Hollands most renowned authors, namely Godfried Bomans (1913–1971): the world asks for a policy that accepts that it should be limited (see Bomans 1961, pp. 80–83).

Compare Dawkins (2006), p. 18; Hoefnagels (1975), pp. 12 a.f.

[7]See Berend (2006), pp. 233 a.f.; Vandewalle (1976), p. 247.

operational funds (both on the level of allocations to the national authorities of the countries participating in the NMWO, as on the level of money creation on behalf of the private sectors).[8] Provided that the increased purchasing power deriving from more available funds is used in a fair and intelligent way, this could generate an important dynamic for the development of the national economies of these developing countries[9], but at the same time also of the economies of other countries (which, for instance, would be able to contribute on a much larger scale in helping to build up the infrastructures of said developing countries). In this process, the global efforts of the world economy would gradually serve towards the creation of a world which will be humane for everyone everywhere (and which would no longer mainly exist for the benefit of enriching a few individuals).[10]

12 This re-orientation of the world monetary order and hence of the world economy itself, will obviously need to be sufficiently drastic.

It can indeed not be considered sufficient that, from time to time, a multi-billionaire, probably out of remorse about how his own selfish craving for ever more money and power negatively effects the world, donates a few millions (expressed in whatever currency) to charity[11], while at the same time aspiring to keep the existing economic and monetary world system in place[12], especially given the fact that this prevailing economic and monetary world system, namely capitalism, inherently results in a fundamentally unfair distribution of the world's riches, including the stockpiling of mega fortunes in the hands of a happy few to the detriment, through poverty and exploitation, of a large part of the rest of the world's population.

It should, on the contrary, become the aspiration to completely turn around the underlying values driving the world economy and to resolutely replace the principle of unbridled selfishness which, especially since Smith, is considered as the sole value determining economic processes, by its opposite value, namely that of radical altruism.

---

[8]Compare Stiglitz (2012), pp. 216 a.f. and pp. 234 a.f.

[9]Compare Stiglitz (2012), p. 236.

[10]On the importance of government spending to stimulate the economy, especially in times of crisis, see *e.g.* Stiglitz (2012), pp. 234 a.f.

[11]One nevertheless should also admire the charity works of some of the world's richest people, such as Bill Gates and his spouse (see Baer 2014).

[12]See, for instance, the famous reaction of Bill Gates to the findings of Thomas Piketty as quoted by the latter himself:

> "I had this discussion with Bill Gates a couple of weeks ago," Piketty, the author of "Capital in the Twenty-First Century," said today at an economics conference in Boston. "He told me, 'I love everything that's in your book, but I don't want to pay more tax." A tax on wealth is one of Piketty's key recommendations for addressing inequality.
>
> "I understand his point," said Piketty, who teaches at the Paris School of Economics. "I think he sincerely believes he's more efficient than the government, and you know, maybe he is sometimes." (See http://www.forbes.com/sites/timworstall/2015/01/04/as-thomas-piketty-says-of-course-bill-gates-is-more-efficient-than-the-government/; last consulted on February 22nd 2016).

As proposed in the present book, such a drastic re-orientation of the world's monetary system could imply a first, albeit huge step in this direction.

If the global community were ever willing to further reflect about the installation 13
of the new monetary system proposed here which would be based on altruistic principles (or at least on a more or less similar (more) "altruistic" monetary system), then, obviously, settling existing monetary reserves and (monetary) debts will most likely be a particularly problematic issue.

In a truly (radical) altruistic perception, countries (or states themselves, but also national entities such as "sovereign funds"[13]), in addition to supranational institutions, such as the IMF and the World Bank, should be more than willing to renounce their receivable positions to other countries (or other supranational entities) in return for being allowed to participate in a truly fair world monetary system, as this would promote the interests of all countries of the world in a fair and equal way.

Altogether, this "price" for building a truly just, fair and enduring world monetary system based upon altruistic principles could turn out to be low in comparison to the cost of a full collapse of the world economy and its monetary and financial system (and hence of global peace) to which the blind continuation of the prevailing free market system could lead (whereby debt and/or reserve positions could *de facto* become a dead letter).[14]

A further question when implementing the proposed New Monetary World 14
Order is in what way one will be able to ensure the conversion of existing monetary positions (in addition to other positions measured in money, such as those laid down in securities and other types of financial instruments), including those that are in the hands of private individuals and companies.

As was done when the euro was first introduced, one way of handling this issue could consist at first of calculating and then, during a preparation phase, freezing the exchange rates of the currencies of the countries which participate in the NMWO. After that, possibly spread over time, all outstanding monetary positions and other positions expressed in a monetary value could be converted to this New Currency in accordance with these fixed exchange rates.

Furthermore, upon the introduction of the New Monetary World System, one could decide which positions should be reduced entirely to zero, for instance, in the

[13]See Bassan (2011), p. 171.

[14]As has been suggested earlier in this text (see above, at marg. 120 a.f. of Chap. 4 of this book), a method of bringing such an aspiration in practical reach of the (rich) countries disposing of (huge) monetary (and other) reserves in foreign currencies, respectively the (poor) debt countries, could be that the allocation policy of the new monetary authorities would take into account the existence of reserve and debt positions of the past. For instance, past reserve positions (as these would be entirely abolished when first implementing the NMWO) could during a certain period of time lead to higher allocations of allocations, while past debt positions (also entirely to be abolished) could result in lower allocations. As such a system would obviously lead to inequalities in the allocation policy, a sufficient degree of caution will have to be kept in place, whereby the aspiration of creating a truly fair and just world monetary order should be preferred above a policy of precise measurements aimed at ensuring that every existing reserve or debt position of the past would be taken into account to the last dollar or euro.

"public sphere", the mutual reserve and debt positions between the countries participating in the NMWO (possibly in addition to those between other national and supranational public entities) (see above, under Sect. 2.7 of Chap. 2 of this book).

A further question arises whether or not to deal with the existing positions of private individuals in a similar way (for instance by reducing some of them to zero).[15]

As regards such private debts and claims, probably the most simple approach would be to, at the date of introduction of the NMWO, simply convert (and hence provisionally retain) all such private positions and only later, by means of transparent and legally secured fiscal (and "parafiscal") mechanisms, work towards the underlying objective of a better re-distribution of the world's resources.

An exception may however be considered with regards to the claims of the private banking system on states (and other public national and supranational institutions). As regards such banking claims, one could also consider an immediate cancellation (albeit possibly in return for some type of compensation), taking into consideration that it is mainly because of the techniques of credit lending (and the interest mechanism), in addition to similar practices of the banking sector, that the world community has been burdened with so many socioeconomic problems.

15 If the world community were ever and effectively to become willing to adhere to the fundamental re-orientation of the global monetary system proposed here, it should be also clear that its introduction will need to take place in a sufficiently prudent way.

Needless to say that such an introduction of the New Monetary World Order should first be adequately studied and prepared, whereby a great deal of attention should be paid to the required preparatory financial calculations in addition to the drafting of the legal framework (including the treaty (ies) which will govern the NMWO and the other regulatory texts), the establishment of the NMWI (which, as suggested above, could perhaps be the result of a thorough reformation of the IMF; see above, at marg. 2–3 of Chap. 5 of this book); the preparation of the network of national central banks that together will form the NGSCB, etc.[16]

16 The proposed creation of a new monetary and financial system based on altruistic principles rather than on the (neo)liberal ideal of a world dominated by greed could, furthermore, be just a first step in the right direction towards a global economy based on altruistic goals.

Indeed, if the global community were found willing to put into effect the here proposed monetary system based on altruistic principles (or a sufficiently similar one), this should not necessarily represent the final phase in promoting an economy based on altruism.

---

[15] Compare Middelkoop (2014), p. 167.

[16] The experiences with the establishment of the Eurozone and of the ECB and the ESCB could probably also here be an important source of inspiration.

Hence, in a later phase of re-orientation of the global economy towards a more altruistic system, one could, for instance, advocate a fairer organization of the business world, whereby the development of mechanisms rewarding labor above capital should be one of the central themes, in addition to the development of fairer and more transparent pricing methods regarding all transactions of goods and services.

First and foremost, every human being, in his combined roles of global citizen, consumer and laborer, should gradually come to the very basic understanding that any enterprise (regardless of its legal form) making enormous profits is doing this merely due to the fact(s) that: **17**

(i) its consumers are (and remain) willing to continue to pay way too much for its products and services, as we all can experience this (basic) truth for ourselves in our various daily expenses, going from expenses for basic goods, such as food, to expenses for computer software licenses and telephone and internet services, in addition to other even more luxurious expenses (such as perfume and luxury clothing).[17]

Hence, it should not come as too big a surprise that the owners of some of the enterprises providing such (basic) goods and services, in addition to those in the financial sector itself, belong to the richest people on earth (see for instance Bill Gates (computer software); Carlos Slim (telephone and related products); the Walton and Ortega families (retail); Stefan Persson (clothing); Liliane Bettencourt (cosmetics);. . .).

and,

(ii) its employees (in the broad sense of the word) remain operative under the rule of the (already ancient) "*Iron Law of the Wages*".

In addition to the intrinsically unfair mechanisms of private money creation based on interest credits by private banks, and of fiscal and parafiscal skimming of the average incomes (and assets) of the middle and poor(er) classes by national governments, the said pricing and wage polices are precisely two of the main building blocks of the current unfair world economy, characterized by an ever wider and deeper gap between the rich and the poor (see above, under Sect. 3.4.8 of Chap. 3 of this book).

Coming to this awareness, while at the same time taking into further consideration the detrimental impact of the free market mechanisms (or, otherwise put, of the capitalist system) on mankind and on the planet it inhabits, one can but recognize that the ideologies advocating the free market have utterly failed, and it is from this awareness that the proposals as described in the current book have been drafted.

The question will certainly be raised whether the proposals as described in this book are (or can be) realistic in the actual world, and whether it is, simply put, **18**

[17]For an enlightening overview (albeit already of the year 2012) of the American retail market, see https://nrf.com/resources/top-retailers-list//top-100-retailers-2012; last consulted on December 8th 2014).

not too late to deploy another economic system than the prevailing free market or capitalist economic system itself.

In anthropological terms, this raises a so-called "TINA"-question (where "TINA" stands for "*There is no alternative*").[18]

19 According to Belgian anthropologist Rik Pinxten, this type of argumentation is typical for people pleading for the adherence to the free market(s) and the mechanisms through which this (these) operate(s)[19], hence for the adepts of the school of economic (neo)liberalism.[20]

20 The question returning to the aforementioned TINA-question (see above, at marg. 18 of Chap. 6 of this book) then becomes how realistic it can be to allow the new neoliberal feudal system as driven by the invisible forces of the free market (or is it by the "*selfish genes*" of the rich and powerful of the planet) to continue to proceed in the way it is today.

21 What will be needed in the first place in order to ensure that mankind starts its search for a more just and fair global social and economic order, for instance by establishing the here proposed monetary and financial system, is a sufficient willingness to fundamentally re-orientate their economic thinking and action.

As regards more specifically the monetary and financial systems, the basic underlying question should therefore be what future effect mankind wants to give to the social contract at the basis of the global monetary system, namely the ideal of a world where (unbridled) selfishness and greed can continue to grow and determine man's fate, or rather one of a world advocating a fair and just socioeconomic order in a spirit of true altruism.

---

[18]Pinxten (2014), p. 16.

[19]See Pinxten (2014), pp. 16 a.f. See also Ongenae (2014), pp. 44–45.

Pinxten has in this regard pointed out that particularly since the 1980s (*ergo* since the rise of neoliberal ideologies), the world has been heading towards a new feudal system in which a small elite of extremely rich people is (socioeconomically) repressing and exploiting the rest of the world's population, a development in which the financial crisis of 2008 itself (and the principle of "*privatization of gains and socialization of losses*") has only had a catalytic effect. According to Pinxten, it is to maintain and ever more enhance this new feudal system that neoliberal thinkers have systematically aimed at rejecting anyone who has dared to express different economic ideas as being "irrational", "irrelevant" or bluntly "idiotic". Pinxten convincingly argues that, especially in light of the state the world is in, this approach hardly makes any sense and that mankind must dare again to "*re-invent the world*", whereby one should aspire to a new social and economic project in which the values of freedom, equality and fraternity/solidarity are effectively given a true meaning once again.

See even John Paul II (2005), pp. 121 a.f., in this regard also having pointed out that

> the capitalism of the early industrial revolution did violence to liberty, equality and fraternity in various way, allowing the exploitation of man in defence to the law of the markets. (p. 123)

[20]See also Galbraith 1994, p. xiii:

> It is my introductory and, I trust, guiding confession that I believe the greatest error in economics is in seeing the economy as a stable, immutable structure.

Already the so-called "*hunger*" (or "*food paradox*") (see above, at marg. 174 of Chap. 3 of this book and under Further Illustration 3.12 in Chap. 3 of this book) speaks for itself. 22

In a world where over 800 million people are hungry[21], albeit enough food is produced to feed everyone, and whereby this situation is only the result of the current socioeconomic system,[22] including its money creation and distribution mechanisms, it could even be considered criminal *not* to search for alternative mechanisms to create and distribute money than the current ones of (mainly) private money creation based on capitalist principles.[23]

Furthermore, from a historical perspective, up till today, not a single system of socioeconomic and political (or other) order has been perpetual, so, why should this be the case with the prevailing capitalist system. 23

The question then becomes in what way the transit to another socioeconomic order should be introduced, namely either starting by introducing a new global social contract regarding (the creation, distribution and use of) money, or by taking refuge in other solutions which have too often been applied in the past (such as, in extreme cases, revolution and war).

With this question in mind, the essential question becomes why mankind should even want to continue to maintain capitalism, with all its excesses and adverse effects, including its intrinsically unjust method of money creation.

Even so, through the course of monetary history, several earlier monetary systems have been witnessed to collapse. 24

In recent history this has for instance been the case with the (nineteenth century) gold standard and with the Bretton Woods-"dollar standard" as it functioned in the period 1944–1971 within the framework of the IMF.[24]

Further back, history on several occasion has witnessed the need to counteract the private banking system itself, for instance when gradually, from the (late)

---

[21]As explained above, hunger is even so becoming even more and more manifest in traditional "prosperous" countries where, under the dictates of economic neo-liberalism, poverty has been increasing during the past decades and the gaps between the rich and the poor are becoming ever deeper and larger. (For further details, see Sect. 3.4.8 of Chap. 3 of this book.)

[22]See *e.g.* Koba (2013).

[23]Van Erp (2014).

[24]See Pettifor (2014):

> The gold standard was largely designed to protect the interests of moneylenders concerned to protect the value of their assets – loans – and to ensure their assets were not eroded by inflation. To this end it was argued that society could only afford, or be trusted to employ a fixed sum of economic activity – equal and limited to a quantity of scarce lumps of gold dug out of the earth – and used by moneylenders as collateral. And so it was that the gold standard operated as a fantastic machinery for protecting the interests of creditors, while constraining and depressing economic activity, in particular employment. That is, until society rebelled against the moneylenders and demanded change. Change was duly brought about in the UK in 1931 and the US in 1933: first as a result of the influence of Keynes and then as a result of the leadership of President Roosevelt.

seventeenth century on, but increasingly in the course of the eighteenth and nineteenth centuries, in most of the (then existing) European countries, it was decided that private banking, because of past excesses, was no longer allowed to issue paper bank notes, albeit at that time the (relatively) "newly" emerging technique of scriptural money creation escaped policy attention, a historical mistake which stands corrected for too long already.

25 "*The Dhammapada*", a collection of sayings attributed to Buddha, starts with the following verses[25]:

> All that we are is the result of what we have thought: it is
> founded on our thoughts, it is made up of our thoughts.[26]

Irrespective of whether these verses indicate that every human being perceives the world through his own thought system (or "*ego*"), or that the world is shaped because the thoughts (of people) precede (their) actions, or (probably) both of the aforementioned meanings, this eternal "Buddhist" truth can easily be extended to the sphere of the collective processes which shape society.

Applied to the monetary system, all of mankind should become fully aware that the monetary system as it is today is indeed nothing more than an (extremely poor) product of men's thoughts, which has on many occasions in the past demonstrated many flaws.

26 To the extent that the entire socioeconomic order is also but a product of the human mind, the question whether or not the search for a fairer and more just system of money creation and distribution should be undertaken can therefore but be answered affirmatively here.

The question may then even become why mankind would not advocate replacing the current clearly intrinsically unjust and unfair functioning mechanism of money creation by a system that does aim at establishing a greater fairness in the socio-economic dimension.

At the very least, from the academic world, there should be a call for more reflection on this subject, which has been one of the key objectives of the present book.

---

[25]Byrom (1994), p. 17.

[26]Translation of F.M. Muller, at http://www.fullbooks.com/The-Dhammapada.html (last consulted on December 1st 2015).

Compare Vivekananda 1989, pp. 25–118, especially p. 30:

> All the actions that we see in the world, all the movements in human society, all the works that we have around us, are simply the display of thought, the manifestations of the will of man.

References

Baer D (2014) 21 insightful quotes from Bill Gates, who just turned 59. http://www.businessinsider.com/quotes-from-bill-gates-the-worlds-richest-man-2014-10. Last consulted 29 Oct 2014

Bassan F (2011) The law of sovereign wealth funds. Edward Elgar, Cheltenham

Berend I (2006) An economic history of twentieth-century Europe. Cambridge University Press, Cambridge

Brook Y, Watkins D (2012) Free market revolution – how Ayn Rand's ideas can end big government. Palgrave Macmillan, New York

Bomans G (1961) Het is de hoogste tijd. In: Noten kraken. Zuid-Nederlandsche Drukkerij nv, 's Hertogenbosch

Buddha. (trans: Muller FM) The Dhammapada. http://www.fullbooks.com/The-Dhammapada.html. Last consulted 1 Dec 2015

Byrom T (1994) De Dhammapada – De woorden van Boeddha. Altamira, Heemstede

Dawkins R (2006) The selfish gene. Oxford University Press, Oxford

Galbraith JK (1994) A journey through economic time – a firsthand view. Houghton Mifflin Company, Boston

Galbraith JK (1996) The good society – the humane agenda. Houghton Mifflin Company, Boston

Hoefnagels HJM (1975) De toekomst staat op het spel. De Nederlandsche boekhandel, Kapellen

John Paul II (2005) Memory & identity. Personal reflections, Hachette, UK

Koba M (2013) A hungry world: Lots of food, in too few places. http://www.cnbc.com/id/100893540#. Last consulted 24 Oct 2014

Middelkoop W (2014) The big reset – war on gold and the financial endgame. AUP, Amsterdam

Ongenae C (2014) Antropoloog Rik Pinxten roept op tot verzet – Het oude kastendenken is terug. In: Knack November 26th 2014, pp 44–45

Oxfam (2014) Even it up – time to end extreme inequality. Oxfam GB, Oxford

Pettifor (2014) The power to 'create money out of thin air'. https://www.opendemocracy.net/ourkingdom/ann-pettifor/power-to-create-money-out-of-thin-air. Last consulted 18 Nov 2014

Pinxten R (2014) Schoon protest (want er is wel een alternatief). EPO Berchem

Stiglitz J (2012) The price of inequality. Allen Lane (an imprint of Penguin Books), London

Vandewalle G (1976) De geschiedenis van het economisch denken. Kluwer, Deventer

Van Erp A (2014) Wereldvoedseldag: Er is voldoende voedsel beschikbaar, niemand zou honger moeten lijden. http://m.knack.be/nieuws/planet-earth/wereldvoedseldag-er-is-voldoende-voedsel-beschikbaar-niemand-zou-honger-moeten-lijden/article-normal-443595.html. Last consulted 16 Oct 2014

Vivekananda (1989) Karma yoga. In: The complete works of Swami Vivekanda (Mayavati Memorial Edition), Advaita Ashrama, Kolkata, Volume I

Kolibri 360 GmbH
Ferdinand-Jühlke-Straße 7
99095 Erfurt, Deutschland
produktsicherheit@kolibri360.de